GOT
QUESTIONS?

www.GotQuestions.org

GOT
QUESTIONS?

BIBLE QUESTIONS ANSWERED
ANSWERS TO THE QUESTIONS PEOPLE ARE REALLY ASKING

S. MICHAEL HOUDMANN
GENERAL EDITOR

Pleasant Word
A Division of WinePress Group
PW

Hard Cover:
ISBN 13: 978-1-4141-1202-2
ISBN 10: 1-4141-1202-5

Soft Cover:
ISBN 13: 978-1-4141-1208-4
ISBN 10: 1-4141-1208-4

Library of Congress Catalog Card Number: 2009921025

CONTENTS

Acknowledgments vii

Preface ix

Introduction: The Ultimate Question xi

Chapter 1: Questions about God 1
Chapter 2: Questions about Jesus Christ 37
Chapter 3: Questions about the Holy Spirit 77
Chapter 4: Questions about Salvation 103
Chapter 5: Questions about the Bible 135
Chapter 6: Questions about the Church 171
Chapter 7: Questions about the End Times 207
Chapter 8: Questions about Angels and Demons 233
Chapter 9: Questions about Humanity 253
Chapter 10: Questions about Theology 277
Chapter 11: Questions about the Christian Life 305
Chapter 12: Questions about Prayer 337
Chapter 13: Questions about Sin 363
Chapter 14: Questions about Heaven, Hell, and Eternity 385

Chapter 15: Questions about Marriage .405

Chapter 16: Questions about Relationships 427

Chapter 17: Questions about Family and Parenting 445

Chapter 18: Questions about Creation 465

Chapter 19: Questions about Cults and Religions 489

Chapter 20: Questions about False Doctrine 527

Chapter 21: Questions about Life Decisions 553

Chapter 22: Topical Bible Questions .581

Chapter 23: Miscellaneous Bible Questions 607

Appendix: Statement of Faith 659

Topical Index 663

Scripture Index 671

ACKNOWLEDGMENTS

THIS BOOK IS dedicated to the more than 300 individuals who have served as volunteer writers for Got Questions Ministries in the past seven years. Their hard work, commitment and passion are what make this ministry possible.

Special thanks goes to Dolores Kimball, Kevin Stone, and MeLissa Houdmann, who contributed greatly to this volume in writing, editing, organizing, and indexing.

Further thanks goes to the volunteer writers whose efforts are included in this volume: Aaron Heath, Alan Hutchins, Andy O'Dwyer, Bill Stowe, Carl Gobelman, Carl Tebeau, Clair Drake, Damon Duehring, Daniel Grimes, Darline Metsker, Dennis LeFleur, Doug Beaumont, Gloria Small, Greg Spencer, Gregg Cudworth, Harvey Katzen, James Whiteside, Jan Kolar, Jeff Laird, Jim Braden, Jonathan McLatchie, Kari Hutson, Lana Brogan, Margaret Newton, Marilyn McClintock, Michael Blunk, Michael Burkett, Paul Bawden, R.Y. Costain, Randall Niles, Randall DeVille, Robin Schumacher, Rosemary Cross, Scott Owen, Sheila Irvine, Thomas Stegall, Tiffany Wismer, Tom Neven, Vera Rudolph, Vic Borden, and William Stewart.

PREFACE

EVERY DAY, MORE and more people are going to the internet to find answers to their questions about spiritual matters. Topics related to spirituality are the second most searched-for subjects online. Sadly, websites that present false teachings far outnumber those that proclaim the truth of God's Word.

In February of 2002, www.gotquestions.org was launched to help fill this gap and meet the needs of millions of spiritually-minded web surfers. Since our launch, we have personally answered over 200,000 questions that have been submitted to us. Tens of millions of people have found answers to their questions via our Frequently Asked Questions archives, giving us a unique understanding of what questions are truly on people's minds.

This volume is a collection of the most important and/or most frequently asked questions. Each question is answered directly from the Bible if the Bible specifically addresses the particular issue. Where the Bible is silent on an issue, biblical principles are used to lead to a solid and correct understanding of the issue. The Lord Jesus Christ is our passion, and declaring His Word is our mission.

Mission Statement of Got Questions Ministries:

"Got Questions Ministries seeks to glorify the Lord Jesus Christ by providing biblical, applicable and timely answers to spiritually-related questions."

INTRODUCTION

THE ULTIMATE QUESTION

Question: What does it mean to accept Jesus as your personal Savior?

Answer: Have you accepted Jesus Christ as your personal Savior? To properly understand this question, you must first understand the terms "Jesus Christ," "personal," and "Savior."

Who is Jesus Christ? Many people will acknowledge Jesus Christ as a good man, a great teacher, or even a prophet of God. These things are definitely true of Jesus, but they do not fully define who He truly is. The Bible tells us that Jesus is God in the flesh, God in human form (see John 1:1, 14). God came to earth to teach us, heal us, correct us, forgive us—and die for us! Jesus Christ is God, the Creator, the sovereign Lord. Have you accepted this Jesus?

What is a Savior, and why do we need a Savior? The Bible tells us that we have all sinned; we have all committed evil acts (Romans 3:10-18). As a result of our sin, we deserve God's anger and judgment. The only just punishment for sins committed against an infinite and eternal God is an infinite punishment (Romans 6:23; Revelation 20:11-15). That is why we need a Savior!

Jesus Christ came to earth and died in our place. Jesus' death was an infinite payment for our sins (2 Corinthians 5:21). Jesus died to pay the penalty for our sins (Romans 5:8). Jesus paid the price so that we would not have to. Jesus' resurrection from the dead proved that His death was sufficient to pay the penalty for our sins. That is why Jesus is the one and only Savior (John 14:6; Acts 4:12)! Are you trusting in Jesus as your Savior?

Is Jesus your "personal" Savior? Many people view Christianity as attending church, performing rituals, and/or not committing certain sins. That is not Christianity. True Christianity is a personal relationship with Jesus Christ. Accepting Jesus as your personal Savior means placing your own personal faith and trust in Him. No one is saved by the faith of others. No one is forgiven by doing certain deeds. The only way to be saved is to personally accept Jesus as your Savior, trusting in His death as the payment for your sins and His resurrection as your guarantee of eternal life (John 3:16). Is Jesus personally your Savior?

If you want to accept Jesus Christ as your personal Savior, say the following words to God. Remember, saying this prayer or any other prayer will not save you. Only believing in Jesus Christ and His finished work on the cross for you can save you from sin. This prayer is simply a way to express to God your faith in Him and thank Him for providing for your salvation. "God, I know that I have sinned against You and deserve punishment. But I believe Jesus Christ took the punishment I deserve so that through faith in Him I could be forgiven. I receive Your offer of forgiveness and place my trust in You for salvation. I accept Jesus as my personal Savior! Thank You for Your wonderful grace and forgiveness—the gift of eternal life! Amen!"

Have you made a decision to receive Jesus Christ as your personal Savior because of what you have read here? If so, please send us an email at questions@gotquestions.org.

Chapter 1

QUESTIONS ABOUT GOD

CONTENTS

Does God exist? Is there evidence for the existence of God? 2

Who is God? 4

What are the attributes of God? What is God like? 6

What does the Bible teach about the Trinity? 8

Who created God? Where did God come from? 11

Why does God allow bad things to happen to good people? 12

Did God create evil? 13

Why is God so different in the Old Testament than He is in the New
    Testament? 14

What does it mean that God is love? 16

Does God still speak to us today? 17

What does it mean to have the fear of God? 18

Does God change His mind? 19

Does God love everyone or just Christians? 21

Is God male or female? 22

Does God still perform miracles? 24

Why does God allow natural disasters? 26

Is God sexist? 27

Does God answer the prayers of an unbeliever? 29

Why is God a jealous God? 30

Can monotheism be proven? 31

Is it wrong to question God? 34

Has anyone ever seen God? 35

Question: Does God exist? Is there evidence for the existence of God?

Answer: The existence of God cannot be proved or disproved. The Bible says that we must accept by faith the fact that God exists: "And without faith it is impossible to please God, because anyone who comes to Him must believe that He exists and that He rewards those who earnestly seek Him" (Hebrews 11:6). If God so desired, He could simply appear and prove to the whole world that He exists. But if He did that, there would be no need for faith. "Then Jesus told him, 'Because you have seen me, you have believed; blessed are those who have not seen and yet have believed'" (John 20:29).

That does not mean, however, that there is no evidence of God's existence. The Bible states, "The heavens declare the glory of God; the skies proclaim the work of His hands. Day after day they pour forth speech; night after night they display knowledge. There is no speech or language where their voice is not heard. Their voice goes out into all the earth, their words to the ends of the world" (Psalm 19:1-4). Looking at the stars, understanding the vastness of the universe, observing the wonders of nature, seeing the beauty of a sunset—all of these things point to a Creator God. If these were not enough, there is also evidence of God in our own hearts. Ecclesiastes 3:11 tells us, "...He has also set eternity in the hearts of men." Deep within us is the recognition that there is something beyond this life and someone beyond this world. We can deny this knowledge intellectually, but God's presence in us and all around us is still obvious. Despite this, the Bible warns that some will still deny God's existence: "The fool says in his heart, 'There is no God'" (Psalm 14:1). Since the vast majority of people throughout history, in all cultures, in all civilizations, and on all continents believe in the existence of some kind of God, there must be something (or someone) causing this belief.

In addition to the biblical arguments for God's existence, there are logical arguments. First, there is the ontological argument. The most popular form of the ontological argument uses the concept of God to prove God's existence. It begins with the definition of God as "a being than which no greater can be conceived." It is then argued that to exist is greater than to not exist, and therefore the greatest conceivable being must exist. If God did not exist, then God would not be the greatest conceivable being, and that would contradict the very definition of God.

A second argument is the teleological argument. The teleological argument states that since the universe displays such an amazing design, there must have been a divine Designer. For example, if the Earth were even a few hundred miles closer or farther away from the sun, it would not be capable of supporting much of the life it currently does. If the elements in our atmosphere were even a few percentage points different, nearly every living thing on earth would die. The odds of a single protein molecule forming by chance is 1 in 10243 (that is a 10 followed by 243 zeros). A single cell is comprised of millions of protein molecules.

A third logical argument for God's existence is called the cosmological argument. Every effect must have a cause. This universe and everything in it is an effect. There must be something that caused everything to come into existence. Ultimately, there must be something "un-caused" in order to cause everything else to come into existence. That "un-caused" cause is God.

A fourth argument is known as the moral argument. Every culture throughout history has had some form of law. Everyone has a sense of right and wrong. Murder, lying, stealing, and immorality are almost universally rejected. Where did this sense of right and wrong come from if not from a holy God?

Despite all of this, the Bible tells us that people will reject the clear and undeniable knowledge of God and believe a lie instead. Romans 1:25 declares, "They exchanged the truth of God for a lie, and worshiped and served created things rather than the Creator—who is forever praised. Amen." The Bible also proclaims that people are without excuse for not believing in God: "For since the creation of the world God's invisible qualities—His eternal power and divine nature—have been clearly seen, being understood from what has been made, so that men are without excuse" (Romans 1:20).

People claim to reject God's existence because it is "not scientific" or "because there is no proof." The true reason is that once they admit that there is a God, they also must realize that they are responsible to God and in need of forgiveness from Him (Romans 3:23, 6:23). If God exists, then we are accountable to Him for our actions. If God does not exist, then we can do whatever we want without having to worry about God judging us. That is why many of those who deny the existence of God cling strongly to the theory of naturalistic evolution—it gives them an alternative to believing in a Creator God. God exists and ultimately everyone knows that He exists. The very fact that some attempt so aggressively to disprove His existence is in fact an argument for His existence.

How do we know God exists? As Christians, we know God exists because we speak to Him every day. We do not audibly hear Him speaking to us, but we sense His presence, we feel His leading, we know His love, we desire His grace. Things have occurred in our lives that have no possible explanation other than God. God has so miraculously saved us and changed our lives that we cannot help but acknowledge and praise His existence. None of these arguments can persuade anyone who refuses to acknowledge what is already obvious. In the end, God's existence must be accepted by faith (Hebrews 11:6). Faith in God is not a blind leap into the dark; it is safe step into a well-lit room where the vast majority of people are already standing.

Question: Who is God?

Answer: Who is God? What is God? How can we know God?

The Fact

The fact of God's existence is so conspicuous, both through creation and through man's conscience, that the Bible calls the atheist a "fool" (Psalm 14:1). Accordingly, the Bible never attempts to prove the existence of God; rather, it assumes His existence from the very beginning (Genesis 1:1). What the Bible does is reveal the nature, character, and work of God.

The Definition

Thinking correctly about God is of utmost importance because a false idea about God is idolatry. In Psalm 50:21, God reproves the wicked man with this accusation: "You thought I was altogether like you." To start with, a good summary definition of God is "the

Supreme Being; the Creator and Ruler of all that is; the Self-existent One who is perfect in power, goodness, and wisdom."

His Nature

We know certain things to be true of God for one reason: in His mercy He has condescended to reveal some of His qualities to us. God is spirit, by nature intangible (John 4:24). God is One, but He exists as three Persons—God the Father, God the Son, and God the Holy Spirit (Matthew 3:16-17). God is infinite (1 Timothy 1:17), incomparable (2 Samuel 7:22), and unchanging (Malachi 3:6). God exists everywhere (Psalm 139:7-12), knows everything (Matthew 11:21), and has all power and authority (Ephesians 1; Revelation 19:6).

His Character

Here are some of God's characteristics as revealed in the Bible: God is just (Acts 17:31), loving (Ephesians 2:4-5), truthful (John 14:6), and holy (1 John 1:5). God shows compassion (2 Corinthians 1:3), mercy (Romans 9:15), and grace (Romans 5:17). God judges sin (Psalm 5:5) but also offers forgiveness (Psalm 130:4).

His Work

We cannot understand God apart from His works, because what God does flows from who He is. Here is an abbreviated list of God's works, past, present, and future: God created the world (Genesis 1:1; Isaiah 42:5); He actively sustains the world (Colossians 1:17); He is executing His eternal plan (Ephesians 1:11) which involves the redemption of man from the curse of sin and death (Galatians 3:13-14); He draws people to Christ (John 6:44); He disciplines His children (Hebrews 12:6); and He will judge the world (Revelation 20:11-15).

A Relationship with Him

In the Person of the Son, God became incarnate (John 1:14). The Son of God became the Son of Man and is therefore the "bridge" between God and man (John 14:6; 1 Timothy 2:5). It is only through the Son that we can have forgiveness of sins (Ephesians 1:7), reconciliation with God (John 15:15; Romans 5:10), and eternal salvation (2 Timothy 2:10). In Jesus Christ "all the fullness of the Deity lives in bodily form" (Colossians 2:9). So, to really know who God is, all we have to do is look at Jesus.

Question: What are the attributes of God? What is God like?

Answer: The Bible, God's Word, tells us what God is like and what He is not like. Without the authority of the Bible, any attempt to explain God's attributes would be no better than an opinion, which by itself is often incorrect, especially in understanding God (Job 42:7). To say that it is important for us to try to understand what God is like is a huge understatement. Failure to do so can cause us to set up, chase after, and worship false gods contrary to His will (Exodus 20:3-5).

Only what God has chosen to reveal of Himself can be known. One of God's attributes or qualities is "light," meaning that He is self-revealing in information of Himself (Isaiah 60:19; James 1:17). The fact that God has revealed knowledge of Himself should not be neglected (Hebrews 4:1). Creation, the Bible, and the Word made flesh (Jesus Christ) will help us to know what God is like.

Let's start by understanding that God is our Creator and that we are a part of His creation (Genesis 1:1; Psalm 24:1) and are created in His image. Man is above the rest of creation and was given dominion over it (Genesis 1:26-28). Creation is marred by the fall but still offers a glimpse of God's works (Genesis 3:17-18; Romans 1:19-20). By considering creation's vastness, complexity, beauty, and order, we can have a sense of the awesomeness of God.

Reading through some of the names of God can be helpful in our search of what God is like. They are as follows:

Elohim - strong One, divine (Genesis 1:1)
Adonai - Lord, indicating a Master-to-servant relationship (Exodus 4:10, 13)
El Elyon - Most High, the strongest One (Genesis 14:20)
El Roi - the strong One who sees (Genesis 16:13)
El Shaddai - Almighty God (Genesis 17:1)
El Olam - Everlasting God (Isaiah 40:28)

Yahweh - Lord "I Am," meaning the eternal self-existent God (Exodus 3:13-14).

God is eternal, meaning He had no beginning and His existence will never end. He is immortal and infinite (Deuteronomy 33:27; Psalm 90:2; 1 Timothy 1:17). God is immutable, meaning He is unchanging; this in turn means that God is absolutely reliable and trustworthy (Malachi 3:6; Numbers 23:19; Psalm 102:26, 27). God is incomparable; there is no one like Him in works or being. He is unequaled and perfect (2 Samuel 7:22; Psalm 86:8; Isaiah 40:25; Matthew 5:48). God is inscrutable, unfathomable, unsearchable, and past finding out as far as understanding Him completely (Isaiah 40:28; Psalm 145:3; Romans 11:33-34).

God is just; He is no respecter of persons in the sense of showing favoritism (Deuteronomy 32:4; Psalm 18:30). God is omnipotent; He is all-powerful and can do anything that pleases Him, but His actions will always be in accord with the rest of His character (Revelation 19:6; Jeremiah 32:17, 27). God is omnipresent, meaning He is present everywhere, but this does not mean that God is everything (Psalm 139:7-13; Jeremiah 23:23). God is omniscient, meaning He knows the past, present, and future, including what we are thinking at any given moment. Since He knows everything, His justice will always be administered fairly (Psalm 139:1-5; Proverbs 5:21).

God is one; not only is there no other, but He is alone in being able to meet the deepest needs and longings of our hearts. God alone is worthy of our worship and devotion (Deuteronomy 6:4). God is righteous, meaning that God cannot and will not pass over wrongdoing. It is because of God's righteousness and justice that, in order for our sins to be forgiven, Jesus had to experience God's wrath when our sins were placed upon Him (Exodus 9:27; Matthew 27:45-46; Romans 3:21-26).

God is sovereign, meaning He is supreme. All of His creation put together cannot thwart His purposes (Psalm 93:1; 95:3; Jeremiah 23:20). God is spirit, meaning He is invisible (John 1:18; 4:24). God is a Trinity. He is three in one, the same in substance, equal in power and glory. God is truth, He will remain incorruptible and cannot lie (Psalm 117:2; 1 Samuel 15:29).

7

God is holy, separated from all moral defilement and hostile toward it. God sees all evil and it angers Him. God is referred to as a consuming fire (Isaiah 6:3; Habakkuk 1:13; Exodus 3:2, 4-5; Hebrews 12:29). God is gracious, and His grace includes His goodness, kindness, mercy, and love. If it were not for God's grace, His holiness would exclude us from His presence. Thankfully, this is not the case, for He desires to know each of us personally (Exodus 34:6; Psalm 31:19; 1 Peter 1:3; John 3:16; 17:3).

Since God is an infinite Being, no human can fully answer this God-sized question, but through God's Word, we can understand much about who God is and what He is like. May we all wholeheartedly continue to seek after Him (Jeremiah 29:13).

Question: What does the Bible teach about the Trinity?

Answer: The most difficult thing about the Christian concept of the Trinity is that there is no way to adequately explain it. The Trinity is a concept that is impossible for any human being to fully understand, let alone explain. God is infinitely greater than we are; therefore, we should not expect to be able to fully understand Him. The Bible teaches that the Father is God, that Jesus is God, and that the Holy Spirit is God. The Bible also teaches that there is only one God. Though we can understand some facts about the relationship of the different Persons of the Trinity to one another, ultimately, it is incomprehensible to the human mind. However, this does not mean the Trinity is not true or that it is not based on the teachings of the Bible.

The Trinity is one God existing in three Persons. Understand that this is not in any way suggesting three Gods. Keep in mind when studying this subject that the word "Trinity" is not found in Scripture. This is a term that is used to attempt to describe the triune God—three coexistent, co-eternal Persons who make up God. Of real importance is that the concept represented by the word "Trinity" does exist in Scripture. The following is what God's Word says about the Trinity:

1. There is one God (Deuteronomy 6:4; 1 Corinthians 8:4; Galatians 3:20; 1 Timothy 2:5).

2. The Trinity consists of three Persons (Genesis 1:1, 26; 3:22; 11:7; Isaiah 6:8, 48:16, 61:1; Matthew 3:16-17, 28:19; 2 Corinthians 13:14). In Genesis 1:1, the Hebrew plural noun *Elohim* is used. In Genesis 1:26, 3:22, 11:7 and Isaiah 6:8, the plural pronoun for "us" is used. The word *Elohim* and the pronoun "us" are plural forms, definitely referring in the Hebrew language to more than two. While this is not an explicit argument for the Trinity, it does denote the aspect of plurality in God. The Hebrew word for God, *Elohim*, definitely allows for the Trinity.

   In Isaiah 48:16 and 61:1, the Son is speaking while making reference to the Father and the Holy Spirit. Compare Isaiah 61:1 to Luke 4:14-19 to see that it is the Son speaking. Matthew 3:16-17 describes the event of Jesus' baptism. Seen in this passage is God the Holy Spirit descending on God the Son while God the Father proclaims His pleasure in the Son. Matthew 28:19 and 2 Corinthians 13:14 are examples of three distinct persons in the Trinity.

3. The members of the Trinity are distinguished one from another in various passages. In the Old Testament, "Lord" is distinguished from "Lord" (Genesis 19:24; Hosea 1:4). The Lord has a Son (Psalm 2:7, 12; Proverbs 30:2-4). The Spirit is distinguished from the "Lord" (Numbers 27:18) and from "God" (Psalm 51:10-12). God the Son is distinguished from God the Father (Psalm 45:6-7; Hebrews 1:8-9). In the New Testament, Jesus speaks to the Father about sending a Helper, the Holy Spirit (John 14:16-17). This shows that Jesus did not consider Himself to be the Father or the Holy Spirit. Consider also all the other times in the Gospels where Jesus speaks to the Father. Was He speaking to Himself? No. He spoke to another person in the Trinity—the Father.

4. Each member of the Trinity is God. The Father is God (John 6:27; Romans 1:7; 1 Peter 1:2). The Son is God (John 1:1, 14; Romans 9:5; Colossians 2:9; Hebrews 1:8; 1 John 5:20). The Holy Spirit is God (Acts 5:3-4; 1 Corinthians 3:16).

5. There is subordination within the Trinity. Scripture shows that the Holy Spirit is subordinate to the Father and the Son,

and the Son is subordinate to the Father. This is an internal relationship and does not deny the deity of any person of the Trinity. This is simply an area which our finite minds cannot understand concerning the infinite God. Concerning the Son see Luke 22:42, John 5:36, John 20:21, and 1 John 4:14. Concerning the Holy Spirit see John 14:16, 14:26, 15:26, 16:7, and especially John 16:13-14.

6. The individual members of the Trinity have different tasks. The Father is the ultimate source or cause of the universe (1 Corinthians 8:6; Revelation 4:11); divine revelation (Revelation 1:1); salvation (John 3:16-17); and Jesus' human works (John 5:17, 14:10). The Father initiates all of these things.

The Son is the agent through whom the Father does the following works: the creation and maintenance of the universe (1 Corinthians 8:6; John 1:3; Colossians 1:16-17); divine revelation (John 1:1; 16:12-15; Matthew 11:27; Revelation 1:1); and salvation (2 Corinthians 5:19; Matthew 1:21; John 4:42). The Father does all these things through the Son, who functions as His agent.

The Holy Spirit is the means by whom the Father does the following works: creation and maintenance of the universe (Genesis 1:2; Job 26:13; Psalm 104:30); divine revelation (John 16:12-15; Ephesians 3:5; 2 Peter 1:21); salvation (John 3:6; Titus 3:5; 1 Peter 1:2); and Jesus' works (Isaiah 61:1; Acts 10:38). Thus the Father does all these things by the power of the Holy Spirit.

There have been many attempts to develop illustrations of the Trinity. However, none of the popular illustrations are completely accurate. The egg (or apple) fails in that the shell, white, and yolk are parts of the egg, not the egg in themselves, just as the skin, flesh, and seeds of the apple are parts of it, not the apple itself. The Father, Son, and Holy Spirit are not parts of God; each of them is God. The water illustration is somewhat better, but it still fails to adequately describe the Trinity. Liquid, vapor, and ice are forms of water. The Father, Son, and Holy Spirit are not forms of God, each of them is God. So, while these illustrations may give us a picture of the Trinity, the picture is not entirely accurate. An infinite God cannot be fully described by a finite illustration.

The doctrine of the Trinity has been a divisive issue throughout the entire history of the Christian church. While the core aspects of the Trinity are clearly presented in God's Word, some of the side issues are not as explicitly clear. The Father is God, the Son is God, and the Holy Spirit is God—but there is only one God. That is the biblical doctrine of the Trinity. Beyond that, the issues are, to a certain extent, debatable and non-essential. Rather than attempting to fully define the Trinity with our finite human minds, we would be better served by focusing on the fact of God's greatness and His infinitely higher nature. "Oh, the depth of the riches of the wisdom and knowledge of God! How unsearchable his judgments, and his paths beyond tracing out! Who has known the mind of the Lord? Or who has been his counselor?" (Romans 11:33-34).

Question: Who created God? Where did God come from?

Answer: A common argument from atheists and skeptics is that if all things need a cause, then God must also need a cause. The conclusion is that if God needed a cause, then God is not God (and if God is not God, then of course there is no God). This is a slightly more sophisticated form of the basic question "Who made God?" Everyone knows that something does not come from nothing. So, if God is a "something," then He must have a cause, right?

The question is tricky because it sneaks in the false assumption that God came from somewhere and then asks where that might be. The answer is that the question does not even make sense. It is like asking, "What does blue smell like?" Blue is not in the category of things that have a smell, so the question itself is flawed. In the same way, God is not in the category of things that are created or caused. God is uncaused and uncreated—He simply exists.

How do we know this? We know that from nothing, nothing comes. So, if there were ever a time when there was absolutely nothing in existence, then nothing would have ever come into existence. But things do exist. Therefore, since there could never have been absolutely nothing, something had to have always been in existence. That ever-existing thing is what we call God. God is the uncaused Being that caused everything else to come into existence. God is the uncreated Creator who created the universe and everything in it.

Question: Why does God allow bad things to happen to good people?

Answer: This is one of the most difficult questions in all of theology. God is eternal, infinite, omniscient, omnipresent, and omnipotent. Why should human beings (not eternal, infinite, omniscient, omnipresent, or omnipotent) expect to be able to fully understand God's ways? The book of Job deals with this issue. God had allowed Satan to do everything he wanted to Job except kill him. What was Job's reaction? "Though he slay me, yet will I hope in him" (Job 13:15). "The LORD gave and the LORD has taken away; may the name of the LORD be praised" (Job 1:21). Job did not understand why God had allowed the things He did, but he knew God was good and therefore continued to trust in Him. Ultimately, that should be our reaction as well.

Why do bad things happen to good people? The biblical answer is there are no "good" people. The Bible makes it abundantly clear that all of us are tainted by and infected with sin (Ecclesiastes 7:20; Romans 6:23; 1 John 1:8). Romans 3:10-18 could not be clearer about the non-existence of "good" people: "There is no one righteous, not even one; there is no one who understands, no one who seeks God. All have turned away, they have together become worthless; there is no one who does good, not even one. Their throats are open graves; their tongues practice deceit. The poison of vipers is on their lips. Their mouths are full of cursing and bitterness. Their feet are swift to shed blood; ruin and misery mark their ways, and the way of peace they do not know. There is no fear of God before their eyes." Every human being on this planet deserves to be thrown into hell at this very moment. Every second we spend alive is only by the grace and mercy of God. Even the most terrible misery we could experience on this planet is merciful compared to what we deserve, eternal hell in the lake of fire.

A better question would be "Why does God allow good things to happen to bad people?" Romans 5:8 declares, "But God demonstrates his own love for us in this: While we were still sinners, Christ died for us." Despite the evil, wicked, sinful nature of the people of this world, God still loves us. He loved us enough to die to take the penalty for our sins (Romans 6:23). If we receive Jesus Christ as Savior (John 3:16;

Romans 10:9), we will be forgiven and promised an eternal home in heaven (Romans 8:1). What we deserve is hell. What we are given is eternal life in heaven if we come to Christ in faith.

Yes, sometimes bad things happen to people who seem undeserving of them. But God allows things to happen for His reasons, whether or not we understand them. Above all, however, we must remember that God is good, just, loving, and merciful. Often things happen to us that we simply cannot understand. However, instead of doubting God's goodness, our reaction should be to trust Him. "Trust in the LORD with all your heart and lean not on your own understanding; in all your ways acknowledge Him, and He will make your paths straight" (Proverbs 3:5-6).

Question: Did God create evil?

Answer: At first it might seem that if God created all things, then evil must have been created by God. However, evil is not a "thing" like a rock or electricity. You cannot have a jar of evil. Evil has no existence of its own; it is really the absence of good. For example, holes are real but they only exist in something else. We call the absence of dirt a hole, but it cannot be separated from the dirt. So when God created, it is true that all He created was good. One of the good things God made was creatures who had the freedom to choose good. In order to have a real choice, God had to allow there to be something besides good to choose. So, God allowed these free angels and humans to choose good or reject good (evil). When a bad relationship exists between two good things we call that evil, but it does not become a "thing" that required God to create it.

Perhaps a further illustration will help. If a person is asked, "Does cold exist?" the answer would likely be "yes." However, this is incorrect. Cold does not exist. Cold is the absence of heat. Similarly, darkness does not exist; it is the absence of light. Evil is the absence of good, or better, evil is the absence of God. God did not have to create evil, but rather only allow for the absence of good.

God did not create evil, but He does allow evil. If God had not allowed for the possibility of evil, both mankind and angels would be serving God out of obligation, not choice. He did not want "robots" that simply did what He wanted them to do because of their "programming." God allowed for the possibility of evil so that we could genuinely have a free will and choose whether or not we wanted to serve Him.

As finite human beings, we can never fully understand an infinite God (Romans 11:33-34). Sometimes we think we understand why God is doing something, only to find out later that it was for a different purpose than we originally thought. God looks at things from a holy, eternal perspective. We look at things from a sinful, earthly, and temporal perspective. Why did God put man on earth knowing that Adam and Eve would sin and therefore bring evil, death, and suffering on all mankind? Why didn't He just create us all and leave us in heaven where we would be perfect and without suffering? These questions cannot be adequately answered this side of eternity. What we can know is whatever God does is holy and perfect and ultimately will glorify Him. God allowed for the possibility of evil in order to give us a true choice in regards to whether we worship Him. God did not create evil, but He allowed it. If He had not allowed evil, we would be worshipping Him out of obligation, not by a choice of our own will.

Question: Why is God so different in the Old Testament than He is in the New Testament?

Answer: At the very heart of this question lies a fundamental misunderstanding of what both the Old and New Testaments reveal about the nature of God. Another way of expressing this same basic thought is when people say, "The God of the Old Testament is a God of wrath while the God of the New Testament is a God of love." The fact that the Bible is God's progressive revelation of Himself to us through historical events and through His relationship with people throughout history might contribute to misconceptions about what God is like in the Old Testament as compared to the New Testament. However, when one reads both the Old and the New Testaments, it becomes evident that God is not different from one testament to another and that God's wrath and His love are revealed in both testaments.

For example, throughout the Old Testament, God is declared to be a "compassionate and gracious God, slow to anger, abounding in love and faithfulness," (Exodus 34:6; Numbers 14:18; Deuteronomy 4:31;

Nehemiah 9:17; Psalm 86:5, 15; 108:4; 145:8; Joel 2:13). Yet in the New Testament, God's loving-kindness and mercy are manifested even more fully through the fact that "God so loved the world that he gave his one and only Son, that whoever believes in him shall not perish but have eternal life" (John 3:16). Throughout the Old Testament, we also see God dealing with Israel the same way a loving father deals with a child. When they willfully sinned against Him and began to worship idols, God would punish them. Yet, each time He would deliver them once they had repented of their idolatry. This is much the same way God deals with Christians in the New Testament. For example, Hebrews 12:6 tells us that "the Lord disciplines those he loves, and he punishes everyone he accepts as a son."

In a similar way, throughout the Old Testament we see God's judgment and wrath poured out on sin. Likewise, in the New Testament we see that the wrath of God is still "being revealed from heaven against all the godlessness and wickedness of men who suppress the truth by their wickedness" (Romans 1:18). So, clearly, God is no different in the Old Testament than He is in the New Testament. God by His very nature is immutable (unchanging). While we might see one aspect of His nature revealed in certain passages of Scripture more than other aspects, God Himself does not change.

As we read and study the Bible, it becomes clear that God is the same in the Old and New Testaments. Even though the Bible is 66 individual books written on two (or possibly three) continents, in three different languages, over a period of approximately 1500 years by more than 40 authors, it remains one unified book from beginning to end without contradiction. In it we see how a loving, merciful, and just God deals with sinful men in all kinds of situations. Truly, the Bible is God's love letter to mankind. God's love for His creation, especially for mankind, is evident all through Scripture. Throughout the Bible we see God lovingly and mercifully calling people into a special relationship with Himself, not because they deserve it, but because He is a gracious and merciful God, slow to anger and abundant in loving-kindness and truth. Yet we also see a holy and righteous God who is the Judge of all those who disobey His Word and refuse to worship Him, turning instead to worship gods of their own creation (Romans chapter 1).

Because of God's righteous and holy character, all sin—past, present, and future—must be judged. Yet God in His infinite love has provided a payment for sin and a way of reconciliation so that sinful man can escape His wrath. We see this wonderful truth in verses like 1 John 4:10: "This is love: not that we loved God, but that he loved us and sent his Son as an atoning sacrifice for our sins." In the Old Testament, God provided a sacrificial system whereby atonement could be made for sin. However, this sacrificial system was only temporary and merely looked forward to the coming of Jesus Christ who would die on the cross to make a complete substitutionary atonement for sin. The Savior who was promised in the Old Testament is fully revealed in the New Testament. Only envisioned in the Old Testament, the ultimate expression of God's love, the sending of His Son Jesus Christ, is revealed in all its glory in the New Testament. Both the Old and the New Testaments were given "to make us wise unto salvation" (2 Timothy 3:15). When we study the Testaments closely, it is evident that God "does not change like shifting shadows" (James 1:17).

Question: What does it mean that God is love?

Answer: Let's look at how the Bible describes love, and then we will see a few ways in which God is the essence of love. "Love is patient, love is kind. It does not envy, it does not boast, it is not proud. It is not rude, it is not self-seeking, it is not easily angered, it keeps no record of wrongs. Love does not delight in evil but rejoices with the truth. It always protects, always trusts, always hopes, always perseveres. Love never fails" (1 Corinthians 13:4-8a). This is God's description of love, and because God is love (1 John 4:8), this is what He is like.

Love (God) does not force Himself on anyone. Those who come to Him do so in response to His love. Love (God) shows kindness to all. Love (Jesus) went about doing good to everyone without partiality. Love (Jesus) did not covet what others had, living a humble life without complaining. Love (Jesus) did not brag about who He was in the flesh, although He could have overpowered anyone He ever came in contact with. Love (God) does not demand obedience. God did not demand obedience from His Son, but rather, Jesus willingly obeyed His Father in heaven. "The world must learn that I love the Father and that I do exactly what my Father has commanded me" (John 14:31). Love (Jesus) was/is always looking out for the interests of others.

The greatest expression of God's love is communicated to us in John 3:16: "For God so loved the world that he gave his one and only Son, that whoever believes in him shall not perish but have eternal life." Romans 5:8 proclaims the same message: "But God demonstrates his own love for us in this: While we were still sinners, Christ died for us." We can see from these verses that it is God's greatest desire that we join Him in His eternal home, heaven. He has made the way possible by paying the price for our sins. He loves us because He chose to as an act of His will. Love forgives. "If we confess our sins, he is faithful and just and will forgive us our sins and purify us from all unrighteousness" (1 John 1:9).

So, what does it mean that God is love? Love is an attribute of God. Love is a core aspect of God's character, His Person. God's love is in no sense in conflict with His holiness, righteousness, justice, or even His wrath. All of God's attributes are in perfect harmony. Everything God does is loving, just as everything He does is just and right. God is the perfect example of true love. Amazingly, God has given those who receive His Son Jesus as their personal Savior the ability to love as He does, through the power of the Holy Spirit (John 1:12; 1 John 3:1, 23-24).

Question: Does God still speak to us today?

Answer: The Bible records God speaking audibly to people many times (Exodus 3:14; Joshua 1:1; Judges 6:18; 1 Samuel 3:11; 2 Samuel 2:1; Job 40:1; Isaiah 7:3; Jeremiah 1:7; Acts 8:26; 9:15 – this is just a small sampling). There is no biblical reason why God could not or would not speak to a person audibly today. With the hundreds of times the Bible records God speaking, we have to remember that they occur over the course of 4,000 years of human history. God speaking audibly is the exception, not the rule. Even in the biblically recorded instances of God speaking, it is not always clear whether it was an audible voice, an inner voice, or a mental impression.

God does speak to people today. First, God speaks to us through His Word (2 Timothy 3:16-17). Isaiah 55:11 tells us, "So is my word that goes out from my mouth: it will not return to me empty, but

17

will accomplish what I desire and achieve the purpose for which I sent it." The Bible records God's words, everything we need to know in order to be saved and live the Christian life. Second Peter 1:3 declares, "His divine power has given us everything we need for life and godliness through our knowledge of Him who called us by his own glory and goodness."

Second, God speaks through impressions, events, and thoughts. God helps us to discern right from wrong through our consciences (1 Timothy 1:5; 1 Peter 3:16). God is in the process of conforming our minds to think His thoughts (Romans 12:2). God allows events to occur in our lives to direct us, change us, and help us to grow spiritually (James 1:2-5; Hebrews 12:5-11). First Peter 1:6-7 reminds us, "In this you greatly rejoice, though now for a little while you may have had to suffer grief in all kinds of trials. These have come so that your faith—of greater worth than gold, which perishes even though refined by fire—may be proved genuine and may result in praise, glory and honor when Jesus Christ is revealed."

Finally, God may sometimes speak audibly to people. It is highly doubtful, though, that this occurs as often as some people claim it does. Again, even in the Bible, God speaking audibly is the exception, not the ordinary. If anyone claims that God has spoken to him/her, always compare what is said with what the Bible says. If God were to speak today, His words would be in full agreement with what He has said in the Bible (2 Timothy 3:16-17). God does not contradict Himself.

Question: What does it mean to have the fear of God?

Answer: For the unbeliever, the fear of God is the fear of the judgment of God and eternal death, which is eternal separation from God (Luke 12:5; Hebrews 10:31). For the believer, the fear of God is something much different. The believer's fear is reverence of God. Hebrews 12:28-29 is a good description of this: "Therefore, since we are receiving a kingdom that cannot be shaken, let us be thankful, and so worship God acceptably with reverence and awe, for our 'God is a consuming fire.'" This reverence and awe is exactly what the fear of God means for Christians. This is the motivating factor for us to surrender to the Creator of the Universe.

Proverbs 1:7 declares, "The fear of the Lord is the beginning of knowledge." Until we understand who God is and develop a reverential fear of Him, we cannot have true wisdom. True wisdom comes only from understanding who God is and that He is holy, just, and righteous. Deuteronomy 10:12, 20-21 records, "And now, O Israel, what does the Lord your God ask of you but to fear the Lord your God, to walk in all his ways, to love him, to serve the Lord your God with all your heart and with all your soul. Fear the Lord your God and serve him. Hold fast to him and take your oaths in his name. He is your praise; he is your God, who performed for you those great and awesome wonders you saw with your own eyes." The fear of God is the basis for our walking in His ways, serving Him, and, yes, loving Him.

Some redefine the fear of God for believers to "respecting" Him. While respect is definitely included in the concept of fearing God, there is more to it than that. A biblical fear of God, for the believer, includes understanding how much God hates sin and fearing His judgment on sin—even in the life of a believer. Hebrews 12:5-11 describes God's discipline of the believer. While it is done in love (Hebrews 12:6), it is still a fearful thing. As children, the fear of discipline from our parents no doubt prevented some evil actions. The same should be true in our relationship with God. We should fear His discipline, and therefore seek to live our lives in such a way that pleases Him.

Believers are not to be scared of God. We have no reason to be scared of Him. We have His promise that nothing can separate us from His love (Romans 8:38-39). We have His promise that He will never leave us or forsake us (Hebrews 13:5). Fearing God means having such a reverence for Him that it has a great impact on the way we live our lives. The fear of God is respecting Him, obeying Him, submitting to His discipline, and worshipping Him in awe.

Question: Does God change His mind?

Answer: Malachi 3:6 declares, "I the Lord do not change. So you, O descendants of Jacob, are not destroyed." Similarly, James 1:17 tells us, "Every good and perfect gift is from above, coming down from the Father of the heavenly lights, who does not change like shifting shadows." The meaning of Numbers 23:19 could not be more clear: "God is not a man, that He should lie, nor a son of man, that He should change His mind. Does He speak and then not act? Does He promise and not fulfill?" No, God does not change His mind. These verses assert that God is unchanging and unchangeable.

How then do we explain verses such as Genesis 6:6, "The LORD was grieved that He had made man on the earth, and His heart was filled with pain"? Also, Jonah 3:10, which says, "When God saw what they did and how they turned from their evil ways, He had compassion and did not bring upon them the destruction He had threatened." Similarly, Exodus 32:14 proclaims, "Then the LORD relented and did not bring on His people the disaster He had threatened." These verses speak of the Lord "repenting" of something and seem to contradict the doctrine of God's immutability. However, close examination of these passages reveals that these are not truly indications that God is capable of changing. In the original language, the word that is translated as "repent" or "relent" is the Hebrew expression "to be sorry for." Being sorry for something does not mean that a change has occurred; it simply means there is regret for something that has taken place.

Consider Genesis 6:6: "…the LORD was grieved that He had made man on the earth." This verse even goes on to say "His heart was filled with pain." This verse declares that God had regret for creating man. However, obviously He did not reverse His decision. Instead, through Noah, He allowed man to continue to exist. The fact that we are alive today is proof that God did not change His mind about creating man. Also, the context of this passage is a description of the sinful state in which man was living, and it is man's sinfulness that triggered God's sorrow, not man's existence. Consider Jonah 3:10: "…He had compassion and did not bring upon them the destruction He had threatened." Again, the same Hebrew word is used, which translates "to be sorry for." Why was God sorry for what He had planned for the Ninevites? Because they had a change in heart and as a result changed their ways from disobedience to obedience. God is entirely consistent. God was going to judge Nineveh because of its evil. However, Nineveh repented and changed its ways. As a result, God had mercy on Nineveh, which is entirely consistent with His character.

Romans 3:23 teaches us that all men sin and fall short of God's standard. Romans 6:23 states that the consequence for this is death (spiritual and physical). So the people of Nineveh were deserving of punishment. All of us face this same situation; it is man's choosing to sin that separates us from God. Man cannot hold God responsible for his own predicament. So it would be contrary to the character of God to not punish the Ninevites had they continued in sin. However, the people of Nineveh turned to obedience, and for that the Lord chose not to punish them as He had originally intended. Did the change on the part of the Ninevites obligate God to do what He did? Absolutely not! God cannot be placed in a position of obligation to man. God is good and righteous, and chose not to punish the Ninevites as a result of their change of heart. If anything, what this passage does is point to the fact that God does not change, because had the Lord not preserved the Ninevites, it would have been contrary to His character.

The Scriptures that are interpreted as God seeming to change His mind are human attempts to explain the actions of God. God was going to do something, but instead did something else. To us, that sounds like a change. But to God, who is omniscient and sovereign, it is not a change. God always knew what He was going to do. God does what He needs to do to cause humanity to fulfill His perfect plan. "…declaring the end from the beginning, and from the past things which were not done, saying, My purpose shall stand, and I will do all My pleasure … What I have said, that will I bring about; what I have planned, that will I do" (Isaiah 46:10-11). God threatened Nineveh with destruction, knowing that it would cause Nineveh to repent. God threatened Israel with destruction, knowing that Moses would intercede. God does not regret His decisions, but He is saddened by some of what man sometimes does in response to His decisions. God does not change His mind but rather acts consistently with His Word in response to our actions.

Question: Does God love everyone or just Christians?

Answer: There is a sense in which God loves everyone in the whole world (John 3:16; 1 John 2:2; Romans 5:8). This love in not conditional—it is based only on the fact that God is a God of love (1 John 4:8, 16). God's love for all of mankind results in the fact that

God shows His mercy by not immediately punishing people for their sins (Romans 3:23; 6:23). God's love for the world is manifested in the fact that He gives people the opportunity to repent (2 Peter 3:9). However, God's love for the world does not mean He will ignore sin. God is also a God of justice (2 Thessalonians 1:6). Sin cannot go unpunished forever (Romans 3:25-26).

The most loving act of eternity is described in Romans 5:8, "But God demonstrates His own love for us in this: While we were still sinners, Christ died for us." Anyone who ignores God's love, who rejects Christ as Savior, who denies the Savior who bought him (2 Peter 2:1) will be subject to God's wrath for eternity (Romans 1:18), not His love (Romans 6:23). God loves everyone unconditionally in that He shows mercy to everyone by not destroying them immediately because of sin. At the same time, God only has "covenant love" for those who place their faith in Jesus Christ for salvation (John 3:36). Only those who believe in Jesus Christ as their Lord and Savior will experience God's love for eternity.

Does God love everyone? Yes. Does God love Christians more than He loves non-Christians? No. Does God love Christians to a different extent than He loves non-Christians? Yes. God loves everyone equally in that He is merciful to all. God only loves Christians in that only Christians have His eternal grace and mercy and the promise of His forever love in heaven. The unconditional love God has for everyone should bring us to faith in Him, receiving in thankfulness the great conditional love He grants all those who receive Jesus Christ as Savior.

Question: Is God male or female?

Answer: In examining Scripture, two facts become clear. First, God is a Spirit and does not possess human characteristics or limitations. Second, all the evidence contained in Scripture agrees that God revealed Himself to mankind in a male form. To begin, God's true nature needs to be understood. God is a Person, obviously, because God exhibits all the characteristics of personhood: God has a mind, a will, an intellect, and emotions. God communicates and He has relationships, and God's personal actions are evidenced throughout Scripture.

As John 4:24 states, "God is spirit, and his worshipers must worship in spirit and in truth." Since God is a spiritual being, He does not possess physical human characteristics. However, sometimes figurative language used in Scripture assigns human characteristics to God in order to make it possible for man to understand God. This assignment of human characteristics to describe God is called "anthropomorphism." Anthropomorphism is simply a means for God (a spiritual being) to communicate truth about His nature to humanity, physical beings. Since humanity is physical, we are limited in our understanding of those things beyond the physical realm; therefore, anthropomorphism in Scripture helps us to understand who God is.

Some of the difficulty comes in examining the fact that humanity is created in God's image. Genesis 1:26-27 says, "Then God said, 'Let us make man in our image, in our likeness, and let them rule over the fish of the sea and the birds of the air, over the livestock, over all the earth, and over all the creatures that move along the ground.' So God created man in his own image, in the image of God he created him; male and female he created them."

Both man and woman are created in the image of God, in that they are greater than all the other creations as they, like God, have a mind, will, intellect, emotions, and moral capacity. Animals do not possess a moral capacity and do not possess an immaterial component like humanity does. The image of God is the spiritual component that humanity alone possesses. God created humanity to have a relationship with Him. Humanity is the only creation designed for that purpose.

That said, man and woman are only patterned after the image of God—they are not tiny "copies" of God. The fact that there are men and women does not require God to have male and female features. Remember, being made in the image of God has nothing to do with physical characteristics.

We know that God is a spiritual being and does not possess physical characteristics. This does not limit, however, how God may choose to reveal Himself to humanity. Scripture contains all the revelation God gave to humanity about Himself, and so it is the only objective source of information about God. In looking at what

Scripture tells us, there are several observations of evidence about the form in which God revealed Himself to humanity.

Scripture contains approximately 170 references to God as the "Father." By necessity, one cannot be a father unless one is male. If God had chosen to be revealed to man in a female form, then the word "mother" would have occurred in these places, not "father." In the Old and New Testaments, masculine pronouns are used over and over again in reference to God.

Jesus Christ referred to God as the Father several times and in other cases used masculine pronouns in reference to God. In the Gospels alone, Christ uses the term "Father" in direct reference to God nearly 160 times. Of particular interest is Christ's statement in John 10:30: "I and the Father are one." Obviously, Jesus Christ came in the form of a human man to die on the cross as payment for the sins of the world. Like God the Father, Jesus was revealed to humanity in a male form. Scripture records numerous other instances where Christ utilized masculine nouns and pronouns in reference to God.

The New Testament Epistles (from Acts to Revelation) also contain nearly 900 verses where the word *theos*—a masculine noun in the Greek—is used in direct reference to God. In countless references to God in Scripture, there is clearly a consistent pattern of His being referred to with masculine titles, nouns, and pronouns. While God is not a man, He chose a masculine form in order to reveal Himself to humanity. Likewise, Jesus Christ, who is constantly referred to with masculine titles, nouns, and pronouns, took a male form while He walked on the earth. The prophets of the Old Testament and the apostles of the New Testament refer to both God and Jesus Christ with masculine names and titles. God chose to be revealed in this form in order for man to more easily grasp who He is. While God makes allowances in order to help us understand Him, it is important to not try to "force God into a box," so to speak, by placing limitations on Him that are not appropriate to His nature.

Question: Does God still perform miracles?

Answer: Many people desire God to perform miracles to "prove" Himself to them. "If only God would perform a miracle, sign, or wonder, then I would believe!" This idea, though, is contradicted by Scripture. When God performed amazing and powerful miracles for the Israelites, did that cause them to obey Him? No, the Israelites constantly disobeyed and rebelled against God even though they saw all the miracles. The same people who saw God part the Red Sea later doubted whether God was able to conquer the inhabitants of the Promised Land. This truth is explained in Luke 16:19-31. In the story, a man in hell asks Abraham to send Lazarus back from the dead to warn his brothers. Abraham informed the man, "If they do not listen to Moses and the Prophets, they will not be convinced even if someone rises from the dead" (Luke 16:31).

Jesus performed countless miracles, yet the vast majority of people did not believe in Him. If God performed miracles today as He did in the past, the result would be the same. People would be amazed and would believe in God for a short time. That faith would be shallow and would disappear the moment something unexpected or frightening occurred. A faith based on miracles is not a mature faith. God performed the greatest miracle of all time in coming to earth as the Man Jesus Christ to die on the cross for our sins (Romans 5:8) so that we could be saved (John 3:16). God does still perform miracles—many of them simply go unnoticed or are denied. However, we do not need more miracles. What we need is to believe in the miracle of salvation through faith in Jesus Christ.

The purpose of miracles was to authenticate the performer of the miracles. Acts 2:22 declares, "Men of Israel, listen to this: Jesus of Nazareth was a man accredited by God to you by miracles, wonders and signs, which God did among you through him, as you yourselves know." The same is said of the apostles, "The things that mark an apostle—signs, wonders and miracles—were done among you with great perseverance" (2 Corinthians 12:12). Speaking of the gospel, Hebrews 2:4 proclaims, "God also testified to it by signs, wonders and various miracles, and gifts of the Holy Spirit distributed according to His will." We now have the truth of Jesus recorded in Scripture. We now have the writings of the apostles recorded in Scripture. Jesus and His apostles, as recorded in Scripture, are the cornerstone and foundation of our faith (Ephesians 2:20). In this sense, miracles are no longer necessary, as the message of Jesus and His apostles has already been attested to and accurately recorded in the Scriptures. Yes, God still performs miracles. At the same time, we should not necessarily expect miracles to occur today just as they did in Bible times.

Question: Why does God allow natural disasters?

Answer: Why does God allow earthquakes, tornados, hurricanes, tsunamis, typhoons, cyclones, mudslides, and other natural disasters? The late 2004 tsunami tragedy in Asia, Hurricane Katrina in 2005 in the southeastern United States, and the 2008 cyclone in Myanmar had many people questioning God's goodness. It is distressing that natural disasters are often termed "acts of God" while no "credit" is given to God for years, decades, or even centuries of peaceful weather. God created the whole universe and the laws of nature (Genesis 1:1). Most natural disasters are a result of these laws at work. Hurricanes, typhoons, and tornados are the results of divergent weather patterns colliding. Earthquakes are the result of the earth's plate structure shifting. A tsunami is caused by an underwater earthquake.

The Bible proclaims that Jesus Christ holds all of nature together (Colossians 1:16-17). Could God prevent natural disasters? Absolutely! Does God sometimes influence the weather? Yes, as we see in Deuteronomy 11:17 and James 5:17. Numbers 16:30-34 shows us that God sometimes causes natural disasters as a judgment against sin. The book of Revelation describes many events which could definitely be described as natural disasters (Revelation chapters 6, 8, and 16). Is every natural disaster a punishment from God? Absolutely not.

In much the same way that God allows evil people to commit evil acts, God allows the earth to reflect the consequences sin has had on creation. Romans 8:19-21 tells us, "The creation waits in eager expectation for the sons of God to be revealed. For the creation was subjected to frustration, not by its own choice, but by the will of the one who subjected it, in hope that the creation itself will be liberated from its bondage to decay and brought into the glorious freedom of the children of God." The fall of humanity into sin had effects on everything, including the world we inhabit. Everything in creation is subject to "frustration" and "decay." Sin is the ultimate cause of natural disasters just as it is the cause of death, disease, and suffering.

We can understand why natural disasters occur. What we do not understand is why God allows them to occur. Why did God allow the tsunami to kill over 225,000 people in Asia? Why did God allow Hurricane Katrina to destroy the homes of thousands of people? For one thing, such events shake our confidence in this life and force us to think about eternity. Churches are usually filled after disasters as people realize how tenuous their lives really are and how life can be taken away in an instant. What we do know is this: God is good! Many amazing miracles occurred during the course of natural disasters that prevented even greater loss of life. Natural disasters cause millions of people to reevaluate their priorities in life. Hundreds of millions of dollars in aid is sent to help the people who are suffering. Christian ministries have the opportunity to help, minister, counsel, pray, and lead people to saving faith in Christ! God can, and does, bring great good out of terrible tragedies (Romans 8:28).

Question: Is God sexist?

Answer: Sexism is one gender, usually male, having dominance over the other gender, usually female. The Bible contains many references to women that, to our modern mindset, sound discriminatory towards women. But we have to remember that when the Bible describes an action, it does not necessarily mean that the Bible endorses that action. The Bible describes men treating women as little more than property, but that does not mean God approves of that action. The Bible is far more focused on reforming our souls than our societies. God knows that a changed heart will result in a changed behavior.

During Old Testament times, virtually every culture in the entire world was patriarchal in structure. That status of history is very clear—not only in Scripture but also in the rules that governed most societies. By modern value systems and worldly human viewpoint, that is called "sexist." God ordained the order in society, not man, and He is the author of the establishment principles of authority. However, like everything else, fallen man has corrupted this order. That has resulted in the inequality of the standing of men and women throughout history. The exclusion and the discrimination that we find in our world is nothing new. It is the result of the fall of man and the introduction of sin. Therefore, we can rightly say that the term and the practice of "sexism" is a result of sin. The progressive revelation of the Bible leads us to the cure for sexism and indeed all the sinful practices of the human race.

To find and maintain a spiritual balance between the God-ordained positions of authority, we must look to Scripture. The New Testament is the fulfillment of the Old, and in it we find principles that tell us the correct line of authority and the cure for sin, the ill of all humanity, and that includes discrimination based upon gender.

The cross of Christ is the great equalizer. John 3:16 says, "Whoever believes," and that is an all-inclusive statement that leaves no one out on the basis of position in society, mental capacity, or gender. We also find a passage in Galatians that speaks of our equal opportunity for salvation. "You are all sons of God through faith in Christ Jesus, for all of you who were baptized into Christ have clothed yourselves with Christ. There is neither Jew nor Greek, slave nor free, male nor female, for you are all one in Christ Jesus" (Galatians 3:26-28). There is no sexism at the cross.

The Bible is not sexist in its accurate portrayal of the results of sin in both men and women. The Bible records all kinds of sin: slavery and bondage and the failures of its greatest heroes. Yet it also gives us the answer and the cure for those sins against God and His established order—a right relationship with God. The Old Testament was looking forward to the supreme sacrifice, and each time a sacrifice for sin was made, it was teaching the need for reconciliation to God. In the New Testament, the "Lamb that takes away the sin of the world" was born, died, was buried and rose again, and then ascended to His place in heaven, and there He intercedes for us. It is through belief in Him that the cure for sin is found, and that includes the sin of sexism.

The charge of sexism in the Bible is based upon a lack of knowledge of Scripture. When men and women of all ages have taken their God-ordained places and lived according to "thus says the LORD," then there is a wonderful balance between the genders. That balance is what God began with, and it is what He will end with. There is an inordinate amount of attention paid to the various products of sin and not to the root of it. It is only when there is personal reconciliation with God through the Lord Jesus Christ that we find true equality. "Then you will know the truth, and the truth will set you free" (John 8:32).

It is also very important to understand that the Bible's ascribing different roles to men and women does not constitute sexism. The Bible makes it abundantly clear that God expects men to take the leadership role in the church and the home. Does this make women inferior? Absolutely not. Does this mean women are less intelligent, less capable, or viewed as less in God's eyes? Absolutely not! What it means is that in our sin-stained world, there has to be structure and authority. God has instituted the roles of authority for our good. Sexism is the abuse of these roles, not the existence of these roles.

Question: Does God answer the prayers of an unbeliever?

Answer: John 9:31 declares, "We know that God does not listen to sinners. He listens to the godly man who does his will." It has also been said that "the only prayer that God hears from a sinner is the prayer for salvation." As a result, some believe that God does not hear and/or will never answer the prayers of an unbeliever. In context, though, John 9:31 is saying that God does not perform miracles through an unbeliever. First John 5:14-15 tells us that God answers prayers based on whether they are asked according to His will. This principle, perhaps, applies to unbelievers. If an unbeliever asks a prayer of God that is according to His will, nothing prevents God from answering such a prayer—according to His will.

Some Scriptures describe God hearing and answering the prayers of unbelievers. In most of these cases, prayer was involved. In one or two, God responded to the cry of the heart (it is not stated whether that cry was directed toward God). In some of these cases, the prayer seems to be combined with repentance. But in other cases, the prayer was simply for an earthly need or blessing, and God responded either out of compassion or in response to the genuine seeking or the faith of the person. Here are some passages dealing with prayer by an unbeliever:

The people of Nineveh prayed that Nineveh might be spared (Jonah 3:5-10). God answered this prayer and did not destroy the city of Nineveh as He had threatened.

Hagar asked God to protect her son Ishmael (Genesis 21:14-19). God not only protected Ishmael, God blessed him exceedingly.

In 1 Kings 21:17-29, especially verses 27-29, Ahab fasts and mourns over Elijah's prophecy concerning his posterity. God responds by not bringing about the calamity in Ahab's time.

The Gentile woman from the Tyre and Sidon area prayed that Jesus would deliver her daughter from a demon (Mark 7:24-30). Jesus cast the demon out of the woman's daughter.

Cornelius, the Roman centurion in Acts 10, had the apostle Peter sent to him in response to Cornelius being a righteous man. Acts 10:2 tells us that Cornelius "prayed to God regularly."

God does make promises that are applicable to all (saved and unsaved alike) such as Jeremiah 29:13: "You will seek me and find me when you seek me with all your heart." This was the case for Cornelius in Acts 10:1-6. But there are many promises that, according to the context of the passages, are for Christians alone. Because Christians have received Jesus as the Savior, they are encouraged to come boldly to the throne of grace to find help in time of need (Hebrews 4:14-16). We are told that when we ask for anything according to God's will, He hears and gives us what we ask for (1 John 5:14-15). There are many other promises for Christians concerning prayer (Matthew 21:22; John 14:13, 15:7). So, yes, there are instances in which God does not answer the prayers of an unbeliever. At the same time, in His grace and mercy, God can intervene in the lives of unbelievers in response to their prayers.

Question: Why is God a jealous God?

Answer: It is important to understand how the word "jealous" is used. Its use in Exodus 20:5 to describe God is different from how it is used to describe the sin of jealousy (Galatians 5:20). When we use the word "jealous," we use it in the sense of being envious of someone who has something we do not have. A person might be jealous or envious of another person because he or she has a nice car or home (possessions). Or a person might be jealous or envious of another person because of some ability or skill that other person has (such as athletic ability). Another example would be that one person might be jealous or envious of another because of his or her beauty.

In Exodus 20:5, it is not that God is jealous or envious because someone has something He wants or needs. Exodus 20:4-5 says, "You shall not make for yourself an idol in the form of anything in heaven above or on the earth beneath or in the waters below. You shall not bow down to them or worship them; for I, the LORD your God, am a jealous God..." Notice that God is jealous when someone gives to another something that rightly belongs to Him.

In these verses, God is speaking of people making idols and bowing down and worshiping those idols instead of giving God the worship that belongs to Him alone. God is possessive of the worship and service that belong to Him. It is a sin (as God points out in this commandment) to worship or serve anything other than God. It is a sin when we desire, or we are envious, or we are jealous of someone because he has something that we do not have. It is a different use of the word "jealous" when God says He is jealous. What He is jealous of belongs to Him; worship and service belong to Him alone, and are to be given to Him alone.

Perhaps a practical example will help us understand the difference. If a husband sees another man flirting with his wife, he is right to be jealous, for only he has the right to flirt with his wife. This type of jealousy is not sinful. Rather, it is entirely appropriate. Being jealous for something that God declares to belong to you is good and appropriate. Jealousy is a sin when it is a desire for something that does not belong to you. Worship, praise, honor, and adoration belong to God alone, for only He is truly worthy of it. Therefore, God is rightly jealous when worship, praise, honor, or adoration is given to idols. This is precisely the jealousy the apostle Paul described in 2 Corinthians 11:2, "I am jealous for you with a godly jealousy..."

Question: Can monotheism be proven?

Answer: The word "monotheism" comes from two words, "mono" meaning "single" and "theism" meaning "belief in God." Specifically, monotheism is the belief in one true God who is the only creator, sustainer, and judge of all creation. Monotheism differs from "henotheism," which is the belief in multiple gods with one supreme God over all. It is also opposed to polytheism, which is the belief in the existence of more than one god.

There are many arguments for monotheism, including those from special revelation (Scripture), natural revelation (philosophy), as well as historical anthropology. These will only be explained briefly below, and this should not in any way be considered an exhaustive list.

Biblical arguments for Monotheism - Deuteronomy 4:35: "You were shown these things so that you might know that the LORD is God; besides Him there is no other." Deuteronomy 6:4: "Hear, O Israel: The LORD our God, the LORD is one." Malachi 2:10a, "Have we not all one Father? Did not one God create us?" 1 Corinthians 8:6: "Yet for us there is but one God, the Father, from whom all things came and for whom we live; and there is but one Lord, Jesus Christ, through whom all things came and through whom we live." Ephesians 4:6: "One God and Father of all, who is over all and through all and in all." 1 Timothy 2:5: "For there is one God and one mediator between God and men, the man Christ Jesus." James 2:19: "You believe that there is one God. Good! Even the demons believe that—and shudder."

Obviously, for many people, it wouldn't suffice to simply say that there is only one God because the Bible says so. This is because without God there is no way to prove that the Bible is His Word in the first place. However, one might argue that since the Bible has the most reliable supernatural evidence confirming what it teaches, monotheism can be affirmed on these grounds. A similar argument would be the beliefs and teaching of Jesus Christ, who proved that He was God (or at the very least approved by God) by His miraculous birth, life, and the miracle of His resurrection. God cannot lie or be deceived; therefore, what Jesus believed and taught was true. Therefore, monotheism, which Jesus believed and taught, is true. This argument may not be very impressive to those unfamiliar with the case for the supernatural confirmations of Scripture and Christ, but this is a good place to start for one who is familiar with its strength.

Historical arguments for Monotheism - Arguments based on popularity are notoriously suspect, but it is interesting just how much monotheism has affected world religions. The popular evolutionary theory of religious development stems from an evolutionary view of reality in general, and the presupposition of evolutionary anthropology which sees "primitive" cultures as representing the earlier stages of religious development. But the problems with this evolutionary theory are several. 1) The kind of development it describes has never been observed; in fact, there seems to be no upward development toward monotheism within any culture—actually the opposite seems to be the case. 2) The anthropological method's definition of "primitive" equates to technological development, yet this is hardly a satisfactory criterion as there are so many components to a given culture. 3) The alleged stages are often missing or skipped. 4) Finally, most polytheistic cultures show vestiges of monotheism early in their development.

What we find is a monotheistic God who is personal, masculine, lives in the sky, has great knowledge and power, created the world, is the author of a morality to which we are accountable, and whom we have disobeyed and are thus estranged from, but who has also provided a way of reconciliation. Virtually every religion carries a variation of this God at some point in its past before devolving into the chaos of polytheism. Thus, it seems that most religions have begun in monotheism and "devolved" into polytheism, animism, and magic—not vice versa. (Islam is a very rare case, having come full circle back into a monotheistic belief.) Even with this movement, polytheism is often functionally monotheistic or henotheistic. It is a rare polytheistic religion which does not hold one of its gods as sovereign over the rest, with the lesser gods only functioning as intermediaries.

Philosophical/Theological arguments for Monotheism - There are many philosophical arguments for the impossibility of there being more than one God in existence. Many of these depend a great deal on one's metaphysical position concerning the nature of reality. Unfortunately, in an article this short it would be impossible to argue for these basic metaphysical positions and then go on to show what they point to regarding monotheism, but rest assured that there are strong philosophical and theological grounds for these truths that go back millennia (and most are fairly self-evident). Briefly, then, here are three arguments one might choose to explore:

1. If there were more than one God, the universe would be in disorder because of multiple creators and authorities, but it is not in disorder; therefore, there is only one God.

33

2. Since God is a completely perfect being, there cannot be a second God, for they would have to differ in some way, and to differ from complete perfection is to be less than perfect and not be God.

3. Since God is infinite in His existence, He cannot have parts (for parts cannot be added to reach infinity). If God's existence is not just a part of Him (which it is for all things which can have existence or not), then He must have infinite existence. Therefore, there cannot be two infinite beings, for one would have to differ from the other.

Someone may wish to argue that many of these would not rule out a sub-class of "gods," and that is fine. Although we know this to be untrue biblically, there is nothing wrong with it in theory. In other words, God could have created a sub-class of "gods," but it just happens to be the case that He did not. If He had, these "gods" would only be limited, created things—probably a lot like angels (Psalm 82). This does not hurt the case for monotheism, which does not say that there cannot be any other spirit beings—only that there cannot be more than one God.

Question: Is it wrong to question God?

Answer: At issue is not whether we should question God, but in what manner—and for what reason—we question Him. To question God is not in itself wrong. The prophet Habakkuk had questions for God concerning the timing and agency of the Lord's plan. Habakkuk, rather than being rebuked for his questions, is patiently answered, and the prophet ends his book with a song of praise to the Lord. Many questions are put to God in the Psalms (Psalms 10, 44, 74, 77). These are the cries of the persecuted who are desperate for God's intervention and salvation. Although God does not always answer our questions in the way we want, we conclude from these passages that a sincere question from an earnest heart is welcomed by God.

Insincere questions, or questions from a hypocritical heart, are a different matter. "And without faith it is impossible to please God, because anyone who comes to him must believe that he exists and that he rewards those who earnestly seek him" (Hebrews 11:6). After King

Saul had disobeyed God, his questions went unanswered (1 Samuel 28:6). It is entirely different to wonder why God allowed a certain event than it is to directly question God's goodness. Having doubts is different from questioning God's sovereignty and attacking His character. In short, an honest question is not a sin, but a bitter, untrusting, or rebellious heart is. God is not intimidated by questions. God invites us to enjoy close fellowship with Him. When we "question God," it should be from a humble spirit and open mind. We can question God, but we should not expect an answer unless we are genuinely interested in His answer. God knows our hearts, and knows whether we are genuinely seeking Him to enlighten us. Our heart attitude is what determines whether it is right or wrong to question God.

Question: Has anyone ever seen God?

Answer: The Bible tells us that no one has ever seen God (John 1:18) except the Lord Jesus Christ. In Exodus 33:20, God declares, "You cannot see my face, for no one may see me and live." These Scriptures seem to contradict other Scriptures which describe various people "seeing" God. For example, Exodus 33:19-23 describes Moses speaking to God "face to face." How could Moses speak with God "face to face" if no one can see God's face and live? In this instance, the phrase "face to face" is a figure of speech indicating they were in very close communion. God and Moses were speaking to each other as if they were two human beings having a close conversation.

In Genesis 32:30, Jacob saw God appearing as an angel; he did not truly see God. Samson's parents were terrified when they realized they had seen God (Judges 13:22), but they had only seen Him appearing as an angel. Jesus was God in the flesh (John 1:1, 14) so when people saw Him, they were seeing God. So, yes, God can be "seen" and many people have "seen" God. At the same time, no one has ever seen God revealed in all His glory. In our fallen human condition, if God were to fully reveal Himself to us, we would be consumed and destroyed. Therefore, God veils Himself and appears in forms in which we can "see" Him. However, this is different than seeing God with all His glory and holiness displayed. People have seen visions of God, images of God, and appearances of God, but no one has ever seen God in all His fullness (Exodus 33:20).

Chapter 2

QUESTIONS ABOUT

JESUS CHRIST

CONTENTS

Who is Jesus Christ? 38

Is Jesus God? Did Jesus ever claim to be God?......................... 40

Is the deity of Christ biblical?... 41

Did Jesus really exist? Is there any historical evidence of Jesus Christ?.... 43

Is Jesus a myth? Is Jesus just a copy of the pagan gods of other ancient
    religions?... 46

Is the resurrection of Jesus Christ true? 51

What does it mean that Jesus is the Son of God? 53

Why is the virgin birth so important?.................................. 54

Did Jesus go to hell between His death and resurrection? 54

Was Jesus crucified on a Friday? If so, how did He spend three days in
    the tomb if He was resurrected on Sunday?......................... 56

Was Jesus ever angry? 59

Could Jesus have sinned?.. 60

Why are Jesus' genealogies in Matthew and Luke so different? 62

What is the hypostatic union? How can Jesus be both God and man at
    the same time? 63

Was Jesus Christ married? 64

If Jesus was God, how could He pray to God? Was Jesus praying to
    Himself?... 65

Did Jesus have brothers and sisters?................................... 67

Why did Jesus have to experience so much suffering?................... 68

What does it mean that Jesus is the Lamb of God? 69

Where does the Old Testament predict the coming of Christ?........... 70

What does it mean that Jesus is the Son of Man?...................... 72

Why did God send Jesus when He did? Why not earlier or later?........... 72

Question: Who is Jesus Christ?

Answer: Unlike the question "Does God exist?" very few people question whether Jesus Christ existed. It is generally accepted that Jesus was truly a man who walked on the earth in Israel 2000 years ago. The debate begins when the subject of Jesus' full identity is discussed. Almost every major religion teaches that Jesus was a prophet or a good teacher or a godly man. The problem is that the Bible tells us that Jesus was infinitely more than a prophet, a good teacher, or a godly man.

C.S. Lewis in his book *Mere Christianity* writes the following: "I am trying here to prevent anyone from saying the really foolish thing that people often say about Him [Jesus Christ]: 'I'm ready to accept Jesus as a great moral teacher, but I don't accept his claim to be God.' That is the one thing we must not say. A man who was merely a man and said the sort of things Jesus said would not be a great moral teacher. He would either be a lunatic—on a level with a man who says he is a poached egg—or else he would be the Devil of hell. You must make your choice. Either this man was, and is, the Son of God, or else a madman or something worse. You can shut him up for fool, you can spit at him and kill him as a demon; or you can fall at his feet and call him Lord and God. But let us not come up with any patronizing nonsense about his being a great human teacher. He has not left that option open to us. He did not intend to."

So, who did Jesus claim to be? Who does the Bible say He is? First, let's look at Jesus' words in John 10:30, "I and the Father are one." At first glance, this might not seem to be a claim to be God. However, look at the Jews' reaction to His statement, "'We are not stoning you for any of these,' replied the Jews, 'but for blasphemy, because you, a mere man, claim to be God'" (John 10:33). The Jews understood Jesus' statement as a claim to be God. In the following verses, Jesus never corrects the Jews by saying, "I did not claim to be God." That indicates Jesus was truly saying He was God by declaring, "I and the Father are one" (John 10:30). John 8:58 is another example: "'I tell you the truth,' Jesus answered, 'before Abraham was born, I am!'" Again, in response, the Jews took up stones in an attempt to stone Jesus (John 8:59). Jesus' announcing His identity as "I am" is a direct application of the Old Testament name for God (Exodus 3:14). Why would the Jews again want to stone Jesus if He had not said something they believed to be blasphemous, namely, a claim to be God?

John 1:1 says "the Word was God." John 1:14 says "the Word became flesh." This clearly indicates that Jesus is God in the flesh. Thomas the disciple declared to Jesus, "My Lord and my God" (John 20:28). Jesus does not correct him. The apostle Paul describes Him as, "...our great God and Savior, Jesus Christ" (Titus 2:13). The apostle Peter says the same, "...our God and Savior Jesus Christ" (2 Peter 1:1). God the Father is witness of Jesus' full identity as well, "But about the Son he says, 'Your throne, O God, will last forever and ever, and righteousness will be the scepter of your kingdom.'" Old Testament prophecies of Christ announce His deity, "For to us a child is born, to us a son is given, and the government will be on his shoulders. And he will be called Wonderful Counselor, Mighty God, Everlasting Father, Prince of Peace" (Isaiah 9:6).

So, as C.S. Lewis argued, believing Jesus to be only a good teacher is not an option. Jesus clearly and undeniably claimed to be God. If He is not God, then He is a liar, and therefore not a prophet, good teacher, or godly man. In attempts to explain away the words of Jesus, modern "scholars" claim the "true historical Jesus" did not say many of the things the Bible attributes to Him. Who are we to argue with God's Word concerning what Jesus did or did not say? How can a "scholar" two thousand years removed from Jesus have better insight into what Jesus did or did not say than those who lived with, served with, and were taught by Jesus Himself (John 14:26)?

Why is the question over Jesus' true identity so important? Why does it matter whether or not Jesus is God? The most important reason that Jesus has to be God is that if He is not God, His death would not have been sufficient to pay the penalty for the sins of the whole world (1 John 2:2). Only God could pay such an infinite penalty (Romans 5:8; 2 Corinthians 5:21). Jesus had to be God so that He could pay our debt. Jesus had to be man so He could die. Salvation is available only through faith in Jesus Christ. Jesus' deity is why He is the only way of salvation. Jesus' deity is why He proclaimed, "I am the way and the truth and the life. No one comes to the Father except through me" (John 14:6).

Question: Is Jesus God? Did Jesus ever claim to be God?

Answer: Jesus is never recorded in the Bible as saying the precise words, "I am God." That does not mean, however, that He did not proclaim that He is God. Take for example Jesus' words in John 10:30, "I and the Father are one." We need only to look at the Jews' reaction to His statement to know He was claiming to be God. They tried to stone Him for this very reason. "… you, a mere man, claim to be God" (John 10:33). The Jews understood exactly what Jesus was claiming—deity. Notice that Jesus does not deny His claim to be God. When Jesus declared, "I and the Father are one" (John 10:30), He was saying that He and the Father are of one nature and essence. John 8:58 is another example. Jesus declared, "I tell you the truth, before Abraham was born, I am!" The response of the Jews who heard this statement was to take up stones to kill Him for blasphemy, as the Mosaic Law commanded them to do (Leviticus 24:15).

John reiterates the concept of Jesus' deity: "the Word was God" and "the Word became flesh" (John 1:1, 14). These verses clearly indicate that Jesus is God in the flesh. Acts 20:28 tells us, "Be shepherds of the church of God, which he bought with his own blood." Who bought the church—the church of God—with His own blood? Jesus Christ. Acts 20:28 declares that God purchased His church with *His own* blood. Therefore, Jesus is God!

Thomas the disciple declared concerning Jesus, "My Lord and my God" (John 20:28). Jesus does not correct him. Titus 2:13 encourages us to wait for the coming of our God and Savior, Jesus Christ (see also 2 Peter 1:1). In Hebrews 1:8, the Father declares of Jesus, "But about the Son He says, 'Your throne, O God, will last forever and ever, and righteousness will be the scepter of your kingdom.'" The Father refers to Jesus as "O God" indicating that Jesus is indeed God.

In Revelation, an angel instructed the apostle John to only worship God (Revelation 19:10). Several times in Scripture Jesus receives worship (Matthew 2:11, 14:33, 28:9, 17; Luke 24:52; John 9:38). He never rebukes people for worshiping Him. If Jesus were not God, He would have told people to not worship Him, just as the angel in Revelation did. There are many other verses and passages of Scripture that argue for Jesus' deity.

The most important reason that Jesus has to be God is that if He is not God, His death would not have been sufficient to pay the penalty for the sins of the world (1 John 2:2). A created being, which Jesus would be if He were not God, could not pay the infinite penalty required for sin against an infinite God. Only God could pay such an infinite penalty. Only God could take on the sins of the world (2 Corinthians 5:21), die, and be resurrected, proving His victory over sin and death.

Question: Is the deity of Christ biblical?

Answer: In addition to Jesus' specific claims about Himself, His disciples also acknowledged the deity of Christ. They claimed that Jesus had the right to forgive sins—something only God can do—as it is God who is offended by sin (Acts 5:31; Colossians 3:13; Psalm 130:4; Jeremiah 31:34). In close connection with this last claim, Jesus is also said to be the one who will "judge the living and the dead" (2 Timothy 4:1). Thomas cried out to Jesus, "My Lord and my God!" (John 20:28). Paul calls Jesus "great God and Savior" (Titus 2:13) and points out that prior to His incarnation Jesus existed in the "form of God" (Philippians 2:5-8). God the Father says regarding Jesus: "Your throne, O God, will last forever and ever" (Hebrews 1:8). John states that "in the beginning was the Word, and the Word was with God, and the Word [Jesus] was God" (John 1:1). Examples of Scriptures that teach the deity of Christ are many (see Revelation 1:17, 2:8, 22:13; 1 Corinthians 10:4; 1 Peter 2:6-8; Psalm 18:2, 95:1; 1 Peter 5:4; Hebrews 13:20), but even one of these is enough to show that Christ was considered to be God by His followers.

Jesus is also given titles that are unique to YHWH (the formal name of God) in the Old Testament. The Old Testament title "redeemer" (Psalm 130:7; Hosea 13:14) is used of Jesus in the New Testament (Titus 2:13; Revelation 5:9). Jesus is called Immanuel—"God with us"—in Matthew 1. In Zechariah 12:10, it is YHWH who says, "They will look on me, the one they have pierced." But the New Testament applies this to Jesus' crucifixion (John 19:37; Revelation 1:7). If it is YHWH who is pierced and looked upon, and Jesus was the one pierced and looked upon, then Jesus is YHWH. Paul interprets Isaiah 45:22-23 as applying to Jesus in Philippians 2:10-11. Further, Jesus' name is used alongside God's in prayer "Grace and peace to you from God our Father and the Lord Jesus Christ" (Galatians 1:3; Ephesians 1:2). This would be blasphemy if Christ were not deity. The name of Jesus appears with God's in Jesus' commanded to baptize "in the name [singular] of the Father and of the Son and of the Holy Spirit" (Matthew 28:19; see also 2 Corinthians 13:14).

Actions that can be accomplished only by God are credited to Jesus. Jesus not only raised the dead (John 5:21, 11:38-44) and forgave sins (Acts 5:31, 13:38), He created and sustains the universe (John 1:2; Colossians 1:16-17). This becomes even clearer when one considers YHWH said He was alone during creation (Isaiah 44:24). Further, Christ possesses attributes that only deity can have: eternality (John 8:58), omnipresence (Matthew 18:20, 28:20), omniscience (Matthew 16:21), and omnipotence (John 11:38-44).

Now, it is one thing to claim to be God or to fool someone into believing it is true, and something else entirely to prove it to be so. Christ offered many miracles as proof of His claim to deity. Just a few of Jesus' miracles include turning water to wine (John 2:7), walking on water (Matthew 14:25), multiplying physical objects (John 6:11), healing the blind (John 9:7), the lame (Mark 2:3), and the sick (Matthew 9:35; Mark 1:40-42), and even raising people from the dead (John 11:43-44; Luke 7:11-15; Mark 5:35). Moreover, Christ Himself rose from the dead. Far from the so-called dying and rising gods of pagan mythology, nothing like the resurrection is seriously claimed by other religions, and no other claim has as much extra-scriptural confirmation.

There are at least twelve historical facts about Jesus that even non-Christian critical scholars will admit:

1. Jesus died by crucifixion.
2. He was buried.
3. His death caused the disciples to despair and lose hope.
4. Jesus' tomb was discovered (or was claimed to be discovered) to be empty a few days later.
5. The disciples believed they experienced appearances of the risen Jesus.
6. After this, the disciples were transformed from doubters into bold believers.

7. This message was the center of preaching in the early Church.
8. This message was preached in Jerusalem.
9. As a result of this preaching, the Church was born and it grew.
10. Resurrection day, Sunday, replaced the Sabbath (Saturday) as the primary day of worship.
11. James, a skeptic, was converted when he also believed that he saw the resurrected Jesus.
12. Paul, an enemy of Christianity, was converted by an experience which he believed to be an appearance of the risen Jesus.

Even if someone were to object to this specific list, only a few are needed to prove the resurrection and establish the gospel: Jesus' death, burial, resurrection, and appearances (1 Corinthians 15:1-5). While there may be some theories to explain one or two of the above facts, only the resurrection explains and accounts for them all. Critics admit that the disciples claimed they saw the risen Jesus. Neither lies nor hallucinations can transform people the way the resurrection did. First, what would they have had to gain? Christianity was not popular and it certainly did not make them any money. Second, liars do not make good martyrs. There is no better explanation than the resurrection for the disciples' willingness to die horrible deaths for their faith. Yes, many people die for lies that they think are true, but people do not die for what they know is untrue.

In conclusion, Christ claimed He was YHWH, that He was deity (not just "a god" but the one true God); His followers (Jews who would have been terrified of idolatry) believed Him and referred to Him as God. Christ proved His claims to deity through miracles, including the world-altering resurrection. No other hypothesis can explain these facts. Yes, the deity of Christ is biblical.

Question: Did Jesus really exist? Is there any historical evidence of Jesus Christ?

Answer: Typically, when this question is asked, the person asking qualifies the question with "outside of the Bible." We do not grant this idea that the Bible cannot be considered a source of evidence for the existence of Jesus. The New Testament contains hundreds of references to Jesus Christ. There are those who date the writing of the Gospels to the second century A.D., more than 100 years after Jesus' death. Even if this were the case (which we strongly dispute), in terms of ancient evidences, writings less than 200 years after events took place are considered very reliable evidences. Further, the vast majority of scholars (Christian and non-Christian) will grant that the Epistles of Paul (at least some of them) were in fact written by Paul in the middle of the first century A.D., less than 40 years after Jesus' death. In terms of ancient manuscript evidence, this is extraordinarily strong proof of the existence of a man named Jesus in Israel in the early first century A.D.

It is also important to recognize that in A.D. 70, the Romans invaded and destroyed Jerusalem and most of Israel, slaughtering its inhabitants. Entire cities were literally burned to the ground. We should not be surprised, then, if much evidence of Jesus' existence was destroyed. Many of the eyewitnesses of Jesus would have been killed. These facts likely limited the amount of surviving eyewitness testimony of Jesus.

Considering that Jesus' ministry was largely confined to a relatively unimportant area in a small corner of the Roman Empire, a surprising amount of information about Jesus can be drawn from secular historical sources. Some of the more important historical evidences of Jesus include the following:

The first-century Roman Tacitus, who is considered one of the more accurate historians of the ancient world, mentioned superstitious "Christians" (from *Christus,* which is Latin for Christ), who suffered under Pontius Pilate during the reign of Tiberius. Suetonius, chief secretary to Emperor Hadrian, wrote that there was a man named Chrestus (or Christ) who lived during the first century (*Annals* 15.44).

Flavius Josephus is the most famous Jewish historian. In his *Antiquities* he refers to James, "the brother of Jesus, who was called Christ." There is a controversial verse (18:3) that says, "Now there was about this time Jesus, a wise man, if it be lawful to call him a man. For he was one who wrought surprising feats....He was [the] Christ...he appeared to them alive again the third day, as the divine prophets had foretold these and ten thousand other wonderful things concerning him." One version reads, "At this time there was a wise man named Jesus. His conduct was good and [he] was known to be virtuous. And many people from among the Jews and the other nations became his disciples. Pilate condemned him to be crucified and to die. But those who became his disciples did not abandon his discipleship. They reported that he had appeared to them three days after his crucifixion, and that he was alive; accordingly he was perhaps the Messiah, concerning whom the prophets have recounted wonders."

Julius Africanus quotes the historian Thallus in a discussion of the darkness which followed the crucifixion of Christ (*Extant Writings*, 18).

Pliny the Younger, in *Letters* 10:96, recorded early Christian worship practices including the fact that Christians worshiped Jesus as God and were very ethical, and he includes a reference to the love feast and Lord's Supper.

The *Babylonian Talmud* (Sanhedrin 43a) confirms Jesus' crucifixion on the eve of Passover and the accusations against Christ of practicing sorcery and encouraging Jewish apostasy.

Lucian of Samosata was a second-century Greek writer who admits that Jesus was worshiped by Christians, introduced new teachings, and was crucified for them. He said that Jesus' teachings included the brotherhood of believers, the importance of conversion, and the importance of denying other gods. Christians lived according to Jesus' laws, believed themselves to be immortal, and were characterized by contempt for death, voluntary self-devotion, and renunciation of material goods.

Mara Bar-Serapion confirms that Jesus was thought to be a wise and virtuous man, was considered by many to be the king of Israel, was put to death by the Jews, and lived on in the teachings of His followers.

Then we have all the Gnostic writings (*The Gospel of Truth, The Apocryphon of John, The Gospel of Thomas, The Treatise on Resurrection,* etc.) that all mention Jesus.

In fact, we can almost reconstruct the gospel just from early non-Christian sources: Jesus was called the Christ (Josephus), did "magic," led Israel into new teachings, and was hanged on Passover for them (*Babylonian Talmud*) in Judea (Tacitus), but claimed to be God and would return (Eliezar), which his followers believed, worshipping Him as God (Pliny the Younger).

There is overwhelming evidence for the existence of Jesus Christ, both in secular and biblical history. Perhaps the greatest evidence that Jesus did exist is the fact that literally thousands of Christians in the first century A.D., including the twelve apostles, were willing to give their lives as martyrs for Jesus Christ. People will die for what they believe to be true, but no one will die for what they know to be a lie.

Question: Is Jesus a myth? Is Jesus just a copy of the pagan gods of other ancient religions?

Answer: There are a number of voices claiming that the accounts of Jesus as recorded in the New Testament are simply myths and are the result of the writers borrowing stories from pagan mythology, such as the stories of Osiris, Dionysus, Adonis, Attis, and Mithras. The claim is that these mythological figures are essentially the same story that the New Testament ascribes to Jesus Christ of Nazareth. As Dan Brown claims in *The Da Vinci Code*, "Nothing in Christianity is original."

However, once the facts are examined, these claims are proven false. To discover the truth about these particular claims and others like them, it is important to 1) unearth the history behind the assertions, 2) examine the actual historical portrayals of the false gods being compared to Christ, 3) expose the logical fallacies that the authors are making, and 4) look at why the New Testament Gospels can be trusted as accurately depicting the true and historical Jesus Christ.

First, the claims of Jesus as a myth or an exaggeration originated in the writings of nineteenth century liberal German theologians. Their claim was essentially that Jesus was nothing more than a copy of the dying-and-rising fertility gods in various places—Tammuz in Mesopotamia, Adonis in Syria, Attis in Asia Minor, and Osiris in Egypt. None of these works ever advanced in the realms of academia and religious thought because their assertions were investigated by theologians and scholars and determined to be completely false and baseless. It has only been in the late twentieth and early twenty-first centuries that these assertions have been resurrected, primarily due to the rise of the internet and the mass distribution of false information with no accountability.

This leads us to the next area of investigation—do the mythological gods of antiquity really mirror the person of Jesus Christ? As an example, *Zeitgeist: the Movie* makes these claims about the Egyptian god Horus:

- He was born on December 25 of a virgin, "Isis Mary"
- A star in the east proclaimed his arrival
- Three kings came to adore the newborn "savior"
- He became a child prodigy teacher at age 12
- At age 30 he was "baptized" and began a "ministry"
- Horus had twelve "disciples"
- Horus was betrayed
- He was crucified
- He was buried for three days
- He was resurrected after three days

However, when the actual writings about Horus are competently examined, this is what we find in comparison to Jesus Christ:

- Horus was born to Isis; there is no mention in history of her being called "Mary." Moreover, "Mary" is our anglicized form of her real name, 'Miryam' or Miriam. "Mary" was not even used in the original texts of Scripture.
- Isis was not a virgin; she was the widow of Osiris and conceived Horus with Osiris.
- Horus was born during month of Khoiak (October/ November), not December 25. Further, there is no mention in the Bible of Christ's actual birth date.
- There is no record of three kings visiting Horus at his birth. The Bible never states the actual number of magi that came to see Christ.
- Horus is not a "savior" in any way; he did not die for anyone.

- There are no accounts of Horus' being a teacher at the age of 12.
- Horus was not "baptized." The only account of Horus that involves water is one story in which Horus is torn to pieces, with Isis requesting the crocodile god to fish him out of the water.
- Horus did not have a "ministry."
- Horus did not have 12 disciples. According to the Horus accounts, Horus had four semi-gods that were his followers, and there are some indications of 16 human followers and an unknown number of blacksmiths that went into battle with him.
- There is no account of Horus being betrayed by a friend.
- Horus did not die by crucifixion. There are various accounts of Horus' death, but none of them involve crucifixion.
- There is no account of Horus being buried for three days.
- Horus was not resurrected. There is no account of Horus coming out of the grave with the body he went in with. Some accounts have Horus/Osiris being brought back to life by Isis and becoming the lord of the underworld.

When compared side-by-side, Jesus and Horus bear little, if any, resemblance to one another.

Those who claim that Jesus Christ is a myth also like to compare Jesus and Mithras. All the above claims of Horus are applied to Mithras (e.g., being born of a virgin, being crucified, rising in three days, etc.). But what does history say about the myths of Mithras?

- He was born out of a rock and not from any woman.
- He battled first with the sun and then with a primeval bull, thought to be the first act of creation. Mithras killed the bull, which then became the ground of life for the human race.
- Mithras' birth was celebrated on December 25, along with winter solstice.
- There is no mention of his being a great teacher.
- There is no mention of Mithras having 12 disciples. The idea that Mithras had 12 disciples may have come from a mural

in which Mithras is surrounded by the twelve signs of the Zodiac.

- Mithras had no bodily resurrection. The myth is told that Mithras completed his earthly mission then was taken to paradise in a chariot, alive and well. The early Christian writer Tertullian did write about Mithras-believers re-enacting resurrection scenes, but he wrote about this occurring well after New Testament times, so if any copycatting was done, it was the cult of Mithras copying from Christianity.

More examples can be cited of Krishna, Attis, Dionysus, and other mythological gods, but the result is the same. In the end, the historical Jesus as portrayed in the Bible is thoroughly unique. The claimed similarities are greatly exaggerated. Further, while belief in Horus, Mithras, and others pre-dated Christianity, there is very little historical record of the pre-Christian beliefs of those religions. Most of the earliest writings about these religions are dated to the third and fourth centuries A.D. It is illogical and unhistorical to claim the pre-Christian beliefs in these religions (of which there is no record) were identical to the post-Christian beliefs in these groups (of which there is record). It is more historically valid to attribute any similarities between these religions and Christianity to the false religions' copying Christian beliefs about Jesus and placing those attributes on their own gods/saviors/founders in an attempt to stop the rapid growth of Christianity.

This leads us to the next area to examine: the logical fallacies committed by those claiming that Christianity borrowed from pagan mystery religions. Two fallacies in particular are obvious—the fallacy of the false cause and the terminological fallacy. If one thing precedes another, it does not mean that the first caused the second. This is the fallacy of the false cause. Even if pre-Christian accounts of mythological gods closely resembled Christ (and they do not), it does not mean they caused the gospel writers to invent a false Jesus. Claiming such a thing would be like saying the TV series Star Trek caused the NASA Space Shuttle program.

The terminological fallacy occurs when terms are redefined to prove a point. For example, the Zeitgeist movie says that Horus "began his ministry," but Horus had no actual ministry—nothing comparable to Christ's. Those claiming Mithras and Jesus are the same talk about the "baptism" that initiated prospects into the Mithras cult, but what was it actually? The Mithras priests (using a ritual also performed by followers of Attis) would suspend a bull over a pit, place those wanting to join the cult into the pit, and slit the bull's stomach, which then covered the initiates in blood. Such a thing has no resemblance whatsoever to Christian baptism—a person going under water (symbolizing the death of Christ) and then coming back out of the water (symbolizing Christ's resurrection). But advocates of the mythological-Jesus position deceptively use the same term to describe both in hopes of linking the two together.

The last issue to examine is the truthfulness of the New Testament itself. While much has been written on this topic, no work from antiquity has more evidence with respect to historical veracity than the New Testament. The New Testament has more writers (nine), better writers, and earlier writers than any other document from that era. Further, history testifies to the fact that these writers went to their deaths claiming that Jesus had risen from the dead. While some may die for a lie they think is true, no person dies for a lie he knows to be false. Think about it—if someone was about to crucify you upside down, as happened to the apostle Peter, and all you had to do to save your life was renounce a lie you had knowingly told, what would you do?

In addition, history has shown that it takes at least two generations to pass before myth can enter into a historical account. Why? Because eyewitnesses can refute error put in print. Those living at the time can refute the errors of an author and expose a work as being false. All the Gospels of the New Testament were written during the lifetime of the eyewitnesses, with some of Paul's epistles having been written as early as A.D. 50. That early dating acts as a key protective mechanism to prevent falsehood from being accepted and circulated.

Finally, the New Testament attests to the fact that the portrayal of Jesus was not mistaken for that of any other god. When faced with Paul's teaching, the elite thinkers of Athens said this: "He seems to be a proclaimer of strange deities"—because he was preaching Jesus and the resurrection. And they brought him to the Areopagus saying, "May we know what this new teaching is which you are proclaiming? For you are bringing some strange things to our ears; so we want to know what these things mean" (Acts 17:18-20). Clearly, if the accounts of Jesus were simply rehashing stories of other gods, the Athenians would not have referred to them as "new" teaching. If dying and rising gods were plentiful in the first century, why, when the apostle Paul preached Jesus rising from the dead in Acts 17, did the Epicureans and Stoics not remark, "Ah, just like Horus and Mithras"?

In conclusion, the claims that Jesus is nothing more than a myth, a copy of mythological gods, originated from authors whose works have been discounted by academia, commit logical fallacies that undermine their veracity, and cannot compare to the New Testament Gospels which have withstood nearly 2,000 years of intense scrutiny. The alleged parallels disappear when they are compared with the original historical texts. Similarities between Jesus and the various mythological gods can only be argued by employing selective and misleading descriptions.

Jesus Christ stands unique in history, with His voice rising above all false gods and continuing to ask the question that ultimately determines a person's eternal destiny: "Who do you say that I am?" (Matthew 16:15).

Question: Is the resurrection of Jesus Christ true?

Answer: Scripture presents conclusive evidence that Jesus Christ was in fact resurrected from the dead. Christ's resurrection is recorded in Matthew 28:1-20; Mark 16:1-20; Luke 24:1-53; and John 20:1–21:25. The resurrected Christ also appeared in the Book of Acts (Acts 1:1-11). From these passages you can gain several "proofs" of Christ's resurrection. First is the dramatic change in the disciples. They went from a group of men frightened and in hiding to strong, courageous witnesses sharing the gospel throughout the world. What else could explain this dramatic change other than the risen Christ appearing to them?

Second is the life of the apostle Paul. What changed him from being a persecutor of the church into an apostle for the church? It was when the risen Christ appeared to him on the road to Damascus (Acts 9:1-6). A third convincing proof is the empty tomb. If Christ were not raised, then where is His body? The disciples and others saw the tomb where He was buried. When they returned, His body was not there. Angels declared that He had been raised from the dead as He had promised (Matthew 28:5-7). Fourth, additional evidence of His resurrection is the many people He appeared to (Matthew 28:5, 9, 16-17; Mark 16:9; Luke 24:13-35; John 20:19, 24, 26-29, 21:1-14; Acts 1:6-8; 1 Corinthians 15:5-7).

Another proof of the resurrection of Jesus is the great amount of weight the apostles gave to Jesus' resurrection. A key passage on Christ's resurrection is 1 Corinthians 15. In this chapter, the apostle Paul explains why it is crucial to understand and believe in Christ's resurrection. The resurrection is important for the following reasons: 1) If Christ was not raised from the dead, believers will not be either (1 Corinthians 15:12-15). 2) If Christ was not raised from the dead, His sacrifice for sin was not sufficient (1 Corinthians 15:16-19). Jesus' resurrection proved that His death was accepted by God as the atonement for our sins. If He had simply died and stayed dead, that would indicate His sacrifice was not sufficient. As a result, believers would not be forgiven for their sins, and they would remain dead after they die (1 Corinthians 15:16-19). There would be no such thing as eternal life (John 3:16). "But now Christ has been raised from the dead, the first fruits of those who are asleep" (1 Corinthians 15:20 NAS).

Finally, Scripture is clear that all those who believe in Jesus Christ will be raised to eternal life just as He was (1 Corinthians 15:20-23). First Corinthians 15 goes on to describe how Christ's resurrection proves His victory over sin and provides us the power to live victoriously over sin (1 Corinthians 15:24-34). It describes the glorious nature of the resurrection body we will receive (1 Corinthians 15:35-49). It proclaims that, as a result of Christ's resurrection, all who believe in Him have ultimate victory over death (1 Corinthians 15:50-58).

What a glorious truth the resurrection of Christ is! "Therefore, my dear brothers, stand firm. Let nothing move you. Always give yourselves fully to the work of the Lord, because you know that your labor in the Lord is not in vain" (1 Corinthians 15:58). According to the Bible, the resurrection of Jesus Christ is most definitely true.

The Bible records Christ's resurrection, records that it was witnessed by over 400 people, and proceeds to build crucial Christian doctrine on the historical fact of Jesus' resurrection.

Question: What does it mean that Jesus is the Son of God?

Answer: Jesus is not God's Son in the sense of a human father and a son. God did not get married and have a son. God did not mate with Mary and, together with her, produce a son. Jesus is God's Son in the sense that He is God made manifest in human form (John 1:1, 14). Jesus is God's Son in that He was conceived in Mary by the Holy Spirit. Luke 1:35 declares, "The angel answered, 'The Holy Spirit will come upon you, and the power of the Most High will overshadow you. So the holy one to be born will be called the Son of God.'"

During His trial before the Jewish leaders, the High Priest demanded of Jesus, "I charge you under oath by the living God: Tell us if you are the Christ, the Son of God" (Matthew 26:63). "'Yes, it is as you say,' Jesus replied. 'But I say to all of you: In the future you will see the Son of Man sitting at the right hand of the Mighty One and coming on the clouds of heaven'" (Matthew 26:64). The Jewish leaders responded by accusing Jesus of blasphemy (Matthew 26:65-66). Later, before Pontius Pilate, "The Jews insisted, 'We have a law, and according to that law He must die, because He claimed to be the Son of God'" (John 19:7). Why would His claiming to be the Son of God be considered blasphemy and be worthy of a death sentence? The Jewish leaders understood exactly what Jesus meant by the phrase "Son of God." To be the Son of God is to be of the same nature as God. The Son of God is "of God." The claim to be of the same nature as God—to in fact be God—was blasphemy to the Jewish leaders; therefore, they demanded Jesus' death, in keeping with Leviticus 24:15. Hebrews 1:3 expresses this very clearly, "The Son is the radiance of God's glory and the exact representation of His being."

Another example can be found in John 17:12 where Judas is described as the "son of perdition." John 6:71 tells us that Judas was the son of Simon. What does John 17:12 mean by describing Judas as the "son of perdition"? The word *perdition* means "destruction, ruin, waste." Judas was not the literal son of "ruin, destruction, and

53

waste," but those things were the identity of Judas' life. Judas was a manifestation of perdition. In this same way, Jesus is the Son of God. The Son of God is God. Jesus is God made manifest (John 1:1, 14).

Question: Why is the virgin birth so important?

Answer: The doctrine of the virgin birth is crucially important (Isaiah 7:14; Matthew 1:23; Luke 1:27, 34). First, let's look at how Scripture describes the event. In response to Mary's question, "How will this be?" (Luke 1:34), Gabriel says, "The Holy Spirit will come upon you, and the power of the Most High will overshadow you" (Luke 1:35). The angel encourages Joseph to not fear marrying Mary with these words: "What is conceived in her is from the Holy Spirit" (Matthew 1:20). Matthew states that the virgin "was found to be with child through the Holy Spirit" (Matthew 1:18). Galatians 4:4 also teaches the Virgin Birth: "God sent His Son, born of a woman."

From these passages, it is certainly clear that Jesus' birth was the result of the Holy Spirit working within Mary's body. The immaterial (the Spirit) and the material (Mary's womb) were both involved. Mary, of course, could not impregnate herself, and in that sense she was simply a "vessel." Only God could perform the miracle of the Incarnation.

However, denying a physical connection between Mary and Jesus would imply that Jesus was not truly human. Scripture teaches that Jesus was fully human, with a physical body like ours. This He received from Mary. At the same time, Jesus was fully God, with an eternal, sinless nature (John 1:14; 1 Timothy 3:16; Hebrews 2:14-17.)

Jesus was not born in sin; that is, He had no sin nature (Hebrews 7:26). It would seem that the sin nature is passed down from generation to generation through the father (Romans 5:12, 17, 19). The Virgin Birth circumvented the transmission of the sin nature and allowed the eternal God to become a perfect man.

Question: Did Jesus go to hell between His death and resurrection?

Answer: There is a great deal of confusion in regards to this question. This concept comes primarily from the Apostles' Creed, which states, "He descended into hell." There are also a few Scriptures which, depending on how they are translated, describe Jesus going to "hell." In studying this issue, it is important to first understand what the Bible teaches about the realm of the dead.

In the Hebrew Scriptures, the word used to describe the realm of the dead is *sheol*. It simply means the "place of the dead" or the "place of departed souls/spirits." The New Testament Greek word that is used for hell is "hades," which also refers to "the place of the dead." Other Scriptures in the New Testament indicate that sheol/hades is a temporary place, where souls are kept as they await the final resurrection and judgment. Revelation 20:11-15 gives a clear distinction between the two. Hell (the lake of fire) is the permanent and final place of judgment for the lost. Hades is a temporary place. So, no, Jesus did not go to hell because hell is a future realm, only put into effect after the Great White Throne Judgment (Revelation 20:11-15).

Sheol/hades is a realm with two divisions (Matthew 11:23, 16:18; Luke 10:15, 16:23; Acts 2:27-31), the abodes of the saved and the lost. The abode of the saved was called "paradise" and "Abraham's bosom." The abodes of the saved and the lost are separated by a "great chasm" (Luke 16:26). When Jesus ascended to heaven, He took the occupants of paradise (believers) with Him (Ephesians 4:8-10). The lost side of sheol/hades has remained unchanged. All unbelieving dead go there awaiting their final judgment in the future. Did Jesus go to sheol/hades? Yes, according to Ephesians 4:8-10 and 1 Peter 3:18-20.

Some of the confusion has arisen from such passages as Psalm 16:10-11 as translated in the King James Version, "For thou wilt not leave my soul in hell; neither wilt thou suffer thine Holy One to see corruption....Thou wilt show me the path of life." "Hell" is not a correct translation of this verse. A correct reading would be "the grave" or "sheol." Jesus said to the thief beside Him, "Today you will be with me in paradise" (Luke 23:43). Jesus' body was in the tomb; His soul/spirit went to the "paradise" side of sheol/hades. He then removed all the righteous dead from paradise and took them with Him to heaven. Unfortunately, in many translations of the Bible, translators are not consistent, or correct, in how they translate the Hebrew and Greek words for "sheol," "hades," and "hell."

Some have the viewpoint that Jesus went to "hell" or the suffering side of sheol/hades in order to further be punished for our sins. This idea is completely unbiblical. It was the death of Jesus on the cross and His suffering in our place that sufficiently provided for our redemption. It was His shed blood that effected our own cleansing from sin (1 John 1:7-9). As He hung there on the cross, He took the sin burden of the whole human race upon Himself. He became sin for us: "God made him who had no sin to be sin for us, so that in him we might become the righteousness of God" (2 Corinthians 5:21). This imputation of sin helps us understand Christ's struggle in the garden of Gethsemane with the cup of sin which would be poured out upon Him on the cross.

When Jesus cried upon the cross, "Oh, Father, why have you forsaken me?" (Matthew 27:46), it was then that He was separated from the Father because of the sin poured out upon Him. As He gave up His spirit, He said, "Father, into your hands I commit my spirit" (Luke 23:46). His suffering in our place was completed. His soul/spirit went to the paradise side of hades. Jesus did not go to hell. Jesus' suffering ended the moment He died. The payment for sin was paid. He then awaited the resurrection of His body and His return to glory in His ascension. Did Jesus go to hell? No. Did Jesus go to sheol/hades? Yes.

Question: Was Jesus crucified on a Friday? If so, how did He spend three days in the tomb if He was resurrected on Sunday?

Answer: The Bible does not explicitly state on which day of the week Jesus was crucified. The two most widely held views are Friday and Wednesday. Some, however, using a synthesis of both the Friday and Wednesday arguments, argue for Thursday as the day.

Jesus said in Matthew 12:40, "For as Jonah was three days and three nights in the belly of a huge fish, so the Son of Man will be three days and three nights in the heart of the earth." Those who argue for a Friday crucifixion say that there is still a valid way in which He could have been considered in the grave for three days. In the Jewish mind of the first century, a part of day was considered as a full day. Since Jesus was in the grave for part of Friday, all of Saturday, and part of Sunday—He could be considered to have been in the grave

56

for three days. One of the principal arguments for Friday is found in Mark 15:42, which notes that Jesus was crucified "the day before the Sabbath." If that was the weekly Sabbath, i.e. Saturday, then that fact leads to a Friday crucifixion. Another argument for Friday says that verses such as Matthew 16:21 and Luke 9:22 teach that Jesus would rise on the third day; therefore, He would not need to be in the grave a full three days and nights. But while some translations use "on the third day" for these verses, not all do, and not everyone agrees that "on the third day" is the best way to translate these verses. Furthermore, Mark 8:31 says that Jesus will be raised "after" three days.

The Thursday argument expands on the Friday view and argues mainly that there are too many events (some count as many as twenty) happening between Christ's burial and Sunday morning to occur from Friday evening to Sunday morning. Proponents of the Thursday view point out that this is especially a problem when the only full day between Friday and Sunday was Saturday, the Jewish Sabbath. An extra day or two eliminates that problem. The Thursday advocates could reason thus: suppose you haven't seen a friend since Monday evening. The next time you see him it is Thursday morning and you say, "I haven't seen you in three days" even though it had technically only been 60 hours (2.5 days). If Jesus was crucified on Thursday, this example shows how it could be considered three days.

The Wednesday opinion states that there were two Sabbaths that week. After the first one (the one that occurred on the evening of the crucifixion [Mark 15:42; Luke 23:52-54]), the women purchased spices—note that they made their purchase after the Sabbath (Mark 16:1). The Wednesday view holds that this "Sabbath" was the Passover (see Leviticus 16:29-31, 23:24-32, 39, where high holy days that are not necessarily the seventh day of the week are referred to as the Sabbath). The second Sabbath that week was the normal weekly Sabbath. Note that in Luke 23:56, the women who had purchased spices after the first Sabbath returned and prepared the spices, then "rested on the Sabbath" (Luke 23:56). The argument states that they could not purchase the spices after the Sabbath, yet prepare those spices before the Sabbath—unless there were two Sabbaths. With the two-Sabbath view, if Christ was crucified on Thursday, then the high holy Sabbath (the Passover) would have begun Thursday at sundown and ended at Friday sundown—at the beginning of the weekly Sabbath or Saturday. Purchasing the spices after the first Sabbath (Passover) would have meant they purchased them on Saturday and were breaking the Sabbath.

Therefore, according to the Wednesday viewpoint, the only explanation that does not violate the biblical account of the women and the spices and holds to a literal understanding of Matthew 12:40, is that Christ was crucified on Wednesday. The Sabbath that was a high holy day (Passover) occurred on Thursday, the women purchased spices (after that) on Friday and returned and prepared the spices on the same day, they rested on Saturday which was the weekly Sabbath, then brought the spices to the tomb early Sunday. Jesus was buried near sundown on Wednesday, which began Thursday in the Jewish calendar. Using a Jewish calendar, you have Thursday night (night one), Thursday day (day one), Friday night (night two), Friday day (day two), Saturday night (night three), Saturday day (day three). We do not know exactly when He rose, but we do know that it was before sunrise on Sunday (John 20:1, Mary Magdalene came "while it was still dark"), so He could have risen as early as just after sunset Saturday evening, which began the first day of the week to the Jews.

A possible problem with the Wednesday view is that the disciples who walked with Jesus on the road to Emmaus did so on "the same day" of His resurrection (Luke 24:13). The disciples, who do not recognize Jesus, tell Him of Jesus' crucifixion (24:21) and say that "today is the third day since these things happened" (24:22). Wednesday to Sunday is four days. A possible explanation is that they may have been counting since Wednesday evening at Christ's burial, which begins the Jewish Thursday, and Thursday to Sunday could be counted as three days.

In the grand scheme of things, it is not all that important to know what day of the week Christ was crucified. If it were very important, then God's Word would have clearly communicated the day and timeframe. What is important is that He did die and that He physically, bodily rose from the dead. What is equally important is the reason He died—to take the punishment that all sinners deserve. John 3:16 and 3:36 both proclaim that putting your trust in Him results in eternal life! This is equally true whether He was crucified on a Wednesday, Thursday, or Friday.

Question: Was Jesus ever angry?

Answer: When Jesus cleared the temple of the moneychangers and animal-sellers, He showed great emotion and anger (Matthew 21:12-13; Mark 11:15-18; John 2:13-22). Jesus' emotion was described as "zeal" for God's house (John 2:17). His anger was pure and completely justified because at its root was concern for God's holiness and worship. Because these were at stake, Jesus took quick and decisive action. Another time Jesus showed anger was in the synagogue of Capernaum. When the Pharisees refused to answer Jesus' questions, "He looked around at them in anger, deeply distressed at their stubborn hearts" (Mark 3:5).

Many times, we think of anger as a selfish, destructive emotion that we should eradicate from our lives altogether. However, the fact that Jesus did sometimes become angry indicates that anger itself, as an emotion, is amoral. This is borne out elsewhere in the New Testament. Ephesians 4:26 instructs us "in your anger do not sin" and not to let the sun go down on our anger. The command is not to "avoid anger" (or suppress it or ignore it) but to deal with it properly, in a timely manner. We note the following facts about Jesus' displays of anger:

1. His anger had the proper motivation. In other words, He was angry for the right reasons. Jesus' anger did not arise from petty arguments or personal slights against Him. There was no selfishness involved.
2. His anger had the proper focus. He was not angry at God or at the "weaknesses" of others. His anger targeted sinful behavior and true injustice.
3. His anger had the proper supplement. Mark 3:5 says that His anger was attended by grief over the Pharisees' lack of faith. Jesus' anger stemmed from love for the Pharisees and concern for their spiritual condition. It had nothing to do with hatred or ill will.

4. His anger had the proper control. Jesus was never out of control, even in His wrath. The temple leaders did not like His cleansing of the temple (Luke 19:47), but He had done nothing sinful. He controlled His emotions; His emotions did not control Him.

5. His anger had the proper duration. He did not allow His anger to turn into bitterness; He did not hold grudges. He dealt with each situation properly, and He handled anger in good time.

6. His anger had the proper result. Jesus' anger had the inevitable consequence of godly action. Jesus' anger, as with all His emotions, was held in check by the Word of God; thus, Jesus' response was always to accomplish God's will.

When we get angry, too often we have improper control or an improper focus. We fail in one or more of the above points. This is the wrath of man, of which we are told "Everyone should be quick to listen, slow to speak and slow to become angry, for man's anger does not bring about the righteous life that God desires" (James 1:19-20). Jesus did not exhibit man's anger, but the righteous indignation of God.

Question: Could Jesus have sinned?

Answer: There are two sides to this interesting question. It is important to remember that this is not a question of whether Jesus sinned. Both sides agree, as the Bible clearly says, that Jesus did not sin (2 Corinthians 5:21; 1 Peter 2:22). The question is whether Jesus *could* have sinned. Those who hold to "impeccability" believe that Jesus could not have sinned. Those who hold to "peccability" believe that Jesus could have sinned, but did not. Which view is correct? The clear teaching of Scripture is that Jesus was impeccable—Jesus could not have sinned. If He could have sinned, He would still be able to sin today because He retains the same essence He did while living on earth. He is the God-Man and will forever remain so, having full deity and full humanity so united in one person as to be indivisible. To believe that Jesus could sin is to believe that God could sin. "For God was pleased to have all his fullness dwell in him" (Colossians 1:19).

Colossians 2:9 adds, "For in Christ all the fullness of the Deity lives in bodily form."

Although Jesus is fully human, He was not born with the same sinful nature that we are born with. He certainly was tempted in the same way we are, in that temptations were put before Him by Satan, yet He remained sinless because God is incapable of sinning. It is against His very nature (Matthew 4:1; Hebrews 2:18, 4:15; James 1:13). Sin is by definition a trespass of the Law. God created the Law, and the Law is by nature what God would or would not do; therefore, sin is anything that God would not do by His very nature.

To be tempted is not, in and of itself, sinful. A person could tempt you with something you have no desire to do, such as committing murder or participating in sexual perversions. You probably have no desire whatsoever to take part in these actions, but you were still tempted because someone placed the possibility before you. There are at least two definitions for the word "tempted":

1. To have a sinful proposition suggested to you by someone or something outside yourself or by your own sin nature.
2. To consider actually participating in a sinful act and the possible pleasures and consequences of such an act to the degree that the act is already taking place in your mind.

The first definition does not describe a sinful act/thought; the second does. When you dwell upon a sinful act and consider how you might be able to bring it to pass, you have crossed the line of sin. Jesus was tempted in the fashion of definition one except that He was never tempted by a sin nature because it did not exist within Him. Satan proposed certain sinful acts to Jesus, but He had no inner desire to participate in the sin. Therefore, He was tempted like we are but remained sinless.

Those who hold to peccability believe that, if Jesus could not have sinned, He could not have truly experienced temptation, and therefore could not truly empathize with our struggles and temptations against sin. We have to remember that one does not have to experience something in order to understand it. God knows everything about everything. While God has never had the desire to sin, and has most definitely never sinned, God knows and understands what sin is. God knows and understands what it is like to be tempted. Jesus can empathize with our temptations because He knows, not because He has "experienced" all the same things we have.

Jesus knows what it is like to be tempted, but He does not know what it is like to sin. This does not prevent Him from assisting us. We are tempted with sins that are common to man (1 Corinthians 10:13). These sins generally can be boiled down to three different types: "the lust of the eyes, the lust of the flesh, and the pride of life" (1 John 2:16 NKJV). Examine the temptation and sin of Eve, as well as the temptation of Jesus, and you will find that the temptations for each came from these three categories. Jesus was tempted in every way and in every area that we are, but remained perfectly holy. Although our corrupt natures will have the inner desire to participate in some sins, we have the ability, through Christ, to overcome sin because we are no longer slaves to sin but rather slaves of God (Romans 6, especially verses 2 and 16-22).

Question: Why are Jesus' genealogies in Matthew and Luke so different?

Answer: Jesus' genealogy is given in two places in Scripture: Matthew 1 and Luke 3:23-38. Matthew traces the genealogy from Jesus to Abraham. Luke traces the genealogy from Jesus to Adam. However, there is good reason to believe that Matthew and Luke are in fact tracing entirely different genealogies. For example, Matthew gives Joseph's father as Jacob (Matthew 1:16), while Luke gives Joseph's father as Heli (Luke 3:23). Matthew traces the line through David's son Solomon (Matthew 1:6), while Luke traces the line through David's son Nathan (Luke 3:31). In fact, between David and Jesus, the only names the genealogies have in common are Shealtiel and Zerubbabel (Matthew 1:12; Luke 3:27).

Some point to these differences as evidence of errors in the Bible. However, the Jews were meticulous record keepers, especially in regard to genealogies. It is inconceivable that Matthew and Luke could build two entirely contradictory genealogies of the same lineage. Again, from David through Jesus, the genealogies are completely different. Even the reference to Shealtiel and Zerubbabel likely refer to different individuals of the same names. Matthew gives Shealtiel's father as Jeconiah while Luke gives Shealtiel's father as Neri. It would be normal for a man named Shealtiel to name his son Zerubbabel in light of the famous individuals of those names (see the books of Ezra and Nehemiah).

Another explanation is that Matthew is tracing the primary lineage while Luke is taking into account the occurrences of "levirate marriage." If a man died without having any sons, it was tradition for the man's brother to marry his wife and have a son who would carry on the man's name. While possible, this view is unlikely as every generation from David to Jesus would have had a "levirate marriage" in order to account for the differences in every generation. This is highly unlikely.

With these concepts in view, most conservative Bible scholars assume Luke is recording Mary's genealogy and Matthew is recording Joseph's. Matthew is following the line of Joseph (Jesus' legal father), through David's son Solomon, while Luke is following the line of Mary (Jesus' blood relative), though David's son Nathan. There was no Greek word for "son-in-law," and Joseph would have been considered a son of Heli through marrying Heli's daughter Mary. Through either line, Jesus is a descendant of David and therefore eligible to be the Messiah. Tracing a genealogy through the mother's side is unusual, but so was the virgin birth. Luke's explanation is that Jesus was the son of Joseph, "so it was thought" (Luke 3:23).

Question: What is the hypostatic union? How can Jesus be both God and man at the same time?

Answer: The hypostatic union is the term used to describe how God the Son, Jesus Christ, took on a human nature, yet remained fully God at the same time. Jesus always had been God (John 8:58, 10:30), but at the incarnation Jesus became a human being (John 1:14). The addition of the human nature to the divine nature is Jesus, the God-man. This is the hypostatic union, Jesus Christ, one Person, fully God and fully man.

Jesus' two natures, human and divine, are inseparable. Jesus will forever be the God-man, fully God and fully human, two distinct natures in one Person. Jesus' humanity and divinity are not mixed, but

63

are united without loss of separate identity. Jesus sometimes operated with the limitations of humanity (John 4:6, 19:28) and other times in the power of His deity (John 11:43; Matthew 14:18-21). In both, Jesus' actions were from His one Person. Jesus had two natures, but only one personality.

The doctrine of the hypostatic union is an attempt to explain how Jesus could be both God and man at the same time. It is ultimately, though, a doctrine we are incapable of fully understanding. It is impossible for us to fully understand how God works. We, as human beings with finite minds, should not expect to totally comprehend an infinite God. Jesus is God's Son in that He was conceived by the Holy Spirit (Luke 1:35). But that does not mean Jesus did not exist before He was conceived. Jesus has always existed (John 8:58, 10:30). When Jesus was conceived, He became a human being in addition to being God (John 1:1, 14).

Jesus is both God and man. Jesus has always been God, but He did not become a human being until He was conceived in Mary. Jesus became a human being in order to identify with us in our struggles (Hebrews 2:17) and, more importantly, so that He could die on the cross to pay the penalty for our sins (Philippians 2:5-11). In summary, the hypostatic union teaches that Jesus is both fully human and fully divine, that there is no mixture or dilution of either nature, and that He is one united Person, forever.

Question: Was Jesus Christ married?

Answer: Jesus Christ was definitely not married. There are popular myths today that speak of Christ being married to Mary Magdalene. This myth is absolutely false and has no basis theologically, historically, or biblically. While a couple of the Gnostic gospels mention Jesus having a close relationship with Mary Magdalene, none of them specifically states that Jesus was married to Mary Magdalene, or had any romantic involvement with her. The closest any of them come is saying that Jesus kissed Mary Magdalene, which just as easily could be a reference to a "friendly kiss." Further, even if the Gnostic gospels directly stated that Jesus was married to Mary Magdalene, they would have no authority, as the Gnostic gospels have all been proven to be forgeries invented to create a Gnostic view of Jesus.

If Jesus had been married, the Bible would have told us so, or there would be some unambiguous statement to that fact. Scripture would not be completely silent on such an important issue. The Bible mentions Jesus' mother, adoptive father, half-brothers, and half-sisters. Why would it neglect to mention the fact that Jesus had a wife? Those who believe/teach that Jesus was married are doing so in an attempt to "humanize" Him, to make Him more ordinary, more like everyone else. People simply do not want to believe that Jesus was God in the flesh (John 1:1, 14; 10:30). So, they invent and believe myths about Jesus being married, having children, and being an ordinary human being.

A secondary question would be, "Could Jesus Christ have been married?" There is nothing sinful about being married. There is nothing sinful about having sexual relations in marriage. So, yes, Jesus could have been married and still be the sinless Lamb of God and Savior of the world. At the same time, there is no biblical reason for Jesus to marry. That is not the point in this debate. Those who believe Jesus was married do not believe that He was sinless, or that He was the Messiah. Getting married and having children is not why God sent Jesus. Mark 10:45 tells us why Jesus came, "For even the Son of Man did not come to be served, but to serve, and to give his life as a ransom for many."

Question: If Jesus was God, how could He pray to God? Was Jesus praying to Himself?

Answer: To understand Jesus as God on earth praying to His Father in heaven, we need to realize that the eternal Father and the eternal Son had an eternal relationship before Jesus took upon Himself the form of a man. Please read John 5:19-27, particularly verse 23 where Jesus teaches that the Father sent the Son (also see John 15:10). Jesus did not become the Son of God when He was born in Bethlehem. He has always been the Son of God from eternity past, still is the Son of God, and always will be.

Isaiah 9:6 tells us that the Son was given and the Child was born. Jesus was always part of the tri-unity, along with the Holy Spirit. The tri-unity always existed, the Father God, the Son God, and the Spirit God, not three gods, but one God existing as three persons. Jesus taught that He and His Father are one (John 10:30), meaning that He and His Father are of the same substance and the same essence. The Father, Son and Spirit are three co-equal persons existing as God. These three had, and continue to have, an eternal relationship.

When Jesus, the eternal Son of God, took upon Himself sinless humanity He also took on the form of a servant, giving up His heavenly glory (Philippians 2:5-11). As the God-man, He had to learn obedience (Hebrews 5:8) to His Father as He was tempted by Satan, accused falsely by men, rejected by His people, and eventually crucified. His praying to His heavenly Father was to ask for power (John 11:41-42) and wisdom (Mark 1:35, 6:46). His praying showed His dependence upon His Father in His humanity to carry out His Father's plan of redemption, as evidenced in Christ's high priestly prayer in John 17. His praying demonstrated that He ultimately submitted to His Father's will, which was to go to the cross and pay the penalty (death) for our breaking God's law (Matthew 26:31-46). Of course, He rose bodily from the grave, winning forgiveness and eternal life for those who repent of sin and believe in Him as the Savior.

There is no problem with God the Son praying or talking to God the Father. As mentioned, they had an eternal relationship before Christ became a man. This relationship is depicted in the Gospels so we can see how the Son of God in His humanity carried out His Father's will, and in doing so, purchased redemption for His children (John 6:38). Christ's continual submission to His heavenly Father was empowered and kept focused through His prayer life. Christ's example of prayer is ours to follow.

Jesus Christ was no less God on earth when praying to His Father in heaven. He was depicting how even in sinless humanity it is necessary to have a vital prayer life in order to do His Father's will. Jesus' praying to the Father was a demonstration of His relationship within the Trinity and an example for us that we must rely on God through prayer for the strength and wisdom we need. Since Christ, as the God-man, needed to have a vibrant prayer life, so should the follower of Christ today.

Question: Did Jesus have brothers and sisters?

Answer: Jesus' brothers are mentioned in several Bible verses. Matthew 12:46, Luke 8:19, and Mark 3:31 say that Jesus' mother and brothers came to see Him. The Bible tells us that Jesus had four brothers: James, Joseph, Simon, and Judas (Matthew 13:55). The Bible also tells us that Jesus had sisters, but they are not named or numbered (Matthew 13:56). In John 7:1-10, His brothers go on to the festival while Jesus stays behind. In Acts 1:14, His brothers and mother are described as praying with the disciples. Galatians 1:19 mentions that James was Jesus' brother. The most natural conclusion of these passages is to interpret that Jesus had actual blood half-siblings.

Some Roman Catholics claim that these "brothers" were actually Jesus' cousins. However, in each instance, the specific Greek word for "brother" is used. While the word can refer to other relatives, its normal and literal meaning is a physical brother. There was a Greek word for "cousin," and it was not used. Further, if they were Jesus' cousins, why would they so often be described as being with Mary, Jesus' mother? There is nothing in the context of His mother and brothers coming to see Him that even hints that they were anyone other than His literal, blood-related, half-brothers.

A second Roman Catholic argument is that Jesus' brothers and sisters were the children of Joseph from a previous marriage. An entire theory of Joseph's being significantly older than Mary, having been previously married, having multiple children, and then being widowed before marrying Mary is invented without any biblical basis. The problem with this is that the Bible does not even hint that Joseph was married or had children before he married Mary. If Joseph had at least six children before he married Mary, why are they not mentioned in Joseph and Mary's trip to Bethlehem (Luke 2:4-7) or their trip to Egypt (Matthew 2:13-15) or their trip back to Nazareth (Matthew 2:20-23)?

There is no biblical reason to believe that these siblings are anything other than the actual children of Joseph and Mary. Those who oppose the idea that Jesus had half-brothers and half-sisters do so, not from a reading of Scripture, but from a preconceived concept of the perpetual virginity of Mary, which is itself clearly unbiblical: "But he (Joseph) had no union with her (Mary) *until* she gave birth to a son. And he gave Him the name Jesus" (Matthew 1:25). Jesus had half-siblings, half-brothers and half-sisters, who were the children of Joseph and Mary. That is the clear and unambiguous teaching of God's Word.

Question: Why did Jesus have to experience so much suffering?

Answer: Isaiah 52:14 declares, "Just as there were many who were appalled at Him—His appearance was so disfigured beyond that of any man and his form marred beyond human likeness." Jesus suffered most severely throughout the trials, torture, and crucifixion (Matthew 27; Mark 15; Luke 23; John 19). As horrible as His physical suffering was, it was nothing compared to the spiritual suffering He went through. Second Corinthians 5:21 says, "God made him who had no sin to be sin for us, so that in him we might become the righteousness of God." Jesus had the weight of the sins of the entire world on Him (1 John 2:2). It was sin that caused Jesus to cry out, "My God, my God, why have you forsaken me?" (Matthew 27:46). So, as brutal as Jesus' physical suffering was, it was nothing compared to His having to bear our sins and die to pay the penalty for them (Romans 5:8).

Isaiah predicts Jesus' suffering in clear language: "He was despised and rejected by men, a man of sorrows, and familiar with suffering. Like one from whom men hide their faces he was despised, and we esteemed him not. But he was pierced for our transgressions, he was crushed for our iniquities; the punishment that brought us peace was upon him, and by his wounds we are healed" (Isaiah 53:3, 5). Psalm 22:14-18 is another powerful passage predicting the suffering of the Messiah: "I am poured out like water, and all my bones are out of joint. My heart has turned to wax; it has melted away within me. My strength is dried up like a potsherd, and my tongue sticks to the roof of my mouth; you lay me in the dust of death. Dogs have surrounded me; a band of evil men has encircled me, they have pierced my hands and my feet. I can count all my bones; people stare and gloat over me. They divide my garments among them and cast lots for my clothing."

Why did Jesus have to suffer so badly? Some think that Jesus' physical torture was part of His punishment for our sins. To some extent, this is true. At the same time, the torture Jesus underwent speaks more of the hatred and cruelty of humanity than it does of God's punishment for sin. Satan's absolute hatred of God and Jesus was surely a part of the motivation behind the relentless torture and abuse. The suffering heaped on Jesus is the ultimate example of the hatred and rage sinful man feels toward a holy God (Romans 3:10-18).

Question: What does it mean that Jesus is the Lamb of God?

Answer: When Jesus is called the Lamb of God in John 1:29 and John 1:36, it is referring to Him as the perfect and ultimate sacrifice for sin. In order to understand who Christ was and what He did, we must begin with the Old Testament, which contains prophecies concerning the coming of Christ as a "guilt offering" (Isaiah 53:10). In fact, the whole sacrificial system established by God in the Old Testament set the stage for the coming of Jesus Christ, who is the perfect sacrifice God would provide as atonement for the sins of His people (Romans 8:3; Hebrews 10).

The sacrifice of lambs played a very important role in the Jewish religious life and sacrificial system. When John the Baptist referred to Jesus as the "Lamb of God who takes away the sin of the world" (John 1:29), the Jews who heard him might have immediately thought of any one of several important sacrifices. With the time of the Passover feast being very near, the first thought might be the sacrifice of the Passover lamb. The Passover feast was one of the main Jewish holidays and a celebration in remembrance of God's deliverance of the Israelites from bondage in Egypt. In fact, the slaying of the Passover lamb and the applying of the blood to doorposts of the houses (Exodus 12:11-13) is a beautiful picture of Christ's atoning work on the cross. Those for whom He died are covered by His blood, protecting us from the angel of (spiritual) death.

Another important sacrifice involving lambs was the daily sacrifice at the temple in Jerusalem. Every morning and evening, a lamb was sacrificed in the temple for the sins of the people (Exodus 29:38-42). These daily sacrifices, like all others, were simply to point people towards the perfect sacrifice of Christ on the cross. In fact, the time of Jesus' death on the cross corresponds to the time the evening sacrifice was being made in the temple. The Jews at that time would have also been familiar with the Old Testament prophets Jeremiah and Isaiah, who foretold the coming of One who would be brought "like a lamb led to the slaughter" (Jeremiah 11:19; Isaiah 53:7) and whose sufferings and sacrifice would provide redemption for Israel. Of course, that person was none other than Jesus Christ, "the Lamb of God."

While the idea of a sacrificial system might seem strange to us today, the concept of payment or restitution is still one we can easily understand. We know that the wages of sin is death (Romans 6:23) and that our sin separates us from God. We also know the Bible teaches we are all sinners and none of us is righteous before God (Romans 3:23). Because of our sin, we are separated from God, and we stand guilty before Him. Therefore, the only hope we can have is if He provides a way for us to be reconciled to Himself, and that is what He did in sending His Son Jesus Christ to die on the cross. Christ died to make atonement for sin and to pay the penalty of the sins of all who believe in Him.

It is through His death on the cross as God's perfect sacrifice for sin and His resurrection three days later that we can now have eternal life if we believe in Him. The fact that God Himself has provided the offering that atones for our sin is part of the glorious good news of the gospel that is so clearly declared in 1 Peter 1:18-21: "For you know that it was not with perishable things such as silver or gold that you were redeemed from the empty way of life handed down to you from your forefathers, but with the precious blood of Christ, a lamb without blemish or defect. He was chosen before the creation of the world, but was revealed in these last times for your sake. Through him you believe in God, who raised him from the dead and glorified him, and so your faith and hope are in God."

Question: Where does the Old Testament predict the coming of Christ?

Answer: There are many Old Testament prophecies about Jesus Christ. Some interpreters place the number of Messianic prophecies in the hundreds. The following are those that are considered the clearest and most important.

Regarding Jesus' birth—Isaiah 7:14: "Therefore the Lord himself will give you a sign: The virgin will be with child and will give birth to a son, and will call him Immanuel." Isaiah 9:6: "For to us a child is born, to us a son is given, and the government will be on his shoulders. And he will be called Wonderful Counselor, Mighty God, Everlasting Father, Prince of Peace." Micah 5:2: "But you, Bethlehem Ephrathah, though you are small among the clans of Judah, out of you will come for me one who will be ruler over Israel, whose origins are from of old, from ancient times."

Concerning Jesus' ministry and death—Zechariah 9:9: "Rejoice greatly, O Daughter of Zion! Shout, Daughter of Jerusalem! See, your king comes to you, righteous and having salvation, gentle and riding on a donkey, on a colt, the foal of a donkey." Psalm 22:16-18: "Dogs have surrounded me; a band of evil men has encircled me, they have pierced my hands and my feet. I can count all my bones; people stare and gloat over me. They divide my garments among them and cast lots for my clothing."

Likely the clearest prophecy about Jesus is the entire 53rd chapter of Isaiah. Isaiah 53:3-7 is especially unmistakable: "He was despised and rejected by men, a man of sorrows, and familiar with suffering. Like one from whom men hide their faces he was despised, and we esteemed him not. Surely he took up our infirmities and carried our sorrows, yet we considered him stricken by God, smitten by him, and afflicted. But he was pierced for our transgressions, he was crushed for our iniquities; the punishment that brought us peace was upon him, and by his wounds we are healed. We all, like sheep, have gone astray, each of us has turned to his own way; and the LORD has laid on him the iniquity of us all. He was oppressed and afflicted, yet he did not open his mouth; he was led like a lamb to the slaughter, and as a sheep before her shearers is silent, so he did not open his mouth."

The "seventy sevens" prophecy in Daniel chapter 9 predicted the precise date that Jesus, the Messiah, would be "cut off." Isaiah 50:6 accurately describes the beating that Jesus endured. Zechariah 12:10 predicts the "piercing" of the Messiah, which occurred after Jesus died on the cross. Many more examples could be provided, but these will suffice. The Old Testament most definitely prophesies the coming of Jesus as the Messiah.

Question: What does it mean that Jesus is the Son of Man?

Answer: Jesus is referred to as the "Son of Man" 88 times in the New Testament. A first meaning of the phrase "Son of Man" is as a reference to the prophecy of Daniel 7:13-14, "In my vision at night I looked, and there before me was one like a son of man, coming with the clouds of heaven. He approached the Ancient of Days and was led into his presence. He was given authority, glory and sovereign power; all peoples, nations and men of every language worshiped him. His dominion is an everlasting dominion that will not pass away, and his kingdom is one that will never be destroyed." The description "Son of Man" was a Messianic title. Jesus is the One who was given dominion and glory and a kingdom. When Jesus used this phrase, He was assigning the Son of Man prophecy to Himself. The Jews of that era would have been intimately familiar with the phrase and to whom it referred. Jesus was proclaiming Himself as the Messiah.

A second meaning of the phrase "Son of Man" is that Jesus was truly a human being. God called the prophet Ezekiel "son of man" 93 times. God was simply calling Ezekiel a human being. A son of a man is a man. Jesus was fully God (John 1:1), but He was also a human being (John 1:14). First John 4:2 tells us, "This is how you can recognize the Spirit of God: Every spirit that acknowledges that Jesus Christ has come in the flesh is from God." Yes, Jesus was the Son of God—He was in His essence God. Yes, Jesus was also the Son of Man—He was in His essence a human being. In summary, the phrase "Son of Man" indicates that Jesus is the Messiah and that He is truly a human being.

Question: Why did God send Jesus when He did? Why not earlier? Why not later?

Answer: "But when the time had fully come, God sent his Son, born of a woman, born under law" (Galatians 4:4). This verse declares that God the Father sent His Son when "the time had fully come." There were many things occurring at the time of the first century that, at least by human reasoning, seem to make it ideal for Christ to come then.

1. There was a great anticipation among the Jews of that time that the Messiah would come. The Roman rule over Israel made the Jews hungry for the Messiah's coming.
2. Rome had unified much of the world under its government, giving a sense of unity to the various lands. Also, because the empire was relatively peaceful, travel was possible, allowing the early Christians to spread the gospel. Such freedom to travel would have been impossible in other eras.
3. While Rome had conquered militarily, Greece had conquered culturally. A "common" form of the Greek language (different from classical Greek) was the trade language and was spoken throughout the empire, making it possible to communicate the gospel to many different people groups through one common language.
4. The fact that the many false idols had failed to give them victory over the Roman conquerors caused many to abandon the worship of those idols. At the same time, in the more "cultured" cities, the Greek philosophy and science of the time left others spiritually empty in the same way that the atheism of communist governments leaves a spiritual void today.
5. The mystery religions of the time emphasized a savior-god and required worshipers to offer bloody sacrifices, thus making the gospel of Christ which involved one ultimate sacrifice believable to them. The Greeks also believed in the immortality of the soul (but not of the body).
6. The Roman army recruited soldiers from among the provinces, introducing these men to Roman culture and to ideas (such as the gospel) that had not reached those outlying provinces yet. The earliest introduction of the gospel to Britain was the result of the efforts of Christian soldiers stationed there.

The above statements are based on men looking at that time and speculating about why that particular point in history was a good time for Christ to come. But we understand that God's ways are not our ways (Isaiah 55:8), and these may or may not have been some reasons for why He chose that particular time to send His Son. From the context of Galatians 3 and 4, it is evident that God sought to lay a foundation through the Jewish Law that would prepare for the coming of the Messiah. The Law was meant to help people understand the depth of their sinfulness (in that they were incapable of keeping the Law) so that they might more readily accept the cure for that sin through Jesus the Messiah (Galatians 3:22-23; Romans 3:19-20). The Law was also "put in charge" (Galatians 3:24) to lead people to Jesus as the Messiah. It did this through its many prophecies concerning the Messiah which Jesus fulfilled. Add to this the sacrificial system that pointed to the need for a sacrifice for sin as well as its own inadequacy (with each sacrifice always requiring later additional ones). Old Testament history also painted pictures of the person and work of Christ through several events and religious feasts (such as the willingness of Abraham to offer up Isaac, or the details of the Passover during the exodus from Egypt, etc.).

Finally, Christ came when He did in fulfillment of specific prophecy. Daniel 9:24-27 speaks of the "seventy weeks" or the seventy "sevens." From the context, these "weeks" or "sevens" refer to groups of seven years, not seven days. We can examine history and line up the details of the first sixty-nine weeks (the seventieth week will take place at a future point). The countdown of the seventy weeks begins with "the going forth of the command to restore and build Jerusalem" (v. 25). This command was given by Artaxerxes Longimanus in 445 B.C (see Nehemiah 2:5). After seven "sevens" plus 62 "sevens," or 69 x 7 years, the prophecy states, "the Anointed One will be cut off and will have nothing. The people of the ruler who will come will destroy the city and the sanctuary" and that the "end will come like a flood" (meaning major destruction) (v. 26). Here we have an unmistakable reference to the Savior's death on the cross. A century ago in his book *The Coming Prince*, Sir Robert Anderson gave detailed calculations of the sixty-nine weeks, using 'prophetic years,' allowing for leap years, errors in the calendar, the change from B.C to A.D., etc., and figured that the sixty-nine weeks ended on the very day of Jesus' triumphal entry into Jerusalem, five days before His death. Whether one uses this timetable or not, the point is that the timing of Christ's incarnation ties in with this detailed prophecy recorded by Daniel over five hundred years beforehand.

The timing of Christ's incarnation was such that the people of that time were prepared for His coming. The people of every century since then have more than sufficient evidence that Jesus was indeed the promised Messiah through His fulfillment of the Scriptures that pictured and prophesied His coming in great detail.

Chapter 3

QUESTIONS ABOUT

THE HOLY SPIRIT

CONTENTS

Who is the Holy Spirit? 78
When/How do we receive the Holy Spirit? 78
What is the blasphemy against the Holy Spirit? 79
What is the baptism of the Holy Spirit? 80
How can I be filled with the Holy Spirit? 81
How do I identify my spiritual gift? 83
How does God distribute spiritual gifts? Will God give me the spiritual
    gift I ask for? 83
Is a believer supposed to be able to feel the Holy Spirit? 85
What is the filioque clause? 87
What is the fruit of the Holy Spirit? 88
What does it mean to grieve/quench the Holy Spirit? 89
What is the role of the Holy Spirit in our lives today? 90
Is being slain in the Spirit biblical? 91
Will the Holy Spirit ever leave a believer? 92
What is the difference between a talent and a spiritual gift? 94
Are the miraculous gifts of the Spirit for today? 95
What is the gift of speaking in tongues? 96
What is praying in tongues? Is praying in tongues a prayer language
    between a believer and God? 98
Is speaking in tongues evidence for having the Holy Spirit? 101

Question: Who is the Holy Spirit?

Answer: There are many misconceptions about the identity of the Holy Spirit. Some view the Holy Spirit as a mystical force. Others understand the Holy Spirit as the impersonal power that God makes available to followers of Christ. What does the Bible say about the identity of the Holy Spirit? Simply put, the Bible declares that the Holy Spirit is God. The Bible also tells us that the Holy Spirit is a divine person, a being with a mind, emotions, and a will.

The fact that the Holy Spirit is God is clearly seen in many Scriptures, including Acts 5:3-4. In this verse Peter confronts Ananias as to why he lied to the Holy Spirit and tells him that he had "not lied to men but to God." It is a clear declaration that lying to the Holy Spirit is lying to God. We can also know that the Holy Spirit is God because He possesses the characteristics of God. For example, His omnipresence is seen in Psalm 139:7-8, "Where can I go from your Spirit? Where can I flee from your presence? If I go up to the heavens, you are there; if I make my bed in the depths, you are there." Then in 1 Corinthians 2:10-11, we see the characteristic of omniscience in the Holy Spirit. "But God has revealed it to us by his Spirit. The Spirit searches all things, even the deep things of God. For who among men knows the thoughts of a man except the man's spirit within him? In the same way no one knows the thoughts of God except the Spirit of God."

We can know that the Holy Spirit is indeed a divine person because He possesses a mind, emotions, and a will. The Holy Spirit thinks and knows (1 Corinthians 2:10). The Holy Spirit can be grieved (Ephesians 4:30). The Spirit intercedes for us (Romans 8:26-27). He makes decisions according to His will (1 Corinthians 12:7-11). The Holy Spirit is God, the third Person of the Trinity. As God, the Holy Spirit can truly function as the Comforter and Counselor that Jesus promised He would be (John 14:16, 26, 15:26).

Question: When/How do we receive the Holy Spirit?

Answer: The apostle Paul clearly taught that we receive the Holy Spirit the moment we receive Jesus Christ as our Savior. First Corinthians 12:13 declares, "For we were all baptized by one Spirit into one body—whether Jews or Greeks, slave or free—and we were all given the one Spirit to drink." Romans 8:9 tells us that if a person does not possess the Holy Spirit, he or she does not belong to Christ: "You, however, are controlled not by the sinful nature but by the Spirit, if the Spirit of God lives in you. And if anyone does not have the Spirit of Christ, he does not belong to Christ." Ephesians 1:13-14 teaches us that the Holy Spirit is the seal of salvation for all those who believe: "Having believed, you were marked in him with a seal, the promised Holy Spirit, who is a deposit guaranteeing our inheritance until the redemption of those who are God's possession—to the praise of his glory."

These three passages make it clear that the Holy Spirit is received at the moment of salvation. Paul could not say that we all were baptized by one Spirit and all given one Spirit to drink if not all of the Corinthian believers possessed the Holy Spirit. Romans 8:9 is even stronger, stating that if a person does not have the Spirit, he does not belong to Christ. Therefore, the possession of the Spirit is an identifying factor of the possession of salvation. Further, the Holy Spirit could not be the "seal of salvation" (Ephesians 1:13-14) if He is not received at the moment of salvation. Many scriptures make it abundantly clear that our salvation is secured the moment we receive Christ as Savior.

This discussion is controversial because the ministries of the Holy Spirit are often confused. The receiving/indwelling of the Spirit occurs at the moment of salvation. The filling of the Spirit is an ongoing process in the Christian life. While we hold that the baptism of the Spirit also occurs at the moment of salvation, some Christians do not. This sometimes results in the baptism of the Spirit being confused with "receiving the Spirit" as an act subsequent to salvation.

In conclusion, how do we receive the Holy Spirit? We receive the Holy Spirit by simply receiving the Lord Jesus Christ as our Savior (John 3:5-16). When do we receive the Holy Spirit? The Holy Spirit becomes our permanent possession the moment we believe.

Question: What is the blasphemy against the Holy Spirit?

Answer: The concept of "blasphemy against the Spirit" is mentioned in Mark 3:22-30 and Matthew 12:22-32. The term *blasphemy* may be generally defined as "defiant irreverence." The term can be applied to such sins as cursing God or willfully degrading things relating to God. It is also attributing some evil to God, or denying Him some good that we should attribute to Him. This case of blasphemy, however, is a specific one, called "the blasphemy against the Holy Spirit" in Matthew 12:31. In Matthew 12:31-32, the Pharisees, having witnessed irrefutable proof that Jesus was working miracles in the power of the Holy Spirit, claimed instead that the Lord was possessed by the demon "Beelzebub" (Matthew 12:24). Now notice that in Mark 3:30 Jesus is very specific about what they did to commit "blasphemy against the Holy Spirit."

This blasphemy has to do with someone accusing Jesus Christ of being demon-possessed instead of Spirit-filled. As a result, this particular incidence of blasphemy against the Holy Spirit cannot be duplicated today. Jesus Christ is not on earth—He is seated at the right hand of God. No one can witness Jesus Christ performing a miracle and then attribute that power to Satan instead of the Spirit. The closest example today would be attributing the miracle of a redeemed person's changed life to Satan's power rather than to the effects of the indwelling Holy Spirit.

The blasphemy of the Spirit today, which is the same as the unpardonable sin, is the state of continued unbelief. There is no pardon for a person who dies in unbelief. Continual rejection of the Holy Spirit's promptings to trust in Jesus Christ is the unpardonable blasphemy against Him. Remember what is stated in John 3:16: "For God so loved the world that he gave his one and only Son, that whoever believes in him shall not perish but have eternal life." Further on in the same chapter is the verse "Whoever believes in the Son has eternal life, but whoever rejects the Son will not see life, for God's wrath remains on him" (John 3:36). The only condition wherein someone would have no forgiveness is if he is not among the "whoever believes in Him," for it is he who "rejects the Son."

Question: What is the baptism of the Holy Spirit?

Answer: The baptism of the Holy Spirit may be defined as that work whereby the Spirit of God places the believer into union with Christ and into union with other believers in the body of Christ at the moment of salvation. First Corinthians 12:12-13 is the central passage in the Bible regarding the baptism of the Holy Spirit: "For we were all baptized by one Spirit into one body—whether Jews or Greeks, slave or free—and we were all given the one Spirit to drink" (1 Corinthians 12:13). While Romans 6:1-4 does not mention specifically the Spirit of God, it does describe the believer's position before God in language similar to the 1 Corinthians passage: "What shall we say, then? Shall we go on sinning so that grace may increase? By no means! We died to sin; how can we live in it any longer? Or don't you know that all of us who were baptized into Christ Jesus were baptized into his death? We were therefore buried with him through baptism into death in order that, just as Christ was raised from the dead through the glory of the Father, we too may live a new life."

The following facts are necessary to help solidify our understanding of Spirit baptism: First, 1 Corinthians 12:13 clearly states that all have been baptized, just as all been given the Spirit to drink (the indwelling of the Spirit). Second, nowhere in Scripture are believers told to be baptized with, in or by the Spirit, or in any sense to seek the baptism of the Holy Spirit. This indicates that all believers have had this experience. Third, Ephesians 4:5 seems to refer to Spirit baptism. If this is the case, Spirit baptism is the reality for every believer, just as "one faith" and "one Father" are.

In conclusion, the baptism of the Holy Spirit does two things, 1) it joins us to the body of Christ, and 2) it actualizes our co-crucifixion with Christ. Being in His body means we are risen with Him to newness of life (Romans 6:4). We should then exercise our spiritual gifts to keep that body functioning properly as stated in the context of 1 Corinthians 12:13. Experiencing the one Spirit baptism serves as the basis for keeping the unity of the church, as in the context of Ephesians 4:5. Being associated with Christ in His death, burial, and resurrection through Spirit baptism establishes the basis for our separation from the power of indwelling sin and our walk in newness of life (Romans 6:1-10; Colossians 2:12).

Question: How can I be filled with the Holy Spirit?

Answer: An important verse in understanding the filling of the Holy Spirit is John 14:16, where Jesus promised the Spirit would indwell believers and that the indwelling would be permanent. It is important to distinguish the indwelling from the filling of the Spirit. The permanent indwelling of the Spirit is not for a select few believers, but for all believers. There are a number of references in Scripture that support this conclusion. First, the Holy Spirit is a gift given to all believers in Jesus without exception, and no conditions are placed upon this gift except faith in Christ (John 7:37-39). Second, the Holy Spirit is given at the moment of salvation (Ephesians 1:13). Galatians 3:2 emphasizes this same truth, saying that the sealing and indwelling of the Spirit took place at the time of believing. Third, the Holy Spirit indwells believers permanently. The Holy Spirit is given to believers as a down payment, or verification of their future glorification in Christ (2 Corinthians 1:22; Ephesians 4:30).

This is in contrast to the filling of the Spirit referred to in Ephesians 5:18. We should be so completely yielded to the Holy Spirit that He can possess us fully and, in that sense, fill us. Romans 8:9 and Ephesians 1:13-14 states that He dwells within every believer, but He can be grieved (Ephesians 4:30), and His activity within us can be quenched (1 Thessalonians 5:19). When we allow this to happen, we do not experience the fullness of the Spirit's working and His power in and through us. To be filled with the Spirit implies freedom for Him to occupy every part of our lives, guiding and controlling us. Then His power can be exerted through us so that what we do is fruitful to God. The filling of the Spirit does not apply to outward acts alone; it also applies to the innermost thoughts and motives of our actions. Psalm 19:14 says, "May the words of my mouth and the meditation of my heart be pleasing in your sight, O Lord, my Rock and my Redeemer."

Sin is what hinders the filling of the Holy Spirit, and obedience to God is how the filling of the Spirit is maintained. Ephesians 5:18 commands that we be filled with the Spirit; however, it is not praying for the filling of the Holy Spirit that accomplishes the filling. Only our obedience to God's commands allows the Spirit freedom to work within us. Because we are still infected with sin, it is impossible to be filled with the Spirit all of the time. When we sin, we should immediately confess it to God and renew our commitment to being Spirit-filled and Spirit-led.

Question: How do I identify my spiritual gift?

Answer: There is no magic formula or definitive test that can tell us exactly what our spiritual gifts are. The Holy Spirit distributes the gifts as He determines (1 Corinthians 12:7-11). A common problem for Christians is the temptation to get so caught up in our spiritual gift that we only seek to serve God in the area in which we feel we have been gifted. That is not how the spiritual gifts work. God calls us to obediently serve Him in all things. He will equip us with whatever gift or gifts we need to accomplish the task He has called us to.

Identifying our spiritual giftedness can be accomplished in various ways. Spiritual gift tests or inventories, while not to be fully relied upon, can definitely help us understand where our gifting might be. Confirmation from others also gives light to our spiritual giftedness. Other people who see us serving the Lord can often identify a spiritual gift in use that we might take for granted or not recognize. Prayer is also important. The one person who knows exactly how we are spiritually gifted is the gift-giver Himself—the Holy Spirit. We can ask God to show us how we are gifted in order to better use our spiritual gifts for His glory.

Yes, God calls some to be teachers and gives them the gift of teaching. God calls some to be servants and blesses them with the gift of helps. However, specifically knowing our spiritual gift does not excuse us from serving God in areas outside our gifting. Is it beneficial to know what spiritual gift(s) God has given us? Of course it is. Is it wrong to focus so much on spiritual gifts that we miss other opportunities to serve God? Yes. If we are dedicated to being used by God, He will equip us with the spiritual gifts we need.

Question: How does God distribute spiritual gifts? Will God give me the spiritual gift I ask for?

Answer: Romans 12:3-8 and 1 Corinthians chapter 12 make it clear that each Christian is given spiritual gifts according to the Lord's choice. Spiritual gifts are given for the edification of the body of Christ (1 Corinthians 12:7, 14:12). The exact timing of the giving of these gifts is not specifically mentioned. Most assume that spiritual gifts are given at the time of spiritual birth (the moment of salvation).

However, there are some verses that may indicate God gives spiritual gifts later as well. Both 1 Timothy 4:14 and 2 Timothy 1:6 refer to a gift that Timothy had received at the time of his ordination "by prophecy." This likely indicates that one of the elders at Timothy's ordination spoke about a spiritual gift that Timothy would have to enable his future ministry.

We are also told in 1 Corinthians 12:28-31 and in 1 Corinthians 14:12-13 that it is God (not us) who chooses the gifts. These passages also indicate that not everyone will have a particular gift. Paul tells the Corinthian believers that if they are going to covet or long after spiritual gifts, they should strive after the more edifying gifts, such as prophesying (speaking forth the word of God for the building up of others). Now, why would Paul tell them to strongly desire the "greater" gifts if they already had been given all they would be given, and there was no further opportunity of gaining these greater gifts? It may lead one to believe that even as Solomon sought wisdom from God in order to be a good ruler over God's people, so God will grant to us those gifts we need in order to be of greater benefit to His church.

Having said this, it still remains that these gifts are distributed according to God's choosing, not our own. If every Corinthian strongly desired a particular gift, such as prophesying, God would not give everyone that gift simply because they strongly desired it. If He did, then who would serve in all of the other functions of the body of Christ?

There is one thing that is abundantly clear—God's command is God's enablement. If God commands us to do something (such as witness, love the unlovely, disciple the nations, etc.), He will enable us to do it. Some may not be as gifted at evangelism as others, but God commands all Christians to witness and disciple (Matthew 28:18-20; Acts 1:8). We are all called to evangelize whether or not we have the spiritual gift of evangelism. A determined Christian who strives to learn the Word and develop his teaching ability may become a better teacher than one who may have the spiritual gift of teaching, but who neglects the gift.

Are spiritual gifts given to us when we receive Christ, or are they cultivated through our walk with God? The answer is both. Normally, spiritual gifts are given at salvation, but also need to be cultivated through spiritual growth. Can a desire in your heart be pursued and developed into your spiritual gift? Can you seek after certain spiritual gifts? First Corinthians 12:31 seems to indicate that this is possible: "earnestly desire the best gifts." You can seek a spiritual gift from God and be zealous after it by seeking to develop that area. At the same time, if it is not God's will, you will not receive a certain spiritual gift no matter how strongly you seek after it. God is infinitely wise, and He knows through which gifts you will be most productive for His kingdom.

No matter how much we have been gifted with one gift or another, we are all called upon to develop a number of areas mentioned in the lists of spiritual gifts: to be hospitable, to show acts of mercy, to serve one another, to evangelize, etc. As we seek to serve God out of love for the purpose of building up others for His glory, He will bring glory to His name, grow His church, and reward us (1 Corinthians 3:5-8, 12:31–14:1). God promises that as we make Him our delight, He will give us the desires of our heart (Psalm 37:4-5). This would surely include preparing us to serve Him in a way that will bring us purpose and satisfaction.

Question: Is a believer supposed to be able to feel the Holy Spirit?

Answer: While certain ministries of the Holy Spirit may involve a feeling, such as conviction of sin, comfort, and empowerment, Scripture does not instruct us to base our relationship with the Holy Spirit on how or what we feel. Every born-again believer has the indwelling Holy Spirit. Jesus told us that when the Comforter has come He will be with us and in us. "And I will ask the Father, and he will give you another Counselor to be with you forever—the Spirit of truth. The world cannot accept him, because it neither sees him nor knows him. But you know him, for he lives with you and will be in you" (John 14:16-17). In other words, Jesus is sending one like Himself to be with us and in us.

We know the Holy Spirit is with us because God's Word tells us that it is so. Every born-again believer is indwelt by the Holy Spirit, but not every believer is controlled by the Holy Spirit, and there is a distinct difference. When we step out in our flesh, we are not under the control of the Holy Spirit even though we are still indwelt by Him. The apostle Paul comments on this truth, and he uses an illustration that helps us to understand. "Do not get drunk on wine, which leads to debauchery. Instead, be filled with the Spirit" (Ephesians 5:18). Many people read this verse and interpret it to mean that the apostle Paul is speaking against wine. However, the context of this passage is the walk and the warfare of the Spirit-filled believer. Therefore, there is something more here than just a warning about drinking too much wine.

When people are drunk with too much wine, they exhibit certain characteristics: they become clumsy, their speech is slurred, and their judgment is impaired. The apostle Paul sets up a comparison here. Just as there are certain characteristics that identify someone who is controlled by too much wine, there should also be certain characteristics that identify someone who is controlled by the Holy Spirit. We read in Galatians 5:22-24 about the fruit of the Spirit. This is the Holy Spirit's fruit, and it is exhibited by the born-again believer who is under His control.

The verb tense in Ephesians 5:18 indicates a continual process of "being filled" by the Holy Spirit. Since it is an exhortation, it follows that it is also possible to not be filled or controlled by the Spirit. The rest of Ephesians 5 gives us the characteristics of a Spirit-filled believer. "Speak to one another with psalms, hymns and spiritual songs. Sing and make music in your heart to the Lord, always giving thanks to God the Father for everything, in the name of our Lord Jesus Christ. Submit to one another out of reverence for Christ" (Ephesians 5:19-21).

We are not filled with the Spirit because we feel we are, but because this is the privilege and possession of the Christian. Being filled or controlled by the Spirit is the result of walking in obedience to the Lord. This is a gift of grace and not an emotional feeling. Emotions can and will deceive us, and we can work ourselves up into an emotional frenzy that is purely from the flesh and not of the Holy Spirit. "So I say, live by the Spirit, and you will not gratify the desires of the sinful nature … Since we live by the Spirit, let us keep in step with the Spirit" (Galatians 5:16, 25).

Having said that, we cannot deny that there are times when we can be overwhelmed by the presence and the power of the Spirit, and this is often an emotional experience. When that happens, it is a joy like no other. King David "danced with all his might" (2 Samuel 6:14) when they brought up the Ark of the Covenant to Jerusalem. Experiencing joy by the Spirit is the understanding that as children of God we are being blessed by His grace. So, absolutely, the ministries of the Holy Spirit can involve our feelings and emotions. At the same time, we are not to base the assurance of our possession of the Holy Spirit on how we feel.

Question: What is the filioque clause?

Answer: The filioque clause was, and still is, a controversy in the church in relation to the Holy Spirit. The question is, "from whom did the Holy Spirit proceed, the Father, or the Father and the Son?" The word *filioque* means "and son" in Latin. It is referred to as the "filioque clause" because the phrase "and son" was added to the Nicene Creed, indicating that the Holy Spirit proceeded from the Father "and Son." There was so much contention over this issue that it eventually led to the split between the Roman Catholic and Eastern Orthodox churches in A. D. 1054. The two churches are still not in agreement on the filioque clause.

John 14:26 tells us, "But the Counselor, the Holy Spirit, whom the Father will send in my name..." John 15:26 tells us, "When the Counselor comes, whom I will send to you from the Father, the Spirit of truth who goes out from the Father, He will testify about me." See also John 14:16 and Philippians 1:19. These Scriptures seem to indicate that the Spirit is sent out by both the Father and the Son. The essential matter in the filioque clause is a desire to protect the deity of the Holy Spirit. The Bible clearly teaches that the Holy Spirit is God (Acts 5:3-4). Those who oppose the filioque clause object because they believe the Holy Spirit proceeding from the Father and the Son makes the Holy Spirit "subservient" to the Father and Son. Those who uphold the filioque clause believe that the Holy Spirit proceeding from both the Father and the Son does not impact the Spirit being equally God with the Father and the Son.

The filioque clause controversy likely involves an aspect of God's person that we will never be able to fully grasp. God, who is an infinite being, is ultimately incomprehensible to our finite human minds. The Holy Spirit is God, and He was sent by God as Jesus Christ's "replacement" here on earth. The question of whether the Holy Spirit was sent by the Father, or by the Father and the Son, likely cannot be decisively answered, nor does it absolutely *need* to be. The filioque clause will perhaps have to remain a controversy.

Question: What is the fruit of the Holy Spirit?

Answer: Galatians 5:22-23 tells us, "But the fruit of the Spirit is love, joy, peace, patience, kindness, goodness, faithfulness, gentleness and self-control." The fruit of the Holy Spirit is the result of the Holy Spirit's presence in the life of a Christian. The Bible makes it clear that everyone receives the Holy Spirit the moment he or she believes in Jesus Christ (Romans 8:9; 1 Corinthians 12:13; Ephesians 1:13-14). One of the primary purposes of the Holy Spirit coming into a Christian's life is to change that life. It is the Holy Spirit's job to conform us to the image of Christ, making us more like Him.

The fruit of the Holy Spirit is in direct contrast with the acts of the sinful nature in Galatians 5:19-21, "The acts of the sinful nature are obvious: sexual immorality, impurity and debauchery; idolatry and witchcraft; hatred, discord, jealousy, fits of rage, selfish ambition, dissensions, factions and envy; drunkenness, orgies, and the like. I warn you, as I did before, that those who live like this will not inherit the kingdom of God." This passage describes all people, to varying degrees, when they do not know Christ and therefore are not under the influence of the Holy Spirit. Our sinful flesh produces certain types of fruit that reflect our nature, and the Holy Spirit produces types of fruit that reflect His nature.

The Christian life is a battle of the sinful flesh against the new nature given by Christ (2 Corinthians 5:17). As fallen human beings, we are still trapped in a body that desires sinful things (Romans 7:14-25). As Christians, we have the Holy Spirit producing His fruit in us and we have the Holy Spirit's power available to conquer the acts of the sinful nature (2 Corinthians 5:17; Philippians 4:13). A Christian will never be completely victorious in always demonstrating the fruits of the Holy Spirit. It is one of the main purposes of the Christian life, though, to progressively allow the Holy Spirit to produce more and more of His fruit in our lives—and to allow the Holy Spirit to conquer the opposing sinful desires. The fruit of the Spirit is what God desires our lives to exhibit and, with the Holy Spirit's help, it is possible!

Question: What does it mean to grieve/quench the Holy Spirit?

Answer: When the word "quench" is used in Scripture, it is speaking of suppressing fire. When believers put on the shield of faith, as part of their armor of God (Ephesians 6:16), they are extinguishing the power of the fiery darts from Satan. Christ described hell as a place where the fire would not be "quenched" (Mark 9:44, 46, 48). Likewise, the Holy Spirit is a fire dwelling in each believer. He wants to express Himself in our actions and attitudes. When believers do not allow the Spirit to be seen in our actions, when we do what we know is wrong, we suppress or quench the Spirit. We do not allow the Spirit to reveal Himself the way that He wants to.

To understand what it means to grieve the Spirit, we must first understand that this indicates the Spirit possesses personality. Only a person can be grieved; therefore, the Spirit must be a divine person in order to have this emotion. Once we understand this, we can better understand how He is grieved, mainly because we too are grieved. Ephesians 4:30 tells us that we should not grieve the Spirit. We grieve the Spirit by living like the pagans (4:17-19), by lying (4:25), by being angry (4:26-27), by stealing (4:28), by cursing (4:29), by being bitter (4:31), by being unforgiving (4:32), and by being sexually immoral (5:3-5). To grieve the Spirit is to act out in a sinful manner, whether it is in thought only or in both thought and deed.

Both quenching and grieving the Spirit are similar in their effects. Both hinder a godly lifestyle. Both happen when a believer sins against God and follows his or her own worldly desires. The only correct road to follow is the road that leads the believer closer to God and purity, and farther away from the world and sin. Just as we do not like to be grieved, and just as we do not seek to quench what is good—so we should not grieve or quench the Holy Spirit by refusing to follow His leading.

Question: What is the role of the Holy Spirit in our lives today?

Answer: Of all the gifts given to mankind by God, there is none greater than the presence of the Holy Spirit. The Spirit has many functions, roles, and activities. First, He does a work in the hearts of all people everywhere. Jesus told the disciples that He would send the Spirit into the world to "convict the world of guilt in regard to sin and righteousness and judgment" (John 16:7-11). Everyone has a "God consciousness," whether or not they admit it. The Spirit applies the truths of God to minds of men to convince them by fair and sufficient arguments that they are sinners. Responding to that conviction brings men to salvation.

Once we are saved and belong to God, the Spirit takes up residence in our hearts forever, sealing us with the confirming, certifying, and assuring pledge of our eternal state as His children. Jesus said He would send the Spirit to us to be our Helper, Comforter, and Guide. "And I will ask the Father, and he will give you another Counselor to be with you forever" (John 14:16). The Greek word translated here "Counselor" means "one who is called alongside" and has the idea of someone who encourages and exhorts. The Holy Spirit takes up permanent residence in the hearts of believers (Romans 8:9; 1 Corinthians 6:19-20, 12:13). Jesus gave the Spirit as a "compensation" for His absence, to perform the functions toward us which He would have done if He had remained personally with us.

Among those functions is that of revealer of truth. The Spirit's presence within us enables us to understand and interpret God's Word. Jesus told His disciples that "when He, the Spirit of Truth, comes, He will guide you into all truth" (John 16:13). He reveals to our minds the whole counsel of God as it relates to worship, doctrine, and Christian living. He is the ultimate guide, going before, leading the way, removing obstructions, opening the understanding, and making all things plain and clear. He leads in the way we should go in all spiritual things. Without such a guide, we would be apt to fall into error. A crucial part of the truth He reveals is that Jesus is who He said He is (John 15:26; 1 Corinthians 12:3). The Spirit convinces us of Christ's deity and incarnation, His being the Messiah, His suffering and death, His resurrection and ascension, His exaltation at the right hand of God, and His role as the judge of all. He gives glory to Christ in all things (John 16:14).

Another one of the Holy Spirit's roles is that of gift-giver. First Corinthians 12 describes the spiritual gifts given to believers in order that we may function as the body of Christ on earth. All these gifts, both great and small, are given by the Spirit so that we may be His ambassadors to the world, showing forth His grace and glorifying Him.

The Spirit also functions as fruit-producer in our lives. When He indwells us, He begins the work of harvesting His fruit in our lives—love, joy, peace, patience, kindness, goodness, faithfulness, gentleness and self-control (Galatians 5:22-23). These are not works of our flesh, which is incapable of producing such fruit, but they are products of the Spirit's presence in our lives.

The knowledge that the Holy Spirit of God has taken up residence in our lives, that He performs all these miraculous functions, that He dwells with us forever, and that He will never leave or forsake us is cause for great joy and comfort. Thank God for this precious gift—the Holy Spirit and His work in our lives!

Question: Is being slain in the Spirit biblical?

Answer: Most commonly, being "slain in the Spirit" happens when a minister lays hands on someone, and that person collapses to the floor, supposedly overcome by the power of the Holy Spirit. Those who practice slaying in the Spirit use Bible passages that talk about people becoming "as dead" (Revelation 1:17) or of falling upon their face (Ezekiel 1:28; Daniel 8:17-18, 10:7-9). However, there are a number of contrasts between this biblical falling on one's face and the practice of being slain in the Spirit.

1. The biblical falling down was a person's reaction to what he saw in a vision or an event beyond ordinary happenings, such as at the transfiguration of Christ (Matthew 17:6). In the unbiblical practice of being slain in the Spirit, the person responds to another's touch or to the motion of the speaker's arm.

2. The biblical instances were few and far between, and they occurred only rarely in the lives of a few people. In the slain in the Spirit phenomenon, falling down is a repeated event and an experience that happens to many.

3. In the biblical instances, the people fall upon their face in awe at either what or whom they see. In the slain in the Spirit counterfeit, they fall backwards, either in response to the wave of the speaker's arm or as a result of a church leader's touch (or push in some cases).

We are not claiming that all examples of being slain in the Spirit are fakes or responses to a touch or push. Many people claim to experience an energy or a force that causes them to fall back. However, we find no biblical basis for this concept. Yes, there may be some energy or force involved, but if so, it is very likely not of God and not the result of the working of the Holy Spirit.

It is unfortunate that people look to such bizarre counterfeits that produce no spiritual fruit, rather than pursuing the practical fruit which the Spirit gives us for the purpose of glorifying Christ with our lives (Galatians 5:22-23). Being filled with the Spirit is not evidenced by such counterfeits, but by a life that overflows with the Word of God in such a way that it spills over in praise, thanksgiving, and obedience to God.

Question: Will the Holy Spirit ever leave a believer?

Answer: Simply put, no, the Holy Spirit will never leave a true believer. This is revealed in many different passages in the New Testament. For example, Romans 8:9 tells us, "…if anyone does not have the Spirit of Christ, he does not belong to Christ." This verse very clearly states that if someone does not have the indwelling presence of the Holy Spirit, then that person is not saved. Therefore, if the Holy Spirit were to leave a believer, that person would have lost the saving relationship with Christ. Yet this is contrary to what the Bible teaches about the eternal security of Christians. Another verse that speaks to the permanence of the Holy Spirit's indwelling presence in the life of believers is John 14:16. Here Jesus states that the Father will give another Helper "to be with you forever."

The fact that the Holy Spirit will never leave a believer is also seen in Ephesians 1:13-14 where believers are said to be "sealed" with the Holy Spirit, "who is a deposit guaranteeing our inheritance until the redemption of those who are God's possession—to the praise of his glory." The picture of being sealed with the Spirit is one of ownership and possession. God has promised eternal life to all who believe in Christ, and as a guarantee that He will keep His promise, He has sent the Holy Spirit to indwell the believer until the day of redemption. Similar to making a down payment on a car or a house, God has provided all believers with a down payment on their future relationship with Him by sending the Holy Spirit to indwell them. The fact that all believers are sealed with the Spirit is also seen in 2 Corinthians 1:22 and Ephesians 4:30.

Prior to Christ's death, resurrection, and ascension into heaven, the Holy Spirit had a "come and go" relationship with people. The Holy Spirit indwelt King Saul, but then departed from him (1 Samuel 16:14). Instead, the Spirit came upon David (1 Samuel 16:13). After his adultery with Bathsheba, David feared that the Holy Spirit would be taken from him (Psalm 51:11). The Holy Spirit filled Bezaleel to enable him to produce the items needed for the tabernacle (Exodus 31:2-5), but this is not described as a permanent relationship. All of this changed after Jesus' ascension into heaven. Beginning on the day of Pentecost, the Holy Spirit began permanently indwelling believers (Acts 2). The permanent indwelling of the Holy Spirit is the fulfillment of God's promise to always be with us and never forsake us.

While the Holy Spirit will never leave a believer, it is possible for our sin to "quench the Holy Spirit" (1 Thessalonians 5:19) or "grieve the Holy Spirit" (Ephesians 4:30). Sin always has consequences in our relationship with God. While our relationship with God is secure in Christ, unconfessed sin in our lives can hinder our fellowship with God and effectively quench the Holy Spirit's working in our lives. That is why it is so important to confess our sins because God is "faithful and just and will forgive us our sins and purify us from all unrighteousness" (1 John 1:9). So, while the Holy Spirit will never leave us, the benefits and joy of His presence can in fact depart from us.

Question: What is the difference between a talent and a spiritual gift?

Answer: There are similarities and differences between talents and spiritual gifts. Both are gifts from God. Both grow in effectiveness with use. Both are intended to be used on behalf of others, not for selfish purposes. First Corinthians 12:7 states that spiritual gifts are given to benefit others and not ourselves. As the two great commandments deal with loving God and others, it follows that one should use his talents for those purposes. But to whom and when talents and spiritual gifts are given differs. A person (regardless of his belief in God or in Christ) is given a natural talent as a result of a combination of genetics (some have natural ability in music, art, or mathematics) and surroundings (growing up in a musical family will aid one in developing a talent for music), or because God desired to endow certain individuals with certain talents (for example, Bazeleel in Exodus 31:1-6). Spiritual gifts are given to all believers by the Holy Spirit (Romans 12:3, 6) at the time they place their faith in Christ for the forgiveness of their sins. At that moment, the Holy Spirit gives to the new believer the spiritual gift(s) He desires the believer to have (1 Corinthians 12:11).

Romans 12:3-8 lists the spiritual gifts as follows: prophecy, serving others (in a general sense), teaching, exhorting, generosity, leadership, and showing mercy. First Corinthians 12:8-11 lists the gifts as the word of wisdom (ability to communicate spiritual wisdom), the word of knowledge (ability to communicate practical truth), faith (unusual reliance upon God), the working of miracles, prophecy, discerning of spirits, tongues (ability to speak in a language that one has not studied), and interpretation of tongues. The third list is found in Ephesians 4:10-12, which speaks of God giving to His church apostles, prophets, evangelists, and pastor-teachers. There is also a question as to how many spiritual gifts there are, as no two lists are the same. It is also possible that the biblical lists are not exhaustive, that there are additional spiritual gifts beyond the ones the Bible mentions.

While one may develop his talents and later direct his profession or hobby along those lines, spiritual gifts were given by the Holy Spirit for the building up of Christ's church. In that, all Christians are to play an active part in the furtherance of the gospel of Christ. All are called and equipped to be involved in the "work of the ministry" (Ephesians 4:12). All are gifted so that they can contribute to the cause of Christ out of gratitude for all He has done for them. In doing so, they also find fulfillment in life through their labor for Christ. It is the job of the church leaders to help build up the saints so they can be further equipped for the ministry to which God has called them. The intended result of spiritual gifts is that the church as a whole can grow, being strengthened by the combined supply of each member of Christ's body.

To summarize the differences between spiritual gifts and talents: 1) A talent is the result of genetics and/or training, while a spiritual gift is the result of the power of the Holy Spirit. 2) A talent can be possessed by anyone, Christian or non-Christian, while spiritual gifts are only possessed by Christians. 3) While both talents and spiritual gifts should be used for God's glory and to minister to others, spiritual gifts are focused on these tasks, while talents can be used entirely for non-spiritual purposes.

Question: Are the miraculous gifts of the Spirit for today?

Answer: First, it is important to recognize that this is not a question of whether God still performs miracles today. It would be foolish and unbiblical to claim God does not heal people, speak to people, and perform miraculous signs and wonders today. The question is whether the miraculous gifts of the Spirit, described primarily in 1 Corinthians 12–14, are still active in the church today. This is also not a question of *can* the Holy Spirit give someone a miraculous gift. The question is *whether* the Holy Spirit still dispenses the miraculous gifts today. Above all else, we entirely recognize that the Holy Spirit is free to dispense gifts according to His will (1 Corinthians 12:7-11).

In the book of Acts and the Epistles, the vast majority of miracles are performed by the apostles and their close associates. Paul gives us the reason why: "The things that mark an apostle—signs, wonders and miracles—were done among you with great perseverance" (2 Corinthians 12:12). If every believer in Christ was equipped with the ability to perform signs, wonders, and miracles, then signs, wonders, and miracles could in no way be the identifying marks of an apostle. Acts 2:22 tells us that Jesus was "accredited" by "miracles, wonders, and signs." Similarly, the apostles were "marked" as genuine messengers from God by the miracles they performed. Acts 14:3 describes the gospel message being "confirmed" by the miracles Paul and Barnabas performed.

Chapters 12–14 of 1 Corinthians deal primarily with the subject of the gifts of the Spirit. It seems from that text "ordinary" Christians were sometimes given miraculous gifts (12:8-10, 28-30). We are not told how commonplace this was. From what we learned above, that the apostles were "marked" by signs and wonders, it would seem that miraculous gifts being given to "ordinary" Christians was the exception, not the rule. Beside the apostles and their close associates, the New Testament nowhere specifically describes individuals exercising the miraculous gifts of the Spirit.

It is also important to realize that the early church did not have the completed Bible, as we do today (2 Timothy 3:16-17). Therefore, the gifts of prophecy, knowledge, wisdom, etc. were necessary in order for the early Christians to know what God would have them do. The gift of prophecy enabled believers to communicate new truth and revelation from God. Now that God's revelation is complete in the Bible, the "revelatory" gifts are no longer needed, at least not in the same capacity as they were in the New Testament.

God miraculously heals people every day. God still speaks to us today, whether in an audible voice, in our minds, or through impressions and feelings. God still does amazing miracles, signs, and wonders and sometimes performs those miracles through a Christian. However, these things are not necessarily the miraculous gifts of the Spirit. The primary purpose of the miraculous gifts was to prove that the gospel was true and that the apostles were truly God's messengers. The Bible does not say outright that the miraculous gifts have ceased, but it does lay the foundation for why they might no longer occur to the same extent as they did as recorded in the New Testament.

Question: What is the gift of speaking in tongues?

Answer: The first occurrence of speaking in tongues occurred on the day of Pentecost in Acts 2:1-4. The apostles went out and shared the gospel with the crowds, speaking to them in their own languages:

"We hear them declaring the wonders of God in our own tongues!" (Acts 2:11). The Greek word translated tongues literally means "languages." Therefore, the gift of tongues is speaking in a language a person does not know in order to minister to someone who does speak that language. In 1 Corinthians chapters 12–14, Paul discusses miraculous gifts, saying, "Now, brothers, if I come to you and speak in tongues, what good will I be to you, unless I bring you some revelation or knowledge or prophecy or word of instruction?" (1 Corinthians 14:6). According to the apostle Paul, and in agreement with the tongues described in Acts, speaking in tongues is valuable to the one hearing God's message in his or her own language, but it is useless to everyone else unless it is interpreted/translated.

A person with the gift of interpreting tongues (1 Corinthians 12:30) could understand what a tongues-speaker was saying even though he did not know the language that was being spoken. The tongues interpreter would then communicate the message of the tongues speaker to everyone else, so all could understand. "For this reason anyone who speaks in a tongue should pray that he may interpret what he says" (1 Corinthians 14:13). Paul's conclusion regarding tongues that were not interpreted is powerful: "But in the church I would rather speak five intelligible words to instruct others than ten thousand words in a tongue" (1 Corinthians 14:19).

Is the gift of tongues for today? First Corinthians 13:8 mentions the gift of tongues ceasing, although it connects the ceasing with the arrival of the "perfect" in 1 Corinthians 13:10. Some point to a difference in the tense of the Greek verbs referring to prophecy and knowledge "ceasing" and that of tongues "being ceased" as evidence for tongues ceasing before the arrival of the "perfect." While possible, this is not explicitly clear from the text. Some also point to passages such as Isaiah 28:11 and Joel 2:28-29 as evidence that speaking in tongues was a sign of God's oncoming judgment. First Corinthians 14:22 describes tongues as a "sign to unbelievers." According to this argument, the gift of tongues was a warning to the Jews that God was going to judge Israel for rejecting Jesus Christ as Messiah. Therefore, when God did in fact judge Israel (with the destruction of Jerusalem by the Romans in A.D. 70), the gift of tongues would no longer serve its intended purpose. While this view is possible, the primary purpose of tongues being fulfilled does not necessarily demand its cessation. Scripture does not conclusively assert that the gift of speaking in tongues has ceased.

At the same time, if the gift of speaking in tongues were active in the church today, it would be performed in agreement with Scripture. It would be a real and intelligible language (1 Corinthians 14:10). It would be for the purpose of communicating God's Word with a person of another language (Acts 2:6-12). It would be in agreement with the command God gave through the apostle Paul, "If anyone speaks in a tongue, two—or at the most three—should speak, one at a time, and someone must interpret. If there is no interpreter, the speaker should keep quiet in the church and speak to himself and God" (1 Corinthians 14:27-28). It would also be in accordance with 1 Corinthians 14:33, "For God is not the author of confusion, but of peace, as in all churches of the saints."

God most definitely can give a person the gift of speaking in tongues to enable him or her to communicate with a person who speaks another language. The Holy Spirit is sovereign in the dispersion of the spiritual gifts (1 Corinthians 12:11). Just imagine how much more productive missionaries could be if they did not have to go to language school, and were instantly able to speak to people in their own language. However, God does not seem to be doing this. Tongues does not seem to occur today in the manner it did in the New Testament, despite the fact that it would be immensely useful. The vast majority of believers who claim to practice the gift of speaking in tongues do not do so in agreement with the Scriptures mentioned above. These facts lead to the conclusion that the gift of tongues has ceased or is at least a rarity in God's plan for the church today.

Question: What is praying in tongues? Is praying in tongues a prayer language between a believer and God?

Answer: There are four primary Scripture passages that are cited as evidence for praying in tongues: Romans 8:26; 1 Corinthians 14:4-17; Ephesians 6:18; and Jude verse 20. Ephesians 6:18 and Jude 20 mention "praying in the Spirit." However, tongues as a prayer language is not a likely interpretation of "praying in the Spirit."

Romans 8:26 teaches us, "In the same way, the Spirit helps us in our weakness. We do not know what we ought to pray for, but the Spirit himself intercedes for us with groans that words cannot express." Two key points make it highly unlikely that Romans 8:26 is referring to tongues as a prayer language. First, Romans 8:26 states that it is the Spirit who "groans," not believers. Second, Romans 8:26 states that the "groans" of the Spirit "cannot be expressed." The very essence of speaking in tongues is uttering words.

That leaves us with 1 Corinthians 14:4-17 and verse 14 especially: "For if I pray in a tongue, my spirit prays, but my mind is unfruitful." First Corinthians 14:14 distinctly mentions "praying in tongues." What does this mean? First, studying the context is immensely valuable. First Corinthians chapter 14 is primarily a comparison/contrast of the gift of speaking in tongues and the gift of prophecy. Verses 2-5 make it clear that Paul views prophecy as a gift superior to tongues. At the same time, Paul exclaims the value of tongues and declares that he is glad that he speaks in tongues more than anyone (verse 18).

Acts chapter 2 describes the first occurrence of the gift of tongues. On the day of Pentecost, the apostles spoke in tongues. Acts chapter 2 makes it clear that the apostles were speaking in a human language (Acts 2:6-8). The word translated "tongues" in both Acts chapter 2 and 1 Corinthians chapter 14 is *glossa* which means "language." It is the word from which we get our modern English word "glossary." Speaking in tongues was the ability to speak in a language the speaker does not know, in order to communicate the gospel to someone who does speak that language. In the multicultural area of Corinth, it seems that the gift of tongues was especially valuable and prominent. The Corinthians believers were able to better communicate the gospel and God's Word as a result of the gift of tongues. However, Paul made it abundantly clear that even in this usage of tongues, it was to be interpreted or "translated" (1 Corinthians 14:13, 27). A Corinthian believer would speak in tongues, proclaiming God's truth to someone who spoke that language, and then that believer, or another believer in the church, was to interpret what was spoken so that the entire assembly could understand what was said.

What, then, is praying in tongues, and how is it different than speaking in tongues? First Corinthians 14:13-17 indicates that praying in tongues is also to be interpreted. As a result, it seems that praying in tongues was offering a prayer to God. This prayer would minister to someone who spoke that language, but would also need to be interpreted so that the entire body could be edified.

This interpretation does not agree with those who view praying in tongues as a prayer language. This alternate understanding can be summarized as follows: praying in tongues is a personal prayer language between a believer and God (1 Corinthians 13:1) that a believer uses to edify himself (1 Corinthians 14:4). This interpretation is unbiblical for the following reasons: 1) How could praying in tongues be a private prayer language if it is to be interpreted (1 Corinthians 14:13-17)? 2) How could praying in tongues be for self-edification when Scripture says that the spiritual gifts are for the edification of the church, not the self (1 Corinthians 12:7). 3) How can praying in tongues be a private prayer language if the gift of tongues is a "sign to unbelievers" (1 Corinthians 14:22)? 4) The Bible makes it clear that not everyone possesses the gift of tongues (1 Corinthians 12:11, 28-30). How could tongues be a gift for self-edification if not every believer can possess it? Do we not all need to be edified?

Some understand praying in tongues to be a "secret code language" that prevents Satan and his demons from understanding our prayers and thereby gaining an advantage over us. This interpretation is unbiblical for the following reasons: 1) The New Testament consistently describes tongues as a human language. It is unlikely that Satan and his demons are unable to understand human languages. 2) The Bible records countless believers praying in their own language, out loud, with no concern of Satan intercepting the prayer. Even if Satan and/or his demons hear and understand the prayers we pray, they have absolutely no power to prevent God from answering the prayers according to His will. We know that God hears our prayers, and that fact makes it irrelevant whether Satan and his demons hear and understand our prayers.

What do we say, then, about the many Christians who have experienced praying in tongues and find it to be very personally edifying? First, we must base our faith and practice on Scripture, not experience. We must view our experiences in light of Scripture, not interpret Scripture in light of our experiences. Second, many of the cults and world religions also report occurrences of speaking in tongues/praying in tongues. Obviously the Holy Spirit is not gifting these unbelieving individuals. So, it seems that the demons are able to counterfeit the gift of speaking in tongues. This should cause us to compare even more carefully our experiences with Scripture. Third, studies have shown how speaking/praying in tongues can be a learned behavior. Through hearing and observing others speak in tongues, a person can learn the procedure, even subconsciously. This is the most likely explanation for the vast majority of instances of speaking/praying in tongues among Christians. Fourth, the feeling of "self-edification" is natural. The human body produces adrenaline and endorphins when it experiences something new, exciting, emotional, and/or disconnected from rational thought.

Praying in tongues is most definitely an issue on which Christians can respectfully and lovingly agree to disagree. Praying in tongues is not what determines salvation. Praying in tongues is not what separates a mature Christian from an immature Christian. Whether or not there is such a thing as praying in tongues as a personal prayer language is not a fundamental of the Christian faith. So, while we believe the biblical interpretation of praying in tongues leads away from the idea of a private prayer language for personal edification, we also recognize that many who practice such are our brothers and sisters in Christ and are worthy of our love and respect.

Question: Is speaking in tongues evidence for having the Holy Spirit?

Answer: There are three occasions in the book of Acts where speaking in tongues accompanied the receiving of the Holy Spirit—Acts 2:4, 10:44-46, and 19:6. However, these three occasions are the only places in the Bible where speaking in tongues is an evidence of receiving the Holy Spirit. Throughout the book of Acts, thousands of people believe in Jesus and nothing is said about them speaking in tongues (Acts 2:41, 8:5-25, 16:31-34, 21:20). Nowhere in the New Testament is it taught that speaking in tongues is the only evidence a person has received the Holy Spirit. In fact, the New Testament teaches the opposite. We are told that every believer in Christ has the Holy Spirit

(Romans 8:9; 1 Corinthians 12:13; Ephesians 1:13-14), but not every believer speaks in tongues (1 Corinthians 12:29-31).

So, why was speaking in tongues the evidence of the Holy Spirit in those three passages in Acts? Acts 2 records the apostles being baptized in the Holy Spirit and empowered by Him to proclaim the gospel. The apostles were enabled to speak in other languages (tongues) so they could share the truth with people in their own languages. Acts 10 records the apostle Peter being sent to share the gospel with non-Jewish people. Peter and the other early Christians, being Jews, would have a hard time accepting Gentiles (non-Jewish people) into the church. God enabled the Gentiles to speak in tongues to demonstrate that they had received the same Holy Spirit the apostles had received (Acts 10:47, 11:17).

Acts 10:44-47 describes this: "While Peter was still speaking these words, the Holy Spirit came on all who heard the message. The circumcised believers who had come with Peter were astonished that the gift of the Holy Spirit had been poured out even on the Gentiles. For they heard them speaking in tongues and praising God. Then Peter said, 'Can anyone keep these people from being baptized with water? They have received the Holy Spirit just as we have.'" Peter later refers back to this occasion as proof that God was indeed saving the Gentiles (Acts 15:7-11).

Speaking in tongues is nowhere presented as something all Christians should expect when they receive Jesus Christ as their Savior and are therefore baptized in the Holy Spirit. In fact, out of all the conversion accounts in the New Testament, only two record speaking in tongues in that context. Tongues was a miraculous gift that had a specific purpose for a specific time. It was not, and never has been, the only evidence of receiving the Holy Spirit.

Chapter 4

··

QUESTIONS ABOUT SALVATION

CONTENTS

What is the way of salvation?...104

What is salvation? What is the Christian doctrine of salvation?.............105

Is salvation by faith alone, or by faith plus works? 106

Can a Christian lose salvation? 107

How can salvation be not of works when faith is required? Isn't believing
    a work? 110

How can I have assurance of my salvation? 111

What is the substitutionary atonement? 112

How were people saved before Jesus died for our sins? 113

What happens to those who have never heard about Jesus? 115

Is eternal security a "license" to sin? 116

How does God's sovereignty and humanity's free will work together in
    salvation? 117

What happens to babies and young children when they die? Where do I
    find the age of accountability in the Bible? 118

Why did God require animal sacrifices in the Old Testament? 120

If our salvation is eternally secure, why does the Bible warn so strongly
    against apostasy? 122

Do Christians have to keep asking for forgiveness for their sins?............124

Is baptism necessary for salvation? What is baptismal regeneration? 126

What is justification?...127

What is Christian reconciliation? Why do we need to be reconciled to
    God?...128

What is the meaning of Christian redemption? 129

What is repentance and is it necessary for salvation? 130

Why is the resurrection of Jesus Christ important to salvation?.............132

Question: What is the way of salvation?

Answer: Are you hungry? Not physically hungry, but do you have a hunger for something more in life? Is there something deep inside of you that never seems to be satisfied? If so, Jesus is the way! Jesus said, "I am the bread of life. He who comes to me will never go hungry, and he who believes in me will never be thirsty" (John 6:35).

Are you confused? Can you never seem to find a path or purpose in life? Does it seem like someone has turned out the lights and you cannot find the switch? If so, Jesus is the way! Jesus proclaimed, "I am the light of the world. Whoever follows me will never walk in darkness, but will have the light of life" (John 8:12).

Do you ever feel like you are locked out of life? Have you tried so many doors, only to find that what is behind them is empty and meaningless? Are you looking for an entrance into a fulfilling life? If so, Jesus is the way! Jesus declared, "I am the gate; whoever enters through me will be saved. He will come in and go out, and find pasture" (John 10:9).

Do other people always let you down? Have your relationships been shallow and empty? Does it seem like everyone is trying to take advantage of you? If so, Jesus is the way! Jesus said, "I am the good shepherd. The good shepherd lays down his life for the sheep. I am the good shepherd; I know my sheep and my sheep know me" (John 10:11, 14).

Do you wonder what happens after this life? Are you tired of living your life for things that only rot or rust? Do you sometimes doubt whether life has any meaning? Do you want to live after you die? If so, Jesus is the way! Jesus declared, "I am the resurrection and the life. He who believes in me will live, even though he dies; and whoever lives and believes in me will never die" (John 11:25-26).

What is the way? What is the truth? What is the life? Jesus answered, "I am the way and the truth and the life. No one comes to the Father except through me" (John 14:6).

The hunger that you feel is a spiritual hunger, and can only be filled by Jesus. Jesus is the only one who can lift the darkness. Jesus is the door to a satisfying life. Jesus is the friend and shepherd that you have been looking for. Jesus is the life—in this world and the next. Jesus is the way of salvation!

The reason you feel hungry, the reason you seem to be lost in darkness, the reason you cannot find meaning in life, is that you are separated from God. The Bible tells us that we have all sinned, and are therefore separated from God (Ecclesiastes 7:20; Romans 3:23). The void you feel in your heart is God missing from your life. We were created to have a relationship with God. Because of our sin, we are separated from that relationship. Even worse, our sin will cause us to be separated from God for all of eternity, in this life and the next (Romans 6:23; John 3:36).

How can this problem be solved? Jesus is the way! Jesus took our sin upon Himself (2 Corinthians 5:21). Jesus died in our place (Romans 5:8), taking the punishment that we deserve. Three days later, Jesus rose from the dead, proving His victory over sin and death (Romans 6:4-5). Why did He do it? Jesus answered that question Himself: "Greater love has no one than this, that he lay down his life for his friends" (John 15:13). Jesus died so that we could live. If we place our faith in Jesus, trusting His death as the payment for our sins, all of our sins are forgiven and washed away. We will then have our spiritual hunger satisfied. The lights will be turned on. We will have access to a fulfilling life. We will know our true best friend and good shepherd. We will know that we will have life after we die—a resurrected life in heaven for eternity with Jesus!

"For God so loved the world that he gave his one and only Son, that whoever believes in him shall not perish but have eternal life" (John 3:16).

Have you made a decision to receive Jesus Christ as your Savior because of what you have read here? If so, please send us an email at questions@gotquestions.org.

Question: What is salvation? What is the Christian doctrine of salvation?

Answer: Salvation is deliverance from danger or suffering. To save is to deliver or protect. The word carries the idea of victory, health, or preservation. Sometimes, the Bible uses the words *saved* or *salvation* to refer to temporal, physical deliverance, such as Paul's deliverance from prison (Philippians 1:19).

More often, the word "salvation" concerns an eternal, spiritual deliverance. When Paul told the Philippian jailer what he must do to be saved, he was referring to the jailer's eternal destiny (Acts 16:30-31). Jesus equated being saved with entering the kingdom of God (Matthew 19:24-25).

What are we saved *from*? In the Christian doctrine of salvation, we are saved from "wrath," that is, from God's judgment of sin (Romans 5:9; 1 Thessalonians 5:9). Our sin has separated us from God, and the consequence of sin is death (Romans 6:23). Biblical salvation refers to our deliverance from the consequence of sin and therefore involves the removal of sin.

Who does the saving? Only God can remove sin and deliver us from sin's penalty (2 Timothy 1:9; Titus 3:5).

How does God save? In the Christian doctrine of salvation, God has rescued us through Christ (John 3:17). Specifically, it was Jesus' death on the cross and subsequent resurrection that achieved our salvation (Romans 5:10; Ephesians 1:7). Scripture is clear that salvation is the gracious, undeserved gift of God (Ephesians 2:5, 8) and is only available through faith in Jesus Christ (Acts 4:12).

How do we receive salvation? We are saved by *faith*. First, we must *hear* the gospel—the good news of Jesus' death and resurrection (Ephesians 1:13). Then, we must *believe*—fully trust the Lord Jesus (Romans 1:16). This involves repentance, a changing of mind about sin and Christ (Acts 3:19), and calling on the name of the Lord (Romans 10:9-10, 13).

A definition of the Christian doctrine of salvation would be "The deliverance, by the grace of God, from eternal punishment for sin which is granted to those who accept by faith God's conditions of repentance and faith in the Lord Jesus." Salvation is available in Jesus alone (John 14:6; Acts 4:12) and is dependent on God alone for provision, assurance, and security.

Question: Is salvation by faith alone, or by faith plus works?

Answer: This is perhaps the most important question in all of Christian theology. This question is the cause of the Reformation, the split between the Protestant churches and Catholic Church. This question is a key difference between biblical Christianity and most of the "Christian" cults. Is salvation by faith alone, or by faith plus works? Am I saved just by believing in Jesus, or do I have to believe in Jesus and do certain things?

The question of faith alone or faith plus works is made difficult by some hard-to-reconcile Bible passages. Compare Romans 3:28, 5:1 and Galatians 3:24 with James 2:24. Some see a difference between Paul (salvation is by faith alone) and James (salvation is by faith plus works). Paul dogmatically says that justification is by faith alone (Ephesians 2:8-9), while James appears to be saying that justification is by faith plus works. This apparent problem is answered by examining what exactly James is talking about. James is refuting the belief that a person can have faith without producing any good works (James 2:17-18). James is emphasizing the point that genuine faith in Christ will produce a changed life and good works (James 2:20-26). James is not saying that justification is by faith plus works, but rather that a person who is truly justified by faith will have good works in his/her life. If a person claims to be a believer, but has no good works in his/her life, then he/she likely does not have genuine faith in Christ (James 2:14, 17, 20, 26).

Paul says the same thing in his writings. The good fruit believers should have in their lives is listed in Galatians 5:22-23. Immediately after telling us that we are saved by faith, not works (Ephesians 2:8-9), Paul informs us that we were created to do good works (Ephesians 2:10). Paul expects just as much of a changed life as James does: "Therefore, if anyone is in Christ, he is a new creation; the old has gone, the new has come" (2 Corinthians 5:17). James and Paul do not disagree in their teaching regarding salvation. They approach the same subject from different perspectives. Paul simply emphasized that justification is by faith alone while James put emphasis on the fact that genuine faith in Christ produces good works.

Question: Can a Christian lose salvation?

Answer: Before this question is answered, the term "Christian" must be defined. A "Christian" is not a person who has said a prayer, or walked down an aisle, or been raised in a Christian family. While each of these things can be a part of the Christian experience, they are not what "makes" a Christian. A Christian is a person who has, by faith, received and fully trusted in Jesus Christ as the only Savior (John 3:16; Acts 16:31; Ephesians 2:8-9).

So, with this definition in mind, can a Christian lose salvation? Perhaps the best way to answer this crucially important question is to examine what the Bible says occurs at salvation, and to study what losing salvation would therefore entail. Here are a few examples:

A Christian is a new creation. "Therefore, if anyone is in Christ, he is a new creation; the old has gone, the new has come!" (2 Corinthians 5:17). This verse speaks of a person becoming an entirely new creature as a result of being "in Christ." For a Christian to lose salvation, the new creation would have to be canceled and reversed.

A Christian is redeemed. "For you know that it was not with perishable things such as silver or gold that you were redeemed from the empty way of life handed down to you from your forefathers, but with the precious blood of Christ, a lamb without blemish or defect" (1 Peter 1:18-19). The word "redeemed" refers to a purchase being made, a price being paid. For a Christian to lose salvation, God Himself would have to revoke His purchase that He paid for with the precious blood of Christ.

A Christian is justified. "Therefore, since we have been justified through faith, we have peace with God through our Lord Jesus Christ" (Romans 5:1). To "justify" means to "declare righteous." All those who receive Jesus as Savior are "declared righteous" by God. For a Christian to lose salvation, God would have to go back on His Word and "un-declare" what He had previously declared.

A Christian is promised eternal life. "For God so loved the world that he gave his one and only Son, that whoever believes in him shall not perish but have eternal life" (John 3:16). Eternal life is a promise of eternity (forever) in heaven with God. God promises, "Believe and you will have eternal life." For a Christian to lose salvation, eternal life would have to be taken away. If a Christian is promised to live forever, how then can God break this promise by taking away eternal life?

A Christian is guaranteed glorification. "And those he predestined, he also called; those he called, he also justified; those he justified, he also glorified" (Romans 8:30). As we learned in Romans 5:1, justification is declared at the moment of faith. According to Romans 8:30, glorification is guaranteed for all those whom God justifies. Glorification refers to a Christian receiving a perfect resurrection body in heaven. If a Christian can lose salvation, then Romans 8:30 is in error, because God could not guarantee glorification for all those whom He predestines, calls, and justifies.

Many more illustrations of what occurs at salvation could be shared. Even these few make it abundantly clear that a Christian cannot lose salvation. Most, if not all, of what the Bible says happens to us when we receive Jesus Christ as Savior would be invalidated if salvation could be lost. Salvation cannot be reversed. A Christian cannot be un-newly created. Redemption cannot be undone. Eternal life cannot be lost and still be considered eternal. If a Christian can lose salvation, God would have to go back on His Word and change His mind—two things that Scripture tells us God never does.

The most frequent objections to the belief that a Christian cannot lose salvation are 1) What about those who are Christians and continually live an immoral lifestyle? 2) What about those who are Christians but later reject the faith and deny Christ? The problem with these two objections is the phrase "who are Christians." The Bible declares that a true Christian will not live a continually immoral lifestyle (1 John 3:6). The Bible declares that anyone who departs the faith is demonstrating that he never truly was a Christian (1 John 2:19). Therefore, neither objection is valid. Christians do not continually live immoral lifestyles, nor do they reject the faith and deny Christ. Such actions are proof that they were never redeemed.

No, a Christian cannot lose salvation. Nothing can separate a Christian from God's love (Romans 8:38-39). Nothing can remove a Christian from God's hand (John 10:28-29). God is both willing and able to guarantee and maintain the salvation He has given us. Jude 24-25, "To Him who is able to keep you from falling and to present you before his glorious presence without fault and with great joy—to the only God our Savior be glory, majesty, power and authority, through Jesus Christ our Lord, before all ages, now and forevermore! Amen."

Question: How can salvation be not of works when faith is required? Isn't believing a work?

Answer: Our salvation depends solely upon Jesus Christ. He is our substitute, taking sin's penalty (2 Corinthians 5:21); He is our Savior from sin (John 1:29); He is the author and finisher of our faith (Hebrews 12:2). The work necessary to provide salvation was fully accomplished by Jesus Himself, who lived a perfect life, took God's judgment for sin, and rose again from the dead (Hebrews 10:12).

The Bible is quite clear that our own works do not help merit salvation. We are saved "not because of righteous things we had done" (Titus 3:5). "Not by works" (Ephesians 2:9). "There is no one righteous, not even one" (Romans 3:10). This means that offering sacrifices, keeping the commandments, going to church, being baptized, and other good deeds are incapable of saving anyone. No matter how "good" we are, we can never measure up to God's standard of holiness (Romans 3:23; Matthew 19:17; Isaiah 64:6).

The Bible is just as clear that salvation is conditional; God does not save everyone. The one condition for salvation is faith in Jesus Christ. Nearly 200 times in the New Testament, faith (or belief) is declared to be the sole condition for salvation (John 1:12; Acts 16:31).

One day, some people asked Jesus what they could do to please God: "What must we do to do the works God requires?" Jesus immediately points them to faith: "The work of God is this: to believe in the one he has sent" (John 6:28-29). So, the question is about God's requirements (plural), and Jesus' answer is that God's requirement (singular) is that you *believe* in Him.

Grace is God's giving us something we cannot earn or deserve. According to Romans 11:6, "works" of any kind destroys grace—the idea is that a worker earns payment, while the recipient of grace simply receives it, unearned. Since salvation is all of grace, it cannot be earned. Faith, therefore, is a non-work. Faith cannot truly be considered a "work," or else it would destroy grace. (See also Romans 4—Abraham's salvation was dependent on faith in God, as opposed to any work he performed.)

Suppose someone anonymously sent me a check for $1,000,000. The money is mine if I want it, but I still must endorse the check. In no way can signing my name be considered earning the million dollars—the endorsement is a non-work. I can never boast about becoming a millionaire through sheer effort or my own business savvy. No, the million dollars was simply a gift, and signing my name was the only way to receive it. Similarly, exercising faith is the only way to receive the generous gift of God, and faith cannot be considered a work worthy of the gift.

True faith cannot be considered a work because true faith involves a cessation of our works in the flesh. True faith has as its object Jesus and His work on our behalf (Matthew 11:28-29; Hebrews 4:10).

To take this a step further, true faith cannot be considered a work because even faith is a gift from God, not something we produce on our own. "For it is by grace you have been saved, through faith—and this not from yourselves, it is the gift of God" (Ephesians 2:8). "No one can come to me unless the Father who sent me draws him" (John 6:44). Praise the Lord for His power to save and for His grace to make salvation a reality!

Question: How can I have assurance of my salvation?

Answer: How can you know for sure if you are saved? Consider 1 John 5:11-13: "And this is the testimony: God has given us eternal life, and this life is in his Son. He who has the Son has life; he who does not have the Son of God does not have life. I write these things to you who believe in the name of the Son of God so that you may know that you have eternal life." Who is it that has the Son? It is those who have believed in Him and accepted Him (John 1:12). If you have Jesus, you have life. Not temporary life, but eternal.

God wants us to have assurance of our salvation. We cannot live our Christian lives wondering and worrying each day whether or not we are truly saved. That is why the Bible makes the plan of salvation so clear. Believe in Jesus Christ and you will be saved (John 3:16; Acts 16:31). Do you believe that Jesus is the Savior, that He died to pay the penalty for your sins (Romans 5:8; 2 Corinthians 5:21)? Are you trusting Him alone for salvation? If your answer is yes, you are saved! Assurance means "having been put beyond all doubt." By taking God's Word to heart, you can "put beyond all doubt" the fact and reality of your eternal salvation.

Jesus Himself affirms this regarding those who have believed in Him: "I give them eternal life, and they shall never perish; no one can snatch them out of my hand. My Father, who has given them to me, is greater than all; no one can snatch them out of my Father's hand" (John 10:28-29). Eternal life is just that—eternal. There is no one, not even yourself, who can take Christ's God-given gift of salvation away from you.

We hide God's Word in our hearts so that we do not sin against Him (Psalm 119:11), and this includes the sin of doubt. Take joy in what God's Word is saying to you, that instead of doubting we can live with confidence! We can have the assurance from Christ's own Word that our salvation will never be in question. Our assurance is based on God's love for us through Jesus Christ.

Question: What is the substitutionary atonement?

Answer: The substitutionary atonement refers to Jesus Christ dying as a substitute for sinners. The Scriptures teach that all men are sinners (Romans 3:9-18, 23). The penalty for our sinfulness is death. Romans 6:23 reads, "For the wages of sin is death, but the gift of God is eternal life in Christ Jesus our Lord."

That verse teaches us several things. Without Christ, we are going to die and spend an eternity in hell as payment for our sins. Death in the Scriptures refers to a "separation." Everyone will die, but some will live in heaven with the Lord for eternity, while others will live a life in hell for eternity. The death spoken of here refers to the life in hell. However, the second thing this verse teaches us is that eternal life is available through Jesus Christ. This is His substitutionary atonement.

Jesus Christ died in our place when He was crucified on the cross. We deserved to be the ones placed on that cross to die because we are the ones who live sinful lives. But Christ took the punishment on Himself in our place—He substituted Himself for us and took what we rightly deserved. "God made him who had no sin to be sin for us, so that in him we might become the righteousness of God" (2 Corinthians 5:21).

"He himself bore our sins in his body on the tree, so that we might die to sins and live for righteousness; by his wounds you have been healed" (1 Peter 2:24). Here again we see that Christ took the sins we committed onto Himself to pay the price for us. A few verses later we read, "For Christ died for sins once for all, the righteous for the unrighteous, to bring you to God. He was put to death in the body but made alive by the Spirit" (1 Peter 3:18). Not only do these verses teach us about the substitute that Christ was for us, but they also teach that He was the atonement, meaning He satisfied the payment due for the sinfulness of man.

One more passage that talks about the substitutionary atonement is Isaiah 53:5. This verse talks about the coming Christ who was to die on the cross for our sins. The prophecy is very detailed, and the crucifixion happened just as it was foretold. "But he was pierced for our transgressions, he was crushed for our iniquities; the punishment that brought us peace was upon him, and by his wounds we are healed." Notice the substitution. Here again we see that Christ paid the price for us!

We can only pay the price of sin on our own by being punished and placed in hell for all eternity. But God's Son, Jesus Christ, came to earth to pay for the price of our sins. Because He did this for us, we now have the opportunity to not only have our sins forgiven, but to spend eternity with Him. In order to do this we must place our faith in what Christ did on the cross. We cannot save ourselves; we need a substitute to take our place. The death of Jesus Christ is the substitutionary atonement.

Question: How were people saved before Jesus died for our sins?

Answer: Since the fall of man, the basis of salvation has always been the death of Christ. No one, either prior to the cross or since the cross, would ever be saved without that one pivotal event in the history of the world. Christ's death paid the penalty for past sins of Old Testament saints and future sins of New Testament saints.

The requirement for salvation has always been faith. The object of one's faith for salvation has always been God. The psalmist wrote, "Blessed are all who take refuge in him" (Psalm 2:12). Genesis 15:6 tells us that Abraham believed God and that was enough for God to credit it to him for righteousness (see also Romans 4:3-8). The Old Testament sacrificial system did not take away sin, as Hebrews 10:1-10 clearly teaches. It did, however, point to the day when the Son of God would shed His blood for the sinful human race.

What has changed through the ages is the content of a believer's faith. God's requirement of what must be believed is based on the amount of revelation He has given mankind up to that time. This is called progressive revelation. Adam believed the promise God gave in Genesis 3:15 that the Seed of the woman would conquer Satan. Adam believed Him, demonstrated by the name he gave Eve (v. 20) and the Lord indicated His acceptance immediately by covering them with coats of skin (v. 21). At that point that is all Adam knew, but he believed it.

Abraham believed God according to the promises and new revelation God gave him in Genesis 12 and 15. Prior to Moses, no Scripture was written, but mankind was responsible for what God had revealed. Throughout the Old Testament, believers came to salvation because they believed that God would someday take care of their sin problem. Today, we look back, believing that He has already taken care of our sins on the cross (John 3:16; Hebrews 9:28).

What about believers in Christ's day, prior to the cross and resurrection? What did they believe? Did they understand the full picture of Christ dying on a cross for their sins? Late in His ministry, "Jesus began to explain to his disciples that he must go to Jerusalem and suffer many things at the hands of the elders, chief priests and teachers of the law, and that he must be killed and on the third day be raised to life" (Matthew 16:21-22). What was the reaction of His disciples to this message? "Then Peter took him aside and began to rebuke him. 'Never, Lord!' he said. 'This shall never happen to you!'" Peter and the other disciples did not know the full truth, yet they were saved because they believed that God would take care of their sin problem. They didn't exactly know how He would accomplish that, any more than Adam, Abraham, Moses, or David knew how, but they believed God.

Today, we have more revelation than the people living before the resurrection of Christ; we know the full picture. "In the past God spoke to our forefathers through the prophets at many times and in various ways, but in these last days he has spoken to us by his Son, whom he appointed heir of all things, and through whom he made the universe" (Hebrews 1:1-2). Our salvation is still based on the death of Christ, our faith is still the requirement for salvation, and the object of our faith is still God. Today, for us, the content of our faith is that Jesus Christ died for our sins, He was buried, and He rose the third day (1 Corinthians 15:3-4).

Question: What happens to those who have never heard about Jesus?

Answer: All people are accountable to God whether or not they have "heard about Him." The Bible tells us that God has clearly revealed Himself in nature (Romans 1:20) and in the hearts of people (Ecclesiastes 3:11). The problem is that the human race is sinful; we all reject this knowledge of God and rebel against Him (Romans 1:21-23). If it were not for God's grace, we would be given over to the sinful desires of our hearts, allowing us to discover how useless and miserable life is apart from Him. He does this for those who continually reject Him (Romans 1:24-32).

In reality, it is not that some people have not heard about God. Rather, the problem is that they have rejected what they have heard and what is readily seen in nature. Deuteronomy 4:29 proclaims, "But if from there you seek the LORD your God, you will find him if you look for him with all your heart and with all your soul." This verse teaches an important principle—everyone who truly seeks after God will find Him. If a person truly desires to know God, God will make Himself known.

The problem is "there is no one who understands, no one who seeks God" (Romans 3:11). People reject the knowledge of God that is present in nature and in their own hearts, and instead decide to worship a "god" of their own creation. It is foolish to debate the fairness of God sending someone to hell who never had the opportunity to hear the gospel of Christ. People are responsible to God for what God has already revealed to them. The Bible says that people reject this knowledge, and therefore God is just in condemning them to hell.

Instead of debating the fate of those who have never heard, we, as Christians, should be doing our best to make sure they do hear. We are called to spread the gospel throughout the nations (Matthew 28:19-20;

Acts 1:8). We know people reject the knowledge of God revealed in nature, and that must motivate us to proclaim the good news of salvation through Jesus Christ. Only by accepting God's grace through the Lord Jesus Christ can people be saved from their sins and rescued from an eternity apart from God.

If we assume that those who never hear the gospel are granted mercy from God, we will run into a terrible problem. If people who never hear the gospel are saved, it is logical that we should make sure no one ever hears the gospel. The worst thing we could do would be to share the gospel with a person and have him or her reject it. If that were to happen, he or she would be condemned. People who do not hear the gospel must be condemned, or else there is no motivation for evangelism. Why run the risk of people possibly rejecting the gospel and condemning themselves when they were previously saved because they had never heard the gospel?

Question: Is eternal security a "license" to sin?

Answer: The most frequent objection to the doctrine of eternal security is that it supposedly allows people to live any way that they want and still be saved. While this may be "technically" true, it is not true in reality. A person who has truly been redeemed by Jesus Christ will not live a life characterized by continuous, willful sin. We must draw a distinction between how a Christian should live and what a person must do in order to receive salvation.

The Bible is clear that salvation is by grace alone, through faith alone, in Jesus Christ alone (John 3:16; Ephesians 2:8-9; John 14:6). The moment a person truly believes in Jesus Christ, he or she is saved and secure in that salvation. Salvation is not gained by faith, but then maintained by works. The apostle Paul addresses this issue in Galatians 3:3 when he asks, "Are you so foolish? After beginning with the Spirit, are you now trying to attain your goal by human effort?" If we are saved by faith, our salvation is also maintained and secured by faith. We cannot earn our own salvation. Therefore, neither can we earn the maintenance of our salvation. It is God who maintains our salvation (Jude 24). It is God's hand that holds us firmly in His grasp (John 10:28-29). It is God's love that nothing can separate us from (Romans 8:38-39).

QUESTIONS ABOUT SALVATION

Any denial of eternal security is, in its essence, a belief that we must maintain our own salvation by our own good works and efforts. This is completely antithetical to salvation by grace. We are saved because of Christ's merits, not our own (Romans 4:3-8). To claim that we must obey God's Word or live a godly life to maintain our salvation is saying that Jesus' death was not sufficient to pay the penalty for our sins. Jesus' death was absolutely sufficient to pay for all of our sins—past, present, and future, pre-salvation and post-salvation (Romans 5:8; 1 Corinthians 15:3; 2 Corinthians 5:21).

Does this mean that a Christian can live any way he wants to and still be saved? This is essentially a hypothetical question, because the Bible makes it clear that a true Christian will not live "any way he wants to." Christians are new creations (2 Corinthians 5:17). Christians demonstrate the fruit of the Spirit (Galatians 5:22-23), not the acts of the flesh (Galatians 5:19-21). First John 3:6-9 clearly states that a true Christian will not live in continual sin. In response to the accusation that grace promotes sin, the apostle Paul declared, "What shall we say, then? Shall we go on sinning so that grace may increase? By no means! We died to sin; how can we live in it any longer?" (Romans 6:1-2).

Eternal security is not a license to sin. Rather, it is the security of knowing that God's love is guaranteed for those who trust in Christ. Knowing and understanding God's tremendous gift of salvation accomplishes the opposite of giving a license to sin. How could anyone, knowing the price Jesus Christ paid for us, go on to live a life of sin (Romans 6:15-23)? How could anyone who understands God's unconditional and guaranteed love for those who believe, take that love and throw it back in God's face? Such a person is demonstrating not that eternal security has given him a license to sin, but rather that he or she has not truly experienced salvation through Jesus Christ. "No one who lives in him keeps on sinning. No one who continues to sin has either seen him or known him" (1 John 3:6).

Question: How does God's sovereignty and humanity's free will work together in salvation?

Answer: It is impossible for us to fully understand the relationship between God's sovereignty and man's free will and responsibility. Only God truly knows how they work together in His plan of salvation.

With this doctrine, probably more so than with any other, it is crucially important to admit our inability to fully grasp the nature of God and our relationship with Him. Going too far to either side results in a distorted understanding of salvation.

Scripture is clear that God determines who will be saved (Romans 8:29; 1 Peter 1:2). Ephesians 1:4 tells us that God chose us "before the creation of the world." The Bible repeatedly describes believers as the "chosen" (Romans 8:33, 11:5; Ephesians 1:11; Colossians 3:12; 1 Thessalonians 1:4; 1 Peter 1:2, 2:9) and the "elect" (Matthew 24:22, 31; Mark 13:20, 27; Romans 11:7; 1 Timothy 5:21; 2 Timothy 2:10; Titus 1:1; 1 Peter 1:1). The fact that believers are predestined (Romans 8:29-30; Ephesians 1:5, 11) and elected for salvation (Romans 9:11, 11:28; 2 Peter 1:10) is clear.

The Bible also says that we are responsible for receiving Christ as Savior. If we believe in Jesus Christ we will be saved (John 3:16; Romans 10:9-10). God knows who will be saved and God chooses who will be saved, and we must choose Christ in order to be saved. How these facts work together is impossible for a finite mind to comprehend (Romans 11:33-36). Our responsibility is to take the gospel to the world (Matthew 28:18-20; Acts 1:8). We should leave foreknowledge, election, and predestination up to God and simply be obedient in sharing the gospel.

Question: What happens to babies and young children when they die? Where do I find the age of accountability in the Bible?

Answer: Frequently lost in the discussion regarding the age of accountability is the fact that children, no matter how young, are not "innocent" in the sense of being sinless. The Bible tells us that even if an infant or child has not committed personal sin, all people, including infants and children, are guilty before God because of inherited and imputed sin. Inherited sin is that which is passed on from our parents. In Psalm 51:5, David wrote, "Surely I was sinful at birth, sinful from the time my mother conceived me." David recognized that even at conception, he was a sinner. The very sad fact that infants sometimes die demonstrates that even infants are impacted by Adam's sin, since physical and spiritual death were the results of Adam's original sin.

Each person, infant or adult, stands guilty before God; each person has offended the holiness of God. The only way God can be just and at the same time declare a person righteous is for that person to have received forgiveness by faith in Christ. Christ is the only way. John 14:6 records what Jesus said: "I am the way, and the truth, and the life; no one comes to the Father, except through Me." Also, Peter states in Acts 4:12, "Salvation is found in no one else, for there is no other name under heaven given to men by which we must be saved." Salvation is an individual choice.

What about babies and young children who never reach the ability to make this individual choice? The age of accountability is a concept that teaches those who die before reaching the age of accountability are automatically saved, by God's grace and mercy. The age of accountability is a belief that God saves all those who die before reaching the ability to make a decision for or against Christ. Thirteen is the most common number given for the age of accountability, based on the Jewish custom that a child becomes an adult at the age of 13. However, the Bible gives no direct support to the age of 13 always being the age of accountability. It likely varies from child to child. A child has passed the age of accountability once he or she is capable of making a faith decision for or against Christ.

With the above in mind, also consider this: Christ's death is presented as sufficient for all of mankind. First John 2:2 says Jesus is "the atoning sacrifice for our sins, and not only for ours but also for the sins of the whole world." This verse is clear that Jesus' death was sufficient for all sins, not just the sins of those who specifically have come to Him in faith. The fact that Christ's death was sufficient for all sin would allow the possibility of God's applying that payment to those who were never capable of believing.

The one passage that seems to identify with this topic more than any other is 2 Samuel 12:21-23. The context of these verses is that King David committed adultery with Bathsheba, with a resulting pregnancy. The prophet Nathan was sent by the Lord to inform David that because of his sin, the Lord would take the child in death. David responded to this by grieving, mourning, and praying for the child. But once the child was taken, David's mourning ended. David's servants were surprised to hear this. They said to King David, "What is this thing that you have done? While the child was alive, you fasted and wept; but when the child died, you arose and ate food." David's response was, "While the child was still alive, I fasted and wept; for I said, 'Who knows, the LORD may be gracious to me, that the child may live.' But now he has died; why should I fast? Can I bring him back again? I shall go to him, but he will not return to me." David's response indicates that those who cannot believe are safe in the Lord. David said that he could go to the child, but that he could not bring the child back to him. Also, and just as important, David seemed to be comforted over this. In other words, David seemed to be saying that he would see the child (in heaven), though he could not bring him back.

Although it is possible that God applies Christ's payment for sin to those who cannot believe, the Bible does not specifically say that He does this. Therefore, this is a subject about which we should not be adamant or dogmatic. God's applying Christ's death to those who cannot believe would seem consistent with His love and mercy. It is our position that God applies Christ's payment for sin to young children and those who are mentally handicapped, since they were not mentally capable of understanding their sinful state and their need for the Savior, but again we cannot be dogmatic. Of this we are certain: God is loving, holy, merciful, just, and gracious. Whatever He does is *always* right and good.

Question: Why did God require animal sacrifices in the Old Testament?

Answer: God required animal sacrifices to provide temporary forgiveness of sins and to foreshadow the perfect and complete sacrifice of Jesus Christ (Leviticus 4:35, 5:10). Animal sacrifice is an important theme found throughout Scripture because "without the shedding of blood there is no forgiveness" (Hebrews 9:22). When Adam and Eve sinned, animals were killed by God to provide clothing for them (Genesis 3:21). Cain and Abel brought sacrifices to the Lord. Cain's was unacceptable because he brought fruit, while Abel's was acceptable because it was the "firstborn of his flock" (Genesis 4:4-5). After the flood receded, Noah sacrificed animals to God (Genesis 8:20-21).

God commanded the nation of Israel to perform numerous sacrifices according to certain procedures prescribed by God. First, the animal had to be spotless. Second, the person offering the sacrifice had to identify with the animal. Third, the person offering the animal had to inflict death upon it. When done in faith, this sacrifice provided forgiveness of sins. Another sacrifice called for on the Day of Atonement, described in Leviticus 16, demonstrates forgiveness and the removal of sin. The high priest was to take two male goats for a sin offering. One of the goats was sacrificed as a sin offering for the people of Israel (Leviticus 16:15), while the other goat was released into the wilderness (Leviticus 16:20-22). The sin offering provided forgiveness, while the other goat provided the removal of sin.

Why, then, do we no longer offer animal sacrifices today? Animal sacrifices have ended because Jesus Christ was the ultimate and perfect sacrifice. John the Baptist recognized this when he saw Jesus coming to be baptized and said, "Look, the lamb of God who takes away the sin of the world!" (John 1:29). You may be asking yourself, why animals? What did they do wrong? That is the point—since the animals did no wrong, they died in place of the one performing the sacrifice. Jesus Christ also did no wrong but willingly gave Himself to die for the sins of mankind (1 Timothy 2:6). Jesus Christ took our sin upon Himself and died in our place. As 2 Corinthians 5:21 says, "God made him [Jesus] who had no sin to be sin for us, so that in him we might become the righteousness of God." Through faith in what Jesus Christ accomplished on the cross, we can receive forgiveness.

In summation, animal sacrifices were commanded by God so that the individual could experience forgiveness of sin. The animal served as a substitute—that is, the animal died in place of the sinner, but only temporarily, which is why the sacrifices needed to be offered over and over. Animal sacrifices have stopped with Jesus Christ. Jesus Christ was the ultimate sacrificial substitute once for all time (Hebrews 7:27) and is now the only mediator between God and humanity (1 Timothy 2:5). Animal sacrifices foreshadowed Christ's sacrifice on our behalf. The only basis on which an animal sacrifice could provide forgiveness of sins is Christ who would sacrifice Himself for our sins, providing the forgiveness that animal sacrifices could only illustrate and foreshadow.

Question: If our salvation is eternally secure, why does the Bible warn so strongly against apostasy?

Answer: The reason the Bible warns us so strongly against apostasy is that true conversion is measured by visible fruit. When John the Baptist was baptizing people in the Jordan River, he warned those who thought they were righteous to "produce fruit in keeping with repentance" (Matthew 3:7). Jesus warned those who were listening to Him while He was giving the Sermon on the Mount that every tree can be known by its fruit (Matthew 7:16) and that every tree that does not bear good fruit will be cut down and thrown into the fire (Matthew 7:19).

The purpose behind these warnings is to counter what some people would call "easy-believism." In other words, following Jesus is more than saying you are a Christian. Anyone can claim Christ as Savior, but those who are truly saved will bear visible fruit. Now, one may ask the question, "What is meant by fruit?" The clearest example of Christian fruit can be found in Galatians 5:22-23 where Paul describes the fruit of the Holy Spirit: love, joy, peace, patience, kindness, goodness, faithfulness, gentleness, and self-control. There are other types of Christian fruit (such as praise, winning souls for Christ), but this list provides us with a good summary of Christian attitudes. True believers will manifest these attitudes in their lives to an increasing degree as they progress in their Christian walk (2 Peter 1:5-8).

It is these true, fruit-bearing disciples who have the guarantee of eternal security, and they will persevere to the end. There are many Scriptures that bear this out. Romans 8:29-30 outlines the "golden chain" of salvation by pointing out that those who were foreknown by God were predestined, called, justified, and glorified—there is no loss along the way. Philippians 1:6 tells us that the work God began in us, He will also finish. Ephesians 1:13-14 teaches that God has sealed us with the Holy Spirit as a guarantee of our inheritance until we possess it. John 10:29 affirms that no one is able to take God's sheep out of His hand. There are many other Scriptures that say the same thing—true believers are eternally secure in their salvation.

The passages warning against apostasy serve two primary purposes. First, they exhort true believers to make sure of their "calling and election." Paul tells us in 2 Corinthians 13:5 to examine ourselves to see whether we are in the faith. If true believers are fruit-bearing followers of Jesus Christ, then we should be able to see the evidence of salvation. Christians bear fruit in varying degrees based on their level of obedience and their spiritual gifts, but all Christians bear fruit; and we should see the evidence of that upon self-examination.

There will be periods in a Christian's life where there is no visible fruit. These would be times of sin and disobedience. What happens during these times of prolonged disobedience is that God removes from us the *assurance* of our salvation. That is why David prayed in Psalm 51 to restore to him the "joy of salvation" (Psalm 51:12). We lose the joy of our salvation when we live in sin. That is why the Bible tells us to "examine yourselves to see whether you are in the faith; test yourselves" (2 Corinthians 13:5). When a true Christian examines himself and sees no recent fruitfulness, it should lead to serious repentance and turning to God.

The second reason for the passages on apostasy is to point out apostates so that we may recognize them. An apostate is someone who abandons his religious faith. It is clear from the Bible that apostates are people who made professions of faith in Jesus Christ, but never genuinely received Him as Savior. Matthew 13:1-9 (the Parable of the Sower) illustrates this point perfectly. In that parable, a sower sows seed, symbolizing the Word of God, onto four types of soil: hard soil, rocky soil, weed-choked soil, and freshly tilled soil. These soils represent four types of responses to the gospel. The first one is pure rejection, whereas the other three represent various levels of acceptance. The rocky soil and the weed-choked soil represent people who initially respond favorably to the gospel, but when persecution comes (rocky soil) or the cares of the world bear down (weed-choked soil), they turn away. Jesus makes it clear with these two types of responses that, although they initially "accepted" the gospel, they never bore any fruit because the seed (of the gospel) never penetrated the soil of the heart. Only the fourth soil, which was "prepared" by God, was able to receive the seed and bear fruit. Again, Jesus says in the Sermon on the Mount, "Not everyone who says to me, 'Lord, Lord,' will enter the kingdom of heaven" (Matthew 7:21).

It may seem unusual for the Bible to warn against apostasy and at the same time say that a true believer will never apostatize. However, this is what Scripture says. First John 2:19 specifically states that those who apostatize are demonstrating that they were not true believers. The biblical warnings against apostasy, therefore, must be a warning to those who are "in the faith" without ever truly having received it. Scriptures such as Hebrews 6:4-6 and Hebrews 10:26-29 are warnings to "pretend" believers that they need to examine themselves and realize that if they are considering apostatizing, they are not truly saved. Matthew 7:22-23 indicates that those "pretend believers" whom God rejects are rejected not because of having lost faith, but because of the fact that God never knew them.

There are many people who are willing to identify with Jesus. Who doesn't want eternal life and blessing? However, Jesus warns us to count the cost of discipleship (Luke 9:23-26, 14:25-33). True believers have counted those costs, whereas apostates have not. Apostates are people who, when they leave the faith, give evidence they were never saved in the first place (1 John 2:19). Apostasy is not a loss of salvation, but rather a demonstration that salvation was never truly possessed.

Question: Do Christians have to keep asking for forgiveness for their sins?

Answer: A frequent question is "what happens if I sin, and then I die before I have an opportunity to confess that sin to God?" Another common question is "what happens if I commit a sin, but then forget about it and never remember to confess it to God?" Both of these questions rest on a faulty assumption. Salvation is not a matter of believers trying to confess and repent from every sin they commit before they die. Salvation is not based on whether a Christian has confessed and repented of every sin. Yes, we should confess our sins to God as soon as we are aware that we have sinned. However, we do not always need to be asking God for forgiveness. When we place our faith in Jesus Christ for salvation, *all* of our sins are forgiven. That includes past, present, and future, big or small. Believers do not have to keep asking for forgiveness or repenting in order to have their sins forgiven. Jesus died to pay the penalty for all of our sins, and when they are forgiven, they are all forgiven (Colossians 1:14; Acts 10:43).

What we are to do is confess our sins: "If we confess our sins, He is faithful and just and will forgive us our sins and purify us from all unrighteousness" (1 John 1:9). What this verse tells us to do is "confess" our sins to God. The word "confess" means "to agree with." When we confess our sins to God, we are agreeing with God that we were wrong, that we have sinned. God forgives us, through confession, on an ongoing basis because of the fact that He is "faithful and just." How is God "faithful and just"? He is faithful by forgiving sins, which He has promised to do for all those who receive Christ as Savior. He is just by applying Christ's payment for our sins, recognizing that the sins have indeed been atoned for.

At the same time, 1 John 1:9 does indicate that somehow forgiveness is dependent on our confessing our sins to God. How does this work if all of our sins are forgiven the moment we receive Christ as Savior? It seems that what the apostle John is describing here is "relational" forgiveness. All of our sins are forgiven "positionally" the moment we receive Christ as Savior. This positional forgiveness guarantees our salvation and promise of an eternal home in heaven. When we stand before God after death, God will not deny us entrance into heaven because of our sins. That is positional forgiveness. The concept of relational forgiveness is based on the fact that when we sin, we offend God and grieve His Spirit (Ephesians 4:30). While God has ultimately forgiven us of the sins we commit, they still result in a blocking or hindrance in our relationship with God. A young boy who sins against his father is not cast out of the family. A godly father will forgive his children unconditionally. At the same time, a good relationship between father and son cannot be achieved until the relationship is restored. This can only occur when a child confesses his mistakes to his father and apologizes. That is why we confess our sins to God—not to maintain our salvation, but to bring ourselves back into close fellowship with the God who loves us and has already forgiven us.

Question: Is baptism necessary for salvation? What is baptismal regeneration?

Answer: Baptismal regeneration is the belief that a person must be baptized in order to be saved. It is our contention that baptism is an important step of obedience for a Christian, but we adamantly reject baptism as being required for salvation. We strongly believe that each and every Christian should be water baptized by immersion. Baptism illustrates a believer's identification with Christ's death, burial, and resurrection. Romans 6:3-4 declares, "Or don't you know that all of us who were baptized into Christ Jesus were baptized into His death? We were therefore buried with him through baptism into death in order that, just as Christ was raised from the dead through the glory of the Father, we too may live a new life." The action of being immersed in the water illustrates dying and being buried with Christ. The action of coming out of the water pictures Christ's resurrection.

Requiring anything in addition to faith in Jesus Christ for salvation is a works-based salvation. To add *anything* to the gospel is to say that Jesus' death on the cross was not sufficient to purchase our salvation. To say we must be baptized in order to be saved is to say we must add our own good works and obedience to Christ's death in order to make it sufficient for salvation. Jesus' death alone paid for our sins (Romans 5:8; 2 Corinthians 5:21). Jesus' payment for our sins is appropriated to our "account" by faith alone (John 3:16; Acts 16:31; Ephesians 2:8-9). Therefore, baptism is an important step of obedience after salvation but cannot be a requirement for salvation.

Yes, there are some verses that seem to indicate baptism as a necessary requirement for salvation. However, since the Bible so clearly tells us that salvation is received by faith alone (John 3:16; Ephesians 2:8-9; Titus 3:5), there must be a different interpretation of those verses. Scripture does not contradict Scripture. In Bible times, a person who converted from one religion to another was often baptized to identify conversion. Baptism was the means of making a decision public. Those who refused to be baptized were saying they did not truly believe. So, in the minds of the apostles and early disciples, the idea of an un-baptized believer was unheard of. When a person claimed to believe in Christ, yet was ashamed to proclaim his faith in public, it indicated that he did not have true faith.

If baptism is necessary for salvation, why would Paul have said, "I am thankful that I did not baptize any of you except Crispus and Gaius" (1 Corinthians 1:14)? Why would he have said, "For Christ did not send me to baptize, but to preach the gospel—not with words of human wisdom, lest the cross of Christ be emptied of its power" (1 Corinthians 1:17)? Granted, in this passage Paul is arguing against the divisions that plagued the Corinthian church. However, how could Paul possibly say, "I am thankful that I did not baptize…" or "For Christ did not send me to baptize…" if baptism were necessary for salvation? If baptism is necessary for salvation, Paul would literally be saying, "I am thankful that you were not saved…" and "For Christ did not send me to save…" That would be an unbelievably ridiculous statement for Paul to make. Further, when Paul gives a detailed outline of what he considers the gospel (1 Corinthians 15:1-8), why does he neglect to mention baptism? If baptism is a requirement for salvation, how could any presentation of the gospel lack a mention of baptism?

Baptismal regeneration is not a biblical concept. Baptism does not save from sin but from a bad conscience. In 1 Peter 3:21, Peter clearly taught that baptism was not a ceremonial act of physical purification, but the pledge of a good conscience toward God. Baptism is the symbol of what has already occurred in the heart and life of one who has trusted Christ as Savior (Romans 6:3-5; Galatians 3:27; Colossians 2:12). Baptism is an important step of obedience that every Christian should take. Baptism cannot be a requirement for salvation. To make it such is an attack on the sufficiency of the death and resurrection of Jesus Christ.

Question: What is justification?

Answer: Simply put, to justify is to declare righteous, to make one right with God. Justification is God's declaring those who receive Christ to be righteous, based on Christ's righteousness being imputed to the accounts of those who receive Christ (2 Corinthians 5:21). Though justification as a principle is found throughout Scripture, the main passage describing justification in relation to believers is Romans 3:21-26: "But now a righteousness from God, apart from law, has been made known, to which the Law and the prophets testify.

This righteousness from God comes through faith in Jesus Christ to all who believe. There is no difference, for all have sinned and fall short of the glory of God, and are justified freely by his grace through the redemption that came by Christ Jesus. God presented him as a sacrifice of atonement, through faith in his blood. He did this to demonstrate his justice, because in his forbearance he had left the sins committed beforehand unpunished—he did it to demonstrate his justice at the present time, so as to be just and the one who justifies those who have faith in Jesus."

We are justified, declared righteous, at the moment of our salvation. Justification does not make us righteous, but rather pronounces us righteous. Our righteousness comes from placing our faith in the finished work of Jesus Christ. His sacrifice covers our sin, allowing God to see us as perfect and unblemished. Because as believers we are in Christ, God sees Christ's own righteousness when He looks at us. This meets God's demands for perfection; thus, He declares us righteous—He justifies us.

Romans 5:18-19 sums it up well: "Consequently, just as the result of one trespass was condemnation for all men, so also the result of one act of righteousness was justification that brings life for all men. For just as through the disobedience of the one man the many were made sinners, so also through the obedience of the one man the many will be made righteous." It is because of justification that the peace of God can rule in our lives. It is because of justification that believers can have assurance of salvation. It is the fact of justification that enables God to begin the process of sanctification—the process by which God makes us in reality what we already are positionally. "Therefore, since we have been justified through faith, we have peace with God through our Lord Jesus Christ" (Romans 5:1).

Question: What is Christian reconciliation? Why do we need to be reconciled to God?

Answer: Imagine two friends who have a fight or argument. The good relationship they once enjoyed is strained to the point of breaking. They cease speaking to each other; communication is deemed too awkward. The friends gradually become strangers. Such estrangement can only be reversed by reconciliation. To be reconciled is to be restored to friendship or harmony. When old friends resolve their differences and restore their relationship, reconciliation has occurred. Second Corinthians 5:18-19 declares, "All this is from God, who reconciled us to himself through Christ and gave us the ministry of reconciliation: that God was reconciling the world to himself in Christ, not counting men's sins against them. And he has committed to us the message of reconciliation."

The Bible says that Christ reconciled us to God (Romans 5:10; 2 Corinthians 5:18; Colossians 1:20-21). The fact that we needed reconciliation means that our relationship with God was broken. Since God is holy, we were the ones to blame. Our sin alienated us from Him. Romans 5:10 says that we were enemies of God: "For if, when we were God's enemies, we were reconciled to him through the death of his Son, how much more, having been reconciled, shall we be saved through his life!"

When Christ died on the cross, He satisfied God's judgment and made it possible for God's enemies, us, to find peace with Him. Our "reconciliation" to God, then, involves the exercise of His grace and the forgiveness of our sin. The result of Jesus' sacrifice is that our relationship has changed from enmity to friendship. "I no longer call you servants ... Instead, I have called you friends" (John 15:15). Christian reconciliation is a glorious truth! We were God's enemies, but are now His friends. We were in a state of condemnation because of our sins, but we are now forgiven. We were at war with God, but now have the peace that transcends all understanding (Philippians 4:7).

Question: What is the meaning of Christian redemption?

Answer: Everyone is in need of redemption. Our natural condition was characterized by guilt: "all have sinned and fall short of the glory of God" (Romans 3:23). Christ's redemption has freed us from guilt, being "justified freely by His grace through the redemption that is in Christ Jesus" (Romans 3:24).

The benefits of redemption include eternal life (Revelation 5:9-10), forgiveness of sins (Ephesians 1:7), righteousness (Romans 5:17), freedom from the law's curse (Galatians 3:13), adoption into God's family (Galatians 4:5), deliverance from sin's bondage (Titus 2:14; 1 Peter 1:14-18), peace with God (Colossians 1:18-20), and the indwelling of the Holy Spirit (1 Corinthians 6:19-20). To be redeemed, then, is to be forgiven, holy, justified, free, adopted, and reconciled. See also Psalm 130:7-8; Luke 2:38; and Acts 20:28.

The word redeem means "to buy out." The term was used specifically in reference to the purchase of a slave's freedom. The application of this term to Christ's death on the cross is quite telling. If we are "redeemed," then our prior condition was one of slavery. God has purchased our freedom, and we are no longer in bondage to sin or to the Old Testament law. This metaphorical use of "redemption" is the teaching of Galatians 3:13 and 4:5.

Related to the Christian concept of redemption is the word ransom. Jesus paid the price for our release from sin and its consequences (Matthew 20:28; 1 Timothy 2:6). His death was in exchange for our life. In fact, Scripture is quite clear that redemption is only possible "through His blood," that is, by His death (Colossians 1:14).

The streets of heaven will be filled with former captives who, through no merit of their own, find themselves redeemed, forgiven, and free. Slaves to sin have become saints. No wonder we will sing a new song—a song of praise to the Redeemer who was slain (Revelation 5:9). We were slaves to sin, condemned to eternal separation from God. Jesus paid the price to redeem us, resulting in our freedom from slavery to sin and our rescue from the eternal consequences of that sin.

Question: What is repentance and is it necessary for salvation?

Answer: Many understand the term repentance to mean "turning from sin." This is not the biblical definition of repentance. In the Bible, the word repent means "to change one's mind." The Bible also tells us that true repentance will result in a change of actions (Luke 3:8-14; Acts 3:19). Acts 26:20 declares, "I preached that they should repent and turn to God and prove their repentance by their deeds." The full biblical definition of repentance is a change of mind that results in a change of action.

What, then, is the connection between repentance and salvation? The Book of Acts seems to especially focus on repentance in regards to salvation (Acts 2:38; 3:19; 11:18; 17:30; 20:21; 26:20). To repent, in relation to salvation, is to change your mind in regard to Jesus

Christ. In Peter's sermon on the day of Pentecost (Acts chapter 2), he concludes with a call for the people to repent (Acts 2:38). Repent from what? Peter is calling the people who rejected Jesus (Acts 2:36) to change their minds about Him, to recognize that He is indeed "Lord and Christ" (Acts 2:36). Peter is calling the people to change their minds from rejection of Christ as the Messiah to faith in Him as both Messiah and Savior.

Repentance and faith can be understood as "two sides of the same coin." It is impossible to place your faith in Jesus Christ as the Savior without first changing your mind about who He is and what He has done. Whether it is repentance from willful rejection or repentance from ignorance or disinterest, it is a change of mind. Biblical repentance, in relation to salvation, is changing your mind from rejection of Christ to faith in Christ.

It is crucially important that we understand repentance is not a work we do to earn salvation. No one can repent and come to God unless God pulls that person to Himself (John 6:44). Acts 5:31 and 11:18 indicate that repentance is something God gives—it is only possible because of His grace. No one can repent unless God grants repentance. All of salvation, including repentance and faith, is a result of God drawing us, opening our eyes, and changing our hearts. God's longsuffering leads us to repentance (2 Peter 3:9), as does His kindness (Romans 2:4).

While repentance is not a work that earns salvation, repentance unto salvation does result in works. It is impossible to truly and fully change your mind without that causing a change in action. In the Bible, repentance results in a change in behavior. That is why John the Baptist called people to "produce fruit in keeping with repentance" (Matthew 3:8). A person who has truly repented from rejection of Christ to faith in Christ will give evidence of a changed life (2 Corinthians 5:17; Galatians 5:19-23; James 2:14-26). Repentance, properly defined, is necessary for salvation. Biblical repentance is changing your mind about Jesus Christ and turning to God in faith for salvation (Acts 3:19). Turning from sin is not the definition of repentance, but it is one of the results of genuine, faith-based repentance towards the Lord Jesus Christ.

Question: Why is the resurrection of Jesus Christ important to salvation?

Answer: The resurrection of Jesus is important for several reasons. First, it witnesses to the immense power of God Himself. To believe in the resurrection is to believe in God. If God exists, and if He created the universe and has power over it, He has power to raise the dead. If He does not have such power, He is not a God worthy of our faith and worship. Only He who created life can resurrect it after death, only He can reverse the hideousness that is death itself, and only He can remove the sting that is death and the victory that is the grave's (1 Corinthians 15:54-55). In resurrecting Jesus from the grave, God reminds us of His absolute sovereignty over life and death.

Second, the resurrection of Jesus is a testimony to the resurrection of human beings, which is a basic tenet of the Christian faith. Unlike all other religions, Christianity alone possesses a founder who transcends death and who promises that His followers will do the same. All other religions were founded by men and prophets whose end was the grave. As Christians, we take comfort in the fact that our God became man, died for our sins, and was resurrected the third day. The grave could not hold Him. He lives, and He sits today at the right hand of God the Father in heaven.

In 1 Corinthians 15, Paul explains in detail the importance of the resurrection of Christ. Some in Corinth did not believe in the resurrection of the dead, and in this chapter Paul gives six disastrous consequences if there were no resurrection: 1) preaching Christ would be senseless (v. 14); 2) faith in Christ would be useless (v. 14); 3) all the witnesses and preachers of the resurrection would be liars (v. 15); 4) no one would be redeemed from sin (v. 17); 5) all former believers would have perished (v.18); and 6) Christians would be the most pitiable people on the earth (v. 19). But Christ indeed has risen from the dead and "has become the first-fruits of those who have fallen asleep" (v. 20), assuring that we will follow Him in resurrection.

The inspired Word of God guarantees the believer's resurrection at the coming of Jesus Christ for His Body (the Church) at the Rapture. Such hope and assurance results in a great song of triumph as Paul writes in 1 Corinthians 15:55, "Where, O death, is your victory? Where, O death, is your sting?"

How do these concluding verses relate to the importance of the resurrection? Paul answers, "...you know that your labor in the Lord is not in vain" (v. 58). He reminds us that because we know we will be resurrected to new life, we can suffer persecution and danger for Christ's sake (vv. 29-31), just as He did. We can follow the example of the thousands of martyrs through history who gladly traded their earthly lives for everlasting life via the resurrection.

The resurrection is the triumphant and glorious victory for every believer. Jesus Christ died, was buried, and rose the third day according to the Scripture. And, He is coming again! The dead in Christ will be raised up, and those who remain and are alive at His coming will be changed and receive new, glorified bodies (1 Thessalonians 4:13-18). Why is the resurrection of Jesus Christ important to salvation? It demonstrated that God accepted Jesus' sacrifice on our behalf. It proves that God has the power to raise us from the dead. It guarantees that those who believe in Christ will not remain dead, but will be resurrected unto eternal life. That is our blessed hope!

Chapter 5

QUESTIONS ABOUT THE BIBLE

CONTENTS

What is the Bible?..136

Is the Bible truly God's Word? 138

Does the Bible contain errors, contradictions, or discrepancies?............142

Is the Bible relevant for today?..143

What is the canon of Scripture? 144

How and when was the canon of the Bible put together?........................146

What does it mean that the Bible is inspired? 147

What is the proper way to study the Bible?....................................149

Why should we study the Bible?..150

Who were the authors of the books of the Bible? 153

Why is it important to believe in biblical inerrancy? 154

Is it possible that more books could be added to the Bible? 157

Has the Bible been corrupted, altered, edited, revised, or tampered with? 158

Old Testament vs. New Testament - what are the differences?................159

Why did God give us four Gospels? 161

Do I have to believe the Bible is inerrant to be saved? 164

What are the lost books of the Bible? 165

What is sola scriptura?..166

Where is a good place to start reading the Bible?........................169

Question: What is the Bible?

Answer: The word "Bible" comes from the Latin and Greek words meaning "book," a fitting name, since the Bible is the book for all people, for all time. It's a book like no other, in a class by itself.

Sixty-six different books comprise the Bible. They include books of law, such as Leviticus and Deuteronomy; historical books, such as Ezra and Acts; books of poetry, such as Psalms and Ecclesiastes; books of prophecy, such as Isaiah and Revelation; biographies, such as Matthew and John; and epistles (formal letters) such as Titus and Hebrews.

The Authors

About 40 different human authors contributed to the Bible, which was written over a period of about 1500 years. The authors were kings, fishermen, priests, government officials, farmers, shepherds, and doctors. From all this diversity comes an incredible unity, with common themes woven throughout.

The Bible's unity is due to the fact that, ultimately, it has one Author—God Himself. The Bible is "God-breathed" (2 Timothy 3:16). The human authors wrote exactly what God wanted them to write, and the result was the perfect and holy Word of God (Psalm 12:6; 2 Peter 1:21).

The Divisions

The Bible is divided into two main parts: the Old Testament and the New Testament. In short, the Old Testament is the story of a nation, and the New Testament is the story of a Man. The nation was God's way of bringing the Man—Jesus Christ—into the world.

The Old Testament describes the founding and preservation of the nation of Israel. God promised to use Israel to bless the whole world (Genesis 12:2-3). Once Israel was established as a nation, God raised up a family within that nation through whom the blessing would come: the family of David (Psalm 89:3-4). Then, from the family of David was promised one Man who would bring the promised blessing (Isaiah 11:1-10).

The New Testament details the coming of that promised Man. His name was Jesus, and He fulfilled the prophecies of the Old Testament as He lived a perfect life, died to become the Savior, and rose from the dead.

The Central Character

Jesus is the central character in the Bible—the whole book is really about Him. The Old Testament predicts His coming and sets the stage for His entrance into the world. The New Testament describes His coming and His work to bring salvation to our sinful world.

Jesus is more than a historical figure; in fact, He is more than a man. He is God in the flesh, and His coming was the most important event in the history of the world. God Himself became a man in order to give us a clear, understandable picture of who He is. What is God like? He is like Jesus; Jesus is God in human form (John 1:14, 14:9).

A Brief Summary

God created man and placed him in a perfect environment; however, man rebelled against God and fell from what God intended him to be. God placed the world under a curse because of sin but immediately set in motion a plan to restore humanity and all creation to its original glory.

As part of His plan of redemption, God called Abraham out of Babylonia into Canaan (about 2000 B.C). God promised Abraham, his son Isaac, and his grandson Jacob (also called Israel) that He would bless the world through a descendant of theirs. Israel's family emigrated from Canaan to Egypt, where they grew to be a nation.

About 1400 B.C, God led Israel's descendants out of Egypt under the direction of Moses and gave them the Promised Land, Canaan, as their own. Through Moses, God gave the people of Israel the Law and made a covenant (testament) with them. If they would remain faithful to God and not follow the idolatry of the surrounding nations, then they would prosper. If they forsook God and followed idols, then God would destroy their nation.

About 400 years later, during the reigns of David and his son Solomon, Israel was solidified into a great and powerful kingdom. God promised David and Solomon that a descendant of theirs would rule as an everlasting king.

After Solomon's reign, the nation of Israel was divided. The ten tribes to the north were called "Israel," and they lasted about 200 years before God judged them for their idolatry. Assyria took Israel captive about 721 B.C The two tribes in the south were called "Judah," and they lasted a little longer, but eventually they, too, turned from God. Babylon took them captive about 600 B.C

About 70 years later, God graciously brought a remnant of the captives back into their own land. Jerusalem, the capital, was rebuilt about 444 B.C, and Israel once again established a national identity. Thus, the Old Testament closes.

The New Testament opens about 400 years later with the birth of Jesus Christ in Bethlehem. Jesus was the descendant promised to Abraham and David, the One to fulfill God's plan to redeem mankind and restore creation. Jesus faithfully completed His work—He died for sin and rose from the dead. The death of Christ is the basis for a new covenant (testament) with the world. All who have faith in Jesus will be saved from sin and live eternally.

After His resurrection, Jesus sent His disciples to spread the news everywhere of His life and His power to save. Jesus' disciples went in every direction spreading the good news of Jesus and salvation. They traveled through Asia Minor, Greece, and all the Roman Empire. The New Testament closes with a prediction of Jesus' return to judge the unbelieving world and free creation from the curse.

Question: Is the Bible truly God's Word?

Answer: Our answer to this question will not only determine how we view the Bible and its importance to our lives, but also it will ultimately have an eternal impact on us. If the Bible is truly God's Word, then we should cherish it, study it, obey it, and fully trust it. If the Bible is the Word of God, then to dismiss it is to dismiss God Himself.

The fact that God gave us the Bible is an evidence and illustration of His love for us. The term "revelation" simply means that

God communicated to mankind what He is like and how we can have a right relationship with Him. These are things that we could not have known had God not divinely revealed them to us in the Bible. Although God's revelation of Himself in the Bible was given progressively over approximately 1500 years, it has always contained everything man needs to know about God in order to have a right relationship with Him. If the Bible is truly the Word of God, then it is the final authority for all matters of faith, religious practice, and morals.

The question we must ask ourselves is how can we know that the Bible is the Word of God and not just a good book? What is unique about the Bible that sets it apart from all other religious books ever written? Is there any evidence that the Bible is truly God's Word? These types of questions must be seriously examined if we are to determine the validity of the Bible's claim to be the very Word of God, divinely inspired, and totally sufficient for all matters of faith and practice. There can be no doubt that the Bible does claim to be the very Word of God. This is clearly seen in Paul's commendation to Timothy: "… from infancy you have known the holy Scriptures, which are able to make you wise for salvation through faith in Christ Jesus. All Scripture is God-breathed and is useful for teaching, rebuking, correcting and training in righteousness, so that the man of God may be thoroughly equipped for every good work" (2 Timothy 3:15-17).

There are both internal and external evidences that the Bible is truly God's Word. The internal evidences are those things within the Bible that testify of its divine origin. One of the first internal evidences that the Bible is truly God's Word is seen in its unity. Even though it is really sixty-six individual books, written on three continents, in three different languages, over a period of approximately 1500 years, by more than 40 authors who came from many walks of life, the Bible remains one unified book from beginning to end without contradiction. This unity is unique from all other books and is evidence of the divine origin of the words which God moved men to record.

Another of the internal evidences that indicates the Bible is truly God's Word is the prophecies contained within its pages. The Bible contains hundreds of detailed prophecies relating to the future of individual nations including Israel, certain cities, and mankind. Other prophecies concern the coming of One who would be the Messiah, the Savior of all who would believe in Him. Unlike the prophecies found in other religious books or those by men such as Nostradamus, biblical prophecies are extremely detailed. There are over three hundred prophecies concerning Jesus Christ in the Old Testament. Not only was it foretold where He would be born and His lineage, but also how He would die and that He would rise again. There simply is no logical way to explain the fulfilled prophecies in the Bible other than by divine origin. There is no other religious book with the extent or type of predictive prophecy that the Bible contains.

A third internal evidence of the divine origin of the Bible is its unique authority and power. While this evidence is more subjective than the first two, it is no less a powerful testimony of the divine origin of the Bible. The Bible's authority is unlike any other book ever written. This authority and power are best seen in the way countless lives have been transformed by the supernatural power of God's Word. Drug addicts have been cured by it, homosexuals set free by it, derelicts and deadbeats transformed by it, hardened criminals reformed by it, sinners rebuked by it, and hate turned to love by it. The Bible does possess a dynamic and transforming power that is only possible because it is truly God's Word.

There are also external evidences that indicate the Bible is truly the Word of God. One is the historicity of the Bible. Because the Bible details historical events, its truthfulness and accuracy are subject to verification like any other historical document. Through both archaeological evidences and other writings, the historical accounts of the Bible have been proven time and time again to be accurate and true. In fact, all the archaeological and manuscript evidence supporting the Bible makes it the best-documented book from the ancient world. The fact that the Bible accurately and truthfully records historically verifiable events is a great indication of its truthfulness when dealing with religious subjects and doctrines and helps substantiate its claim to be the very Word of God.

Another external evidence that the Bible is truly God's Word is the integrity of its human authors. As mentioned earlier, God used men from many walks of life to record His words. In studying the lives of these men, we find them to be honest and sincere. The fact that they were willing to die often excruciating deaths for what they believed testifies that these ordinary yet honest men truly believed God had spoken to them. The men who wrote the New Testament and many hundreds of other believers (1 Corinthians 15:6) knew the truth of their message because they had seen and spent time with Jesus Christ after He had risen from the dead. Seeing the risen Christ had a tremendous impact on them. They went from hiding in fear to being willing to die for the message God had revealed to them. Their lives and deaths testify to the fact that the Bible truly is God's Word.

A final external evidence that the Bible is truly God's Word is the indestructibility of the Bible. Because of its importance and its claim to be the very Word of God, the Bible has suffered more vicious attacks and attempts to destroy it than any other book in history. From early Roman Emperors like Diocletian, through communist dictators and on to modern-day atheists and agnostics, the Bible has withstood and outlasted all of its attackers and is still today the most widely published book in the world.

Throughout time, skeptics have regarded the Bible as mythological, but archeology has confirmed it as historical. Opponents have attacked its teaching as primitive and outdated, but its moral and legal concepts and teachings have had a positive influence on societies and cultures throughout the world. It continues to be attacked by pseudo-science, psychology, and political movements, yet it remains just as true and relevant today as it was when it was first written. It is a book that has transformed countless lives and cultures throughout the last 2000 years. No matter how its opponents try to attack, destroy, or discredit it, the Bible remains; its veracity and impact on lives is unmistakable. The accuracy which has been preserved despite every attempt to corrupt, attack, or destroy it is clear testimony to the fact that the Bible is truly God's Word and is supernaturally protected by Him. It should not surprise us that, no matter how the Bible is attacked, it always comes out unchanged and unscathed. After all, Jesus said, "Heaven and earth will pass away, but my words will never pass away" (Mark 13:31). After looking at the evidence, one can say without a doubt that, yes, the Bible is truly God's Word.

Question: Does the Bible contain errors, contradictions, or discrepancies?

Answer: If we read the Bible at face value, without a preconceived bias for finding errors, we will find it to be a coherent, consistent, and relatively easy-to-understand book. Yes, there are difficult passages. Yes, there are verses that appear to contradict each other. We must remember that the Bible was written by approximately 40 different authors over a period of around 1500 years. Each writer wrote with a different style, from a different perspective, to a different audience, for a different purpose. We should expect some minor differences. However, a difference is not a contradiction. It is only an error if there is absolutely no conceivable way the verses or passages can be reconciled. Even if an answer is not available right now, that does not mean an answer does not exist. Many have found a supposed error in the Bible in relation to history or geography only to find out that the Bible is correct once further archaeological evidence is discovered.

We often receive questions along the lines of "Explain how these verses do not contradict!" or "Look, here is an error in the Bible!" Admittedly, some of the things people bring up are difficult to answer. However, it is our contention that there are viable and intellectually plausible answers to every supposed Bible contradiction and error. There are books and websites available that list "all the errors in the Bible." Most people simply get their ammunition from these places; they do not find supposed errors on their own. There are also books and websites available that refute every one of these supposed errors. The saddest thing is that most people who attack the Bible are not truly interested in an answer. Many "Bible attackers" are even aware of these answers, but they continue to use the same old shallow attacks again and again.

So, what are we to do when someone approaches us with an alleged Bible error? 1) Prayerfully study the Scriptures and see if there is a simple solution. 2) Do some research using some of the fine Bible commentaries, "Bible defense" books, and biblical research websites. 3) Ask our pastors/church leaders to see if they can find a solution. 4) If there is still no clear answer after steps 1), 2), and 3) are followed, we trust God that His Word is truth and that there is a solution that just simply has not been realized yet (2 Timothy 2:15, 3:16-17).

Question: Is the Bible relevant for today?

Answer: Hebrews 4:12 says, "For the word of God is living and active. Sharper than any double-edged sword, it penetrates even to dividing soul and spirit, joints and marrow; it judges the thoughts and attitudes of the heart." While the Bible was completed approximately 1900 years ago, its accuracy and relevance for today remain unchanged. The Bible is the sole objective source of all the revelation God has given us about Himself and His plan for humanity.

The Bible contains a great deal of information about the natural world that has been confirmed by scientific observations and research. Some of these passages include Leviticus 17:11; Ecclesiastes 1:6-7; Job 36:27-29; Psalm 102:25-27 and Colossians 1:16-17. As the Bible's story of God's redemptive plan for humanity unfolds, many different characters are vividly described. In those descriptions, the Bible provides a great deal of information about human behavior and tendencies. Our own day-to-day experience shows us that this information is more accurate and descriptive of the human condition than any psychology textbook. Many historical facts recorded in the Bible have been confirmed by extra-biblical sources. Historical research often shows a great deal of agreement between biblical accounts and extra-biblical accounts of the same events.

However, the Bible is not a history book, a psychology text, or a scientific journal. The Bible is the description God gave us about who He is, and His desires and plans for humanity. The most significant component of this revelation is the story of our separation from God by sin and God's provision for restoration of fellowship through the sacrifice of His Son, Jesus Christ, on the cross. Our need for redemption does not change. Neither does God's desire to reconcile us to Himself.

The Bible contains a great deal of accurate and relevant information. The Bible's most important message—redemption—is universally and perpetually applicable to humanity. God's Word will never be outdated, superseded, or improved upon. Cultures change, laws change, generations come and go, but the Word of God is as relevant today as it was when it was first written. Not all of Scripture necessarily applies explicitly to us today, but all Scriptures contain truth that we can, and should, apply to our lives today.

Question: What is the canon of Scripture?

Answer: The word "canon" comes from the rule of law that was used to determine if a book measured up to a standard. It is important to note that the writings of Scripture were canonical at the moment they were written. Scripture was Scripture when the pen touched the parchment. This is very important because Christianity does not start by defining God, or Jesus Christ, or salvation. The basis of Christianity is found in the authority of Scripture. If we cannot identify what Scripture is, then we cannot properly distinguish any theological truth from error.

What measure or standard was used to determine which books should be classified as Scripture? A key verse to understanding the process and purpose, and perhaps the timing of the giving of Scripture, is Jude 3 which states that a Christian's faith "was once for all entrusted to the saints." Since our faith is defined by Scripture, Jude is essentially saying that Scripture was given once for the benefit of all Christians. Isn't it wonderful to know that there are no hidden or lost manuscripts yet to be found, there are no secret books only familiar to a select few, and there are no people alive who have special revelation requiring us to trek up a Himalayan mountain in order to be enlightened? We can be confident that God has not left us without a witness. The same supernatural power God used to produce His Word has also been used to preserve it.

Psalm 119:160 states that the entirety of God's Word is truth. Starting with that premise, we can compare writings outside the accepted canon of Scripture to see if they meet the test. As an example, the Bible claims that Jesus Christ is God (Isaiah 9:6-7; Matthew 1:22-23; John 1:1, 2, 14, 20:28; Acts 16:31, 34; Philippians 2:5-6; Colossians 2:9; Titus 2:13; Hebrews 1:8; 2 Peter 1:1). Yet many extra-biblical texts, claiming to be Scripture, argue that Jesus is not God. When clear contradictions exist, the established Bible is to be trusted, leaving the others outside the sphere of Scripture.

In the early centuries of the church, Christians were sometimes put to death for possessing copies of Scripture. Because of this persecution, the question soon came up, "What books are worth dying for?" Some books may have contained sayings of Jesus, but were they inspired as stated in 2 Timothy 3:16? Church councils played a role in publicly recognizing the canon of Scripture, but often an individual church or groups of churches recognized a book as inspired from its writing (e.g., Colossians 4:16; 1 Thessalonians 5:27). Throughout the early centuries of the church, few books were ever disputed and the list was basically settled by A.D. 303.

When it came to the Old Testament, three important facts were considered: 1) The New Testament quotes from or alludes to every Old Testament book but two. 2) Jesus effectively endorsed the Hebrew canon in Matthew 23:35 when He cited one of the first narratives and one of the last in the Scriptures of His day. 3) The Jews were meticulous in preserving the Old Testament Scriptures, and they had few controversies over what parts belong or do not belong. The Roman Catholic Apocrypha did not measure up and fell outside the definition of Scripture and has never been accepted by the Jews.

Most questions about which books belong in the Bible dealt with writings from the time of Christ and forward. The early church had some very specific criteria in order for books to be considered as part of the New Testament. These included: Was the book written by someone who was an eyewitness of Jesus Christ? Did the book pass the "truth test"? (i.e., did it concur with other, already agreed-upon Scripture?). The New Testament books they accepted back then have endured the test of time and Christian orthodoxy has embraced these, with little challenge, for centuries.

Confidence in the acceptance of specific books dates back to the first century recipients who offered firsthand testimony as to their authenticity. Furthermore, the end-time subject matter of the book of Revelation, and the prohibition of adding to the words of the book in Revelation 22:18, argue strongly that the canon was closed at the time of its writing (c. A.D. 95).

There is an important theological point that should not be missed. God has used His word for millennia for one primary purpose—to reveal Himself and communicate to mankind. Ultimately, the church councils did not decide if a book was Scripture; that was decided when the human author was chosen by God to write. In order to accomplish the end result, including the preservation of His Word through the centuries, God guided the early church councils in their recognition of the canon.

The acquisition of knowledge regarding such things as the true nature of God, the origin of the universe and life, the purpose and meaning of life, the wonders of salvation, and future events (including the destiny of mankind) are beyond the natural observational and scientific capacity of mankind. The already-delivered Word of God, valued and personally applied by Christians for centuries, is sufficient to explain to us everything we need to know of Christ (John 5:18; Acts 18:28; Galatians 3:22; 2 Timothy 3:15) and to teach us, correct us, and instruct us into all righteousness (2 Timothy 3:16).

Question: How and when was the canon of the Bible put together?

Answer: The term "canon" is used to describe the books that are divinely inspired and therefore belong in the Bible. The difficulty in determining the biblical canon is that the Bible does not give us a list of the books that belong in the Bible. Determining the canon was a process conducted first by Jewish rabbis and scholars and later by early Christians. Ultimately, it was God who decided what books belonged in the biblical canon. A book of Scripture belonged in the canon from the moment God inspired its writing. It was simply a matter of God's convincing His human followers which books should be included in the Bible.

Compared to the New Testament, there was very little controversy over the canon of the Old Testament. Hebrew believers recognized God's messengers and accepted their writings as inspired of God. While there was undeniably some debate in regards to the Old Testament canon, by A.D. 250 there was nearly universal agreement on the canon of Hebrew Scripture. The only issue that remained was the Apocrypha, with some debate and discussion continuing today. The vast majority of Hebrew scholars considered the Apocrypha to be good historical and religious documents, but not on the same level as the Hebrew Scriptures.

For the New Testament, the process of the recognition and collection began in the first centuries of the Christian church. Very early on, some of the New Testament books were being recognized. Paul considered Luke's writings to be as authoritative as the Old Testament (1 Timothy 5:18; see also Deuteronomy 25:4 and Luke 10:7). Peter recognized Paul's writings as Scripture (2 Peter 3:15-16). Some of the books of the New Testament were being circulated among the churches (Colossians 4:16; 1 Thessalonians 5:27). Clement of Rome mentioned at least eight New Testament books (A.D. 95). Ignatius of Antioch acknowledged about seven books (A.D. 115). Polycarp, a disciple of John the apostle, acknowledged 15 books (A.D. 108). Later, Irenaeus mentioned 21 books (A.D. 185). Hippolytus recognized 22 books (A.D. 170-235). The New Testament books receiving the most controversy were Hebrews, James, 2 Peter, 2 John, and 3 John.

The first "canon" was the Muratorian Canon, which was compiled in A.D. 170. The Muratorian Canon included all of the New Testament books except Hebrews, James, and 3 John. In A.D. 363, the Council of Laodicea stated that only the Old Testament (along with the Apocrypha) and the 27 books of the New Testament were to be read in the churches. The Council of Hippo (A.D. 393) and the Council of Carthage (A.D. 397) also affirmed the same 27 books as authoritative.

The councils followed something similar to the following principles to determine whether a New Testament book was truly inspired by the Holy Spirit: 1) Was the author an apostle or have a close connection with an apostle? 2) Is the book being accepted by the body of Christ at large? 3) Did the book contain consistency of doctrine and orthodox teaching? 4) Did the book bear evidence of high moral and spiritual values that would reflect a work of the Holy Spirit? Again, it is crucial to remember that the church did not determine the canon. No early church council decided on the canon. It was God, and God alone, who determined which books belonged in the Bible. It was simply a matter of God's imparting to His followers what He had already decided. The human process of collecting the books of the Bible was flawed, but God, in His sovereignty, and despite our ignorance and stubbornness, brought the early church to the recognition of the books He had inspired.

Question: What does it mean that the Bible is inspired?

Answer: When people speak of the Bible as inspired, they are referring to the fact that God divinely influenced the human authors of the Scriptures in such a way that what they wrote was the very Word of God. In the context of the Scriptures, the word "inspiration" simply means "God-breathed." Inspiration means the Bible truly is the Word of God and makes the Bible unique among all other books.

While there are different views as to the extent to which the Bible is inspired, there can be no doubt that the Bible itself claims that every word in every part of the Bible comes from God (1 Corinthians 2:12-13; 2 Timothy 3:16-17). This view of the Scriptures is often referred to as "verbal plenary" inspiration. That means the inspiration extends to the very words themselves (verbal)—not just concepts or ideas—and that the inspiration extends to all parts of Scripture and all subject matters of Scripture (plenary). Some people believe only parts of the Bible are inspired or only the thoughts or concepts that deal with religion are inspired, but these views of inspiration fall short of the Bible's claims about itself. Full verbal plenary inspiration is an essential characteristic of the Word of God.

The extent of inspiration can be clearly seen in 2 Timothy 3:16, "All Scripture is God-breathed and is useful for teaching, rebuking, correcting and training in righteousness, so that the man of God may be thoroughly equipped for every good work." This verse tells us that God inspired all Scripture and that it is profitable to us. It is not just the parts of the Bible that deal with religious doctrines that are inspired, but each and every word from Genesis to Revelation. Because it is inspired by God, the Scriptures are therefore authoritative when it comes to establishing doctrine, and sufficient for teaching man how be in a right relationship with God. The Bible claims not only to be inspired by God, but also to have the supernatural ability to change us and make us "complete." What more can we need?

Another verse that deals with the inspiration of the Scriptures is 2 Peter 1:21. This verse helps us to understand that even though God used men with their distinctive personalities and writing styles, God divinely inspired the very words they wrote. Jesus Himself confirmed the verbal plenary inspiration of the Scriptures when He said, "Do not think that I have come to abolish the Law or the Prophets; I have not come to abolish them but to fulfill them. I tell you the truth, until heaven and earth disappear, not the smallest letter, not the least stroke of a pen, will by any means disappear from the Law..." (Matthew 5:17-18). In these verses, Jesus is reinforcing the accuracy of the Scriptures down to the smallest detail and the slightest punctuation mark, because it is the very Word of God.

Because the Scriptures are the inspired Word of God, we can conclude that they are also inerrant and authoritative. A correct view of God will lead us to a correct view of His Word. Because God is all-powerful, all-knowing, and completely perfect, His Word will by its very nature have the same characteristics. The same verses that establish the inspiration of the Scriptures also establish that it is both inerrant and authoritative. Without a doubt the Bible is what it claims to be—the undeniable, authoritative, Word of God to humanity.

Question: What is the proper way to study the Bible?

Answer: Determining the meaning of Scripture is one of the most important tasks a believer has in this life. God does not tell us that we must simply read the Bible. We must study it and handle it correctly (2 Timothy 2:15). Studying the Scriptures is hard work. A cursory or brief scanning of Scripture can sometimes yield very wrong conclusions. Therefore, it is crucial to understand several principles for determining the correct meaning of Scripture.

First, the Bible student must pray and ask the Holy Spirit to impart understanding, for that is one of His functions. "But when he, the Spirit of truth, comes, he will guide you into all truth. He will not speak on his own; he will speak only what he hears, and he will tell you what is yet to come" (John 16:13). Just as the Holy Spirit guided the apostles in the writing of the New Testament, He also guides us in the understanding of Scripture. Remember, the Bible is God's book, and we need to ask Him what it means. If you are a Christian, the author of Scripture—the Holy Spirit—dwells inside you, and He wants you to understand what He wrote.

Second, we are not to pull a scripture out of the verses that surround it and try to determine the meaning of the verse outside of the context. We should always read the surrounding verses and chapters to discern the context. While all of Scripture comes from God (2 Timothy 3:16; 2 Peter 1:21), God used men to write it down. These men had a theme in mind, a purpose for writing, and a specific issue they were addressing. We should read the background of the book of the Bible we are studying to find out who wrote the book, to whom it was written, when it was written, and why it was written. Also, we should take care to let the text speak for itself. Sometimes people will assign their own meanings to words in order to get the interpretation they desire.

Third, we must not attempt to be totally independent in our studying of the Bible. It is arrogant to think that we cannot gain understanding through the lifelong work of others who have studied Scripture. Some people, in error, approach the Bible with the idea that they will depend on the Holy Spirit alone and they will discover all the hidden truths of Scripture. Christ, in the giving of the Holy Spirit, has given people with spiritual gifts to the body of Christ. One of these spiritual gifts is that of teaching (Ephesians 4:11-12; 1 Corinthians 12:28). These teachers are given by the Lord to help us to correctly understand and obey Scripture. It is always wise to study the Bible with other believers, assisting each other in understanding and applying the truth of God's Word.

So, in summary, what is the proper way to study the Bible? First, through prayer and humility, we must rely on the Holy Spirit to give us understanding. Second, we should always study Scripture in its context, recognizing that the Bible explains itself. Third, we should respect the efforts of other Christians, past and present, who have also sought to properly study the Bible. Remember, God is the author of the Bible, and He wants us to understand it.

Question: Why should we study the Bible?

Answer: We should read and study the Bible because it is God's Word to us. The Bible is literally "God-breathed" (2 Timothy 3:16). In other words, it is God's very words to us. There are so many questions that philosophers have asked that God answers for us in Scripture. What is the purpose to life? Where did I come from? Is there life after death? How do I get to heaven? Why is the world full of evil? Why do I struggle to do good? In addition to these "big" questions, the Bible gives much practical advice in areas such as: What do I look for in a mate? How can I have a successful marriage? How can I be a good friend? How can I be a good parent? What is success and how do I achieve it? How can I change? What really matters in life? How can I live so that I do not look back with regret? How can I handle the unfair circumstances and bad events of life victoriously?

We should read and study the Bible because it is totally reliable and without error. The Bible is unique among so-called "holy" books in that it does not merely give moral teaching and say, "Trust me." Rather, we have the ability to test it by checking the hundreds of detailed prophecies that it makes, by checking the historical accounts it records, and by checking the scientific facts it relates. Those who say the Bible has errors have their ears closed to the truth. Jesus once asked which is easier to say, "Your sins are forgiven you," or "Rise, take up your bed and walk." Then He proved He had the ability to forgive sins (something we cannot see with our eyes) by healing the paralytic (something those around Him could test with their eyes). Similarly, we are given assurance that God's Word is true when it discusses spiritual areas that we cannot test with our senses by showing itself true in those areas that we can test, such as historical accuracy, scientific accuracy, and prophetic accuracy.

We should read and study the Bible because God does not change and because mankind's nature does not change; it is as relevant for us as it was when it was written. While technology changes, mankind's nature and desires do not change. We find, as we read the pages of biblical history, that whether we are talking about one-on-one relationships or societies, "there is nothing new under the sun" (Ecclesiastes 1:9). And while mankind as a whole continues to seek love and satisfaction in all of the wrong places, God—our good and gracious Creator—tells us what will bring us lasting joy. His revealed Word, the Bible, is so important that Jesus said of it, "Man does not live on bread alone, but by every word that comes from the mouth of God" (Matthew 4:4). In other words, if we want to live life to the fullest, as God intended, we must listen to and heed God's written Word.

We should read and study the Bible because there is so much false teaching. The Bible gives us the measuring stick by which we can distinguish truth from error. It tells us what God is like. To have a wrong impression of God is to worship an idol or false god. We are worshiping something that He is not. The Bible tells us how one truly gets to heaven, and it is not by being good or by being baptized or by anything else we do (John 14:6; Ephesians 2:1-10; Isaiah 53:6; Romans 3:10-18, 5:8, 6:23, 10:9-13). Along this line,

God's Word shows us just how much God loves us (Romans 5:6-8; John 3:16). And it is in learning this that we are drawn to love Him in return (1 John 4:19).

The Bible equips us to serve God (2 Timothy 3:17; Ephesians 6:17; Hebrews 4:12). It helps us know how to be saved from our sin and its ultimate consequence (2 Timothy 3:15). Meditating on God's Word and obeying its teachings will bring success in life (Joshua 1:8; James 1:25). God's Word helps us see sin in our lives and helps us get rid of it (Psalm 119:9, 11). It gives us guidance in life, making us wiser than our teachers (Psalm 32:8, 119:99; Proverbs 1:6). The Bible keeps us from wasting years of our lives on that which does not matter and will not last (Matthew 7:24-27).

Reading and studying the Bible helps us see beyond the attractive "bait" to the painful "hook" in sinful temptations, so that we can learn from others' mistakes rather than making them ourselves. Experience is a great teacher, but when it comes to learning from sin, it is a terribly hard teacher. It is so much better to learn from others' mistakes. There are so many Bible characters to learn from, some of whom can serve as both positive and negative role models at different times in their lives. For example, David, in his defeat of Goliath, teaches us that God is greater than anything He asks us to face (1 Samuel 17), while his giving in to the temptation to commit adultery with Bathsheba reveals just how long-lasting and terrible the consequences of a moment's sinful pleasure can be (2 Samuel 11).

The Bible is a book that is not merely for reading. It is a book for studying so that it can be applied. Otherwise, it is like swallowing food without chewing and then spitting it back out again—no nutritional value is gained by it. The Bible is God's Word. As such, it is as binding as the laws of nature. We can ignore it, but we do so to our own detriment, just as we would if we ignored the law of gravity. It cannot be emphasized strongly enough just how important the Bible is to our lives. Studying the Bible can be compared to mining for gold. If we make little effort and merely "sift through the pebbles in a stream," we will only find a little gold dust. But the more we make an effort to really dig into it, the more reward we will gain for our effort.

Question: Who were the authors of the books of the Bible?

Answer: Ultimately, above the human authors, the Bible was written by God. Second Timothy 3:16 tells us that the Bible was "breathed out" by God. God superintended the human authors of the Bible so that, while using their own writing styles and personalities, they still recorded exactly what God intended. The Bible was not dictated by God, but it was perfectly guided and entirely inspired by Him.

Humanly speaking, the Bible was written by approximately 40 men of diverse backgrounds over the course of 1500 years. Isaiah was a prophet, Ezra was a priest, Matthew was a tax-collector, John was a fisherman, Paul was a tentmaker, Moses was a shepherd, Luke was a physician. Despite being penned by different authors over 15 centuries, the Bible does not contradict itself and does not contain any errors. The authors all present different perspectives, but they all proclaim the same one true God, and the same one way of salvation— Jesus Christ (John 14:6; Acts 4:12). Few of the books of the Bible specifically name their author. Here are the books of the Bible along with the name of who is most assumed by biblical scholars to be the author, along with the approximate date of authorship:

Genesis, Exodus, Leviticus, Numbers, Deuteronomy = Moses - 1400 B.C

Joshua = Joshua - 1350 B.C

Judges, Ruth, 1 Samuel, 2 Samuel = Samuel/Nathan/Gad - 1000 - 900 B.C

1 Kings, 2 Kings = Jeremiah - 600 B.C

1 Chronicles, 2 Chronicles, Ezra, Nehemiah = Ezra - 450 B.C

Esther = Mordecai - 400 B.C

Job = Moses - 1400 B.C

Psalms = several different authors, mostly David - 1000 - 400 B.C

Proverbs, Ecclesiastes, Song of Solomon = Solomon - 900 B.C

Isaiah = Isaiah - 700 B.C

Jeremiah, Lamentations = Jeremiah - 600 B.C

Ezekiel = Ezekiel - 550 B.C

Daniel = Daniel - 550 B.C

Hosea = Hosea - 750 B.C

Joel = Joel - 850 B.C

Amos = Amos - 750 B.C

Obadiah = Obadiah - 600 B.C

Jonah = Jonah - 700 B.C

Micah = Micah - 700 B.C

Nahum = Nahum - 650 B.C

Habakkuk = Habakkuk - 600 B.C

Zephaniah = Zephaniah - 650 B.C

Haggai = Haggai - 520 B.C

Zechariah = Zechariah - 500 B.C

Malachi = Malachi - 430 B.C

Matthew = Matthew - A.D. 55

Mark = John Mark - A.D. 50

Luke = Luke - A.D. 60

John = John - A.D. 90

Acts = Luke - A.D. 65

Romans, 1 Corinthians, 2 Corinthians, Galatians, Ephesians, Philippians, Colossians, 1 Thessalonians, 2 Thessalonians, 1 Timothy, 2 Timothy, Titus, Philemon = Paul - A.D. 50-70

Hebrews = unknown, mostly likely Paul, Luke, Barnabas, or Apollos - A.D. 65

James = James - A.D. 45

1 Peter, 2 Peter = Peter - A.D. 60

1 John, 2 John, 3 John = John - A.D. 90

Jude = Jude - A.D. 60

Revelation = John - A.D. 90

Question: Why is it important to believe in biblical inerrancy?

Answer: We live in a time that tends to shrug its shoulders when confronted with error. Instead of asking, like Pilate, "What is truth?" postmodern man says, "Nothing is truth" or perhaps "There is truth, but we cannot know it." We've grown accustomed to being lied to, and many people seem comfortable with the false notion that the Bible, too, contains errors.

The doctrine of biblical inerrancy is an extremely important one because the truth does matter. This issue reflects on the character of God and is foundational to our understanding of everything the Bible teaches. Here are some reasons why we should absolutely believe in biblical inerrancy:

1. The Bible itself claims to be perfect. "And the words of the Lord are flawless, like silver refined in a furnace of clay, purified seven times" (Psalm 12:6). "The law of the Lord is perfect" (Psalm 19:7). "Every word of God is pure" (Proverbs 30:5 KJV). These claims of purity and perfection are absolute statements. Note that it doesn't say God's Word is "mostly" pure or scripture is "nearly" perfect. The Bible argues for complete perfection, leaving no room for "partial perfection" theories.

2. The Bible stands or falls as a whole. If a major newspaper were routinely discovered to contain errors, it would be quickly discredited. It would make no difference to say, "All the errors are confined to page three." For a paper to be reliable in any of its parts, it must be factual throughout. In the same way, if the Bible is inaccurate when it speaks of geology, why should its theology be trusted? It is either a trustworthy document, or it is not.

3. The Bible is a reflection of its Author. All books are. The Bible was written by God Himself as He worked through human authors in a process called "inspiration." "All scripture is God-breathed" (1 Timothy 3:16). See also 2 Peter 1:21 and Jeremiah 1:2.

   We believe that the God who created the universe is capable of writing a book. And the God who is perfect is capable of writing a perfect book. The issue is not simply "Does the Bible have a mistake?" but "Can God make a mistake?" If the Bible contains factual errors, then God is not omniscient and is capable of making errors Himself. If the Bible contains misinformation, then God is not truthful but is instead a liar. If the Bible contains contradictions, then God is the author of confusion. In other words, if biblical inerrancy is not true, then God is not God.

4. The Bible judges us, not vice versa. "For the word of God... judges the thoughts and attitudes of the heart" (Hebrews 4:12). Notice the relationship between "the heart" and "the Word." The Word examines; the heart is being examined. To discount parts of the Word for any reason is to reverse this process. We become the examiners, and the Word must submit to our "superior insight." Yet God says, "But who are you, O man, to talk back to God?" (Romans 9:20).

5. The Bible's message must be taken as a whole. It is not a mixture of doctrine that we are free to select from. Many people like the verses that say God loves them, but they dislike the verses that say God will judge sinners. But we simply cannot pick and choose what we like about the Bible and throw the rest away. If the Bible is wrong about hell, for example, then who is to say it is right about heaven—or about anything else? If the Bible cannot get the details right about creation, then maybe the details about salvation cannot be trusted either. If the story of Jonah is a myth, then perhaps so is the story of Jesus. On the contrary, God has said what He has said, and the Bible presents us a full picture of who God is. "Your word, O Lord, is eternal; it stands firm in the heavens" (Psalm 119:89).

6. The Bible is our only rule for faith and practice. If it is not reliable, then on what do we base our beliefs? Jesus asks for our trust, and that includes trust in what He says in His Word. John 6:67-69 is a beautiful passage. Jesus had just witnessed the departure of many who had claimed to follow Him. Then He turns to the twelve apostles and asks, "You do not want to leave too, do you?" At this, Peter speaks for the rest when he says, "Lord, to whom shall we go? You have the words of eternal life." May we have the same trust in the Lord and in His words of life.

None of what we have presented here should be taken as a rejection of true scholarship. Biblical inerrancy does not mean that we are to stop using our minds or accept what the Bible says blindly. We are commanded to study the Word (2 Timothy 2:15), and those who search it out are commended (Acts 17:11). Also, we recognize that there are difficult passages in the Bible, as well as sincere disagreements over interpretation. Our goal is to approach Scripture reverently and prayerfully, and when we find something we do not understand, we pray harder, study more, and—if the answer still eludes us—humbly acknowledge our own limitations in the face of the perfect Word of God.

Question: Is it possible that more books could be added to the Bible?

Answer: There is no reason to believe that God would present further revelation to add to His Word. The Bible begins with the very beginning of humanity—Genesis—and ends with the end of humanity as we know it—Revelation. Everything in between is for our benefit as believers, to be empowered with God's truth in our daily living. We know this from 2 Timothy 3:16-17, "All Scripture is God-breathed and is useful for teaching, rebuking, correcting and training in righteousness, so that the man of God may be thoroughly equipped for every good work."

If further books were added to the Bible, that would equate to saying that the Bible we have today is incomplete—that it does not tell us everything we need to know. Although it only applies directly to the book of Revelation, Revelation 22:18-20 teaches us an important truth about adding to God's Word: "I warn everyone who hears the words of the prophecy of this book: If anyone adds anything to them, God will add to him the plagues described in this book. And if anyone takes words away from this book of prophecy, God will take away from him his share in the tree of life and in the holy city...'"

We have all that we need in the current 66 books of the Bible. There is not a single situation in life that cannot be addressed by Scripture. What was begun in Genesis finds conclusion in Revelation. The Bible is absolutely complete and sufficient. Could God add to the Bible? Of course He could. However, there is no reason, biblically or theologically, to believe that He is going to do so, or that there is any need for Him to do so.

Question: Has the Bible been corrupted, altered, edited, revised, or tampered with?

Answer: The books of the Old Testament were written from approximately 1400 B.C to 400 B.C The books of the New Testament were written from approximately A.D. 40 to A.D. 90. So, anywhere between 3400 to 1900 years have passed since a book of the Bible was written. In this time, the original manuscripts have been lost. They very likely no longer exist. Also during this time, the books of the Bible have been copied again and again. Copies of copies of copies have been made. In view of this, can we still trust the Bible?

When God originally inspired men to write His Word, it was God-breathed and inerrant (2 Timothy 3:16-17; John 17:17). The Bible nowhere applies this to copies of the original manuscripts. As meticulous as scribes were with the replication of the Scriptures, no one is perfect. As a result, minor differences arose in the various copies of the Scriptures. Of all of the thousands of Greek and Hebrew manuscripts that are in existence, no two were identical until the printing press was invented in the A.D. 1500s.

However, any unbiased document scholar will agree that the Bible has been remarkably well-preserved over the centuries. Copies of the Bible dating to the 14th century A.D. are nearly identical in content to copies from the 3rd century A.D. When the Dead Sea Scrolls were discovered, scholars were shocked to see how similar they were to other ancient copies of the Old Testament, even though the Dead Sea Scrolls were hundreds of years older than anything previously discovered. Even many hardened skeptics and critics of the Bible admit that the Bible has been transmitted over the centuries far more accurately than any other ancient document.

There is absolutely no evidence that the Bible has been revised, edited, or tampered with in any systematic manner. The sheer volume of biblical manuscripts makes it simple to recognize any attempts to distort God's Word. There is no major doctrine of the Bible that is put in doubt as a result of the minor differences that exist between manuscripts.

Again, the question, can we trust the Bible? Absolutely! God has preserved His Word despite the unintentional failings and intentional attacks of human beings. We can have utmost confidence that the Bible we have today is the same Bible that was originally written. The Bible is God's Word, and we can trust it (2 Timothy 3:16; Matthew 5:18).

Question: Old Testament vs. New Testament - what are the differences?

Answer: The Old Testament lays the foundation for the teachings and events found in the New Testament. The Bible is a progressive revelation. If you skip the first half of any good book and try to finish it, you will have a hard time understanding the characters, the plot, and the ending. In the same way, the New Testament is only completely understood when it is seen as a fulfillment of the events, characters, laws, sacrificial system, covenants, and promises of the Old Testament.

If we only had the New Testament, we would come to the gospels and not know why the Jews were looking for a Messiah (a Savior King). Without the Old Testament, we would not understand why this Messiah was coming (see Isaiah 53), and we would not have been able to identify Jesus of Nazareth as the Messiah through the many detailed prophecies that were given concerning Him, e.g., His birthplace (Micah 5:2); His manner of death (Psalm 22, especially vv. 1, 7-8, 14-18; Psalm 69:21), His resurrection (Psalm 16:10), and many more details of His ministry (Isaiah 52:19, 9:2).

Without the Old Testament, we would not understand the Jewish customs that are mentioned in passing in the New Testament. We would not understand the perversions that the Pharisees had made to God's law as they added their traditions to it. We would not understand why Jesus was so upset as He cleansed the temple courtyard. We would not understand that we can make use of the same wisdom that Christ used in His many replies to His adversaries.

The New Testament Gospels and the Acts of the apostles record many of the fulfillments of prophecies that were recorded hundreds of years earlier in the Old Testament. In the circumstances of Jesus' birth, life, miracles, death, and resurrection as found in the Gospels, we find the fulfillment of the Old Testament prophecies that relate to the Messiah's first coming. It is these details that validate Jesus' claim to be the promised Christ. And even the prophecies in the New Testament (many of which are in the book of Revelation) are built upon earlier prophecies found in Old Testament books. These New Testament prophecies relate to events surrounding the second coming of Christ. Roughly two out of three verses in Revelation are based on or related to Old Testament verses.

Also, because the revelation in Scripture is progressive, the New Testament brings into focus teachings that were only alluded to in the Old Testament. The book of Hebrews describes how Jesus is the true High Priest and how His one sacrifice replaces all of the previous sacrifices, which were mere portrayals. The Old Testament gives the Law, which has two parts: the commandments and the blessing/curse that comes from obedience or disobedience to those commands. The New Testament clarifies that God gave those commandments to show men their need of salvation; they were never intended to be a means of salvation (Romans 3:19).

The Old Testament describes the sacrificial system God gave the Israelites to temporarily cover their sins. The New Testament clarifies that this system alluded to the sacrifice of Christ through whom alone salvation is found (Acts 4:12; Hebrews 10:4-10). The Old Testament saw paradise lost; the New Testament shows how paradise was regained for mankind through the second Adam (Christ) and how it will one day be restored. The Old Testament declares that man was separated from God through sin (Genesis chapter 3), and the New Testament declares that man can now be restored in his relationship to God (Romans chapters 3–6). The Old Testament predicted the Messiah's life. The Gospels primarily record Jesus' life, and the Epistles interpret His life and how we are to respond to all He has done.

Without the Old Testament we would not understand the promises God will yet fulfill to the Jewish nation. As a result, we would not properly see that the tribulation period is a seven-year period in which He will specifically be working with the Jewish nation who rejected His first coming but who will receive Him at His second coming. We would not understand how Christ's future 1000-year reign fits in with His promises to the Jews, or how Gentiles will fit in. Nor would we see how the end of the Bible ties up the loose ends that were unraveled in the beginning of the Bible, restoring the paradise that God originally created this world to be.

In summary, the Old Testament lays the foundation for, and was meant to prepare the Israelites for, the coming of the Messiah who would sacrifice Himself for the sins of the whole world (1 John 2:2). The New Testament shares the life of Jesus Christ and then looks back on what He did and how we are to respond to His gift of eternal life and live our lives in gratitude for all He has done for us (Romans 12). Both testaments reveal the same holy, merciful, and righteous God who must condemn sin but who desires to bring to Himself a fallen human race of sinners through the forgiveness only possible through Christ's atoning sacrifice. In both testaments, God reveals Himself to us and how we are to come to Him through Jesus Christ. In both testaments, we find all we need for eternal life and godly living (2 Timothy 3:15-17).

Question: Why did God give us four Gospels?

Answer: Here are some reasons why God gave four Gospels instead of just one:

1. **To give a more complete picture of Christ.** While the entire Bible is inspired by God (2 Timothy 3:16), He used human authors with different backgrounds and personalities to accomplish His purposes through their writing. Each of the gospel authors had a distinct purpose behind his gospel and in carrying out those purposes, each emphasized different aspects of the person and ministry of Jesus Christ.

Matthew was writing to a Hebrew audience, and one of his purposes was to show from Jesus' genealogy and fulfillment of Old Testament prophecies that He was the long-expected Messiah, and thus should be believed in. Matthew's emphasis is that Jesus is the promised King, the "Son of David," who would forever sit upon the throne of Israel (Matthew 9:27; 21:9).

Mark, a cousin of Barnabas (Colossians 4:10), was an eyewitness to the events in the life of Christ as well as being a friend of the apostle Peter. Mark wrote for a Gentile audience, as is brought out by his not including things important to Jewish readers (genealogies, Christ's controversies with Jewish leaders of His day, frequent references to the Old Testament, etc.). Mark emphasizes Christ as the suffering Servant, the One who came not to be served, but to serve and give His life a ransom for many (Mark 10:45).

161

Luke, the "beloved physician" (Colossians 4:14 KJV), evangelist, and companion of the apostle Paul, wrote both the gospel of Luke and the Acts of the apostles. Luke is the only Gentile author of the New Testament. He has long been accepted as a diligent master historian by those who have used his writings in geological and historical studies. As a historian, he states that it is his intent to write down an orderly account of the life of Christ based on the reports of those who were eyewitnesses (Luke 1:1-4). Because he specifically wrote for the benefit of Theophilus, apparently a Gentile of some stature, his gospel was composed with a Gentile audience in mind, and his intent is to show that a Christian's faith is based upon historically reliable and verifiable events. Luke often refers to Christ as the "Son of Man," emphasizing His humanity, and he shares many details that are not found in the other gospel accounts.

The gospel of John, written by John the apostle, is distinct from the other three Gospels and contains much theological content in regard to the person of Christ and the meaning of faith. Matthew, Mark, and Luke are referred to as the "Synoptic Gospels" because of their similar styles and content and because they give a synopsis of the life of Christ. The gospel of John begins not with Jesus' birth or earthly ministry but with the activity and characteristics of the Son of God before He became man (John 1:14). The gospel of John emphasizes the deity of Christ, as is seen in his use of such phrases as "the Word was God" (John 1:1), "the Savior of the World" (John 4:42), the "Son of God" (used repeatedly), and "Lord and...God" (John 20:28). In John's gospel, Jesus also affirms His deity with several "I Am" statements; most notable among them is John 8:58, in which He states that "...before Abraham was, I Am" (compare to Exodus 3:13-14). But John also emphasizes the fact of Jesus' humanity, desiring to show the error of a religious sect of his day, the Gnostics, who did not believe in Christ's humanity. John's gospel spells out his overall purpose for writing: "Jesus did many other miraculous signs in the presence of his disciples, which are not recorded in this book. But these are written that you may believe that Jesus is the Christ, the Son of God, and that by believing you may have life in his name" (John 20:30-31).

Thus, in having four distinct and yet equally accurate accounts of Christ, different aspects of His person and ministry are revealed. Each account becomes like a different-colored thread in a tapestry woven together to form a more complete picture of this One who is beyond description. And while we will never fully understand everything about Jesus Christ (John 20:30), through the four Gospels we can know enough of Him to appreciate who He is and what He has done for us so that we may have life through faith in Him.

2. **To enable us to objectively verify the truthfulness of their accounts.** The Bible, from earliest times, states that judgment in a court of law was not to be made against a person based on the testimony of a single eyewitness but that two or three as a minimum number were required (Deuteronomy 19:15). Even so, having different accounts of the person and earthly ministry of Jesus Christ enables us to assess the accuracy of the information we have concerning Him.

Simon Greenleaf, a well-known and accepted authority on what constitutes reliable evidence in a court of law, examined the four Gospels from a legal perspective. He noted that the type of eyewitness accounts given in the four Gospels—accounts which agree, but with each writer choosing to omit or add details different from the others—is typical of reliable, independent sources that would be accepted in a court of law as strong evidence. Had the Gospels contained exactly the same information with the same details written from the same perspective, it would indicate collusion, i.e., of there having been a time when the writers got together beforehand to "get their stories straight" in order to make their writings seem credible. The differences between the Gospels, even the apparent contradictions of details upon first examination, speak to the independent nature of the writings. Thus, the independent nature of the four Gospel accounts, agreeing in their information but differing in perspective, amount of detail, and which events were recorded, indicate that the record that we have of Christ's life and ministry as presented in the Gospels is factual and reliable.

3. **To reward those who are diligent seekers.** Much can be gained by an individual study of each of the Gospels. But still more can be gained by comparing and contrasting the different accounts of specific events of Jesus' ministry. For instance, in Matthew 14 we are given the account of the feeding of the 5000 and Jesus walking on the water. In Matthew 14:22 we are told that "Jesus made the disciples get into

the boat and go on ahead of him to the other side, while he dismissed the crowd." One may ask, why did He do this? There is no apparent reason given in Matthew's account. But when we combine it with the account in Mark 6, we see that the disciples had come back from casting out demons and healing people through the authority He had given them when He sent them out two-by-two. But they returned with "big heads," forgetting their place and ready now to instruct Him (Matthew 14:15). So, in sending them off in the evening to go to the other side of the Sea of Galilee, Jesus reveals two things to them. As they struggle against the wind and waves in their own self-reliance until the early hours of the morning (Mark 6:48-50), they begin to see that 1) they can achieve nothing for God in their own ability and 2) nothing is impossible if they call upon Him and live in dependence upon His power. There are many passages containing similar "jewels" to be found by the diligent student of the Word of God who takes the time to compare Scripture with Scripture.

Question: Do I have to believe the Bible is inerrant to be saved?

Answer: We are not saved by believing in the inspiration or inerrancy of the Bible. We are saved by believing in the Lord Jesus Christ as our Savior from sin (John 3:16; Ephesians 2:8-9; Romans 10:9-10). At the same time, though, it is only through the Bible that we learn about Jesus Christ and His death and resurrection on our behalf (2 Corinthians 5:21; Romans 5:8). We do not have to believe everything in the Bible in order to be saved—but we do have to believe in Jesus Christ, who is proclaimed by the Bible. We should definitely hold to the Bible as the Word of God and we should absolutely believe everything the Bible teaches.

When people are first saved, they generally know very little about the Bible. Salvation is a process that begins with an understanding of our sinful state, not an understanding of the inerrancy of the Bible. Our consciences tell us that we are not able to stand before a holy God on our own merits. We know that we are not righteous enough to do that, so we turn to Him and accept the sacrifice of His Son on the cross in payment of our sin. We place our full trust in Him. From that point on, we have a completely new nature, pure and undefiled by sin. God's Holy Spirit lives within our hearts, sealing us for eternity.

We go forward from that point, loving and obeying God more and more each day. Part of this "going forward" is feeding daily on His Word to grow and strengthen our walk with Him. The Bible alone has the power to perform this miracle in our lives.

If we believe and trust in the Person and work of the Lord Jesus Christ, as taught in the Bible, we are saved. When we trust in Jesus Christ, though, the Holy Spirit will work on our hearts and minds—and will convince us that the Bible is true and is to be believed (2 Timothy 3:16-17). If there are doubts in our minds about the inerrancy of Scripture, the best way to handle that is to ask God to give us assurance about His Word and confidence in His Word. He is more than willing to answer those who seek Him honestly and with their whole hearts (Matthew 7:7-8).

Question: What are the lost books of the Bible?

Answer: There are no "lost books" of the Bible or books that were taken out of the Bible. There are many legends and rumors of lost books, but there is no truth whatsoever to these stories. Every book that God intended and inspired to be in the Bible is in the Bible. There are literally hundreds of religious books that were written in the same time period as the books of the Bible. Some of these books contain true accounts of things that actually occurred (1 Maccabees, for example). Some contain good spiritual teaching (the Wisdom of Solomon, for example). However, these books are not inspired by God. If we read any of these books, the Apocrypha as an example, we have to treat them as fallible historical books, not as the inspired, inerrant Word of God (2 Timothy 3:16-17).

The gospel of Thomas, for example, was a forgery written in the 3rd or 4th century A.D., claiming to have been written by the apostle Thomas. It was not written by Thomas. The early church fathers almost universally rejected the gospel of Thomas as heretical. It contains many false and heretical things that Jesus supposedly said and did. None of it (or at best very little of it) is true. The epistle of Barnabas was not written by the biblical Barnabas, but by an imposter. The same can be said of the gospel of Philip, the apocalypse of Peter, etc.

There is one God. The Bible has one Creator. It is one book. It has one plan of grace, recorded from initiation, through execution, to consummation. From predestination to glorification, the Bible is the story of God redeeming His chosen people for the praise of His glory. As God's redemptive purposes and plan unfold in Scripture, the recurring themes constantly emphasized are the character of God, the judgment for sin and disobedience, the blessing for faith and obedience, the Lord Savior and sacrifice for sin, and the coming kingdom and glory. It is God's intention that we know and understand these five themes because our lives and eternal destinies depend upon them. It is therefore unthinkable that God would allow some of this vital information to be "lost" in any way. The Bible is complete, in order that we who read and understand it might also be "complete, and equipped for every good work" (2 Timothy 3:16-17).

Question: What is *sola scriptura*?

Answer: The phrase *sola scriptura* is from the Latin: *sola* having the idea of "alone," "ground," "base," and the word *scriptura* meaning "writings"—referring to the Scriptures. *Sola scriptura* means that Scripture alone is authoritative for the faith and practice of the Christian. The Bible is complete, authoritative, and true. "All Scripture is God-breathed and is useful for teaching, rebuking, correcting and training in righteousness" (2 Timothy 3:16).

Sola scriptura was the rallying cry of the Protestant Reformation. For centuries the Roman Catholic Church had made its traditions superior in authority to the Bible. This resulted in many practices that were in fact contradictory to the Bible. Some examples are prayer to saints and/or Mary, the immaculate conception, transubstantiation, infant baptism, indulgences, and papal authority. Martin Luther, the founder of the Lutheran Church and father of the Protestant Reformation, was publicly rebuking the Catholic Church for its unbiblical teachings. The Catholic Church threatened Martin Luther with excommunication (and death) if he did not recant. Martin Luther's reply was, "Unless therefore I am convinced by the testimony of Scripture, or by the clearest reasoning, unless I am persuaded by means of the passages I have quoted, and unless they thus render my conscience bound by the Word of God, I cannot and will not retract, for it is unsafe for a Christian to speak against his conscience. Here I stand, I can do no other; may God help me! Amen!"

The primary Catholic argument against *sola scriptura* is that the Bible does not explicitly teach *sola scriptura*. Catholics argue that the Bible nowhere states that it is the *only* authoritative guide for faith and practice. While this is true, they fail to recognize a crucially important issue. We know that the Bible is the Word of God. The Bible declares itself to be God-breathed, inerrant, and authoritative. We also know that God does not change His mind or contradict Himself. So, while the Bible itself may not explicitly argue for *sola scriptura*, it most definitely does not allow for traditions that contradict its message. *Sola scriptura* is not as much of an argument against tradition as it is an argument against unbiblical, extra-biblical and/or anti-biblical doctrines. The only way to know for sure what God expects of us is to stay true to what we know He has revealed—the Bible. We can know, beyond the shadow of any doubt, that Scripture is true, authoritative, and reliable. The same cannot be said of tradition.

The Word of God is the only authority for the Christian faith. Traditions are valid only when they are based on Scripture and are in full agreement with Scripture. Traditions that contradict the Bible are not of God and are not a valid aspect of the Christian faith. *Sola scriptura* is the only way to avoid subjectivity and keep personal opinion from taking priority over the teachings of the Bible. The essence of *sola scriptura* is basing your spiritual life on the Bible alone and rejecting any tradition or teaching that is not in full agreement with the Bible. Second Timothy 2:15 declares, "Do your best to present yourself to God as one approved, a workman who does not need to be ashamed and who correctly handles the word of truth."

Sola scriptura does not nullify the concept of church traditions. Rather, *sola scriptura* gives us a solid foundation on which to base church traditions. There are many practices, in both Catholic and Protestant churches, that are the result of traditions, not the explicit teaching of Scripture. It is good, and even necessary, for the church to have traditions. Traditions play an important role in clarifying and organizing Christian practice. At the same time, in order for these traditions to be valid, they must not be in disagreement with God's Word. They must be based on the solid foundation of the teaching of Scripture. The problem with the Roman Catholic Church, and many other churches, is that they base traditions on traditions which are based on traditions which are based on traditions, often with the initial tradition not being in full harmony with the Scriptures. That is why Christians must always go back to *sola scriptura*, the authoritative Word of God, as the only solid basis for faith and practice.

On a practical matter, a frequent objection to the concept of *sola scriptura* is the fact that the canon of the Bible was not officially agreed upon for at least 250 years after the church was founded. Further, the Scriptures were not available to the masses for over 1500 years after the church was founded. How, then, were early Christians to use *sola scriptura*, when they did not even have the full Scriptures? And how were Christians who lived before the invention of the printing press supposed to base their faith and practice on Scripture alone if there was no way for them to have a complete copy of the Scriptures? This issue is further compounded by the very high rates of illiteracy throughout history. How does the concept of *sola scriptura* handle these issues?

The problem with this argument is that it essentially says that Scripture's authority is based on its availability. This is not the case. Scripture's authority is universal; because it is God's Word, it is His authority. The fact that Scripture was not readily available, or that people could not read it, does not change the fact that Scripture is God's Word. Further, rather than this being an argument against *sola scriptura*, it is actually an argument for what the church should have done, instead of what it did. The early church should have made producing copies of the Scriptures a high priority. While it was unrealistic for every Christian to possess a complete copy of the Bible, it was possible that every church could have some, most, or all of the Scriptures available to it. Early church leaders should have made studying the Scriptures their highest priority so they could accurately teach it. Even if the Scriptures could not be made available to the masses, at least church leaders could be well-trained in the Word of God. Instead of building traditions upon traditions and passing them on from generation to generation, the church should have copied the Scriptures and taught the Scriptures (2 Timothy 4:2).

Again, traditions are not the problem. Unbiblical traditions are the problem. The availability of the Scriptures throughout the centuries is not the determining factor. The Scriptures themselves are the determining factor. We now have the Scriptures readily available to us. Through the careful study of God's Word, it is clear that many church traditions which have developed over the centuries are in fact contradictory to the Word of God. This is where *sola scriptura* applies. Traditions that are based on, and in agreement with, God's Word can be maintained. Traditions that are not based on, and/or disagree with, God's Word must be rejected. *Sola scriptura* points us back to what God has revealed to us in His Word. *Sola scriptura* ultimately points us back to the God who always speaks the truth, never contradicts Himself, and always proves Himself to be dependable.

Question: Where is a good place to start reading the Bible?

Answer: For starters, it is important realize that the Bible is not an ordinary book that reads smoothly from cover to cover. It is actually a library, or collection, of books written by different authors in several languages over 1500 years. Martin Luther said that the Bible is the "cradle of Christ" because all biblical history and prophecy ultimately point to Jesus. Therefore, any first reading of the Bible should begin with the Gospels. The gospel of Mark is quick and fast-paced and is a good place to start. Then you might want to go on to the gospel of John, which focuses on the things Jesus claimed about Himself. Mark tells about what Jesus did, while John tells about what Jesus said and who Jesus was. In John are some of the simplest and clearest passages, but also some of the deepest and most profound passages. Reading the Gospels (Matthew, Mark, Luke, John) will familiarize you with Christ's life and ministry.

After that, read through some of the Epistles (Romans, Ephesians, Philippians). They teach us how to live our lives in a way that is honoring to God. When you start reading the Old Testament, read the book of Genesis. It tells us how God created the world and how mankind fell into sin, as well as the impact that fall had on the world. Exodus, Leviticus, Numbers, and Deuteronomy can be hard to read because they get into all the laws God required the Jews to live by. While you should not avoid these books, they are perhaps better left for later study. In any case, try not to get bogged down in them. Read Joshua through Chronicles to get a good history of Israel. Reading Psalms through Song of Solomon will give you a good feel for Hebrew poetry and wisdom. The prophetic books, Isaiah through Malachi, can be hard to understand as well. Remember, the key to understanding the Bible is asking God for wisdom (James 1:5). God is the author of the Bible, and He wants you to understand His Word.

It is important to know that not everyone can be a successful Bible student. Only those with the necessary "qualifications" for studying the Word can do so with God's blessings:

Are you saved by faith in Jesus Christ (1 Corinthians 2:14-16)?

Are you hungering for God's Word (1 Peter 2:2)?

Are you diligently searching God's Word (Acts 17:11)?

If you answered "yes" to these three questions, you can be sure that God will bless your efforts to know Him and His Word, no matter where you start and no matter what your method of study. If you are not sure that you are a Christian—that you have been saved by faith in Christ and have the Holy Spirit within you—you will find it impossible to understand the meaning of the words of Scripture. The truths of the Bible are hidden from those who have not come to faith in Christ, but they are life itself to those who believe (1 Corinthians 2:13-14; John 6:63).

Chapter 6

....

QUESTIONS ABOUT

THE CHURCH

CONTENTS

What is the church?.. 172

What is the purpose of the church? 173

What is the importance of Christian baptism? 174

What is the importance of the Lord's Supper/Christian Communion?.... 175

Women pastors/preachers? What does the Bible say about women in ministry? 177

Why is church attendance important? 180

What should I be looking for in a church?............................... 180

Why should I believe in organized religion?............................ 182

What is biblical separation? 183

What does the Bible say about church discipline/excommunication?...... 185

What does the Bible say about the form of church government? 186

What does the Bible say about church growth? 188

Why are there so many Christian denominations?................... 189

Why are there so many different Christian interpretations? 191

Why are so many evangelical Christian leaders caught in scandals? 194

What is the history of Christianity?... 196

What does the "husband of one wife" in 1 Timothy 3:2 mean? Can a divorced man serve as a pastor, elder, or deacon? 200

What is the proper mode of baptism?...................................... 201

Does God require Sabbath-keeping of Christians? 202

What are appropriate reasons for missing church?................... 203

Question: What is the church?

Answer: Many people today understand the church as a building. This is not a biblical understanding of the church. The word "church" comes from the Greek word *ekklesia* which is defined as "an assembly" or "called-out ones." The root meaning of "church" is not that of a building, but of people. It is ironic that when you ask people what church they attend, they usually identify a building. Romans 16:5 says "… greet the church that is in their house." Paul refers to the church in their house—not a church building, but a body of believers.

The church is the body of Christ, of which He is the head. Ephesians 1:22-23 says, "And God placed all things under his feet and appointed him to be head over everything for the church, which is his body, the fullness of him who fills everything in every way." The body of Christ is made up of all believers in Jesus Christ from the day of Pentecost (Acts chapter 2) until Christ's return. The body of Christ is comprised of two aspects:

1. The universal church consists of all those who have a personal relationship with Jesus Christ. "For we were all baptized by one Spirit into one body—whether Jews or Greeks, slave or free—and we were all given the one Spirit to drink" (1 Corinthians 12:13). This verse says that anyone who believes is part of the body of Christ and has received the Spirit of Christ as evidence. The universal church of God is all those who have received salvation through faith in Jesus Christ.

2. The local church is described in Galatians 1:1-2: "Paul, an apostle … and all the brothers with me, to the churches in Galatia." Here we see that in the province of Galatia there were many churches—what we call local churches. A Baptist church, Lutheran church, Catholic church, etc., is not *the* church, as in the universal church—but rather is a local church, a local body of believers. The universal church is comprised of those who belong to Christ and who have trusted Him for salvation. These members of the universal church should seek fellowship and edification in a local church.

In summary, the church is not a building or a denomination. According to the Bible, the church is the body of Christ—all those who have placed their faith in Jesus Christ for salvation (John 3:16; 1 Corinthians 12:13). Local churches are gatherings of members of the universal church. The local church is where the members of the universal church can fully apply the "body" principles of 1 Corinthians chapter 12: encouraging, teaching, and building one another up in the knowledge and grace of the Lord Jesus Christ.

Question: What is the purpose of the church?

Answer: Acts 2:42 could be considered a purpose statement for the church: "They devoted themselves to the apostles' teaching and to the fellowship, to the breaking of bread and to prayer." According to this verse, the purposes/activities of the church should be 1) teaching biblical doctrine, 2) providing a place of fellowship for believers, 3) observing the Lord's supper, and 4) praying.

The church is to teach biblical doctrine so we can be grounded in our faith. Ephesians 4:14 tells us, "Then we will no longer be infants, tossed back and forth by the waves, and blown here and there by every wind of teaching and by the cunning and craftiness of men in their deceitful scheming." The church is to be a place of fellowship, where Christians can be devoted to one another and honor one another (Romans 12:10), instruct one another (Romans 15:14), be kind and compassionate to one another (Ephesians 4:32), encourage one another (1 Thessalonians 5:11), and most importantly, love one another (1 John 3:11).

The church is to be a place where believers can observe the Lord's Supper, remembering Christ's death and shed blood on our behalf (1 Corinthians 11:23-26). The concept of "breaking bread" (Acts 2:42) also carries the idea of having meals together. This is another example of the church promoting fellowship. The final purpose of the church according to Acts 2:42 is prayer. The church is to be a place that promotes prayer, teaches prayer, and practices prayer. Philippians 4:6-7 encourages us, "Do not be anxious about anything, but in everything, by prayer and petition, with thanksgiving, present your requests to God. And the peace of God, which transcends all understanding, will guard your hearts and your minds in Christ Jesus."

Another commission given to the church is proclaiming the gospel of salvation through Jesus Christ (Matthew 28:18-20; Acts 1:8). The church is called to be faithful in sharing the gospel through word and deed. The church is to be a "lighthouse" in the community, pointing people toward our Lord and Savior Jesus Christ. The church is to both promote the gospel and prepare its members to proclaim the gospel (1 Peter 3:15).

Some final purposes of the church are given in James 1:27: "Religion that God our Father accepts as pure and faultless is this: to look after orphans and widows in their distress and to keep oneself from being polluted by the world." The church is to be about the business of ministering to those in need. This includes not only sharing the gospel, but also providing for physical needs (food, clothing, shelter) as necessary and appropriate. The church is also to equip believers in Christ with the tools they need to overcome sin and remain free from the pollution of the world. This is done by biblical teaching and Christian fellowship.

So, what is the purpose of the church? Paul gave an excellent illustration to the believers in Corinth. The church is God's hands, mouth, and feet in this world—the body of Christ (1 Corinthians 12:12-27). We are to be doing the things that Jesus Christ would do if He were here physically on the earth. The church is to be "Christian," "Christ-like," and Christ-following.

Question: What is the importance of Christian baptism?

Answer: Christian baptism is, according to the Bible, an outward testimony of what has occurred inwardly in a believer's life. Christian baptism illustrates a believer's identification with Christ's death, burial, and resurrection. The Bible declares, "Or don't you know that all of us who were baptized into Christ Jesus were baptized into his death? We were therefore buried with Him through baptism into death in order that, just as Christ was raised from the dead through the glory of the Father, we too may live a new life" (Romans 6:3-4). In Christian baptism, the action of being immersed in the water symbolizes dying and being buried with Christ. The action of coming out of the water pictures Christ's resurrection.

In Christian baptism, there are two requirements before a person is baptized: 1) the person being baptized must have trusted in Jesus Christ as Savior, and 2) the person must understand what baptism signifies. If a person knows the Lord Jesus as Savior, understands that Christian baptism is a step of obedience in publicly proclaiming his faith in Christ, and desires to be baptized, then there is no reason to prevent the believer from being baptized. According to the Bible, Christian baptism is important because it is a step of obedience—publicly declaring faith in Christ and commitment to Him—an identification with Christ's death, burial, and resurrection.

Question: What is the importance of the Lord's Supper/Christian Communion?

Answer: A study of the Lord's Supper is a soul-stirring experience because of the depth of meaning it contains. It was during the age-old celebration of the Passover on the eve of His death that Jesus instituted a significant new fellowship meal that we observe to this day. It is an integral part of Christian worship. It causes us to remember our Lord's death and resurrection and to look for His glorious return in the future.

The Passover was the most sacred feast of the Jewish religious year. It commemorated the final plague on Egypt when the firstborn of the Egyptians died and the Israelites were spared because of the blood of a lamb that was sprinkled on their doorposts. The lamb was then roasted and eaten with unleavened bread. God's command was that throughout the generations to come the feast would be celebrated. The story is recorded in Exodus 12.

During the Last Supper—a Passover celebration—Jesus took a loaf of bread and gave thanks to God. As He broke it and gave it to His disciples, He said, "'This is my body given for you; do this in remembrance of me.' In the same way, after the supper he took the cup, saying, 'This cup is the new covenant in my blood, which is poured out for you'" (Luke 22:19-21). He concluded the feast by singing a hymn (Matthew 26:30), and they went out into the night to the Mount of Olives. It was there that Jesus was betrayed, as predicted, by Judas. The following day He was crucified.

The accounts of the Lord's Supper are found in the Gospels (Matthew 26:26-29; Mark 14:17-25; Luke 22:7-22; and John 13:21-30). The apostle Paul wrote concerning the Lord's Supper in 1 Corinthians 11:23-29. Paul includes a statement not found in the Gospels: "Therefore, whoever eats the bread or drinks the cup of the Lord in an unworthy manner will be guilty of sinning against the body and blood of the Lord. A man ought to examine himself before he eats of the bread and drinks of the cup. For anyone who eats and drinks without recognizing the body of the Lord eats and drinks judgment on himself" (1 Corinthians 11:27-29). We may ask what it means to partake of the bread and the cup "in an unworthy manner." It may mean to disregard the true meaning of the bread and cup and to forget the tremendous price our Savior paid for our salvation. Or it may mean to allow the ceremony to become a dead and formal ritual or to come to the Lord's Supper with unconfessed sin. In keeping with Paul's instruction, we should examine ourselves before eating the bread and drinking the cup.

Another statement Paul made that is not included in the gospel accounts is "For whenever you eat this bread and drink this cup, you proclaim the Lord's death until He comes" (1 Corinthians 11:26). This places a time limit on the ceremony—until our Lord's return. From these brief accounts we learn how Jesus used two of the frailest of elements as symbols of His body and blood and initiated them to be a monument to His death. It was not a monument of carved marble or molded brass, but of bread and wine.

He declared that the bread spoke of His body which would be broken. There was not a broken bone, but His body was so badly tortured that it was hardly recognizable (Psalm 22:12-17; Isaiah 53:4-7). The wine spoke of His blood, indicating the terrible death He would soon experience. He, the perfect Son of God, became the fulfillment of the countless Old Testament prophecies concerning a Redeemer (Genesis 3:15; Psalm 22; Isaiah 53). When He said, "Do this in remembrance of me," He indicated this was a ceremony that must be continued in the future. It indicated also that the Passover, which required the death of a lamb and looked forward to the coming of the Lamb of God who would take away the sin of the world, was fulfilled in the Lord's Supper. The New Covenant replaced the Old

Covenant when Christ, the Passover Lamb (1 Corinthians 5:7), was sacrificed (Hebrews 8:8-13). The sacrificial system was no longer needed (Hebrews 9:25-28). The Lord's Supper/Christian Communion is a remembrance of what Christ did for us and a celebration of what we receive as a result of His sacrifice.

Question: Women pastors/preachers? What does the Bible say about women in ministry?

Answer: There is perhaps no more hotly debated issue in the church today than the issue of women serving as pastors/preachers. As a result, it is very important to not see this issue as men versus women. There are women who believe women should not serve as pastors and that the Bible places restrictions on the ministry of women, and there are men who believe women can serve as preachers and that there are no restrictions on women in ministry. This is not an issue of chauvinism or discrimination. It is an issue of biblical interpretation.

The Word of God proclaims, "A woman should learn in quietness and full submission. I do not permit a woman to teach or to have authority over a man; she must be silent" (1 Timothy 2:11-12). In the church, God assigns different roles to men and women. This is a result of the way mankind was created and the way in which sin entered the world (2 Timothy 2:13-14). God, through the apostle Paul, restricts women from serving in roles of teaching and/or having spiritual authority over men. This precludes women from serving as pastors, which definitely includes preaching to, teaching, and having spiritual authority over men.

There are many "objections" to this view of women in ministry. A common one is that Paul restricts women from teaching because in the first century, women were typically uneducated. However, 1 Timothy 2:11-14 nowhere mentions educational status. If education were a qualification for ministry, the majority of Jesus' disciples would not have been qualified. A second common objection is that Paul only restricted the women of Ephesus from teaching (1 Timothy was written to Timothy, who was the pastor of the church in Ephesus). The city of Ephesus was known for its temple to Artemis, a false Greek/Roman goddess. Women were the authority in the worship of Artemis. However, the book of 1 Timothy nowhere mentions Artemis, nor does Paul mention Artemis worship as a reason for the restrictions in 1 Timothy 2:11-12.

A third common objection is that Paul is only referring to husbands and wives, not men and women in general. The Greek words in the passage could refer to husbands and wives; however, the basic meaning of the words refers to men and women. Further, the same Greek words are used in verses 8-10. Are only husbands to lift up holy hands in prayer without anger and disputing (verse 8)? Are only wives to dress modestly, have good deeds, and worship God (verses 9-10)? Of course not. Verses 8-10 clearly refer to all men and women, not only husbands and wives. There is nothing in the context that would indicate a switch to husbands and wives in verses 11-14.

Yet another frequent objection to this interpretation of women in ministry is in relation to women who held positions of leadership in the Bible, specifically Miriam, Deborah, and Huldah in the Old Testament. This objection fails to note some significant factors. First, Deborah was the only female judge among 13 male judges. Huldah was the only female prophet among dozens of male prophets mentioned in the Bible. Miriam's only connection to leadership was being the sister of Moses and Aaron. The two most prominent women in the times of the Kings were Athaliah and Jezebel—hardly examples of godly female leadership. Most significantly, though, the authority of women in the Old Testament is not relevant to the issue. The book of 1 Timothy and the other Pastoral Epistles present a new paradigm for the church—the body of Christ—and that paradigm involves the authority structure for the church, not for the nation of Israel or any other Old Testament entity.

Similar arguments are made using Priscilla and Phoebe in the New Testament. In Acts 18, Priscilla and Aquila are presented as faithful ministers for Christ. Priscilla's name is mentioned first, perhaps indicating that she was more "prominent" in ministry than her husband. However, Priscilla is nowhere described as participating in a ministry activity that is in contradiction to 1 Timothy 2:11-14. Priscilla and Aquila brought Apollos into their home and they both discipled him, explaining the Word of God to him more accurately (Acts 18:26).

In Romans 16:1, even if Phoebe is considered a "deaconess" instead of a "servant," that does not indicate that Phoebe was a teacher in the church. "Able to teach" is given as a qualification for elders, but not deacons (1 Timothy 3:1-13; Titus 1:6-9). Elders/bishops/deacons are described as the "husband of one wife," "a man whose children believe," and "men worthy of respect." Clearly the indication is that these qualifications refer to men. In addition, in 1 Timothy 3:1-13 and Titus 1:6-9, masculine pronouns are used exclusively to refer to elders/bishops/deacons.

The structure of 1 Timothy 2:11-14 makes the "reason" perfectly clear. Verse 13 begins with "for" and gives the "cause" of Paul's statement in verses 11-12. Why should women not teach or have authority over men? Because "Adam was created first, then Eve. And Adam was not the one deceived; it was the woman who was deceived." God created Adam first and then created Eve to be a "helper" for Adam. This order of creation has universal application in the family (Ephesians 5:22-33) and the church. The fact that Eve was deceived is also given as a reason for women not serving as pastors or having spiritual authority over men. This leads some to believe that women should not teach because they are more easily deceived. That concept is debatable, but if women are more easily deceived, why should they be allowed to teach children (who are easily deceived) and other women (who are supposedly more easily deceived)? That is not what the text says. Women are not to teach men or have spiritual authority over men because Eve was deceived. As a result, God has given men the primary teaching authority in the church.

Many women excel in gifts of hospitality, mercy, teaching, and helps. Much of the ministry of the local church depends on women. Women in the church are not restricted from public praying or prophesying (1 Corinthians 11:5), only from having spiritual teaching authority over men. The Bible nowhere restricts women from exercising the gifts of the Holy Spirit (1 Corinthians 12). Women, just as much as men, are called to minister to others, to demonstrate the fruit of the Spirit (Galatians 5:22-23), and to proclaim the gospel to the lost (Matthew 28:18-20; Acts 1:8; 1 Peter 3:15).

God has ordained that only men are to serve in positions of spiritual teaching authority in the church. This is not because men are necessarily better teachers, or because women are inferior or less intelligent (which is not the case). It is simply the way God designed the church to function. Men are to set the example in spiritual leadership—in their lives and through their words. Women are to take a less authoritative role. Women are encouraged to teach other women (Titus 2:3-5). The Bible also does not restrict women from teaching children. The only activity women are restricted from is teaching men or having spiritual authority over them. This logically would preclude women from serving as pastors/preachers. This does not make women less important, by any means, but rather gives them a ministry focus more in agreement with God's plan and His gifting of them.

Question: Why is church attendance important?

Answer: The Bible tells us we need to attend church so we can worship God with other believers and be taught His Word for our spiritual growth (Acts 2:42; Hebrews 10:25). Church is the place where believers can love one another (1 John 4:12), encourage one another (Hebrews 3:13), "spur" one another (Hebrews 10:24), serve one another (Galatians 5:13), instruct one another (Romans 15:14), honor one another (Romans 12:10), and be kind and compassionate to one another (Ephesians 4:32).

When a person trusts Jesus Christ for salvation, he or she is made a member of the body of Christ (1 Corinthians 12:27). For a church body to function properly, all of its "body parts" need to be present (1 Corinthians 12:14-20). Likewise, a believer will never reach full spiritual maturity without the assistance and encouragement of other believers (1 Corinthians 12:21-26). For these reasons, church attendance, participation, and fellowship should be regular aspects of a believer's life. Weekly church attendance is in no sense "required" for believers, but someone who belongs to Christ should have a desire to worship God, receive His Word, and fellowship with other believers.

Question: What should I be looking for in a church?

Answer: In order to know what to look for in a local church, we must first understand God's purpose for the church—the body of Christ—in general. There are two outstanding truths about the church. First, "the church of the living God [is] the pillar and foundation of the truth" (1 Timothy 3:15). Second, Christ alone is the head of the church (Ephesians 1:22; 4:15; Colossians 1:18).

In regard to the truth, the local church is a place where the Bible (God's only Truth) has complete authority. The Bible is the only infallible rule of faith and practice (2 Timothy 3:15-17). Therefore, when seeking a church to attend, we should find one where, according to biblical standards, the gospel is preached, sin is condemned, worship is from the heart, the teaching is biblical, and opportunities to minister to others exist. Consider the model of the early church found in Acts 2:42-47, "They devoted themselves to the apostles' teaching and to the fellowship, to the breaking of bread and to prayer…They broke bread in their homes and ate together with glad and sincere hearts, praising God and enjoying the favor of all the people. And the Lord added to their number daily those who were being saved."

In regard to the second truth about the church, Christians should attend a local fellowship that declares Christ's headship in all matters of doctrine and practice. No man—whether pastor, priest, or pope—is the head of the church. All men die—how can the living church of the living God have a dead head? It cannot. Christ is the church's one supreme authority, and all church leadership, gifts, order, discipline, and worship are appointed through His sovereignty, as found in the Scriptures.

Once these two fundamentals are in place, the rest of the factors (buildings, worship styles, activities, programs, location, etc.) are merely a matter of personal taste. Before even setting foot inside a church, some homework is in order. Doctrinal statements, purpose statements, mission statements, or anything that will give insight into what a church believes should be carefully looked over. Many churches have websites where one can get a feel for what they believe regarding the Bible, God, the Trinity, Jesus Christ, sin, and salvation.

Next should be visits to the churches that seem to have the fundamentals in place. Attendance at two or three services at each church will be helpful. Any literature they have for visitors should be scrutinized, paying close attention to belief statements. Church evaluation should be based on the principles outlined above. Is the

Bible held as the only authority? Is Christ exalted as head of the church? Does the church focus on discipleship? Were you led to worship God? What types of ministries does the church involve itself in? Was the message biblical and evangelical? How was the fellowship? You also need to feel comfortable—were you made to feel welcome? Is the congregation comprised of true worshippers?

Finally, remember that no church is perfect. At best, it is still filled with saved sinners whose flesh and spirits are continually at war. Also, do not forget the importance of prayer. Praying about the church God would have you attend is crucial throughout the decision-making process.

Question: Why should I believe in organized religion?

Answer: A dictionary definition of "religion" would be something similar to "belief in God or gods to be worshipped, usually expressed in conduct and ritual; any specific system of belief, worship, etc., often involving a code of ethics." In light of this definition, the Bible does speak of organized religion, but in many cases the purpose and impact of "organized religion" are not something that God is pleased with.

In Genesis chapter 11, perhaps the first instance of organized religion, the descendents of Noah organized themselves to build the tower of Babel instead of obeying God's command to fill the entire earth. They believed that their unity was more important than their relationship with God. God stepped in and confused their languages, thus breaking up this organized religion.

In Exodus chapter 6 and following, God "organized" a religion for the nation of Israel. The Ten Commandments, the laws regarding the tabernacle, and the sacrificial system were all instituted by God and were to be followed by the Israelites. Further study of the New Testament clarifies that the intent of this religion was to point to the need for a Savior-Messiah (Galatians 3; Romans 7). However, many have misunderstood this and have worshipped the rules and rituals rather than God.

Throughout Israel's history, many of the conflicts experienced by the Israelites involved conflict with organized religions. Examples include the worship of Baal (Judges 6; 1 Kings 18), Dagon (1 Samuel 5), and

Molech (2 Kings 23:10). God defeated the followers of these religions, displaying His sovereignty and omnipotence.

In the Gospels, the Pharisees and Sadducees are depicted as the representatives of organized religion at the time of Christ. Jesus constantly confronted them about their false teachings and hypocritical lifestyles. In the Epistles, there were organized groups that mixed the gospel with certain lists of required works and rituals. They also sought to put pressure on believers to change and accept these "Christianity plus" religions. Galatians and Colossians give warnings about such religions. In the book of Revelation, organized religion will have an impact on the world as the Antichrist sets up a one-world religion.

In many cases, the end result of organized religion is a distraction from the intent of God. However, the Bible does speak of organized believers who are part of His plan. God calls these groups of organized believers "churches." The descriptions from the book of Acts and the Epistles indicate that the church is to be organized and interdependent. The organization leads to protection, productivity, and outreach (Acts 2:41-47). In the case of the church, it could better be called an "organized relationship."

Religion is man's attempt to have communion with God. The Christian faith is a relationship with God because of what He has done for us through the sacrifice of Jesus Christ. There is no plan to reach God (He has reached out to us—Romans 5:8). There is no pride (all is received by grace—Ephesians 2:8-9). There should be no conflict over leadership (Christ is the head—Colossians 1:18). There should be no prejudice (we are all one in Christ—Galatians 3:28). Being organized is not the problem. Focusing on the rules and rituals of a religion is the problem.

Question: What is biblical separation?

Answer: Biblical separation is the recognition that God has called believers out of the world and into a personal and corporate purity in the midst of sinful cultures. Biblical separation is usually considered in two areas: personal and ecclesiastical.

Personal separation involves an individual's commitment to a godly standard of behavior. Daniel practiced personal separatism when he "resolved not to defile himself with the royal food and wine" (Daniel 1:8). His was a biblical separatism because his standard was based on God's revelation in the Mosaic law.

A modern example of personal separation could be the decision to decline invitations to parties where alcohol is served. Such a decision might be made in order to circumvent temptation (Romans 13:14), to avoid "every kind of evil" (1 Thessalonians 5:22), or simply to be consistent with a personal conviction (Romans 14:5).

The Bible clearly teaches that the child of God is to be separate from the world. "Do not be yoked together with unbelievers. For what do righteousness and wickedness have in common? Or what fellowship can light have with darkness? What harmony is there between Christ and Belial? What does a believer have in common with an unbeliever? What agreement is there between the temple of God and idols? For we are the temple of the living God. As God has said: 'I will live with them and walk among them, and I will be their God, and they will be my people.' Therefore come out from them and be separate, says the Lord" (2 Corinthians 6:14-17; see also 1 Peter 1:14-16).

Ecclesiastical separation involves the decisions of a church concerning its ties to other organizations, based on their theology or practices. Separatism is implied in the very word "church," which comes from the Greek word *ekklesia* meaning "a called-out assembly." In Jesus' letter to the church of Pergamum, He warned against tolerating those who taught false doctrine (Revelation 2:14-15). The church was to be separate, breaking ties with heresy. A modern example of ecclesiastical separation could be a denomination's stance against ecumenical alliances which would unite the church with apostates.

Biblical separation does not require Christians to have no contact with unbelievers. Like Jesus, we should befriend the sinner without partaking of the sin (Luke 7:34). Paul expresses a balanced view of separatism: "I have written you in my letter not to associate with sexually immoral people—not at all meaning the people of this world who are immoral, or the greedy and swindlers, or idolaters. In that case you would have to leave this world" (1 Corinthians 5:9-10). In other words, we are in the world, but not of it.

We are to be light to the world without allowing the world to diminish our light. "You are the light of the world. A city on a hill cannot be hidden. Neither do people light a lamp and put it under a bowl. Instead they put it on its stand, and it gives light to everyone in the house. In the same way, let your light shine before men, that they may see your good deeds and praise your Father in heaven" (Matthew 5:14-16).

Question: What does the Bible say about church discipline/ excommunication?

Answer: Excommunication is the formal removal of an individual from church membership and the informal separation from that individual. Matthew 18:15-20 gives the procedure and authority for a church to do this. It instructs us that one individual (usually the offended party) is to go to the offending individual. If he/she does not repent, then two or three go to confirm the situation and the refusal to repent. If there is still no repentance, it is taken before the church. This process is never "desirable," just as a father never delights in having to discipline his children. Often, though, it is necessary. The purpose is not to be mean-spirited or to display a "holier than thou" attitude. Rather, the goal is the restoration of the individual to full fellowship with both God and other believers. It is to be done in love toward the individual, in obedience and honor to God, and in godly fear for the sake of others in the church.

The Bible gives an example of the necessity of excommunication in a local church—the church at the city of Corinth (1 Corinthians 5:1-13). In this passage, the apostle Paul also gives some purposes behind the biblical use of excommunication. One reason (not directly found in the passage) is for the sake of the testimony of Christ Jesus (and His church) before unbelievers. When David sinned with Bathsheba, one of the consequences of his sin was that the name of the one true God was blasphemed by God's enemies (2 Samuel 12:14). A second reason is that sin is like a cancer; if allowed to exist, it spreads to those nearby in the same way that "a little yeast works through the whole batch of dough" (1 Corinthians 5:6-7). Also, Paul explains that Jesus saved us so that we might be set apart from sin, that we might be "unleavened" or free from that which causes spiritual decay (1 Corinthians 5:7-8). Christ's desire for His bride, the church, is that she might be pure and undefiled (Ephesians 5:25-27).

Excommunication is also for the long-term welfare of the one being disciplined by the church. Paul, in 1 Corinthians 5:5, states that excommunication is a way of delivering the unrepentant sinner "over to Satan, so that the sinful nature may be destroyed and his spirit saved on the day of the Lord." This means that excommunication can somehow involve God's using Satan (or one of his demons) as a disciplinary tool to work in the sinner's life physically to bring about true repentance in his/her heart.

Hopefully the disciplinary action of the church is successful in bringing about godly sorrow and true repentance. When this occurs, the individual can be restored to fellowship. The man involved in the 1 Corinthians 5 passage repented, and Paul encouraged the church to restore him to fellowship with the church (2 Corinthians 2:5-8). Unfortunately, disciplinary action, even when done in love and in the correct manner, is not always successful in bringing about such restoration. But even when church discipline fails to achieve its goal of bringing repentance, it is still needed to accomplish the other good purposes mentioned above.

We have all likely witnessed the behavior of a young boy who has been allowed to do as he pleases with no consistent discipline. It is not a pretty sight. Nor is such parenting loving, for it dooms the child to a dismal future. Such behavior will keep the child from forming meaningful relationships and performing well in any kind of setting. Similarly, discipline in the church, while never enjoyable or easy, is not only necessary, but loving as well. Moreover, it is commanded by God.

Question: What does the Bible say about the form of church government?

Answer: The Lord was very clear in His Word about how He wishes His church on earth to be organized and managed. First, Christ is the head of the church and its supreme authority (Ephesians 1:22; 4:15; Colossians 1:18). Second, the local church is to be autonomous, free from any external authority or control, with the right of self-government and freedom from the interference of any hierarchy of individuals or organizations (Titus 1:5). Third, the church is to be governed by spiritual leadership consisting of two main offices—elders and deacons.

"Elders" were a leading body among the Israelites since the time of Moses. We find them making political decisions (2 Samuel 5:3; 2 Samuel 17:4, 15), advising the king in later history (1 Kings 20:7), and representing the people concerning spiritual matters (Exodus 7:17; 24:1, 9; Numbers 11:16, 24-25). The early Greek translation of the Old Testament, the Septuagint, used the Greek word *presbuteros* for "elder." This is the same Greek word used in the New Testament that is also translated "elder."

The New Testament refers a number of times to elders who served in the role of church leadership (Acts 14:23, 15:2, 20:17; Titus 1:5; James 5:14) and apparently each church had more than one, as the word is usually found in the plural. The only exceptions refer to cases in which one elder is being singled out for some reason (1 Timothy 5:1, 19). In the Jerusalem church, elders were part of the leadership along with the apostles (Acts 15:2-16:4).

It seems that the position of elder was equal to the position of *episkopos*, translated "overseer" or "bishop" (Acts 11:30; 1 Timothy 5:17). The term "elder" may refer to the dignity of the office, while the term "bishop/overseer" describes its authority and duties (1 Peter 2:25, 5:1-4). In Philippians 1:1, Paul greets the bishops and deacons but does not mention the elders, presumably because the elders are the same as the bishops. Likewise, 1 Timothy 3:2, 8 gives the qualifications of bishops and deacons but not of elders. Titus 1:5-7 seems also to tie these two terms together.

The position of "deacon," from *diakonos*, meaning "through the dirt," was one of servant leadership to the church. Deacons are separate from elders, while having qualifications that are in many ways similar to those of elders (1 Timothy 3:8-13). Deacons assist the church in whatever is needed, as recorded in Acts chapter 6.

Concerning the word *poimen*, translated "pastor" in reference to a human leader of a church, it is found only once in the New Testament, in Ephesians 4:11: "It was he who gave some to be apostles, some to be prophets, some to be evangelists, and some to be pastors and teachers." Most associate the two terms "pastors" and "teachers" as referring to a single position, a pastor-teacher. It is likely that a pastor-teacher was the spiritual shepherd of a particular local church.

It would seem from the above passages that there was always a plurality of elders, but this does not negate God's gifting particular elders with the teaching gifts while gifting others with the gift of administration, prayer, etc. (Romans 12:3-8; Ephesians 4:11). Nor does it negate God's calling them into a ministry in which they will use those gifts (Acts 13:1). Thus, one elder may emerge as the "pastor," another may do the majority of visiting members because he has the gift of compassion, while another may "rule" in the sense of handling the organizational details. Many churches that are organized with a pastor and deacon board perform the functions of a plurality of elders in that they share the ministry load and work together in some decision making. In Scripture there was also much congregational input into decisions. Thus, a "dictator" leader who makes the decisions (whether called elder, or bishop, or pastor) is unscriptural (Acts 1:23, 26; 6:3, 5; 15:22, 30; 2 Corinthians 8:19). So, too, is a congregation-ruled church that does not give weight to the elders' or church leaders' input.

In summary, the Bible teaches a leadership consisting of a plurality of elders (bishops/overseers) along with a group of deacons who serve the church. But it is not contrary to this plurality of elders to have one of the elders serving in the major "pastoral" role. God calls some as "pastor/teachers" (even as He called some to be missionaries in Acts 13) and gives them as gifts to the church (Ephesians 4:11). Thus, a church may have many elders, but not all elders are called to serve in the pastoral role. But, as one of the elders, the pastor or "teaching elder" has no more authority in decision making than does any other elder.

Question: What does the Bible say about church growth?

Answer: Although the Bible does not specifically address church growth, the principle of church growth is the understanding that Jesus said, "I will build my church, and the gates of Hades will not overcome it" (Matthew 16:18). Paul confirmed that the church has its foundation in Jesus Christ (1 Corinthians 3:11). Jesus Christ is also the head of the church (Ephesians 1:18-23) and the church's life (John 10:10). Having said that, it should be remembered that "growth" can be a relative term. There are different kinds of growth, some of which have nothing to do with numbers.

A church can be alive and growing even though the number of members/attendees is not changing. If those in the church are growing in the grace and knowledge of the Lord Jesus, submitting to His will for their lives, both individually and corporately, that is a church that is experiencing true growth. At the same time, a church can be adding to its rolls weekly, have huge numbers, and still be spiritually stagnant.

Growth of any kind follows a typical pattern. As with a growing organism, the local church has those who plant the seed (evangelists), those who water the seed (pastor/teachers), and others who use their spiritual gifts for the growth of those in the local church. But note that it is God who gives the increase (1 Corinthians 3:7). Those who plant and those who water will each receive their own reward according to their labor (1 Corinthians 3:8).

There has to be a balance between planting and watering for a local church to grow, which means that in a healthy church each person must know what his/her spiritual gift is so that he/she can function within in the body of Christ. If the planting and watering get out of balance, the church will not prosper as God intended. Of course, there has to be daily dependence upon and obedience to the Holy Spirit so His power can be released in those who plant and water in order for God's increase to come.

Finally, the description of a living and growing church is found in Acts 2:42-47 where the believers "devoted themselves to the apostles' teaching and to the fellowship, to the breaking of bread and to prayer." They were serving one another and reaching out to those who needed to know the Lord, for the Lord "added to their number daily those who were being saved." When these things are present, the church will experience spiritual growth, whether or not there is numerical increase.

Question: Why are there so many Christian denominations?

Answer: To answer this question, we must first differentiate between denominations within the body of Christ and non-Christian cults and false religions. Presbyterians and Lutherans are examples of Christian denominations. Mormons and Jehovah's Witnesses are examples of cults (groups claiming to be Christian but denying one or more of the essentials of the Christian faith). Islam and Buddhism are entirely separate religions.

The rise of denominations within the Christian faith can be traced back to the Protestant Reformation, the movement to "reform" the Roman Catholic Church during the 16th century, out of which four major divisions or traditions of Protestantism would emerge: Lutheran, Reformed, Anabaptist, and Anglican. From these four, other denominations grew over the centuries.

The Lutheran denomination was named after Martin Luther and was based on his teachings. The Methodists got their name because their founder, John Wesley, was famous for coming up with "methods" for spiritual growth. Presbyterians are named for their view on church leadership—the Greek word for elder is *presbyteros*. Baptists got their name because they have always emphasized the importance of baptism. Each denomination has a slightly different doctrine or emphasis from the others, such as the method of baptism; the availability of the Lord's Supper to all or just to those whose testimonies can be verified by church leaders; the sovereignty of God vs. free will in the matter of salvation; the future of Israel and the church; pre-tribulation vs. post-tribulation rapture; the existence of the "sign" gifts in the modern era, and so on. The point of these divisions is never Christ as Lord and Savior, but rather honest differences of opinion by godly, albeit flawed, people seeking to honor God and retain doctrinal purity according to their consciences and their understanding of His Word.

Denominations today are many and varied. The original "mainline" denominations mentioned above have spawned numerous offshoots such as Assemblies of God, Christian and Missionary Alliance, Nazarenes, Evangelical Free, independent Bible churches, and others. Some denominations emphasize slight doctrinal differences, but more often they simply offer different styles of worship to fit the differing tastes and preferences of Christians. But make no mistake: as believers, we must be of one mind on the essentials of the faith, but beyond that there is great deal of latitude in how Christians should worship in a corporate setting. This latitude is what causes so many different "flavors" of Christianity. A Presbyterian church in Uganda will have a style of worship much different from a Presbyterian church in Colorado, but their doctrinal stand will be, for the most part, the same. Diversity is a good thing, but disunity is not. If two churches disagree doctrinally, debate and dialogue over the Word may be called for. This type of "iron sharpening iron" (Proverbs 27:17) is beneficial to all. If they disagree on style and form, however, it is fine for them to remain separate. This separation, though, does not lift the responsibility Christians have to love one another (1 John 4:11-12) and ultimately be united as one in Christ (John 17:21-22).

Question: Why are there so many different Christian interpretations?

Answer: Scripture says there is "one Lord, one faith, one baptism" (Ephesians 4:5). This passage emphasizes the unity that should exist in the body of Christ as we are indwelt by "one Spirit" (verse 4). In verse 3, Paul makes an appeal to humility, meekness, patience, and love—all of which are necessary to preserve unity. According to 1 Corinthians 2:10-13, the Holy Spirit knows the mind of God (verse 11), which He reveals (verse 10) and teaches (verse 13) to those whom He indwells. This activity of the Holy Spirit is called illumination.

In a perfect world, every believer would dutifully study the Bible (2 Timothy 2:15) in prayerful dependence upon the Holy Spirit's illumination. As can be clearly seen, this is not a perfect world. Not everyone who possesses the Holy Spirit actually listens to the Holy Spirit. There are Christians who grieve Him (Ephesians 4:30). Ask any educator—even the best classroom teacher has his share of wayward students who seem to resist learning, no matter what the teacher does. So, one reason different people have different interpretations of the Bible is simply that some do not listen to the Teacher—the Holy Spirit. Following are some other reasons for the wide divergence of beliefs among those who teach the Bible.

1. **Unbelief.** The fact is that many who claim to be Christians have never been born again. They wear the label of "Christian," but there has been no true change of heart. Many who do not even believe the Bible to be true presume to teach it. They claim to speak for God yet live in a state of unbelief. Most false interpretations of Scripture come from such sources.

It is impossible for an unbeliever to correctly interpret Scripture. "The man without the Spirit does not accept the things that come from the Spirit of God, for they are foolishness to him, and he cannot understand them, because they are spiritually discerned" (1 Corinthians 2:14). An unsaved man cannot understand the truth of the Bible. He has no illumination. Further, even being a pastor or theologian does not guarantee one's salvation.

An example of the chaos created by unbelief is found in John 12:28-29. Jesus prays to the Father, saying, "Father, glorify your name." The Father responds with an audible voice from heaven, which everyone nearby hears. Notice, however, the difference in interpretation: "The crowd that was there and heard it said it had thundered; others said an angel had spoken to him." Everyone heard the same thing—an intelligible statement from heaven—yet everyone heard what he wanted to hear.

2. **Lack of training.** The apostle Peter warns against those who misinterpret the Scriptures. He attributes their spurious teachings in part to the fact that they are "ignorant" (2 Peter 3:16). Timothy is told to "Do your best to present yourself to God as one approved, a workman who does not need to be ashamed and who correctly handles the word of truth" (2 Timothy 2:15). There is no shortcut to proper biblical interpretation; we are constrained to study.

3. **Poor hermeneutics.** Much error has been promoted because of a simple failure to apply good hermeneutics (the science of interpreting Scripture). Taking a verse out of its immediate context can do great damage to the intent of the verse. Ignoring the wider context of the chapter and book, or failing to understand the historical/cultural context will also lead to problems.

4. **Ignorance of the whole Word of God.** Apollos was a powerful and eloquent preacher, but he only knew the baptism of John. He was ignorant of Jesus and His provision of salvation, so his message was incomplete. Aquila and Priscilla took him aside and "explained to him the way of

God more adequately" (Acts 18:24-28). After that, Apollos preached Jesus Christ. Some groups and individuals today have an incomplete message because they concentrate on certain passages to the exclusion of others. They fail to compare Scripture with Scripture.

5. **Selfishness and pride.** Sad to say, many interpretations of the Bible are based on an individual's own personal biases and pet doctrines. Some people see an opportunity for personal advancement by promoting a "new perspective" on Scripture. (See the description of false teachers in Jude's epistle.)

6. **Failure to mature.** When Christians are not maturing as they should, their handling of the Word of God is affected. "I gave you milk, not solid food, for you were not yet ready for it. Indeed, you are still not ready. You are still worldly" (1 Corinthians 3:2-3). An immature Christian is not ready for the "meat" of God's Word. Note that the proof of the Corinthians' carnality is a division in their church (verse 4).

7. **Undue emphasis on tradition.** Some churches claim to believe the Bible, but their interpretation is always filtered through the established traditions of their church. Where tradition and the teaching of the Bible are in conflict, tradition is given precedence. This effectively negates the authority of the Word and grants supremacy to the church leadership.

On the essentials, the Bible is abundantly clear. There is nothing ambiguous about the deity of Christ, the reality of heaven and hell, and salvation by grace through faith. On some issues of less importance, however, the teaching of Scripture is less clear, and this naturally leads to different interpretations. For example, we have no direct biblical command governing the frequency of communion or the style of music to use. Honest, sincere Christians can have differing interpretations of the passages concerning these peripheral issues.

The important thing is to be dogmatic where Scripture is and to avoid being dogmatic where Scripture is not. Churches should strive to follow the model of the early church in Jerusalem: "They devoted themselves to the apostles' teaching and to the fellowship, to the breaking of bread and to prayer" (Acts 2:42). There was unity in the early church because they were steadfast in the apostles' doctrine. There will be unity in the church again when we get back to the apostles' doctrine and forego the other doctrines, fads, and gimmicks that have crept into the church.

Question: Why are so many evangelical Christian leaders caught in scandals?

Answer: First, it is important to point out that "so many" is not an accurate characterization. It may seem like many evangelical Christian leaders are caught in scandals, but this is due to the vast amount of attention such scandals are given. There are thousands of evangelical Christian leaders, pastors, professors, missionaries, writers, and evangelists who have never participated in anything "scandalous." The vast majority of evangelical Christian leaders are men and women who love God, are faithful to their spouses and families, and handle their activities with the utmost honesty and integrity. The failures of a few should not be used to attack the character of all.

With that said, there is still the problem that scandals do sometimes occur among those claiming to be evangelical Christians. Prominent Christian leaders have been exposed for committing adultery or participating in prostitution. Some evangelical Christians have been convicted of tax fraud and other financial illegalities. Why does this occur? There are at least three primary explanations: 1) Some of those claiming to be evangelical Christians are unbelieving charlatans, 2) some evangelical Christian leaders allow their position to result in pride, and 3) Satan and his demons more aggressively attack and tempt those in Christian leadership because they know that a scandal involving a leader can have devastating results, on both Christians and non-Christians.

1. Some "evangelical Christians" who are caught in scandals are unredeemed charlatans and false prophets. Jesus warned, "Watch out for false prophets. They come to you in sheep's clothing, but inwardly they are ferocious wolves … Therefore by their fruits you will know them" (Matthew 7:15-20). False prophets pretend to be godly men and women and appear to be solid evangelical leaders. However, their "fruit"

(scandals) eventually reveals them to be the opposite of what they claimed to be. In this, they follow the example of Satan, "And no wonder, for Satan himself masquerades as an angel of light. It is not surprising, then, if his servants masquerade as servants of righteousness. Their end will be what their actions deserve" (2 Corinthians 11:14-15).

2. The Bible makes it clear that "pride goes before destruction, a haughty spirit before a fall" (Proverbs 16:18). James 4:6 reminds us that "God opposes the proud but gives grace to the humble." The Bible repeatedly warns against pride. Many Christian leaders begin a ministry in a spirit of humility and reliance upon God, but as the ministry grows and thrives, they are tempted to take some of this glory for themselves. Some evangelical Christian leaders, while paying lip-service to God, actually attempt to manage and build the ministry in their own strength and wisdom. This type of pride leads to a fall. God, through the prophet Hosea, warned, "When I fed them, they were satisfied; when they were satisfied, they became proud; then they forgot me" (Hosea 13:6).

3. Satan knows that by instigating a scandal with an evangelical Christian leader, he can have a powerful impact. Just as King David's adultery with Bathsheba and arranged murder of Uriah caused great damage to David's family and the entire nation of Israel, so has many a church or ministry been damaged or destroyed by the moral failure of its leader. Many Christians have had their faith weakened as a result of seeing a leader fall. Non-Christians use the failure of "Christian" leaders as a reason to reject Christianity. Satan and his demons know this, and therefore direct more of their attacks against those in leadership roles. The Bible warns us all, "Be self-controlled and alert. Your enemy the devil prowls around like a roaring lion looking for someone to devour" (1 Peter 5:8).

How are we to respond when an evangelical Christian leader is accused of or caught in a scandal? 1) Do not listen to or accept baseless and unfounded accusations (Proverbs 18:8, 17; 1 Timothy 5:19). 2) Take appropriate biblical measures to rebuke those who sin (Matthew 18:15-17; 1 Timothy 5:20). If the sin is proven and severe, permanent removal from ministry leadership should be enforced (1 Timothy 3:1-13). 3) Forgive those who sin (Ephesians 4:32; Colossians 3:13), and when repentance is proven, restore them to fellowship (Galatians 6:1; 1 Peter 4:8) but not to leadership. 4) Be faithful in praying for our leaders. Knowing the problems they deal with, the temptations they suffer, and the stress they must endure, we should be praying for our leaders, asking God to strengthen them, protect them, and encourage them. 5) Most importantly, take the failure of an evangelical Christian leader as a reminder to put your ultimate faith in God and God alone. God never fails, never sins, and never lies. "Holy, holy, holy is the LORD Almighty; the whole earth is full of His glory" (Isaiah 6:3).

Question: What is the history of Christianity?

Answer: The history of Christianity is really the history of Western civilization. Christianity has had an all-pervasive influence on society at large—art, language, politics, law, family life, calendar dates, music, and the very way we think have all been colored by Christian influence for nearly two millennia. The story of the church, therefore, is an important one to know.

The Beginning of the Church

The church began 50 days after Jesus' resurrection (c. A.D. 35). Jesus had promised that He would build His church (Matthew 16:18), and with the coming of the Holy Spirit on the day of Pentecost (Acts 2:1-4), the church—*ekklesia* (the "called-out assembly")—officially began. Three thousand people responded to Peter's sermon that day and chose to follow Christ.

The initial converts to Christianity were Jews or proselytes to Judaism, and the church was centered in Jerusalem. Because of this, Christianity was seen at first as a Jewish sect, akin to the Pharisees, the Sadducees, or the Essenes. However, what the apostles preached was radically different from what other Jewish groups were teaching. Jesus was the Jewish Messiah (the anointed King) who had come to fulfill the Law (Matthew 5:17) and institute a new covenant based on

His death (Mark 14:24). This message, with its charge that they had killed their own Messiah, infuriated many Jewish leaders, and some, like Saul of Tarsus, took action to stamp out "the Way" (Acts 9:1-2).

It is quite proper to say that Christianity has its roots in Judaism. The Old Testament laid the groundwork for the New, and it is impossible to fully understand Christianity without a working knowledge of the Old Testament (see the books of Matthew and Hebrews). The Old Testament explains the necessity of a Messiah, contains the history of the Messiah's people, and predicts the Messiah's coming. The New Testament, then, is all about the coming of Messiah and His work to save us from sin. In His life, Jesus fulfilled over 300 specific prophecies, proving that He was the One the Old Testament had anticipated.

The Growth of the Early Church

Not long after Pentecost, the doors to the church were opened to non-Jews. The evangelist Philip preached to the Samaritans (Acts 8:5), and many of them believed in Christ. The apostle Peter preached to the Gentile household of Cornelius (Acts 10), and they, too, received the Holy Spirit. The apostle Paul (the former persecutor of the church) spread the gospel all over the Greco-Roman world, reaching as far as Rome itself (Acts 28:16) and possibly all the way to Spain.

By A.D. 70, the year Jerusalem was destroyed, most of the books of the New Testament had been completed and were circulating among the churches. For the next 240 years, Christians were persecuted by Rome—sometimes at random, sometimes by government edict.

In the 2nd and 3rd centuries, the church leadership became more and more hierarchical as numbers increased. Several heresies were exposed and refuted during this time, and the New Testament canon was agreed upon. Persecution continued to intensify.

The Rise of the Roman Church

In A.D. 312, the Roman Emperor Constantine claimed to have had a conversion experience. About 70 years later, during the reign of Theodosius, Christianity became the official religion of the Roman Empire. Bishops were given places of honor in the government, and by A.D. 400, the terms "Roman" and "Christian" were virtually synonymous.

197

After Constantine, then, Christians were no longer persecuted. In time, it was the pagans who came under persecution unless they "converted" to Christianity. Such forced conversions led to many people entering the church without a true change of heart. The pagans brought with them their idols and the practices they were accustomed to, and the church changed; icons, elaborate architecture, pilgrimages, and the veneration of saints were added to the simplicity of early church worship. About this same time, some Christians retreated from Rome, choosing to live in isolation as monks, and infant baptism was introduced as a means of washing away original sin.

Through the next centuries, various church councils were held in an attempt to determine the church's official doctrine, to censure clerical abuses, and to make peace between warring factions. As the Roman Empire grew weaker, the church became more powerful, and many disagreements broke out between the churches in the West and those in the East. The Western (Latin) church, based in Rome, claimed apostolic authority over all other churches. The bishop of Rome had even begun calling himself the "Pope" (the Father). This did not sit well with the Eastern (Greek) church, based in Constantinople. Theological, political, procedural, and linguistic divides all contributed to the Great Schism in 1054, in which the Roman Catholic ("Universal") Church and the Eastern Orthodox Church excommunicated each other and broke all ties.

The Middle Ages

During the Middle Ages in Europe, the Roman Catholic Church continued to hold power, with the popes claiming authority over all levels of life and living as kings. Corruption and greed in the church leadership was commonplace. From 1095 to 1204 the popes endorsed a series of bloody and expensive crusades in an effort to repel Muslim advances and liberate Jerusalem.

The Reformation

Through the years, several individuals had tried to call attention to the theological, political, and human rights abuses of the Roman Church. All had been silenced in one way or another. But in 1517, a

German monk named Martin Luther took a stand against the church, and everyone heard. With Luther came the Protestant Reformation, and the Middle Ages were brought to a close.

The Reformers, including Luther, Calvin, and Zwingli, differed in many finer points of theology, but they were consistent in their emphasis on the Bible's supreme authority over church tradition and the fact that sinners are saved by grace through faith alone apart from works (Ephesians 2:8-9).

Although Catholicism made a comeback in Europe, and a series of wars between Protestants and Catholics ensued, the Reformation had successfully dismantled the power of the Roman Catholic Church and helped open the door to the modern age.

The Age of Missions

From 1790 to 1900, the church showed an unprecedented interest in missionary work. Colonization had opened eyes to the need for missions, and industrialization had provided people with the financial ability to fund the missionaries. Missionaries went around the world preaching the gospel, and churches were established throughout the world.

The Modern Church

Today, the Roman Catholic Church and the Eastern Orthodox Church have taken steps to mend their broken relationship, as have Catholics and Lutherans. The evangelical church is strongly independent and rooted firmly in Reformed theology. The church has also seen the rise of Pentecostalism, the charismatic movement, ecumenicalism, and various cults.

What We Learn from Our History

If we learn nothing else from church history, we should at least recognize the importance of letting "the word of Christ dwell in [us] richly" (Colossians 3:16). Each of us is responsible to know what the Scripture says and to live by it. When the church forgets what the Bible teaches and ignores what Jesus taught, chaos reigns.

There are many churches today, but only one gospel. It is "the faith that was once for all entrusted to the saints" (Jude 3). May we be careful to preserve that faith and pass it on without alteration, and the Lord will continue to fulfill His promise to build His church.

Question: What does the "husband of one wife" in 1 Timothy 3:2 mean? Can a divorced man serve as a pastor, elder, or deacon?

Answer: There are at least three possible interpretations of the phrase "husband of one wife" in 1 Timothy 3:2. 1) It could simply be saying that a polygamist is not qualified to be an elder, a deacon or a pastor. This is the most literal interpretation of the phrase, but seems somewhat unlikely considering that polygamy was quite rare in the time that Paul was writing. 2) The phrase could also be translated "one-woman man." This would indicate that a bishop must be absolutely loyal to the woman he is married to. This interpretation focuses more on moral purity than marital status. 3) The phrase could also be understood to declare that in order to be an elder/deacon/ pastor, a man can only have been married once, other than in the case of a remarried widower.

Interpretations 2) and 3) are the most prevalent today. Interpretation 2) seems to be the strongest, primarily because Scripture seems to allow for divorce in exceptional circumstances (Matthew 19:9; 1 Corinthians 7:12-16). It would also be important to differentiate between a man who was divorced and remarried before he became a Christian from a man who was divorced and remarried after becoming a Christian. An otherwise qualified man should not be excluded from church leadership because of actions he took prior to coming to know the Lord Jesus Christ as his Savior. Although 1 Timothy 3:2 does not necessarily exclude a divorced or remarried man from serving as an elder/deacon/pastor, there are other issues to consider.

The first qualification of an elder/deacon/pastor is to be "above reproach" (1 Timothy 3:2). If the divorce and/or remarriage results in a poor testimony for the man in the church or community, it may be the "above reproach" qualification that excludes him rather than the "husband of one wife" requirement. An elder/deacon/pastor is to be a man that the church and community can look up to as an example of Christ-likeness and godly leadership. If his divorce and/ or remarriage situation detracts from this purpose, perhaps he should not serve in the position of elder/deacon/pastor. It is important to remember, though, that just because a man is disqualified from serving as an elder/deacon/pastor, he is still a valuable member of the body of Christ. Every Christian possesses spiritual gifts (1 Corinthians 12:4-7) and is called to participate in edifying other believers with those gifts (1 Corinthians 12:7). A man who is disqualified from the position of elder/deacon/pastor can still teach, preach, serve, pray, worship, and play an important role in the church.

Question: What is the proper mode of baptism?

Answer: The simplest answer to this question is found in the meaning of the word "baptize." It comes from a Greek word which means "to submerge in water." Therefore, baptism by sprinkling or by pouring is an oxymoron, something that self-contradictory. Baptism by sprinkling would mean "submerging someone in water by sprinkling water on them." Baptism, by its inherent definition, must be an act of immersion in water.

Baptism illustrates a believer's identification with Christ's death, burial, and resurrection. "Or don't you know that all of us who were baptized into Christ Jesus were baptized into his death? We were therefore buried with him through baptism into death in order that, just as Christ was raised from the dead through the glory of the Father, we too may live a new life" (Romans 6:3-4). The action of being immersed in the water pictures dying and being buried with Christ. The action of coming out of the water illustrates Christ's resurrection. As a result, baptism by immersion is the only method of baptism which illustrates being buried with Christ and being raised with Him. Baptism by sprinkling and/or pouring came into practice as a result of the unbiblical practice of infant baptism.

Baptism by immersion, while it is the most biblical mode of identifying with Christ, is not (as some believe) a prerequisite for salvation. It is rather an act of obedience, a public proclamation of faith in Christ and identification with Him. Baptism is a picture of our leaving our old life and becoming a new creation (2 Corinthians 5:17). Baptism by immersion is the only mode that fully illustrates this radical change.

Question: Does God require Sabbath-keeping of Christians?

Answer: In Colossians 2:16-17, the apostle Paul declares, "Therefore do not let anyone judge you by what you eat or drink, or with regard to a religious festival, a New Moon celebration or a Sabbath day. These are a shadow of the things that were to come; the reality, however, is found in Christ." Similarly, Romans 14:5 states, "One man considers one day more sacred than another; another man considers every day alike. Each one should be fully convinced in his own mind." These Scriptures make it clear that, for the Christian, Sabbath-keeping is a matter of spiritual freedom, not a command from God. Sabbath-keeping is an issue on which God's Word instructs us not to judge each other. Sabbath-keeping is a matter about which each Christian needs to be fully convinced in his/her own mind.

In the early chapters of the book of Acts, the first Christians were predominantly Jews. When Gentiles began to receive the gift of salvation through Jesus Christ, the Jewish Christians had a dilemma. What aspects of the Mosaic Law and Jewish tradition should Gentile Christians be instructed to obey? The apostles met and discussed the issue in the Jerusalem council (Acts 15). The decision was, "It is my judgment, therefore, that we should not make it difficult for the Gentiles who are turning to God. Instead we should write to them, telling them to abstain from food polluted by idols, from sexual immorality, from the meat of strangled animals and from blood" (Acts 15:19-20). Sabbath-keeping was not one of the commands the apostles felt was necessary to force on Gentile believers. It is inconceivable that the apostles would neglect to include Sabbath-keeping if it was God's command for Christians to observe the Sabbath day.

A common error in the Sabbath-keeping debate is the concept that the Sabbath was the day of worship. Groups such as the Seventh Day Adventists hold that God requires the church service to be held on Saturday, the Sabbath day. That is not what the Sabbath command was. The Sabbath command was to do no work on the Sabbath day (Exodus 20:8-11). Nowhere in Scripture is the Sabbath day commanded to be the day of worship. Yes, Jews in Old Testament, New Testament, and modern times use Saturday as the day of worship, but that is not the essence of the Sabbath command. In the book of

Acts, whenever a meeting is said to be on the Sabbath, it is a meeting of Jews, not Christians.

When did the early Christians meet? Acts 2:46-47 gives us the answer, "Every day they continued to meet together in the temple courts. They broke bread in their homes and ate together with glad and sincere hearts, praising God and enjoying the favor of all the people. And the Lord added to their number daily those who were being saved." If there was a day that Christians met regularly, it was the first day of the week (our Sunday), not the Sabbath day (our Saturday) (Acts 20:7; 1 Corinthians 16:2). In honor of Christ's resurrection on Sunday, the early Christians observed Sunday not as the "Christian Sabbath" but as a day to especially worship Jesus Christ.

Is there anything wrong with worshipping on Saturday, the Jewish Sabbath? Absolutely not! We should worship God every day, not just on Saturday or Sunday! Many churches today have both Saturday and Sunday services. There is freedom in Christ (Romans 8:21; 2 Corinthians 3:17; Galatians 5:1). Should a Christian practice Sabbath-keeping, that is, not working on Saturdays? If a Christian feels led to do so, absolutely, yes (Romans 14:5). However, those who choose to practice Sabbath-keeping should not judge those who do not keep the Sabbath (Colossians 2:16). Further, those who do not keep the Sabbath should avoid being a stumbling block (1 Corinthians 8:9) to those who do keep the Sabbath. Galatians 5:13-15 sums up the whole issue: "You, my brothers, were called to be free. But do not use your freedom to indulge the sinful nature; rather, serve one another in love. The entire law is summed up in a single command: 'Love your neighbor as yourself.' If you keep on biting and devouring each other, watch out or you will be destroyed by each other."

Question: What are appropriate reasons for missing church?

Answer: Many people have an improper and/or unbiblical understanding of church attendance. Some people feel that they must attend church legalistically, being at church virtually every time there is any kind of service or meeting. Some people experience a feeling of guilt whenever they miss a Sunday morning service. Sadly, some churches encourage this guilt by putting excessive pressure on people to attend regularly. In the matter of church attendance, the most crucial thing

203

to understand is that the quality of a person's relationship with God is not determined by how often he/she is in church. Similarly, God's love for His children is not based on the number of times they attend formal services.

There is no doubt that Christians, followers of Jesus Christ, should attend church. It should be the desire of each and every Christian to worship corporately (Ephesians 5:19-20), to fellowship with and encourage other Christians (1 Thessalonians 5:11), and to be taught God's Word (2 Timothy 3:16-17). Attending church should be a joy, not a dreaded and dreary assignment. Just as God loves a cheerful giver (2 Corinthians 9:7), so He is pleased with a genuinely cheerful church attendee (Hebrews 10:24-25).

What then are appropriate reasons for missing church? Is it acceptable to miss church to attend a sporting event? Yes. Is it acceptable to miss church while on vacation? Yes. Is it acceptable to miss church when you are sick/ill? Yes. Is it acceptable to miss church because you are tired from a difficult week? Yes. Is it acceptable to miss church simply because you do not feel like attending? Yes. Like so many other issues in the Christian life, church attendance can become legalistic instead of a matter of grace. A person does not *have* to attend church to be saved, to be a good Christian, to grow spiritually, etc. Rather, a Christian *should* attend church to learn about the greatness of God's gift of salvation, to learn how to become more like Christ, and to have opportunities to minister to others.

Why do you attend church? Is it to make yourself appear spiritual? Is it to interact with possible business contacts? Is it out of legalistic thinking that says the more frequently you walk through the doors of a church, the more God is pleased with you? Is your Sunday morning filled with family strife, arguing, and screaming, followed by attending church with pasted-on smiling, happy faces? In such an instance, it would be better to stay home and work on biblically resolving the conflict in your family, instead of making a token appearance at church.

It all comes down to perspective and priorities. The busyness of many people's lives makes church attendance more of a chore than a blessing. If attending church is not important enough, or valuable enough, to make it a priority, either something is wrong with your church or something is wrong with your attitude about church. Is your church attendance nothing more than arriving one minute before the service starts, sitting bored and inattentively through the worship and sermon, and then leaving immediately after the service ends? If so, you might as well have missed church, as you did not take anything from it, and you contributed nothing to it.

We should want to attend church so we can fellowship with others who have also experienced the amazing grace of Jesus Christ. We should avoid missing church, whenever possible, because we recognize the importance of hearing God's Word, applying it to our lives, and sharing it with others. We should attend church, not to collect spiritual bonus points, but because we love God and recognize what His Word says about the importance of corporate fellowship and worship (Hebrews 10:24-25). Every Christian should attend church regularly. At the same time, missing church for a good reason is in no sense a sin or something that should cause feelings of guilt.

When you *miss* (do not attend) church, do you *miss* (have a longing for) church? If so, that is a sign you have a good and biblical connection with church. If not, that is a sign you need to re-evaluate your choice of church and/or participation in church. God knows our hearts. God is not impressed by a person attending every Sunday morning service, Sunday evening service, mid-week service, and Bible study opportunity a church offers. God's desire is that we utilize the local church for our own spiritual edification and the use of our spiritual gifts to minister to others.

Chapter 7

QUESTIONS ABOUT

THE END TIMES

CONTENTS

What is going to happen according to end times prophecy? 208

What signs indicate that the end times are approaching? 209

What is the rapture of the church?...210

What is the tribulation? How do we know the tribulation will last seven
years? 210

When is the rapture going to occur in relation to the tribulation?...........212

What is the second coming of Jesus Christ?..214

What is the Millennial Kingdom? 215

Who is the Antichrist?...216

Who are the 144,000? 217

What is the abomination of desolation?...219

What is the Apocalypse? 220

What is the battle of Armageddon?...221

What is the day of the Lord? 222

What is the difference between the rapture and the second coming? 223

Who are the four horsemen of the Apocalypse? 225

How are we to live our lives in light of Christ's return? 226

What is the mark of the beast (666)?...227

What are the seven seals, trumpets, and bowls in the book of
Revelation? 228

How can I understand the book of Revelation? 229

Question: What is going to happen according to end times prophecy?

Answer: The Bible has a lot to say about the end times. Nearly every book of the Bible contains prophecy regarding the end times. Taking all of these prophecies and organizing them can be difficult. Following is a very brief summary of what the Bible declares will happen in the end times.

Christ will remove all born-again believers from the earth in an event known as the rapture (1 Thessalonians 4:13-18; 1 Corinthians 15:51-54). At the judgment seat of Christ, these believers will be rewarded for good works and faithful service during their time on earth or will lose rewards, but not eternal life, for lack of service and obedience (1 Corinthians 3:11-15; 2 Corinthians 5:10).

The Antichrist (the beast) will come into power and will sign a covenant with Israel for seven years (Daniel 9:27). This seven-year period of time is known as the "tribulation." During the tribulation, there will be terrible wars, famines, plagues, and natural disasters. God will be pouring out His wrath against sin, evil, and wickedness. The tribulation will include the appearance of the four horsemen of the Apocalypse, and the seven seal, trumpet, and bowl judgments.

About halfway through the seven years, the Antichrist will break the peace covenant with Israel and make war against it. The Antichrist will commit "the abomination of desolation" and set up an image of himself to be worshipped in the Jerusalem temple (Daniel 9:27; 2 Thessalonians 2:3-10), which will have been rebuilt. The second half of the tribulation is known as "the great tribulation" (Revelation 7:14) and "the time of Jacob's trouble" (Jeremiah 30:7).

At the end of the seven-year tribulation, the Antichrist will launch a final attack on Jerusalem, culminating in the battle of Armageddon. Jesus Christ will return, destroy the Antichrist and his armies, and cast them into the lake of fire (Revelation 19:11-21). Christ will then bind Satan in the Abyss for 1000 years and He will rule His earthly kingdom for this thousand-year period (Revelation 20:1-6).

At the end of the thousand years, Satan will be released, defeated again, and then cast into the lake of fire (Revelation 20:7-10) for eternity. Christ then judges all unbelievers (Revelation 20:10-15) at the great white throne judgment, casting them all into the lake of fire. Christ will then usher in a new heaven and new earth and the

New Jerusalem—the eternal dwelling place of believers. There will be no more sin, sorrow, or death (Revelation 21–22).

Question: What signs indicate that the end times are approaching?

Answer: Matthew 24:5-8 gives us some important clues so we can discern the approach of the end times, "For many will come in my name, claiming, 'I am the Christ,' and will deceive many. You will hear of wars and rumors of wars, but see to it that you are not alarmed. Such things must happen, but the end is still to come. Nation will rise against nation, and kingdom against kingdom. There will be famines and earthquakes in various places." An increase in false messiahs, an increase in warfare, and increases in famines, plagues, and natural disasters—these are signs of the end times. In this passage, though, we are given a warning: we are not to be deceived, because these events are only the beginning of birth pains; the end is still to come.

Some interpreters point to every earthquake, every political upheaval, and every attack on Israel as a sure sign that the end times are rapidly approaching. While the events may signal the approach of the last days, they are not necessarily indicators that the end times have arrived. The apostle Paul warned that the last days would bring a marked increase in false teaching. "The Spirit clearly says that in later times some will abandon the faith and follow deceiving spirits and things taught by demons" (1 Timothy 4:1). The last days are described as "perilous times" because of the increasingly evil character of man and people who actively "resist the truth" (2 Timothy 3:1-9; see also 2 Thessalonians 2:3).

Other possible signs would include a rebuilding of a Jewish temple in Jerusalem, increased hostility towards Israel, and advances toward a one-world government. The most prominent sign of the end times, however, is the nation of Israel. In 1948, Israel was recognized as a sovereign state, essentially for the first time since A.D. 70. God promised Abraham that his posterity would have Canaan as "an everlasting possession" (Genesis 17:8), and Ezekiel prophesied a physical and spiritual resuscitation of Israel (Ezekiel chapter 37). Having Israel as a nation in its own land is important in light of end times prophecy because of Israel's prominence in eschatology (Daniel 10:14; 11:41; Revelation 11:8).

With these signs in mind, we can be wise and discerning in regard to the expectation of the end times. We should not, however, interpret any of these singular events as a clear indication of the soon arrival of the end times. God has given us enough information that we can be prepared, and that is what we are called to be.

Question: What is the rapture of the church?

Answer: The word "rapture" does not occur in the Bible. The concept of the rapture, though, is clearly taught in Scripture. The rapture of the church is the event in which God removes all believers from the earth in order to make way for His righteous judgment to be poured out on the earth during the tribulation period. The rapture is described primarily in 1 Thessalonians 4:13-18 and 1 Corinthians 15:50-54. God will resurrect all believers who have died, give them glorified bodies, and take them from the earth, along with those believers who are still alive and who will at that time also be given glorified bodies. "For the Lord Himself will come down from heaven, with a loud command, with the voice of the archangel and with the trumpet call of God, and the dead in Christ will rise first. After that, we who are still alive and are left will be caught up together with them in the clouds to meet the Lord in the air. And so we will be with the Lord forever" (1 Thessalonians 4:16-17).

The rapture will be instantaneous in nature, and we will receive glorified bodies at that time. "Listen, I tell you a mystery: We will not all sleep, but we will all be changed—in a flash, in the twinkling of an eye, at the last trumpet. For the trumpet will sound, the dead will be raised imperishable, and we will be changed" (1 Corinthians 15:51-52). The rapture is the glorious event we should all be longing for. We will finally be free from sin. We will be in God's presence forever. There is far too much debate over the meaning and scope of the rapture. This is not God's intent. Rather, in regard to the rapture, God wants us to "encourage each other with these words" (1 Thessalonians 4:18).

Question: What is the tribulation? How do we know the tribulation will last seven years?

Answer: The tribulation is a future seven-year period of time when God will finish His discipline of Israel and finalize His judgment of the unbelieving world. The church, made up of all who have trusted in the person and work of the Lord Jesus to save them from being punished for sin, will not be present during the tribulation. The church will be removed from the earth in an event known as the rapture (1 Thessalonians 4:13-18; 1 Corinthians 15:51-53). The church is saved from the wrath to come (1 Thessalonians 5:9). Throughout Scripture, the tribulation is referred to by other names such as the Day of the Lord (Isaiah 2:12; 13:6-9; Joel 1:15; 2:1-31; 3:14; 1 Thessalonians 5:2); trouble or tribulation (Deuteronomy 4:30; Zephaniah 1:1); the great tribulation, which refers to the more intense second half of the seven-year period (Matthew 24:21); time or day of trouble (Daniel 12:1; Zephaniah 1:15); time of Jacob's trouble (Jeremiah 30:7).

An understanding of Daniel 9:24-27 is necessary in order to understand the purpose and time of the tribulation. This passage speaks of 70 weeks that have been declared against "your people." Daniel's people are the Jews, the nation of Israel, and Daniel 9:24 speaks of a period of time that God has given "to finish transgression, to put an end to sin, to atone for wickedness, to bring in everlasting righteousness, to seal up vision and prophecy and to anoint the most holy." God declares that "seventy sevens" will fulfill all these things. This is 70 sevens of years, or 490 years. (Some translations refer to 70 weeks of years.) This is confirmed by another part of this passage in Daniel. In verses 25 and 26, Daniel is told that the Messiah will be cut off after "seven sevens and sixty-two sevens" (69 total), beginning with the decree to rebuild Jerusalem. In other words, 69 sevens of years (483 years) after the decree to rebuild Jerusalem, the Messiah will be cut off. Biblical historians confirm that 483 years passed from the time of the decree to rebuild Jerusalem to the time when Jesus was crucified. Most Christian scholars, regardless of their view of eschatology (future things/events), have the above understanding of Daniel's 70 sevens.

With 483 years having passed from the decree to rebuild Jerusalem to the cutting off of the Messiah, this leaves one seven-year period to be fulfilled in terms of Daniel 9:24: "to finish transgression, to put an end to sin, to atone for wickedness, to bring in everlasting righteousness, to seal up vision and prophecy and to anoint the most holy." This final seven-year period is known as the tribulation period—it is a time when God finishes judging Israel for its sin.

Daniel 9:27 gives a few highlights of the seven-year tribulation period: "He will confirm a covenant with many for one 'seven.' In the middle of the 'seven' he will put an end to sacrifice and offering. And on a wing of the temple he will set up an abomination that causes desolation, until the end that is decreed is poured out on him." The person of whom this verse speaks is the person Jesus calls the "abomination that causes desolation" (Matthew 24:15) and is called "the beast" in Revelation 13. Daniel 9:27 says that the beast will make a covenant for seven years, but in the middle of this week (3 1/2 years into the tribulation), he will break the covenant, putting a stop to sacrifice. Revelation 13 explains that the beast will place an image of himself in the temple and require the world to worship him. Revelation 13:5 says that this will go on for 42 months, which is 3 1/2 years. Since Daniel 9:27 says that this will happen in the middle of the week, and Revelation 13:5 says that the beast will do this for a period of 42 months, it is easy to see that the total length of time is 84 months or seven years. Also see Daniel 7:25, where the "time, times, and half a time" (time=1 year; times=2 years; half a time=1/2 year; total of 3 1/2 years) also refers to "great tribulation," the last half of the seven-year tribulation period when the beast will be in power.

For further references about the tribulation, see Revelation 11:2-3, which speaks of 1260 days and 42 months, and Daniel 12:11-12, which speaks of 1290 days and 1335 days. These days have a reference to the midpoint of the tribulation. The additional days in Daniel 12 may include the time at the end for the judgment of the nations (Matthew 25:31-46) and time for the setting up of Christ's millennial kingdom (Revelation 20:4-6).

Question: When is the rapture going to occur in relation to the tribulation?

Answer: The timing of the rapture in relation to the tribulation is one of the most controversial issues in the church today. The three primary views are pre-tribulational (the rapture occurs before the tribulation), mid-tribulational (the rapture occurs at or near the mid-point of the tribulation), and post-tribulational (the rapture occurs at the end of the tribulation). A fourth view, commonly known as pre-wrath, is a slight modification of the mid-tribulational position.

First, it is important to recognize the purpose of the tribulation. According to Daniel 9:27, there is a seventieth "seven" (seven years) that is still yet to come. Daniel's entire prophecy of the seventy sevens (Daniel 9:20-27) is speaking of the nation of Israel. It is a time period in which God focuses His attention especially on Israel. The seventieth seven, the tribulation, must also be a time when God deals specifically with Israel. While this does not necessarily indicate that the church could not also be present, it does bring into question why the church would need to be on the earth during that time.

The primary Scripture passage on the rapture is 1 Thessalonians 4:13-18. It states that all living believers, along with all believers who have died, will meet the Lord Jesus in the air and will be with Him forever. The rapture is God's removing His people from the earth. A few verses later, in 1 Thessalonians 5:9, Paul says, "For God did not appoint us to suffer wrath but to receive salvation through our Lord Jesus Christ." The book of Revelation, which deals primarily with the time period of the tribulation, is a prophetic message of how God will pour out His wrath upon the earth during the tribulation. It seems inconsistent for God to promise believers that they will not suffer wrath and then leave them on the earth to suffer through the wrath of the tribulation. The fact that God promises to deliver Christians from wrath shortly after promising to remove His people from the earth seems to link those two events together.

Another crucial passage on the timing of the rapture is Revelation 3:10, in which Christ promises to deliver believers from the "hour of trial" that is going to come upon the earth. This could mean two things. Either Christ will protect believers in the midst of the trials, or He will deliver believers out of the trials. Both are valid meanings of the Greek word translated "from." However, it is important to recognize what believers are promised to be kept from. It is not just the trial, but the "hour" of trial. Christ is promising to keep believers from the very time period that contains the trials, namely the tribulation. The purpose of the tribulation, the purpose of the rapture, the meaning of 1 Thessalonians 5:9, and the interpretation of Revelation 3:10 all give clear support to the pre-tribulational position. If the Bible is interpreted literally and consistently, the pre-tribulational position is the most biblically-based interpretation.

Question: What is the second coming of Jesus Christ?

Answer: The second coming of Jesus Christ is the hope of believers that God is in control of all things, and is faithful to the promises and prophecies in His Word. In His first coming, Jesus Christ came to earth as a baby in a manger in Bethlehem, just as prophesied. Jesus fulfilled many of the prophecies of the Messiah during His birth, life, ministry, death, and resurrection. However, there are some prophecies regarding the Messiah that Jesus has not yet fulfilled. The second coming of Christ will be the return of Christ to fulfill these remaining prophecies. In His first coming, Jesus was the suffering Servant. In His second coming, Jesus will be the conquering King. In His first coming, Jesus arrived in the most humble of circumstances. In His second coming, Jesus will arrive with the armies of heaven at His side.

The Old Testament prophets did not make clearly this distinction between the two comings. This can be seen in Isaiah 7:14, 9:6-7 and Zechariah 14:4. As a result of the prophecies seeming to speak of two individuals, many Jewish scholars believed there would be both a suffering Messiah and a conquering Messiah. What they failed to understand is that there is only one Messiah and He would fulfill both roles. Jesus fulfilled the role of the suffering servant (Isaiah chapter 53) in His first coming. Jesus will fulfill the role of Israel's deliverer and King in His second coming. Zechariah 12:10 and Revelation 1:7, describing the second coming, look back to Jesus being pierced. Israel, and the whole world, will mourn for not having accepted the Messiah the first time He came.

After Jesus ascended into heaven, the angels declared to the apostles, "'Men of Galilee,' they said, 'why do you stand here looking into the sky? This same Jesus, who has been taken from you into heaven, will come back in the same way you have seen him go into heaven'" (Acts 1:11). Zechariah 14:4 identifies the location of the second coming as the Mount of Olives. Matthew 24:30 declares, "At that time the sign of the Son of Man will appear in the sky, and all the nations of the earth will mourn. They will see the Son of Man coming on the clouds of the sky, with power and great glory." Titus 2:13 describes the second coming as a "glorious appearing."

The second coming is spoken of in greatest detail in Revelation 19:11-16, "I saw heaven standing open and there before me was a white horse, whose rider is called Faithful and True. With justice he judges and makes war. His eyes are like blazing fire, and on his head are many crowns. He has a name written on him that no one knows but he himself. He is dressed in a robe dipped in blood, and his name is the Word of God. The armies of heaven were following him, riding on white horses and dressed in fine linen, white and clean. Out of his mouth comes a sharp sword with which to strike down the nations. 'He will rule them with an iron scepter.' He treads the winepress of the fury of the wrath of God Almighty. On his robe and on his thigh he has this name written: KING OF KINGS AND LORD OF LORDS."

Question: What is the Millennial Kingdom, and should it be understood literally?

Answer: The millennial kingdom is the title given to the 1000-year reign of Jesus Christ on the earth. Some seek to interpret the 1000 years in an allegorical manner. Some understand the 1000 years as merely a figurative way of saying "a long period of time," not a literal, physical reign of Jesus Christ on the earth. However, six times in Revelation 20:2-7, the millennial kingdom is specifically said to be 1000 years in length. If God wished to communicate "a long period of time," He could have easily done so without explicitly and repeatedly mentioning an exact time frame.

The Bible tells us that when Christ returns to earth He will establish Himself as King in Jerusalem, sitting on the throne of David (Luke 1:32-33). The unconditional covenants demand a literal, physical return of Christ to establish the kingdom. The Abrahamic covenant promised Israel a land, a posterity and ruler, and a spiritual blessing (Genesis 12:1-3). The Palestinian covenant promised Israel a restoration to the land and occupation of the land (Deuteronomy 30:1-10). The Davidic covenant promised Israel forgiveness—the means whereby the nation could be blessed (Jeremiah 31:31-34).

At the second coming, these covenants will be fulfilled as Israel is re-gathered from the nations (Matthew 24:31), converted (Zechariah 12:10-14), and restored to the land under the rule of the Messiah,

Jesus Christ. The Bible speaks of the conditions during the millennium as a perfect environment physically and spiritually. It will be a time of peace (Micah 4:2-4; Isaiah 32:17-18), joy (Isaiah 61:7, 10), comfort (Isaiah 40:1-2), and no poverty or sickness (Amos 9:13-15; Joel 2:28-29). The Bible also tells us that only believers will enter the millennial kingdom. Because of this, it will be a time of complete righteousness (Matthew 25:37; Psalm 24:3-4), obedience (Jeremiah 31:33), holiness (Isaiah 35:8), truth (Isaiah 65:16), and fullness of the Holy Spirit (Joel 2:28-29). Christ will rule as king (Isaiah 9:3-7; 11:1-10), with David as regent (Jeremiah 33:15-21; Amos 9:11). Nobles and governors will also rule (Isaiah 32:1; Matthew 19:28), and Jerusalem will be the political center of the world (Zechariah 8:3).

Revelation 20:2-7 gives the precise time period of the millennial kingdom. Even without these scriptures, there are countless others that point to a literal reign of the Messiah on the earth. The fulfillment of many of God's covenants and promises rests on a literal, physical, future kingdom. There is no solid basis to deny the literal interpretation of the millennial kingdom and its duration being 1000 years.

Question: Who is the Antichrist?

Answer: There is much speculation about the identity of the Antichrist. Some of the more popular targets are Vladimir Putin, Mahmoud Ahmadinejad, and Pope Benedict XVI. In the United States, former Presidents Bill Clinton and George W. Bush, and current President Barack Obama, are the most frequent candidates. So, who is the Antichrist, and how will we recognize him?

The Bible really does not say anything specific about where the Antichrist will come from. Many Bible scholars speculate that he will come from a confederacy of ten nations and/or a reborn Roman empire (Daniel 7:24-25; Revelation 17:7). Others see him as having to be a Jew in order to claim to be the Messiah. It is all just speculation since the Bible does not specifically say where the Antichrist will come from or what race he will be. One day, the Antichrist will be revealed. Second Thessalonians 2:3-4 tells us how we will recognize the Antichrist: "Don't let anyone deceive you in any way, for that day will not come until the rebellion occurs and the man of lawlessness is revealed, the man doomed to destruction. He will oppose and will exalt himself over everything that is called God or is worshiped, so that he sets himself up in God's temple, proclaiming himself to be God."

It is likely that most people who are alive when the Antichrist is revealed will be very surprised at his identity. The Antichrist may or may not be alive today. Martin Luther was convinced that the pope in his time was the Antichrist. During the 1940's, many believed Adolph Hitler was the Antichrist. Others who have lived in the past few hundred years have been equally sure as to the identity of the Antichrist. So far, they have all been incorrect. We should put the speculations behind us and focus on what the Bible actually says about the Antichrist. Revelation 13:5-8 declares, "The beast was given a mouth to utter proud words and blasphemies and to exercise his authority for forty-two months. He opened his mouth to blaspheme God, and to slander his name and his dwelling place and those who live in heaven. He was given power to make war against the saints and to conquer them. And he was given authority over every tribe, people, language and nation. All inhabitants of the earth will worship the beast—all whose names have not been written in the book of life belonging to the Lamb that was slain from the creation of the world."

Question: Who are the 144,000?

Answer: The book of Revelation has always presented the interpreter with challenges. The book is steeped in vivid imagery and symbolism which people have interpreted differently depending on their pre-conceptions of the book as a whole. There are four main interpretive approaches to the book of Revelation: 1) preterist (which sees all or most of the events in Revelation as having already occurred by the end of the 1st century); 2) historicist (which sees Revelation as a survey of church history from apostolic times to the present); 3) idealist (which sees Revelation as a depiction of the struggle between good and evil); 4) futurist (which sees Revelation as prophecy of events to come). Of the four, only the futurist approach interprets Revelation in the same grammatical-historical method as the rest of Scripture. It is also a better fit with Revelation's own claim to be prophecy (Revelation 1:3; 22:7, 10, 18, 19).

So the answer to the question "who are the 144,000?" will depend on which interpretive approach you take to the book of Revelation. With the exception of the futurist approach, all of the other approaches interpret the 144,000 symbolically, as representative of the church and the number 144,000 being symbolic of the totality—i.e., the complete number—of the church. Yet when taken at face value: "Then I heard the number of those who were sealed: 144,000 from all the tribes of Israel" (Revelation 7:4), nothing in the passage leads to interpreting the 144,000 as anything but a literal number of Jews—12,000 taken from every tribe of the "sons of Israel." The New Testament offers no clear cut text replacing Israel with the church.

These Jews are "sealed," which means they have the special protection of God from all of the divine judgments and from the Antichrist to perform their mission during the tribulation period (see Revelation 6:17, in which people will wonder who can stand from the wrath to come). The tribulation period is a future seven-year period of time in which God will enact divine judgment against those who reject Him and will complete His plan of salvation for the nation of Israel. All of this is according to God's revelation to the prophet Daniel (Daniel 9:24-27). The 144,000 Jews are a sort of "first fruits" (Revelation 14:4) of a redeemed Israel which has been previously prophesied (Zechariah 12:10; Romans 11:25-27), and their mission is to evangelize the post-rapture world and proclaim the gospel during the tribulation period. As a result of their ministry, millions—"a great multitude that no one could count, from every nation, tribe, people and language" (Revelation 7:9)—will come to faith in Christ.

Much of the confusion regarding the 144,000 is a result of the false doctrine of the Jehovah's Witnesses. The Jehovah's Witnesses claim that 144,000 is a limit to the number of people who will reign with Christ in heaven and spend eternity with God. The 144,000 have what the Jehovah's Witnesses call the heavenly hope. Those who are not among the 144,000 will enjoy what they call the earthly hope—a paradise on earth ruled by Christ and the 144,000. Clearly, we can see that Jehovah's Witness teaching sets up a caste society in the afterlife with a ruling class (the 144,000) and those who are ruled. The Bible teaches no such "dual class" doctrine. It is true that according to Revelation 20:4 there will be people ruling in the millennium with Christ. These people will be comprised of the church (believers in Jesus Christ), Old Testament saints (believers who died before Christ's first advent), and tribulation saints (those who accept Christ during the tribulation). Yet the Bible places no numerical limit on this group of people. Furthermore, the millennium is different from the eternal state, which will take place at the completion of the millennial period. At that time, God will dwell with us in the New Jerusalem. He will be our God and we will be His people (Revelation 21:3). The inheritance promised to us in Christ and sealed by the Holy Spirit (Ephesians 1:13-14) will become ours, and we will all be co-heirs with Christ (Romans 8:17).

Question: What is the abomination of desolation?

Answer: The phrase "abomination of desolation" refers to Matthew 24:15 (KJV): "So when you see standing in the holy place 'the abomination that causes desolation,' spoken of through the prophet Daniel—let the reader understand." This is referring to Daniel 9:27, "He will confirm a covenant with many for one 'seven.' In the middle of the 'seven' he will put an end to sacrifice and offering. And on a wing [of the temple] he will set up an abomination that causes desolation, until the end that is decreed is poured out on him." In 167 B.C a Greek ruler by the name of Antiochus Epiphanies set up an altar to Zeus over the altar of burnt offerings in the Jewish temple in Jerusalem. He also sacrificed a pig on the altar in the Temple in Jerusalem. This event is known as the abomination of desolation.

In Matthew 24:15, Jesus was speaking some 200 years after the abomination of desolation described above had already occurred. So, Jesus must have been prophesying that some time in the future another abomination of desolation would occur in a Jewish temple in Jerusalem. Most Bible prophecy interpreters believe that Jesus was referring to the Antichrist who will do something very similar to what Antiochus Epiphanies did. This is confirmed by the fact that some of what Daniel prophesied in Daniel 9:27 did not occur in 167 B.C with Antiochus Epiphanies. Antiochus did not confirm a covenant with Israel for seven years. It is the Antichrist who, in the end times, will establish a covenant with Israel for seven years and then break it by doing something similar to the abomination of desolation in the Jewish temple in Jerusalem.

Whatever the future abomination of desolation is, it will leave no doubt in anyone's mind that the one perpetrating it is the person known as the Antichrist. Revelation 13:14 describes him making some kind of image which all are forced to worship. Turning the temple of the living God into a place of worship for the Antichrist is truly an "abomination." Those who are alive and remain during the tribulation should be watchful and recognize that this event is the beginning of 3 1/2 years of the worst of the tribulation period and that the return of the Lord Jesus is imminent. "Be always on the watch, and pray that you may be able to escape all that is about to happen, and that you may be able to stand before the Son of Man" (Luke 21:36).

Question: What is the Apocalypse?

Answer: The word "apocalypse" comes from the Greek word *apocalupsis* which means "revealing, disclosure, to take off the cover." The book of Revelation is sometimes referred to as the "Apocalypse of John" because it is God's revealing of the end times to the apostle John. Further, the Greek word for "apocalypse" is the very first word in the Greek text of the book of Revelation. The phrase "apocalyptic literature" is used to describe the use of symbols, images, and numbers to depict future events. Outside of Revelation, examples of apocalyptic literature in the Bible are Daniel chapters 7–12, Isaiah chapters 24–27, Ezekiel chapters 37–41, and Zechariah chapters 9–12.

Why was apocalyptic literature written with such symbolism and imagery? The apocalyptic books were written when it was more prudent to disguise the message in images and symbolism than to give the message in plain language. Further, the symbolism created an element of mystery about details of time and place. The purpose of such symbolism, however, was not to cause confusion, but rather to instruct and encourage followers of God in difficult times.

Beyond the specifically biblical meaning, the term "apocalypse" is often used to refer to the end times in general, or to the last end times events specifically. End-times events such as the second coming of Christ and the battle of Armageddon are sometimes referred to as the Apocalypse. The Apocalypse will be the ultimate revealing of God, His wrath, His justice, and, ultimately, His love. Jesus Christ is the supreme "apocalypse" of God, as He revealed God to us (John 14:9; Hebrews 1:2).

Question: What is the battle of Armageddon?

Answer: The word "Armageddon" comes from a Hebrew word *Har-Magedone,* which means "Mount Megiddo" and has become synonymous with the future battle in which God will intervene and destroy the armies of the Antichrist as predicted in biblical prophecy (Revelation 16:16; 20:1-3, 7-10). There will be a multitude of people engaged in the battle of Armageddon, as all the nations gather together to fight against Christ.

The exact location of the valley of Armageddon is unclear because there is no mountain called Meggido. However, since "Har" can also mean hill, the most likely location is the hill country surrounding the plain of Meggido, some sixty miles north of Jerusalem. More than two hundred battles have been fought in that region. The plain of Megiddo and the nearby plain of Esdraelon will be the focal point for the battle of Armadeggon, which will rage the entire length of Israel as far south as the Edomite city of Bozrah (Isaiah 63:1). The valley of Armageddon was famous for two great victories in Israel's history: 1) Barak's victory over the Canaanites (Judges 4:15) and 2) Gideon's victory over the Midianites (Judges 7). Armageddon was also the site for two great tragedies: 1) the death of Saul and his sons (1 Samuel 31:8) and 2) the death of King Josiah (2 Kings 23:29-30; 2 Chronicles 35:22).

Because of this history, the valley of Armageddon became a symbol of the final conflict between God and the forces of evil. The word "Armageddon" only occurs in Revelation 16:16, "Then they gathered the kings together to the place that in Hebrew is called Armageddon." This speaks of the kings who are loyal to the Antichrist gathering together for a final assault on Israel. At Armageddon "the cup filled with the wine of the fury of [God's] wrath" (Revelation 16:19) will be delivered, and the Antichrist and his followers will be overthrown and defeated. "Armageddon" has become a general term that refers to the end of the world, not exclusively to the battle that takes place in the plain of Megiddo.

Question: What is the day of the Lord?

Answer: The phrase "day of the Lord" usually identifies events that take place at the end of history (Isaiah 7:18-25) and is often closely associated with the phrase "that day." One key to understanding these phrases is to note that they always identify a span of time during which God personally intervenes in history, directly or indirectly, to accomplish some specific aspect His plan.

Most people associate the day of the Lord with a period of time or a special day that will occur when God's will and purpose for His world and for mankind will be fulfilled. Some scholars believe that the day of the Lord will be a longer period of time than a single day—a period of time when Christ will reign throughout the world before He cleanses heaven and earth in preparation for the eternal state of all mankind. Other scholars believe the day of the Lord will be an instantaneous event when Christ returns to earth to redeem His faithful believers and send unbelievers to eternal damnation.

The phrase "the day of the Lord" is used nineteen times in the Old Testament (Isaiah 2:12; 13:6, 9; Ezekiel 13:5, 30:3; Joel 1:15, 2:1, 11, 31; 3:14; Amos 5:18, 20; Obadiah 15; Zephaniah 1:7,14; Zechariah 14:1; Malachi 4:5) and four times in the New Testament (Acts 2:20; 2 Thessalonians 2:2; 2 Peter 3:10). It is also alluded to in other passages (Revelation 6:17; 16:14).

The Old Testament passages dealing with the day of the Lord often convey a sense of imminence, nearness, and expectation: "Wail, for the day of the Lord is near!" (Isaiah 13:6); "For the day is near, even the day of the Lord is near" (Ezekiel 30:3); "Let all who live in the land tremble, for the day of the Lord is coming. It is close at hand" (Joel 2:1); "Multitudes, multitudes in the valley of decision! For the day of the Lord is near in the valley of decision" (Joel 3:14); "Be silent before the Lord God! For the day of the Lord is near" (Zephaniah 1:7). This is because the Old Testament passages referring to the day of the Lord often speak of both a near and a far fulfillment, as does much of Old Testament prophecy. Some Old Testament passages that refer to the day of the Lord describe historical judgments that have already been fulfilled in some sense (Isaiah 13:6-22; Ezekiel 30:2-19; Joel 1:15, 3:14; Amos 5:18-20; Zephaniah 1:14-18), while others refers to divine judgments that will take place toward the end of the age (Joel 2:30-32; Zechariah 14:1; Malachi 4:1, 5).

The New Testament calls it a day of "wrath," a day of "visitation," and the "great day of God Almighty" (Revelation 16:4) and refers to a still future fulfillment when God's wrath is poured out on unbelieving Israel (Isaiah 22; Jeremiah 30:1-17; Joel 1-2; Amos 5; Zephaniah 1) and on the unbelieving world (Ezekiel 38–39; Zechariah 14). The Scriptures indicate that "the day of the Lord" will come quickly, like a thief in the night (Zephaniah 1:14-15; 2 Thessalonians 2:2), and therefore Christians must be watchful and ready for the coming of Christ at any moment.

Besides being a time of judgment, it will also be a time of salvation as God will deliver the remnant of Israel, fulfilling His promise that "all of Israel will be saved" (Romans 11:26), forgiving their sins and restoring His chosen people to the land He promised to Abraham (Isaiah 10:27; Jeremiah 30:19-31, 40; Micah 4; Zechariah 13). The final outcome of the day of the Lord will be that "the arrogance of man will be brought low and the pride of men humbled; the Lord alone will be exalted in that day" (Isaiah 2:17). The ultimate or final fulfillment of the prophecies concerning the day of the Lord will come at the end of history when God, with wondrous power, will punish evil and fulfill all His promises.

Question: What is the difference between the rapture and the second coming?

Answer: The rapture and the second coming of Christ are often confused. Sometimes it is difficult to determine whether a scripture verse is referring to the rapture or the second coming. However, in studying end-times Bible prophecy, it is very important to differentiate between the two.

The rapture is when Jesus Christ returns to remove the church (all believers in Christ) from the earth. The rapture is described in 1 Thessalonians 4:13-18 and 1 Corinthians 15:50-54. Believers who have died will have their bodies resurrected and, along with believers who are still living, will meet the Lord in the air. This will all occur in a moment, in a twinkling of an eye. The second coming is when Jesus returns to defeat the Antichrist, destroy evil, and establish His millennial kingdom. The second coming is described in Revelation 19:11-16.

The important differences between the rapture and second coming are as follows:

1. At the rapture, believers meet the Lord in the air (1 Thessalonians 4:17). At the second coming, believers return with the Lord to the earth (Revelation 19:14).
2. The second coming occurs after the great and terrible tribulation (Revelation chapters 6–19). The rapture occurs before the tribulation (1 Thessalonians 5:9; Revelation 3:10).
3. The rapture is the removal of believers from the earth as an act of deliverance (1 Thessalonians 4:13-17, 5:9). The second coming includes the removal of unbelievers as an act of judgment (Matthew 24:40-41).
4. The rapture will be secret and instant (1 Corinthians 15:50-54). The second coming will be visible to all (Revelation 1:7; Matthew 24:29-30).
5. The second coming of Christ will not occur until after certain other end-times events take place (2 Thessalonians 2:4; Matthew 24:15-30; Revelation chapters 6–18). The rapture is imminent; it could take place at any moment (Titus 2:13; 1 Thessalonians 4:13-18; 1 Corinthians 15:50-54).

Why is it important to keep the rapture and the second coming distinct?

1. If the rapture and the second coming are the same event, believers will have to go through the tribulation (1 Thessalonians 5:9; Revelation 3:10).
2. If the rapture and the second coming are the same event, the return of Christ is not imminent—there are many things which must occur before He can return (Matthew 24:4-30).
3. In describing the tribulation period, Revelation chapters 6–19 nowhere mentions the church. During the tribulation—also called "the time of trouble for Jacob" (Jeremiah 30:7)—God

will again turn His primary attention to Israel (Romans 11:17-31).

The rapture and second coming are similar but separate events. Both involve Jesus returning. Both are end-times events. However, it is crucially important to recognize the differences. In summary, the rapture is the return of Christ in the clouds to remove all believers from the earth before the time of God's wrath. The second coming is the return of Christ to the earth to bring the tribulation to an end and to defeat the Antichrist and his evil world empire.

Question: Who are the four horsemen of the Apocalypse?

Answer: The four horsemen of the Apocalypse are described in Revelation chapter 6, verses 1-8. The four horsemen are symbolic descriptions of different events which will take place in the end times. The first horseman of the Apocalypse is mentioned in Revelation 6:2: "I looked, and there before me was a white horse! Its rider held a bow, and he was given a crown, and he rode out as a conqueror bent on conquest." This first horseman likely refers to the Antichrist, who will be given authority and will conquer all who oppose him. The antichrist is the false imitator of the true Christ, who will also return on a white horse (Revelation 19:11-16).

The second horseman of the Apocalypse appears in Revelation 6:4, "Then another horse came out, a fiery red one. Its rider was given power to take peace from the earth and to make men slay each other. To him was given a large sword." The second horseman refers to terrible warfare that will break out in the end times. The third horseman is described in Revelation 6:5-6, "...and there before me was a black horse! Its rider was holding a pair of scales in his hand. Then I heard what sounded like a voice among the four living creatures, saying, 'A quart of wheat for a day's wages, and three quarts of barley for a day's wages, and do not damage the oil and the wine!'" The third horseman of the Apocalypse refers to a great famine that will take place, likely as a result of the wars from the second horseman.

The fourth horseman is mentioned in Revelation 6:8, "I looked, and there before me was a pale horse! Its rider was named Death, and Hades was following close behind him. They were given power over a fourth of the earth to kill by sword, famine and plague, and by the wild beasts of the earth." The fourth horseman of the Apocalypse is symbolic of death and devastation. It seems to be a combination of the previous horsemen. The fourth horseman of the Apocalypse will bring further warfare and terrible famines along with awful plagues and diseases. What is most amazing, or perhaps terrifying, is that the four horsemen of the Apocalypse are just "precursors" of even worse judgments that come later in the tribulation (Revelation chapters 8–9 and 16).

Question: How are we to live our lives in light of Christ's return?

Answer: We believe that the return of Jesus Christ is imminent, that is, His return could occur at any moment. We, with the apostle Paul, look for "the blessed hope—the glorious appearing of our great God and Savior, Jesus Christ" (Titus 2:13). Knowing that the Lord could come back today, some are tempted to stop what they are doing and just "wait" for Him.

However, there is a big difference between knowing that Jesus could return today and knowing that He will return today. Jesus said, "No one knows about that day or hour" (Matthew 24:36). The time of His coming is something God has not revealed to anyone, and so, until He calls us to Himself, we should continue serving Him. In Jesus' parable of the ten talents, the departing king instructs his servants to "occupy till I come" (Luke 19:13 KJV).

The return of Christ is always presented in Scripture as a great motivation to action, not as a reason to cease from action. In 1 Corinthians 15:58, Paul wraps up his teaching on the rapture by saying, "Always give yourselves fully to the work of the Lord." In 1 Thessalonians 5:6, Paul concludes a lesson on Christ's coming with these words: "So then, let us not be like others, who are asleep, but let us be alert and self-controlled." To retreat and "hold the fort" was never Jesus' intention for us. Instead, we work while we can. "Night is coming, when no one can work" (John 9:4).

The apostles lived and served with the idea that Jesus could return within their lifetime; what if they had ceased from their labors and just "waited"? They would have been in disobedience to Christ's command to "go into all the world and preach the good news to all creation" (Mark 16:15), and the gospel would not have been spread. The apostles understood that Jesus' imminent return meant they must busy themselves with God's work. They lived life to the fullest, as if every day were their last. We, too, should view every day as a gift and use it to glorify God.

Question: What is the mark of the beast (666)?

Answer: The main passage in the Bible that mentions the "mark of the beast" is Revelation 13:15-18. Other references can be found in Revelation 14:9, 11, 15:2, 16:2, 19:20, and 20:4. This mark acts as a seal for the followers of Antichrist and the false prophet (the spokesperson for the Antichrist). The false prophet (the second beast) is the one who causes people to take this mark. The mark is literally placed in the hand or forehead and is not simply a card someone carries.

The recent breakthroughs in medical implant chip technologies have increased interest in the mark of the beast spoken of in Revelation chapter 13. It is possible that the technology we are seeing today represents the beginning stages of what may eventually be used as the mark of the beast. It is important to realize that a medical implant chip is not the mark of the beast. The mark of the beast will be something given only to those who worship the Antichrist. Having a medical or financial microchip inserted into your right hand or forehead is not the mark of the beast. The mark of the beast will be an end-times identification required by the Antichrist in order to buy or sell, and it will be given only to those who worship the Antichrist.

Many good expositors of Revelation differ widely as to the exact nature of the mark of the beast. Besides the implanted chip view, other speculations include an ID card, a microchip, a barcode that is tattooed into the skin, or simply a mark that identifies someone as being faithful to the Antichrist's kingdom. This last view requires the least speculation, since it does not add any more information to what the Bible gives us. In other words, any of these things are possible, but at the same time they are all speculations. We should not spend a lot of time speculating on the precise details.

The meaning of 666 is a mystery as well. Some have speculated that there was a connection to June 6, 2006—06/06/06. However, in Revelation chapter 13, the number 666 identifies a person, not a date. Revelation 13:18 tells us, "This calls for wisdom. If anyone has insight, let him calculate the number of the beast, for it is man's number. His number is 666." Somehow, the number 666 will identify the Antichrist. For centuries Bible interpreters have been trying to identify certain individuals with 666. Nothing is conclusive. That is why Revelation 13:18 says the number requires wisdom. When the Antichrist is revealed (2 Thessalonians 2:3-4), it will be clear who he is and how the number 666 identifies him.

Question: What are the seven seals, trumpets, and bowls in the book of Revelation?

Answer: The seven seals (Revelation 6:1-17, 8:1-5), seven trumpets (Revelation 8:6-21, 11:15-19), and seven bowls (Revelation 16:1-21) are three succeeding series of end-times judgments from God. The judgments get progressively worse and more devastating as the end times progress. The seven seals, trumpets, and bowls are connected to one another. The seventh seal introduces the seven trumpets (Revelation 8:1-5), and the seventh trumpet introduces the seven bowls (Revelation 11:15-19, 15:1-8).

The first four of the seven seals are known as the four horsemen of the Apocalypse. The first seal introduces the Antichrist (Revelation 6:1-2). The second seal causes great warfare (Revelation 6:3-4). The third of the seven seals causes famine (Revelation 6:5-6). The fourth seal brings about plague, further famine, and further warfare (Revelation 6:7-8).

The fifth seal tells us of those who will be martyred for their faith in Christ during the end times (Revelation 6:9-11). God hears their cries for justice and will deliver it in His timing—in the form of the sixth seal, along with the trumpet and bowl judgments. When the sixth of the seven seals is broken, a devastating earthquake occurs, causing massive upheaval and terrible devastation—along with unusual astronomical phenomena (Revelation 6:12-14). Those who survive are right to cry out, "Fall on us and hide us from the face of him who sits on the throne and from the wrath of the Lamb! For the great day of their wrath has come, and who can stand?" (Revelation 6:16-17).

The seven trumpets are described in Revelation 8:6-21. The seven trumpets are the "contents" of the seventh seal (Revelation 8:1-5).

The first trumpet causes hail and fire that destroys much of the plant life in the world (Revelation 8:7). The second trumpet brings about what seems to be a meteor hitting the oceans and causing the death of much of the world's sea life (Revelation 8:8-9). The third trumpet is similar to the second, except it affects the world's lakes and rivers instead of the oceans (Revelation 8:10-11).

The fourth of the seven trumpets causes the sun and moon to be darkened (Revelation 8:12). The fifth trumpet results in a plague of "demonic locusts" that attack and torture humanity (Revelation 9:1-11). The sixth trumpet releases a demonic army that kills a third of humanity (Revelation 9:12-21). The seventh trumpet calls forth the seven angels with the seven bowls of God's wrath (Revelation 11:15-19, 15:1-8).

The seven bowl judgments are described in Revelation 16:1-21. The seven bowl judgments are called forth by the seventh trumpet. The first bowl causes painful sores to break out on humanity (Revelation 16:2). The second bowl results in the death of every living thing in the sea (Revelation 16:3). The third bowl causes the rivers to turn into blood (Revelation 16:4-7). The fourth of the seven bowls results in the sun's heat being intensified and causing great pain (Revelation 16:8-9). The fifth bowl causes great darkness and an intensification of the sores from the first bowl (Revelation 16:10-11). The sixth bowl results in the Euphrates River being dried up and the armies of the Antichrist being gathered together to wage the battle of Armageddon (Revelation 16:12-14). The seventh bowl results in a devastating earthquake followed by giant hailstones (Revelation 16:15-21).

Revelation 16:5-7 declares of God, "You are just in these judgments, you who are and who were, the Holy One, because you have so judged; for they have shed the blood of your saints and prophets, and you have given them blood to drink as they deserve. ... Yes, Lord God Almighty, true and just are your judgments."

Question: How can I understand the book of Revelation?

Answer: The key to Bible interpretation, especially for the book of Revelation, is to have a consistent hermeneutic. Hermeneutics is the study of the principles of interpretation. In other words, it is the way you interpret Scripture. A normal hermeneutic or normal interpretation of Scripture means that unless the verse or passage clearly indicates the author was using figurative language, it should be understood it in its normal sense. We are not to look for other meanings if the natural meaning of the sentence makes sense. Also, we are not to spiritualize Scripture by assigning meanings to words or phrases when it is clear the author, under the guidance of the Holy Spirit, meant it to be understood as it is written.

One example is Revelation 20. Many will assign various meanings to references to a thousand-year period. Yet, the language does not imply in any way that the references to the thousand years should be taken to mean anything other than a literal period of one thousand years.

A simple outline for the book of Revelation is found in Revelation 1:19. In the first chapter, the risen and exalted Christ is speaking to John. Christ tells John to "write, therefore, what you have seen, what is now and what will take place later." The things John had already seen are recorded in chapter 1. The "things which are" (that were present in John's day) are recorded in chapters 2–3 (the letters to the churches). The "things that will take place" (future things) are recorded in chapters 4–22.

Generally speaking, chapters 4–18 of Revelation deal with God's judgments on the people of the earth. These judgments are not for the church (1 Thessalonians 5:2, 9). Before the judgments begin, the church will have been removed from the earth in an event called the rapture (1 Thessalonians 4:13-18; 1 Corinthians 15:51-52). Chapters 4–18 describe a time of "Jacob's trouble"—trouble for Israel (Jeremiah 30:7; Daniel 9:12, 12:1). It is also a time when God will judge unbelievers for their rebellion against Him.

Chapter 19 describes Christ's return with the church, the bride of Christ. He defeats the beast and the false prophet and casts them into the lake of fire. In Chapter 20, Christ has Satan bound and cast in the Abyss. Then Christ sets up His kingdom on earth that will last 1000 years. At the end of the 1000 years, Satan is released and he leads a rebellion against God. He is quickly defeated and also cast into the lake of fire. Then the final judgment occurs, the judgment for all unbelievers, when they too are cast into the lake of fire.

Chapters 21 and 22 describe what is referred to as the eternal state. In these chapters God tells us what eternity with Him will be like. The book of Revelation is understandable. God would not have given it to us if its meaning were entirely a mystery. The key to understanding the book of Revelation is to interpret it as literally as possible—it says what it means and means what it says.

Chapter 8

QUESTIONS ABOUT
ANGELS AND DEMONS

CONTENTS

What does the Bible say about angels? 234
What does the Bible say about demons?..235
Who is Satan? 235
How, why, and when did Satan fall from heaven? 236
What does the Bible say about demon possession?..............................237
Can a Christian be demon possessed? 239
Who were the sons of God and daughters of men in Genesis 6:1-4? 240
Who/what were the Nephilim?...241
Why did God allow Satan and the demons to sin?..................................243
Who is the angel of the Lord? 244
Are angels male or female?..245
What are archangels?..246
Do we become angels after we die?...246
What are cherubim? Are cherubs angels? 247
What are seraphim? Are seraphs angels?...248
Can a Christian today perform an exorcism?...248
Is there an angel of death?...250
Do we have guardian angels? 250

Question: What does the Bible say about angels?

Answer: Angels are personal spiritual beings who have intelligence, emotions, and will. This is true of both the good and evil angels (demons). Angels possess intelligence (Matthew 8:29; 2 Corinthians 11:3; 1 Peter 1:12), show emotion (Luke 2:13; James 2:19; Revelation 12:17), and exercise will (Luke 8:28-31; 2 Timothy 2:26; Jude 6). Angels are spirit beings (Hebrews 1:14) without true physical bodies. Although they do not have physical bodies, they are still personalities.

Because they are created beings, their knowledge is limited. This means they do not know all things as God does (Matthew 24:36). They do seem to have greater knowledge than humans, however, which may be due to three things. First, angels were created as an order of creatures higher than humans. Therefore, they innately possess greater knowledge. Second, angels study the Bible and the world more thoroughly than humans do and gain knowledge from it (James 2:19; Revelation 12:12). Third, angels gain knowledge through long observation of human activities. Unlike humans, angels do not have to study the past; they have experienced it. Therefore, they know how others have acted and reacted in situations and can predict with a greater degree of accuracy how we may act in similar circumstances.

Though they have wills, angels, like all creatures, are subject to the will of God. Good angels are sent by God to help believers (Hebrews 1:14). Here are some activities the Bible ascribes to angels:

They praise God (Psalm 148:1-2; Isaiah 6:3). They worship God (Hebrews 1:6; Revelation 5:8-13). They rejoice in what God does (Job 38:6-7). They serve God (Psalm 103:20; Revelation 22:9). They appear before God (Job 1:6; 2:1). They are instruments of God's judgments (Revelation 7:1; 8:2). They bring answers to prayer (Acts 12:5-10). They aid in winning people to Christ (Acts 8:26; 10:3). They observe Christian order, work, and suffering (1 Corinthians 4:9; 11:10; Ephesians 3:10; 1 Peter 1:12). They encourage in times of danger (Acts 27:23-24). They care for the righteous at the time of death (Luke 16:22).

Angels are an entirely different order of being than humans. Human beings do not become angels after they die. Angels will never become, and never were, human beings. God created the angels, just as He created humanity. The Bible nowhere states that angels are created in the image and likeness of God, as humans are (Genesis 1:26). Angels are spiritual beings that can, to a certain degree, take on physical form. Humans are primarily physical beings, but with a spiritual aspect. The greatest thing we can learn from the holy angels is their instant, unquestioning obedience to God's commands.

Question: What does the Bible say about demons?

Answer: Revelation 12:9 is the clearest scripture on the identity of demons, "The great dragon was hurled down—that ancient serpent called the devil, or Satan, who leads the whole world astray. He was hurled to the earth, and his angels with him." Satan's fall from heaven is symbolically described in Isaiah 14:12-15 and Ezekiel 28:12-15. Revelation 12:4 seems to indicate that Satan took one-third of the angels with him when he sinned. Jude 6 mentions angels who sinned. The Bible indicates that the demons are fallen angels who, along with Satan, rebelled against God.

Satan and his demons now look to destroy and deceive all those who follow and worship God (1 Peter 5:8; 2 Corinthians 11:14-15). The demons are described as evil spirits (Matthew 10:1), unclean spirits (Mark 1:27), and angels of Satan (Revelation 12:9). Satan and his demons deceive the world (2 Corinthians 4:4), attack Christians (2 Corinthians 12:7; 1 Peter 5:8), and combat the holy angels (Revelation 12:4-9). Demons are spiritual beings, but they can appear in physical forms (2 Corinthians 11:14-15). The demons/fallen angels are enemies of God, but they are defeated enemies. Greater is He who is in us, than those who are in the world (1 John 4:4).

Question: Who is Satan?

Answer: People's beliefs concerning Satan range from the silly to the abstract—from a little red guy with horns who sits on your shoulder urging you to sin, to an expression used to describe the personification of evil. The Bible, however, gives us a clear portrait of who Satan is and how he affects our lives. Put simply, the Bible defines Satan as an angelic being who fell from his position in heaven due to sin and is now completely opposed to God, doing all in his power to thwart God's purposes.

Satan was created as a holy angel. Isaiah 14:12 possibly gives Satan's pre-fall name as Lucifer. Ezekiel 28:12-14 describes Satan as having been created a cherubim, apparently the highest created angel. He became arrogant in his beauty and status and decided he wanted to sit on a throne above that of God (Isaiah 14:13-14; Ezekiel 28:15; 1 Timothy 3:6). Satan's pride led to his fall. Notice the many "I will" statements in Isaiah 14:12-15. Because of his sin, God barred Satan from heaven.

Satan became the ruler of this world and the prince of the power of the air (John 12:31; 2 Corinthians 4:4; Ephesians 2:2). He is an accuser (Revelation 12:10), a tempter (Matthew 4:3; 1 Thessalonians 3:5), and a deceiver (Genesis 3; 2 Corinthians 4:4; Revelation 20:3). His very name means "adversary" or "one who opposes." Another of his titles, the devil, means "slanderer."

Even though he was cast out of heaven, he still seeks to elevate his throne above God. He counterfeits all that God does, hoping to gain the worship of the world and encourage opposition to God's kingdom. Satan is the ultimate source behind every false cult and world religion. Satan will do anything and everything in his power to oppose God and those who follow God. However, Satan's destiny is sealed—an eternity in the lake of fire (Revelation 20:10).

Question: How, why, and when did Satan fall from heaven?

Answer: Satan's fall from heaven is symbolically described in Isaiah 14:12-14 and Ezekiel 28:12-18. While these two passages are referring specifically to the kings of Babylon and Tyre, they also reference the spiritual power behind those kings, namely, Satan. These passages describe why Satan fell, but they do not specifically say when the fall occurred. What we do know is this: the angels were created before the earth (Job 38:4-7). Satan fell before he tempted Adam and Eve in the Garden (Genesis 3:1-14). Satan's fall, therefore, must have occurred somewhere after the time the angels were created and before he tempted Adam and Eve in the Garden of Eden. Whether Satan's fall occurred a few minutes, hours, or days before he tempted Adam and Eve in the Garden, Scripture does not specifically say.

The book of Job tells us that, for a time at least, Satan still had access to heaven and to the throne of God. "One day the angels came to present themselves before the Lᴏʀᴅ, and Satan also came with them. The Lᴏʀᴅ said to Satan, 'Where have you come from?' Satan answered the Lᴏʀᴅ, 'From roaming through the earth and going back and forth in it'" (Job 1:6-7). Apparently at that time, Satan was still moving freely between heaven and earth, speaking to God directly and answering for his activities. At what point God discontinued this access is unknown.

Why did Satan fall from heaven? Satan fell because of pride. He desired to be God, not to be a servant of God. Notice the many "I will..." statements in Isaiah 14:12-15. Ezekiel 28:12-15 describes Satan as an exceedingly beautiful angel. Satan was likely the highest of all angels, the most beautiful of all of God's creations, but he was not content in his position. Instead, Satan desired to be God, to essentially "kick God off His throne" and take over the rule of the universe. Satan wanted to be God, and interestingly enough, that is what Satan tempted Adam and Eve with in the Garden of Eden (Genesis 3:1-5). How did Satan fall from heaven? Actually, a fall is not an accurate description. It would be far more accurate to say God cast Satan out of heaven (Isaiah 14:15; Ezekiel 28:16-17). Satan did not *fall* from heaven; rather, Satan was *pushed* out of heaven.

Question: What does the Bible say about demon possession?

Answer: The Bible gives some examples of people possessed or influenced by demons. From these examples we can find some symptoms of demonic influence and gain insight as to how a demon possesses someone. Here are some of the biblical passages: Matthew 9:32-33; 12:22; 17:18; Mark 5:1-20; 7:26-30; Luke 4:33-36; Luke 22:3; Acts 16:16-18. In some of these passages, the demon possession causes physical ailments such as inability to speak, epileptic symptoms, blindness, etc. In other cases, it causes the individual to do evil, Judas being the main example. In Acts 16:16-18, the spirit apparently gives a slave girl some ability to know things beyond her own learning. The demon-possessed man of the Gadarenes, who was possessed by a multitude of demons (Legion), had superhuman strength and lived naked among the tombstones. King Saul, after rebelling against the LORD, was troubled by an evil spirit (1 Samuel 16:14-15; 18:10-11; 19:9-10) with the apparent effect of a depressed mood and an increased desire to kill David.

Thus, there is a wide variety of possible symptoms of demon possession, such as a physical impairment that cannot be attributed to an actual physiological problem, a personality change such as depression or aggression, supernatural strength, immodesty, antisocial behavior, and perhaps the ability to share information that one has no natural way of knowing. It is important to note that nearly all, if not all, of these characteristics may have other explanations, so it is important not to label every depressed person or epileptic individual as demon-possessed. On the other hand, western cultures probably do not take satanic involvement in people's lives seriously enough.

In addition to these physical or emotional distinctions, one can also look at spiritual attributes showing demonic influence. These may include a refusal to forgive (2 Corinthians 2:10-11) and the belief in and spread of false doctrine, especially concerning Jesus Christ and His atoning work (2 Corinthians 11:3-4, 13-15; 1 Timothy 4:1-5; 1 John 4:1-3).

Concerning the involvement of demons in the lives of Christians, the apostle Peter is an illustration of the fact that a believer can be influenced by the devil (Matthew 16:23). Some refer to Christians who are under a strong demonic influence as being "demonized," but never is there an example in Scripture of a believer in Christ being possessed by a demon. Most theologians believe that a Christian cannot be possessed because he has the Holy Spirit abiding within (2 Corinthians 1:22; 5:5; 1 Corinthians 6:19), and the Spirit of God would not share residence with a demon.

We are not told exactly how one opens himself up for possession. If Judas' case is representative, he opened his heart to evil—in his case by his greed (John 12:6). So it may be possible that if one allows his heart to be ruled by some habitual sin, it becomes an invitation for a demon to enter. From missionaries' experiences, demon possession also seems to be related to the worship of heathen idols and the possession of occult materials. Scripture repeatedly relates idol worship to the actual worship of demons (Leviticus 17:7; Deuteronomy 32:17;

Psalm 106:37; 1 Corinthians 10:20), so it should not be surprising that involvement with idolatry could lead to demon possession.

Based on the above scriptural passages and some of the experiences of missionaries, we can conclude that many people open their lives up to demon involvement through the embracing of some sin or through cultic involvement (either knowingly or unknowingly). Examples may include immorality, drug/alcohol abuse that alters one's state of consciousness, rebellion, bitterness, and transcendental meditation.

There is an additional consideration. Satan and his evil host can do nothing the Lord does not allow them to do (Job 1-2). This being the case, Satan, thinking he is accomplishing his own purposes, is actually accomplishing God's good purposes, as in the case of Judas' betrayal. Some people develop an unhealthy fascination with the occult and demonic activity. This is unwise and unbiblical. If we pursue God, if we are clothing ourselves with His armor and relying upon His strength (Ephesians 6:10-18), we have nothing to fear from the evil ones, for God rules over all!

Question: Can a Christian be demon possessed?

Answer: The Bible does not explicitly state whether a Christian can be possessed by a demon. However, since a Christian is indwelt by the Holy Spirit (Romans 8:9-11; 1 Corinthians 3:16; 6:19), it would seem unlikely that the Holy Spirit would allow a demon to possess the same person He is indwelling. This is sometimes a controversial issue; however, we strongly hold to the belief that a Christian cannot be possessed by a demon. We believe there is a distinct difference between being possessed by a demon and being oppressed or influenced by a demon. Demon possession involves a demon having direct control over the thoughts and/or actions of a person (Luke 4:33-35; 8:27-33; Matthew 17:14-18). Demon oppression or influence involves a demon or demons attacking a person spiritually and/or encouraging him/her into sinful behavior (1 Peter 5:8-9; James 4:7). Notice that in all the New Testament passages dealing with spiritual warfare, we are never told to cast a demon out of a believer (Ephesians 6:10-18). Believers are told to resist the devil (1 Peter 5:8-9; James 4:7), not to cast him out.

It is unthinkable that God would allow one of His children, whom He purchased with the blood of Christ (1 Peter 1:18-19) and made into a new creation (2 Corinthians 5:17), to be possessed and controlled by a demon. Yes, as believers, we wage war with Satan and his demons, but not from within ourselves. The apostle John declares, "You, dear children, are from God and have overcome them, because the One who is in you is greater than the one who is in the world" (1 John 4:4). Who is the One in us? The Holy Spirit. Who is the one in the world? Satan and his demons. Therefore, the believer has overcome the world of demons, and the case for demon possession of a believer cannot be made scripturally.

Question: Who were the sons of God and daughters of men in Genesis 6:1-4?

Answer: Genesis 6:1-4 refers to the sons of God and the daughters of men. There have been several suggestions as to who the sons of God were and why the children they had with daughters of men grew into a race of giants (that is what the word *Nephilim* seems to indicate).

The three primary views on the identity of the sons of God are 1) they were fallen angels, 2) they were powerful human rulers, or 3) they were godly descendants of Seth intermarrying with wicked descendants of Cain. Giving weight to the first theory is the fact that in the Old Testament the phrase "sons of God" always refers to angels (Job 1:6; 2:1; 38:7). A potential problem with this is in Matthew 22:30, which indicates that angels do not marry. The Bible gives us no reason to believe that angels have a gender or are able to reproduce. The other two views do not present this problem.

The weakness of views 2) and 3) is that ordinary human males marrying ordinary human females does not account for why the offspring were "giants" or "heroes of old, men of renown." Further, why would God decide to bring the flood on the earth (Genesis 6:5-7) when God had never forbade powerful human males or descendants of Seth to marry ordinary human females or descendants of Cain? The oncoming judgment of Genesis 6:5-7 is linked to what took place in Genesis 6:1-4. Only the obscene, perverse marriage of fallen angels with human females would seem to justify such a harsh judgment.

As previously noted, the weakness of the first view is that Matthew 22:30 declares, "At the resurrection people will neither marry nor be given in marriage; they will be like the angels in heaven." However, the text does not say "angels are not *able* to marry." Rather, it indicates only that angels do not marry. Second, Matthew 22:30 is referring to the "angels in heaven." It is not referring to fallen angels, who do not care about God's created order and actively seek ways to disrupt God's plan. The fact that God's holy angels do not marry or engage in sexual relations does not mean the same is true of Satan and his demons.

View 1) is the most likely position. Yes, it is an interesting "contradiction" to say that angels are sexless and then to say that the "sons of God" were fallen angels who procreated with human females. However, while angels are spiritual beings (Hebrews 1:14), they can appear in human, physical form (Mark 16:5). The men of Sodom and Gomorrah wanted to have sex with the two angels who were with Lot (Genesis 19:1-5). It is plausible that angels are capable of taking on human form, even to the point of replicating human sexuality and possibly even reproduction. Why do the fallen angels not do this more often? It seems that God imprisoned the fallen angels who committed this evil sin, so that the other fallen angels would not do the same (as described in Jude 6). Earlier Hebrew interpreters and apocryphal and pseudopigraphal writings are unanimous in holding to the view that fallen angels are the "sons of God" mentioned in Genesis 6:1-4. This by no means closes the debate. However, the view that Genesis 6:1-4 involves fallen angels mating with human females has a strong contextual, grammatical, and historical basis.

Question: Who/what were the Nephilim?

Answer: The Nephilim ("fallen ones, giants") were the offspring of sexual relationships between the sons of God and daughters of men in Genesis 6:1-4. There is much debate as to the identity of the "sons of God." It is our contention that the "sons of God" were fallen angels (demons) who mated with human females and/or possessed human males and then mated with human females. These unions resulted in offspring, the Nephilim, that were "heroes of old, men of renown" (Genesis 6:4).

Why would the demons do such a thing? The Bible does not specifically give us the answer. The demons are evil, twisted beings—so nothing they do should surprise us. As to a distinct motivation, the best speculation is that the demons were attempting to pollute the human blood line in order to prevent the coming of the Messiah, Jesus Christ. God had promised that a Messiah would come from the line of Eve (Genesis 3:15) who would crush the head of the serpent, Satan. So, the demons were possibly attempting to prevent this by polluting the human bloodline, making it impossible for a sinless Messiah to one day be born. Again, this is not a specifically biblical answer, but it is plausible and not in contradiction to anything the Bible teaches.

What were the Nephilim? According to Hebraic and other legends (the Book of Enoch and other non-biblical writings), they were a race of giants and super-heroes who did acts of great evil. Their great size and power likely came from the mixture of demonic "DNA" with human genetics. All that the Bible directly says about them is that they were "heroes of old, men of renown" (Genesis 6:4). The Nephilim were not aliens, they were literal, physical beings produced from the union of the sons of God and daughters of men (Genesis 6:1-4).

What happened to the Nephilim? The Nephilim were one of the primary reasons for the great flood in Noah's time. Immediately after the Nephilim are mentioned, God's Word tells us this: "The LORD saw how great man's wickedness on the earth had become, and that every inclination of the thoughts of his heart was only evil all the time. The LORD was grieved that he had made man on the earth, and his heart was filled with pain. So the LORD said, 'I will wipe mankind, whom I have created, from the face of the earth—men and animals, and creatures that move along the ground, and birds of the air—for I am grieved that I have made them'" (Genesis 6:5-7). So, God proceeded to flood the entire earth, killing everyone and everything (including the Nephilim) other than Noah and his family and the animals on the ark (Genesis 6:11-22).

Were there Nephilim after the flood? Genesis 6:4 tells us, "The Nephilim were on the earth in those days — and also afterward." It seems that the demons repeated their sin sometime after the flood as well. However, it likely took place to a much lesser extent than it did prior to the flood. When the Israelites spied out the land of Canaan, they reported back to Moses: "We saw the Nephilim there (the descendants of Anak come from the Nephilim). We seemed like grasshoppers in our own eyes, and we looked the same to them" (Numbers 13:33). Now, this passage does not specifically say that the Nephilim were genuinely there, only that the spies thought they saw the Nephilim. It is more likely that the spies witnessed very large people in Canaan and mistakenly believed them to be the Nephilim. Or, it is possible that after the flood the demons again mated with human females, producing more Nephilim. Whatever the case, these "giants" were destroyed by the Israelites during their invasion of Canaan (Joshua 11:21-22) and later in their history (Deuteronomy 3:11; 1 Samuel 17).

What prevents the demons from producing more Nephilim today? It seems that God put an end to demons mating with humans by placing all the demons who committed such an act in the Abyss. Jude verse 6 tells us, "And the angels who did not keep their positions of authority but abandoned their own home—these he has kept in darkness, bound with everlasting chains for judgment on the great Day." Obviously, not all of the demons are in "prison" today, so there must have been a group of demons who committed further grievous sin beyond the original fall. Presumably, the demons who mated with human females are the ones who are "bound with everlasting chains." This would prevent any more demons from attempting such an act.

Question: Why did God allow Satan and the demons to sin?

Answer: With both the angels and humanity, God chose to present a choice. While the Bible does not give many details regarding the rebellion of Satan and the fallen angels, it seems that Satan—probably the greatest of all the angels (Ezekiel 28:12-18)—in pride chose to rebel against God in order to seek to become his own god. Satan (Lucifer) did not want to worship or obey God; he wanted to be God (Isaiah 14:12-14). Revelation 12:4 is understood to be a figurative description of one third of the angels choosing to follow Satan in his rebellion, becoming the fallen angels—demons.

Unlike humanity, however, the choice the angels had to follow Satan or remain faithful to God was an eternal choice. The Bible presents no opportunity for the fallen angels to repent and be forgiven. Nor does the Bible indicate that it is possible for more of the angels to sin. The angels who remain faithful to God are described as the "elect angels" (1 Timothy 5:21). Satan and the fallen angels knew God in all His glory. For them to rebel, despite what they knew about God, was the utmost of evil. As a result, God does not give Satan and the other fallen angels the opportunity to repent. Further, the Bible gives us no reason to believe they would repent even if God gave them the chance (1 Peter 5:8). God gave Satan and the angels the same choice He gave Adam and Eve, to obey Him or not. The angels had a free-will choice to make; God did not force or encourage any of the angels to sin. Satan and the fallen angels sinned of their own free will and therefore are worthy of God's eternal wrath in the lake of fire.

Why did God give the angels this choice, when He knew what the results would be? God knew that one-third of the angels would rebel and therefore be cursed to the eternal fire. God also knew that Satan would further his rebellion by tempting humanity into sin. So, why did God allow it? The Bible does not explicitly give the answer to this question. The same can be asked of almost any evil action. Why does God allow it? Ultimately, it comes back to God's sovereignty over His creation. The Psalmist tells us, "As for God, His way is *perfect*" (Psalm 18:30). If God's ways are "perfect," then we can trust that whatever He does—and whatever He allows—is also perfect. So the perfect plan from our perfect God was to allow sin. Our minds are not God's mind, nor are our ways His ways, as He reminds us in Isaiah 55:8-9.

Question: Who is the angel of the Lord?

Answer: The precise identity of the "angel of the Lord" is not given in the Bible. However, there are many important "clues" to his identity. There are Old and New Testament references to "angels of the Lord," "*an* angel of the Lord," and "*the* angel of the Lord." It seems when the definite article "the" is used, it is specifying a unique being, separate from the other angels. The angel of the Lord speaks as God, identifies Himself with God, and exercises the responsibilities of God (Genesis 16:7-12; 21:17-18; 22:11-18; Exodus 3:2; Judges 2:1-4; 5:23; 6:11-24;

13:3-22; 2 Samuel 24:16; Zechariah 1:12; 3:1; 12:8). In several of these appearances, those who saw the angel of the Lord feared for their lives because they had "seen the Lord." Therefore, it is clear that in at least some instances, the angel of the Lord is a theophany, an appearance of God in physical form.

The appearances of the angel of the Lord cease after the incarnation of Christ. Angels are mentioned numerous times in the New Testament, but "*the* angel of the Lord" is never mentioned in the New Testament. It is possible that appearances of the angel of the Lord were manifestations of Jesus before His incarnation. Jesus declared Himself to be existent "before Abraham" (John 8:58), so it is logical that He would be active and manifest in the world. Whatever the case, whether the angel of the Lord was a pre-incarnate appearance of Christ (Christophany) or an appearance of God the Father (theophany), it is highly likely that the phrase "the angel of the Lord" usually identifies a physical appearance of God.

Question: Are angels male or female?

Answer: The Bible does not necessarily support the idea of angels being male or female. Whenever gender is specifically "assigned" to an angel in Scripture, it is male (Genesis 19:10-12; Revelation 7:2; 8:3; 10:7). However, this does not necessarily indicate that angels are male. Matthew 22:30 seems to indicate that angels are "sexless," without gender: "At the resurrection people will neither marry nor be given in marriage; they will be like the angels in heaven." If angels do not procreate, there is no need for gender, at least not in the sense of human gender distinctions.

In a similar manner, God always refers to Himself in masculine language, although God is neither male nor female. God uses masculine language when He speaks of Himself because it more adequately describes who He is and what He does, especially in the patriarchal cultures in which the Bible was written. If angels do have a gender in some form, Scripture would indicate that they are predominately or universally male. It is more likely that angels are genderless, just as God is, and that masculine language is used to describe them and their role in serving God.

Question: What are archangels?

Answer: The word "archangel" occurs in only two verses of the Bible. First Thessalonians 4:16 exclaims, "For the Lord Himself will come down from heaven, with a loud command, with the voice of the archangel and with the trumpet call of God, and the dead in Christ will rise first." Jude verse 9 declares, "But even *the* archangel Michael, when he was disputing with the devil about the body of Moses, did not dare to bring a slanderous accusation against him, but said, 'The Lord rebuke you!'" The word "archangel" comes from a Greek word meaning "chief angel." It refers to an angel who seems to be the leader of other angels.

Jude verse 9 uses the definite article "the archangel Michael," which could possibly indicate that Michael is the only archangel. However, Daniel 10:13 describes Michael as "one of the chief princes." This possibly indicates that there is more than one archangel, because it places Michael on the same level as the other "chief princes." So, while it is possible that there are multiple archangels, it is best not to presume upon the Word of God by declaring other angels as archangels. Daniel 10:21 describes Michael the archangel as "your prince," and Daniel 12:1 identifies Michael as "the great prince who protects." Even if there are multiple archangels, it seems that Michael is the chief among them.

Question: Do we become angels after we die?

Answer: Angels are beings created by God (Colossians 1:15-17) and are entirely different from humans. They are God's special agents to carry out His plan and to minister to the followers of Christ (Hebrews 1:13-14). There is no indication that angels were formerly humans or anything else—they were created as angels. Angels have no need of, and cannot experience, the redemption that Christ came to provide for the human race. First Peter 1:12 describes their desire to look into the Gospel, but it is not for them to experience. Had they been formerly humans, the concept of salvation would not be a mystery to them, having experienced it themselves. Yes, they rejoice when a sinner turns to Christ (Luke 15:10), but salvation in Christ is not for them.

Eventually, the body of the believer in Christ will die. What happens then? The spirit of the believer goes to be with Christ

(2 Corinthians 5:8). The believer does not become an angel. It is interesting that both Elijah and Moses were recognizable on the Mount of Transfiguration. They had not transformed into angels, but appeared as themselves—although glorified—and were recognizable to Peter, James and John.

In 1 Thessalonians 4:13-18, Paul tells us that believers in Christ are asleep in Jesus; that is, their bodies are dead, but their spirits are alive. This text tells us that when Christ returns, He will bring with Him those who are asleep in Him, and then their bodies will be raised, made new like Christ's resurrected body, to be joined with their spirits which He brings with Him. All believers in Christ who are living at the return of Christ will have their bodies changed to be like Christ, and they will be completely new in their spirits, no longer having a sin nature.

All the believers in Christ will recognize one another and live with the Lord forever. We will serve Him throughout eternity, not as angels, but along with the angels. Thank the Lord for the living hope He provides for the believer in Jesus Christ.

Question: What are cherubim? Are cherubs angels?

Answer: Cherubim/cherubs are angelic beings involved in the worship and praise of God. The cherubim are first mentioned in the Bible in Genesis 3:24, "After He drove the man out, He placed on the east side of the Garden of Eden cherubim and a flaming sword flashing back and forth to guard the way to the tree of life." Prior to his rebellion, Satan was a cherub (Ezekiel 28:12-15). The tabernacle and temple along with their articles contained many representations of cherubim (Exodus 25:17-22; 26:1, 31; 36:8; 1 Kings 6:23-35; 7:29-36; 8:6-7; 1 Chronicles 28:18; 2 Chronicles 3:7-14; 2 Chronicles 3:10-13; 5:7-8; Hebrews 9:5).

Chapters 1 and 10 of the book of Ezekiel describe the "four living creatures" (Ezekiel 1:5) as the same beings as the cherubim (Ezekiel 10). Each had four faces—that of a man, a lion, an ox, and an eagle (Ezekiel 1:10; also 10:14)—and each had four wings. In their appearance, the cherubim "had the likeness of a man" (Ezekiel 1:5). These cherubim used two of their wings for flying and the other two for covering their bodies (Ezekiel 1:6, 11, 23). Under their wings the cherubim appeared to have the form, or likeness, of a man's hand (Ezekiel 1:8; 10:7-8, 21).

The imagery of Revelation 4:6-9 also seems to be describing cherubim. The cherubim serve the purpose of magnifying the holiness and power of God. This is one of their main responsibilities throughout the Bible. In addition to singing God's praises, they also serve as a visible reminder of the majesty and glory of God and His abiding presence with His people.

Question: What are seraphim? Are seraphs angels?

Answer: The seraphim (fiery, burning ones) are angelic beings associated with the prophet Isaiah's vision of God in the Temple when God called him to his prophetic ministry (Isaiah 6:1-7). Isaiah 6:2-4 records, "Above him were seraphs, each with six wings: With two wings they covered their faces, with two they covered their feet, and with two they were flying. And they were calling to one another: 'Holy, holy, holy is the Lord Almighty; the whole earth is full of his glory.' At the sound of their voices the doorposts and thresholds shook and the temple was filled with smoke." Seraphs are angels who worship God continually.

Isaiah chapter 6 is the only place in the Bible that specifically mentions the seraphim. Each seraph had six wings. They used two to fly, two to cover their feet, and two to cover their faces (Isaiah 6:2). The seraphim flew about the throne on which God was seated, singing His praises as they called special attention to God's glory and majesty. These beings apparently also served as agents of purification for Isaiah as he began his prophetic ministry. One placed a hot coal against Isaiah's lips with the words, "See, this has touched your lips; your guilt is taken away and your sin atoned for" (Isaiah 6:7). Similar to the other types of holy angels, the seraphim are perfectly obedient to God. Similar to the cherubim, the seraphim are particularly focused on worshipping God.

Question: Can a Christian today perform an exorcism?

Answer: Exorcism (commanding demons to leave other people) was practiced by various people in the Gospels and the Book of Acts—the disciples as part of Christ's instructions (Matthew 10); others using

Christ's name (Mark 9:38); the children of the Pharisees (Luke 11:18-19); Paul (Acts 16); and certain exorcists (Acts 19:11-16).

It appears that the purpose of Jesus' disciples performing exorcisms was to show Christ's dominion over the demons (Luke 10:17) and to verify that the disciples were acting in His name and by His authority. It also revealed their faith or lack of faith (Matthew 17:14-21). It was obvious that this act of casting out demons was important to the ministry of the disciples. However, it is unclear what part casting out demons actually played in the discipleship process.

Interestingly, there seems to be a shift in the latter part of the New Testament regarding demonic warfare. The teaching portions of the New Testament (Romans through Jude) refer to demonic activity, yet do not discuss the actions of casting them out, nor are believers exhorted to do so. We are told to put on the armor to stand against them (Ephesians 6:10-18). We are told to resist the devil (James 4:7), be careful of him (1 Peter 5:8), and not give him room in our lives (Ephesians 4:27). However, we are not told how to cast him or his demons out of others, or that we should even consider doing so.

The book of Ephesians gives clear instructions on how we are to have victory in our lives in the battle against the forces of evil. The first step is placing our faith in Christ (2:8-9), which breaks the rule of "the prince of power of the air" (2:2). We are then to choose, again by God's grace, to put off ungodly habits and to put on godly habits (4:17-24). This does not involve casting out demons, but rather renewing our minds (4:23). After several practical instructions on how to obey God as His children, we are reminded that there is a spiritual battle. It is fought with certain armor that allows us to stand against—not cast out—the trickery of the demonic world (6:10). We stand with truth, righteousness, the gospel, faith, salvation, the Word of God, and prayer (6:10-18).

It appears that as the Word of God was completed, the Christians had more weapons with which to battle the spirit world than the early Christians did. The role of casting out demons was replaced, for the most part, with evangelism and discipleship through the Word of God. Since the methods of spiritual warfare in the New Testament do not involve casting out demons, it is difficult to determine instructions on how to do such a thing. If necessary at all, it seems that it is through exposing the individual to the truth of the Word of God and the name of Jesus Christ.

Question: Is there an angel of death?

Answer: The idea of an "angel of death" is present in several religions. The "angel of death" is known as Samael, Sariel, or Azrael in Judaism, as Malak Almawt in Islam, as Yama or Yamaraj in Hinduism, and as the Grim Reaper in popular fiction. In various mythologies, the angel of death is imagined as anything from a cloaked skeletal figure with a sickle, to a beautiful woman, to a small child. While the details vary, the core belief regarding the angel of death is that it is a being who comes to a person at the moment of death, either actually causing death or simply observing it—with the purpose of then taking the person's soul to the abode of the dead.

This "angel of death" concept is not taught in the Bible. The Bible nowhere teaches that there is a particular angel who is in charge of death or who is present whenever a person dies. Second Kings 19:35 describes an angel putting to death 185,000 Assyrians who had invaded Israel. Some also see Exodus chapter 12, the death of the firstborn of Egypt, as the work of an angel. While this is possible, the Bible nowhere attributes the death of the firstborn to an angel. Whatever the case, while the Bible describes angels causing death at the command of the Lord, Scripture nowhere teaches that there is a specific angel of death.

God, and God alone, is sovereign over the timing of our deaths. No angel or demon can in any sense cause our death before the time God has willed it to occur. According to Romans 6:23 and Revelation 20:11-15, death is separation, separation of our soul-spirit from our body (physical death) and, in the case of unbelievers, everlasting separation from God (eternal death). Death is something that occurs. Death is not an angel, a demon, a person, or any other being. Angels can cause death, and may be involved in what happens to us after death—but there is no such thing as the "angel of death."

Question: Do we have guardian angels?

Answer: Matthew 18:10 states, "See that you do not look down on one of these little ones. For I tell you that their angels in heaven always see the face of my Father in heaven." In the context, "these little ones" could either apply to those who believe in Him (v. 6) or it could refer to the little children (vs. 3-5). This is the key passage regarding guardian angels. There is no doubt that good angels help protect (Daniel 6:20-23; 2 Kings 6:13-17), reveal information (Acts 7:52-53; Luke 1:11-20), guide (Matthew 1:20-21; Acts 8:26), provide for (Genesis 21:17-20; 1 Kings 19:5-7), and minister to believers in general (Hebrews 1:14).

The question is whether each person—or each believer—has an angel assigned to him/her. In the Old Testament, the nation of Israel had the archangel (Michael) assigned to it (Daniel 10:21; 12:1), but Scripture nowhere states that an angel is "assigned" to an individual (angels were sometimes sent to individuals, but there is no mention of permanent assignment). The Jews fully developed the belief in guardian angels during the time between the Old and New Testament periods. Some early church fathers believed that each person had not only a good angel assigned to him/her, but a demon as well. The belief in guardian angels has been around for a long time, but there is no explicit scriptural basis for it.

To return to Matthew 18:10, the word "their" is a collective pronoun in the Greek and refers to the fact that believers are served by angels in general. These angels are pictured as "always" watching the face of God so as to hear His command to them to help a believer when it is needed. The angels in this passage do not seem to be guarding a person so much as being attentive to the Father in heaven. The active duty or oversight seems, then, to come more from God than from the angels, which makes perfect sense because God alone is omniscient. He sees every believer at every moment, and He alone knows when one of us needs the intervention of an angel. Because they are continually seeing His face, the angels are at His disposal to help one of His "little ones."

It cannot be emphatically answered from Scripture whether or not each believer has a guardian angel assigned to him/her. But, as stated earlier, God does use angels in ministering to us. It is scriptural to say that He uses them as He uses us; that is, He in no way needs us or them to accomplish His purposes, but chooses to use us and them nevertheless (Job 4:18; 15:15). In the end, whether or not we have an angel assigned to protect us, we have an even greater assurance from God: if we are His children through faith in Christ, He works all things together for good (Romans 8:28-30), and Jesus Christ will never leave us or forsake us (Hebrews 13:5-6). If we have an omniscient, omnipotent, all-loving God with us, does it really matter whether or not there is a finite guardian angel protecting us?

Chapter 9

. . . .

QUESTIONS ABOUT HUMANITY

CONTENTS

What does it mean that man is made in the image of God? 254

Do we have two or three parts? Are we body, soul, and spirit - or - body, soul-spirit? 255

What is the difference between the soul and spirit of man? 256

Why did the people in Genesis live such long lives? 257

What is the origin of the different races? 258

What does the Bible say about racism, prejudice, and discrimination? ... 259

Is there an age limit to how long we can live? 260

Are only Christians God's children? 261

How should Christians view human cloning? 262

What does the Bible say about cremation? Should Christians be cremated? 264

What does the Bible say about euthanasia? 265

What does it mean that we are fearfully and wonderfully made (Psalm 139:14)? 266

Do human beings truly have a free will? 269

Does everyone have a "God-shaped hole"? 270

Can man live without God? 271

How are human souls created? 273

Is the human soul mortal or immortal? 275

Why did God create us? 275

Question: What does it mean that man is made in the image of God?

Answer: On the last day of creation, God said, "Let us make man in our image, in our likeness" (Genesis 1:26). Thus, He finished His work with a "personal touch." God formed man from the dust and gave him life by sharing His own breath (Genesis 2:7). Accordingly, man is unique among all God's creations, having both a material body and an immaterial soul/spirit.

Having the "image" or "likeness" of God means, in the simplest terms, that we were made to resemble God. Adam did not resemble God in the sense of God's having flesh and blood. Scripture says that "God is spirit" (John 4:24) and therefore exists without a body. However, Adam's body did mirror the life of God insofar as it was created in perfect health and was not subject to death.

The image of God refers to the immaterial part of man. It sets man apart from the animal world, fits him for the dominion God intended him to have over the earth (Genesis 1:28), and enables him to commune with his Maker. It is a likeness mentally, morally, and socially.

Mentally, man was created as a rational, volitional agent. In other words, man can reason and man can choose. This is a reflection of God's intellect and freedom. Anytime someone invents a machine, writes a book, paints a landscape, enjoys a symphony, calculates a sum, or names a pet, he or she is proclaiming the fact that we are made in God's image.

Morally, man was created in righteousness and perfect innocence, a reflection of God's holiness. God saw all He had made (mankind included) and called it "very good" (Genesis 1:31). Our conscience or "moral compass" is a vestige of that original state. Whenever someone writes a law, recoils from evil, praises good behavior, or feels guilty, he is confirming the fact that we are made in God's own image.

Socially, man was created for fellowship. This reflects God's triune nature and His love. In Eden, man's primary relationship was with God (Genesis 3:8 implies fellowship with God), and God made the first woman because "it is not good for the man to be alone" (Genesis 2:18). Every time someone marries, makes a friend, hugs a child, or attends church, he is demonstrating the fact that we are made in the likeness of God.

Part of being made in God's image is that Adam had the capacity to make free choices. Although he was given a righteous nature, Adam made an evil choice to rebel against his Creator. In so doing, Adam marred the image of God within himself, and he passed that damaged likeness on to all his descendants (Romans 5:12). Today, we still bear the image of God (James 3:9), but we also bear the scars of sin. Mentally, morally, socially, and physically, we show the effects of sin.

The good news is that when God redeems an individual, He begins to restore the original image of God, creating a "new self, created to be like God in true righteousness and holiness" (Ephesians 4:24). That redemption is only available by God's grace through faith in Jesus Christ as our Savior from the sin that separates us from God (Ephesians 2:8-9). Through Christ, we are made new creations in the likeness of God (2 Corinthians 5:17).

Question: Do we have two or three parts? Are we body, soul, and spirit - or - body, soul-spirit?

Answer: Genesis 1:26-27 indicates that there is something that makes humanity distinct from all the other creations. Human beings were intended to have a relationship with God, and as such, God created us with both material and immaterial parts. The material is obviously that which is tangible: the physical body, bones, organs, etc., and exists as long as the person is alive. The immaterial aspects are those which are intangible: soul, spirit, intellect, will, conscience, etc. These exist beyond the physical lifespan of the individual.

All human beings possess both material and immaterial characteristics. It is clear that all mankind has a body containing flesh, blood, bones, organs, and cells. However, it is the intangible qualities of mankind that are often debated. What does Scripture say about these? Genesis 2:7 states that man was created as a living soul. Numbers 16:22 names God as the "God of the spirits" that are possessed by all mankind. Proverbs 4:23 tells us, "Above all else, guard your heart, for it is the wellspring of life," indicating that the heart is central to man's will and emotions. Acts 23:1 says, "Paul looked straight at the Sanhedrin and said, 'My brothers, I have fulfilled my duty to God in all good conscience to this day.'" Here Paul refers to the conscience, that part of the mind that convicts us of right and wrong. Romans 12:2 states, "Do not conform any longer to the pattern of this world, but be transformed by the renewing of your mind." These verses, and numerous others, refer to the various aspects of the immaterial part of humanity. We all share both material and immaterial qualities.

So, Scripture outlines far more than just soul and spirit. Somehow, the soul, spirit, heart, conscience, and mind are connected and interrelated. The soul and spirit, though, definitely are the primary immaterial aspects of humanity. They likely comprise the other aspects. With this is mind, is humanity dichotomous (cut in two, body/soul-spirit), or trichotomous (cut in three, body/soul/spirit). It is impossible to be dogmatic. There are good arguments for both views. A key verse is Hebrews 4:12: "For the word of God is living and active. Sharper than any double-edged sword, it penetrates even to dividing soul and spirit, joints and marrow; it judges the thoughts and attitudes of the heart." This verse tells us at least two things about this debate. The soul and spirit can be divided, and the division of soul and spirit is something that only God can discern. Rather than focusing on something we cannot know for sure, it is better to focus on the Creator, who has made us "fearfully and wonderfully" (Psalm 139:14).

Question: What is the difference between the soul and spirit of man?

Answer: The soul and the spirit are the two primary immaterial aspects that Scripture ascribes to humanity. It can be confusing to attempt to discern the precise differences between the two. The word "spirit" refers only to the immaterial facet of humanity. Human beings have a spirit, but are we not spirits. However, in Scripture, only believers are said to be spiritually alive (1 Corinthians 2:11; Hebrews 4:12; James 2:26), while unbelievers are spiritually dead (Ephesians 2:1-5; Colossians 2:13). In Paul's writing, the spiritual was pivotal to the life of the believer (1 Corinthians 2:14; 3:1; Ephesians 1:3; 5:19; Colossians 1:9; 3:16). The spirit is the element in humanity which gives us the ability to have an intimate relationship with God. Whenever the word "spirit" is used, it refers to the immaterial part of humanity that "connects" with God, who Himself is spirit (John 4:24).

The word "soul" can refer to both the immaterial and material aspects of humanity. Unlike human beings *having* a spirit, human beings *are* souls. In its most basic sense, the word "soul" means "life." However, beyond this essential meaning, the Bible speaks of the soul in many contexts. One of these is humanity's eagerness to sin (Luke 12:26). Humanity is naturally evil, and our souls are tainted as a result. The life principle of the soul is removed at the time of physical death (Genesis 35:18; Jeremiah 15:2). The soul, as with the spirit, is the center of many spiritual and emotional experiences (Job 30:25; Psalm 43:5; Jeremiah 13:17). Whenever the word "soul" is used, it can refer to the whole person, whether alive or in the afterlife.

The soul and the spirit are connected, but separable (Hebrews 4:12). The soul is the essence of humanity's being; it is who we are. The spirit is the aspect of humanity that connects with God.

Question: Why did the people in Genesis live such long lives?

Answer: It is somewhat of a mystery why people in early chapters of Genesis lived such long lives. There are many theories put forward by biblical scholars. The genealogy in Genesis 5 records the line of the godly descendants of Adam—the line that would eventually produce the Messiah. God possibly blessed this line with especially long life as a result of their godliness and obedience. While this is a possible explanation, the Bible nowhere specifically limits the long lifespans to the individuals mentioned in Genesis chapter 5. Further, other than Enoch, Genesis 5 does not identify any of the individuals as being especially godly. It is likely that everyone at that time period lived several hundred years. Several factors probably contributed to this.

Genesis 1:6-7 mentions the water above the expanse, a canopy of water that surrounded the earth. Such a water canopy would have created a greenhouse effect and would have blocked much of the radiation that now hits the earth. This would have resulted in ideal living conditions. Genesis 7:11 indicates that, at the time of the flood, the water canopy was poured out on the earth, ending the ideal living conditions. Compare the life spans before the flood (Genesis 5:1-32) with those after the flood (Genesis 11:10-32). Immediately after the flood, the ages decreased dramatically.

Another consideration is that in the first few generations after creation, the human genetic code had developed few defects. Adam and Eve were created perfect. They were surely highly resistant to disease and illness. Their descendants would have inherited these advantages, albeit to lesser degrees. Over time, as a result of sin, the human genetic code became increasingly corrupted, and human beings became more and more susceptible to death and disease. This would also have resulted in drastically reduced lifespans.

Question: What is the origin of the different races?

Answer: The Bible does not explicitly give us the origin of the different "races" or skin colors in humanity. In actuality, there is only one race—the human race. Within the human race is diversity in skin color and other physical characteristics. Some speculate that when God confused the languages at the tower of Babel (Genesis 11:1-9), He also created racial diversity. It is possible that God made genetic changes to humanity to better enable people to survive in different ecologies, such as the darker skin of Africans being better equipped genetically to survive the excessive heat in Africa. According to this view, God confused the languages, causing humanity to segregate linguistically, and then created genetic racial differences based on where each racial group would eventually settle. While possible, there is no explicit biblical basis for this view. The races/skin colors of humanity are nowhere mentioned in connection with the tower of Babel.

After the flood, when the different languages came into existence, groups that spoke one language moved away with others of the same language. In doing so, the gene pool for a specific group shrank dramatically as the group no longer had the entire human population to mix with. Closer inbreeding took place, and in time certain features were emphasized in these different groups (all of which were present as a possibility in the genetic code). As further inbreeding occurred through the generations, the gene pool grew smaller and smaller, to the point that people of one language family all had the same or similar features.

Another explanation is that Adam and Eve possessed the genes to produce black, brown, and white offspring (and everything else in between). This would be similar to how a mixed-race couple sometimes has children that vary in color. Since God obviously desired humanity to be diverse in appearance, it makes sense that God would have given Adam and Eve the ability to produce children of different skin tones. Later, the only survivors of the flood were Noah and his wife, Noah's three sons and their wives—eight people in all (Genesis 7:13). Perhaps Noah's daughters-in-law were of different races. It is also possible that Noah's wife was of a different race than Noah. Maybe all eight of them were of mixed race, which would mean they possessed the genetics to produce children of different races. Whatever the explanation, the most important aspect of this question is that we are all the same race, all created by the same God, all created for the same purpose—to glorify Him.

Question: What does the Bible say about racism, prejudice, and discrimination?

Answer: The first thing to understand in this discussion is that there is only one race—the human race. Caucasians, Africans, Asians, Indians, Arabs, and Jews are not different races. Rather, they are different ethnicities of the human race. All human beings have the same physical characteristics (with minor variations, of course). More importantly, all human beings are created in the image and likeness of God (Genesis 1:26-27). God loved the world so much that He sent Jesus to lay down His life for us (John 3:16). The "world" obviously includes all ethnic groups.

God does not show partiality or favoritism (Deuteronomy 10:17; Acts 10:34; Romans 2:11; Ephesians 6:9), and neither should we. James 2:4 describes those who discriminate as "judges with evil thoughts." Instead, we are to love our neighbors as ourselves (James 2:8). In the Old Testament, God divided humanity into two "racial" groups: Jews and Gentiles. God's intent was for the Jews to be a kingdom of priests, ministering to the Gentile nations. Instead, for the most part, the Jews became proud of their status and despised the Gentiles. Jesus Christ put an end to this, destroying the dividing wall of hostility (Ephesians 2:14). All forms of racism, prejudice, and discrimination are affronts to the work of Christ on the cross.

Jesus commands us to love one another as He loves us (John 13:34). If God is impartial and loves us with impartiality, then we need to love others with that same high standard. Jesus teaches in Matthew 25 that whatever we do to the least of His brothers, we do to

Him. If we treat a person with contempt, we are mistreating a person created in God's image; we are hurting somebody whom God loves and for whom Jesus died.

Racism, in varying forms and to various degrees, has been a plague on humanity for thousands of years. Brothers and sisters of all ethnicities, this should not be. Victims of racism, prejudice, and discrimination need to forgive. Ephesians 4:32 declares, "Be kind and compassionate to one another, forgiving each other, just as in Christ God forgave you." Racists may not deserve your forgiveness, but we deserved God's forgiveness far less. Those who practice racism, prejudice, and discrimination need to repent. "Present yourselves to God as being alive from the dead, and your members as instruments of righteousness to God" (Romans 6:13). May Galatians 3:28 be completely realized, "There is neither Jew nor Greek, slave nor free, male nor female, for you are all one in Christ Jesus."

Question: Is there an age limit to how long we can live?

Answer: Many people understand Genesis 6:3 to be a 120-year age limit on humanity, "Then the LORD said, 'My Spirit will not contend with man forever, for he is mortal; his days will be a hundred and twenty years.'" However, Genesis chapter 11 records several people living past the age of 120. As a result, some interpret Genesis 6:3 to mean that, as a general rule, people will no longer live past 120 years of age. After the flood, the life spans began to shrink dramatically (compare Genesis 5 with Genesis 11) and eventually shrank to below 120 (Genesis 11:24). Since that time, very few people have lived past 120 years old.

However, another interpretation, which seems to be more in keeping with the context, is that Genesis 6:3 is God's declaration that the flood would occur 120 years from His pronouncement. Humanity's days being ended is a reference to humanity itself being destroyed in the flood. Some dispute this interpretation due to the fact that God commanded Noah to build the ark when Noah was 500 years old in Genesis 5:32 and Noah was 600 years old when the flood came (Genesis 7:6); only giving 100 years of time, not 120 years. However, the timing of God's pronouncement of Genesis 6:3 is not given. Further, Genesis 5:32 is not the time that God commanded Noah to build the Ark, but rather the age Noah was when he became the father of his three sons. It is perfectly plausible that God determined the flood to occur in 120 years and then waited several years before He commanded Noah to build the ark. Whatever the case, the 100 years between Genesis 5:32 and 7:6 in no way contradicts the 120 years mentioned in Genesis 6:3.

Several hundred years after the flood, Moses declared, "The length of our days is seventy years—or eighty, if we have the strength; yet their span is but trouble and sorrow, for they quickly pass, and we fly away" (Psalm 90:10). Neither Genesis 6:3 nor Psalm 90:10 are God-ordained age limits for humanity. Genesis 6:3 is a prediction of the timetable for the flood. Psalm 90:10 is simply stating that as a general rule, people live 70-80 years (which is still true today).

Question: Are only Christians God's children?

Answer: The Bible is clear that all people are God's creation (Colossians 1:16), and that God loves the entire world (John 3:16), but only those who are born again are children of God (John 1:12; 11:52; Romans 8:16; 1 John 3:1-10).

In Scripture, the lost are never referred to as children of God. Ephesians 2:3 tells us that before we were saved we were "by nature objects of wrath." Romans 9:8 says that "it is not the natural children who are God's children, but it is the children of the promise who are regarded as Abraham's offspring." Instead of being born as God's children, we are born in sin, which separates us from God and aligns us with Satan as God's enemy (James 4:4; 1 John 3:8). Jesus said, "If God were your Father, you would love me, for I came from God and now am here. I have not come on my own; but he sent me" (John 8:42). Then a few verses later in John 8:44, Jesus told the Pharisees that they "belong to your father, the devil, and you want to carry out your father's desire." The fact that those who are not saved are not children of God is also seen in 1 John 3:10: "This is how we know who the children of God are and who the children of the devil are: Anyone who does not do what is right is not a child of God; nor is anyone who does not love his brother."

We become children of God when we are saved because we are adopted into God's family through our relationship with Jesus Christ

(Galatians 4:5-6; Ephesians 1:5). This can be clearly seen in verses like Romans 8:14-17: "...because those who are led by the Spirit of God are sons of God. For you did not receive a spirit that makes you a slave again to fear, but you received the Spirit of sonship. And by him we cry, 'Abba, Father.' The Spirit himself testifies with our spirit that we are God's children. Now if we are children, then we are heirs—heirs of God and co-heirs with Christ, if indeed we share in his sufferings in order that we may also share in his glory." Those who are saved are children "of God through faith in Christ Jesus" (Galatians 3:26) because God has "predestined us to be adopted as his sons through Jesus Christ, in accordance with his pleasure and will" (Ephesians 1:5).

Question: How should Christians view human cloning?

Answer: While the Bible does not specifically deal with the subject of human cloning, there are principles in Scripture which may shed more light on the concept. Cloning requires both DNA and embryo cells. First, DNA is removed from the nucleus of a creature's cell. The material, bearing coded genetic information, is then placed in the nucleus of an embryonic cell. The cell receiving the new genetic information would have had its own DNA removed in order to accept the new DNA. If the cell accepts the new DNA, a duplicate embryo is formed. However, the embryo cell may reject the new DNA and die. Also, it is very possible that the embryo may not survive having the original genetic material removed from its nucleus. In many cases, when cloning is attempted, several embryos are used in order to increase the odds of a successful implantation of new genetic material. While it is possible for a duplicate creature to be created in this manner (for example, Dolly the sheep), the chances of successfully duplicating a creature without variations, and without complication, are extremely slim.

The Christian view of the process of human cloning can be stated in light of several scriptural principles. First, human beings are created in the image of God and, therefore, are unique. Genesis 1:26-27 asserts that man is created in God's image and likeness and is unique among all creations. Clearly, human life is something to be valued and not treated like a commodity to be bought and sold. Some people have promoted human cloning for the purpose of creating replacement organs for people in need of transplants who cannot find a suitable donor. The thinking is that to take one's own DNA and create a duplicate organ composed of that DNA would greatly reduce the chances of organ rejection. While this may be true, the problem is that doing so cheapens human life. The process of cloning requires human embryos to be used. While cells can be generated to make new organs, it is necessary to kill several embryos to obtain the required DNA. In essence the cloning would "throw away" many human embryos as "waste material," eliminating the chance for those embryos to grow into full maturity.

Many people believe that life does not begin at conception with the formation of the embryo, and therefore embryos are not really human beings. The Bible teaches differently. Psalm 139:13-16 says, "For you created my inmost being; you knit me together in my mother's womb. I praise you because I am fearfully and wonderfully made; your works are wonderful, I know that full well. My frame was not hidden from you when I was made in the secret place. When I was woven together in the depths of the earth, your eyes saw my unformed body. All the days ordained for me were written in your book before one of them came to be." The writer, David, declares that he was known personally by God before he was born, meaning that at his conception he was a human being with a God-ordained future.

Further, Isaiah 49:1-5 speaks of God calling Isaiah to his ministry as a prophet while he was still in his mother's womb. Also, John the Baptist was filled with the Holy Spirit while he was still in the womb (Luke 1:15). All of this points to the Bible's stand on life beginning at conception. In light of this, human cloning, with its destruction of human embryos, would not be consistent with the Bible's view of human life.

In addition, if humanity was created, then there must be a Creator, and humanity is therefore subject and accountable to that Creator. Although popular thinking—secular psychology and humanistic thought—would have one believe that man is accountable to no one but himself and that man is the ultimate authority, the Bible teaches differently. God created man and gave him responsibility over the earth (Genesis 1:28-29, 9:1-2). With this responsibility comes accountability to God. Man is not the ultimate authority over himself, and he is therefore not in a position to make decisions about the value of human life. Neither, then, is science the authority by which the ethics of human cloning, abortion, or euthanasia are decided. According to the Bible, God is the only one who rightfully exercises sovereign control over human life. To attempt to control such things is to place oneself in God's position. Clearly, man is not to do this.

If we view man as simply another creature and not as the unique creation he is, it is not difficult to see human beings as mere mechanisms needing maintenance and repair. But we are not just a collection of molecules and chemicals. The Bible teaches that God created each of us and has a specific plan for each of us. Further, He seeks a personal relationship with each of us through His Son, Jesus Christ. While there are aspects of human cloning which may seem beneficial, mankind has no control over where cloning technology may go. It is foolish to assume that only good intentions will direct the utilization of cloning. Man is not in a position to exercise the responsibility or judgment that would be required to govern the cloning of human beings.

A frequent question is whether a cloned human being, assuming that human cloning is one day successful, would have a soul. Genesis 2:7 says, "And the LORD God formed man of the dust of the ground, and breathed into his nostrils the breath of life; and man became a living soul." Here is the description of God creating a living, human soul. Souls are what we are, not what we have (1 Corinthians 15:45). The question is what kind of living soul would be created by human cloning? That is not a question that can be conclusively answered. It seems, though, that if a human being were successfully cloned, the clone would be just as much of a human being, including having an eternal soul, as any other human being.

Question: What does the Bible say about cremation? Should Christians be cremated?

Answer: The Bible does not give any specific teaching about cremation. There are occurrences in the Old Testament of people being burned to death (1 Kings 16:18; 2 Kings 21:6) and of human bones being burned (2 Kings 23:16-20), but these are not examples of cremation. It is interesting to note that in 2 Kings 23:16-20, burning human bones on an altar desecrated the altar. At the same time, the Old Testament law nowhere commands that a deceased human body not be burned, nor does it attach any curse or judgment on someone who is cremated.

Cremation was practiced in biblical times, but it was not commonly practiced by the Israelites or by New Testament believers. In the cultures of Bible times, burial in a tomb, cave, or in the ground was the common way to dispose of a human body (Genesis 23:19; 35:4; 2 Chronicles 16:14; Matthew 27:60-66). While burial was the common practice, the Bible nowhere commands burial as the only allowed method of disposing of a body.

Is cremation something a Christian can consider? Again, there is no explicit scriptural command against cremation. Some believers object to the practice of cremation on the basis it does not recognize that one day God will resurrect our bodies and re-unite them with our soul/spirit (1 Corinthians 15:35-58; 1 Thessalonians 4:16). However, the fact that a body has been cremated does not make it any more difficult for God to resurrect that body. The bodies of Christians who died a thousand years ago have, by now, completely turned into dust. This will in no way prevent God from being able to resurrect their bodies. He created them in the first place; He will have no difficulty re-creating them. Cremation does nothing but "expedite" the process of turning a body into dust. God is equally able to raise a person's remains that have been cremated as He is the remains of a person who was not cremated. The question of burial or cremation is within the realm of Christian freedom. A person or a family considering this issue should pray for wisdom (James 1:5) and follow the conviction that results.

Question: What does the Bible say about euthanasia?

Answer: Euthanasia can be a very difficult issue. There are two sides that are difficult to balance. On one end, we do not want to take a person's life into our own hands and end it prematurely. On the other end, at what point do we simply allow a person to die and take no further action to preserve life?

The overriding truth that drives the conclusion that God is opposed to euthanasia is His sovereignty. We know that physical death is inevitable (Psalm 89:48; Hebrews 9:27). However, God alone is sovereign over when and how a person's death occurs. Job testifies in Job 30:23, "I know you will bring me down to death, to the place appointed for all the living." Ecclesiastes 8:8a declares, "No man has power over the wind to contain it; so no one has power over the day of his death." God has the final say over death (see also 1 Corinthians 15:26, 54-56; Hebrews 2:9, 14-15; Revelation 21:4). Euthanasia is man's way of trying to usurp that authority from God.

Death is a natural occurrence. Sometimes God allows a person to suffer for a long time before death occurs; other times, the person's suffering is cut short. No one enjoys suffering, but that does not make it right to determine that a person is ready to die. Often God's purposes are made known through a person's suffering. "When times are good, be happy; but when times are bad, consider: God has made the one as well as the other…" (Ecclesiastes 7:14). Romans 5:3 teaches that tribulations bring about perseverance. God cares about those who are crying out for death to end their suffering. God gives purpose to life even to the end. Only God knows what is best, and His timing, even in the matter of one's death, is perfect.

At the same time, the Bible does not command us to do everything we can to keep a person alive. If a person is being kept alive only by machines, it is not immoral to turn off the machines and allow the person to die. If a person has been in a persistent vegetative state for a prolonged period of time, it would not be an offense to God to remove whatever tubes/machines that are keeping the person's body alive. Should God desire to keep a person alive, He is perfectly capable of doing so without the help of feeding tubes and/or machines.

Making a decision like this one is very difficult and painful. It is never easy to tell a doctor to end the life support of a loved one. We should never seek to prematurely end a life, but at the same time, neither do we have to go to extraordinary means to preserve a life. The best advice to anyone facing this decision is to pray to God for wisdom (James 1:5).

Question: What does it mean that we are fearfully and wonderfully made (Psalm 139:14)?

Answer: Psalm 139:14 declares, "I praise you because I am fearfully and wonderfully made; your works are wonderful, I know that full well." The context of this verse is the incredible nature of our physical bodies. The human body is the most complex and unique organism in the world, and that complexity and uniqueness speaks volumes about the mind of its Creator. Every aspect of the body, down to the tiniest microscopic cell, reveals that it is fearfully and wonderfully made.

Engineers understand how to design strong yet light beams by putting the strong material toward the outside edges of a cross-section and filling the inside with lighter, weaker material. This is done because the greatest amounts of stress occur on the surfaces of a structure when handling common bending or stresses. A cross section of a human bone reveals that the strong material is on the outside and the inside is used as a factory for blood cells of various kinds. When you examine a sophisticated camera with its ability to let in more or less light as needed and its ability to focus automatically over a vast range of field, you find repeated imitations of the operation of the human eye. And yet, having two eyeballs, we also have depth perception which gives us the ability to judge how far away an object is.

The human brain is also an amazing organ, fearfully and wonderfully made. It has the ability to learn, reason, and control so many automatic functions of the body such as heart rate, blood pressure, and breathing, and to maintain balance to walk, run, stand, and sit, all while concentrating on something else. Computers can outdo the human brain in raw calculating power but are primitive when it comes to performing most reasoning tasks. The brain also has an amazing ability to adapt. In an experiment, when people put on glasses that made the world seem upside down, their brains quickly reinterpreted the information they were being given to perceive the world as "right-side-up." When others were blindfolded for long periods of time, the "vision center" of the brain soon began to be used for other functions. When people move to a house near a railroad, soon the sound of the trains is filtered out by their brains, and they lose conscious thought of the noise.

When it comes to miniaturization, the human body is also a marvel fearfully and wonderfully made. For instance, information needed for the replication of an entire human body, with every detail covered, is stored in the double-helix DNA strand found in the nucleus of each of the billions of cells in the human body. And the system of information and control represented by our nervous system is amazingly compact in comparison to man's clumsy inventions of wires and optical cables. Each cell, once called a "simple" cell, is a tiny factory not yet fully understood by man. As microscopes become more and more powerful, the incredible vistas of the human cell begin to come into focus.

Consider the single fertilized cell of a newly conceived human life. From that one cell within the womb develop all the different kinds of tissues, organs, and systems, all working together at just the right time in an amazingly coordinated process. An example is the hole in the septum between the two ventricles in the heart of the newborn infant. This hole closes up at exactly the right time during the birth process to allow for the oxygenation of the blood from the lungs, which does not occur while the baby is in the womb and is receiving oxygen through the umbilical cord.

Further, the body's immune system is able to fight off so many enemies and restore itself from the smallest repair (even repairing bad portions of DNA) to the largest (mending bones and recovering from major accidents). Yes, there are diseases that will eventually overcome the body as we age, but we have no idea how many times through a lifetime that our immune systems have saved us from certain death.

The functions of the human body are also incredible. The ability to handle large, heavy objects and to also carefully manipulate a delicate object without breaking it is also amazing. We can shoot a bow with the arrow repeatedly hitting a distant target, peck away quickly at a computer keyboard without thinking about the keys, crawl, walk, run, twirl around, climb, swim, do somersaults and flips, and perform "simple" tasks such as unscrewing a light bulb, brushing our teeth, and lacing up our shoes—again without thinking. Indeed, these are "simple" things, but man has yet to design and program a robot that is able to perform such a vast range of tasks and motions.

The function of the digestive tract and the related organs, the longevity of the heart, the formation and function of nerves and of blood vessels, the cleansing of the blood through the kidneys, the complexity of the inner and middle ear, the sense of taste and smell, and so many other things we barely understand—each one is a marvel and beyond man's ability to duplicate. Truly, we are fearfully and wonderfully made. How grateful we are to know the Creator—through His Son, Jesus Christ—and to marvel not only at His knowledge but also at His love (Psalm 139:17-24).

Question: Do human beings truly have a free will?

Answer: If "free will" means that God gives humans the opportunity to make choices that genuinely affect their destiny, then yes, human beings do have a free will. The world's current sinful state is directly linked to choices made by Adam and Eve. God created mankind in His own image, and that included the ability to choose.

However, free will does not mean that mankind can do anything he pleases. Our choices are limited to what is in keeping with our nature. For example, a man may choose to walk across a bridge or not to walk across it; what he may *not* choose is to fly over the bridge—his nature prevents him from flying. In a similar way, a man cannot choose to make himself righteous—his (sin) nature prevents him from canceling his guilt (Romans 3:23). So, free will is limited by nature.

This limitation does not mitigate our accountability. The Bible is clear that we not only have the *ability* to choose, we also have the *responsibility* to choose wisely. In the Old Testament, God chose a nation (Israel), but individuals within that nation still bore an obligation to choose obedience to God. And individuals outside of Israel were able to choose to believe and follow God as well (e.g., Ruth and Rahab).

In the New Testament, sinners are commanded over and over to "repent" and "believe" (Matthew 3:2; 4:17; Acts 3:19; 1 John 3:23). Every call to repent is a call to choose. The command to believe assumes that the hearer can choose to obey the command.

Jesus identified the problem of some unbelievers when He told them, "You refuse to come to me to have life" (John 5:40). Clearly, they could have come if they wanted to; their problem was they chose not to. "A man reaps what he sows" (Galatians 6:7), and those who are outside of salvation are "without excuse" (Romans 1:20-21).

But how can man, limited by a sin nature, ever choose what is good? It is only through the grace and power of God that free will truly becomes "free" in the sense of being able to choose salvation (John 15:16). It is the Holy Spirit who works in and through a person's will to regenerate that person (John 1:12-13) and give him/her a new nature "created to be like God in true righteousness and holiness" (Ephesians 4:24). Salvation is God's work. At the same time, our motives, desires, and actions are voluntary, and we are rightly held responsible for them.

Question: Does everyone have a "God-shaped hole"?

Answer: The "God-shaped hole" concept states that every person has a void in his soul/spirit/life that can only be filled by God. The "God-shaped hole" is the innate longing of the human heart for something outside itself, something transcendent, something "other." Ecclesiastes 3:11 refers to God's placing of "eternity in man's heart." God made humanity for His eternal purpose, and only God can fulfill our desire for eternity. All religion is based on the innate desire to "connect" with God. This desire can only be fulfilled by God, and therefore can be likened to a "God-shaped hole."

The problem, though, is that humanity ignores this hole or attempts to fill it with things other than God. Jeremiah 17:9 describes the condition of our hearts: "The heart is deceitful above all things and beyond cure. Who can understand it?" Solomon reiterates the same concept: "The hearts of men, moreover, are full of evil and there is madness in their hearts while they live…" (Ecclesiastes 9:3). The New Testament concurs: "The sinful mind is hostile to God. It does not submit to God's law, nor can it do so" (Romans 8:7). Romans 1:18-22 describes humanity ignoring what can be known about God, including presumably the "God-shaped hole," and instead worshipping anything and everything other than God.

Sadly, too many spend their lives looking for something other than God to fill their longing for meaning—business, family, sports, etc. But in pursuing these things that are not eternal, they remain unfulfilled and wonder why their lives never seem satisfactory. There is no doubt that many people pursuing things other than God achieve a measure of "happiness" for a time. But when we consider Solomon, who had all the riches, success, esteem, and power in the world—in short, all that men seek after in this life—we see that none of it fulfilled the longing for eternity. He declared it all "vanity," meaning that he sought after these things in vain because they did not satisfy. In the end he said, "Now all has been heard; here is the conclusion of the matter: Fear God and keep his commandments, for this is the whole [duty] of man" (Ecclesiastes 12:13).

Just as a square peg cannot fill a round hole, neither can the "God-shaped hole" inside each of us be filled by anyone or anything other than God. Only through a personal relationship with God through faith in Jesus Christ can the "God-shaped hole" be filled and the desire for eternity fulfilled.

Question: Can man live without God?

Answer: Contrary to the claims of atheists and agnostics through the centuries, man cannot live without God. Man can have a mortal existence without acknowledging God, but not without the fact of God.

As the Creator, God originated human life. To say that man can exist apart from God is to say that a watch can exist without a watchmaker or a story can exist without a storyteller. We owe our being to the God in whose image we are made (Genesis 1:27). Our existence depends on God, whether we acknowledge His existence or not.

As the Sustainer, God continuously confers life (Psalm 104:10-32). He is life (John 14:6), and all creation is held together by the power of Christ (Colossians 1:17). Even those who reject God receive their sustenance from Him: "He causes his sun to rise on the evil and the good, and sends rain on the righteous and the unrighteous" (Matthew 5:45). To think that man can live without God is to suppose a sunflower can continue to live without light or a rose without water.

As the Savior, God gives eternal life to those who believe. In Christ is life, which is the light of men (John 1:4). Jesus came that we may have life "and have it to the full" (John 10:10). All who place their trust in Him are promised eternity with Him (John 3:15-16). For man to live—truly live—he must know Christ (John 17:3).

271

Without God, man has physical life only. God warned Adam and Eve that on the day they rejected Him they would "surely die" (Genesis 2:17). As we know, they did disobey, but they did not die physically that day; rather, they died spiritually. Something inside them died—the spiritual life they had known, the communion with God, the freedom to enjoy Him, the innocence and purity of their soul—it was all gone.

Adam, who had been created to live and fellowship with God, was cursed with a completely carnal existence. What God had intended to go from dust to glory now was to go from dust to dust. Just like Adam, the man without God today still functions in an earthly existence. Such a person may seem to be happy; after all, there is enjoyment and pleasure to be had in this life. But even those enjoyments and pleasures cannot be fully received without a relationship with God.

Some who reject God live lives of diversion and merriment. Their fleshly pursuits seem to yield a carefree and gratified existence. The Bible says there is a certain measure of delight to be had in sin (Hebrews 11:25). The problem is that it is temporary; life in this world is short (Psalm 90:3-12). Sooner or later, the hedonist, like the prodigal son in the parable, finds that worldly pleasure is unsustainable (Luke 15:13-15).

Not everyone who rejects God is an empty pleasure-seeker, however. There are many unsaved people who live disciplined, sober lives—happy and fulfilled lives, even. The Bible presents certain moral principles which will benefit anyone in this world—fidelity, honesty, self-control, etc. But, again, without God man has only this world. Getting smoothly through this life is no guarantee that we are ready for the afterlife. See the parable of the rich farmer in Luke 12:16-21 and Jesus' exchange with the rich (but very moral) young man in Matthew 19:16-23.

Without God, man is unfulfilled, even in his mortal life. Man is not at peace with his fellow man because he is not at peace with himself. Man is restless with himself because he has no peace with God. The pursuit of pleasure for pleasure's sake is a sign of inner turmoil. Pleasure seekers throughout history have found over and over that the temporary diversions of life give way to a deeper despair. The nagging feeling that "something is wrong" is hard to shake off.

King Solomon gave himself to a pursuit of all this world has to offer, and he recorded his findings in the book of Ecclesiastes.

Solomon discovered that knowledge, in and of itself, is futile (Ecclesiastes 1:12-18). He found that pleasure and wealth are futile (2:1-11), materialism is folly (2:12-23), and riches are fleeting (chapter 6).

Solomon concludes that life is God's gift (3:12-13) and the only wise way to live is to fear God: "Let us hear the conclusion of the whole matter: Fear God, and keep His commandments: for this is the whole duty of man. For God shall bring every work into judgment, with every secret thing, whether it be good, or whether it be evil" (12:13-14).

In other words, there is more to life than the physical dimension. Jesus stresses this point when He says, "Man does not live on bread alone, but on every word that comes from the mouth of God" (Matthew 4:4). Not bread (the physical) but God's Word (the spiritual) keeps us alive. It is useless for us to search within ourselves for the cure to all our miseries. Man can only find life and fulfillment when he acknowledges God.

Without God, man's destiny is hell. The man without God is spiritually dead; when his physical life is over, he faces eternal separation from God. In Jesus' narrative of the rich man and Lazarus (Luke 16:19-31), the rich man lives a pleasurable life of ease without a thought of God, while Lazarus suffers through his life but knows God. It is after their deaths that both men truly comprehend the gravity of the choices they made in life. The rich man realized, too late, that there is more to life than the pursuit of wealth. Meanwhile, Lazarus is comforted in paradise. For both men, the short duration of their earthly existence paled in comparison to the permanent state of their souls.

Man is a unique creation. God has set a sense of eternity in our hearts (Ecclesiastes 3:11), and that sense of timeless destiny can only find its fulfillment in God Himself.

Question: How are human souls created?

Answer: There are two biblically plausible views on how the human soul is created. Traducianism is the theory that a soul is generated

273

by the physical parents along with the physical body. Support for Traducianism is as follows: (A) In Genesis 2:7, God breathed the breath of life into Adam, causing Adam to become a "living soul." Scripture nowhere records God performing this action again. (B) Adam had a son in his own likeness (Genesis 5:3). Adam's descendants seem to be "living souls" without God breathing into them. (C) Genesis 2:2-3 seems to indicate that God ceased His creative work. (D) Adam's sin affects all men—both physically and spiritually—this makes sense if the body and soul both come from the parents. The weakness of Traducianism is that it is unclear how an immaterial soul can be generated through an entirely physical process. Traducianism can only be true if the body and soul are inextricably connected.

Creationism is the view that God creates a new soul when a human being is conceived. Creationism was held by many early church fathers and also has scriptural support. First, Scripture differentiates the origin of the soul from the origin of the body (Ecclesiastes 12:7; Isaiah 42:5; Zechariah 12:1; Hebrews 12:9). Second, if God creates each individual soul at the moment it is needed, the separation of soul and body is held firm. The weakness of Creationism is that it has God continually creating new human souls, while Genesis 2:2-3 indicates that God ceased creating. Also, since the entire human existence—body, soul, and spirit—are infected by sin and God creates a new soul for every human being, how is that soul then infected with sin?

A third view, but one that lacks biblical support, is the concept that God created all human souls at the same time, and "attaches" a soul to a human being at the moment of conception. This view holds that there is sort of a "warehouse of souls" in heaven where God stores souls that await a human body to be attached to. Again, this view has no biblical support, and is usually held by those of a "new age" or reincarnation mindset.

Whether the Traducianist view or the Creationist view is correct, both agree that the soul does not exist prior to conception. This seems to be the clear teaching of the Bible. Whether God creates a new human soul at the moment of conception, or whether God designed the human reproductive process to also reproduce a soul, God is ultimately responsible for the creation of each and every human soul.

Question: Is the human soul mortal or immortal?

Answer: Without a doubt the human soul is immortal. This is clearly seen in many Scriptures in both the Old and New Testaments: Psalm 22:26; 23:6; 49:7-9; Ecclesiastes 12:7; Daniel 12:2-3; Matthew 25:46; and 1 Corinthians 15:12-19. Daniel 12:2 says, "Multitudes who sleep in the dust of the earth will awake: some to everlasting life, others to shame and everlasting contempt." Similarly, Jesus Himself said that the wicked "will go away to eternal punishment, but the righteous to eternal life" (Matthew 25:46). With the same Greek word used to refer to both "punishment" and "life," it is clear that both the wicked and the righteous have an eternal/immortal soul.

The unmistakable teaching of the Bible is that all people, whether they are saved or lost, will exist eternally, in either heaven or hell. True life or spiritual life does not cease when our fleshly bodies pass away in death. Our souls will live forever, either in the presence of God in heaven if we are saved, or in punishment in hell if we reject God's gift of salvation. In fact, the promise of the Bible is that not only will our souls live forever, but also that our bodies will be resurrected. This hope of a bodily resurrection is at the very heart of the Christian faith (1 Corinthians 15:12-19).

While all souls are immortal, it is important to remember that we are not eternal in the same way that God is. God is the only truly eternal being in that He alone is without a beginning or end. God has always existed and will always continue to exist. All other sentient creatures, whether they are human or angelic, are finite in that they had a beginning. While our souls will live forever once we come into being, the Bible does not support the concept that our souls have always existed. Our souls are immortal, as that is how God created them, but they did have a beginning; there was a time they did not exist.

Question: Why did God create us?

Answer: The short answer to the question "why did God create us?" is "for His pleasure." Revelation 4:11 says, "You are worthy, our Lord and God, to receive glory and honor and power, for you created all things, and by your will they were created and have their being." Colossians 1:16 reiterates the point: "All things were created by him and for him." Being created for God's pleasure does not mean humanity was made to entertain God or provide Him with amusement. God is a creative Being, and it gives Him pleasure to create. God is a personal Being, and it gives Him pleasure to have other beings He can have a genuine relationship with.

Being made in the image and likeness of God (Genesis 1:27), human beings have the ability to know God and therefore love Him, worship Him, serve Him, and fellowship with Him. God did not create human beings because He needed them. As God, He needs nothing. In all eternity past, He felt no loneliness, so He was not looking for a "friend." He loves us, but this is not the same as needing us. If we had never existed, God would still be God—the unchanging One (Malachi 3:6). The I AM (Exodus 3:14) was never dissatisfied with His own eternal existence. When He made the universe, He did what pleased Himself, and since God is perfect, His action was perfect. "It was very good" (Genesis 1:31).

Also, God did not create "peers" or beings equal to Himself. Logically, He could not do so. If God were to create another being of equal power, intelligence, and perfection, then He would cease to be the one true God for the simple reason that there would be two gods—and that would be an impossibility. "The LORD is God; besides him there is no other" (Deuteronomy 4:35). Anything that God creates must of necessity be lesser than He. The thing made can never be greater than, or as great as, the One who made it.

Recognizing the complete sovereignty and holiness of God, we are amazed that He would take man and crown him "with glory and honor" (Psalm 8:5) and that He would condescend to call us "friends" (John 15:14-15). Why did God create us? God created us for His pleasure and so that we, as His creation, would have the pleasure of knowing Him.

Chapter 10

··

QUESTIONS ABOUT THEOLOGY

CONTENTS

What is the definition of theology? 278

What is systematic theology? 279

What is a Christian worldview? 280

Calvinism vs. Arminianism—which view is correct? 281

What is predestination? Is predestination biblical? 282

What is dispensationalism and is it biblical? 284

What is premillennialism? 285

What is amillennialism? 288

What is postmillennialism? 290

What are the various theories on the atonement? 291

What is Christian apologetics? 294

What is Christian ethics? 295

What is divine providence? 297

What is general revelation and special revelation? 299

What is Trinitarianism? Is Trinitarianism biblical? 301

What is replacement theology? 302

Question: What is the definition of theology?

Answer: The word "theology" comes from two Greek words that combined mean "the study of God." Christian theology is simply an attempt to understand God as He is revealed in the Bible. No theology will ever fully explain God and His ways because God is infinitely and eternally higher than we are. Therefore, any attempt to describe Him will fall short (Romans 11:33-36). However, God does want us to know Him insofar as we are able, and theology is the art and science of knowing what we can know and understand about God in an organized and understandable manner. Some people try to avoid theology because they believe it is divisive. Properly understood, though, theology is uniting. Proper, biblical theology is a good thing; it is the teaching of God's Word (2 Timothy 3:16-17).

The study of theology, then, is nothing more than digging into God's Word to discover what He has revealed about Himself. When we do this, we come to know Him as Creator of all things, Sustainer of all things, and Judge of all things. He is the Alpha and Omega, the beginning and end of all things. When Moses asked who was sending him to Pharaoh, God replied "I AM WHO I AM" (Exodus 3:14). The name I AM indicates personality. God has a name, even as He has given names to others. The name I AM stands for a free, purposeful, self-sufficient personality. God is not an ethereal force or a cosmic energy. He is the almighty, self-existing, self-determining Being with a mind and a will—the "personal" God who has revealed Himself to humanity through His Word, and through His Son, Jesus Christ.

To study theology is to get to know God in order that we may glorify Him through our love and obedience. Notice the progression here: we must get to know Him before we can love Him, and we must love Him before we can desire to obey Him. As a byproduct, our lives are immeasurably enriched by the comfort and hope He imparts to those who know, love, and obey Him. Poor theology and a superficial, inaccurate understanding of God will only make our lives worse instead of bringing the comfort and hope we long for. Knowing about God is crucially important. We are cruel to ourselves if we try to live in this world without knowing about God. The world is a painful place, and life in it is disappointing and unpleasant. Reject theology and you doom yourself to life with no sense of direction. Without theology, we waste our lives and lose our souls.

All Christians should be consumed with theology—the intense, personal study of God—in order to know, love, and obey the One with whom we will joyfully spend eternity.

Question: What is systematic theology?

Answer: "Systematic" refers to something being put into a system. Systematic theology is, therefore, the division of theology into systems that explain its various areas. For example, many books of the Bible give information about the angels. No one book gives all the information about the angels. Systematic theology takes all the information about angels from all the books of the Bible and organizes it into a system called angelology. That is what systematic theology is all about—organizing the teachings of the Bible into categorical systems.

Theology Proper or Paterology is the study of God the Father. Christology is the study of God the Son, the Lord Jesus Christ. Pneumatology is the study of God the Holy Spirit. Bibliology is the study of the Bible. Soteriology is the study of salvation. Ecclesiology is the study of the church. Eschatology is the study of the end times. Angelology is the study of angels. Christian Demonology is the study of demons from a Christian perspective. Christian Anthropology is the study of humanity from a Christian perspective. Hamartiology is the study of sin. Systematic theology is an important tool in helping us to understand and teach the Bible in an organized manner.

In addition to systematic theology, there are other ways that theology can be divided. Biblical theology is the study of a certain book (or books) of the Bible and emphasizing the different aspects of theology it focuses on. For example, the Gospel of John is very Christological since it focuses so much on the deity of Christ (John 1:1, 14; 8:58; 10:30; 20:28). Historical theology is the study of doctrines and how they have developed over the centuries of the Christian church. Dogmatic theology is the study of the doctrines of certain Christian groups that have systematized doctrine—for example, Calvinistic theology and dispensational theology. Contemporary theology is the study of doctrines that have developed or come into focus in recent times. No matter what method of theology is studied, what is important is that theology is studied.

Question: What is a Christian worldview?

Answer: A "worldview" refers to a comprehensive conception of the world from a specific standpoint. A "Christian worldview," then, is a comprehensive conception of the world from a Christian standpoint. An individual's worldview is his "big picture," a harmony of all his beliefs about the world. It is his way of understanding reality. One's worldview is the basis for making daily decisions and is therefore extremely important.

An apple sitting on a table is seen by several people. A botanist looking at the apple classifies it. An artist sees a still-life and draws it. A grocer sees an asset and inventories it. A child sees lunch and eats it. How we look at any situation is influenced by how we look at the world at large. Every worldview, Christian and non-Christian, deals with at least these three questions:

1. Where did we come from? (and why are we here?)
2. What is wrong with the world?
3. How can we fix it?

A prevalent worldview today is naturalism, which answers the three questions like this: 1) We are the product of random acts of nature with no real purpose. 2) We do not respect nature as we should. 3) We can save the world through ecology and conservation. A naturalistic worldview generates many related philosophies such as moral relativism, existentialism, pragmatism, and utopianism.

A Christian worldview, on the other hand, answers the three questions biblically: 1) We are God's creation, designed to govern the world and fellowship with Him (Genesis 1:27-28; 2:15). 2) We sinned against God and subjected the whole world to a curse (Genesis 3). 3) God Himself has redeemed the world through the sacrifice of His Son, Jesus Christ (Genesis 3:15; Luke 19:10), and will one day restore creation to its former perfect state (Isaiah 65:17-25). A Christian worldview leads us to believe in moral absolutes, miracles, human dignity, and the possibility of redemption.

It is important to remember that a worldview is comprehensive. It affects every area of life, from money to morality, from politics to art. True Christianity is more than a set of ideas to use at church. Christianity as taught in the Bible is itself a worldview. The Bible never distinguishes between a "religious" and a "secular" life; the Christian life is the only life there is. Jesus proclaimed Himself "the way, the truth, and the life" (John 14:6) and, in doing so, became our worldview.

Question: Calvinism vs. Arminianism—which view is correct?

Answer: Calvinism and Arminianism are two systems of theology that attempt to explain the relationship between God's sovereignty and man's responsibility in the matter of salvation. Calvinism is named for John Calvin, a French theologian who lived from 1509-1564. Arminianism is named for Jacobus Arminius, a Dutch theologian who lived from 1560-1609.

Both systems can be summarized with five points. Calvinism holds to the total depravity of man while Arminianism holds to partial depravity. Total depravity states that every aspect of humanity is tainted by sin; therefore, human beings are unable to come to God on their own accord. Partial depravity states that every aspect of humanity is tainted by sin, but not to the extent that they are unable to place faith in God of their own accord.

Calvinism includes the belief that election is unconditional, while Arminianism believes in conditional election. Unconditional election is the view that God elects individuals to salvation based entirely on His will alone, not on anything inherently worthy in the individual. Conditional election states that God elects individuals to salvation based on His foreknowledge of who will believe in Christ unto salvation, thereby on the condition that the individual chooses God.

Calvinism sees the atonement as limited, while Arminianism sees it as unlimited. This is the most controversial of the five points. Limited atonement is the belief that Jesus only died for the elect. Unlimited atonement is the belief that Jesus died for all, but that His death is not effectual until a person receives Him by faith.

Calvinism includes the belief that God's grace is irresistible, while Arminianism says that an individual can resist the grace of God. Irresistible grace argues that when God calls a person to salvation, that person will inevitably come to salvation. Resistible grace states that God calls all to salvation, but that many people resist and reject this call.

Calvinism holds to perseverance of the saints while Arminianism holds to conditional salvation. Perseverance of the saints refers to the concept that a person who is elected by God will persevere in faith and will not permanently deny Christ or turn away from Him. Conditional salvation is the view that a believer in Christ can, of his/her own free will, turn away from Christ and thereby lose salvation.

So, in the Calvinism vs. Arminianism debate, who is correct? It is interesting to note that in the diversity of the body of Christ, there are all sorts of mixtures of Calvinism and Arminianism. There are five-point Calvinists and five-point Arminians, and at the same time three-point Calvinists and two-point Arminians. Many believers arrive at some sort of mixture of the two views. Ultimately, it is our view that both systems fail in that they attempt to explain the unexplainable. Human beings are incapable of fully grasping a concept such as this. Yes, God is absolutely sovereign and knows all. Yes, human beings are called to make a genuine decision to place faith in Christ unto salvation. These two facts seem contradictory to us, but in the mind of God they make perfect sense.

Question: What is predestination? Is predestination biblical?

Answer: Romans 8:29-30 tells us, "For those God foreknew he also predestined to be conformed to the likeness of his Son, that he might be the firstborn among many brothers. And those he predestined, he also called; those he called, he also justified; those he justified, he also glorified." Ephesians 1:5 and 11 declare, "He predestined us to be adopted as his sons through Jesus Christ, in accordance with his pleasure and will…In him we were also chosen, having been predestined according to the plan of him who works out everything in conformity with the purpose of his will." Many people have a strong hostility to the doctrine of predestination. However, predestination is a biblical doctrine. The key is understanding what predestination means, biblically.

The words translated "predestined" in the Scriptures referenced above are from the Greek word *proorizo*, which carries the meaning of "determine beforehand," "ordain," "to decide upon ahead of time." So, predestination is God determining certain things to occur ahead of time. What did God determine ahead of time? According to Romans 8:29-30, God predetermined that certain individuals would be conformed to the likeness of His Son, be called, justified, and glorified. Essentially, God predetermines that certain individuals will be saved. Numerous scriptures refer to believers in Christ being chosen (Matthew 24:22, 31; Mark 13:20, 27; Romans 8:33, 9:11, 11:5-7, 28; Ephesians 1:11; Colossians 3:12; 1 Thessalonians 1:4; 1 Timothy 5:21; 2 Timothy 2:10; Titus 1:1; 1 Peter 1:1-2, 2:9; 2 Peter 1:10). Predestination is the biblical doctrine that God in His sovereignty chooses certain individuals to be saved.

The most common objection to the doctrine of predestination is that it is unfair. Why would God choose certain individuals and not others? The important thing to remember is that no one deserves to be saved. We have all sinned (Romans 3:23), and are all worthy of eternal punishment (Romans 6:23). As a result, God would be perfectly just in allowing all of us to spend eternity in hell. However, God chooses to save some of us. He is not being unfair to those who are not chosen, because they are receiving what they deserve. God's choosing to be gracious to some is not unfair to the others. No one deserves anything from God; therefore, no one can object if he does not receive anything from God. An illustration would be a man randomly handing out money to five people in a crowd of twenty. Would the fifteen people who did not receive money be upset? Probably so. Do they have a right to be upset? No, they do not. Why? Because the man did not owe anyone money. He simply decided to be gracious to some.

If God is choosing who is saved, doesn't that undermine our free will to chose and believe in Christ? The Bible says that we have the choice—all who believe in Jesus Christ will be saved (John 3:16; Romans 10:9-10). The Bible never describes God rejecting anyone who believes in Him or turning away anyone who is seeking Him (Deuteronomy 4:29). Somehow, in the mystery of God, predestination works hand-in-hand with a person being drawn by God (John 6:44) and believing unto salvation (Romans 1:16). God predestines who will be saved, and we must choose Christ in order to be saved. Both facts are equally true. Romans 11:33 proclaims, "Oh, the depth of the riches of the wisdom and knowledge of God! How unsearchable his judgments, and his paths beyond tracing out!"

Question: What is dispensationalism and is it biblical?

Answer: Dispensationalism is a system of theology that has two primary distinctives. 1) A consistently literal interpretation of Scripture, especially Bible prophecy. 2) A distinction between Israel and the church in God's program.

Dispensationalists claim that their principle of hermeneutics is that of literal interpretation, which means giving each word the meaning it would commonly have in everyday usage. Symbols, figures of speech and types are all interpreted plainly in this method, and this is in no way contrary to literal interpretation. Even symbols and figurative sayings have literal meanings behind them.

There are at least three reasons why this is the best way to view Scripture. First, philosophically, the purpose of language itself seems to require that we interpret it literally. Language was given by God for the purpose of being able to communicate with man. The second reason is biblical. Every prophecy about Jesus Christ in the Old Testament was fulfilled literally. Jesus' birth, Jesus' ministry, Jesus' death, and Jesus' resurrection all occurred exactly and literally as the Old Testament predicted. There is no non-literal fulfillment of these prophecies in the New Testament. This argues strongly for the literal method. If literal interpretation is not used in studying the Scriptures, there is no objective standard by which to understand the Bible. Each and every person would be able to interpret the Bible as he saw fit. Biblical interpretation would devolve into "what this passage says to me..." instead of "the Bible says..." Sadly, this is already the case in much of what is called biblical interpretation today.

Dispensational theology teaches that there are two distinct peoples of God: Israel and the church. Dispensationalists believe that salvation has always been by faith—in God in the Old Testament and specifically in God the Son in the New Testament. Dispensationalists hold that the church has not replaced Israel in God's program and the Old Testament promises to Israel have not been transferred to the church. They believe that the promises God made to Israel (for land, many descendants, and blessings) in the Old Testament will be ultimately fulfilled in the 1000-year period spoken of in Revelation chapter 20. Dispensationalists believe that just as God is in this age focusing His attention on the church, He will again in the future focus His attention on Israel (Romans 9-11).

Using this system as a basis, dispensationalists understand the Bible to be organized into seven dispensations: Innocence (Genesis 1:1–3:7), conscience (Genesis 3:8–8:22), human government (Genesis 9:1–11:32), promise (Genesis 12:1–Exodus 19:25), law (Exodus 20:1–Acts 2:4), grace (Acts 2:4–Revelation 20:3), and the millennial kingdom (Revelation 20:4-6). Again, these dispensations are not paths to salvation, but manners in which God relates to man. Dispensationalism, as a system, results in a premillennial interpretation of Christ's second coming and usually a pretribulational interpretation of the rapture. To summarize, dispensationalism is a theological system that emphasizes the literal interpretation of Bible prophecy, recognizes a clear distinction between Israel and the church, and organizes the Bible into the different dispensations it presents.

Question: What is premillennialism?

Answer: Premillennialism is the view that Christ's second coming will occur prior to His millennial kingdom, and that the millennial kingdom is a literal 1000-year reign of Christ on earth. In order to understand and interpret the passages in Scripture that deal with end-times events, there are two things that must be clearly understood: a proper method of interpreting Scripture and the distinction between Israel (the Jews) and the church (the body of all believers in Jesus Christ).

First, a proper method of interpreting Scripture requires that Scripture be interpreted in a way that is consistent with its context. This means that a passage must be interpreted in a way that is consistent with the audience to which it is written, those it is written about, whom it is written by, and so on. It is critical to know the author, intended audience, and historical background of each passage one interprets. The historical and cultural setting will often reveal the correct meaning of a passage. It is also important to remember that

Scripture interprets Scripture. That is, often a passage will cover a topic or subject that is also addressed elsewhere in the Bible. It is important to interpret all of these passages consistently with one another.

Finally, and most importantly, passages must always be taken in their normal, regular, plain, literal meaning unless the context of the passage indicates that it is figurative in nature. A literal interpretation does not eliminate the possibility of figures of speech being used. Rather, it encourages the interpreter to not read figurative language into the meaning of a passage unless it is appropriate for that context. It is crucial to never seek a "deeper, more spiritual" meaning than is presented. Spiritualizing a passage is dangerous because it moves the basis for accurate interpretation from Scripture to the mind of the reader. Then, there can be no objective standard of interpretation; instead, Scripture becomes subject to each person's own impression of what it means. Second Peter 1:20-21 reminds us that "no prophecy of Scripture came about by the prophet's own interpretation. For prophecy never had its origin in the will of man, but men spoke from God as they were carried along by the Holy Spirit."

Applying these principles of biblical interpretation, it must be seen that Israel (Abraham's physical descendants) and the church (all New Testament believers) are two distinct groups. It is crucial to recognize that Israel and the church are distinct because, if this is misunderstood, Scripture will be misinterpreted. Especially prone to misinterpretation are passages that deal with promises made to Israel (both fulfilled and unfulfilled). Such promises should not be applied to the church. Remember, the context of the passage will determine to whom it is addressed and will point to the most correct interpretation.

With those concepts in mind, we can look at various passages of Scripture that produce the premillennial view. Genesis 12:1-3: "The Lord had said to Abram, 'Leave your country, your people and your father's household and go to the land I will show you. I will make you into a great nation and I will bless you; I will make your name great, and you will be a blessing. I will bless those who bless you, and whoever curses you I will curse; and all peoples on earth will be blessed through you.'"

God promises Abraham three things here: Abraham would have many descendants, this nation would own and occupy a land, and a universal blessing will come to all mankind out of Abraham's line (the Jews). In Genesis 15:9-17, God ratifies His covenant with Abraham. By the way this is done, God places sole responsibility for the covenant upon Himself. That is, there was nothing Abraham could do or fail to do that would void the covenant God made. Also in this passage, the boundaries are set for the land that the Jews will eventually occupy. For a detailed list of the boundaries, see Deuteronomy 34. Other passages that deal with the promise of land are Deuteronomy 30:3-5 and Ezekiel 20:42-44.

In 2 Samuel 7:10-17, we see the promise made by God to King David. Here, God promises David that he will have descendants, and out of those descendants God will establish an eternal kingdom. This is referring to the rule of Christ during the millennium and forever. It is important to keep in mind that this promise must be fulfilled literally and has not yet taken place. Some would believe that the rule of Solomon was the literal fulfillment of this prophecy, but there is a problem with that. The territory over which Solomon ruled is not held by Israel today, and neither does Solomon rule over Israel today. Remember that God promised Abraham that his descendants would possess a land forever. Also, 2 Samuel 7 says that God would establish a king who would rule for eternity. Solomon could not be a fulfillment of the promise made to David. Therefore, this is a promise that has yet to be fulfilled.

Now, with all this in mind, examine what is recorded in Revelation 20:1-7. The thousand years which is repeatedly mentioned in this passage corresponds to Christ's literal 1000-year reign on the earth. Recall that the promise made to David regarding a ruler had to be fulfilled literally and has not yet taken place. Premillennialism sees this passage as describing the future fulfillment of that promise with Christ on the throne. God made unconditional covenants with both Abraham and David. Neither of these covenants has been fully or permanently fulfilled. A literal, physical rule of Christ is the only way the covenants can be fulfilled as God promised they would.

Applying a literal method of interpretation to Scripture results in the pieces of the puzzle coming together. All of the Old Testament prophecies of Jesus' first coming were fulfilled literally. Therefore, we should expect the prophecies regarding His second coming to be fulfilled literally as well. Premillennialism is the only system that agrees with a literal interpretation of God's covenants and end-times prophecy.

Question: What is amillennialism?

Answer: Amillennialism is the name given to the belief that there will not be a literal 1000-year reign of Christ. The people who hold to this belief are called amillennialists. The prefix "a-" in amillennialism means "no" or "not." Hence, "amillennialism" means "no millennium." This differs from the most widely accepted view called premillennialism (the view that Christ's second coming will occur prior to His millennial kingdom and that the millennial kingdom is a literal 1000-year reign) and from the less-widely accepted view called postmillennialism (the belief that Christ will return after Christians, not Christ Himself, have established the kingdom on this earth).

However, in fairness to amillennialists, they do not believe that there is no millennium at all. They just do not believe in a literal millennium—a literal 1000-year reign of Christ on earth. Instead, they believe that Christ is now sitting on the throne of David and that this present church age is the kingdom over which Christ reigns. There is no doubt that Christ is now sitting on a throne, but this does not mean that it is what the Bible refers to as the throne of David. There is no doubt that Christ now rules, for He is God. Yet this does not mean He is ruling over the millennial kingdom.

In order for God to keep His promises to Israel and His covenant with David (2 Samuel 7:8-16, 23:5; Psalm 89:3-4), there must be a literal, physical kingdom on this earth. To doubt this is to call into question God's desire and/or ability to keep His promises, and this opens up a host of other theological problems. For example, if God would renege on His promises to Israel after proclaiming those promises to be "everlasting," how could we be sure of anything He promises, including the promises of salvation to believers in the Lord Jesus? The only solution is to take Him at His word and understand that His promises will be literally fulfilled.

Clear biblical indications that the kingdom will be a literal, earthly kingdom are

1. Christ's feet will actually touch the Mount of Olives prior to the establishment of His kingdom (Zechariah 14:4, 9);
2. During the kingdom, the Messiah will execute justice and judgment on the earth (Jeremiah 23:5-8);
3. The kingdom is described as being under heaven (Daniel 7:13-14, 27);
4. The prophets foretold of dramatic earthly changes during the kingdom (Acts 3:21; Isaiah 35:1-2, 11:6-9, 29:18, 65:20-22; Ezekiel 47:1-12; Amos 9:11-15); and
5. The chronological order of events in Revelation indicates the existence of an earthly kingdom prior to the conclusion of world history (Revelation 20).

The amillennial view comes from using one method of interpretation for unfulfilled prophecy and another method for non-prophetic Scripture and fulfilled prophecy. Non-prophetic Scripture and fulfilled prophecy are interpreted literally or normally. But, according to the amillennialist, unfulfilled prophecy is to be interpreted spiritually, or non-literally. Those who hold to amillennialism believe that a "spiritual" reading of unfulfilled prophecy is the normal reading of the texts. This is called using a dual hermeneutic. (Hermeneutics is the study of the principles of interpretation.) The amillennialist assumes that most, or all, unfulfilled prophecy is written in symbolic, figurative, spiritual language. Therefore, the amillennialist will assign different meanings to those parts of Scripture instead of the normal, contextual meanings of those words.

The problem with interpreting unfulfilled prophecy in this manner is that this allows for a wide range of meanings. Unless you interpret Scripture in the normal sense, there will not be one meaning. Yet God, the ultimate author of all of Scripture, did have one specific meaning in mind when He inspired the human authors to write. Though there may be many life applications in a passage of Scripture, there is only one meaning, and that meaning is what God intended it to mean. Also, the fact that fulfilled prophecy was fulfilled literally is the best reason of all for assuming that unfulfilled prophecy will also be literally fulfilled. The prophecies concerning Christ's first coming were all fulfilled literally. Therefore, prophecies concerning Christ's second coming should also be expected to be fulfilled literally. For these reasons, an allegorical interpretation of unfulfilled prophecy should be rejected and a literal or normal interpretation of unfulfilled prophecy should be adopted. Amillennialism fails in that it uses inconsistent hermeneutics, namely, interpreting unfulfilled prophecy differently from fulfilled prophecy.

Question: What is postmillennialism?

Answer: Postmillennialism is an interpretation of Revelation chapter 20 which sees Christ's second coming as occurring after the "millennium," a golden age or era of Christian prosperity and dominance. The term includes several similar views of the end times, and it stands in contrast to premillennialism (the view that Christ's second coming will occur prior to His millennial kingdom and that the millennial kingdom is a literal 1000-year reign) and, to a lesser extent, amillennialism (no literal millennium).

Postmillennialism is the belief that Christ returns after a period of time, but not necessarily a literal 1000 years. Those who hold this view do not interpret unfulfilled prophecy using a normal, literal method. They believe that Revelation 20:4-6 should not be taken literally. They believe that "1000 years" simply means "a long period of time." Furthermore, the prefix "post-" in "postmillennialism" denotes the view that Christ will return after Christians (not Christ Himself) have established the kingdom on this earth.

Those who hold to postmillennialism believe that this world will become better and better—all evidence to the contrary notwithstanding—with the entire world eventually becoming "Christianized." After this happens, Christ will return. However, this is not the view of the world in the end times that Scripture presents. From the book of Revelation, it is easy to see that the world will be a terrible place during that future time. Also, in 2 Timothy 3:1-7, Paul describes the last days as "terrible times."

Those who hold to postmillennialism use a non-literal method of interpreting unfulfilled prophecy, assigning their own meanings to words. The problem with this is that when someone starts assigning meanings to words other than their normal meaning, a person can decide that a word, phrase, or sentence means anything he wants it to mean. All objectivity concerning the meaning of words is lost. When words lose their meaning, communication ceases. However, this is not how God has intended for language and communication to be. God communicates to us through His written word, with objective meanings to words, so that ideas and thoughts can be communicated.

A normal, literal interpretation of Scripture rejects postmillennialism and holds to a normal interpretation of all Scripture, including unfulfilled prophecy. We have hundreds of examples in Scripture of prophecies being fulfilled. Take, for example, the prophecies concerning Christ in the Old Testament. Those prophecies were fulfilled literally. Consider the virgin birth of Christ (Isaiah 7:14; Matthew 1:23). Consider His death for our sins (Isaiah 53:4-9; 1 Peter 2:24). These prophecies were fulfilled literally, and that is reason enough to assume that God will continue in the future to literally fulfill His Word. Postmillennialism fails in that it interprets Bible prophecy subjectively and holds that the millennial kingdom will be established by the church, not by Christ Himself.

Question: What are the various theories on the atonement?

Answer: Throughout church history, several different views of the atonement, some true and some false, have been put forth by different individuals or denominations. One of the reasons for the various views is that both the Old and New Testaments reveal many truths about Christ's atonement, making it hard, if not impossible, to find any single "theory" that fully encapsulates or explains the richness of the atonement. What we discover as we study the Scriptures is a rich and multifaceted picture of the atonement as the Bible puts forth many interrelated truths concerning the redemption that Christ has accomplished. Another contributing factor to the many different theories of the atonement is that much of what we can learn about the atonement needs to be understood from the experience and perspective of God's people under the Old Covenant sacrificial system.

The atonement of Christ, its purpose and what it accomplished, is such a rich subject that volumes have been written about it. This article will simply provide a brief overview of many of the theories that have been put forward at one time or another. In looking at the different views of the atonement, we must remember that any view that does not recognize the sinfulness of man or the substitutionary nature of the atonement is deficient at best and heretical at worst.

Ransom to Satan: This view sees the atonement of Christ as a ransom paid to Satan to purchase man's freedom and release him from being enslaved to Satan. It is based on a belief that man's spiritual condition is bondage to Satan and that the meaning of Christ's death was to secure God's victory over Satan. This theory has little, if any, scriptural support and has had few supporters throughout church history. It is unbiblical in that it sees Satan, rather than God, as the one who required that a payment be made for sin. Thus, it completely ignores the demands of God's justice as seen throughout Scripture. It also has a higher view of Satan than it should and views him as having more power than he really does. There is no scriptural support for the idea that sinners owe anything to Satan, but throughout Scripture we see that God is the One who requires a payment for sin.

Recapitulation Theory: This theory states that the atonement of Christ has reversed the course of mankind from disobedience to obedience. It believes that Christ's life recapitulated all the stages of human life and in doing so reversed the course of disobedience initiated by Adam. This theory cannot be supported scripturally.

Dramatic Theory: This view sees the atonement of Christ as securing the victory in a divine conflict between good and evil and winning man's release from bondage to Satan. The meaning of Christ's death was to ensure God's victory over Satan and to provide a way to redeem the world out of its bondage to evil.

Mystical Theory: The mystical theory sees the atonement of Christ as a triumph over His own sinful nature through the power of the Holy Spirit. Those who hold this view believe that knowledge of this will mystically influence man and awake his "god-consciousness." They also believe that man's spiritual condition is not the result of sin but simply a lack of "god-consciousness." Clearly, this is unbiblical. To believe this, one must believe that Christ had a sin nature, while Scripture is clear that Jesus was the perfect God-man, sinless in every aspect of His nature (Hebrews 4:15).

Moral Influence Theory: This is the belief that the atonement of Christ is a demonstration of God's love which causes man's heart to soften and repent. Those who hold this view believe that man is spiritually sick and in need of help and that man is moved to accept God's forgiveness by seeing God's love for man. They believe that the purpose and meaning of Christ's death was to demonstrate God's love toward man. While it is true that Christ's atonement is the ultimate example of the love of God, this view is unbiblical because it denies the true spiritual condition of man—dead in transgressions and sins (Ephesians 2:1)—and denies that God actually requires a payment for sin. This view of Christ's atonement leaves mankind without a true sacrifice or payment for sin.

Example Theory: This view sees the atonement of Christ as simply providing an example of faith and obedience to inspire man to be obedient to God. Those who hold this view believe that man is spiritually alive and that Christ's life and atonement were simply an example of true faith and obedience and should serve as inspiration to men to live a similar life of faith and obedience. This and the moral influence theory are similar in that they both deny that God's justice actually requires payment for sin and that Christ's death on the cross was that payment. The main difference between the moral influence theory and the example theory is that the moral influence theory says that Christ's death teaches us how much God loves us and the example theory says that Christ's death teaches how to live. Of course, it is true that Christ is an example for us to follow, even in His death, but the example theory fails to recognize man's true spiritual condition and that God's justice requires payment for sin which man is not capable of paying.

Commercial Theory: The commercial theory views the atonement of Christ as bringing infinite honor to God. This resulted in God giving Christ a reward which He did not need, and Christ passed that reward on to man. Those who hold this view believe that man's spiritual condition is that of dishonoring God and so Christ's death, which brought infinite honor to God, can be applied to sinners for salvation. This theory, like many of the others, denies the true spiritual state of unregenerate sinners and their need of a completely new nature, available only in Christ (2 Corinthians 5:17).

293

Governmental Theory: This view sees the atonement of Christ as demonstrating God's high regard for His law and His attitude toward sin. It is through Christ's death that God has a reason to forgive the sins of those who repent and accept Christ's substitutionary death. Those who hold this view believe that man's spiritual condition is as one who has violated God's moral law and that the meaning of Christ's death was to be a substitute for the penalty of sin. Because Christ paid the penalty for sin, it is possible for God to legally forgive those who accept Christ as their substitute. This view falls short in that it does not teach that Christ actually paid the penalty of the actual sins of any people, but instead His suffering simply showed mankind that God's laws were broken and that some penalty was paid.

Penal Substitution Theory: This theory sees the atonement of Christ as being a vicarious, substitutionary sacrifice that satisfied the demands of God's justice upon sin. With His sacrifice, Christ paid the penalty of man's sin, bringing forgiveness, imputing righteousness, and reconciling man to God. Those who hold this view believe that every aspect of man—his mind, will, and emotions—have been corrupted by sin and that man is totally depraved and spiritually dead. This view holds that Christ's death paid the penalty for sin and that through faith man can accept Christ's substitution as payment for sin. This view of the atonement aligns most accurately with Scripture in its view of sin, the nature of man, and the results of the death of Christ on the cross.

Question: What is Christian apologetics?

Answer: The English word "apology" comes from a Greek word which basically means "to give a defense." Christian apologetics, then, is the science of giving a defense of the Christian faith. There are many skeptics who doubt the existence of God and/or attack belief in the God of the Bible. There are many critics who attack the inspiration and inerrancy of the Bible. There are many false teachers who promote false doctrines and deny the key truths of the Christian faith. The mission of Christian apologetics is to combat these movements and instead promote the Christian God and Christian truth.

Probably the key verse for Christian apologetics is 1 Peter 3:15, "But in your hearts set apart Christ as Lord. Always be prepared to give an answer to everyone who asks you to give the reason for the hope that you have. But do this with gentleness and respect..." There is no excuse for a Christian to be completely unable to defend his or her faith. Every Christian should be able to give a reasonable presentation of his or her faith in Christ. No, not every Christian needs to be an expert in apologetics. Every Christian, though, should know what he believes, why he believes it, how to share it with others, and how to defend it against lies and attacks.

A second aspect of Christian apologetics that is often ignored is the second half of 1 Peter 3:15, "but do this with gentleness and respect..." Defending the Christian faith with apologetics should never involve being rude, angry, or disrespectful. While practicing Christian apologetics, we should strive to be strong in our defense and at the same time Christ-like in our presentation. If we win a debate but turn a person even further away from Christ by our attitude, we have lost the true purpose of Christian apologetics.

There are two primary methods of Christian apologetics. The first, commonly known as classical apologetics, involves sharing proofs and evidences that the Christian message is true. The second, commonly known as "presuppositional" apologetics, involves confronting the presuppositions (preconceived ideas, assumptions) behind anti-Christian positions. Proponents of the two methods of Christian apologetics often debate each other as to which method is most effective. It would seem to be far more productive to be using both methods, depending on the person and situation.

Christian apologetics is simply presenting a reasonable defense of the Christian faith and truth to those who disagree. Christian apologetics is a necessary aspect of the Christian life. We are all commanded to be ready and equipped to proclaim the gospel and defend our faith (Matthew 28:18-20; 1 Peter 3:15). That is the essence of Christian apologetics.

Question: What is Christian ethics?

Answer: Christian ethics is well summarized by Colossians 3:1-6: "Since, then, you have been raised with Christ, set your hearts on things above, where Christ is seated at the right hand of God. Set your minds on things above, not on earthly things. For you died, and your life is now hidden with Christ in God. When Christ, who is your life, appears, then you also will appear with him in glory. Put to death, therefore, whatever belongs to your earthly nature: sexual immorality, impurity, lust, evil desires and greed, which is idolatry. Because of these, the wrath of God is coming."

While more than just a list of "do's" and "don'ts," the Bible does give us detailed instructions on how we should live. The Bible is all we need to know about how to live the Christian life. However, the Bible does not explicitly cover every situation we will face in our lives. How then is it sufficient for the all the ethical dilemmas we face? That is where Christian ethics comes in.

Science defines ethics as "a set of moral principles, the study of morality." Therefore, Christian ethics would be the principles derived from the Christian faith by which we act. While God's Word may not cover every situation we face throughout our lives, its principles give us the standards by which we must conduct ourselves in those situations where there are no explicit instructions.

For example, the Bible does not say anything explicitly about the use of illegal drugs, yet based on the principles we learn through Scripture, we can know that it is wrong. For one thing, the Bible tells us that the body is a temple of the Holy Spirit and that we should honor God with it (1 Corinthians 6:19-20). Knowing what drugs do to our bodies—the harm they cause to various organs—we know that by using them we would be destroying the temple of the Holy Spirit. That is certainly not honoring to God. The Bible also tells us that we are to follow the authorities that God Himself has put into place (Romans 13:1). Given the illegal nature of the drugs, by using them we are not submitting to the authorities but are rebelling against them. Does this mean if illegal drugs were legalized it would be ok? Not without violating the first principle.

By using the principles we find in Scripture, Christians can determine the ethical course for any given situation. In some cases it will be simple, like the rules for Christian living we find in Colossians, chapter 3. In other cases, however, we need to do a little digging. The best way to do that is to pray over God's Word. The Holy Spirit indwells every believer, and part of His role is teaching us how to live: "But the Counselor, the Holy Spirit, whom the Father will send in my name, will teach you all things and will remind you of everything I have said to you" (John 14:26). "As for you, the anointing you received from him remains in you, and you do not need anyone to teach you. But as his anointing teaches you about all things and as that anointing is real, not counterfeit—just as it has taught you, remain in him" (1 John 2:27). So, when we pray over Scripture, the Spirit will guide us and teach us. He will show us the principles we need to stand on for any given situation.

While God's Word does not cover every situation we will face in our lives, it is all-sufficient for living a Christian life. For most things, we can simply see what the Bible says and follow the proper course based on that. In ethical questions where Scripture does not give explicit instructions, we need to look for principles that can be applied to the situation. We must pray over His Word, and open ourselves to His Spirit. The Spirit will teach us and guide us through the Bible to find the principles on which we need to stand so we may live as a Christian should.

Question: What is divine providence?

Answer: Divine providence is the means by and through which God governs all things in the universe. The doctrine of divine providence asserts that God is in complete control of all things. This includes the universe as a whole (Psalm 103:19), the physical world (Matthew 5:45), the affairs of nations (Psalm 66:7), human birth and destiny (Galatians 1:15), human successes and failures (Luke 1:52), and the protection of His people (Psalm 4:8). This doctrine stands in direct opposition to the idea that the universe is governed by chance or fate.

The purpose, or goal, of divine providence is to accomplish the will of God. To ensure that His purposes are fulfilled, God governs the affairs of men and works through the natural order of things. The laws of nature are nothing more than a depiction of God at work in the universe. The laws of nature have no inherent power, nor do they work independently. The laws of nature are the rules and principles that God set in place to govern how things work.

The same goes for human choice. In a very real sense we are not free to choose or act apart from God's will. Everything we do and everything we choose is in full accordance to God's will—even our sinful choices (Genesis 50:20). The bottom line is that God controls our choices and actions (Genesis 45:5; Deuteronomy 8:18; Proverbs 21:1), yet He does so in such a way that does not violate our responsibility as free moral agents, nor does it negate the reality of our choice.

The doctrine of divine providence can be succinctly summarized this way: "God in eternity past, in the counsel of His own will, ordained everything that will happen; yet in no sense is God the author of sin; nor is human responsibility removed." The primary means by which God accomplishes His will is through secondary causes (e.g., laws of nature, human choice). In other words, God works indirectly through these secondary causes to accomplish His will.

God also sometimes works directly to accomplish His will. These works are what we would call miracles (i.e., supernatural events as opposed to natural). A miracle is God's circumventing, for a short period of time, the natural order of things to accomplish His will and purpose. Two examples from the book of Acts should serve to highlight God directly and indirectly working to accomplish His will. In Acts 9 we see the conversion of Saul of Tarsus. In a blinding flash of light and in a voice that only Saul/Paul heard, God changed his life forever. It was God's will to use Paul to further accomplish His will, and God used direct means to convert Paul. Talk to anyone who converted to Christianity, and you will more than likely never hear a story quite like this. Most of us come to Christ through hearing a sermon preached or reading a book or the persistent witness of a friend or family member. In addition to that, there are usually life circumstances that prepare the way—loss of a job, loss of a family member, failed marriage, chemical addiction. Paul's conversion was direct and supernatural.

In Acts 16:6-10, we see God accomplishing His will indirectly. This takes place during Paul's second missionary journey. God wanted Paul and his company to go to Troas, but when Paul left Antioch of Pisidia, he wanted to go east into Asia. The Bible says that the Holy Spirit forbade them to speak the word in Asia. Then they wanted to go west into Bythinia, but the Spirit of Christ prevented them, so they ended up going to Troas. This was written in retrospect, but at the time there were probably some logical explanations as to why they could not go into those two regions. However, after the fact, they realized that it was God directing them where He wanted them to go—that is providence. Proverbs 16:9 speaks to this: "The heart of a man plans his way, but the Lord establishes his steps."

On the other hand, there are those who will say that the concept of God directly or indirectly orchestrating all things destroys any possibility of free will. If God is in complete control, how can we be truly free in the decisions we make? In other words, for free will to be meaningful, there must be some things which are outside of God's sovereign control—e.g., the contingency of human choice. Let us assume for the sake of argument that this is true. What then? If God is not in complete control of all contingencies, then how could He guarantee our salvation? Paul says in Philippians 1:6 that "He who began a good work in you will bring it to completion at the day of Christ Jesus." If God is not in control of all things, then this promise, and all other biblical promises, are invalid. We could not have complete security that the good work of salvation that was begun in us will be brought to completion.

Furthermore, if God is not in control of all things, then He is not sovereign, and if He is not sovereign, then He is not God. So, the price of maintaining contingencies outside of God's control results in a God who is no God at all. And if our "free" will can supersede divine providence, then who ultimately is God? We are. That is, obviously, unacceptable to anyone with a Christian and biblical worldview. Divine providence does not destroy our freedom. Rather, divine providence is what enables us to properly use that freedom.

Question: What is general revelation and special revelation?

Answer: General revelation and special revelation are the two ways God has chosen to reveal Himself to humanity. General revelation refers to the general truths that can be known about God through nature. Special revelation refers to the more specific truths that can be known about God through the supernatural.

In regard to general revelation, Psalm 19:1-4 declares, "The heavens declare the glory of God; the skies proclaim the work of His hands. Day after day they pour forth speech; night after night they display knowledge. There is no speech or language where their voice is not heard. Their voice goes out into all the earth, their words to the ends of the world." According to this passage, God's existence and power can be clearly seen through observing the universe. The order, intricacy, and wonder of creation speak to the existence of a powerful and glorious Creator.

General revelation is also taught in Romans 1:20, "For since the creation of the world God's invisible qualities—His eternal power and divine nature—have been clearly seen, being understood from what has been made, so that men are without excuse." Like Psalm 19, Romans 1:20 teaches that God's eternal power and divine nature are "clearly seen" and "understood" from what has been made, and that there is no excuse for denying these facts. With these Scriptures in mind, perhaps a working definition of general revelation would be "the revelation of God to all people, at all times, and in all places that proves that God exists and that He is intelligent, powerful, and transcendent."

Special revelation is how God has chosen to reveal Himself through miraculous means. Special revelation includes physical appearances of God, dreams, visions, the written Word of God, and most importantly—Jesus Christ. The Bible records God appearing in physical form many times (Genesis 3:8, 18:1; Exodus 3:1-4, 34:5-7), and the Bible records God speaking to people through dreams (Genesis 28:12, 37:5; 1 Kings 3:5; Daniel 2) and visions (Genesis 15:1; Ezekiel 8:3-4; Daniel 7; 2 Corinthians 12:1-7).

Of primary importance in the revealing of God is His Word, the Bible, which is also a form of special revelation. God miraculously guided the authors of Scripture to correctly record His message to mankind, while still using their own styles and personalities. The Word of God is living and active (Hebrews 4:12). The Word of God is inspired, profitable, and sufficient (2 Timothy 3:16-17). God determined to have the truth regarding Him recorded in written form because He knew the inaccuracy and unreliability of oral tradition. He also understood that the dreams and visions of man can be misinterpreted. God decided to reveal everything that humanity needs to know about Him, what He expects, and what He has done for us in the Bible.

The ultimate form of special revelation is the Person of Jesus Christ. God became a human being (John 1:1, 14). Hebrews 1:1-3 summarizes it best, "In the past God spoke to our forefathers through the prophets at many times and in various ways, but in these last days he has spoken to us by his Son … The Son is the radiance of God's glory and the exact representation of his being." God became a human being, in the Person of Jesus Christ, to identify with us, to set an example for us, to teach us, to reveal Himself to us, and, most importantly, to provide salvation for us by humbling Himself in death on the cross (Philippians 2:6-8). Jesus Christ is the ultimate "special revelation" from God.

Question: What is Trinitarianism? Is Trinitarianism biblical?

Answer: Trinitarianism is the teaching that God is triune, that He has revealed Himself in three co-equal and co-eternal Persons. For a detailed biblical presentation of the Trinity, please see our article on what the Bible teaches about the Trinity. The purpose of this article is to discuss the importance of Trinitarianism in regard to salvation and the Christian life.

We are often asked the question, "Do I have to believe in the Trinity to be saved?" The answer is yes and no. Does a person have to fully understand and agree with every aspect of Trinitarianism to be saved? No. Are there some aspects of Trinitarianism that play key roles in salvation? Yes. For example, the deity of Christ is crucially important to the doctrine of salvation. If Jesus were not God, His death could not have paid the infinite penalty of sin. Only God is infinite—He had no beginning, and He has no end. All other creatures, including angels, are finite; they were created at some point. Only the death of an infinite Being could atone for the sin of mankind throughout eternity. If Jesus were not God, He could not be the Savior, the Messiah, the Lamb of God who takes away the sin of the world (John 1:29). An unbiblical view of Jesus' divine nature results in an errant view of salvation. Every "Christian" cult that denies the true deity of Christ also teaches that we must add our own works to Christ's death in order to be saved. The true and full deity of Christ, an aspect of Trinitarianism, refutes this concept.

At the same time, we recognize that there are some genuine believers in Christ who do not hold to full Trinitarianism. While we reject modalism, we do not deny that a person can be saved while holding that God is not three Persons, but rather simply revealed Himself in three "modes." The Trinity is a mystery, which no finite human being can fully, or perfectly, understand. For salvation to be received, God requires us to trust in Jesus Christ, God incarnate, as the Savior. For salvation to be received, God does not require complete adherence to every precept of sound biblical theology. No, full understanding and agreement with all aspects of Trinitarianism is not required for salvation.

We strongly hold that Trinitarianism is a biblically-based doctrine. We dogmatically proclaim that understanding and believing in biblical Trinitarianism is crucially important to understanding God, salvation, and the ongoing work of God in the lives of believers. At the same time, there have been godly men, genuine followers of Christ, who have had some disagreements with aspects of Trinitarianism. It is important to remember that we are not saved by having perfect doctrine. We are saved by trusting in our perfect Savior (John 3:16). Do we have to believe in some aspects of Trinitarianism to be saved? Yes. Do we have to fully agree with all areas of Trinitarianism to be saved? No.

Question: What is replacement theology?

Answer: Replacement theology essentially teaches that the church has replaced Israel in God's plan. Adherents of replacement theology believe the Jews are no longer God's chosen people, and God does not have specific future plans for the nation of Israel. All the different views of the relationship between the church and Israel can be divided into two camps: either the church is a continuation of Israel (replacement/covenant theology), or the church is completely different and distinct from Israel (dispensationalism/premillennialism).

Replacement theology teaches that the church is the replacement for Israel and that the many promises made to Israel in the Bible are fulfilled in the Christian church, not in Israel. So, the prophecies in Scripture concerning the blessing and restoration of Israel to the Promised Land are "spiritualized" or "allegorized" into promises of

302

God's blessing for the church. Major problems exist with this view, such as the continuing existence of the Jewish people throughout the centuries and especially with the revival of the modern state of Israel. If Israel has been condemned by God, and there is no future for the Jewish nation, how do we explain the supernatural survival of the Jewish people over the past 2000 years despite the many attempts to destroy them? How do we explain why and how Israel reappeared as a nation in the 20th century after not existing for 1900 years?

The view that Israel and the church are different is clearly taught in the New Testament. Biblically speaking, the church is completely different and distinct from Israel, and the two are never to be confused or used interchangeably. We are taught from Scripture that the church is an entirely new creation that came into being on the day of Pentecost and will continue until it is taken to heaven at the rapture (Ephesians 1:9-11; 1 Thessalonians 4:13-17). The church has no relationship to the curses and blessings for Israel. The covenants, promises, and warnings are valid only for Israel. Israel has been temporarily set aside in God's program during these past 2000 years of dispersion.

After the rapture (1 Thessalonians 4:13-18), God will restore Israel as the primary focus of His plan. The first event at this time is the tribulation (Revelation chapters 6-19). The world will be judged for rejecting Christ, while Israel is prepared through the trials of the great tribulation for the second coming of the Messiah. Then, when Christ does return to the earth, at the end of the tribulation, Israel will be ready to receive Him. The remnant of Israel which survives the tribulation will be saved, and the Lord will establish His kingdom on this earth with Jerusalem as its capital. With Christ reigning as King, Israel will be the leading nation, and representatives from all nations will come to Jerusalem to honor and worship the King—Jesus Christ. The church will return with Christ and will reign with Him for a literal thousand years (Revelation 20:1-5).

Both the Old Testament and the New Testament support a premillennial/dispensational understanding of God's plan for Israel. Even so, the strongest support for premillennialism is found in the clear teaching of Revelation 20:1-7, where it says six times that Christ's kingdom will last 1000 years. After the tribulation the Lord will return and establish His kingdom with the nation of Israel, Christ will reign over the whole earth, and Israel will be the leader of the nations. The church will reign with Him for a literal thousand years. The church has not replaced Israel in God's plan. While God may be focusing His attention primarily on the church in this dispensation of grace, God has not forgotten Israel and will one day restore Israel to His intended role as the nation He has chosen (Romans 11).

Chapter 11

· ·

QUESTIONS ABOUT THE

CHRISTIAN LIFE

CONTENTS

What is a Christian? 306

What is the meaning of life? 307

How can I know God's will for my life? What does the Bible say about knowing God's will? 310

Do Christians have to obey the Old Testament law? 310

How can I overcome sin in my Christian life? 311

What does the Bible say about Christian tithing? 314

How can I evangelize my friends and family? 315

Christian fasting—what does the Bible say? 316

How can I forgive those who sin against me? 317

What is spiritual growth? 318

What does the Bible say about spiritual warfare? 319

How can we recognize the voice of God? 321

What is a carnal Christian? 322

Why are all Christians hypocrites? 323

How can I experience joy in my Christian life? 325

What is Christian meditation? 326

What is Christian spirituality? 327

Why do we need to confess our sins if they have already been forgiven (1 John 1:9)? 328

If I am saved and all of my sins are forgiven, why not continue to sin? ...329

When, why, and how does the Lord God discipline us when we sin? 331

How should a Christian deal with feelings of guilt regarding past sins, whether pre- or post-salvation? 331

What does the Bible say about legalism? 333

Who am I in Christ? 334

Question: What is a Christian?

Answer: A dictionary definition of a Christian would be something similar to "a person professing belief in Jesus as the Christ or in the religion based on the teachings of Jesus." While this is a good starting point, like many dictionary definitions, it falls somewhat short of really communicating the biblical truth of what it means to be a Christian. The word "Christian" is used three times in the New Testament (Acts 11:26; 26:28; 1 Peter 4:16). Followers of Jesus Christ were first called "Christians" in Antioch (Acts 11:26) because their behavior, activity, and speech were like Christ. The word "Christian" literally means, "belonging to the party of Christ" or a "follower of Christ."

Unfortunately over time, the word "Christian" has lost a great deal of its significance and is often used of someone who is religious or has high moral values but who may or may not be a true follower of Jesus Christ. Many people who do not believe and trust in Jesus Christ consider themselves Christians simply because they go to church or they live in a "Christian" nation. But going to church, serving those less fortunate than you, or being a good person does not make you a Christian. Going to church does not make you a Christian anymore than going to a garage makes you an automobile. Being a member of a church, attending services regularly, and giving to the work of the church does not make you a Christian.

The Bible teaches that the good works we do cannot make us acceptable to God. Titus 3:5 says, "He saved us, not because of righteous things we had done, but because of his mercy. He saved us through the washing of rebirth and renewal by the Holy Spirit." So, a Christian is someone who has been born again by God (John 3:3; John 3:7; 1 Peter 1:23) and has put faith and trust in Jesus Christ. Ephesians 2:8 tells us that it is "...by grace you have been saved, through faith—and this not from yourselves, it is the gift of God."

A true Christian is a person who has put faith and trust in the person and work of Jesus Christ, including His death on the cross as payment for sins and His resurrection on the third day. John 1:12 tells us, "Yet to all who received him, to those who believed in his name, he gave the right to become children of God." The mark of a true Christian is love for others and obedience to God's Word (1 John 2:4, 10). A true

306

Christian is indeed a child of God, a part of God's true family, and one who has been given new life in Jesus Christ.

Question: What is the meaning of life?

Answer: What is the meaning of life? How can purpose, fulfillment, and satisfaction in life be found? How can something of lasting significance be achieved? So many people have never stopped to consider these important questions. They look back years later and wonder why their relationships have fallen apart and why they feel so empty, even though they may have achieved what they set out to accomplish. An athlete who had reached the pinnacle of his sport was once asked what he wished someone would have told him when he first started playing his sport. He replied, "I wish that someone would have told me that when you reach the top, there's nothing there." Many goals reveal their emptiness only after years have been wasted in their pursuit.

In our humanistic culture, people pursue many things, thinking that in them they will find meaning. Some of these pursuits include business success, wealth, good relationships, sex, entertainment, and doing good to others. People have testified that while they achieved their goals of wealth, relationships, and pleasure, there was still a deep void inside, a feeling of emptiness that nothing seemed to fill.

The author of the biblical book of Ecclesiastes describes this feeling when he says, "Meaningless! Meaningless! ...Utterly meaningless! Everything is meaningless" (Ecclesiastes 1:2). King Solomon, the writer of Ecclesiastes, had wealth beyond measure, wisdom beyond any man of his time or ours, hundreds of women, palaces and gardens that were the envy of kingdoms, the best food and wine, and every form of entertainment available. He said at one point that anything his heart wanted, he pursued. And yet he summed up "life under the sun"—life lived as though all there is to life is what we can see with our eyes and experience with our senses—is meaningless. Why is there such a void? Because God created us for something beyond what we can experience in the here-and-now. Solomon said of God, "He has also set eternity in the hearts of men..." (Ecclesiastes 3:11). In our hearts we are aware that the "here-and-now" is not all that there is.

In Genesis, the first book of the Bible, we find that God created mankind in His image (Genesis 1:26). This means that we are more like God than we are like anything else (any other life form). We also find that before mankind fell into sin and the curse of sin came upon the earth, the following things were true: 1) God made man a social creature (Genesis 2:18-25); 2) God gave man work (Genesis 2:15); 3) God had fellowship with man (Genesis 3:8); and 4) God gave man dominion over the earth (Genesis 1:26). What is the significance of these things? God intended for each of these to add to our fulfillment in life, but all of these (especially man's fellowship with God) were adversely affected by man's fall into sin and the resulting curse upon the earth (Genesis 3).

In Revelation, the last book of the Bible, God reveals that He will destroy this present earth and heavens and usher in the eternal state by creating a new heaven and a new earth. At that time, He will restore full fellowship with redeemed mankind, while the unredeemed will have been judged unworthy and cast into the lake of fire (Revelation 20:11-15). The curse of sin will be done away with; there will be no more sin, sorrow, sickness, death, or pain (Revelation 21:4). God will dwell with them, and they shall be His sons (Revelation 21:7). Thus, we come full circle: God created us to have fellowship with Him, man sinned, breaking that fellowship, God restores that fellowship fully in the eternal state. To go through life achieving everything only to die separated from God for eternity would be worse than futile! But God has made a way to not only make eternal bliss possible (Luke 23:43) but also life on earth satisfying and meaningful. How is this eternal bliss and "heaven on earth" obtained?

Meaning of life restored through Jesus Christ

Real meaning in life, both now and in eternity, is found in the restoration of the relationship with God that was lost with Adam and Eve's fall into sin. That relationship with God is only possible through His Son, Jesus Christ (Acts 4:12; John 1:12; 14:6). Eternal life is gained when we repent of our sin (no longer want to continue in it) and Christ changes us, making of us new creations, and we rely on Jesus Christ as Savior.

Real meaning in life is not found only in accepting Jesus as Savior, as wonderful as that is. Rather, real meaning in life is when one begins to follow Christ as His disciple, learning of Him, spending time with Him in His Word, communing with Him in prayer, and in walking with Him in obedience to His commands. If you are not a Christian (or perhaps a new believer), you might be saying to yourself, "That does not sound very exciting or fulfilling to me!" But Jesus made the following statements:

"Come to me, all you who are weary and burdened, and I will give you rest. Take my yoke upon you and learn from me, for I am gentle and humble in heart, and you will find rest for your souls. For my yoke is easy and my burden is light" (Matthew 11:28-30). "I have come that they may have life, and have it to the full" (John 10:10b). "If anyone would come after me, he must deny himself and take up his cross and follow me. For whoever wants to save his life will lose it, but whoever loses his life for me will find it" (Matthew 16:24-25). "Delight yourself in the LORD and he will give you the desires of your heart" (Psalm 37:4).

What all of these verses are saying is that we have a choice. We can continue to seek to guide our own lives, which results in emptiness, or we can choose to pursue God and His will for our lives with a whole heart, which will result in living life to the full, having the desires of our hearts met, and finding contentment and satisfaction. This is so because our Creator loves us and desires the best for us (not necessarily the easiest life, but the most fulfilling).

The Christian life can be compared to the choice of whether to purchase the expensive seats at a sporting event that are close to the action, or pay less and watch the game from a distance. Watching God work "from the front row" is what we should choose but, sadly, is not what most people choose. Watching God work firsthand is for whole-hearted disciples of Christ who have truly stopped pursuing their own desires to pursue instead God's purposes. They have paid the price (complete surrender to Christ and His will); they are experiencing life to its fullest; and they can face themselves, their fellow man, and their Maker with no regrets. Have you paid the price? Are you willing to? If so, you will not hunger after meaning or purpose again.

Question: How can I know God's will for my life? What does the Bible say about knowing God's will?

Answer: There are two keys to knowing God's will for a given situation: 1) Make sure what you are asking for or considering doing is not something the Bible forbids. 2) Make sure what you are asking for or considering doing will glorify God and help you grow spiritually. If these two things are true and God still is not giving you what you are asking, then it is likely not God's will for you to have what you are asking for. Or, perhaps you just need to wait a while longer for it. Knowing God's will is sometimes difficult. People want God to tell them specifically what to do—where to work, where to live, whom to marry, etc. God rarely gives people information that direct and specific. God allows us to make choices regarding those things.

Romans 12:2 tells us, "Do not conform any longer to the pattern of this world, but be transformed by the renewing of your mind. Then you will be able to test and approve what God's will is—His good, pleasing and perfect will." The only decision God does not want us to make is the decision to sin or resist His will. God wants us to make choices that are in agreement with His will. So, how do you know what God's will is for you? If you are walking closely with the Lord and truly desiring His will for your life, God will place His desires on your heart. The key is wanting God's will, not your own. "Delight yourself in the LORD and He will give you the desires of your heart" (Psalm 37:4). If the Bible does not speak against it and it can genuinely benefit you spiritually, then the Bible gives you the "permission" to make decisions and to follow your heart. If you truly seek God's will with a humble spirit and an open mind, He will reveal His will to you.

Question: Do Christians have to obey the Old Testament law?

Answer: The key to understanding this issue is knowing that the Old Testament law was given to the nation of Israel, not to Christians. Some of the laws were to reveal to the Israelites how to obey and please God (the Ten Commandments, for example). Some of the laws were to show the Israelites how to worship God and atone for sin (the sacrificial system). Some of the laws were intended to make the Israelites distinct from other nations (the food and clothing rules).

None of the Old Testament law is binding on us today. When Jesus died on the cross, He put an end to the Old Testament law (Romans 10:4; Galatians 3:23-25; Ephesians 2:15).

In place of the Old Testament law, we are under the law of Christ (Galatians 6:2), which is to "love the Lord your God with all your heart and with all your soul and with all your mind…and to love your neighbor as yourself" (Matthew 22:37-39). If we obey those two commands, we will be fulfilling all that Christ requires of us: "All the Law and the Prophets hang on these two commandments" (Matthew 22:40). Now, this does not mean the Old Testament law is irrelevant today. Many of the commands in the Old Testament law fall into the categories of "loving God" and "loving your neighbor." The Old Testament law can be a good guidepost for knowing how to love God and knowing what goes into loving your neighbor. At the same time, to say that the Old Testament law applies to Christians today is incorrect. The Old Testament law is a unit (James 2:10). Either all of it applies, or none of it applies. If Christ fulfilled some it, such as the sacrificial system, He fulfilled all of it.

"This is love for God: to obey his commands. And his commands are not burdensome" (1 John 5:3). The Ten Commandments were essentially a summary of the entire Old Testament law. Nine of the Ten Commandments are clearly repeated in the New Testament (all except the command to observe the Sabbath day). Obviously, if we are loving God, we will not be worshipping false gods or bowing down before idols. If we are loving our neighbors, we will not be murdering them, lying to them, committing adultery against them, or coveting what belongs to them. The purpose of the Old Testament law is to convict people of our inability to keep the law and point us to our need for Jesus Christ as Savior (Romans 7:7-9; Galatians 3:24). The Old Testament law was never intended by God to be the universal law for all people for all of time. We are to love God and love our neighbors. If we obey those two commands faithfully, we will be upholding all that God requires of us.

Question: How can I overcome sin in my Christian life?

Answer: The Bible presents several different resources to aid us in our effort to overcome sin. In this lifetime, we will never be perfectly victorious over sin (1 John 1:8), but that should still be our goal. With God's help, and by following the principles of His Word, we can progressively overcome sin and become more and more like Christ.

The first resource the Bible mentions in our effort to overcome sin is the Holy Spirit. God has given us the Holy Spirit so we can be victorious in Christian living. God contrasts the deeds of the flesh with the fruit of the Spirit in Galatians 5:16-25. In that passage we are called upon to walk in the Spirit. All believers already possess the Holy Spirit, but this passage tells us that we need to walk in the Spirit, yielding to His control. This means choosing to consistently follow the Holy Spirit's prompting in our lives rather than following the flesh.

The difference the Holy Spirit can make is demonstrated in the life of Peter, who, before being filled with the Holy Spirit, denied Jesus three times—and this after he had said he would follow Christ to the death. After being filled with the Spirit, he spoke openly and strongly to the Jews at Pentecost.

We walk in the Spirit as we try not to quench the Spirit's promptings (as spoken of in 1 Thessalonians 5:19) and seek instead to be filled with the Spirit (Ephesians 5:18-21). How is one filled with the Holy Spirit? First of all, it is of God's choosing even as it was in the Old Testament. He selected individuals to accomplish a work that He wanted done and filled them with His Spirit (Genesis 41:38; Exodus 31:3; Numbers 24:2; 1 Samuel 10:10). There is evidence in Ephesians 5:18-21 and Colossians 3:16 that God chooses to fill those who are filling themselves with the Word of God. This leads us to the second resource.

The Word of God, the Bible, says that God has given us His Word to equip us for every good work (2 Timothy 3:16-17). It teaches us how to live and what to believe, it reveals to us when we have chosen wrong paths, it helps us get back on the right path, and it helps us to stay on that path. Hebrews 4:12 tells us that the Word of God is living and powerful, able to penetrate to our hearts to root out and overcome the deepest sins of heart and attitude. The psalmist talks about its life-changing power in-depth in Psalm 119. Joshua was told that the key to success in overcoming his enemies was not to forget this resource but instead to meditate on it day and night and obey it. This he did, even when what God commanded did not make sense militarily, and this was the key to his victory in his battles for the Promised Land.

The Bible is a resource that we too often treat lightly. We give token service to it by carrying our Bibles to church or reading a daily devotional or a chapter a day, but we fail to memorize it, meditate on it, or apply it to our lives; we fail to confess the sins it reveals or praise God for the gifts it reveals to us. When it comes to the Bible, we are often either anorexic or bulimic. We either take in just enough to keep us alive spiritually by eating from the Word (but never ingesting enough to be healthy, thriving Christians), or we come to feed often but never meditate on it long enough to get spiritual nutrition from it.

It is important, if you have not made a habit of daily studying and memorizing God's Word, that you begin to do so. Some find it helpful start a journal. Make it a habit not to leave the Word until you have written down something you have gained from it. Some record prayers to God, asking Him to help them change in the areas that He has spoken to them about. The Bible is the tool the Spirit uses in our lives (Ephesians 6:17), an essential and major part of the armor that God gives us to fight our spiritual battles (Ephesians 6:12-18).

A third crucial resource in our battle against sin is prayer. Again, it is a resource that Christians often give lip service to but make poor use of. We have prayer meetings, times of prayer, etc., but we do not use prayer in the same way as the early church (Acts 3:1; 4:31; 6:4; 13:1-3). Paul repeatedly mentions how he prayed for those he ministered to. God has given us wonderful promises concerning prayer (Matthew 7:7-11; Luke 18:1-8; John 6:23-27; 1 John 5:14-15), and Paul includes prayer in his passage on preparing for spiritual battle (Ephesians 6:18).

How important is prayer to overcoming sin in our lives? We have Christ's words to Peter in the Garden of Gethsemane, just before Peter's denial. As Jesus prays, Peter is sleeping. Jesus wakes him and says, "Watch and pray so that you will not fall into temptation. The spirit is willing, but the body is weak" (Matthew 26:41). We, like Peter, want to do what is right but are not finding the strength. We need to follow God's admonition to keep seeking, keep knocking, keep asking—and He will give us the strength that we need (Matthew 7:7). Prayer is not a magic formula. Prayer is simply acknowledging our own limitations and God's inexhaustible power and turning to Him for that strength to do what He wants us to do, not what *we* want to do (1 John 5:14-15).

A fourth resource in our war to conquer sin is the church, the fellowship of other believers. When Jesus sent His disciples out, He sent them out two-by-two (Matthew 10:1). The missionaries in Acts did not go out one at a time, but in groups of two or more. Jesus commands us not to forsake the assembling of ourselves together but to use that time for encouraging one another in love and good works (Hebrews 10:24). He tells us to confess our faults to one another (James 5:16). In the wisdom literature of the Old Testament, we are told that as iron sharpens iron, so one man sharpens another (Proverbs 27:17). There is strength in numbers (Ecclesiastes 4:11-12).

Many Christians find that having an accountability partner can be a huge benefit in overcoming stubborn sins. Having another person who can talk with you, pray with you, encourage you, and even rebuke you is of great value. Temptation is common to us all (1 Corinthians 10:13). Having an accountability partner or an accountability group can give us the final dose of encouragement and motivation we need to overcome even the most stubborn of sins.

Sometimes victory over sin comes quickly. Other times, victory comes more slowly. God has promised that as we make use of His resources, He will progressively bring about change in our lives. We can persevere in our efforts to overcome sin because we know that He is faithful to His promises.

Question: What does the Bible say about Christian tithing?

Answer: Many Christians struggle with the issue of tithing. In some churches tithing is over-emphasized. At the same time, many Christians refuse to submit to the biblical exhortations about making offerings to the Lord. Tithing/giving is intended to be a joy and a blessing. Sadly, that is sometimes not the case in the church today.

Tithing is an Old Testament concept. The tithe was a requirement of the law in which all Israelites were to give 10 percent of everything they earned and grew to the Tabernacle/Temple (Leviticus 27:30; Numbers 18:26; Deuteronomy 14:24; 2 Chronicles 31:5). In fact, the Old Testament Law required multiple tithes which would have pushed the total to around 23.3 percent, not the 10 percent which is generally considered the tithe amount today. Some understand the Old Testament tithe as a method of taxation to provide for the needs of the priests and Levites in the sacrificial system. The New Testament nowhere commands, or even recommends, that Christians submit to a legalistic tithe system. Paul states that believers should set aside a portion of their income in order to support the church (1 Corinthians 16:1-2).

The New Testament nowhere designates a percentage of income a person should set aside, but only says it is to be "in keeping with income" (1 Corinthians 16:2). Some in the Christian church have taken the 10 percent figure from the Old Testament tithe and applied it as a "recommended minimum" for Christians in their giving. The New Testament talks about the importance and benefits of giving. We are to give as we are able. Sometimes that means giving more than 10 percent; sometimes that may mean giving less. It all depends on the ability of the Christian and the needs of the church. Every Christian should diligently pray and seek God's wisdom in the matter of participating in tithing and/or how much to give (James 1:5). Above all, all tithes and offerings should be given with pure motives and an attitude of worship to God and service to the body of Christ. "Each man should give what he has decided in his heart to give, not reluctantly or under compulsion, for God loves a cheerful giver" (2 Corinthians 9:7).

Question: How can I evangelize my friends and family without pushing them away?

Answer: At some point, every Christian has had a family member, a friend, co-worker, or acquaintance who is not a Christian. Sharing the gospel with others can be difficult, and it can become even more difficult when it involves someone with whom you have close emotional ties. The Bible tells us that some people will be offended at the gospel (Luke 12:51-53). However, we are commanded to share the gospel, and there is no excuse for not doing so (Matthew 28:19-20; Acts 1:8; 1 Peter 3:15).

So, how can we evangelize our family members, friends, co-workers, and acquaintances? The most important thing we can do is pray for them. Pray that God would change their hearts and open their eyes (2 Corinthians 4:4) to the truth of the gospel. Pray that God would convince them of His love for them and their need for salvation through Jesus Christ (John 3:16). Pray for wisdom as to how you can minister to them (James 1:5). In addition to praying, we must also live godly Christian lives in front of them, so they can see the change God has made in our own lives (1 Peter 3:1-2). As Saint Francis of Assisi once said, "Preach the gospel at all times and when necessary use words."

Finally, we must be willing and bold in our actual sharing of the gospel. Proclaim the message of salvation through Jesus Christ to your friends and family (Romans 10:9-10). Always be prepared to speak of your faith (1 Peter 3:15), doing so with gentleness and respect. Ultimately, we must leave the salvation of our loved ones up to God. It is God's power and grace that saves people, not our efforts. The best and most we can do is pray for them, witness to them, and live the Christian life in front of them.

Question: Christian fasting—what does the Bible say?

Answer: Scripture does not command Christians to fast. God does not require or demand it of Christians. At the same time, the Bible presents fasting as something that is good, profitable, and beneficial. The book of Acts records believers fasting before they made important decisions (Acts 13:4, 14:23). Fasting and prayer are often linked together (Luke 2:37; 5:33). Too often, the focus of fasting is on the lack of food. Instead, the purpose of fasting should be to take your eyes off the things of this world to focus completely on God. Fasting is a way to demonstrate to God, and to ourselves, that we are serious about our relationship with Him. Fasting helps us gain a new perspective and a renewed reliance upon God.

Although fasting in Scripture is almost always a fasting from food, there are other ways to fast. Anything given up temporarily in order to focus all our attention on God can be considered a fast (1 Corinthians 7:1-5). Fasting should be limited to a set time, especially when fasting from food. Extended periods of time without eating can be harmful to the body. Fasting is not intended to punish the flesh, but to redirect attention to God. Fasting should not be considered a "dieting method" either. The purpose of a biblical fast is not to lose weight, but rather to gain deeper fellowship with God. Anyone can fast, but some may not be able to fast from food (diabetics, for example). Everyone can temporarily give up something in order to draw closer to God.

By taking our eyes off the things of this world, we can more successfully turn our attention to Christ. Fasting is not a way to get God to do what we want. Fasting changes us, not God. Fasting is not a way to appear more spiritual than others. Fasting is to be done in a spirit of humility and a joyful attitude. Matthew 6:16-18 declares, "When you fast, do not look somber as the hypocrites do, for they disfigure their faces to show men they are fasting. I tell you the truth, they have received their reward in full. But when you fast, put oil on your head and wash your face, so that it will not be obvious to men that you are fasting, but only to your Father, who is unseen; and your Father, who sees what is done in secret, will reward you."

Question: How can I forgive those who sin against me?

Answer: Everyone has been wronged, offended, and sinned against at some point. How are Christians to respond when such offenses occur? According to the Bible, we are to forgive. Ephesians 4:32 declares, "Be kind and compassionate to one another, forgiving each other, just as in Christ God forgave you." Similarly, Colossians 3:13 proclaims, "Bear with each other and forgive whatever grievances you may have against one another. Forgive as the Lord forgave you." The key in both Scriptures is that we are to forgive others as God has forgiven us. Why do we forgive? Because we have been forgiven! Those who are not Christians, however, have not been forgiven by God and have neither the power nor the desire to forgive others.

Forgiveness would be simple if we only had to grant it to those who come asking for it in sorrow and repentance. The Bible tells us that we are to forgive, without condition, those who sin against us. Refusing to truly forgive a person demonstrates resentment, bitterness, and anger, none of which are the traits of a true Christian. In the Lord's Prayer, we ask God to forgive us our sins, just as we forgive those who sin against us (Matthew 6:12). Jesus said in Matthew 6:14-15, "If you forgive those who sin against you, your heavenly Father will forgive you. But if you refuse to forgive others, your Father will not forgive your sins." In light of other Scriptures that speak of God's forgiveness, Matthew 6:14-15 is best understood to be saying that people who refuse to forgive others have not truly experienced God's forgiveness themselves.

Whenever we disobey one of God's commands, we sin against Him. Whenever we wrong another person, we not only sin against that person, but also against God. When we consider the extent to which God forgives *all* our transgressions, we realize that we do not have the right to withhold this grace from others. We have sinned against God infinitely more than any person can sin against us. If God forgives us of so much, how can we refuse to forgive others of so little? Jesus' parable in Matthew 18:23-35 is a powerful illustration of this truth. God promises that when we come to Him asking for forgiveness, He freely grants it (1 John 1:9). The forgiveness we extend should know no limits, in the same way that God's forgiveness is limitless (Luke 17:3-4).

Question: What is spiritual growth?

Answer: Spiritual growth is the process of becoming more and more like Jesus Christ. When we place our faith in Jesus, the Holy Spirit begins the process of making us more like Him, conforming us to His image. Spiritual growth is perhaps best described in 2 Peter 1:3-8, which tells us that by God's power we have "everything we need" to live lives of godliness, which is the goal of spiritual growth. Notice that what we need comes "through our knowledge of Him," which is the key to obtaining everything we need. Our knowledge of Him comes from the Word, given to us for our edification and growth.

There are two lists in Galatians 5:19-23. Verses 19-21 list the "acts of the flesh." These are the things that identified our lives before we came to Christ for salvation. The acts of the flesh are the activities we are to confess, repent of, and, with God's help, overcome. As we experience spiritual growth, fewer and fewer of the "acts of the flesh" will be evident in our lives. The second list is the "fruit of the Spirit" (verses 22-23). These are what should characterize our lives now that we have experienced salvation in Jesus Christ. Spiritual growth is identified by the fruit of the Spirit becoming increasingly evident in a believer's life.

When the transformation of salvation takes place, spiritual growth begins. The Holy Spirit indwells us (John 14:16-17). We are new creatures in Christ (2 Corinthians 5:17). The old nature is replaced with a new one (Romans 6-7). Spiritual growth is a life-long process that depends on our study and application of God's Word (2 Timothy 3:16-17) and our walk in the Spirit (Galatians 5:16-26). As we seek spiritual growth, we should pray to God and ask for wisdom concerning the areas He desires us to grow in. We can ask God to increase our faith and knowledge of Him. God desires for us to grow spiritually, and He has given us all we need to experience spiritual growth. With the Holy Spirit's help, we can overcome sin and steadily become more like our Savior, the Lord Jesus Christ.

Question: What does the Bible say about spiritual warfare?

Answer: There are two primary errors when it comes to spiritual warfare—over-emphasis and under-emphasis. Some blame every sin, every conflict, and every problem on demons that need to be cast out. Others completely ignore the spiritual realm and the fact that the Bible tells us our battle is against spiritual powers. The key to successful spiritual warfare is finding the biblical balance. Jesus sometimes cast demons out of people and sometimes healed people with no mention of the demonic. The apostle Paul instructs Christians to wage war against the sin in themselves (Romans 6) and to wage war against the evil one (Ephesians 6:10-18).

Ephesians 6:10-12 declares, "Finally, be strong in the Lord and in his mighty power. Put on the full armor of God so that you can take your stand against the devil's schemes. For our struggle is not against flesh and blood, but against the rulers, against the authorities, against the powers of this dark world and against the spiritual forces of evil in the heavenly realms." This text teaches some crucial truths: we can only be strong in the Lord's power, it is God's armor that protects us, and our battle is against spiritual forces of evil in the world.

A powerful example of someone strong in the Lord's power is Michael, the archangel, in Jude 9. Michael, likely the most powerful of all of God's angels, did not rebuke Satan in his own power, but said, "The Lord rebuke you!" Revelation 12:7-8 records that in the end times Michael will defeat Satan. Still, when it came to his conflict with Satan, Michael rebuked Satan in God's name and authority, not his own. It is only through our relationship with Jesus Christ that Christians have any authority over Satan and his demons. It is only in His Name that our rebuke has any power.

Ephesians 6:13-18 gives a description of the spiritual armor God gives us. We are to stand firm with the belt of truth, the breastplate of righteousness, the gospel of peace, the shield of faith, the helmet of salvation, the sword of the Spirit, and by praying in the Spirit. What do these pieces of spiritual armor represent in spiritual warfare? We are to speak the truth against Satan's lies. We are to rest in the fact that we are declared righteous because of Christ's sacrifice for us. We are to proclaim the gospel no matter how much resistance we receive. We are not to waver in our faith, no matter how strongly we are attacked. Our ultimate defense is the assurance we have of our salvation, an assurance that no spiritual force can take away. Our offensive weapon is the Word of God, not our own opinions and feelings. We are to follow Jesus' example in recognizing that some spiritual victories are only possible through prayer.

Jesus is our ultimate example for spiritual warfare. Observe how Jesus handled direct attacks from Satan when He was tempted by him in the wilderness (Matthew 4:1-11). Each temptation was answered the same way—with the words "It is written." Jesus knew the Word of the living God is the most powerful weapon against the temptations of the devil. If Jesus Himself used the Word to counter the devil, do we dare to use anything less?

The ultimate example of how not to engage in spiritual warfare is the seven sons of Sceva. "Some Jews who went around driving out evil spirits tried to invoke the name of the Lord Jesus over those who were demon-possessed. They would say, 'In the name of Jesus, whom Paul preaches, I command you to come out.' Seven sons of Sceva, a Jewish chief priest, were doing this. One day the evil spirit answered them, 'Jesus I know, and I know about Paul, but who are you?' Then the man who had the evil spirit jumped on them and overpowered them all. He gave them such a beating that they ran out of the house naked and bleeding" (Acts 19:13-16). The seven sons of Sceva were using Jesus' name. That is not enough. The seven sons of Sceva did not have a relationship with Jesus; therefore, their words were void of any power or authority. The seven sons of Sceva were relying on a methodology. They were not relying on Jesus as their Lord and Savior, and they were not employing the Word of God in their spiritual warfare. As a result, they received a humiliating beating. May we learn from their bad example and conduct spiritual warfare as the Bible instructs.

In summary, what are the keys to success in spiritual warfare? First, we rely on God's power, not our own. Second, we rebuke in Jesus' Name, not our own. Third, we protect ourselves with the full armor of God. Fourth, we wage warfare with the sword of the Spirit—the Word of God. Finally, we remember that while we wage spiritual warfare against Satan and his demons, not every sin or problem is a demon that needs to be rebuked.

Question: How can we recognize the voice of God?

Answer: This question has been asked by countless people through-out the ages. Samuel heard the voice of God, but did not recognize it until he was instructed by Eli (1 Samuel 3:1-10). Gideon had a physical revelation from God, and he still doubted what he had heard to the point of asking for a sign, not once, but three times (Judges 6:17-22, 36-40). When we are listening for God's voice, how can we know that He is the one speaking? First of all, we have something that Gideon and Samuel did not. We have the complete Bible, the inspired Word of God, to read, study, and meditate on. "All Scripture is God-breathed and is useful for teaching, rebuking, correcting and training in righteousness, so that the man of God may be thoroughly equipped for every good work" (2 Timothy 3:16-17). When we have a question about a certain topic or decision in our lives, we should see what the Bible has to say about it. God will never lead us or direct us contrary to what He has taught or promised in His Word (Titus 1:2).

Second, to hear God's voice we must recognize it. Jesus said, "My sheep listen to my voice; I know them, and they follow me" (John 10:27). Those who hear God's voice are those who belong to

Him—those who have been saved by His grace through faith in the Lord Jesus. These are the sheep who hear and recognize His voice, because they know Him as their Shepherd and they know His voice. If we are to recognize God's voice, we must belong to Him.

Third, we hear His voice when we spend time in prayer, Bible study, and quiet contemplation of His Word. The more time we spend intimately with God and His Word, the easier it is to recognize His voice and His leading in our lives. Employees at a bank are trained to recognize counterfeits by studying genuine money so closely that it is easy to spot a fake. We should be so familiar with God's Word that when God does speak to us or lead us, it is clear that it is God. God speaks to us so that we may understand truth. While God can speak audibly to people, He speaks primarily through His Word, and sometimes through the Holy Spirit to our consciences, through circumstances, and through other people. By applying what we hear to the truth of Scripture, we can learn to recognize His voice.

Question: What is a carnal Christian?

Answer: Can a true Christian be carnal? In answering this question, let's first define the term "carnal." The word "carnal" is translated from the Greek word *sarkikos*, which literally means "fleshly." This descriptive word is seen in the context of Christians in 1 Corinthians 3:1-3. In this passage, the apostle Paul is addressing the readers as "brethren," a term he uses almost exclusively to refer to other Christians; he then goes on to describe them as "carnal." Therefore, we can conclude that Christians can be carnal. The Bible is absolutely clear that no one is sinless (1 John 1:8). Every time we sin, we are acting carnally.

The key thing to understand is that while a Christian can be, for a time, carnal, a true Christian will not remain carnal for a lifetime. Some have abused the idea of a "carnal Christian" by saying that it is possible for people to come to faith in Christ and then proceed to live the rest of their lives in a completely carnal manner, with no evidence of being born again or a new creation (2 Corinthians 5:17). Such a concept is completely unbiblical. James 2 makes it abundantly clear that genuine faith will always result in good works. Ephesians 2:8-10 declares that while we are saved by grace alone through faith alone, that salvation will result in works. Can a Christian, in a time of failure and/or rebellion, appear to be carnal? Yes. Will a true Christian remain carnal? No.

Since eternal security is a fact of Scripture, even the carnal Christian is still saved. Salvation cannot be lost, because salvation is a gift of God that He will not take away (see John 10:28; Romans 8:37-39; 1 John 5:13). Even in 1 Corinthians 3:15, the carnal Christian is assured of salvation: "If anyone's work is burned, he will suffer loss; but he himself will be saved, yet so as through fire." The question is not whether a person who claims to be a Christian but lives carnally has lost his salvation, but whether that person was truly saved in the first place (1 John 2:19).

Christians who become carnal in their behavior can expect God to lovingly discipline them (Hebrews 12:5-11) so they can be restored to close fellowship with Him and be trained to obey Him. God's desire in saving us is that we would progressively grow closer to the image of Christ (Romans 12:1-2), becoming increasingly spiritual and decreasingly carnal, a process known as sanctification. Until we are delivered from our sinful flesh, there will be outbreaks of carnality. For a genuine believer in Christ, though, these outbreaks of carnality will be the exception, not the rule.

Question: Why are all Christians hypocrites?

Answer: Perhaps no accusation is more provocative than that of "hypocrite." Unfortunately, some feel justified in their view that all Christians are hypocrites. The term "hypocrite" enjoys a rich heritage in the English language. The term comes to us via the Latin *hypocrisies* meaning "play-acting, pretense." Further back, the word occurs in both classical and New Testament Greek and has the very same idea—to play a part, pretend.

This is the way the Lord Jesus employed the term. For example, when Christ taught the significance of prayer, fasting, and alms-giving for kingdom people, He discouraged us from following the examples of those who are hypocrites (Matthew 6:2, 5, 16). By making long public prayers, employing extreme measures to ensure others noticed their fasts, and parading their gifts to the Temple and the poor, they revealed only an outward attachment to the Lord. While the Pharisees performed well their dramatic role as public examples of religious virtue, they failed miserably in the inner world of the heart where true virtue resides (Matthew 23:13-33; Mark 7:20-23).

Jesus never called His disciples hypocrites. That name was given only to misguided religious zealots. Rather, He called His own "followers," "babes," "sheep," and His "church." In addition, there is a warning in the New Testament about the sin of hypocrisy (1 Peter 2:1), which Peter calls "insincerity." Also, two blatant examples of hypocrisy are recorded in the church. In Acts 5:1-10, two disciples are exposed for pretending to be more generous than they were. The consequence was severe. And, of all people, Peter is charged with leading a group of hypocrites in their treatment of Gentile believers (Galatians 2:13).

From the New Testament teaching, then, we may draw at least two conclusions. First, hypocrites do exist among professing Christians. They were present in the beginning, and, according to Jesus' parable of the tares and wheat, they will certainly exist until the end of the age (Matthew 13:18-30). In addition, if even an apostle may be guilty of hypocrisy, there is no reason to believe "ordinary" Christians will be free from it. We must always be on our guard that we do not fall into the very same temptations (1 Corinthians 10:12).

Of course, not everyone who claims to be a Christian is truly a Christian. Perhaps all or most of the famous hypocrites among Christians were in fact pretenders and deceivers. To this day, prominent Christian leaders have fallen into terrible sins. Financial and sexual scandals sometimes seem to plague the Christian community. However, instead of taking the actions of a few and using them to denigrate the whole community of Christians, we need to ask whether all those who claim to be Christians really are. Numerous biblical passages confirm that those who truly belong to Christ will exhibit the fruit of the Spirit (Galatians 5:22-23). Jesus' parable of the seed and the soils in Matthew 13 makes it clear that not all professions of faith in Him are genuine. Sadly, many who profess to belong to Him will be stunned one day to hear Him say to them, "I never knew you. Away from me, you evildoers!" (Matthew 7:23).

Second, while it should not surprise us that people who pretend to be more holy than they are claim to be Christians, we cannot conclude that the church is made up almost entirely of hypocrites. One surely may concede that all of us who name the name of Jesus Christ remain sinners even after our sin is forgiven. That is, even though we are saved from sins' eternal penalty (Romans 5:1; 6:23), we are yet to be saved and delivered from the presence of sin in our lives (1 John 1:8-9), including the sin of hypocrisy. Through our living faith in the Lord Jesus, we continually overcome sin's power until we are finally delivered (1 John 5:4-5).

All Christians fail to perfectly live up to the standard the Bible teaches. No Christian has ever been perfectly Christ-like. However, there are many Christians who are genuinely seeking to live the Christian life and are relying more and more on the Holy Spirit to convict, change, and empower them. There have been multitudes of Christians who have lived their lives free from scandal. No Christian is perfect, but making a mistake and failing to reach perfection in this life is not the same thing as being a hypocrite.

Question: How can I experience joy in my Christian life?

Answer: Periods of sadness and depression can enter the life of even the most devout Christian. We see many examples of this in the Bible. Job wished he had never been born (Job 3:11). David prayed to be taken away to a place where he would not have to deal with reality (Psalm 55:6-8). Elijah, even after defeating 450 prophets of Baal with fire called down from heaven (1 Kings 18:16-46), fled into the desert and asked God to take his life (1 Kings 19:3-5).

So how can we overcome these periods of joylessness? We can see how these same people overcame their bouts of depression. Job said that, if we pray and remember our blessings, God will restore us to joy and righteousness (Job 33:26). David wrote that the study of God's Word can bring us joy (Psalm 19:8). David also realized that he needed to praise God even in the midst of despair (Psalm 42:5). In Elijah's case, God let him rest for a time and then sent a man, Elisha, to help him (1 Kings 19:19-21). We also need friends that we can share our hurts and pains with (Ecclesiastes 4:9-12). It may be helpful to share our feelings with a fellow Christian. We may be surprised to find that he or she has struggled with some of the same things that we are going through.

Most importantly, it is certain that dwelling on ourselves, our problems, our hurts, and especially our pasts will *never* produce true spiritual joy. Joy is not found in materialism, it is not found in psychotherapy, and it most certainly is not found in obsession with ourselves. It is found in Christ. We who belong to the Lord "glory in Christ Jesus, and put no confidence in the flesh" (Philippians 3:3). To know Christ is to come to have a true sense of ourselves, and true spiritual insight, making it impossible to glory in ourselves, in our wisdom, strength, riches, or goodness, but in Christ—in His wisdom and strength, in His riches and goodness, and in His person only. If we remain in Him, immerse ourselves in His Word, and seek to know Him more intimately, our "joy will be full" (John 15:1-11).

Finally, remember that it is only through God's Holy Spirit that we can find true joy (Psalm 51:11-12; Galatians 5:22; 1 Thessalonians 1:6). We can do nothing apart from the power of God (2 Corinthians 12:10, 13:4). Indeed, the harder we try to be joyful through our own efforts, the more miserable we can become. Rest in the Lord's arms (Matthew 11:28-30) and seek His face through prayer and Scripture. "May the God of hope fill you with all joy and peace as you trust in Him, so that you may overflow with hope by the power of the Holy Spirit" (Romans 15:13).

Question: What is Christian meditation?

Answer: Psalm 19:14 states, "May the words of my mouth and the *meditation* of my heart be pleasing in your sight, O Lord, my Rock and my Redeemer." What, then, is Christian meditation, and how should Christians meditate? Unfortunately, the word "meditation" can carry the connotation of something mystical. For some, meditation is clearing the mind while sitting in an unusual position. For others, meditation is communing with the spirit world around us. Concepts such as these most definitely do not characterize Christian meditation.

Christian meditation has nothing to do with practices that have Eastern mysticism as their foundation. Such practices include lectio divina, transcendental meditation, and many forms of what is called contemplative prayer. These have at their core a dangerous premise that we need to "hear God's voice," not through His Word, but through personal revelation through meditation. Some churches are filled with people who think they are hearing a "word from the Lord," often contradicting one another and therefore causing endless divisions within the body of Christ. Christians are not to abandon God's Word, which is "God-breathed and is useful for teaching, rebuking, correcting and training in righteousness, so that the man of God may be thoroughly equipped for every good work" (2 Timothy 3:16-17). If the Bible is sufficient to thoroughly equip us for every good work, how could we think we need to seek a mystical experience instead of or in addition to it?

Christian meditation is to be solely on the Word of God and what it reveals about Him. David found this to be so, and he describes the man who is "blessed" as one whose "delight is in the law of the LORD, and on his law he *meditates* day and night" (Psalm 1:2). True Christian meditation is an active thought process whereby we give ourselves to the study of the Word, praying over it and asking God to give us understanding by the Spirit, who has promised to lead us "into all truth" (John 16:13). Then we put this truth into practice, committing ourselves to the Scriptures as the rule for life and practice as we go about our daily activities. This causes spiritual growth and maturing in the things of God as we are taught by His Holy Spirit.

Question: What is Christian spirituality?

Answer: When we are born again, we receive the Holy Spirit who seals us for the day of redemption (Ephesians 1:13; 4:30). Jesus promised that the Holy Spirit would lead us "into all truth" (John 16:13). Part of that truth is taking the things of God and applying them to our lives. When that application is made, the believer then makes a choice to allow the Holy Spirit to control him/her. True Christian spirituality is based upon the extent to which a born-again believer allows the Holy Spirit to lead and control his or her life.

The apostle Paul tells believers to be filled with the Holy Spirit. "Do not get drunk on wine, which leads to debauchery. Instead, be filled with the Spirit" (Ephesians 5:18). The tense in this passage is continual and therefore means "keep on being filled with the Spirit." Being filled with the Spirit is simply allowing the Holy Spirit to control us rather than yielding to the desires of our own carnal nature. In this passage Paul is making a comparison. When someone is controlled by wine, he is drunk and exhibits certain characteristics such as slurred speech, unsteady walk, and impaired decision making. Just as you can tell when a person is drunk because of the characteristics he displays, so a born-again believer who is controlled by the Holy Spirit will display His characteristics. We find those characteristics in Galatians 5:22-23 where they are called the "fruit of the Spirit." This is true Christian spirituality, produced by the Spirit working in and through the believer. This character is not produced by self effort. A born-again believer who is controlled by the Holy Spirit will exhibit sound speech, a consistent spiritual walk, and decision making based on the Word of God.

Therefore, Christian spirituality involves a choice we make to "know and grow" in our daily relationship with the Lord Jesus Christ by submitting to the ministry of the Holy Spirit in our lives. This means that, as believers, we make a choice to keep our communication with the Spirit clear through confession (1 John 1:9). When we grieve the Spirit by sin (Ephesians 4:30; 1 John 1:5-8), we erect a barrier between ourselves and God. When we submit to the Spirit's ministry, our relationship is not interrupted (1 Thessalonians 5:19). Christian spirituality is a consciousness of fellowship with the Spirit of Christ, uninterrupted by carnality and sin. Christian spirituality develops when a born-again believer makes a consistent and ongoing choice to surrender to the ministry of the Holy Spirit.

Question: Why do we need to confess our sins if they have already been forgiven (1 John 1:9)?

Answer: The apostle Paul wrote, "To the praise of his glorious grace, which he has freely given us in the One he loves. In him we have redemption through his blood, the forgiveness of sins, in accordance with the riches of God's grace that he lavished on us with all wisdom and understanding" (Ephesians 1:6-8). This forgiveness is referring to salvation, in which God has taken our sins and removed them from us "as far as the east is from the west" (Psalm 103:12). This is the judicial forgiveness that God gives us upon receiving Jesus Christ as Savior. All our past, present, and future sins are forgiven on a judicial basis, meaning that we will not suffer eternal judgment for our sins.

We still often suffer consequences of sin while we are here on earth, however, which brings us to the question at hand.

The difference between Ephesians 1:6-8 and 1 John 1:9 is that John is dealing with what we call "relational," or "familial," forgiveness—like that of a father and a son. For example, if a son does something wrong to his father—falling short of his expectations or rules—the son has hindered his fellowship with his father. He remains the son of his father, but the relationship suffers. Their fellowship will be hindered until the son admits to his father that he has done wrong. It works the same way with God; our fellowship with Him is hindered until we confess our sin. When we confess our sin to God, the fellowship is restored. This is relational forgiveness.

"Positional" forgiveness, or judicial forgiveness, is that which is obtained by every believer in Christ. In our position as members of the body of Christ, we have been forgiven of every sin we have ever committed or ever will commit. The price paid by Christ on the cross has satisfied God's wrath against sin, and no further sacrifice or payment is necessary. When Jesus said, "It is finished," He meant it. Our positional forgiveness was obtained then and there.

Confession of sin will help to keep us from the discipline of the Lord. If we fail to confess sin, the discipline of the Lord is sure to come until we do confess it. As stated previously, our sins are forgiven at salvation (positional forgiveness), but our daily fellowship with God needs to stay in good standing (relational forgiveness). Proper fellowship with God cannot happen with unconfessed sin in our lives. Therefore, we need to confess our sins to God as soon as we are aware that we have sinned, in order to maintain close fellowship with God.

Question: If I am saved and all of my sins are forgiven, why not continue to sin?

Answer: The apostle Paul answered a very similar question in Romans 6:1-2, "What shall we say, then? Shall we go on sinning so that grace may increase? By no means! We died to sin; how can we live in it any longer?" The idea that a person could "trust in Jesus Christ" for salvation and then go on living just as he/she lived before, is absolutely foreign to the Bible. Believers in Christ are new creations

(2 Corinthians 5:17). The Holy Spirit changes us from producing the acts of the flesh (Galatians 5:19-21) to producing the fruit of the Spirit (Galatians 5:22-23). The Christian life is a changed life because the Christian is changed.

What differentiates Christianity from every other religion is that Christianity is based on what God has done for us through Jesus Christ—divine accomplishment. Every other world religion is based on what we must do to earn God's favor and forgiveness—human achievement. Every other religion teaches that we must do certain things and stop doing certain other things in order to earn God's love and mercy. Christianity, faith in Christ, teaches that we do certain things and stop doing certain things *because* of what Christ has done for us.

How could anyone, having been delivered from sin's penalty, eternity in hell, go back to living the same life that had him on the path to hell in the first place? How could anyone, having been cleansed from the defilement of sin, desire to go back to the same cesspool of depravity? How could anyone, knowing what Jesus Christ did on our behalf, go on living as if He were not important? How could anyone, realizing how much Christ suffered for our sins, continue sinning as if those sufferings were meaningless?

Romans 6:11-15 declares, "In the same way, count yourselves dead to sin but alive to God in Christ Jesus. Therefore do not let sin reign in your mortal body so that you obey its evil desires. Do not offer the parts of your body to sin, as instruments of wickedness, but rather offer yourselves to God, as those who have been brought from death to life; and offer the parts of your body to him as instruments of righteousness. For sin shall not be your master, because you are not under law, but under grace. What then? Shall we sin because we are not under law but under grace? By no means!"

For the truly converted, then, continuing to live sinfully is not an option. Because our conversion resulted in a completely new nature, our desire is to no longer live in sin. Yes, we still sin, but instead of wallowing in it as we once did, we now hate it and wish to be delivered from it. The idea of "taking advantage" of Christ's sacrifice on our behalf by continuing to live sinfully is unthinkable. If a person believes himself to be a Christian and still desires to live the old, sinful life, he has reason to doubt his salvation. "Examine yourselves to see whether you are in the faith; test yourselves. Do you not realize that Christ Jesus is in you—unless, of course, you fail the test?" (2 Corinthians 13:5).

Question: When, why, and how does the Lord God discipline us when we sin?

Answer: The Lord's discipline is an often-ignored fact of life for believers. We often complain about our circumstances without realizing that they are the consequences of our own sin and are a part of the Lord's loving and gracious discipline for that sin. This self-centered ignorance can contribute to the formation of habitual sin in a believer's life, incurring even greater discipline.

Discipline is not to be confused with cold-hearted punishment. The Lord's discipline is a response of His love for us and His desire for each of us to be holy. "My son, do not despise the LORD's discipline and do not resent his rebuke, because the LORD disciplines those he loves, as a father the son he delights in" (Proverbs 3:11-12; see also Hebrews 12:5-11). God will use testing, trials, and various predicaments to bring us back to Himself in repentance. The result of His discipline is a stronger faith and a renewed relationship with God (James 1:2-4), not to mention destroying the hold that particular sin had over us.

The Lord's discipline works for our own good, that He might be glorified with our lives. He wants us to exhibit lives of holiness, lives that reflect the new nature that God has given us: "As obedient children, do not conform to the evil desires you had when you lived in ignorance. But just as he who called you is holy, so be holy in all you do; for it is written: 'Be holy, because I am holy'" (1 Peter 1:15-16).

Question: How should a Christian deal with feelings of guilt regarding past sins, whether pre- or post-salvation?

Answer: Everyone has sinned, and one of the results of sin is guilt. We can be thankful for guilty feelings because they drive us to seek forgiveness. The moment a person turns from sin to Jesus Christ in faith, his sin is forgiven. Repentance is part of the faith that leads to salvation (Matthew 3:2; 4:17; Acts 3:19).

In Christ, even the most heinous sins are blotted out (see 1 Corinthians 6:9-11 for a list of unrighteous acts that can be forgiven). Salvation is by grace, and grace forgives. After a person is saved, he will still sin, and when he does, God still promises forgiveness. "But if anybody does sin, we have one who speaks to the Father in our defense—Jesus Christ, the Righteous One" (1 John 2:1).

Freedom from sin, however, does not always mean freedom from guilty feelings. Even when our sins are forgiven, we still remember them. Also, we have a spiritual enemy, called "the accuser of our brothers" (Revelation 12:10) who relentlessly reminds us of our failures, faults, and sins. When a Christian experiences feelings of guilt, he or she should do the following things:

1. Confess all known, previously unconfessed sin. In some cases, feelings of guilt are appropriate because confession is needed. Many times, we feel guilty because we are guilty! (See David's description of guilt and its solution in Psalm 32:3-5.)
2. Ask the Lord to reveal any other sin that may need confessing. Have the courage to be completely open and honest before the Lord. "Search me, O God, and know my heart; test me and know my anxious thoughts. See if there is any offensive way in me, and lead me in the way everlasting" (Psalm 139:23-24).
3. Trust the promise of God that He will forgive sin and remove guilt, based on the blood of Christ (1 John 1:9; Psalm 85:2; 86:5; Romans 8:1).
4. On occasions when guilty feelings arise over sins already confessed and forsaken, reject such feelings as false guilt. The Lord has been true to His promise to forgive. Read and meditate on Psalm 103:8-12.
5. Ask the Lord to rebuke Satan, your accuser, and ask the Lord to restore the joy that comes with freedom from guilt (Psalm 51:12).

Psalm 32 is a very profitable study. Although David had sinned terribly, he found freedom from both sin and guilty feelings. He dealt with the cause of guilt and the reality of forgiveness. Psalm 51 is another good passage to investigate. The emphasis here is confession of sin, as David pleads with God from a heart full of guilt and sorrow. Restoration and joy are the results.

Finally, if sin has been confessed, repented of, and forgiven, it is time to move on. Remember that we who have come to Christ have been made new creatures in Him. "Therefore, if anyone is in Christ, he is a new creation; the old has gone, the new has come!" (2 Corinthians 5:17). Part of the "old" which has gone is the remembrance of past sins and the guilt they produced. Sadly, some Christians are prone to wallowing in memories of their former sinful lives, memories which should have been dead and buried long ago. This is pointless and runs counter to the victorious Christian life God wants for us. A wise saying is "If God has saved you out of a sewer, don't dive back in and swim around."

Question: What does the Bible say about legalism?

Answer: The word "legalism" does not occur in the Bible. It is a term Christians use to describe a doctrinal position emphasizing a system of rules and regulations for achieving both salvation and spiritual growth. Legalists believe in and demand a strict literal adherence to rules and regulations. Doctrinally, it is a position essentially opposed to grace. Those who hold a legalistic position often fail to see the real purpose for law, especially the purpose of the Old Testament law of Moses, which is to be our "schoolmaster" or "tutor" to bring us to Christ (Galatians 3:24).

Even true believers can be legalistic. We are instructed, rather, to be gracious to one another: "Accept him whose faith is weak, without passing judgment on disputable matters" (Romans 14:1). Sadly, there are those who feel so strongly about non-essential doctrines that they will run others out of their fellowship, not even allowing the expression of another viewpoint. That, too, is legalism. Many legalistic believers today make the error of demanding unqualified adherence to their own biblical interpretations and even to their own traditions. For example, there are those who feel that to be spiritual one must simply avoid tobacco, alcoholic beverages, dancing, movies, etc. The truth is that avoiding these things is no guarantee of spirituality.

The apostle Paul warns us of legalism in Colossians 2:20-23: "Since you died with Christ to the basic principles of this world, why, as though you still belonged to it, do you submit to its rules: 'Do not handle! Do not taste! Do not touch!'? These are all destined to perish with use, because they are based on human commands and teachings. Such regulations indeed have an appearance of wisdom, with their self-imposed worship, their false humility and their harsh treatment of the body, but they lack any value in restraining sensual indulgence." Legalists may appear to be righteous and spiritual, but legalism ultimately fails to accomplish God's purposes because it is an outward performance instead of an inward change.

To avoid falling into the trap of legalism, we can start by holding fast to the words of the apostle John, "For the law was given through Moses; grace and truth came through Jesus Christ" (John 1:17) and remembering to be gracious, especially to our brothers and sisters in Christ. "Who are you to judge someone else's servant? To his own master he stands or falls. And he will stand, for the Lord is able to make him stand" (Romans 14:4). "You, then, why do you judge your brother? Or why do you look down on your brother? For we will all stand before God's judgment seat" (Romans 14:10).

A word of caution is necessary here. While we need to be gracious to one another and tolerant of disagreement over disputable matters, we cannot accept heresy. We are exhorted to contend for the faith that was once for all entrusted to the saints (Jude 3). If we remember these guidelines and apply them in love and mercy, we will be safe from both legalism and heresy. "Dear friends, do not believe every spirit, but test the spirits to see whether they are from God, because many false prophets have gone out into the world" (1 John 4:1).

Question: Who am I in Christ?

Answer: According to 2 Corinthians 5:17, "If anyone is in Christ, he is a new creation; the old has gone, the new has come!" There are two Greek words which are translated "new" in the Bible. The first, *neos*, refers to something that has just been made, but there are already many others in existence just like it. The word translated "new" in this verse is the word *kainos*, which means "something just made which is unlike anything else in existence." In Christ, we are made an entirely new creation, just as God created the heavens and the earth originally—He made them out of nothing, and so He does with us. He does not merely clean up our old selves; He makes an entirely new self. When we are in Christ, we are "partakers of the divine nature" (2 Peter 1:4 KJV). God Himself, in the person of His Holy Spirit, takes up residence in our hearts. We are in Christ and He is in us.

In Christ, we are regenerated, renewed, and born again, and this new creation is spiritually minded, whereas the old nature is carnally minded. The new nature fellowships with God, obeys His will, and is devoted to His service. These are actions the old nature is incapable of doing or even desiring to do. The old nature is dead to the things of the spirit and cannot revive itself. It is "dead in trespasses and sins" (Ephesians 2:1) and can only be made alive by a supernatural awakening, which happens when we come to Christ and are indwelt by Him. Christ gives us a completely new and holy nature and an incorruptible life. Our old life, previously dead to God because of sin, is buried, and we are raised "to walk in newness of life" with Him (Romans 6:4).

If we belong to Christ, we are united to Him and no longer slaves to sin (Romans 6:5-6); we are made alive with Him (Ephesians 2:5); we are conformed to His image (Romans 8:29); we are free from condemnation and walking not according to the flesh, but according to the Spirit (Romans 8:1); and we are part of the body of Christ with other believers (Romans 12:5). The believer now possesses a new heart (Ezekiel 11:19) and has been blessed "with every spiritual blessing in the heavenly places in Christ Jesus" (Ephesians 1:3).

We might wonder why we so often do not live in the manner described, even though we have given our lives to Christ and are sure of our salvation. This is because our new natures are residing in our old fleshly bodies, and these two are at war with one another. The old nature is dead, but the new nature still has to battle the old "tent" in which it dwells. Evil and sin are still present, but the believer now sees them in a new perspective and they no longer control him as they once did. In Christ, we can now choose to resist sin, whereas the old nature could not. Now we have the choice to either feed the new nature through the Word, prayer, and obedience, or to feed the flesh by neglecting those things.

When we are in Christ, "we are more than conquerors through Him that loved us" (Romans 8:37) and can rejoice in our Savior, who makes all things possible (Philippians 4:13). In Christ we are loved, forgiven, and secure. In Christ we are adopted, justified, redeemed, reconciled, and chosen. In Christ we are victorious, filled with joy and peace, and granted true meaning in life. What a wonderful Savior is Christ!

Chapter 12

QUESTIONS ABOUT PRAYER

CONTENTS

What is the prayer of salvation?..338

Why pray? 339

What is the Lord's Prayer, and should we pray it? 340

What does it mean to pray in Jesus' name? 342

How can I have my prayers answered by God? 342

Is it acceptable to repeatedly pray for the same thing?.......................343

Is corporate prayer important? Is corporate prayer more powerful than
an individual praying alone? 344

Whom are we to pray to—the Father, the Son, or the Holy Spirit? 346

What is the power of prayer? 347

How can I be sure I am praying according to the will of God?..............348

Silent prayer—is it biblical?...350

What is the proper way to pray? 351

What is praying in the Spirit? 352

What is the connection between prayer and fasting? 353

What does it mean to pray without ceasing? 355

What is prayer walking? Is it biblical to go on a prayer walk?..............356

What are some hindrances to effective prayer? 357

What is intercessory prayer?..360

Question: What is the prayer of salvation?

Answer: Many people ask, "Is there a prayer I can pray that will guarantee my salvation?" It is important to remember that salvation is not received by reciting a prayer or uttering certain words. The Bible nowhere records a person's receiving salvation by a prayer. Saying a prayer is not the biblical way of salvation.

The biblical method of salvation is faith in Jesus Christ. John 3:16 tells us, "For God so loved the world that he gave his one and only Son, that whoever believes in him shall not perish but have eternal life." Salvation is gained by faith (Ephesians 2:8), by receiving Jesus as Savior (John 1:12), and by fully trusting Jesus alone (John 14:6; Acts 4:12), not by reciting a prayer.

The biblical message of salvation is simple and clear and amazing at the same time. We have all committed sin against God (Romans 3:23). Other than Jesus Christ, there is no one who has lived an entire life without sinning (Ecclesiastes 7:20). Because of our sin, we have earned judgment from God (Romans 6:23), and that judgment is physical death followed by spiritual death. Because of our sin and its deserved punishment, there is nothing we can do on our own to make ourselves right with God. As a result of His love for us, God became a human being in the Person of Jesus Christ. Jesus lived a perfect life and always taught the truth. However, humanity rejected Jesus and put Him to death by crucifying Him. Through that horrible act, though, Jesus died in our place. Jesus took the burden and judgment of sin on Himself, and He died in our place (2 Corinthians 5:21). Jesus was then resurrected (1 Corinthians 15), proving that His payment for sin was sufficient and that He had overcome sin and death. As a result of Jesus' sacrifice, God offers us salvation as a gift. God calls us all to change our minds about Jesus (Acts 17:30) and to receive Him as the full payment of our sins (1 John 2:2). Salvation is gained by receiving the gift God offers us, not by praying a prayer.

Now, that does not mean prayer cannot be involved in receiving salvation. If you understand the gospel, believe it to be true, and have accepted Jesus as your salvation, it is good and appropriate to express that faith to God in prayer. Communicating with God through prayer can be a way to progress from accepting facts about Jesus to fully trusting in Him as Savior. Prayer can be connected to the act of placing your faith in Jesus alone for salvation.

Again, though, it is crucially important that you do not base your salvation on having said a prayer. Reciting a prayer cannot save you! If you want to receive the salvation that is available through Jesus, place your faith in Him. Fully trust His death as the sufficient sacrifice for your sins. Completely rely on Him alone as your Savior. That is the biblical method of salvation. If you have received Jesus as your Savior, by all means, say a prayer to God. Tell God how thankful you are for Jesus. Offer praise to God for His love and sacrifice. Thank Jesus for dying for your sins and providing salvation for you. That is the biblical connection between salvation and prayer.

Question: Why pray?

Answer: For the Christian, praying is like breathing. It is easier to do it than to not do it. We pray for a variety of reasons. For one thing, prayer is a form of serving God (Luke 2:36-38) and obeying Him. We pray because God commands us to pray (Philippians 4:6-7). Prayer is exemplified for us by Christ and the early church (Mark 1:35; Acts 1:14; 2:42; 3:1; 4:23-31; 6:4; 13:1-3). If Jesus thought it was worthwhile to pray, we should also. If He needed to pray to remain in the Father's will, how much more do we need to pray?

Another reason to pray is that God intends prayer to be the means of obtaining His solutions in a number of situations. We pray in preparation for major decisions (Luke 6:12-13); to overcome demonic barriers (Matthew 17:14-21); to gather workers for the spiritual harvest (Luke 10:2); to gain strength to overcome temptation (Matthew 26:41); and to obtain the means of strengthening others spiritually (Ephesians 6:18-19).

We come to God with our specific requests, and we have God's promise that our prayers are not in vain, even if we do not receive specifically what we asked for (Matthew 6:6; Romans 8:26-27). He has promised that when we ask for things that are in accordance with His will, He will give us what we ask for (1 John 5:14-15). Sometimes He delays His answers according to His wisdom and for our benefit. In these situations, we are to be diligent and persistent in prayer (Matthew 7:7; Luke 18:1-8). Prayer should not be seen as our means of getting God to do our will on earth, but rather as a means of getting God's will done on earth. God's wisdom far exceeds our own.

For situations in which we do not know God's will specifically, prayer is a means of discerning His will. If the Syrian woman with the demon-influenced daughter had not prayed to Christ, her daughter would not have been made whole (Mark 7:26-30). If the blind man outside Jericho had not called out to Christ, he would have remained blind (Luke 18:35-43). God has said that we often go without because we do not ask (James 4:2). In one sense, prayer is like sharing the gospel with people. We do not know who will respond to the message of the gospel until we share it. In the same way, we will never see the results of answered prayer unless we pray.

A lack of prayer demonstrates a lack of faith and a lack of trust in God's Word. We pray to demonstrate our faith in God, that He will do as He has promised in His Word and bless our lives abundantly more than we could ask or hope for (Ephesians 3:20). Prayer is our primary means of seeing God work in others' lives. Because it is our means of "plugging into" God's power, it is our means of defeating Satan and his army that we are powerless to overcome by ourselves. Therefore, may God find us often before His throne, for we have a high priest in heaven who can identify with all that we go through (Hebrews 4:15-16). We have His promise that the fervent prayer of a righteous man accomplishes much (James 5:16-18). May God glorify His name in our lives as we believe in Him enough to come to Him often in prayer.

Question: What is the Lord's Prayer, and should we pray it?

Answer: The Lord's Prayer is a prayer the Lord Jesus taught His disciples in Matthew 6:9-13 and Luke 11:2-4. Matthew 6:9-13 says, "This, then, is how you should pray: 'Our Father in heaven, hallowed be your name, your kingdom come, your will be done on earth as it is in heaven. Give us today our daily bread. Forgive us our debts, as we also have forgiven our debtors. And lead us not into temptation, but deliver us from the evil one.'" Many people misunderstand the Lord's Prayer to be a prayer we are supposed to recite word for word. Some people treat the Lord's Prayer as a magic formula, as if the words themselves have some specific power or influence with God.

The Bible teaches the opposite. God is far more interested in our hearts when we pray than He is in our words. "But when you pray, go into your room, close the door and pray to your Father, who is unseen. Then your Father, who sees what is done in secret, will reward you. And when you pray, do not use vain repetitions as the heathen do. For they think that they will be heard for their many words" (Matthew 6:6-7). In prayer, we are to pour out our hearts to God (Philippians 4:6-7), not simply recite memorized words to God.

The Lord's Prayer should be understood as an example, a pattern, of how to pray. It gives us the "ingredients" that should go into prayer. Here is how it breaks down. "Our Father in heaven" is teaching us whom to address our prayers to—the Father. "Hallowed be your name" is telling us to worship God, and to praise Him for who He is. The phrase "your kingdom come, your will be done on earth as it is in heaven" is a reminder to us that we are to pray for God's plan in our lives and the world, not our own plan. We are to pray for God's will to be done, not for our desires. We are encouraged to ask God for the things we need in "give us today our daily bread." "Forgive us our debts, as we also have forgiven our debtors" reminds us to confess our sins to God and to turn from them, and also to forgive others as God has forgiven us. The conclusion of the Lord's Prayer, "And lead us not into temptation, but deliver us from the evil one" is a plea for help in achieving victory over sin and a request for protection from the attacks of the devil.

So, again, the Lord's Prayer is not a prayer we are to memorize and recite back to God. It is only an example of how we should be praying. Is there anything wrong with memorizing the Lord's Prayer? Of course not! Is there anything wrong with praying the Lord's Prayer back to God? Not if your heart is in it and you truly mean the words you say. Remember, in prayer, God is far more interested in our communicating with Him and speaking from our hearts than He is in the specific words we use. Philippians 4:6-7 declares, "Do not be anxious about anything, but in everything, by prayer and petition, with thanksgiving, present your requests to God. And the peace of God, which transcends all understanding, will guard your hearts and your minds in Christ Jesus."

Question: What does it mean to pray in Jesus' name?

Answer: Prayer in Jesus' name is taught in John 14:13-14, "And I will do whatever you ask in my name, so that the Son may bring glory to the Father. You may ask me for anything in my name, and I will do it." Some misapply this verse, thinking that saying "in Jesus' name" at the end of a prayer results in God's always granting what is asked for. This is essentially treating the words "in Jesus' name" as a magic formula. This is absolutely unbiblical.

Praying in Jesus' name means praying with His authority and asking God the Father to act upon our prayers because we come in the name of His Son, Jesus. Praying in Jesus' name means the same thing as praying according to the will of God, "This is the confidence we have in approaching God: that if we ask anything according to his will, he hears us. And if we know that he hears us—whatever we ask—we know that we have what we asked of him" (1 John 5:14-15). Praying in Jesus' name is praying for things that will honor and glorify Jesus.

Saying "in Jesus' name" at the end of a prayer is not a magic formula. If what we ask for or say in prayer is not for God's glory and according to His will, saying "in Jesus' name" is meaningless. Genuinely praying in Jesus' name and for His glory is what is important, not attaching certain words to the end of a prayer. It is not the words in the prayer that matter, but the purpose behind the prayer. Praying for things that are in agreement with God's will is the essence of praying in Jesus' name.

Question: How can I have my prayers answered by God?

Answer: Many people believe answered prayer is God granting a prayer request that is offered to Him. If a prayer request is not granted, it is understood as an "unanswered" prayer. However, this is an incorrect understanding of prayer. God answers every prayer that is lifted to Him. Sometimes God answers "no" or "wait." God only promises to grant our prayers when we ask according to His will. "This is the confidence we have in approaching God: that if we ask anything according to his will, he hears us. And if we know that he hears us—whatever we ask—we know that we have what we asked of him" (1 John 5:14-15).

What does it mean to pray according to God's will? Praying according to God's will is praying for things that honor and glorify God and/or praying for what the Bible clearly reveals God's will to be. If we pray for something that is not honoring to God or not God's will for our lives, God will not give what we ask for. How can we know what God's will is? God promises to give us wisdom when we ask for it. James 1:5 proclaims, "If any of you lacks wisdom, he should ask God, who gives generously to all without finding fault, and it will be given to him." A good place to start is 1 Thessalonians 5:12-24, which outlines many things that are God's will for us. The better we understand God's Word, the better we will know what to pray for (John 15:7). The better we know what to pray for, the more often God will answer "yes" to our requests.

Question: Is it acceptable to repeatedly pray for the same thing?

Answer: In Luke 18:1-7, Jesus uses a parable to illustrate the importance of persevering in prayer. He tells the story of a widow who came to an unjust judge seeking justice against her adversary. Because of her persistence in prayer, the judge relented. Jesus' point is that if an unjust judge will grant the petition of someone who perseveres in a request for justice, how much more will the God who loves us—"his chosen ones" (v. 7)—answer our prayer when we keep praying? The parable does not teach, as is mistakenly thought, that if we pray for something over and over, God is obligated to give it to us. Rather, God promises to avenge His own, to vindicate them, right their wrongs, do them justice, and deliver them from their adversaries. He does this because of His justice, His holiness, and His hatred of sin; in answering prayer, He keeps His promises and displays His power.

Jesus gives another illustration of prayer in Luke 11:5-12. Similar to the parable of the unjust judge, Jesus' message in this passage is that if a man will inconvenience himself to provide for a needy friend, God will provide for our needs far more, since no request is an inconvenience to Him. Here again, the promise is not that we will receive whatever we ask if we just keep asking. God's promise to His children is a promise to meet our needs, not our wants. And He knows our needs better than we do. The same promise is reiterated in

Matthew 7:7-11 and in Luke 11:13, where the "good gift" is further explained to be the Holy Spirit.

Both of these passages encourage us to pray and to keep praying. There is nothing wrong with repeatedly asking for the same thing. As long as what you are praying for is within the will of God (1 John 5:14-15), keep asking until God grants your request or removes the desire from your heart. Sometimes God forces us to wait for an answer to our prayers in order to teach us patience and perseverance. Sometimes we ask for something when granting it is not yet in God's timing for our lives. Sometimes we ask for something that is not God's will for us, and He says "no." Prayer is not only our presenting requests to God; it is God's presenting His will to our hearts. Keep on asking, keep on knocking, and keep on seeking until God grants your request or convinces you that your request is not His will for you.

Question: Is corporate prayer important? Is corporate prayer more powerful than an individual praying alone?

Answer: Corporate prayer is an important part of the life of the church, along with worship, sound doctrine, communion, and fellowship. The early church met regularly to learn the doctrine of the apostles, break bread, and pray together (Acts 2:42). When we pray together with other believers, the effects can be very positive. Corporate prayer edifies and unifies us as we share our common faith. The same Holy Spirit who dwells within each believer causes our hearts to rejoice as we hear praises to our Lord and Savior, knitting us together in a unique bond of fellowship found nowhere else in life.

To those who may be alone and struggling with life's burdens, hearing others lift them up to the throne of grace can be a great encouragement. It also builds in us love and concern for others as we intercede for them. At the same time, corporate prayer will only be a reflection of the hearts of the individuals who participate. We are to come to God in humility (James 4:10), truth (Psalm 145:18), obedience (1 John 3:21-22), with thanksgiving (Philippians 4:6) and confidence (Hebrews 4:16). Sadly, corporate prayer can also become a platform for those whose words are directed not to God, but to their hearers. Jesus warned against such behavior in Matthew 6:5-8 where he exhorts us not to be showy, long-winded, or hypocritical in our prayers, but to pray secretly in our own rooms in order to avoid the temptation of using prayer hypocritically.

There is nothing in Scripture to suggest that corporate prayers are "more powerful" than individual prayers in the sense of moving the hand of God. Far too many Christians equate prayer with "getting things from God," and group prayer becomes mainly an occasion to recite a list of our wants. Biblical prayers, however, are multi-faceted, encompassing the whole of the desire to enter into conscious and intimate communion with our holy, perfect, and righteous God. That such a God would bend an ear to His creatures causes praise and adoration to pour forth in abundance (Psalm 27:4; 63:1-8), produces heartfelt repentance and confession (Psalm 51; Luke 18:9-14), generates an outpouring of gratitude and thanksgiving (Philippians 4:6; Colossians 1:12), and creates sincere intercessory pleas on behalf of others (2 Thessalonians 1:11; 2:16).

Prayer, then, is cooperating with God to bring about His plan, not trying to bend Him to our will. As we abandon our own desires in submission to the One who knows our circumstances far better than we ever could and who "knows what you need before you ask" (Matthew 6:8), our prayers reach their highest level. Prayers offered in submission to the Divine will, therefore, are always answered positively, whether offered by one person or a thousand.

The idea that corporate prayers are more likely to move the hand of God comes largely from a misinterpretation of Matthew 18:19-20, "Again, I tell you that if two of you on earth agree about anything you ask for, it will be done for you by my Father in heaven. For where two or three come together in my name, there am I with them." These verses come from a larger passage which addresses the procedures to be followed in the case of church discipline of a sinning member. To interpret them as promising believers a blank check for anything they might agree to ask God for, no matter how sinful or foolish, not only does not fit the context of church discipline, but it denies the rest of Scripture, especially the sovereignty of God.

In addition, to believe that when "two or three are gathered" to pray, some kind of magical power boost is automatically applied to our prayers is not biblically supportable. Of course Jesus is present when two or three pray, but He is equally present when one believer prays alone, even if that person is separated from others by thousands of miles. Corporate prayer is important because it creates unity (John 17:22-23), and is a key aspect of believers' encouraging one another (1 Thessalonians 5:11) and spurring one another on to love and good deeds (Hebrews 10:24).

Question: Whom are we to pray to—the Father, the Son, or the Holy Spirit?

Answer: All prayer should be directed to our triune God—Father, Son, and Holy Spirit. The Bible teaches that we can pray to one or all three, because all three are one. To the Father we pray with the psalmist, "Listen to my cry for help, my King and my God, for to you I pray" (Psalm 5:2). To the Lord Jesus, we pray as to the Father because they are equal. Prayer to one member of the Trinity is prayer to all. Stephen, as he was being martyred, prayed, "Lord Jesus, receive my spirit" (Acts 7:59). We are also to pray in the name of Christ. Paul exhorted the Ephesian believers to always give "thanks to God the Father for everything, in the name of our Lord Jesus Christ" (Ephesians 5:20). Jesus assured His disciples that whatever they asked in His name—meaning in His will—would be granted (John 15:16; 16:23). Similarly, we are told to pray to the Holy Spirit and in His power. The Spirit helps us to pray, even when we do not know how or what to ask for (Romans 8:26; Jude 20). Perhaps the best way to understand the role of the Trinity in prayer is that we pray to the Father, through (or in the name of) the Son, by the power of the Holy Spirit. All three are active participants in the believer's prayer.

Equally important is whom we are *not* to pray to. Some non-Christian religions encourage their adherents to pray to a pantheon of gods, dead relatives, saints, and spirits. Roman Catholics are taught to pray to Mary and various saints. Such prayers are not scriptural and are, in fact, an insult to our heavenly Father. To understand why, we need only look at the nature of prayer. Prayer has several elements, and if we look at just two of them—praise and thanksgiving—we can see that prayer is, at its very core, worship. When we praise God, we are worshipping Him for His attributes and His work in our lives. When we offer prayers of thanksgiving, we are worshipping His goodness, mercy, and loving-kindness to us. Worship gives glory to God, the only One who deserves to be glorified. The problem with praying to anyone other than God is that He will not share His glory. In fact, praying to anyone or anything other than God is idolatry. "I am the LORD; that is my name! I will not give my glory to another or my praise to idols" (Isaiah 42:8).

Other elements of prayer such as repentance, confession, and petition are also forms of worship. We repent knowing that God is a forgiving and loving God and He has provided a means of forgiveness in the sacrifice of His Son on the cross. We confess our sins because we know "He is faithful and just to forgive us our sins, and to cleanse us from all unrighteousness" (1 John 1:9) and we worship Him for it. We come to Him with our petitions and intercessions because we know He loves us and hears us, and we worship Him for His mercy and kindness in being willing to hear and answer. When we consider all this, it is easy to see that praying to someone other than our triune God is unthinkable because prayer is a form of worship, and worship is reserved for God and God alone. Who are we to pray to? The answer is God. Praying to God, and God alone, is far more important than to which Person of the Trinity we address our prayers.

Question: What is the power of prayer?

Answer: The idea that power is inherent in prayer is a very popular one. According to the Bible, the power of prayer is, quite simply, the power of God, who hears and answers prayer. Consider the following:

1. The Lord God Almighty can do all things; there is nothing impossible for Him (Luke 1:37).
2. The Lord God Almighty invites His people to pray to Him. Prayer to God should be made persistently (Luke 18:1), with thanksgiving (Philippians 4:6), in faith (James 1:5), within the will of God (Matthew 6:10), for the glory of God (John 14:13-14), and from a heart right with God (James 5:16).
3. The Lord God Almighty hears the prayers of His children. He commands us to pray, and He promises to listen when we do. "In my distress I called to the LORD; I cried to my God

for help. From his temple he heard my voice; my cry came before him, into his ears" (Psalm 18:6).

4. The Lord God Almighty answers prayer. "I call on you, O God, for you will answer me" (Psalm 17:6). "The righteous cry out, and the LORD hears them; he delivers them from all their troubles" (Psalm 34:17).

Another popular idea is that the amount of faith we have determines whether or not God will answer our prayers. However, sometimes the Lord answers our prayers in spite of our own lack of faith. In Acts 12, the church prays for Peter's release from prison (v. 5), and God answers their prayer (vv. 7-11). Peter goes to the door of the prayer meeting and knocks, but those who are praying refuse at first to believe that it is really Peter. They prayed he would be released, but they failed to expect an answer to their prayers.

The power of prayer does not flow from us; it is not special words we say or the special way we say them or even how often we say them. The power of prayer is not based on a certain direction we face or a certain position of our bodies. The power of prayer does not come from the use of artifacts or icons or candles or beads. The power of prayer comes from the omnipotent One who hears our prayers and answers them. Prayer places us in contact with Almighty God, and we should expect almighty results, whether or not He chooses to grant our petitions or deny our requests. Whatever the answer to our prayers, the God to whom we pray is the source of the power of prayer, and He can and will answer us, according to His perfect will and timing.

Question: How can I be sure I am praying according to the will of God?

Answer: Man's highest aim should be to bring glory to God (1 Corinthians 10:31), and this includes praying according to His will. First, we must ask for wisdom. "If any of you lacks wisdom, he should ask God, who gives generously to all without finding fault, and it will be given to him" (James 1:5). In asking for wisdom, we must also trust that God is gracious and willing to answer our prayers: "But when he asks, he must believe and not doubt" (James 1:6; see also Mark 11:24). So, praying according to the will of God includes asking for wisdom (to know the will of God) and asking in faith (to trust the will of God).

Here are seven biblical instructions that will guide the believer in praying according to God's will:

1. Pray for the things for which the Bible commands prayer. We are told to pray for our enemies (Matthew 5:44); for God to send missionaries (Luke 10:2); that we do not enter temptation (Matthew 26:41); for ministers of the Word (Colossians 4:3; 2 Thessalonians 3:1); for government authorities (1 Timothy 2:1-3); for relief from affliction (James 5:13); and for the healing of fellow believers (James 5:16). Where God commands prayer, we can pray with confidence that we are praying according to His will.

2. Follow the example of godly characters in Scripture. Paul prayed for the salvation of Israel (Romans 10:1). David prayed for mercy and forgiveness when he sinned (Psalm 51:1-2). The early church prayed for boldness to witness (Acts 4:29). These prayers were according to the will of God, and similar prayers today can be as well. As with Paul and the early church, we should always be praying for the salvation of others. For ourselves, we should pray as David prayed, always aware of our sin and bringing it before God before it hinders our relationship with Him and thwarts our prayers.

3. Pray with the right motivation. Selfish motives will not be blessed by God. "When you ask, you do not receive, because you ask with wrong motives, that you may spend what you get on your pleasures" (James 4:3). We should also pray, not so our lofty words can be heard and we may be seen by others as "spiritual," but mostly in private and in secret, so that our heavenly Father will hear in private and reward us openly (Matthew 6:5-6).

4. Pray with a spirit of forgiveness toward others (Mark 11:25). A spirit of bitterness, anger, revenge or hatred toward others will prevent our hearts from praying in total submission to God. Just as we are told not to give offerings to God while there is conflict between ourselves and another Christian

(Matthew 5:23-24), in the same way God does not want the offering of our prayers until we have reconciled with our brothers and sisters in Christ.

5. Pray with thanksgiving (Colossians 4:2; Philippians 4:6-7). We can always find something to be thankful for, no matter how burdened we are by our wants or needs. The greatest sufferer that lives in this world of redeeming love, and who has the offer of heaven before him, has reason to be grateful to God.

6. Pray with persistence (Luke 18:1; 1 Thessalonians 5:17). We should persevere in prayer and not quit or be dejected because we have not received an immediate answer. Part of praying in God's will is believing that, whether His answer is "yes," "no," or "wait," we accept His judgment, submit to His will, and continue to pray.

7. Rely on the Spirit of God in prayer. This is a wonderful truth: "We do not know what we ought to pray for, but the Spirit himself intercedes for us with groans that words cannot express. And he who searches our hearts knows the mind of the Spirit, because the Spirit intercedes for the saints in accordance with God's will" (Romans 8:26-27). We have the Spirit's help in praying. At the times of our deepest depression or sorrow, those times when we feel that we "just cannot pray," we have the comfort of knowing that the Holy Spirit is actually praying for us! What an amazing God we have!

What assurance we have when we seek to walk in the Spirit and not in the flesh! Then we can have confidence that the Holy Spirit will accomplish His work in presenting our prayers to the Father according to His perfect will and timing, and we can rest in the knowledge that He is working all things together for our good (Romans 8:28).

Question: Silent prayer—is it biblical?

Answer: The Bible may not specifically mention praying silently, but that does not mean it is any less valid than praying out loud. God can hear our thoughts just as easily as He can hear our words (Psalm 139:23; Jeremiah 12:3). Jesus knew the evil thoughts of the

Pharisees (Matthew 12:24-26; Luke 11:7). Nothing we do, say, or think is hidden from God, who does not need to hear our words to know our thoughts. He has access to all prayers directed to Him, whether or not they are spoken.

The Bible does mention praying in private (Matthew 6:6). What would be the difference between praying out loud or silently if you are by yourself? There are some circumstances where only silent prayer is appropriate, e.g., praying for something between you and God only, praying for someone who is present, etc. There is not anything wrong with praying silently, as long as we are not doing it because we are embarrassed to be seen praying.

Perhaps the best verse to indicate the validity of unspoken prayers is 1 Thessalonians 5:17: "Pray without ceasing." To pray unceasingly obviously cannot mean we are praying out loud all of the time. Rather, it means we are to be in a constant state of God-consciousness, where we take every thought captive to Him (2 Corinthians 10:5) and bring every situation, plan, fear, or concern before His throne. Part of unceasing prayer will be prayers that are spoken, whispered, shouted, sung, and silent as we direct our thoughts of praise, petition, supplication, and thanksgiving to God.

Question: What is the proper way to pray?

Answer: Is it best to pray standing up, sitting down, kneeling, or bowing down? Should our hands be open, closed, or lifted up to God? Do our eyes need to be closed when we pray? Is it better to pray in a church building or out in nature? Should we pray in the morning when we get up or at night before we go to bed? Are there certain words we need to say in our prayers? How do we begin our prayers? What is the proper way to close a prayer? These questions, and others, are common questions asked about prayer. What is the proper way to pray? Do any of the above things even matter?

Far too often, prayer is viewed as a "magic formula." Some believe that if we do not say exactly the right things, or pray in the right position, God will not hear and answer our prayer. This is completely unbiblical. God does not answer our prayers based on when we pray, where we are, what position our body is in, or in what order we word our prayers. We are told in 1 John 5:14-15 to have confidence when we come to God in prayer, knowing He hears us and will grant whatever we ask as long as it is in His will. Similarly, John 14:13-14 declares, "And I will do whatever you ask in my name, so that the Son may bring glory to the Father. You may ask me for anything in my name, and I will do it." According to these and many other Scriptures, God answers prayer requests based on whether they are asked according to His will and in the name of Jesus (to bring glory to Jesus).

So, what is the proper way to pray? Philippians 4:6-7 tells us to pray without being anxious, to pray about everything, and to pray with thankful hearts. God will answer all such prayers with the gift of His peace in our hearts. The proper way to pray is to pour out our hearts to God, being honest and open with God, as He already knows us better than we know ourselves. We are to present our requests to God, keeping in mind that God knows what is best and will not grant a request that is not His will for us. We are to express our love, gratitude, and worship to God in prayer without worrying about having just the right words to say. God is more interested in the content of our hearts than the eloquence of our words.

The closest the Bible comes to giving a "pattern" for prayer is the Lord's Prayer in Matthew 6:9-13. Please understand that the Lord's Prayer is not a prayer we are to memorize and recite to God. It is an example of the things that should go into a prayer—worship, trust in God, requests, confession, and submission. We are to pray for the things the Lord's Prayer talks about, using our own words and "customizing" it to our own journey with God. The proper way to pray is to express our hearts to God. Sitting, standing, or kneeling; hands open or closed; eyes opened or closed; in a church, at home, or outside; in the morning or at night—these are all side issues, subject to personal preference, conviction, and appropriateness. God's desire is for prayer to be a real and personal connection between Himself and us.

Question: What is praying in the Spirit?

Answer: Praying in the Spirit is mentioned three times in Scripture. First Corinthians 14:15 says, "So what shall I do? I will pray with my spirit, but I will also pray with my mind; I will sing with my spirit, but I will also sing with my mind." Ephesians 6:18 says, "And pray in the Spirit on all occasions with all kinds of prayers and requests. With this in mind, be alert and always keep on praying for all the saints." Jude 20 says, "But you, dear friends, build yourselves up in your most holy faith and pray in the Holy Spirit." So, what exactly does it mean to pray in the Spirit?

The Greek word translated "pray in" can have several different meanings. It can mean "by means of," "with the help of," "in the sphere of," and "in connection to." Praying in the Spirit does not refer to the words we are saying. Rather, it refers to how we are praying. Praying in the Spirit is praying according to the Spirit's leading. It is praying for things the Spirit leads us to pray for. Romans 8:26 tells us, "In the same way, the Spirit helps us in our weakness. We do not know what we ought to pray for, but the Spirit Himself intercedes for us with groans that words cannot express."

Some, based on 1 Corinthians 14:15, equate praying in the Spirit with praying in tongues. Discussing the gift of tongues, Paul mentions "pray with my spirit." First Corinthians 14:14 states that when a person prays in tongues, he does not know what he is saying, since it is spoken in a language he does not know. Further, no one else can understand what is being said, unless there is an interpreter (1 Corinthians 14:27-28). In Ephesians 6:18, Paul instructs us to "pray in the Spirit on all occasions with all kinds of prayers and requests." How are we to pray with all kinds of prayers and requests and pray for the saints, if no one, including the person praying, understands what is being said? Therefore, praying in the Spirit should be understood as praying in the power of the Spirit, by the leading of the Spirit, and according to His will, not as praying in tongues.

Question: What is the connection between prayer and fasting?

Answer: Although the connection between prayer and fasting is not specifically explained in Scripture, a common thread connecting the two seems to run through all the instances of prayer and fasting that are recorded in the Bible. In the Old Testament, it appears that fasting with prayer had to do with a sense of need and dependence, and/or of abject helplessness in the face of actual or anticipated calamity. Prayer and fasting are combined in the Old Testament in times of mourning, repentance, and/or deep spiritual need.

The first chapter of Nehemiah describes Nehemiah praying and fasting, because of his deep distress over the news that Jerusalem had been desolated. His many days of prayer were characterized by tears, fasting, confession on behalf of his people, and pleas to God for mercy. So intense was the outpouring of his concerns that it's almost inconceivable he could "take a break" in the middle of such prayer to eat and drink. The devastation that befell Jerusalem also prompted Daniel to adopt a similar posture: "So I turned to the Lord God and pleaded with him in prayer and petition, in fasting, and in sackcloth and ashes" (Daniel 9:3). Like Nehemiah, Daniel fasted and prayed that God would have mercy upon the people, saying, "We have been wicked and have rebelled; we have turned away from your commands and laws" (v. 5).

In several instances in the Old Testament, fasting is linked with intercessory prayer. David prayed and fasted over his sick child (2 Samuel 12:16), weeping before the Lord in earnest intercession (vv. 21-22). Esther urged Mordecai and the Jews to fast for her as she planned to appear before her husband the king (Esther 4:16). Clearly, fasting and petition are closely linked.

There are instances of prayer and fasting in the New Testament, but they are not connected with repentance or confession. The prophetess Anna "never left the temple but worshiped night and day, fasting and praying" (Luke 2:37). At age 84, her prayer and fasting were part of her service to the Lord in His temple as she awaited the promised Savior of Israel. Also in the New Testament, the church at Antioch was fasting in connection with their worship when the Holy Spirit spoke to them about commissioning Saul and Barnabas to the Lord's work. At that point, they prayed and fasted, placed their hands on the two men and sent them off. So, we see these examples of prayer and fasting as components of worshipping the Lord and seeking His favor. Nowhere, however, is there any indication that the Lord is more likely to answer prayers if they are accompanied by fasting. Rather, fasting along with prayer seems to indicate the sincerity of the people praying and the critical nature of the situations in which they find themselves.

One thing is clear: the theology of fasting is a theology of priorities in which believers are given the opportunity to express themselves in an undivided and intensive devotion to the Lord and to the concerns of spiritual life. This devotion will be expressed by abstaining for a short while from such normal and good things as food and drink, so as to enjoy a time of uninterrupted communion with our Father. Our "confidence to enter the Most Holy Place by the blood of Jesus" (Hebrews 10:19), whether fasting or not fasting, is one of the most delightful parts of that "better thing" which is ours in Christ. Prayer and fasting should not be a burden or a duty, but rather a celebration of God's goodness and mercy to His children.

Question: What does it mean to pray without ceasing?

Answer: Paul's command in 1 Thessalonians 5:17 to "pray without ceasing," can be confusing. Obviously, it cannot mean we are to be in a head-bowed, eyes-closed posture all day long. Paul is not referring to non-stop talking, but rather an attitude of God-consciousness and God-surrender that we carry with us all the time. Every waking moment is to be lived in an awareness that God is with us and that He is actively involved and engaged in our thoughts and actions.

When our thoughts turn to worry, fear, discouragement, and anger, we are to consciously and quickly turn every thought into prayer and every prayer into thanksgiving. In his letter to the Philippians, Paul commands us to stop being anxious and instead, "in everything, by prayer and petition, with thanksgiving, present your requests to God" (Philippians 4:6). He taught the believers at Colossae to devote themselves "to prayer, being watchful and thankful" (Colossians 4:2). Paul exhorted the Ephesian believers to see prayer as a weapon to use in fighting spiritual battles (Ephesians 6:18). As we go through the day, prayer should be our first response to every fearful situation, every anxious thought, and every undesired task that God commands. A lack of prayer will cause us to depend on ourselves instead of depending on God's grace. Unceasing prayer is, in essence, continual dependence upon and communion with the Father.

For Christians, prayer should be like breathing. You do not have to think to breathe because the atmosphere exerts pressure on your lungs and essentially forces you to breathe. That is why it is more difficult to hold your breath than it is to breathe. Similarly, when we are born into the family of God, we enter into a spiritual atmosphere where God's presence and grace exert pressure, or influence, on our lives. Prayer is the normal response to that pressure. As believers, we have all entered the divine atmosphere to breathe the air of prayer.

Unfortunately, many believers hold their "spiritual breath" for long periods, thinking brief moments with God are sufficient to allow them to survive. But such restricting of their spiritual intake is caused by sinful desires. The fact is that every believer must be continually in the presence of God, constantly breathing in His truths, to be fully functional.

It is easier for Christians to feel secure by presuming on—instead of depending on—God's grace. Too many believers become satisfied with physical blessings and have little desire for spiritual ones. When programs, methods, and money produce impressive results, there is an inclination to confuse human success with divine blessing. When that happens, passionate longing for God and yearning for His help will be missing. Continual, persistent, incessant prayer is an essential part of Christian living and flows out of humility and dependence on God.

Question: What is prayer walking? Is it biblical to go on a prayer walk?

Answer: Prayer walking is the practice of praying on location, a type of intercessory prayer that involves walking to or near a particular place while praying. Some people believe that being close to a location allows them to "pray nearer to pray clearer." Prayer walks are taken by individuals, groups, and even whole churches. They can be as short as a block or as long as many miles. The idea is to use the five senses—sight, hearing, smell, taste, and touch—to increase the intercessor's understanding of prayer needs.

For example, if you walk through your neighborhood looking for things to pray about, you might come across a yard that is extremely untidy and rundown. This might prompt you to pray for the health, both physical and spiritual, of the residents inside. Some groups prayer walk around schools, prompting prayer for the teachers and students inside, for their safety and peace, and for the schemes of the devil in their school to be thwarted. Some people feel they can concentrate and direct their prayers more effectively by walking near the people and places they are praying for.

Prayer walking is a relatively new phenomenon, the origin of which is not clear. There is no biblical model for prayer walking, although since walking was the major mode of transportation in Bible times, clearly people must have walked and prayed at the same time. However, there is no direct command that prayer walking is something we should be doing. To believe that prayers offered in any setting, or while in any position, are more effective than those offered at another time or in another manner is not scriptural. In addition, while we may feel we need to be close to a location or situation to pray more clearly, our heavenly Father, who is everywhere at all times, knows exactly what needs are present and will respond to them in His own perfect will and timing. The fact that He allows us to be part of His plans through our prayers is for our benefit, not His.

We are commanded to "pray without ceasing" (1 Thessalonians 5:17), and since walking is something we do daily, surely part of praying without ceasing is praying while walking. God hears all prayers offered by those who abide in Christ (John 15:7), regardless of time, place, or position. At the same time, there certainly is no command against prayer walking, and anything that prompts us to pray is worthy of consideration.

Question: What are some hindrances to effective prayer?

Answer: The most obvious hindrance to effective prayer is the presence of unconfessed sins in the heart of the one who is praying. Because our God is holy, there is a barrier that exists between Him and us when we come to Him with unconfessed sin in our lives. "But your iniquities have separated you from your God; your sins have hidden his face from you, so that he will not hear" (Isaiah 59:2). David concurred, knowing from experience that God is far from those who try to hide their sin: "If I had cherished sin in my heart, the Lord would not have listened" (Psalm 66:18).

The Bible refers to several areas of sin that are hindrances to effective prayer. First, when we are living according to the flesh, rather than in the Spirit, our desire to pray and our ability to effectively communicate with God are hindered. Although we receive a new

357

nature when we are born again, that new nature still resides in our old flesh, and that old "tent" is corrupt and sinful. The flesh can gain control of our actions, attitudes, and motives unless we are diligent to "put to death the deeds of the body" (Romans 8:13) and be led by the Spirit in a right relationship with God. Only then will we be able to pray in close communion with Him.

One way living in the flesh manifests itself is in selfishness, another hindrance to effective prayer. When our prayers are selfishly motivated, when we ask God for what we want rather than for what He wants, our motives hinder our prayers. "This is the confidence we have in approaching God: that if we ask anything according to his will, he hears us" (1 John 5:14). Asking according to God's will is the same as asking in submission to whatever His will may be, whether or not we know what that will is. As in all things, Jesus is to be our example in prayer. He always prayed in the will of His Father: "Yet not my will, but yours be done" (Luke 22:42). Selfish prayers are always those that are intended to gratify our own selfish desires, and we should not expect God to respond to such prayers. "When you ask, you do not receive, because you ask with wrong motives, that you may spend what you get on your pleasures" (James 4:3).

Living according to selfish, fleshly desires will also hinder our prayers because it produces a hardness of heart toward others. If we are indifferent to the needs of others, we can expect God to be indifferent to our needs. When we go to God in prayer, our first concern should be His will. The second should be the needs of others. This stems from the understanding that we are to consider others better than ourselves and be concerned about their interests over and above our own (Philippians 2:3-4).

A major hindrance to effective prayer is a spirit of unforgiveness toward others. When we refuse to forgive others, a root of bitterness grows up in our hearts and chokes our prayers. How can we expect God to pour out His blessings upon us undeserving sinners if we harbor hatred and bitterness toward others? This principle is beautifully illustrated in the parable of the unforgiving servant in Matthew 18:23-35. This story teaches that God has forgiven us a debt that is beyond measure (our sin), and He expects us to forgive others as we have been forgiven. To refuse to do so will hinder our prayers.

Another major hindrance to effective prayer is unbelief and doubt. This does not mean, as some suggest, that because we come to God convinced that He will grant our requests, He is somehow obligated to do so. Praying without doubt means praying in the secure belief and understanding of God's character, nature, and motives. "And without faith it is impossible to please God, because anyone who comes to him must believe that he exists and that he rewards those who earnestly seek him" (Hebrews 11:6). When we come to God in prayer, doubting His character, purpose, and promises, we insult Him terribly. Our confidence must be in His ability to grant any request that is in accordance with His will and purpose for our lives. We must pray with the understanding that whatever He purposes is the best possible scenario. "But when he asks, he must believe and not doubt, because he who doubts is like a wave of the sea, blown and tossed by the wind. That man should not think he will receive anything from the Lord; he is a double-minded man, unstable in all he does" (James 1:6-7).

Finally, discord in the home is a definite obstacle to prayer. Peter specifically mentions this as a hindrance to the prayers of a husband whose attitude toward his wife is less than godly. "Husbands, in the same way be considerate as you live with your wives, and treat them with respect as the weaker partner and as heirs with you of the gracious gift of life, so that nothing will hinder your prayers" (1 Peter 3:7). Where there is a serious conflict in family relationships and the head of the household is not demonstrating the attitudes Peter mentions, the husband's prayer communication with God is hindered. Likewise, wives are to follow the biblical principles of submission to their husbands' headship if their own prayers are not to be hindered (Ephesians 5:22-24).

Fortunately, all these prayer hindrances can be dealt with at once by coming to God in prayers of confession and repentance. We are assured in 1 John 1:9 that "If we confess our sins, he is faithful and just and will forgive us our sins and purify us from all unrighteousness." Once we have done that, we enjoy a clear and open channel of communication with God, and our prayers will not only be heard and answered, but we will also be filled with a deep sense of joy.

Question: What is intercessory prayer?

Answer: Quite simply, intercessory prayer is the act of praying on behalf of others. The role of mediator in prayer was prevalent in the Old Testament, in the cases of Abraham, Moses, David, Samuel, Hezekiah, Elijah, Jeremiah, Ezekiel, and Daniel. Christ is pictured in the New Testament as the ultimate intercessor, and because of this, *all* Christian prayer becomes intercession since it is offered to God through and by Christ. Jesus closed the gap between us and God when He died on the cross. Because of Jesus' mediation, we can now intercede in prayer on behalf of other Christians or for the lost, asking God to grant their requests according to His will. "For there is one God and one mediator between God and men, the man Christ Jesus" (1 Timothy 2:5). "Who is he that condemns? Christ Jesus, who died—more than that, who was raised to life—is at the right hand of God and is also interceding for us" (Romans 8:34).

A wonderful model of intercessory prayer is found in Daniel 9. It has all the elements of true intercessory prayer. It is in response to the Word (v. 2); characterized by fervency (v. 3) and self-denial (v. 4); identified unselfishly with God's people (v. 5); strengthened by confession (vv. 5-15); dependent on God's character (vv. 4, 7, 9, 15); and has as its goal God's glory (vv. 16-19). Like Daniel, Christians are to come to God on behalf of others in a heartbroken and repentant attitude, recognizing their own unworthiness and with a sense of self-denial. Daniel does not say, "I have a right to demand this out of You, God, because I am one of your special, chosen intercessors." He says, "I'm a sinner," and, in effect, "I do not have a right to demand anything." True intercessory prayer seeks not only to know God's will and see it fulfilled, but to see it fulfilled whether or not it benefits us and regardless of what it costs us. True intercessory prayer seeks God's glory, not our own.

The following is only a partial list of those for whom we are to offer intercessory prayers: all in authority (1 Timothy 2:2); ministers (Philippians 1:19); the church (Psalm 122:6); friends (Job 42:8); fellow countrymen (Romans 10:1); the sick (James 5:14); enemies (Jeremiah 29:7); those who persecute us (Matthew 5:44); those who forsake us (2 Timothy 4:16); and all men (1 Timothy 2:1).

There is an erroneous idea in contemporary Christianity that those who offer up intercessory prayers are a special class of "super-Christians," called by God to a specific ministry of intercession. The Bible is clear that *all* Christians are called to be intercessors. All Christians have the Holy Spirit in their hearts and, just as He intercedes for us in accordance with God's will (Romans 8:26-27), we are to intercede for one another. This is not a privilege limited to an exclusive Christian elite; this is the command to all. In fact, not to intercede for others is sin. "As for me, far be it from me that I should sin against the Lord by failing to pray for you" (1 Samuel 12:23).

Certainly Peter and Paul, when asking others to intercede for them, did not limit their request to those with a special calling to intercession. "So Peter was kept in prison, but the church was earnestly praying to God for him" (Acts 12:5). Notice it was the whole church that prayed for him, not just those with a gift of intercession. In Ephesians 6:16-18, Paul exhorts the Ephesian believers—all of them—on the fundamentals of the Christian life, which includes intercession "on all occasions with all kinds of prayers and requests." Clearly, intercessory prayer is part of the Christian life for all believers.

Further, Paul sought prayer on his behalf from all the Roman believers in Romans 15:30. He also urged the Colossians to intercede for him in Colossians 4:2-3. Nowhere in any biblical request for intercession is there any indication that only a certain group of people could intercede. On the contrary, those who seek others to intercede for them can use all the help they can get! The idea that intercession is the privilege and calling of only some Christians is without biblical basis. Worse, it is a destructive idea that often leads to pride and a sense of superiority.

God calls all Christians to be intercessors. It is God's desire that every believer be active in intercessory prayer. What a wonderful and exalted privilege we have in being able to come boldly before the throne of Almighty God with our prayers and requests!

Chapter 13

· ·

QUESTIONS ABOUT SIN

CONTENTS

What is the definition of sin? 364

How can I know if something is a sin? 366

What are the seven deadly sins? 367

Are all sins equal to God? 368

What does the Bible say about homosexuality? 368

What does the Bible say about pornography? 369

Masturbation—is it a sin according to the Bible? 370

What does the Bible say about tattoos/body piercings? 371

What does the Bible say about drinking alcohol/wine? Is it a sin for a
    Christian to drink alcohol/wine? 372

Is gambling a sin? What does the Bible say about gambling? 374

What is the Christian view of smoking? Is smoking a sin? 375

Is gluttony a sin? What does the Bible say about overeating? 377

Did we all inherit sin from Adam and Eve? 377

What is original sin? 378

Are children punished for the sins of their parents? 380

What is the sin unto death? 381

What is the unpardonable sin/unforgivable sin? 382

Question: What is the definition of sin?

Answer: Sin is described in the Bible as transgression of the law of God (1 John 3:4) and rebellion against God (Deuteronomy 9:7; Joshua 1:18). Sin had its beginning with Lucifer, probably the most beautiful and powerful of the angels. Not content with his position, he desired to be higher than God, and that was his downfall, the beginning of sin (Isaiah 14:12-15). Renamed Satan, he brought sin to the human race in the Garden of Eden, where he tempted Adam and Eve with the same enticement, "you shall be like God." Genesis 3 describes Adam and Eve's rebellion against God and against His command. Since that time, sin has been passed down through all the generations of mankind and we, Adam's descendants, have inherited sin from him. Romans 5:12 tells us that through Adam sin entered the world, and so death was passed on to all men because "the wages of sin is death" (Romans 6:23).

Through Adam, the inherent inclination to sin entered the human race, and human beings became sinners by nature. When Adam sinned, his inner nature was transformed by his sin of rebellion, bringing to him spiritual death and depravity which would be passed on to all who came after him. We are sinners not because we sin; rather, we sin because we are sinners. This passed-on depravity is known as inherited sin. Just as we inherit physical characteristics from our parents, we inherit our sinful natures from Adam. King David lamented this condition of fallen human nature in Psalm 51:5: "Surely I was sinful at birth, sinful from the time my mother conceived me."

Another type of sin is known as imputed sin. Used in both financial and legal settings, the Greek word translated "imputed" means "to take something that belongs to someone and credit it to another's account." Before the Law of Moses was given, sin was not imputed to man, although men were still sinners because of inherited sin. After the Law was given, sins committed in violation of the Law were imputed (accounted) to them (Romans 5:13). Even before transgressions of the law were imputed to men, the ultimate penalty for sin (death) continued to reign (Romans 5:14). All humans, from Adam to Moses, were subject to death, not because of their sinful acts against the Mosaic Law (which they did not have), but because of their own inherited sinful nature. After Moses, humans were subject to death both because of inherited sin from Adam and imputed sin from violating the laws of God.

God used the principle of imputation to benefit mankind when He imputed the sin of believers to the account of Jesus Christ, who paid the penalty for that sin—death—on the cross. Imputing our sin to Jesus, God treated Him as if He were a sinner, though He was not, and had Him die for the sins of the entire world (1 John 2:2). It is important to understand that sin was imputed to Him, but He did not inherit it from Adam. He bore the penalty for sin, but He never became a sinner. His pure and perfect nature was untouched by sin. He was treated as though He were guilty of all the sins ever committed by the human race, even though He committed none. In exchange, God imputed the righteousness of Christ to believers and credited our accounts with His righteousness, just as He had credited our sins to Christ's account (2 Corinthians 5:21).

A third type of sin is personal sin, that which is committed every day by every human being. Because we have inherited a sin nature from Adam, we commit individual, personal sins, everything from seemingly innocent untruths to murder. Those who have not placed their faith in Jesus Christ must pay the penalty for these personal sins, as well as inherited and imputed sin. However, believers have been freed from the eternal penalty of sin—hell and spiritual death—but now we also have the power to resist sinning. Now we can choose whether or not to commit personal sins because we have the power to resist sin through the Holy Spirit who dwells within us, sanctifying and convicting us of our sins when we do commit them (Romans 8:9-11). Once we confess our personal sins to God and ask forgiveness for them, we are restored to perfect fellowship and communion with Him. "If we confess our sins, He is faithful and just to forgive us our sins and cleanse us from all unrighteousness" (1 John 1:9).

We are all three times condemned due to inherited sin, imputed sin, and personal sin. The only just penalty for this sin is death (Romans 6:23), not just physical death but eternal death (Revelation 20:11-15). Thankfully, inherited sin, imputed sin, and personal sin have all been crucified on the cross of Jesus, and now by faith in Jesus Christ as the Savior "we have redemption through His blood, the forgiveness of sins, according to the riches of His grace" (Ephesians 1:7).

Question: How can I know if something is a sin?

Answer: There are two issues involved in this question, the things that the Bible specifically mentions and declares to be sin and those the Bible does not directly address. Scriptural lists of various sins include Proverbs 6:16-19, Galatians 5:19-21, and 1 Corinthians 6:9-10. There can be no doubt that these passages present the activities as sinful, things God does not approve of. Murder, adultery, lying, stealing, etc.—there is no doubt the Bible presents such things as sin. The more difficult issue is in determining what is sinful in areas that the Bible does not directly address. When the Bible does not cover a certain subject, we have some general principles in His Word to guide us.

First, when there is no specific scriptural reference, it is good to ask not whether a certain thing is wrong, but, rather, if it is definitely good. The Bible says, for example, that we are to "make the most of every opportunity" (Colossians 4:5). Our few days here on earth are so short and precious in relation to eternity that we ought never to waste time on selfish things, but to use it only on "what is helpful for building others up according to their needs" (Ephesians 4:29).

A good test is to determine whether we can honestly, in good conscience, ask God to bless and use the particular activity for His own good purposes. "So whether you eat or drink or whatever you do, do it all for the glory of God" (1 Corinthians 10:31). If there is room for doubt as to whether it pleases God, then it is best to give it up. "Everything that does not come from faith is sin" (Romans 14:23). We need to remember that our bodies, as well as our souls, have been redeemed and belong to God. "Do you not know that your body is a temple of the Holy Spirit, who is in you, whom you have received from God? You are not your own; you were bought at a price. Therefore honor God with your body" (1 Corinthians 6:19-20). This great truth should have a real bearing on what we do and where we go.

In addition, we must evaluate our actions not only in relation to God, but also in relation to their effect on our family, our friends, and other people in general. Even if a particular thing may not hurt us personally, if it harmfully influences or affects someone else, it is a sin. "It is better not to eat meat or drink wine or to do anything else that will cause your brother to fall....We who are strong ought to bear with the failings of the weak and not to please ourselves" (Romans 14:21; 15:1).

Finally, remember that Jesus Christ is our Lord and Savior, and nothing else can be allowed to take priority over our conformity to His will. No habit or recreation or ambition can be allowed to have undue control over our lives; only Christ has that authority. "Everything is permissible for me—but not everything is beneficial. Everything is permissible for me—but I will not be mastered by anything" (1 Corinthians 6:12). "And whatever you do, whether in word or deed, do it all in the name of the Lord Jesus, giving thanks to God the Father through him" (Colossians 3:17).

Question: What are the seven deadly sins?

Answer: The seven deadly sins are a list originally used in early Christian teachings to educate and instruct followers concerning fallen man's tendency to sin. The misconception about the list of seven "deadly" sins is that they are sins that God will not forgive. The Bible is clear that the only sin God will not forgive is that of continued unbelief, because it rejects the only means to obtain forgiveness— Jesus Christ and His substitutionary death on the cross.

Is the idea of seven deadly sins biblical? Yes and no. Proverbs 6:16-19 declares, "There are six things the LORD hates, seven that are detestable to him: 1) haughty eyes, 2) a lying tongue, 3) hands that shed innocent blood, 4) a heart that devises wicked schemes, 5) feet that are quick to rush into evil, 6) a false witness who pours out lies, and 7) a man who stirs up dissension among brothers." However, this list is not what most people understand as the seven deadly sins.

According to Pope Gregory the Great in the 6th century, the seven deadly sins are as follows: pride, envy, gluttony, lust, anger, greed, and sloth. Although these are undeniably sins, they are never given the description of "the seven deadly sins" in the Bible. The traditional list of seven deadly sins can function as a good way to categorize the many different sins that exist. Nearly every kind of sin could be placed under one of the seven categories. More importantly, we must realize these seven sins are no more "deadly" than any other sin. All sin results in death (Romans 6:23). Praise be to God, that through Jesus Christ, all of our sins, including the "seven deadly sins," can be forgiven (Matthew 26:28; Acts 10:43; Ephesians 1:7).

Question: Are all sins equal to God?

Answer: In Matthew 5:21-28, Jesus equates committing adultery with having lust in your heart and committing murder with having hatred in your heart. However, this does not mean the sins are equal. What Jesus was trying to get across to the Pharisees is that sin is still sin even if you only want to do the act, without actually carrying it out. The religious leaders of Jesus' day taught that it was okay to think about anything you wanted to, as long as you did not act on those desires. Jesus is forcing them to realize that God judges a person's thoughts as well as his actions. Jesus proclaimed that our actions are the result of what is in our hearts (Matthew 12:34).

So, although Jesus said that lust and adultery are both sins, that does not mean they are equal. It is much worse to actually murder a person than it is to simply hate a person, even though they are both sins in God's sight. There are degrees to sin. Some sins are worse than others. At the same time, in regard to both eternal consequences and salvation, all sins are the same. Every sin will lead to eternal condemnation (Romans 6:23). All sin, no matter how "small," is against an infinite and eternal God, and is therefore worthy of an infinite and eternal penalty. Further, there is no sin too "big" that God cannot forgive it. Jesus died to pay the penalty for sin (1 John 2:2). Jesus died for *all* of our sins (2 Corinthians 5:21). Are all sins equal to God? Yes and no. In severity? No. In penalty? Yes. In forgivability? Yes.

Question: What does the Bible say about homosexuality? Is homosexuality a sin?

Answer: The Bible consistently tells us that homosexual activity is a sin (Genesis 19:1-13; Leviticus 18:22; Romans 1:26-27; 1 Corinthians 6:9). Romans 1:26-27 teaches specifically that homosexuality is a result of denying and disobeying God. When people continue in sin and unbelief, God "gives them over" to even more wicked and depraved sin in order to show them the futility and hopelessness of life apart from God. 1 Corinthians 6:9 proclaims that homosexual "offenders" will not inherit the kingdom of God.

God does not create a person with homosexual desires. The Bible tells us that people become homosexuals because of sin (Romans 1:24-27) and ultimately because of their own choice. A person may be born with a greater susceptibility to homosexuality, just as some people are born with a tendency to violence and other sins. That does not excuse the person's choosing to sin by giving in to sinful desires. If a person is born with a greater susceptibility to anger/rage, does that make it right for him to give into those desires? Of course not! The same is true with homosexuality.

However, the Bible does not describe homosexuality as a "greater" sin than any other. All sin is offensive to God. Homosexuality is just one of the many things listed in 1 Corinthians 6:9-10 that will keep a person from the kingdom of God. According to the Bible, God's forgiveness is just as available to a homosexual as it is to an adulterer, idol worshipper, murderer, thief, etc. God also promises the strength for victory over sin, including homosexuality, to all those who will believe in Jesus Christ for their salvation (1 Corinthians 6:11; 2 Corinthians 5:17; Philippians 4:13).

Question: What does the Bible say about pornography?

Answer: By far, the most searched for terms on the internet are related to pornography. Pornography is rampant in the world today. Perhaps more than anything else, Satan has succeeded in twisting and perverting sex. He has taken what is good and right (loving sex between a husband and wife) and replaced it with lust, pornography, adultery, rape, and homosexuality. Pornography can be the first step on a very slippery slope of ever-increasing wickedness and immorality (Romans 6:19). The addictive nature of pornography is well documented. Just as a drug user must consume greater and more powerful quantities of drugs to achieve the same "high," pornography drags a person deeper and deeper into hard-core sexual addictions and ungodly desires.

The three main categories of sin are the lust of the flesh, the lust of the eyes, and the pride of life (1 John 2:16). Pornography definitely causes us to lust after flesh, and it is undeniably a lust of the eyes. Pornography definitely does not qualify as one of the things we are to think about, according to Philippians 4:8. Pornography is addictive (1 Corinthians 6:12; 2 Peter 2:19), and destructive (Proverbs 6:25-28; Ezekiel 20:30; Ephesians 4:19). Lusting after other people in our minds, which is the essence of pornography, is offensive to God (Matthew 5:28). When habitual devotion to pornography characterizes a person's life, it demonstrates the person is not saved (1 Corinthians 6:9).

For those involved in pornography, God can and will give the victory. Are you involved with pornography and desire freedom from it? Here are some steps to victory: 1) Confess your sin to God (1 John 1:9). 2) Ask God to cleanse, renew, and transform your mind (Romans 12:2). 3) Ask God to fill your mind with Philippians 4:8. 4) Learn to possess your body in holiness (1 Thessalonians 4:3-4). 5) Understand the proper meaning of sex and rely on your spouse alone to meet that need (1 Corinthians 7:1-5). 6) Realize that if you walk in the Spirit, you will not fulfill the lusts of the flesh (Galatians 5:16). 7) Take practical steps to reduce your exposure to graphic images. Install pornography blockers on your computer, limit television and video usage, and find another Christian who will pray for you and help keep you accountable.

Question: Masturbation—is it a sin according to the Bible?

Answer: The Bible never explicitly mentions masturbation or states whether or not masturbation is a sin. The Scripture most frequently pointed to in regards to masturbation is the story of Onan in Genesis 38:9-10. Some interpret this passage as saying that "spilling your seed" on the ground is a sin. However, that is not precisely what the passage is saying. God condemned Onan not for "spilling his seed" but because Onan refused to fulfill his duty to provide an heir for his brother. The passage is not about masturbation, but rather about fulfilling a family duty. A second passage sometimes used as evidence for masturbation's being a sin is Matthew 5:27-30. Jesus speaks against having lustful thoughts and then says, "If your right hand causes you to sin, cut it off and throw it away." While there are parallels between this passage and masturbation, it is unlikely that masturbation was what Jesus was alluding to.

While the Bible nowhere explicitly states that masturbation is a sin, there is no question as to whether the actions that lead to masturbation are sinful. Masturbation is nearly always the result of lustful thoughts, sexual stimulation, and/or pornographic images. It is these problems that need to be dealt with. If the sins of lust, immoral thoughts, and pornography are forsaken and overcome, masturbation will become a non-issue. Many people struggle with guilty feelings concerning masturbation, when in reality, the things that led to the act are far more worthy of repentance.

There are some biblical principles that can be applied to the issue of masturbation. Ephesians 5:3 declares, "Among you there must not be even a hint of sexual immorality, or of any kind of impurity." It is hard to see how masturbating can pass that particular test. The Bible teaches us, "So whether you eat or drink or whatever you do, do it all for the glory of God" (1 Corinthians 10:31). If you cannot give God glory for something, you should not do it. If a person is not fully convinced that an activity is pleasing to God, then it is a sin: "Everything that does not come from faith is sin" (Romans 14:23). Further, we need to remember that our bodies have been redeemed and belong to God. "Do you not know that your body is a temple of the Holy Spirit, who is in you, whom you have received from God? You are not your own; you were bought at a price. Therefore honor God with your body" (1 Corinthians 6:19-20). This great truth should have a real bearing on what we do with our bodies. In light of these principles, the conclusion that masturbation is a sin is biblical. Clearly, masturbation is not glorifying to God; it does not avoid the appearance of immorality, nor does it pass the test of God's having ownership over our bodies.

Question: What does the Bible say about tattoos/body piercings?

Answer: The Old Testament law commanded the Israelites, "Do not cut your bodies for the dead or put tattoo marks on yourselves. I am the LORD" (Leviticus 19:28). So, even though believers today are not under the Old Testament law (Romans 10:4; Galatians 3:23-25; Ephesians 2:15), the fact that there was a command against tattoos should raise some questions. The New Testament does not say anything about whether or not a believer should get a tattoo.

In relation to tattoos and body piercings, a good test is to determine whether we can honestly, in good conscience, ask God to bless and use that particular activity for His own good purposes. "So whether you eat or drink or whatever you do, do it all for the glory of God" (1 Corinthians 10:31). The New Testament does not command against tattoos or body piercings, but it also does not give us any reason to believe God would have us get tattoos or body piercings.

An important scriptural principle on issues the Bible does not specifically address is if there is room for doubt whether it pleases God, then it is best not to engage in that activity. Romans 14:23 reminds us that anything that does not come from faith is sin. We need to remember that our bodies, as well as our souls, have been redeemed and belong to God. Although 1 Corinthians 6:19-20 does not directly apply to tattoos or body piercings, it does give us a principle: "Do you not know that your body is a temple of the Holy Spirit, who is in you, whom you have received from God? You are not your own; you were bought at a price. Therefore honor God with your body." This great truth should have a real bearing on what we do and where we go with our bodies. If our bodies belong to God, we should make sure we have His clear "permission" before we "mark them up" with tattoos or body piercings.

Question: What does the Bible say about drinking alcohol/wine? Is it a sin for a Christian to drink alcohol/wine?

Answer: Scripture has much to say regarding the drinking of alcohol (Leviticus 10:9; Numbers 6:3; Deuteronomy 29:6; Judges 13:4, 7, 14; Proverbs 20:1; 31:4; Isaiah 5:11, 22; 24:9; 28:7; 29:9; 56:12). However, Scripture does not necessarily forbid a Christian from drinking beer, wine, or any other drink containing alcohol. In fact, some Scriptures discuss alcohol in positive terms. Ecclesiastes 9:7 instructs, "Drink your wine with a merry heart." Psalm 104:14-15 states that God gives wine "that makes glad the heart of men." Amos 9:14 discusses drinking wine from your own vineyard as a sign of God's blessing. Isaiah 55:1 encourages, "Yes, come buy wine and milk…"

What God commands Christians regarding alcohol is to avoid drunkenness (Ephesians 5:18). The Bible condemns drunkenness and its effects (Proverbs 23:29-35). Christians are also commanded to not allow their bodies to be "mastered" by anything (1 Corinthians 6:12; 2 Peter 2:19). Drinking alcohol in excess is undeniably addictive. Scripture also forbids a Christian from doing anything that might offend other Christians or encourage them to sin against their conscience (1 Corinthians 8:9-13). In light of these principles, it would be extremely difficult for any Christian to say he is drinking alcohol in excess to the glory of God (1 Corinthians 10:31).

Jesus changed water into wine. It even seems that Jesus drank wine on occasion (John 2:1-11; Matthew 26:29). In New Testament times, the water was not very clean. Without modern sanitation, the water was often filled with bacteria, viruses, and all kinds of contaminants. The same is true in many third-world countries today. As a result, people often drank wine (or grape juice) because it was far less likely to be contaminated. In 1 Timothy 5:23, Paul was instructing Timothy to stop drinking the water (which was probably causing his stomach problems) and instead drink wine. In that day, wine was fermented (containing alcohol), but not necessarily to the degree it is today. It is incorrect to say that it was grape juice, but it is also incorrect to say that it was the same thing as the wine commonly used today. Again, Scripture does not forbid Christians from drinking beer, wine, or any other drink containing alcohol. Alcohol is not, in and of itself, tainted by sin. It is drunkenness and addiction to alcohol that a Christian must absolutely refrain from (Ephesians 5:18; 1 Corinthians 6:12).

Alcohol, consumed in small quantities, is neither harmful nor addictive. In fact, some doctors advocate drinking small amounts of red wine for its health benefits, especially for the heart. Consumption of small quantities of alcohol is a matter of Christian freedom. Drunkenness and addiction are sin. However, due to the biblical concerns regarding alcohol and its effects, due to the easy temptation to consume alcohol in excess, and due to the possibility of causing offense and/or stumbling of others, it is usually best for a Christian to abstain entirely from drinking alcohol.

Question: Is gambling a sin? What does the Bible say about gambling?

Answer: The Bible does not specifically condemn gambling, betting, or the lottery. The Bible does warn us, however, to stay away from the love of money (1 Timothy 6:10; Hebrews 13:5). Scripture also encourages us to stay away from attempts to "get rich quick" (Proverbs 13:11; 23:5; Ecclesiastes 5:10). Gambling most definitely is focused on the love of money and undeniably tempts people with the promise of quick and easy riches.

What is wrong with gambling? Gambling is a difficult issue because if it is done in moderation and only on occasion, it is a waste of money, but it is not necessarily evil. People waste money on all sorts of activities. Gambling is no more or less of a waste of money than seeing a movie (in many cases), eating an unnecessarily expensive meal, or purchasing a worthless item. At the same time, the fact that money is wasted on other things does not justify gambling. Money should not be wasted. Excess money should be saved for future needs or given to the Lord's work, not gambled away.

While the Bible does not explicitly mention gambling, it does mention events of "luck" or "chance." As an example, casting lots is used in Leviticus to choose between the sacrificial goat and the scapegoat. Joshua cast lots to determine the allotment of land to the various tribes. Nehemiah cast lots to determine who would live inside the walls of Jerusalem. The apostles cast lots to determine the replacement for Judas. Proverbs 16:33 says, "The lot is cast in the lap, but its every decision is from the Lord."

What would the Bible say about casinos and lotteries? Casinos use all sorts of marketing schemes to entice gamblers to risk as much money as possible. They often offer inexpensive or even free alcohol, which encourages drunkenness, and thereby a decreased ability to make wise decisions. Everything in a casino is perfectly rigged for taking money in large sums and giving nothing in return, except for fleeting and empty pleasures. Lotteries attempt to portray themselves as a way to fund education and/or social programs. However, studies show that lottery participants are usually those who can least afford to be spending money on lottery tickets. The allure of "getting rich quick" is too great a temptation to resist for those who are desperate.

The chances of winning are infinitesimal, which results in many peoples' lives being ruined.

Can lotto/lottery proceeds please God? Many people claim to be playing the lottery or gambling so that they can give the money to the church or to some other good cause. While this may be a good motive, reality is that few use gambling winnings for godly purposes. Studies show that the vast majority of lottery winners are in an even worse financial situation a few years after winning a jackpot than they were before. Few, if any, truly give the money to a good cause. Further, God does not need our money to fund His mission in the world. Proverbs 13:11 says, "Dishonest money dwindles away, but he who gathers money little by little makes it grow." God is sovereign and will provide for the needs of the church through honest means. Would God be honored by receiving donated drug money or money stolen in a bank robbery? Of course not. Neither does God need or want money that was "stolen" from the poor in the temptation for riches.

First Timothy 6:10 tells us, "For the love of money is a root of all kinds of evil. Some people, eager for money, have wandered from the faith and pierced themselves with many griefs." Hebrews 13:5 declares, "Keep your lives free from the love of money and be content with what you have, because God has said, 'Never will I leave you; never will I forsake you.'" Matthew 6:24 proclaims, "No one can serve two masters. Either he will hate the one and love the other, or he will be devoted to the one and despise the other. You cannot serve both God and Money."

Question: What is the Christian view of smoking? Is smoking a sin?

Answer: The Bible never directly mentions smoking. There are principles, however, that definitely apply to smoking. First, the Bible commands us not to allow our bodies to become "mastered" by anything. "Everything is permissible for me—but not everything is beneficial. Everything is permissible for me—but I will not be mastered by anything" (1 Corinthians 6:12). Smoking is undeniably strongly addictive. Later in the same passage we are told, "Do you not know that your body is a temple of the Holy Spirit, who is in you, whom you have received from God? You are not your own; you were bought at a price. Therefore honor God with your body" (1 Corinthians 6:19-20). Smoking is undoubtedly very bad for your health. Smoking has been proven to damage the lungs and the heart.

Can smoking be considered "beneficial" (1 Corinthians 6:12)? Can it be said that smoking is truly honoring God with your body (1 Corinthians 6:20)? Can a person honestly smoke "for the glory of God" (1 Corinthians 10:31)? We believe that the answer to these three questions is a resounding "no." As a result, we believe that smoking is a sin and therefore should not be practiced by followers of Jesus Christ.

Some argue against this view by pointing to the fact that many people eat unhealthy foods, which can be just as addicting and just as bad for the body. As an example, many people are so helplessly addicted to caffeine that they cannot function without their first cup of coffee in the morning. While this is true, how does that make smoking right? It is our contention that Christians should avoid gluttony and excessively unhealthy eating. Yes, Christians are often hypocritical by condemning one sin and condoning another, but, again, this does not make smoking honoring to God.

Another argument against this view of smoking is that many godly men have been smokers, such as the famous British preacher C.H. Spurgeon, who was known to smoke cigars. Again, we do not believe this argument holds any weight. We believe Spurgeon was wrong for smoking. Was he otherwise a godly man and fantastic teacher of God's Word? Absolutely! Does that make all of his actions and habits honoring to God? No.

In stating that smoking is a sin, we are not stating that all smokers are unsaved. There are many true believers in Jesus Christ who smoke. Smoking does not prevent a person from being saved. Nor does it cause a person to lose salvation. Smoking is no less forgivable than any other sin, whether for a person becoming a Christian or a Christian confessing his/her sin to God (1 John 1:9). At the same time, we firmly believe that smoking is a sin that should be forsaken and, with God's help, overcome.

Question: Is gluttony a sin? What does the Bible say about overeating?

Answer: Gluttony seems to be a sin that Christians like to ignore. We are often quick to label smoking and drinking as sins, but for some reason gluttony is accepted or at least tolerated. Many of the arguments used against smoking and drinking, such as health and addiction, apply equally to overeating. Many believers would not even consider having a glass of wine or smoking a cigarette but have no qualms about gorging themselves at the dinner table. This should not be!

Proverbs 23:20-21 warns us, "Do not join those who drink too much wine or gorge themselves on meat, for drunkards and gluttons become poor, and drowsiness clothes them in rags." Proverbs 28:7 declares, "He who keeps the law is a discerning son, but a companion of gluttons disgraces his father." Proverbs 23:2 proclaims, "Put a knife to your throat if you are given to gluttony."

Physical appetites are an analogy of our ability to control ourselves. If we are unable to control our eating habits, we are probably also unable to control other habits, such as those of the mind (lust, covetousness, anger) and unable to keep our mouths from gossip or strife. We are not to let our appetites control us, but we are to have control over our appetites. (See Deuteronomy 21:20, Proverbs 23:2, 2 Peter 1:5-7, 2 Timothy 3:1-9, and 2 Corinthians 10:5.) The ability to say "no" to anything in excess—self-control—is one of the fruits of the Spirit common to all believers (Galatians 5:22).

God has blessed us by filling the earth with foods that are delicious, nutritious, and pleasurable. We should honor God's creation by enjoying these foods and by eating them in appropriate quantities. God calls us to control our appetites, rather than allowing them to control us.

Question: Did we all inherit sin from Adam and Eve?

Answer: Yes, all people inherited sin from Adam and Eve, specifically from Adam. Sin is described in the Bible as transgression of the law of God (1 John 3:4) and rebellion against God (Deuteronomy 9:7; Joshua 1:18). Genesis 3 describes Adam and Eve's rebellion against

God and His command. Because of Adam and Eve's disobedience, sin has been an "inheritance" for all of their descendants. Romans 5:12 tells us that, through Adam, sin entered the world and so death was passed on to all men because all have sinned. This passed-on sin is known as inherited sin. Just as we inherit physical characteristics from our parents, we inherit our sinful nature from Adam.

Adam and Eve were made in the image and likeness of God (Genesis 1:26-27; 9:6). However, we are also in the image and likeness of Adam (Genesis 5:3). When Adam fell into sin, the result was every one of his descendants also being "infected" with sin. David lamented this fact in one of his Psalms: "Surely I was sinful at birth, sinful from the time my mother conceived me" (Psalm 51:5). This does not mean that his mother bore him illegitimately; rather, his mother had inherited a sin nature from her parents, and they from their parents, and so on. David inherited sin from his parents, just as we all do. Even if we live the best life possible, we are still sinners as a result of inherited sin.

Being born sinners results in the fact that we all sin. Notice the progression in Romans 5:12: sin entered the world through Adam, death follows sin, death comes to all people, all people sin because they inherit sin from Adam. Because "all have sinned and fall short of the glory of God" (Romans 3:23), we need a perfect, sinless sacrifice to wash away our sin, something we are powerless to do on our own. Thankfully, Jesus Christ is the Savior from sin! Our sin has been crucified on the cross of Jesus, and now "in Him we have redemption through His blood, the forgiveness of sins, according to the riches of His grace" (Ephesians 1:7). God, in His infinite wisdom, has provided the remedy for the sin we inherit, and that remedy is available to everyone: "Therefore, my brothers, I want you to know that through Jesus the forgiveness of sins is proclaimed to you" (Acts 13:38).

Question: What is original sin?

Answer: The term "original sin" deals with Adam's sin of disobedience in eating from the Tree of Knowledge of Good and Evil and its effects upon the rest of the human race. Original sin can be defined as "that sin and its guilt that we all possess in God's eyes as a direct result of Adam's sin in the Garden of Eden." The doctrine of original sin focuses particularly on its effects on our nature and our standing before God, even before we are old enough to commit conscious sin. There are three main views that deal with that effect.

Pelagianism: This view says that Adam's sin had no effect upon the souls of his descendants other than his sinful example influencing those who followed after him to also sin. According to this view, man has the ability to stop sinning if he simply chooses to. This teaching runs contrary to a number of passages that indicate man is hopelessly enslaved by his sins (apart from God's intervention) and that his good works are "dead" or worthless in meriting God's favor (Ephesians 2:1-2; Matthew 15:18-19; Romans 7:23; Hebrews 6:1; 9:14).

Arminianism: Arminians believe Adam's sin has resulted in the rest of mankind inheriting a propensity to sin, commonly referred to as having a "sin nature." This sin nature causes us to sin in the same way that a cat's nature causes it to meow—it comes naturally. According to this view, man cannot stop sinning on his own; that is why God gives a universal grace to all to enable us to stop. In Arminianism, this grace is called prevenient grace. According to this view, we are not held accountable for Adam's sin, just our own. This teaching runs contrary to the fact that all bear the punishment for sin, even though all may not have sinned in a manner similar to Adam (1 Corinthians 15:22; Romans 5:12-18). Nor is the teaching of prevenient grace explicitly found in Scripture.

Calvinism: The Calvinistic doctrine states that Adam's sin has resulted not only in our having a sin nature, but also in our incurring guilt before God for which we deserve punishment. Being conceived with original sin upon us (Psalm 51:5) results in our inheriting a sin nature so wicked that Jeremiah 17:9 describes the human heart as "deceitful above all things and beyond cure." Not only was Adam found guilty because he sinned, but his guilt and his punishment (death) belongs to us as well (Romans 5:12, 19). There are two views as to why Adam's guilt should be seen by God as also belonging to us. The first view states that the human race was within Adam in seed form; thus when Adam sinned, we sinned in him. This is similar to the biblical teaching that Levi (a descendent of Abraham) paid tithes to Melchizedek in Abraham (Genesis 14:20; Hebrews 7:4-9), even though Levi was not born until hundreds of years later. The other main view is that Adam served as our representative and so, when he sinned, we were found guilty as well.

The Calvinistic view sees one as unable to overcome his sin apart from the power of the Holy Spirit, a power possessed only when one turns in reliance upon Christ and His atoning sacrifice for sin upon the cross. The Calvinistic view of original sin is most consistent with biblical teaching. However, how can God hold us accountable for a sin we did not personally commit? There is a plausible interpretation that we become responsible for original sin when we choose to accept, and act according to, our sinful nature. There comes a point in our lives when we become aware of our own sinfulness. At that point we should reject the sinful nature and repent of it. Instead, we all "approve" that sinful nature, in effect saying that it is good. In approving our sinfulness, we are expressing agreement with the actions of Adam and Eve in the Garden of Eden. We are therefore guilty of that sin without actually having committed it.

Question: Are children punished for the sins of their parents?

Answer: Children are not punished for the sins committed by their parents; neither are parents punished for the sins of their children. Each of us is responsible for our own sins. Ezekiel 18:20 tells us, "The soul who sins is the one who will die. The son will not share the guilt of the father, nor will the father share the guilt of the son." This verse clearly shows that punishment for one's sins is borne by that person.

There is a verse that has led some to believe the Bible teaches intergenerational punishment for sin, but this interpretation is incorrect. The verse in question is Exodus 20:5, which says in reference to idols, "You shall not bow down to them or worship them; for I, the LORD your God, am a jealous God, punishing the children for the sin of the fathers to the third and fourth generation of those who hate me." This verse is speaking not so much of punishment, but of consequences. It is saying that the consequences of a man's sins can be felt generations later. God was telling the Israelites that their children would feel the impact of their parents' generation as a natural consequence of their disobedience and hatred of God. Children raised in such an environment would practice similar idolatry, thus falling into the established pattern of disobedience. The effect of a disobedient generation was to plant wickedness so deeply that it took several generations to reverse. God does not hold us accountable for the sins of our parents, but we sometimes suffer as a result of the sins our parents committed, as Exodus 20:5 illustrates.

As Ezekiel 18:20 shows, each of us is responsible for his own sins and we must bear the punishment for them. We cannot share our guilt with another, nor can another be held responsible for it. There is, however, one exception to this rule, and it applies to all mankind. One man bore the sins of others and paid the penalty for them so sinners could become completely righteous and pure in the sight of God. That man is Jesus Christ. God sent Jesus into the world to exchange His perfection for our sin. "God made him who had no sin to be sin for us, so that in him we might become the righteousness of God" (2 Corinthians 5:21). Jesus Christ takes away the punishment for sin for those who come to Him in faith.

Question: What is the sin unto death?

Answer: First John 5:16 is one of the most difficult verses in the New Testament to interpret. "If anyone sees his brother commit a sin that does not lead to death, he should pray and God will give him life. I refer to those whose sin does not lead to death. There is a sin that leads to death. I am not saying that he should pray about that." Of all the interpretations out there, none seems to answer all the questions concerning this verse. The best interpretation may be found by comparing this verse to what happened to Ananias and Sapphira in Acts 5:1-10 (see also 1 Corinthians 11:30). The "sin unto death" is deliberate, willful, continuous, unrepentant sin. God, in His grace, allows His children to sin without immediately punishing them. However, there comes a point when God will no longer allow a believer to continue in unrepentant sin. When this point is reached, God sometimes decides to punish a Christian, even to the point of taking his or her life.

That is what He did in Acts 5:1-10 and 1 Corinthians 11:28-32. This is perhaps what Paul described to the Corinthian church in 1 Corinthians 5:1-5. We are to pray for Christians who are sinning. However, there may come a time when God will no longer hear prayers for a sinning believer for whom He has determined that judgment is due. It is difficult to realize there are times when it is just too late to pray for a person. God is good and just, and we will just have to let Him decide when it is too late.

Question: What is the unpardonable sin/unforgivable sin?

Answer: The case of the "unpardonable sin/unforgivable sin" or "blasphemy of the Holy Spirit" is mentioned in Mark 3:22-30 and Matthew 12:22-32. The term "blasphemy" may be generally defined as "defiant irreverence." We would apply the term to such sins as cursing God or willfully degrading things relating to Him. It is also attributing some evil to God, or denying Him some good that we should attribute to Him. This case of blasphemy, however, is a specific one called "the blasphemy against the Holy Spirit" in Matthew 12:31. In this passage, the Pharisees, having witnessed irrefutable proof that Jesus was working miracles in the power of the Holy Spirit, claimed instead that He was possessed by the demon Beelzebub (Matthew 12:24). In Mark 3:30, Jesus is very specific about what exactly they did to commit "the blasphemy against the Holy Spirit."

This blasphemy then has to do with accusing Jesus Christ (in person, on earth) of being demon-possessed. There are other ways to blaspheme the Holy Spirit (such as lying to Him, as in the case of Ananias and Sapphira in Acts 5:1-10), but the accusation against Jesus was *the* blasphemy that was unpardonable. This specific unpardonable sin against the Holy Spirit cannot be duplicated today.

The only unpardonable sin today is that of continued unbelief. There is no pardon for a person who dies in unbelief. John 3:16 tells us, "For God so loved the world that he gave his one and only Son, that whoever believes in him shall not perish but have eternal life." The only condition in which someone would have no forgiveness is if he/she is not among the "whoever" that believes in Him. Jesus said, "I am the way and the truth and the life. No one comes to the Father except through me" (John 14:6). To reject the *only* means of salvation is to condemn oneself to an eternity in hell because to reject the only pardon is, obviously, unpardonable.

Many people fear they have committed some sin that God cannot or will not forgive, and they feel there is no hope for them, no matter what they do. Satan would like nothing better than to keep us laboring under this misconception. The truth is that if a person has this fear, he/she needs only to come before God, confess that sin, repent of it, and accept God's promise of forgiveness. "If we confess our sins, he is faithful and just and will forgive us our sins and purify us from all unrighteousness" (1 John 1:9). This verse assures us that God is ready to forgive any sin—no matter how heinous—if we come to Him in repentance. If you are suffering under a load of guilt today, God is waiting with His arms open in love and compassion for you to come to Him. He will never disappoint or fail to pardon those who do.

Chapter 14

. . . .

QUESTIONS ABOUT HEAVEN,

HELL, AND ETERNITY

CONTENTS

Is there life after death?..386

What happens after death?...388

Can people in heaven look down and see us?...........................389

Will we be able to see and know our friends and family members in
heaven? 390

What are the new heavens and the new earth?.........................391

Is hell real? Is hell eternal?..392

How is eternity in hell a fair punishment for sin? 392

What is the judgment seat of Christ?...394

What is the great white throne judgment?................................395

Do pets/animals go to heaven? Do pets/animals have souls?...................397

Is heaven real? 398

What is heaven like?...399

Are there different levels of heaven? 400

Are there different levels of punishment in hell?....................401

What does the Bible say about soul sleep? 402

Question: Is there life after death?

Answer: The existence of life after death is a universal question. Job speaks for all of us by stating, "Man born of woman is of few days and full of trouble. He springs up like a flower and withers away; like a fleeting shadow, he does not endure....If a man dies, will he live again?" (Job 14:1-2, 14). Like Job, all of us have been challenged by this question. Exactly what happens to us after we die? Do we simply cease to exist? Is life a revolving door of departing and returning to earth in order to eventually achieve personal greatness? Does everyone go to the same place, or do we go to different places? Is there really a heaven and hell?

The Bible tells us that there is not only life after death, but eternal life so glorious that "no eye has seen, no ear has heard, and no mind has imagined what God has prepared for those who love him" (1 Corinthians 2:9). Jesus Christ, God in the flesh, came to the earth to give us this gift of eternal life. "But he was pierced for our transgressions, he was crushed for our iniquities; the punishment that brought us peace was upon him, and by his wounds we are healed" (Isaiah 53:5). Jesus took on the punishment that all of us deserve and sacrificed His life to pay the penalty for our sin. Three days later, He proved Himself victorious over death by rising from the grave. He remained on the earth for forty days and was witnessed by thousands before ascending to heaven. Romans 4:25 says, "He was delivered over to death for our sins and was raised to life for our justification."

The resurrection of the Christ is a well-documented event. The apostle Paul challenged people to question eyewitnesses for its validity, and no one was able to contest its truth. The resurrection is the cornerstone of the Christian faith. Because Christ was raised from the dead, we can have faith that we, too, will be resurrected. The resurrection of Jesus Christ is the ultimate proof of life after death. Christ was only the first of a great harvest of those who will be raised to life again. Physical death came through one man, Adam, to whom we are all related. But all who have been adopted into God's family through faith in Jesus Christ will be given new life (1 Corinthians 15:20-22). Just as God raised up Jesus' body, so will our bodies be resurrected upon Jesus' return (1 Corinthians 6:14).

Although we will all be eventually resurrected, not everyone will go to heaven. A choice must be made by each person in this life, and this choice will determine one's eternal destination. The Bible says that it is appointed for us to die only once, and after that will come judgment (Hebrews 9:27). Those who have been made righteous by faith in Christ will go into eternal life in heaven, but those who reject Christ as Savior will be sent to eternal punishment in hell (Matthew 25:46). Hell, like heaven, is not simply a state of existence, but a literal place. It is a place where the unrighteous will experience never-ending, eternal wrath from God. Hell is described as a bottomless pit (Luke 8:31; Revelation 9:1) and a lake of fire, burning with sulfur, where the inhabitants will be tormented day and night forever and ever (Revelation 20:10). In hell, there will be weeping and gnashing of teeth, indicating intense grief and anger (Matthew 13:42).

God takes no pleasure in the death of the wicked, but desires them to turn from their wicked ways so that they can live (Ezekiel 33:11). But He will not force us into submission; if we choose to reject Him, He accepts our decision to live eternally apart from Him. Life on earth is a test, a preparation for what is to come. For believers, life after death is eternal life in heaven with God. For unbelievers, life after death is eternity in the lake of fire. How can we receive eternal life after death and avoid an eternity in the lake of fire? There is only one way—through faith and trust in Jesus Christ. Jesus said, "I am the resurrection and the life. He who believes in me will live, even though he dies; and whoever lives and believes in me will never die..." (John 11:25-26).

The free gift of eternal life is available to all. "Whoever believes in the Son has eternal life, but whoever rejects the Son will not see life, for God's wrath remains on him" (John 3:36). We will not be given the opportunity to accept God's gift of salvation after death. Our eternal destination is determined in our earthly lifetimes by our reception or rejection of Jesus Christ. "I tell you, now is the time of God's favor, now is the day of salvation" (2 Corinthians 6:2). If we trust the death of Jesus Christ as the full payment for our sin against God, we are guaranteed not only a meaningful life on earth, but also eternal life after death, in the glorious presence of Christ.

Have you made a decision to receive Jesus Christ as your personal Savior because of what you have read here? If so, please send us an email at questions@gotquestions.org.

Question: What happens after death?

Answer: Within the Christian faith, there is a significant amount of confusion regarding what happens after death. Some hold that after death, everyone "sleeps" until the final judgment, after which everyone will be sent to heaven or hell. Others believe that at the moment of death, people are instantly judged and sent to their eternal destinations. Still others claim that when people die, their souls/spirits are sent to a "temporary" heaven or hell, to await the final resurrection, the final judgment, and then the finality of their eternal destination. So, what exactly does the Bible say happens after death?

First, for the believer in Jesus Christ, the Bible tells us that after death believers' souls/spirits are taken to heaven, because their sins are forgiven by having received Christ as Savior (John 3:16, 18, 36). For believers, death is to be "away from the body and at home with the Lord" (2 Corinthians 5:6-8; Philippians 1:23). However, passages such as 1 Corinthians 15:50-54 and 1 Thessalonians 4:13-17 describe believers being resurrected and given glorified bodies. If believers go to be with Christ immediately after death, what is the purpose of this resurrection? It seems that while the souls/spirits of believers go to be with Christ immediately after death, the physical body remains in the grave "sleeping." At the resurrection of believers, the physical body is resurrected, glorified, and then reunited with the soul/spirit. This reunited and glorified body-soul-spirit will be the possession of believers for eternity in the new heavens and new earth (Revelation 21-22).

Second, for those who do not receive Jesus Christ as Savior, death means everlasting punishment. However, similar to the destiny of believers, unbelievers also seem to be sent immediately to a temporary holding place, to await their final resurrection, judgment, and eternal destiny. Luke 16:22-23 describes a rich man being tormented immediately after death. Revelation 20:11-15 describes all the unbelieving dead being resurrected, judged at the great white throne, and then being cast into the lake of fire. Unbelievers, then, are not sent to hell (the lake of fire) immediately after death, but rather are in a temporary realm of judgment and condemnation. However, even though unbelievers are not instantly sent to the lake of fire, their immediate fate after death is not a pleasant one. The rich man cried out, "I am in agony in this fire" (Luke 16:24).

Therefore, after death, a person resides in a "temporary" heaven or hell. After this temporary realm, at the final resurrection, a person's eternal destiny will not change. The precise "location" of that eternal destiny is what changes. Believers will ultimately be granted entrance into the new heavens and new earth (Revelation 21:1). Unbelievers will ultimately be sent to the lake of fire (Revelation 20:11-15). These are the final, eternal destinations of all people—based entirely on whether or not they had trusted Jesus Christ alone for salvation (Matthew 25:46; John 3:36).

Question: Can people in heaven look down and see us?

Answer: Hebrews 12:1 states, "Therefore, since we are surrounded by such a great cloud of witnesses..." Some understand the "cloud of witnesses" to be people looking down on us from heaven. That is not the correct interpretation. Hebrews chapter 11 records many people whom God commended for their faith. It is these people who are the "cloud of witnesses." They are "witnesses" not in that they are watching us, but rather in that they have set an example for us. They are witnesses for Christ and God and truth. Hebrews 12:1 continues, "...let us throw off everything that hinders and the sin that so easily entangles, and let us run with perseverance the race marked out for us." Because of the faith and diligence of Christians who went before us, we should be inspired to follow their example.

The Bible does not specifically say whether or not people in heaven can look down on us who are still on the earth. It is highly unlikely that they can. Why? First, they would sometimes see things that would cause them grief or pain, namely, acts of sin and evil. Since there is no grief, tears, or unhappiness in heaven (Revelation 21:4), it does not seem that observing earthly events would be possible. Second, people in heaven are so preoccupied with worshipping God and enjoying the glories of heaven that it does not seem they would have significant interest in what is happening here on earth. The very fact that they are free from sin and experiencing God's presence in heaven surely is more than enough to captivate their attention. While it is possible that God allows people in heaven to look down upon their loved ones, the Bible gives us no reason to believe this actually occurs.

Question: Will we be able to see and know our friends and family members in heaven?

Answer: Many people say that the first thing they want to do when they arrive in heaven is see all their friends and loved ones who have passed on before them. In eternity, there will be plenty of time to see, know, and spend time with our friends and family members. However, that will not be our primary focus in heaven. We will be far more occupied with worshipping God and enjoying the wonders of heaven. Our reunions with loved ones are more likely to be filled with recounting the grace and glory of God in our lives, His wondrous love, and His mighty works. We will rejoice all the more because we can praise and worship the Lord in the company of other believers, especially those we loved on earth.

What does the Bible say about whether we will be able to recognize people in the afterlife? King Saul recognized Samuel when the witch of Endor summoned Samuel from the realm of the dead (1 Samuel 28:8-17). When David's infant son died, David declared, "I will go to him, but he will not return to me" (2 Samuel 12:23). David assumed that he would be able to recognize his son in heaven, despite the fact that he died as a baby. In Luke 16:19-31, Abraham, Lazarus, and the rich man were all recognizable after death. At the transfiguration, Moses and Elijah were recognizable (Matthew 17:3-4). In these examples, the Bible does seem to indicate that we will be recognizable after death.

The Bible declares that when we arrive in heaven, we will "be like him [Jesus]; for we shall see him as he is" (1 John 3:2). Just as our earthly bodies were of the first man Adam, so will our resurrection bodies be just like Christ's (1 Corinthians 15:47). "And just as we have borne the likeness of the earthly man, so shall we bear the likeness of the man from heaven. For the perishable must clothe itself with the imperishable, and the mortal with immortality" (1 Corinthians 15:49, 53). Many people recognized Jesus after His resurrection (John 20:16, 20; 21:12; 1 Corinthians 15:4-7). If Jesus was recognizable in His glorified body, we also will be recognizable in our glorified bodies. Being able to see our loved ones is a glorious aspect of heaven, but heaven is far more about God, and far less about us. What a pleasure it will be to be reunited with our loved ones and worship God with them for all eternity.

Question: What are the new heavens and the new earth?

Answer: Many people have a misconception of what heaven is truly like. Revelation chapters 21-22 gives us a detailed picture of the new heavens and the new earth. After the events of the end times, the current heavens and earth will be done away with and replaced by the new heavens and new earth. The eternal dwelling place of believers will be the new earth. The new earth is the "heaven" on which we will spend eternity. It is the new earth where the New Jerusalem, the heavenly city, will be located. It is on the new earth that the pearly gates and streets of gold will be.

Heaven—the new earth—is a physical place where we will dwell with glorified physical bodies (1 Corinthians 15:35-58). The concept that heaven is "in the clouds" is unbiblical. The concept that we will be "spirits floating around in heaven" is also unbiblical. The heaven that believers will experience will be a new and perfect planet on which we will dwell. The new earth will be free from sin, evil, sickness, suffering, and death. It will likely be similar to our current earth, or perhaps even a re-creation of our current earth, but without the curse of sin.

What about the new heavens? It is important to remember that in the ancient mind, "heavens" referred to the skies and outer space, as well as the realm in which God dwells. So, when Revelation 21:1 refers to the new heavens, it is likely indicating that the entire universe will be created—a new earth, new skies, a new outer space. It seems as if God's heaven will be recreated as well, to give everything in the universe a "fresh start," whether physical or spiritual. Will we have access to the new heavens in eternity? Possibly, but we will have to wait to find out. May we all allow God's Word to shape our understanding of heaven.

Question: Is hell real? Is hell eternal?

Answer: It is interesting that a much higher percentage of people believe in the existence of heaven than believe in the existence of hell. According to the Bible, though, hell is just as real as heaven. The Bible clearly and explicitly teaches that hell is a real place to which the wicked/unbelieving are sent after death. We have all sinned against God (Romans 3:23). The just punishment for that sin is death (Romans 6:23). Since all of our sin is ultimately against God (Psalm 51:4), and since God is an infinite and eternal Being, the punishment for sin, death, must also be infinite and eternal. Hell is this infinite and eternal death which we have earned because of our sin.

The punishment of the wicked dead in hell is described through-out Scripture as "eternal fire" (Matthew 25:41), "unquenchable fire" (Matthew 3:12), "shame and everlasting contempt" (Daniel 12:2), a place where "the fire is not quenched" (Mark 9:44-49), a place of "torment" and "fire" (Luke 16:23-24), "everlasting destruction" (2 Thessalonians 1:9), a place where "the smoke of torment rises forever and ever" (Revelation 14:10-11), and a "lake of burning sulfur" where the wicked are "tormented day and night forever and ever" (Revelation 20:10).

The punishment of the wicked in hell is as never ending as the bliss of the righteous in heaven. Jesus Himself indicates that punishment in hell is just as everlasting as life in heaven (Matthew 25:46). The wicked are forever subject to the fury and the wrath of God. Those in hell will acknowledge the perfect justice of God (Psalm 76:10). Those who are in hell will know that their punishment is just and that they alone are to blame (Deuteronomy 32:3-5). Yes, hell is real. Yes, hell is a place of torment and punishment that lasts forever and ever, with no end. Praise God that, through Jesus, we can escape this eternal fate (John 3:16, 18, 36).

Question: How is eternity in hell a fair punishment for sin?

Answer: This is an issue that bothers many people who have an incomplete understanding of three things: the nature of God, the nature of man, and the nature of sin. As fallen, sinful human beings, the nature of God is a difficult concept for us to grasp. We tend to see God as a kind, merciful Being whose love for us overrides and overshadows all His other attributes. Of course God is loving, kind, and merciful, but He is first and foremost a holy and righteous God. So holy is He that He cannot tolerate sin. He is a God whose anger burns against the wicked and disobedient (Isaiah 5:25; Hosea 8:5; Zechariah 10:3). He is not only a loving God—He is love itself! But the Bible also tells us that He hates all manner of sin (Proverbs 6:16-19). And while He is merciful, there are limits to His mercy. "Seek the LORD while he may be found; call on him while he is near. Let the wicked forsake his way and the evil man his thoughts. Let him turn to the LORD, and he will have mercy on him, and to our God, for he will freely pardon" (Isaiah 55:6-7).

Humanity is corrupted by sin, and that sin is always directly against God. When David sinned by committing adultery with Bathsheba and having Uriah murdered, he responded with an interesting prayer: "Against you, you only, have I sinned and done what is evil in your sight…" (Psalm 51:4). Since David had sinned against Bathsheba and Uriah, how could he claim to have only sinned against God? David understood that all sin is ultimately against God. God is an eternal and infinite Being (Psalm 90:2). As a result, all sin requires an eternal punishment. God's holy, perfect, and infinite character has been offended by our sin. Although to our finite minds our sin is limited in time, to God—who is outside of time—the sin He hates goes on and on. Our sin is eternally before Him and must be eternally punished in order to satisfy His holy justice.

No one understands this better than someone in hell. A perfect example is the story of the rich man and Lazarus. Both died, and the rich man went to hell while Lazarus went to paradise (Luke 16). Of course, the rich man was aware that his sins were only committed during his lifetime. But, interestingly, he never says, "How did I end up here?" That question is never asked in hell. He does not say, "Did I really deserve this? Don't you think this is a little extreme? A little over the top?" He only asks that someone go to his brothers who are still alive and warn them against his fate.

Like the rich man, every sinner in hell has a full realization that he deserves to be there. Each sinner has a fully informed, acutely aware, and sensitive conscience which, in hell, becomes his own tormenter. This is the experience of torture in hell—a person fully aware of his or her sin with a relentlessly accusing conscience, without relief for even one moment. The guilt of sin will produce shame and everlasting self-hatred. The rich man knew that eternal punishment for a lifetime of sins is justified and deserved. That is why he never protested or questioned being in hell.

The realities of eternal damnation, eternal hell, and eternal punishment are frightening and disturbing. But it is good that we might, indeed, be terrified. While this may sound grim, there is good news. God loves us (John 3:16) and wants us to be saved from hell (2 Peter 3:9). But because God is also just and righteous, He cannot allow our sin to go unpunished. Someone has to pay for it. In His great mercy and love, God provided His own payment for our sin. He sent His Son Jesus Christ to pay the penalty for our sins by dying on the cross for us. Jesus' death was an infinite death because He is the infinite God/man, paying our infinite sin debt, so that we would not have to pay it in hell for eternity (2 Corinthians 5:21). If we confess our sin and place our faith in Christ, asking for God's forgiveness based on Christ's sacrifice, we are saved, forgiven, cleansed, and promised an eternal home in heaven. God loved us so much that He provided the means for our salvation, but if we reject His gift of eternal life, we will face the eternal consequences of that decision.

Question: What is the judgment seat of Christ?

Answer: Romans 14:10-12 says, "For we will all stand before God's judgment seat...so then, each of us will give an account of himself to God." Second Corinthians 5:10 tells us, "For we must all appear before the judgment seat of Christ, that each one may receive what is due him for the things done while in the body, whether good or bad." In the context, it is clear that both scriptures are referring to Christians, not unbelievers. The judgment seat of Christ, therefore, involves believers giving an account of their lives to Christ. The judgment seat of Christ does not determine salvation; that was determined by Christ's sacrifice on our behalf (1 John 2:2) and our faith in Him (John 3:16). All of our sins are forgiven, and we will never be condemned for them (Romans 8:1). We should not look at the judgment seat of Christ as God judging our sins, but rather as God rewarding us for our lives. Yes, as the Bible says, we will have to give an account of ourselves. Part of this is surely answering for the sins we committed. However, that is not going to be the primary focus of the judgment seat of Christ.

At the judgment seat of Christ, believers are rewarded based on how faithfully they served Christ (1 Corinthians 9:4-27; 2 Timothy 2:5). Some of the things we might be judged on are how well we obeyed the Great Commission (Matthew 28:18-20), how victorious we were over sin (Romans 6:1-4), and how well we controlled our tongues (James 3:1-9). The Bible speaks of believers receiving crowns for different things based on how faithfully they served Christ (1 Corinthians 9:4-27; 2 Timothy 2:5). The various crowns are described in 2 Timothy 2:5, 2 Timothy 4:8, James 1:12, 1 Peter 5:4, and Revelation 2:10. James 1:12 is a good summary of how we should think about the judgment seat of Christ: "Blessed is the man who perseveres under trial, because when he has stood the test, he will receive the crown of life that God has promised to those who love him."

Question: What is the great white throne judgment?

Answer: The great white throne judgment is described in Revelation 20:11-15 and is the final judgment prior to the lost being cast into the lake of fire. We know from Revelation 20:7-15 that this judgment will take place after the millennium and after Satan, the beast, and the false prophet are thrown into the lake of fire (Revelation 20:7-10). The books that are opened (Revelation 20:12) contain records of everyone's deeds, whether they are good or evil, because God knows everything that has ever been said, done, or even thought, and He will reward or punish each one accordingly (Psalm 28:4; 62:12; Romans 2:6; Revelation 2:23; 18:6; 22:12).

Also at this time, another book is opened, called the "book of life" (Revelation 20:12). It is this book that determines whether a person will inherit eternal life with God or receive everlasting punishment in the lake of fire. Although Christians are held accountable for their actions, they are forgiven in Christ and their names were written in the "book of life from the creation of the world" (Revelation 17:8). We also know from Scripture that it is at this judgment when the dead will be "judged according to what they had done" (Revelation 20:12) and that "anyone's name" that is not "found written in the book of life" will be "thrown into the lake of fire" (Revelation 20:15).

The fact that there is going to be a final judgment for all men, both believers and unbelievers, is clearly confirmed in many passages of Scripture. Every person will one day stand before Christ and be judged for his or her deeds. While it is very clear that the great white throne judgment is the final judgment, Christians disagree on how it relates to the other judgments mentioned in the Bible, specifically, who will be judged at the great white throne judgment.

Some Christians believe that the Scriptures reveal three different judgments to come. The first is the judgment of the sheep and the goats or a judgment of the nations (Matthew 25:31-36). This takes place after the tribulation period but prior to the millennium; its purpose is to determine who will enter the millennial kingdom. The second is a judgment of believers' works, often referred to as the "judgment seat [*bema*] of Christ" (2 Corinthians 5:10). At this judgment, Christians will receive degrees of reward for their works or service to God. The third is the great white throne judgment at the end of the millennium (Revelation 20:11-15). This is the judgment of unbelievers in which they are judged according to their works and sentenced to everlasting punishment in the lake of fire.

Other Christians believe that all three of these judgments speak of the same final judgment, not of three separate judgments. In other words, the great white throne judgment in Revelation 20:11-15 will be the time that believers and unbelievers alike are judged. Those whose names are found in the book of life will be judged for their deeds in order to determine the rewards they will receive or lose. Those whose names are not in the book of life will be judged according to their deeds to determine the degree of punishment they will receive in the lake of fire. Those who hold this view believe that Matthew 25:31-46 is another description of what takes place at the great white throne judgment. They point to the fact that the result of this judgment is the same as what is seen after the great white throne judgment in Revelation 20:11-15. The sheep (believers) enter into eternal life, while the goats (unbelievers) are cast into "eternal punishment" (Matthew 25:46).

Whichever view one holds of the great white throne judgment, it is important to never lose sight of the facts concerning the coming judgment(s). First, Jesus Christ will be the judge, all unbelievers will be judged by Christ, and they will be punished according to the works they have done. The Bible is very clear that unbelievers are storing up wrath against themselves (Romans 2:5) and that God will "give to each person according to what he has done" (Romans 2:6). Believers will also be judged by Christ, but since Christ's righteousness has been imputed to us and our names are written in the book of life, we will be rewarded, but not punished, according to our deeds. Romans 14:10-12 says that we will all stand before the judgment seat of Christ and that each one of us will give an account to God.

Question: Do pets/animals go to heaven? Do pets/animals have souls?

Answer: The Bible does not give any explicit teaching on whether pets/animals have "souls" or whether pets/animals will be in heaven. However, we can use general biblical principles to develop some clarity on the subject. The Bible states that both man (Genesis 2:7) and animals (Genesis 1:30; 6:17; 7:15, 22) have the breath of life. The primary difference between human beings and animals is that humanity is made in the image and likeness of God (Genesis 1:26-27), while animals are not. Being made in the image and likeness of God means that human beings are like God, capable of spirituality, with mind, emotion, and will, and they have a part of their being that continues after death. If pets/animals do have a "soul" or immaterial aspect, it must therefore be of a different and lesser "quality." This difference possibly means that pet/animal "souls" do not continue in existence after death.

Another factor to consider is that animals are a part of God's creative process in Genesis. God created the animals and said they were good (Genesis 1:25). Therefore, there is no reason why there could not be animals on the new earth (Revelation 21:1). There will most definitely be animals during the millennial kingdom (Isaiah 11:6; 65:25). It is impossible to say definitively whether some of these animals might be the pets we had while here on earth. We do know that God is just and that when we get to heaven we will find

397

ourselves in complete agreement with His decision on this issue, whatever it may be.

Question: Is heaven real?

Answer: Heaven is indeed a real place. The Bible tells us that heaven is God's throne (Isaiah 66:1; Acts 7:48-49; Matthew 5:34-35). After Jesus' resurrection and appearance on earth to His disciples, "He was taken up into heaven and sat at the right hand of God" (Mark 16:19; Acts 7:55-56). "Christ did not enter a man-made sanctuary that was only a copy of the true one; He entered heaven itself, now to appear for us in God's presence" (Hebrews 9:24). Jesus not only went before us, entering on our behalf, but He is alive and has a present ministry in heaven, serving as our high priest in the true tabernacle made by God (Hebrews 6:19-20; 8:1-2).

We are also told by Jesus Himself that there are many rooms in God's house and that He has gone before us to prepare a place for us. We have the assurance of His word that He will one day come back to earth and take us to where He is in heaven (John 14:1-4). Our belief in an eternal home in heaven is based on an explicit promise of Jesus. Heaven is most definitely a real place. Heaven truly does exist.

When people deny the existence of heaven, they deny not only the written Word of God, but they also deny the innermost longings of their own hearts. Paul addressed this issue in his letter to the Corinthians, encouraging them to cling to the hope of heaven so that they would not lose heart. Although we "groan and sigh" in our earthly state, we have the hope of heaven always before us and are eager to get there (2 Corinthians 5:1-4). Paul urged the Corinthians to look forward to their eternal home in heaven, a perspective that would enable them to endure hardships and disappointments in this life. "For our light and momentary troubles are achieving for us an eternal glory that far outweighs them all. So we fix our eyes not on what is seen, but on what is unseen. For what is seen is temporary, but what is unseen is eternal" (2 Corinthians 4:17-18).

Just as God has put in men's hearts the knowledge that He exists (Romans 1:19-20), so are we "programmed" to desire heaven. It is the theme of countless books, songs, and works of art. Unfortunately, our sin has barred the way to heaven. Since heaven is the abode of a holy and perfect God, sin has no place there, nor can it be tolerated. Fortunately, God has provided for us the key to open the doors of heaven—Jesus Christ (John 14:6). All who believe in Him and seek forgiveness for sin will find the doors of heaven swung wide open for them. May the future glory of our eternal home motivate us all to serve God faithfully and wholeheartedly. "Since we have confidence to enter the Most Holy Place by the blood of Jesus by a new and living way opened for us through the curtain, that is his body, and since we have a great high priest over the house of God, let us draw near to God with a sincere heart full of assurance of faith, having our hearts sprinkled to cleanse us from a guilty conscience and having our bodies washed with pure water" (Hebrews 10:19-22).

Question: What is heaven like?

Answer: Heaven is a real place described in the Bible. The word "heaven" is found 276 times in the New Testament alone. Scripture refers to three heavens. The apostle Paul was "caught up to the third heaven," but he was prohibited from revealing what he experienced there (2 Corinthians 12:1-9).

If a third heaven exists, there must also be two other heavens. The first is most frequently referred to in the Old Testament as the "sky" or the "firmament." This is the heaven that contains clouds, the area that birds fly through. The second heaven is interstellar/outer space, which is the abode of the stars, planets, and other celestial objects (Genesis 1:14-18).

The third heaven, the location of which is not revealed, is the dwelling place of God. Jesus promised to prepare a place for true Christians in heaven (John 14:2). Heaven is also the destination of Old Testament saints who died trusting God's promise of the Redeemer (Ephesians 4:8). Whoever believes in Christ shall never perish but have eternal life (John 3:16).

The apostle John was privileged to see and report on the heavenly city (Revelation 21:10-27). John witnessed that heaven (the new earth) possesses the "glory of God" (Revelation 21:11), the very presence of God. Because heaven has no night and the Lord Himself is the light, the sun and moon are no longer needed (Revelation 22:5).

The city is filled with the brilliance of costly stones and crystal clear jasper. Heaven has twelve gates (Revelation 21:12) and twelve foundations (Revelation 21:14). The paradise of the Garden of Eden is restored: the river of the water of life flows freely and the tree of life is available once again, yielding fruit monthly with leaves that "heal the nations" (Revelation 22:1-2). However eloquent John was in his description of heaven, the reality of heaven is beyond the ability of finite man to describe (1 Corinthians 2:9).

Heaven is a place of "no mores." There will be no more tears, no more pain, and no more sorrow (Revelation 21:4). There will be no more separation, because death will be conquered (Revelation 20:6). The best thing about heaven is the presence of our Lord and Savior (1 John 3:2). We will be face to face with the Lamb of God who loved us and sacrificed Himself so that we can enjoy His presence in heaven for eternity.

Question: Are there different levels of heaven?

Answer: The closest thing Scripture says to there being different levels of heaven is found in 2 Corinthians 12:2, "I know a man in Christ who fourteen years ago was caught up to the third heaven. Whether it was in the body or out of the body I do not know—God knows." Some interpret this as indicating that there are three different levels of heaven, a level for "super-committed Christians" or Christians who have obtained a high level of spirituality, a level for "ordinary" Christians, and a level for Christians who did not serve God faithfully. This view has no basis in Scripture.

Paul is not saying that there are three heavens or even three levels of heaven. In many ancient cultures, people used the term "heaven" to describe three different "realms"—the sky, outer space, and then a spiritual heaven. Although the terms are not specifically biblical, these are commonly known as the terrestrial, telestial, and celestial heavens. Paul was saying that God took him to the "celestial" heavens, as in the realm in which God dwells. The concept of different levels of heaven may have come in part from Dante's *Divine Comedy* in which the poet describes both heaven and hell as having nine different levels. The *Divine Comedy*, however, is a fictional work. The idea of different levels of heaven is foreign to Scripture.

Scripture does speak of different rewards in heaven. Jesus said regarding rewards, "Behold, I am coming soon! My reward is with me, and I will give to everyone according to what he has done" (Revelation 22:12). Jesus said that when He comes He will have with Him rewards to give to people on the basis of what they have done. This shows us that there will be a time of reward for believers. In 2 Timothy 4:7-8, we read the words of Paul as he closes out his ministry: "I have fought the good fight, I have finished the race, I have kept the faith. Now there is in store for me the crown of righteousness, which the Lord, the righteous Judge, will award to me on that day — and not only to me, but also to all who have longed for his appearing."

Only those works that survive God's refining fire have eternal value and will be worthy of reward. Those valuable works are referred to as "gold, silver, and costly stones" (1 Corinthians 3:12) and are those things that are built upon the foundation of faith in Christ. Those works that will not be rewarded are called "wood, hay, and stubble;" these are not evil deeds but shallow activities with no eternal value. Rewards will be distributed at the "judgment seat of Christ," a place where believers' lives will be evaluated for the purpose of rewards. "Judgment" of believers never refers to punishment for sin. Jesus Christ was punished for our sin when He died on the cross, and God said about us: "I will forgive their wickedness and will remember their sins no more" (Hebrews 8:12). What a glorious thought! The Christian need never fear punishment, but can look forward to crowns of reward that he can cast at the feet of the Savior. In conclusion, there are not different levels of heaven, but there are different levels of reward in heaven.

Question: Are there different levels of punishment in hell?

Answer: The idea that there are different levels of punishment in hell derives primarily from the *Divine Comedy* written by Dante Alighieri between 1308 and 1321. In it, the Roman poet Virgil guides Dante through the nine circles of hell. The circles are concentric, representing a gradual increase in wickedness, and culminating at the center of the earth, where Satan is held in bondage. Each circle's sinners are punished in a fashion befitting their crimes. Each sinner is afflicted for all of eternity by the chief sin he committed. According to Dante, the circles range from the first circle, where dwell the unbaptized and virtuous pagans, to the very center of hell reserved for those who have committed the ultimate sin—treachery against God.

Although it does not specifically say so, the Bible might seem to indicate that there are different levels of punishment in hell. In Revelation 20:11-15, the people are judged "according to what they had done as recorded in the books" (Revelation 20:12). All the people at this judgment, though, are thrown into the lake of fire (Revelation 20:13-15). So, perhaps, the purpose of the judgment is to determine how severe the punishment in hell will be. Whatever the case, being thrown into a slightly less hot portion of the lake of fire is no consolation to those who are still doomed for eternity. Whatever degrees of punishment hell contains, it is clear that hell is a place to be avoided.

Unfortunately, the Bible states that most people will wind up in hell. "...For wide is the gate and broad is the road that leads to destruction, and many enter through it. But small is the gate and narrow the road that leads to life, and only a few find it" (Matthew 7:13-14). The question one must ask is "which road am I on?" The "many" on the broad road have one thing in common—they have all rejected Christ as the one and only way to heaven. Jesus said, "I am the way and the truth and the life. No one comes to the Father except through me" (John 14:6). When He said He is the only way, that is precisely what He meant. Everyone following another "way" beside Jesus Christ is on the broad road to destruction, and whether or not there are different levels of punishment in hell, the suffering is hideous, dreadful, eternal, and avoidable.

Question: What does the Bible say about soul sleep?

Answer: "Soul sleep" is a belief that after a person dies, his/her soul "sleeps" until the resurrection and final judgment. The concept of "soul sleep" is not biblical. When the Bible describes a person "sleeping" in relation to death (Luke 8:52; 1 Corinthians 15:6), it does not mean literal sleep. Sleeping is just a way to describe death because a dead body appears to be asleep. The moment we die, we face the judgment of God (Hebrews 9:27). For believers, to be absent from the body is to be present with the Lord (2 Corinthians 5:6-8; Philippians 1:23).

For unbelievers, death means everlasting punishment in hell (Luke 16:22-23).

Until the final resurrection, though, there is a temporary heaven—paradise (Luke 23:43; 2 Corinthians 12:4) and a temporary hell—Hades (Revelation 1:18; 20:13-14). As can be clearly seen in Luke 16:19-31, neither in paradise nor in Hades are people sleeping. It could be said, though, that a person's body is "sleeping" while his soul is in paradise or Hades. At the resurrection, this body is "awakened" and transformed into the everlasting body a person will possess for eternity, whether in heaven or hell. Those who were in paradise will be sent to the new heavens and new earth (Revelation 21:1). Those who were in Hades will be thrown into the lake of fire (Revelation 20:11-15). These are the final, eternal destinations of all people—based entirely on whether or not a person trusted in Jesus Christ for salvation.

Chapter 15

QUESTIONS ABOUT MARRIAGE

CONTENTS

What does the Bible say about marriage? 406

Making marriage last—what is the key? 407

What does the Bible say about interracial marriage? 408

What does the Bible say about gay marriage/same sex marriage? 409

What does the Bible say about divorce and remarriage? 411

I am divorced. Can I remarry according to the Bible? 413

Does a wife have to submit to her husband? 414

What constitutes marriage according to the Bible? 415

What does it mean to leave and cleave? 418

Will there be marriage in heaven? 419

What should a Christian do if he/she is married to an unbeliever? 420

What does it mean to be one flesh in a marriage? 421

What is a Christian couple allowed to do in sex? 423

Why did God allow polygamy in the Bible? 423

Question: What does the Bible say about marriage?

Answer: The creation of marriage is recorded in Genesis 2:23-24: "The man said, 'This is now bone of my bones and flesh of my flesh; she shall be called "woman," for she was taken out of man.' For this reason a man will leave his father and mother and be united to his wife, and they will become one flesh." God created man and then made woman to complement him. Marriage is God's "fix" for the fact that "it is not good for the man to be alone" (Genesis 2:18).

The word "helper" used to describe Eve in Genesis 2:20 means "to surround, to protect or aid, help." Eve was created to be alongside Adam as his "other half," to be his aid and his helper. A man and woman, when married, become "one flesh." This oneness is manifested most fully in the physical union of sexual intimacy. The New Testament adds a warning regarding this oneness. "So they are no longer two, but one. Therefore what God has joined together, let man not separate" (Matthew 19:6).

There are several epistles written by the apostle Paul that refer to marriage and how believers are to operate within the marriage relationship. One such passage is 1 Corinthians chapter 7, and another is Ephesians 5:22-33. When studied together, these two passages provide biblical principles that form a framework for a God-pleasing marriage relationship.

The Ephesians passage is especially profound in reference to a successful biblical marriage. "Wives, submit to your husbands as to the Lord. For the husband is the head of the wife as Christ is the head of the church, his body, of which he is the Savior" (Ephesians 5:22-23). "Husbands, love your wives, just as Christ loved the church and gave himself up for her" (Ephesians 5:25). "In this same way, husbands ought to love their wives as their own bodies. He who loves his wife loves himself. After all, no one ever hated his own body, but he feeds and cares for it, just as Christ does the church" (Ephesians 5:28-29). "For this reason a man will leave his father and mother and be united to his wife, and the two will become one flesh" (Ephesians 5:31).

When a believing husband and wife institute God's principles, a biblical marriage results. A biblically-based marriage is one that is in balance, with Christ as the head of the man and the wife together.

The biblical concept of marriage is a oneness between two individuals that pictures the oneness of Christ with His church.

Question: Making marriage last—what is the key?

Answer: The Apostle Paul says that the wife is "bound" to her husband as long as he lives (Romans 7:2). The principle here is that either the husband or wife has to die before the marriage bond is broken. This is God's command, but in our modern society marriage ends in divorce over 51 percent of the time. That means that over half of the couples who make the vow "Till death do us part" break that vow.

What can the married couple do to ensure that their marriage will last? The first and most important issue is one of obedience to God and His Word. This is a principle that should be in force before the marriage. God says, "Do two walk together unless they have agreed to do so?" (Amos 3:3). For the born-again believer, this means not beginning a close relationship with anyone who is not also a believer. "Do not be yoked together with unbelievers. For what do righteousness and wickedness have in common? Or what fellowship can light have with darkness?" (2 Corinthians 6:14). If this one principle were followed, it would save a lot of heartache and suffering later in marriages.

Another principle that would protect the longevity of a marriage is that the husband should obey God and love, honor, and protect his wife as he would his own body (Ephesians 5:25-31). The corresponding principle is that the wife should obey God and submit to her own husband "as to the Lord" (Ephesians 5:22). The marriage between a man and a woman is a picture of the relationship between Christ and the church. Christ gave Himself for the church and He loves, honors, and protects her as His "bride" (Revelation 19:7-9).

When God brought Eve to Adam in the first marriage, she was made from his "flesh and bone" (Genesis 2:31) and they became "one flesh" (Genesis 2:23-24). Becoming one flesh means more than just a physical union. It means a meeting of the mind and soul to form one unit. This relationship goes far beyond sensual or emotional attraction and into the realm of spiritual "oneness" that can only be found as both partners surrender to God and each other. This relationship is not centered on "me and my" but on "us and our." This is one of the secrets to a lasting marriage. Making a marriage last until death is something both partners have to make a priority. Solidifying one's vertical relationship with God goes a long way toward ensuring that the horizontal relationship between a husband and wife is a lasting, and therefore God-honoring, one.

Question: What does the Bible say about interracial marriage?

Answer: The Old Testament Law commanded the Israelites not to engage in interracial marriage (Deuteronomy 7:3-4). However, the reason for this was not primarily racial in nature. Rather, it was religious. The reason God commanded against interracial marriage was that people of other races were idolaters and worshippers of false gods. The Israelites would be led astray from God if they intermarried with idol worshippers, pagans, or heathens. A similar principle is laid out in the New Testament, but at a much different level: "Do not be yoked together with unbelievers. For what do righteousness and wickedness have in common? Or what fellowship can light have with darkness?" (2 Corinthians 6:14). Just as the Israelites (believers in the one true God) were commanded not to marry idolaters, so Christians (believers in the one true God) are commanded not to marry unbelievers. To answer this question specifically, no, the Bible does not say that interracial marriage is wrong.

As Martin Luther King noted, a person should be judged by his or her character, not by skin color. There is no place in the life of the Christian for favoritism based on race (James 2:1-10). When selecting a mate, a Christian should always first find out if the potential spouse is born again by faith in Jesus Christ (John 3:3-5). Faith in Christ, not skin color, is the biblical standard for choosing a spouse. Interracial marriage is not a matter of right or wrong, but of wisdom, discernment, and prayer.

The only reason interracial marriage should be considered carefully is the difficulties a mixed-race couple may experience because of others who have a hard time accepting them. Many interracial couples experience discrimination and ridicule, sometimes even from their own families. Some interracial couples experience difficulties when their children have skin tones of different shades from the parents and/or siblings. An interracial couple needs to take these things into consideration and be prepared for them, should they decide to marry. Again, though, the only biblical restriction placed on whom a Christian may marry is whether the other person is a member of the body of Christ.

Question: What does the Bible say about gay marriage/same sex marriage?

Answer: While the Bible does address homosexuality, it does not explicitly mention gay marriage/same-sex marriage. It is clear, however, that the Bible condemns homosexuality as an immoral and unnatural sin. Leviticus 18:22 identifies homosexual sex as an abomination, a detestable sin. Romans 1:26-27 declares homosexual desires and actions to be shameful, unnatural, lustful, and indecent. First Corinthians 6:9 states that homosexuals are unrighteous and will not inherit the kingdom of God. Since both homosexual desires and actions are condemned in the Bible, it is clear that homosexuals "marrying" is not God's will, and would be, in fact, sinful.

Whenever the Bible mentions marriage, it is between a male and a female. The first mention of marriage, Genesis 2:24, describes it as a man leaving his parents and being united to his wife. In passages that contain instructions regarding marriage, such as 1 Corinthians 7:2-16 and Ephesians 5:23-33, the Bible clearly identifies marriage as being between a man and a woman. Biblically speaking, marriage is the lifetime union of a man and a woman, primarily for the purpose of building a family and providing a stable environment for that family.

The Bible alone, however, does not have to be used to demonstrate this understanding of marriage. The biblical viewpoint of marriage has been the universal understanding of marriage in every human civilization in world history. History argues against gay marriage. Modern secular psychology recognizes that men and women are psychologically and emotionally designed to complement one another. In regard to the family, psychologists contend that a union between a man and woman in which both spouses serve as good gender role models is the best environment in which to raise well-adjusted children. Psychology argues against gay marriage. In nature/physicality, clearly, men and women were designed to "fit" together sexually. With the "natural" purpose of sexual intercourse being procreation, clearly only a sexual relationship between a man and a woman can fulfill this purpose. Nature argues against gay marriage.

So, if the Bible, history, psychology, and nature all argue for marriage being between a man and a woman—why is there such a controversy today? Why are those who are opposed to gay marriage/same-sex marriage labeled as hateful, intolerant bigots, no matter how respectfully the opposition is presented? Why is the gay rights movement so aggressively pushing for gay marriage/same-sex marriage when most people, religious and non-religious, are supportive of—or at least far less opposed to—gay couples having all the same legal rights as married couples with some form of civil union?

The answer, according to the Bible, is that everyone inherently knows that homosexuality is immoral and unnatural, and the only way to suppress this inherent knowledge is by normalizing homosexuality and attacking any and all opposition to it. The best way to normalize homosexuality is by placing gay marriage/same-sex marriage on an equal plane with traditional opposite-gender marriage. Romans 1:18-32 illustrates this. The truth is known because God has made it plain. The truth is rejected and replaced with a lie. The lie is then promoted and the truth suppressed and attacked. The vehemence and anger expressed by many in the gay rights movement to any who oppose them is, in fact, an indication that they know their position is indefensible. Trying to overcome a weak position by raising your voice is the oldest trick in the debating book. There is perhaps no more accurate description of the modern gay rights agenda than Romans 1:31, "they are senseless, faithless, heartless, ruthless."

To give sanction to gay marriage/same-sex marriage would be to give approval to the homosexual lifestyle, which the Bible clearly and consistently condemns as sinful. Christians should stand firmly against the idea of gay marriage/same-sex marriage. Further, there are strong and logical arguments against gay marriage/same-sex marriage from contexts completely separated from the Bible. One does not have to be an evangelical Christian to recognize that marriage is between a man and a woman.

According to the Bible, marriage is ordained by God to be between a man and a woman (Genesis 2:21-24; Matthew 19:4-6). Gay marriage/same-sex marriage is a perversion of the institution of marriage and an offense to the God who created marriage. As Christians, we are not to condone or ignore sin. Rather, we are to share the love of God and the forgiveness of sins that is available to all, including homosexuals, through Jesus Christ. We are to speak the truth in love (Ephesians 4:15) and contend for truth with "gentleness and respect" (1 Peter 3:15). As Christians, when we make a stand for truth and the result is personal attacks, insults, and persecution, we should remember the words of Jesus: "If the world hates you, keep in mind that it hated me first. If you belonged to the world, it would love you as its own. As it is, you do not belong to the world, but I have chosen you out of the world. That is why the world hates you" (John 15:18-19).

Question: What does the Bible say about divorce and remarriage?

Answer: First of all, no matter what view one takes on the issue of divorce, it is important to remember Malachi 2:16: "I hate divorce, says the LORD God of Israel." According to the Bible, marriage is a lifetime commitment. "So they are no longer two, but one. Therefore what God has joined together, let man not separate" (Matthew 19:6). God realizes, though, that since marriages involve two sinful human beings, divorces are going to occur. In the Old Testament, He laid down some laws in order to protect the rights of divorcees, especially women (Deuteronomy 24:1-4). Jesus pointed out that these laws were given because of the hardness of people's hearts, not because they were God's desire (Matthew 19:8).

The controversy over whether divorce and remarriage is allowed according to the Bible revolves primarily around Jesus' words in Matthew 5:32 and 19:9. The phrase "except for marital unfaithfulness" is the only thing in Scripture that possibly gives God's permission for divorce and remarriage. Many interpreters understand this "exception clause" as referring to "marital unfaithfulness" during the "betrothal" period. In Jewish custom, a man and a woman were considered married even while they were still engaged or "betrothed." According to this view, immorality during this "betrothal" period would then be the only valid reason for a divorce.

However, the Greek word translated "marital unfaithfulness" is a word which can mean any form of sexual immorality. It is can mean fornication, prostitution, adultery, etc. Jesus is possibly saying that divorce is permissible if sexual immorality is committed. Sexual relations are an integral part of the marital bond: "the two will become one flesh" (Genesis 2:24; Matthew 19:5; Ephesians 5:31). Therefore, any breaking of that bond by sexual relations outside of marriage might be a permissible reason for divorce. If so, Jesus also has remarriage in mind in this passage. The phrase "and marries another" (Matthew 19:9) indicates that divorce and remarriage are allowed in an instance of the exception clause, whatever it is interpreted to be. It is important to note that only the innocent party is allowed to remarry. Although it is not stated in the text, the allowance for remarriage after a divorce is God's mercy for the one who was sinned against, not for the one who committed the sexual immorality. There may be instances where the "guilty party" is allowed to remarry, but it is not taught in this text.

Some understand 1 Corinthians 7:15 as another "exception," allowing remarriage if an unbelieving spouse divorces a believer. However, the context does not mention remarriage, but only says a believer is not bound to continue a marriage if an unbelieving spouse wants to leave. Others claim that abuse (spousal or child) are valid reasons for divorce even though they are not listed as such in the Bible. While this may very well be the case, it is never wise to presume upon the Word of God.

Sometimes lost in the debate over the exception clause is the fact that whatever "marital unfaithfulness" means, it is an allowance for divorce, not a requirement for it. Even when adultery is committed, a couple can, through God's grace, learn to forgive and begin rebuilding their marriage. God has forgiven us of so much more. Surely we can follow His example and even forgive the sin of adultery (Ephesians 4:32). However, in many instances, a spouse is unrepentant and continues in sexual immorality. That is where Matthew 19:9 can possibly be applied. Many also look to quickly remarry after a divorce when God might desire them to remain single. God sometimes calls people to be single so that their attention is not divided (1 Corinthians 7:32-35). Remarriage after a divorce may be an option in some circumstances, but that does not mean it is the only option.

It is distressing that the divorce rate among professing Christians is nearly as high as that of the unbelieving world. The Bible makes it abundantly clear that God hates divorce (Malachi 2:16) and that reconciliation and forgiveness should be the marks of a believer's life (Luke 11:4; Ephesians 4:32). However, God recognizes that divorce will occur, even among His children. A divorced and/or remarried believer should not feel any less loved by God, even if the divorce and/or remarriage is not covered under the possible exception clause of Matthew 19:9. God often uses even the sinful disobedience of Christians to accomplish great good.

Question: I am divorced. Can I remarry according to the Bible?

Answer: We often receive questions like "I am divorced for such and such a reason. Can I get remarried?" "I have been divorced twice—the first for adultery by my spouse, the second for incompatibility. I am dating a man who has been divorced three times—the first for incompatibility, the second for adultery on his part, the third for adultery on his wife's part. Can we get married to each other?" Questions like these are very difficult to answer because the Bible does not go into great detail regarding to the various scenarios for remarriage after a divorce.

What we can know for sure is that it is God's plan for a married couple to stay married as long as both spouses are alive (Genesis 2:24; Matthew 19:6). The only specific allowance for remarriage after a divorce is for adultery (Matthew 19:9), and even this is debated among Christians. Another possibility is desertion—when an unbelieving spouse leaves a believing spouse (1 Corinthians 7:12-15). This passage, though, does not specifically address remarriage, only being bound to stay in a marriage. It would also seem that physical, sexual, or severe emotional abuse would be a sufficient cause for divorce and possibly remarriage. The Bible does not specifically teach this, however.

We know two things for sure. God hates divorce (Malachi 2:16), and God is merciful and forgiving. Every divorce is a result of sin, either on the part of one spouse or both. Does God forgive divorce? Absolutely! Divorce is no less forgivable than any other sin. Forgiveness of all sins is available through faith in Jesus Christ (Matthew 26:28; Ephesians 1:7). If God forgives the sin of divorce, does that mean you are free to remarry? Not necessarily. God sometimes calls people to remain single (1 Corinthians 7:7-8). Being single should not be viewed as a curse or punishment, but as an opportunity to serve God wholeheartedly (1 Corinthians 7:32-36). God's Word does tell us, though, that it is better to marry than to burn with passion (1 Corinthians 7:9). Perhaps this sometimes applies to remarriage after a divorce.

So, can you or should you get remarried? We cannot answer that question. Ultimately, that is between you, your potential spouse, and, most importantly, God. The only advice we can give is for you to pray to God for wisdom regarding what He would have you do (James 1:5). Pray with an open mind and genuinely ask the Lord to place His desires on your heart (Psalm 37:4). Seek the Lord's will (Proverbs 3:5-6) and follow His leading.

Question: Does a wife have to submit to her husband?

Answer: Submission is a very important issue in relation to marriage. Even before sin entered the world, there was still the principle of headship (1 Timothy 2:13). Adam was created first, and Eve was created to be a "helper" for Adam (Genesis 2:18-20). At the same time, since there was no sin, there was no authority for man to obey except God's authority. When Adam and Eve disobeyed God, sin entered the world, and then authority was needed. Therefore, God established the authority needed to enforce the laws of the land and also to provide us with the protection we need. First, we need to submit to God, which is the only way we can truly obey Him (James 1:21; 4:7). In 1 Corinthians 11:2-3, we find that the husband is to submit to Christ as Christ did to God. Then the verse says that the wife should follow his example and submit to her husband.

Submission is a natural response to loving leadership. When a husband loves his wife as Christ loves the church (Ephesians 5:25-33), then submission is a natural response from a wife to her husband. The Greek word translated "submit," *hupotasso*, is the continuing form of the verb. This means that submitting to God, the government, or a husband is not a one-time act. It is a continual attitude, which becomes a pattern of behavior. The submission talked about in Ephesians 5 is not a one-sided subjection of a believer to a selfish, domineering person. Biblical submission is designed to be between two Spirit-filled believers who are mutually yielded to each other and to God. Submission is a two-way street. Submission is a position of honor and completeness. When a wife is loved as the church is loved by Christ, submission is not difficult. Ephesians 5:24 says, "Now as the church submits to Christ, so also wives should submit to their husbands in everything." This verse is saying that the wife is to submit to her husband in everything that is right and lawful. Therefore, the wife is under no obligation to disobey the law or God in the name of submission.

Matthew Henry wrote: "The woman was made out of Adam's side. She was not made out of his head to rule over him, nor out of his feet to be trampled upon by him, but out of his side to be equal with him, under his arm to be protected, and near his heart to be loved." Believers are to submit to one another out of reverence for Christ (Ephesians 5:21). In context, everything in Ephesians 5:19-33 is a result of being filled with the Spirit. Spirit-filled believers are to be worshipful (5:19), thankful (5:20), and submissive (5:21). Paul then follows his line of thought on Spirit-filled living and applies it to husbands and wives in verses 22-33. A wife should submit to her husband, not because women are inferior, but because that is how God designed the marital relationship to function. Submission is not a wife's being a "doormat" for her husband. Rather, with the help of the Holy Spirit, a wife submits to her husband, and a husband sacrificially loves his wife.

Question: What constitutes marriage according to the Bible?

Answer: This is a difficult question to answer because the Bible nowhere explicitly states at what point God considers a couple to be married. There are three common viewpoints: 1) God only considers a couple married when they are legally married. 2) A couple is married in God's eyes when they have completed some kind of formal wedding ceremony. 3) God considers a couple to be married at the moment the marriage is consummated with sexual intercourse. Let's look at each of the three views and see what strengths and weaknesses each has.

1. God only considers a couple married when they are legally married. The scriptural support typically given to this view is the verses that advocate submission to the government (Romans 13:1-7; 1 Peter 2:17). The argument is that if the government requires certain "paperwork" to be completed before a marriage is recognized, a couple should submit themselves to whatever process the government requires. It is definitely biblical for a couple to submit to the government as long as the requirements do not contradict God's Word and are reasonable. Romans 13:1-2 tells us, "Everyone must submit himself to the governing authorities, for there is no authority except that which God has established. The authorities that exist have been established by God. Consequently, he who rebels against the authority is rebelling against what God has instituted, and those who do so will bring judgment on themselves."

    There are some weaknesses and potential problems with this view. First, there were marriages before any government was organized. For thousands of years, people were getting married with no such thing as a marriage license. Second, even today, there are some countries that have no governmental recognition of marriage, and/or no legal requirements for marriage. Third, there are some governments that place unbiblical requirements on a marriage before it is legally recognized. As an example, there are countries that require a wedding to be held in a Catholic church, according to Catholic teachings, and overseen by a Catholic priest. Obviously, for those who have strong disagreements with the Catholic Church and the Catholic understanding of marriage as a sacrament, it would be unbiblical to submit to being married in the Catholic Church.

2. A couple is married in God's eyes when they have completed some kind of formal wedding ceremony. Similar to the

416

way—in many cultures—a father gives away his daughter at the wedding, some interpreters understand God's bringing Eve to Adam (Genesis 2:22) as God's overseeing the first wedding "ceremony." In John chapter 2, Jesus attended a wedding ceremony. Jesus would not have attended such an event if He did not approve of what was occurring. Jesus' attending a wedding ceremony by no means indicates that God requires a wedding ceremony, but it most definitely does indicate that a wedding ceremony is acceptable in God's sight. Nearly every culture in the history of humanity has had some kind of formal wedding ceremony. In every culture there is an event, action, covenant, or proclamation that is recognized as declaring a man and woman to be married.

3. God considers a couple to be married at the moment the marriage is consummated with sexual intercourse. There are some who argue that if any man and woman have sex, God considers the two of them to be married. Such a viewpoint is not biblically sound. The basis for this argument is the fact that sexual intercourse between a husband and wife is the ultimate fulfillment of the "one flesh" principle (Genesis 2:24; Matthew 19:5; Ephesians 5:31). In this sense, sexual intercourse is the final "seal" on a marriage covenant. However, if a couple is legally and ceremonially married, but for some reason are unable to engage in sexual intercourse, the couple is still considered married.

It is not biblical to consider a couple who have had sexual intercourse—but who have not observed any of the other aspects of a marriage covenant—to be married. Scriptures such as 1 Corinthians 7:2 indicate that sex before marriage is immorality. If sexual intercourse causes a couple to become married, it could not be considered immoral, as the couple would be considered married the moment they engaged in sexual intercourse. There is absolutely no biblical basis for an unmarried couple to have sex and then declare themselves to be married, thereby declaring all future sexual relations to be moral and God-honoring.

So, what constitutes marriage in God's eyes? It would seem that the following principles should be followed: 1) As long as the requirements are reasonable and not against the Bible, a couple should seek whatever formal governmental recognition is available. 2) A couple should follow whatever cultural and familial practices are typically employed to recognize a couple as "officially married." 3) If possible, a couple should consummate the marriage sexually, fulfilling the physical aspect of the "one flesh" principle.

What if one or more of these principles are not fulfilled? Is such a couple still considered married in God's eyes? Ultimately, that is between the couple and God. God knows our hearts (1 John 3:20). God knows the difference between a true marriage covenant and an attempt to justify sexual immorality.

Question: What does it mean to leave and cleave?

Answer: "Therefore shall a man leave his father and his mother, and shall cleave unto his wife: and they shall be one flesh" (Genesis 2:24 KJV). Other translations render "leave and cleave" as "leave and be united" (NIV), "leave and be joined" (NASB), and "leave and hold fast" (ESV). So, what precisely does it mean to leave your father and mother and cleave to your spouse?

As recorded in Genesis chapter 2, God created Adam first, and then Eve. God Himself brought Eve to Adam. God Himself ordained that they would be joined together in holy matrimony. He said that the two of them would become one flesh. This is a picture of marital intimacy—the act of love that is never to involve anyone else. To "cleave" means "to adhere to, stick to, or join with." It is a unique joining of two people into one entity. It means we do not quit when things are not going right. It includes talking things out, praying things through, being patient as you trust God to work in both of your hearts, being willing to admit when you are wrong and asking forgiveness, and seeking God's counsel regularly in His Word.

If either spouse fails to both leave and cleave, problems will result in a marriage. If spouses refuse to truly leave their parents, conflict and stress result. Leaving your parents does not mean ignoring them or not spending any time with them. Leaving your parents means recognizing that your marriage created a new family and that this new family must be a higher priority than your previous family. If spouses neglect to cleave to each other, the result is a lack of intimacy and unity. Cleaving to your spouse does not mean being with your spouse every moment or not having meaningful friendships outside of your marriage. Cleaving to your spouse means recognizing that you are joined, essentially "glued," to your spouse. Cleaving is key in building a marriage that will endure hard times and be the beautiful relationship that God intends it to be.

The "leave and cleave" in the marriage bond is also a picture of the union God wants us to have with Him. "Ye shall walk after the Lord your God, and fear him, and keep his commandments, and obey his voice, and ye shall serve him, and cleave unto him" (Deuteronomy 13:4 KJV). It means we leave all other gods, whatever form they may take, and join to Him alone as our God. We cleave to Him as we read His Word and submit to His authority over us. Then, as we follow Him closely, we find that His instruction to leave father and mother in order to cleave to our spouse is to discover commitment and security, just as He intended. God takes His design for marriage seriously. Leaving and cleaving is God's plan for those who marry. When we follow God's plan, we are never disappointed.

Question: Will there be marriage in heaven?

Answer: The Bible tells us, "At the resurrection people will neither marry nor be given in marriage; they will be like the angels in heaven" (Matthew 22:30). This was Jesus' answer in response to a question concerning a woman who had been married multiple times in her life—whom would she be married to in heaven (Matthew 22:23-28)? Evidently, there will be no such thing as marriage in heaven. This does not mean that a husband and wife will no longer know each other in heaven. This also does not mean that a husband and wife could not still have a close relationship in heaven. What it does seem to indicate, though, is that a husband and wife will no longer be married in heaven.

Most likely, there will be no marriage in heaven simply because there will be no need for it. When God established marriage, He did so to fill certain needs. First, He saw that Adam was in need of a companion. "The Lord God said, 'It is not good for the man to be alone. I will make a helper suitable for him'" (Genesis 2:18). Eve was the solution to the problem of Adam's loneliness, as well as his need for a "helper," someone to come alongside him as his companion and go through life by his side. In heaven, however, there will be no loneliness, nor will there be any need for helpers. We will be surrounded by multitudes of believers and angels (Revelation 7:9), and all our needs will be met, including the need for companionship.

Second, God created marriage as a means of procreation and the filling of the earth with human beings. Heaven, however, will not be populated by procreation. Those who go to heaven will get there by faith in the Lord Jesus Christ; they will not be created there by means of reproduction. Therefore, there is no purpose for marriage in heaven since there is no procreation or loneliness.

Question: What should a Christian do if he/she is married to an unbeliever?

Answer: Being married to an unbeliever can be one of the most difficult challenges in a Christian's life. Marriage is a sacred covenant that joins two people together in one flesh (Matthew 19:5). It can be very difficult for a believer and an unbeliever to live in peaceful harmony (2 Corinthians 6:14-15). If one partner becomes a Christian after the marriage, the inherent struggles of living under two different authorities quickly become apparent.

Often Christians in this situation will look for a way out of the marriage, convinced that this is the only way to truly bring honor to God. His Word, however, says the contrary. It is very important not only to be content in our situation, but also to look for ways to bring glory to Him out of our challenging circumstances (1 Corinthians 7:17). The Bible specifically addresses those who are married to unbelievers in 1 Corinthians 7:12-14: "…If any brother has a wife who is not a believer and she is willing to live with him, he must not divorce her. And if a woman has a husband who is not a believer and he is willing to live with her, she must not divorce him. For the unbelieving husband has been sanctified through his wife, and the unbelieving wife has been sanctified through her believing husband…"

Christians married to unbelievers will need to pray for the power of the Holy Spirit to enable them to profess Christ and live in the light of God's presence (1 John 1:7). They should seek God's transforming power to change their hearts and produce the fruit of the Holy Spirit (Galatians 5:22-23). A Christian wife is obligated to have a submissive heart, even toward her unbelieving husband (1 Peter 3:1), and she will need to remain close to God and rely on His grace to enable her to do so.

Christians are not meant to live solitary lives; they need to find support from outside sources such as the church and Bible study groups. Being married to an unbeliever does not alter the sacredness of the relationship, so it should be the priority of every Christian to pray for his or her spouse and set a good example, allowing Christ's light to shine brightly (Philippians 2:14). May the truth found in 1 Peter 3:1—that an unbelieving spouse is "won over"—be the hope and goal of every Christian who is married to an unbeliever.

Question: What does it mean to be one flesh in a marriage?

Answer: The term "one flesh" comes from the Genesis account of the creation of Eve. Genesis 2:21-24 describes the process by which God created Eve from a rib taken from Adam's side as he slept. Adam recognized that Eve was part of him—they were in fact "one flesh." The term "one flesh" means that just as our bodies are one whole entity and cannot be divided into pieces and still be a whole, so God intended it to be with the marriage relationship. There are no longer two entities (two individuals), but now there is one entity (a married couple). There are a number of aspects to this new union.

As far as emotional attachments are concerned, the new unit takes precedence over all previous and future relationships (Genesis 2:24). Some marriage partners continue to place greater weight upon ties with parents than with the new partner. This is a recipe for disaster in the marriage and is a perversion of God's original intention of "leaving and cleaving." A similar problem can develop when a spouse begins to draw closer to a child to meet emotional needs rather than to his or her partner.

Emotionally, spiritually, intellectually, financially, and in every other way, the couple is to become one. Even as one part of the body cares for the other body parts (the stomach digests food for the body, the brain directs the body for the good of the whole, the hands work for the sake of the body, etc.), so each partner in the marriage is to care for the other. Each partner is no longer to see money earned as "my" money; but rather as "our" money. Ephesians 5:22-33 and Proverbs 31:10-31 give the application of this "oneness" to the role of the husband and to the wife, respectively.

Physically, they become one flesh, and the result of that one flesh is found in the children that their union produces; these children now possess a special genetic makeup, specific to their union. Even in the sexual aspect of their relationship, a husband and wife are not to consider their bodies as their own but as belonging to their partner (1 Corinthians 7:3-5). Nor are they to focus on their own pleasure but rather the giving of pleasure to their spouse.

This oneness and desire to benefit each other is not automatic, especially after mankind's fall into sin. The man, in Genesis 2:24 (KJV), is told to "cleave" to his wife. This word has two ideas behind it. One is to be "glued" to his wife, a picture of how tight the marriage bond is to be. The other aspect is to "pursue hard after" the wife. This "pursuing hard after" is to go beyond the courtship leading to marriage, and is to continue throughout the marriage. The fleshly tendency is to "do what feels good to me" rather than to consider what will benefit the spouse. And this self-centeredness is the rut that marriages commonly fall into once the "honeymoon is over." Instead of each spouse dwelling upon how his or her own needs are not being met, he or she is to remain focused on meeting the needs of the spouse.

As nice as it may be for two people to live together meeting each other's needs, God has a higher calling for the marriage. Even as they were to be serving Christ with their lives before marriage (Romans 12:1-2), now they are to serve Christ together as a unit and raise their children to serve God (1 Corinthians 7:29-34; Malachi 2:15; Ephesians 6:4). Priscilla and Aquila, in Acts 18, would be good examples of this. As a couple pursues serving Christ together, the joy which the Spirit gives will fill their marriage (Galatians 5:22-23). In the Garden of Eden, there were three present (Adam, Eve, and God), and there was joy. So, if God is central in a marriage today, there also will be joy. Without God, a true and full oneness is not possible.

Question: What is a Christian couple allowed to do in sex?

Answer: The Bible says that "Marriage should be honored by all, and the marriage bed kept pure, for God will judge the adulterer and all the sexually immoral" (Hebrews 13:4). Scripture never says what a husband and wife are or are not allowed to do sexually. Husbands and wives are instructed, "Do not deprive each other except by mutual consent and for a time (1 Corinthians 7:5a). This verse perhaps lays down the principle for sexual relations in marriage. Whatever is done, it should be mutually agreed upon. No one should be encouraged or coerced to do something he or she is uncomfortable with or thinks is wrong. If a husband and wife both agree that they want to try something (e.g., oral sex, different positions, sex toys, etc.), then the Bible does not give any reason why they cannot.

There are a few things, though, that are never allowable sexually for a married couple. The practice of "swapping" or "bringing in an extra" (threesomes, foursomes, etc.) is blatant adultery (Galatians 5:19; Ephesians 5:3; Colossians 3:5; 1 Thessalonians 4:3). Adultery is sin even if your spouse allows, approves, or even participates in it. Pornography appeals to the "lust of the flesh and the lust of the eyes" (1 John 2:16) and is therefore condemned by God as well. A husband and wife should never bring pornography into their sexual union. Other than these two items, there is nothing that Scripture explicitly forbids a husband and wife to do with each other as long as it is by mutual consent.

Question: Why did God allow polygamy in the Bible?

Answer: The question of polygamy is an interesting one in that most people today view polygamy as immoral while the Bible nowhere explicitly condemns it. The first instance of polygamy/bigamy in the Bible was that of Lamech in Genesis 4:19: "Lamech married two women." Several prominent men in the Old Testament were polygamists. Abraham, Jacob, David, Solomon, and others all had multiple wives. In 2 Samuel 12:8, God, speaking through the prophet Nathan, said that if David's wives and concubines were not enough, He would have given David even more. Solomon had 700 wives and 300 concubines (essentially wives of a lower status), according to 1 Kings 11:3. What are we to do with these instances of polygamy in the

Old Testament? There are three questions that need to be answered: 1) Why did God allow polygamy in the Old Testament? 2) How does God view polygamy today? 3) Why did it change?

1. Why did God allow polygamy in the Old Testament? The Bible does not specifically say why God allowed polygamy. As we speculate about God's silence, there are a few key factors to consider. First, there have always been more women in the world than men. Current statistics show that approximately 50.5 percent of the world population are women, with men being 49.5 percent. Assuming the same percentages in ancient times, and multiplied by millions of people, there would be tens of thousands more women than men. Second, warfare in ancient times was especially brutal, with an incredibly high rate of fatality. This would have resulted in an even greater percentage of women to men. Third, due to patriarchal societies, it was nearly impossible for an unmarried woman to provide for herself. Women were often uneducated and untrained. Women relied on their fathers, brothers, and husbands for provision and protection. Unmarried women were often subjected to prostitution and slavery. The significant difference between the number of women **and men** would have left many, many women in an undesirable situation.

   So, it seems that God may have allowed polygamy to protect and provide for the women who could not find a husband otherwise. A man would take multiple wives and serve as the provider and protector of all of them. While definitely not ideal, living in a polygamist household was far better than the alternatives: prostitution, slavery, or starvation. In addition to the protection/provision factor, polygamy enabled a much faster expansion of humanity, fulfilling God's command to "be fruitful and increase in number; multiply on the earth" (Genesis 9:7). Men are capable of impregnating multiple women in the same time period, causing humanity to grow much faster than if each man was only producing one child each year.

2. How does God view polygamy today? Even while allowing polygamy, the Bible presents monogamy as the plan which conforms most closely to God's ideal for marriage. The Bible says that God's original intention was for one man to be married to only one woman: "For this reason a man will leave his father and mother and be united to his wife [not wives], and they will become one flesh [not fleshes]" (Genesis 2:24). While Genesis 2:24 is describing what marriage is, rather than how many people are involved, the consistent use of the singular should be noted. In Deuteronomy 17:14-20, God says that the kings were not supposed to multiply wives (or horses or gold). While this cannot be interpreted as a command that the kings must be monogamous, it can be understood as declaring that having multiple wives causes problems. This can be clearly seen in the life of Solomon (1 Kings 11:3-4).

In the New Testament, 1 Timothy 3:2, 12 and Titus 1:6 give "the husband of one wife" in a list of qualifications for spiritual leadership. There is some debate as to what specifically this qualification means. The phrase could literally be translated "a one-woman man." Whether or not this phrase is referring exclusively to polygamy, in no sense can a polygamist be considered a "one-woman man." While these qualifications are specifically for positions of spiritual leadership, they should apply equally to all Christians. Should not all Christians be "above reproach...temperate, self-controlled, respectable, hospitable, able to teach, not given to drunkenness, not violent but gentle, not quarrelsome, not a lover of money" (1 Timothy 3:2-4)? If we are called to be holy (1 Peter 1:16), and if these standards are holy for elders and deacons, then they are holy for all.

Ephesians 5:22-33 speaks of the relationship between husbands and wives. When referring to a husband (singular), it always also refers to a wife (singular). "For the husband is the head of the wife [singular] … He who loves his wife [singular] loves himself. For this reason a man will leave his father and mother and be united to his wife [singular], and the two will become one flesh....Each one of you also must love his wife [singular] as he loves himself, and the wife [singular] must respect her husband [singular]." While a somewhat parallel passage, Colossians 3:18-19, refers to husbands and wives in the plural, it is clear that Paul is addressing all the husbands and wives among the Colossian believers, not stating that a husband might have multiple wives. In contrast, Ephesians 5:22-33 is specifically describing the marital relationship. If polygamy were allowable, the entire illustration of Christ's relationship with His body (the church) and the husband-wife relationship falls apart.

3. Why did it change? It is not so much God's disallowing something He previously allowed as it is God's restoring marriage to His original plan. Even going back to Adam and Eve, polygamy was not God's original intent. God seems to have allowed polygamy to solve a problem, but it is not the ideal. In most modern societies, there is absolutely no need for polygamy. In most cultures today, women are able to provide for and protect themselves—removing the only "positive" aspect of polygamy. Further, most modern nations outlaw polygamy. According to Romans 13:1-7, we are to obey the laws the government establishes. The only instance in which disobeying the law is permitted by Scripture is if the law contradicts God's commands (Acts 5:29). Since God only allows for polygamy, and does not command it, a law prohibiting polygamy should be upheld.

Are there some instances in which the allowance for polygamy would still apply today? Perhaps, but it is unfathomable that there would be no other possible solution. Due to the "one flesh" aspect of marriage, the need for oneness and harmony in marriage, and the lack of any real need for polygamy, it is our firm belief that polygamy does not honor God and is not His design for marriage.

Chapter 16

....

QUESTIONS ABOUT

RELATIONSHIPS

CONTENTS

Is it right for a Christian to date or marry a non-Christian? 428

What does the Bible say about sex before marriage/premarital sex? 428

What is an appropriate level of intimacy before marriage? 430

What does the Bible say about dating/courting? 430

How can I know if I am in love? 431

Is it wrong for a couple to live together before marriage? 432

How can I prepare myself for marriage? 433

Is there such a thing as a soul mate? 434

What should I be looking for in a husband? 435

What should I be looking for in a wife? 436

Are we supposed to be actively looking for a spouse, or waiting for God
    to bring a spouse to us? 438

How will I know when I have found the perfect spouse? 439

When is the right time for marriage? 440

How young is too young to be in a romantic relationship? 442

Question: Is it right for a Christian to date or marry a non-Christian?

Answer: For a Christian, dating a non-Christian is unwise, and marrying one is not an option. Second Corinthians 6:14 (KJV) tells us not to be "unequally yoked" with an unbeliever. The imagery is of two incompatible oxen sharing the same yoke. Instead of working together to pull the load, they would be working against each other. While this passage does not specifically mention marriage, it definitely has implications for marriage. The passage goes on to say that there is no harmony between Christ and Belial (Satan). There can be no spiritual harmony in a marriage between a Christian and a non-Christian. Paul goes on to remind believers that they are the dwelling place of the Holy Spirit, who inhabits their hearts at salvation (2 Corinthians 6:15-17). Because of that, they are to be separate from the world—in the world, but not of the world—and nowhere is that more important than in life's most intimate relationship—marriage.

The Bible also says, "Do not be misled: 'Bad company corrupts good character' (1 Corinthians 15:33). Having any kind of intimate relationship with an unbeliever can quickly turn into something that is a hindrance to your walk with Christ. We are called to evangelize the lost, not be intimate with them. There is nothing wrong with building quality friendships with unbelievers, but that is as far as it should go. If you were dating an unbeliever, what would honestly be your priority, romance or winning a soul for Christ? If you were married to an unbeliever, how would the two of you cultivate a spiritual intimacy in your marriage? How could a quality marriage be built and maintained if you disagree on the most crucial issue in the universe—the Lord Jesus Christ?

Question: What does the Bible say about sex before marriage/premarital sex?

Answer: There is no Hebrew or Greek word used in the Bible that precisely refers to sex before marriage. The Bible undeniably condemns adultery and sexual immorality, but is sex before marriage considered sexually immoral? According to 1 Corinthians 7:2, "yes" is the clear answer: "But since there is so much immorality, each man should have his own wife, and each woman her own husband." In this verse, Paul states that marriage is the "cure" for sexual immorality. First Corinthians 7:2 is essentially saying that, because people cannot control themselves and so many are having immoral sex outside of marriage, people should get married. Then they can fulfill their passions in a moral way.

Since 1 Corinthians 7:2 clearly includes sex before marriage in the definition of sexual immorality, all of the Bible verses that condemn sexual immorality as being sinful also condemn sex before marriage as sinful. Sex before marriage is included in the biblical definition of sexual immorality. There are numerous Scriptures that declare sex before marriage to be a sin (Acts 15:20; 1 Corinthians 5:1; 6:13, 18; 10:8; 2 Corinthians 12:21; Galatians 5:19; Ephesians 5:3; Colossians 3:5; 1 Thessalonians 4:3; Jude 7). The Bible promotes complete abstinence before marriage. Sex between a husband and his wife is the only form of sexual relations of which God approves (Hebrews 13:4).

Far too often we focus on the "recreation" aspect of sex without recognizing that there is another aspect—procreation. Sex within marriage is pleasurable, and God designed it that way. God wants men and women to enjoy sexual activity within the confines of marriage. Song of Solomon and several other Bible passages (such as Proverbs 5:19) clearly describe the pleasure of sex. However, the couple must understand that God's intent for sex includes producing children. Thus, for a couple to engage in sex before marriage is doubly wrong—they are enjoying pleasures not intended for them, and they are taking a chance of creating a human life outside of the family structure God intended for every child.

While practicality does not determine right from wrong, if the Bible's message on sex before marriage were obeyed, there would be far fewer sexually transmitted diseases, far fewer abortions, far fewer unwed mothers and unwanted pregnancies, and far fewer children growing up without both parents in their lives. Abstinence is God's only policy when it comes to sex before marriage. Abstinence saves lives, protects babies, gives sexual relations the proper value, and, most importantly, honors God.

Question: What is an appropriate level of intimacy before marriage?

Answer: Ephesians 5:3 tells us, "But among you there must not be even a hint of sexual immorality, or of any kind of impurity...because these are improper for God's holy people." Anything that even "hints" of sexual immorality is inappropriate for a Christian. The Bible does not give us a list of what qualifies as a "hint" or tell us what physical activities are approved for a couple to engage in before marriage. However, just because the Bible does not specifically address the issue does not mean God approves of "pre-sexual" activity before marriage. By essence, foreplay is designed to get one ready for sex. Logically then, foreplay should be restricted to married couples. Anything that can be considered foreplay should be avoided until marriage.

If there is any doubt whatsoever whether an activity is right for an unmarried couple, it should be avoided (Romans 14:23). Any and all sexual and pre-sexual activity should be restricted to married couples. An unmarried couple should avoid any activity that tempts them toward sex, that gives the appearance of immorality, or that could be considered foreplay. Many pastors and Christian counselors strongly advise a couple to not go beyond holding hands, hugging, and light kissing before marriage. The more a married couple has to share exclusively between themselves, the more special and unique the sexual relationship in that marriage becomes.

Question: What does the Bible say about dating/courting?

Answer: Although the words "courtship" and "dating" are not found in the Bible, we are given some principles that Christians are to go by during the time before marriage. The first is that we must separate from the world's view on dating because God's way contradicts the world's (2 Peter 2:20). While the world's view may be to date around as much as we want, the important thing is to discover the character of a person before making any commitment to him or her. We should find out if the person has been born again in the Spirit of Christ (John 3:3-8) and if he or she shares the same desire toward Christ-likeness (Philippians 2:5). The ultimate goal of dating or courting is finding a life partner. The Bible tells us that, as Christians, we should not marry an unbeliever (2 Corinthians 6:14-15) because this would weaken our relationship with Christ and compromise our morals and standards.

When one is in a committed relationship, whether dating or courting, it is important to remember to love the Lord above all else (Matthew 10:37). To say or believe that another person is "everything" or the most important thing in one's life is idolatry, which is sin (Galatians 5:20; Colossians 3:5). Also, we are not to defile our bodies by having premarital sex (1 Corinthians 6:9, 13; 2 Timothy 2:22). Sexual immorality is a sin not only against God but against our own bodies (1 Corinthians 6:18). It is important to love and honor others as we love yourselves (Romans 12:9-10), and this is certainly true for a courtship or dating relationship. Whether dating or courting, following these biblical principles is the best way to have a secure foundation for a marriage. It is one of the most important decisions we will ever make, because when two people marry, they cleave to one another and become one flesh in a relationship which God intended to be permanent and unbreakable (Genesis 2:24; Matthew 19:5).

Question: How can I know if I am in love?

Answer: Love is a very powerful emotion. It motivates much of our lives. We make many important decisions based on this emotion, and even get married because we feel that we are "in love." This may be the reason about half of all first marriages end in divorce. The Bible teaches us that true love is not an emotion that can come or go, but a decision. We are not just to love those who love us; we should even love those who hate us, the same way that Christ loves the unlovable (Luke 6:35). "Love is patient, love is kind. It does not envy, it does not boast, it is not proud. It is not rude, it is not self-seeking, it is not easily angered, it keeps no record of wrongs. Love does not delight in evil but rejoices with the truth. It always protects, always trusts, always hopes, always perseveres" (1 Corinthians 13:4-7).

It can be very easy to "fall in love" with someone, but there are some questions to ask before deciding if what we are feeling is true love. First, is this person a Christian, meaning has he given his life to Christ? Is he/she trusting Christ alone for salvation? Also, if you are considering giving your heart and emotions to one person, you should ask yourself if you are willing to put that person above all other people and to put your relationship second only to God. The Bible tells us that when two people get married, they become one flesh (Genesis 2:24; Matthew 19:5).

Another thing to consider is whether or not the loved one is a good candidate for being a mate. Has he/she already put God first and foremost in his/her life? Is he/she able to give his/her time and energy to building the relationship into a marriage that will last a lifetime? There is no measuring stick to determine when we are truly in love with someone, but it is important to discern whether we are following our emotions or following God's will for our lives. True love is a decision, not just an emotion. True biblical love is loving someone all of the time, not just when you feel "in love."

Question: Is it wrong for a couple to live together before marriage?

Answer: The answer to this question depends somewhat on what is meant by "living together." If it means having sexual relations, it is definitely wrong. Premarital sex is repeatedly condemned in Scripture, along with all other forms of sexual immorality (Acts 15:20; Romans 1:29; 1 Corinthians 5:1; 6:13, 18; 7:2; 10:8; 2 Corinthians 12:21; Galatians 5:19; Ephesians 5:3; Colossians 3:5; 1 Thessalonians 4:3; Jude 7). The Bible promotes complete abstinence outside of (and before) marriage. Sex before marriage is just as wrong as adultery and other forms of sexual immorality, because they all involve having sex with someone you are not married to.

If "living together" means living in the same house, that is perhaps a different issue. Ultimately, there is nothing wrong with a man and a woman living in the same house—*if* there is nothing immoral taking place. However, the problem arises in that there is still the appearance of immorality (1 Thessalonians 5:22; Ephesians 5:3), and it could be a tremendous temptation for immorality. The Bible tells us to flee immorality, not expose ourselves to constant temptations to immorality (1 Corinthians 6:18). Then there is the problem of appearances. A couple who is living together is assumed to be sleeping together—that is just the nature of things. Even though living in the same house is not sinful in and of itself, the appearance of sin is there. The Bible tells us to avoid the appearance of evil (1 Thessalonians 5:22; Ephesians 5:3), to flee from immorality, and not to cause anyone to stumble or be offended. As a result, it is not honoring to God for a man and a woman to live together outside of marriage.

Question: How can I prepare myself for marriage?

Answer: Preparing oneself for marriage biblically is the same as preparing for any life endeavor. There is a principle that should govern all aspects of our lives as born-again believers: "Love the Lord your God with all your heart and with all your soul and with all your mind" (Matthew 22:37). This is not a flippant command. It is the centerpiece of our lives as believers. It is choosing to focus upon God and upon His Word with our whole heart so that our soul and our mind are occupied with the things that will please Him.

The relationship we have with God through the Lord Jesus Christ is what puts all other relationships into perspective. The marriage relationship is based upon the model of Christ and His church (Ephesians 5:22-33). Every aspect of our lives is governed by our commitment as believers to live according to the commandments and precepts of the Lord. Our obedience to God and to His Word equips us to fulfill our God-given roles in marriage and in the world. And the role of every born-again believer is to glorify God in all things (1 Corinthians 10:31).

In order to prepare yourself for marriage, to walk worthy of your calling in Christ Jesus, and to become intimate with God through His Word (2 Timothy 3:16-17), focus upon obedience in all things. There is no easy plan to learn to walk in obedience to God. It is a choice we must make every day to put aside worldly viewpoints and follow God instead. Walking worthy of Christ is to submit ourselves in humility to the only Way, the only Truth and the only Life on a day-by-day, moment-by-moment basis. That is the preparation every believer needs to be ready for the great gift we call marriage.

A person who is spiritually mature and walking with God is more prepared for marriage than anyone else. Marriage demands commitment, passion, humility, love, and respect. These traits are most evident in a person who has an intimate relationship with God. As you prepare yourself for marriage, focus on allowing God to shape you and mold you into the man or woman He wants you to be (Romans 12:1-2). If you submit yourself to Him, He will enable you to be ready for marriage when that wonderful day arrives.

Question: Is there such a thing as a soul mate?

Answer: The common idea of a "soul mate" is that for every person, there is another person who is a "perfect fit," and if you marry anyone other than this soul mate, you will never be happy. Is this concept of a soul mate biblical? No, it is not. The soul mate concept is often used as an excuse for divorce. People who are unhappy in their marriage sometimes claim that they did not marry their soul mate and therefore should divorce and begin the search for their true soul mate. This is nothing more than an excuse, a blatantly unbiblical excuse. If you are married, the person you are married to is your soul mate. Mark 10:7-9 declares, "A man will leave his father and mother and be united to his wife, and the two will become one flesh. So they are no longer two, but one. Therefore what God has joined together, let man not separate." A husband and wife are "united," "one flesh," "no longer two, but one," and "joined together," i.e., soul mates.

A marriage may not be as unified and joyous as a couple wishes it to be. A husband and wife may not have the physical, emotional, and spiritual unity that they desire. But even in this instance, the husband and wife are still soul mates. A couple in such a situation needs to work on developing true "soul mate" intimacy. By obeying what the Bible teaches about marriage (Ephesians 5:22-33), a couple can develop the intimacy, love, and commitment that being "one flesh" soul mates entails. If you are married, you are married to your soul mate. No matter how disharmonious a marriage is, God can bring healing, forgiveness, restoration, and true marital love and harmony.

Is it possible to marry the wrong person? If we give ourselves to God and seek His guidance, He promises to direct us: "Trust in the LORD with all your heart and lean not on your own understanding; in all your ways acknowledge him and he will make your paths straight" (Proverbs 3:5-6). The implication of Proverbs 3:5-6 is that if you are not trusting in the Lord with all your heart, and are leaning on your own understanding, you can go the wrong direction. Yes, it is possible, in a time of disobedience and lack of close fellowship with God, to marry someone whom He did not desire you to marry. Even in such an instance, though, God is sovereign and in control.

Even if a marriage was not God's desire, it is still within His sovereign will and plan. God hates divorce (Malachi 2:16), and "marrying the wrong person" is never presented in the Bible as grounds for divorce. The claim "I married the wrong person and will never be happy unless I find my true soul mate" is unbiblical in two respects. First, it is a claim that your wrong decision has overridden God's will and destroyed His plan. Second, it is a claim that God is not capable of making a struggling marriage happy, unified, and successful. Nothing we do can disrupt God's sovereign will. God can take any two people, no matter how mismatched, and mold them into two people who are perfect for each other.

If we maintain close fellowship with God, He will lead us and guide us. If a person is walking with the Lord and truly seeking His will, God will lead that person to the spouse He intends. God will lead us to our "soul mate" if we submit to Him and follow Him. However, being soul mates is both a position and a practice. A husband and wife are soul mates in that they are "one flesh," spiritually, physically, and emotionally united to each other. In practice, though, there is a process of taking what a couple is, soul mates, and making that a day-by-day reality. True soul mate oneness is only possible by implementing the biblical pattern of marriage.

Question: What should I be looking for in a husband?

Answer: When a Christian woman is looking for a husband, she should seek a man "after God's own heart" (Acts 13:22). The most important relationship that any of us have is our personal relationship with the Lord Jesus Christ. That relationship comes before all others. If our vertical relationship with the Lord is as it should be, then our horizontal relationships will reflect that reality. Therefore, a potential husband should be a man who has his focus upon walking in obedience to God's Word and who seeks to live so that his life brings glory to God (1 Corinthians 10:31).

What are some other qualities to look for? The apostle Paul gives us the qualities we should look for in a husband in 1 Timothy chapter 3. In this passage are the qualifications for a leader in the church body. However, these qualities should grace the lives of any man who walks "after God's heart." The qualities can be paraphrased as follows: a man should be patient and controlled in his demeanor, not filled with pride but of sober mental attitude, able to master his emotions, given to graciousness to others, able to patiently teach, not given to drunkenness or uncontrolled use of any of God's gifts, not prone to violence, not overly focused upon the details of life but focused upon God, not apt to be a hot-head or be thin-skinned so that he takes offense easily, and grateful for what God has given, rather than envious of what gifts others have received.

The above qualities describe a man who is actively engaged in the process of becoming a mature believer. That is the type of man a woman should look for as a potential husband. Yes, physical attraction, similar interests, complementary strengths and weaknesses, and the desire for children are things to consider. These things, though, must be secondary to the spiritual qualities a woman should look for in a man. A man you can trust, respect, and follow in the path of godliness is of far greater value than a man of good looks, fame, power, or money.

Finally, when "looking" for a husband, we must be surrendered to God's will in our lives. Every woman wants to find her "prince charming," but the reality is that she will probably marry a man with as many flaws as she has. Then, by God's grace, they will spend the rest of their lives together learning how to be a partner to, and servant of, each other. We must enter into the second most-important relationship of our lives (marriage), not under an emotional cloud, but with eyes wide open. Our most important relationship, with our Lord and Savior, has to be the focus of our lives.

Question: What should I be looking for in a wife?

Answer: The most important personal relationship that a man can have, outside of his spiritual relationship with God through the Lord Jesus Christ, is his relationship with his wife. In the process of looking for a wife, the highest principle is to look for a woman with a personal faith in Jesus Christ. The Apostle Paul tells us not to be "unequally yoked" with unbelievers (2 Corinthians 6:14). Unless a man and woman are in full agreement on this most crucial issue, a godly and fulfilling marriage cannot take place.

However, marrying a fellow believer does not guarantee the full experience of being "equally yoked." The fact that a woman is a Christian does not mean she is necessarily a good match for you spiritually. Does she have the same spiritual goals as you? Does she have the same doctrinal beliefs? Does she have the same passion for God? The qualities of a potential wife are crucially important. Far too many men marry for emotional or physical attraction alone, and that can be a recipe for failure.

What are some godly qualities a man can look for in a wife? Scripture gives us some principles we can use to create a picture of a godly woman. She should first be surrendered in her own spiritual relationship with the Lord. The apostle Paul tells the wife that she is to submit to her husband as unto the Lord (Ephesians 5:22-24). If a woman is not surrendered to the Lord, she will not likely see submission to her husband as necessary to her own spiritual well-being. We cannot fulfill the expectations of anyone else without first allowing God to fill us with Himself. A woman with God at the center of her life is a good candidate for a wife.

Paul also gives some character traits for a woman in his instructions about leaders in the church. "In the same way, their wives are to be women worthy of respect, not malicious talkers but temperate and trustworthy in everything" (1 Timothy 3:11). In other words, this is a woman who is not overly proud, knows when to speak and when to be silent, and is able to take her place beside her husband in confidence. She is a woman whose first focus is upon her relationship with the Lord and her own spiritual growth.

The responsibilities of marriage are greater for the husband, for God's order places him as the head of his wife and his family. This headship is modeled after the relationship between Christ and the church (Ephesians 5:25-33). It is a relationship grounded in love. Just as Christ loved the church and gave Himself for it, the husband is to love his wife as he does his own body. Therefore, a man's personal spiritual relationship with the Lord is of supreme importance in the success of his marriage and his family. Willing sacrifice and the strength to choose to be a servant to the betterment of his marriage are the marks of a maturing spiritual man who honors God. Wisely choosing a wife based upon biblical qualities is important, but of equal importance is a man's own ongoing spiritual growth and his surrender to God's will in his life. A man who is seeking to be the man God wants him to be will be able to help his wife be the woman God desires her to be and will be able to build the marriage into the union God, he, and his wife desire it to be.

Question: Are we supposed to be actively looking for a spouse, or waiting for God to bring a spouse to us?

Answer: The answer to both questions is "yes." There is an important balance between the two. We are not to frantically search for a spouse as if it depends solely on our own efforts. Neither are we to be passive, thinking that God will one day cause a spouse to arrive at our door. As Christians, once we have decided that it is time to start looking for a spouse, we should begin the process with prayer. Committing ourselves to God's will for our lives is the first step. "Delight yourself in the LORD and he will give you the desires of your heart" (Psalm 37:4). Delighting in the Lord means we find pleasure in knowing Him and trusting that He will delight us in return. He will put His desires into our hearts, and in the context of seeking a spouse, that means desiring for ourselves the type of spouse He desires for us and who He knows will delight us further. Proverbs 3:6 tells us, "In all your ways acknowledge him, and he will make your paths straight." Acknowledging Him in the search for a spouse means submitting to His sovereign will and telling Him that whatever He decides is best is what you want.

After committing ourselves to God's will, we need to be clear on the characteristics of a godly husband or wife and be seeking someone who qualifies on a spiritual level. It is important to have a clear understanding of these qualities first and then to seek someone who fits them. To "fall in love" with someone and then discover he/she is not spiritually qualified to be our mate is to invite heartache and put ourselves in a very difficult position.

Once we know what the Bible says we should be looking for, we can begin actively looking for a spouse, understanding that God will bring him/her into our lives as we are in the process of looking, according to His perfect will and timing. If we pray, God will lead us to the person He has for us. If we wait for His timing, we will be given the person who fits best with our background, personality, and desires. We have to trust in Him and His timing (Proverbs 3:5), even when His timing is not our timing. Sometimes God calls people not to marry at all (1 Corinthians 7), but in those situations, He makes it clear by removing the desire for marriage. God's timing is perfect, and with faith and patience, we will receive His promises (Hebrews 6:12).

Question: How will I know when I have found the perfect spouse?

Answer: The Bible does not address how to find the "perfect spouse," nor does it get as specific as we might like on the matter of finding the right marriage partner. The one thing God's Word does explicitly tell us is to make sure that we do not marry an unbeliever (2 Corinthians 6:14-15). First Corinthians 7:39 reminds us that, while we are free to marry, we should only marry those who are acceptable to God—in other words, Christians. Beyond this, the Bible is silent about how to know we are marrying the "right" person.

So why doesn't God spell out for us what we should look for in a mate? Why do we not have more specifics about such an important issue? The truth is that the Bible is so clear on what a Christian is and how we are to act that specifics are not necessary. Christians are supposed to be likeminded about important issues, and if two Christians are committed to their marriage and to obeying Christ, they already possess the necessary ingredients for success. However, because our society is inundated with many professing Christians, it would be wise to use discernment before devoting oneself to the lifelong commitment of marriage. Once a prospective mate's priorities are identified—if he or she is truly committed to Christ-likeness—then the specifics are easier to identify and deal with.

First, we should make sure that we are ready to marry. We must have enough maturity to look beyond the here and now and be able to commit ourselves to joining with this one person for the rest of our lives. We must also recognize that marriage requires sacrifice and selflessness. Before marrying, a couple should study the roles and duties of a husband and wife (Ephesians 5:22-31; 1 Corinthians 7:1-16; Colossians 3:18-19; Titus 2:1-5; 1 Peter 3:1-7).

A couple should make sure they know each other for a sufficient amount of time before discussing marriage. They should watch how the other person reacts to different situations, how he behaves around his family and friends, and what kind of people she spends time with. A person's behavior is greatly influenced by those he keeps company with (1 Corinthians 15:33). They should agree on issues such as morality, finances, values, children, church attendance and involvement, relationships with in-laws, and employment. These are areas of potential conflict in marriage and should be carefully considered beforehand.

Finally, any couple considering marriage should first go to premarital counseling with their pastor or another trained Christian counselor. Here they will learn valuable tools for building their marriage on a foundation of faith in Christ, and they will also learn how to deal with inevitable conflicts. After all these criteria have been met, the couple is ready to prayerfully decide if they desire to be joined together in marriage. If we are earnestly seeking the will of God, He will direct our paths (Proverbs 3:5-6).

Question: When is the right time for marriage?

Answer: The right time for marriage is different for each person and unique to each situation. Maturity levels and life experiences are varying factors; some people are ready for marriage at 18, and some are never prepared for it. As the U.S. divorce rate exceeds 50 percent, it is obvious that much of our society does not view marriage as an everlasting commitment. However, this is the world's view, which will usually contradict God's (1 Corinthians 3:18).

A strong foundation is imperative for a successful marriage and should be settled before one even begins to date or court a potential life mate. Our Christian walk should include much more than just attending church on Sundays and being involved in Bible study. We must have a personal relationship with God that comes only through trusting in and obeying Jesus Christ. We must educate ourselves about marriage, seeking God's view on it, before diving in. A person must know what the Bible says about love, commitment, sexual relations, the role of a husband and wife, and His expectations of us before committing to marriage. Having at least one Christian married couple as a role model is also important. An older couple can answer questions about what goes into a successful marriage, how to create intimacy (beyond the physical), how faith is invaluable, etc.

A prospective married couple also needs to make sure that they know each other well. They should know each other's views on marriage, finances, in-laws, child-rearing, discipline, duties of a husband and wife, whether only one of them or both will be working outside the home, and they should know the level of the other person's spiritual maturity. Many people get married taking their partner's word for it that they are a Christian, only to find out later that it was merely lip service. Every couple considering marriage should go through counseling with a Christian marriage counselor or pastor. In fact, many pastors will not perform weddings unless they have met several times with the couple in a counseling setting.

Marriage is not only a commitment, but a covenant with God. It is the promise to remain with that other person for the remainder of your life, no matter whether your spouse is rich, poor, healthy, sick, overweight, underweight, or boring. A Christian marriage should endure through every circumstance, including fighting, anger, devastation, disaster, depression, bitterness, addiction, and loneliness. Marriage should never be entered into with the idea that divorce is an option—not even as the last straw. The Bible tells us that through God all things are possible (Luke 18:27), and this certainly includes marriage. If a couple makes the decision at the beginning to stay committed and to put God first, divorce will not be the inevitable solution to a miserable situation.

It is important to remember that God wants to give us the desires of our heart, but that is only possible if our desires match His. People often get married because it just "feels right." In the early stages of dating, and even of marriage, you see the other person coming, and you get butterflies in your stomach. Romance is at its peak, and you know the feeling of being "in love." Many expect that this feeling will remain forever. The reality is that it does not. The result can be disappointment and even divorce as those feelings fade, but those in successful marriages know that the excitement of being with the other person does not have to end. Instead, the butterflies give way to a deeper love, a stronger commitment, a more solid foundation, and an unbreakable security.

The Bible is clear that love does not rely on feelings. This is evident when we are told to love our enemies (Luke 6:35). True love is possible only when we allow the Holy Spirit to work through us, cultivating the fruit of our salvation (Galatians 5:22-23). It is a decision we make on a daily basis to die to ourselves and our selfishness, and to let God shine through us. Paul tells us how to love others in 1 Corinthians 13:4-7: "Love is patient, love is kind. It does not envy, it does not boast, it is not proud. It is not rude, it is not self-seeking, it is not easily angered, it keeps no record of wrongs. Love does not delight in evil but rejoices with the truth. It always protects, always trusts, always hopes, always perseveres." When we are ready to love another person as 1 Corinthians 13:4-7 describes, that is the right time for marriage.

Question: How young is too young to be in a romantic relationship?

Answer: How young is "too young" to start a relationship depends on the individual's level of maturity, goals, and beliefs. Often, the younger we are, the less mature we are due to a lack of life experience. When we are just beginning to figure out who we are, we may not be firmly grounded enough spiritually to form solid romantic attachments and may be more prone to making unwise decisions that can leave us with emotional, physical, psychological, and spiritual damage.

Being in a relationship puts one in almost constant temptation, especially as emotions begin to develop and the attraction to the other person deepens. Young teens—even older teens—are besieged by hormonal and societal pressures that seem at times almost unbearable. Each day brings new feelings—doubts, fears, and confusion coupled with joys and exhilaration—which can be very confusing. Young people spend much of their time just figuring out who they are and how they relate to the world and the people around them. To add the pressure of a relationship at this stage seems almost too much to ask, especially when the other person is experiencing the same upheaval. Such early relationships make it more difficult to avoid damage to the delicate and still-forming self-image, not to mention the problem of resisting temptation. If being marriage-minded is still far off, it is probably too early to begin dating or courtship. Much safer for all concerned are group activities where young people can develop social skills and friendships without the pressure and inherent difficulties of romantic attachments.

No matter when a person decides to begin a romantic relationship, this should be a time of building on the foundation of faith that he or she has been taught, of growing and figuring out what God wants him or her to do. We are never too young to begin this exciting process. "Don't let anyone look down on you because you are young, but set an example for the believers in speech, in life, in love, in faith and in purity" (1 Timothy 4:12).

Chapter 17

QUESTIONS ABOUT FAMILY

AND PARENTING

CONTENTS

What does the Bible say about being a good parent? 446

What does the Bible say about Christian fathers? 447

What does the Bible say about Christian mothers? 449

How should Christians discipline their children? 450

What should Christian parents do if they have a prodigal son (or daughter)? 452

What does the Bible say about birth control? Should Christians use birth control? 453

What does the Bible say about adoption? 455

What should be the order of priorities in our family? 456

What does it mean to honor my father and mother? 457

How should a Christian deal with infertility? 459

What does the Bible say to do with a rebellious child? 460

What are the roles of the husband and wife in a family? 463

Question: What does the Bible say about being a good parent?

Answer: Parenting can be a difficult and challenging venture, but at the same time can be the most rewarding and fulfilling thing we ever do. The Bible has a great deal to say about the way we can successfully raise our children to be men and women of God. The first thing we must do is teach them the truth about God's Word.

Along with loving God and being a godly example by committing ourselves to His commands, we need to heed the command of Deuteronomy 6:7-9 regarding teaching our children to do the same. This passage emphasizes the ongoing nature of such instruction. It should be done at all times—at home, on the road, at night, and in the morning. Biblical truth should be the foundation of our homes. By following the principles of these commands, we teach our children that worshiping God should be constant, not reserved for Sunday mornings or nightly prayers.

Although our children learn a great deal through direct teaching, they learn much more by watching us. This is why we must be careful in everything we do. We must first acknowledge our God-given roles. Husbands and wives are to be mutually respectful and submissive to each other (Ephesians 5:21). At the same time, God has established a line of authority to keep order. "Now I want you to realize that the head of every man is Christ, and the head of the woman is man, and the head of Christ is God" (1 Corinthians 11:3). We know that Christ is not inferior to God, just as a wife is not inferior to her husband. God recognizes, however, that without submission to authority, there is no order. The husband's responsibility as the head of the household is to love his wife as he loves his own body, in the same sacrificial way that Christ loved the church (Ephesians 5:25-29).

In response to this loving leadership, it is not difficult for the wife to submit to her husband's authority (Ephesians 5:24; Colossians 3:18). Her primary responsibility is to love and respect her husband, live in wisdom and purity, and take care of the home (Titus 2:4-5). Women are naturally more nurturing than men because they were designed to be the primary caretakers of their children.

Discipline and instruction are integral parts of parenting. Proverbs 13:24 says, "He who spares the rod hates his son, but he who loves him is careful to discipline him." Children who grow up in undisciplined households feel unwanted and unworthy. They lack direction and self-control, and as they get older they rebel and have little or no respect for any kind of authority, including God's. "Discipline your son, for in that there is hope; do not be a willing party to his death" (Proverbs 19:18). At the same time, discipline must be balanced with love, or children may grow up resentful, discouraged, and rebellious (Colossians 3:21). God recognizes that discipline is painful when it is happening (Hebrews 12:11), but if followed by loving instruction, it is remarkably beneficial to the child. "Fathers, do not exasperate your children; instead, bring them up in the training and instruction of the Lord" (Ephesians 6:4).

It is important to involve children in the church family and ministry when they are young. Regularly attend a Bible-believing church (Hebrews 10:25), allow them to see you studying the Word, and also study it with them. Discuss with them the world around them as they see it, and teach them about the glory of God through everyday life. "Train a child in the way he should go, and when he is old he will not turn from it" (Proverbs 22:6). Being a good parent is all about raising children who will follow your example in obeying and worshipping the Lord.

Question: What does the Bible say about Christian fathers?

Answer: The greatest commandment in Scripture is this: "Love the LORD your God with all your heart and with all your soul and with all your strength" (Deuteronomy 6:5). Going back to verse 2, we read, "So that you, your children and their children after them may fear the LORD your God as long as you live by keeping all his decrees and commands that I give you, and so that you may enjoy long life." Following Deuteronomy 6:5, we read, "These commandments that I give you today are to be upon your hearts. Impress them on your children. Talk about them when you sit at home and when you walk along the road, when you lie down and when you get up" (vv. 6-7).

Israelite history reveals that the father was to be diligent in instructing his children in the ways and words of the Lord for their own spiritual development and well-being. The father who was obedient to the commands of Scripture did just that. This brings us to Proverbs 22:6, "Train a child in the way he should go, and when he is old he will not turn from it." To "train" indicates the first instruction that a father and mother give to a child, i.e., his early education. The training is designed to make clear to children the manner of life they are intended for. To commence a child's early education in this way is of great importance.

Ephesians 6:4 is a summary of instructions to the father, stated in both a negative and positive way. "Fathers, do not exasperate your children; instead, bring them up in the training and instruction of the Lord." The negative part of this verse indicates that a father is not to foster negativity in his children by severity, injustice, partiality, or unreasonable exercise of authority. Harsh, unreasonable conduct towards a child will only serve to nurture evil in the heart. The word "provoke" means "to irritate, exasperate, rub the wrong way, or incite." This is done by a wrong spirit and wrong methods—severity, unreasonableness, sternness, harshness, cruel demands, needless restrictions, and selfish insistence upon dictatorial authority. Such provocation will produce adverse reactions, deadening children's affection, reducing their desire for holiness, and making them feel that they cannot possibly please their parents. A wise parent seeks to make obedience desirable and attainable by love and gentleness.

The positive part of Ephesians 6:4 is expressed in a comprehensive direction—educate them, bring them up, develop their conduct in all of life by the instruction and admonition of the Lord. This is the whole process of educating and discipline. The word "admonition" carries the idea of reminding the child of faults (constructively) and duties (responsibilities).

The Christian father is really an instrument in God's hand. The whole process of instruction and discipline must be that which God commands and which He administers, so that His authority should be brought into constant and immediate contact with the mind, heart, and conscience of children. The human father should never present himself as the ultimate authority to determine truth and duty. It is only by making God the teacher and ruler on whose authority everything is done that the goals of education can best be attained.

Martin Luther said, "Keep an apple beside the rod to give the child when he does well." Discipline must be exercised with watchful care and constant training with much prayer. Chastening, discipline, and counsel by the Word of God, giving both reproof and encouragement, is at the core of "admonition." The instruction proceeds from the Lord, is learned in the school of Christian experience, and is administered by the parents—primarily the father, but also, under his direction, the mother. Christian discipline is needed to enable children to grow up with reverence for God, respect for parental authority, knowledge of Christian standards, and habits of self-control.

"All Scripture is God-breathed and is useful for teaching, rebuking, correcting and training in righteousness" (2 Timothy 3:16-17). A father's first responsibility is to acquaint his children with Scripture. The means and methods that fathers may use to teach God's truth will vary. As the father is faithful in role modeling, what children learn about God will put them in good standing throughout their earthly lives, no matter what they do or where they go.

Question: What does the Bible say about Christian mothers?

Answer: Being a mother is a very important role that the Lord chooses to give to many women. A Christian mother is told to love her children (Titus 2:4-5), in part so that she does not bring reproach on the Lord and on the Savior whose name she bears.

Children are a gift from the Lord (Psalm 127:3-5). In Titus 2:4, the Greek word *phileoteknos* appears in reference to mothers loving their children. This word represents a special kind of "mother love." The idea that flows out of this word is that of caring for our children, nurturing them, affectionately embracing them, meeting their needs, and tenderly befriending each one as a unique gift from the hand of God.

Several things are commanded of Christian mothers in God's Word:

Availability – morning, noon, and night (Deuteronomy 6:6-7)

Involvement – interacting, discussing, thinking, and processing life together (Ephesians 6:4)

Teaching – the Scriptures and a biblical worldview (Psalm 78:5-6; Deuteronomy 4:10; Ephesians 6:4)

Training – helping a child to develop skills and discover his/her strengths (Proverbs 22:6) and spiritual gifts (Romans 12:3-8 and 1 Corinthians 12)

Discipline – teaching the fear of the Lord, drawing the line consistently, lovingly, firmly (Ephesians 6:4; Hebrews 12:5-11; Proverbs 13:24; 19:18; 22:15; 23:13-14; 29:15-17)

Nurture – providing an environment of constant verbal support, freedom to fail, acceptance, affection, unconditional love (Titus 2:4; 2 Timothy 1:7; Ephesians 4:29-32; 5:1-2; Galatians 5:22; 1 Peter 3:8-9)

Modeling with Integrity – living what you say, being a model from which a child can learn by "catching" the essence of godly living (Deuteronomy 4:9, 15, 23; Proverbs 10:9; 11:3; Psalm 37:18, 37).

The Bible never states that every woman should be a mother. However, it does say that those whom the Lord blesses to be mothers should take the responsibility seriously. Mothers have a unique and crucial role in the lives of their children. Motherhood is not a chore or unpleasant task. Just as a mother bears a child during pregnancy, and just as a mother feeds and cares for a child during infancy, so mothers also play an ongoing role in the lives of their children, whether they are adolescents, teenagers, young adults, or even adults with children of their own. While the role of motherhood must change and develop, the love, care, nurture, and encouragement a mother gives should never cease.

Question: How should Christians discipline their children?

Answer: How to best discipline children can be difficult task to learn, but it is crucially important. Some claim that physical discipline (corporal punishment) such as spanking is the only method the Bible supports. Others insist that "time-outs" and other punishments that do not involve physical discipline are far more effective. What does the Bible say? The Bible teaches that physical discipline is appropriate, beneficial, and necessary.

Do not misunderstand—we are by no means advocating child abuse. A child should never be disciplined physically to the extent that it causes actual physical damage. According to the Bible, though, the appropriate and restrained physical discipline of children is a good thing and contributes to the well-being and correct upbringing of the child.

Many Scriptures do in fact promote physical discipline. "Don't fail to correct your children. They won't die if you spank them. Physical discipline may well save them from death" (Proverbs 23:13-14; see also 13:24; 22:15; 20:30). The Bible strongly stresses the importance of discipline; it is something we must all have in order to be productive people, and it is much more easily learned when we are young. Children who are not disciplined often grow up rebellious, have no respect for authority, and as a result find it difficult to willingly obey and follow God. God Himself uses discipline to correct us and lead us down the right path and to encourage repentance for our wrong actions (Psalm 94:12; Proverbs 1:7; 6:23; 12:1; 13:1; 15:5; Isaiah 38:16; Hebrews 12:9).

In order to apply discipline correctly and according to biblical principles, parents must be familiar with the scriptural advice regarding discipline. The book of Proverbs contains plentiful wisdom regarding the rearing of children, such as, "The rod of correction imparts wisdom, but a child left to himself disgraces his mother" (Proverbs 29:15). This verse outlines the consequences of not disciplining a child—the parents are disgraced. Of course, discipline must have as its goal the good of the child and must never be used to justify the abuse and mistreatment of children. Never should it be used to vent anger or frustration.

Discipline is used to correct and train people to go in the right way. "No discipline seems pleasant at the time, but painful. Later on, however, it produces a harvest of righteousness and peace for those who have been trained by it" (Hebrews 12:11). God's discipline is loving, as should it be between parent and child. Physical discipline should never be used to cause lasting physical harm or pain. Physical punishment should always be followed immediately by comforting the child with assurance that he/she is loved. These moments are the perfect time to teach a child that God disciplines us because He loves us and that, as parents, we do the same for our children.

Can other forms of discipline, such as "time-outs," be used instead of physical discipline? Some parents find that their children do not respond well to physical discipline. Some parents find that "time-outs," grounding, and/or taking something away from the children is more effective in encouraging behavioral change. If that is indeed the case, by all means, a parent should employ the methods that best produce the needed behavioral change. While the Bible undeniably advocates physical discipline, the Bible is more concerned with the goal of building godly character than it is in the precise method used to produce that goal.

Making this issue even more difficult is the fact that governments are beginning to classify all manner of physical discipline as child abuse. Many parents do not spank their children for fear of being reported to the government and risk having their children taken away. What should parents do if a government has made physical discipline of children illegal? According to Romans 13:1-7, parents should submit to the government. A government should never contradict God's Word, and physical discipline is, biblically speaking, in the best interest of children. However, keeping children in families in which they will at least receive some discipline is far better than losing children to the "care" of the government.

In Ephesians 6:4, fathers are told not to exasperate their children. Instead, they are to bring them up in God's ways. Raising a child in the "training and instruction of the Lord" includes restrained, corrective, and, yes, loving physical discipline.

Question: What should Christian parents do if they have a prodigal son (or daughter)?

Answer: There is inherent in the story of the prodigal son (Luke 15:11-32) several principles that believing parents can use to react to and deal with children who walk contrary to the way in which the parents have raised them. Parents need to remember that once their children have reached adulthood, they are no longer under the authority of their parents.

In the story of the prodigal son, the younger son takes his inheritance and goes into a far country and wastes it. In the case of a child who is not a born-again believer, this is just doing what comes naturally. In the case of a child who at one time made a clear profession of faith in Christ, we call this child a "prodigal." The meaning of this word is "a person who has spent his resources wastefully," a good description of a child who leaves home and wastes the spiritual inheritance that his parents have invested in him. All the years of nurture, teaching, love, and care are forgotten as this child rebels against God. For all rebellion is against God first, and is manifested in a rebellion against parents and their authority.

Notice that the father in the parable does not stop his child from leaving. Nor does he follow after his child to try to protect him. Rather, this parent faithfully stays at home and prays, and when that child "comes to his senses" and turns around and heads back, the parent is waiting and watching and runs to greet that child even when he is a "long way off."

When our sons and daughters go off on their own—assuming they are of legal age to do so—and make choices that we know will bring hard consequences, parents must let go and allow them to leave. The parent does not follow after, and the parent does not interfere with the consequences that will come. Rather, the parent stays at home, keeps faithfully praying and watching for the signs of repentance and a change of direction. Until that comes, parents keep to their own counsel, do not support the rebellion, and do not interfere (1 Peter 4:15).

Once children are of an age of legal adulthood, they are subject only to the authority of God and the delegated authority of government (Romans 13:1-7). As parents, we can support our prodigals with love and prayer and be ready to come alongside once they have made their move toward God. God often uses self-inflicted misery to bring us to wisdom, and it is up to each individual to respond correctly. As parents, we cannot save our children—only God can do that. Until that time comes, we must watch, pray, and leave the matter in the hands of God. This may be a painful process, but when carried out biblically, it will bring peace of mind and heart. We cannot judge our children, only God can. In this there is a great comfort: "Will not the Judge of all the earth do right?" (Genesis 18:25b).

Question: What does the Bible say about birth control? Should Christians use birth control?

Answer: Man was commissioned by God "to be fruitful and multiply" (Genesis 1:28). Marriage was instituted by God as a stable environment in which to produce and raise children. Sadly, children today are sometimes considered a nuisance and a burden. They stand in the way of people's career paths and financial goals, and they "crimp your style" socially. Often, this type of selfishness is at the root of contraceptive use.

Contrary to the self-centeredness behind some birth control usage, the Bible presents children as a gift from God (Genesis 4:1; Genesis 33:5). Children are a heritage from the Lord (Psalm 127:3-5). Children are a blessing from God (Luke 1:42). Children are a crown to the aged (Proverbs 17:6). God blesses barren women with children (Psalm 113:9; Genesis 21:1-3; 25:21-22; 30:1-2; 1 Samuel 1:6-8; Luke 1:7, 24-25). God forms children in the womb (Psalm 139:13-16). God knows children before their birth (Jeremiah 1:5; Galatians 1:15).

The closest that Scripture comes to specifically condemning birth control is Genesis chapter 38, the account of Judah's sons Er and Onan. Er married a woman named Tamar, but he was wicked and the Lord put him to death, leaving Tamar with no husband or children. Tamar was given in marriage to Er's brother, Onan, in accordance with the law of levirate marriage in Deuteronomy 25:5-6. Onan did not want to split his inheritance with any child that he might produce on his brother's behalf, so he practiced the oldest form of birth control, withdrawal. Genesis 38:10 says, "What he did was wicked in the Lord's sight; so He put him to death also." Onan's motivation was selfish: he used Tamar for his own pleasure, but refused to perform his legal duty of creating an heir for his deceased brother. This passage is often used as evidence that God does not approve of birth control. However, it was not explicitly the act of contraception that caused the Lord to put Onan to death; it was Onan's selfish motives behind the action.

It is important to view children as God sees them, not as the world tells us we should. Having said that, the Bible does not forbid contraception. Contraception, by definition, is merely the opposite of conception. It is not the act of contraception itself that determines whether it is wrong or right. As we learned from Onan, it is the motivation behind the contraception that determines if it is right or wrong. If a married couple is practicing contraception in order to have more for themselves, then it is wrong. If a couple is practicing contraception in order to temporarily delay children until they are more mature and more financially and spiritually prepared, then it is perhaps acceptable to use contraception for a time. Again, it all comes back to motivation.

The Bible always presents having children as a good thing. The Bible "expects" that a husband and wife will have children. The inability to have children is always presented in Scripture as a bad thing. There is no one in the Bible who expressed a desire not to have any children. At the same time, it cannot be argued from the Bible that it is explicitly wrong to use birth control for a limited time. All married couples should seek the Lord's will in regards to when they should try to have children and how many children they seek to have.

Question: What does the Bible say about adoption?

Answer: Giving children up for adoption can be a loving alternative for parents who may, for various reasons, be unable to care for their own children. It can also be an answer to prayer for many couples who have not been able to have children of their own. Adoption is, for some, a calling to multiply their impact as parents by expanding their family with children who are not their own, biologically. Adoption is spoken of favorably throughout Scripture.

The book of Exodus tells the story of a Hebrew woman named Jochebed who bore a son during a time when Pharaoh had ordered all Hebrew male infants to be put to death (Exodus 1:15-22). Jochebed took a basket, waterproofed it, and sent the baby down the river in the basket. One of Pharaoh's daughters spotted the basket and retrieved the child. She eventually adopted him into the royal family and gave him the name Moses. He went on to become a faithful and blessed servant of God (Exodus 2:1-10).

In the book of Esther, a beautiful girl named Esther, who was adopted by her cousin after her parents' death, became a queen, and God used her to bring deliverance to the Jewish people. In the New Testament, Jesus Christ was conceived through the Holy Spirit instead of through the seed of a man (Matthew 1:18). He was "adopted" and raised by His mother's husband, Joseph, who took Jesus as his own child.

Once we give our hearts to Christ, believing and trusting in Him alone for salvation, God says we become part of His family—not through the natural process of human conception, but through adoption. "For you did not receive a spirit that makes you a slave again to fear, but you received the Spirit of sonship [adoption]. And by him we cry, '*Abba*, Father'" (Romans 8:15). Similarly, bringing a person into a family by means of adoption is done by choice and out of love. "His unchanging plan has always been to adopt us into His own family by bringing us to Himself through Jesus Christ. And this gave Him great pleasure" (Ephesians 1:5). As God adopts those who receive Christ as Savior into His spiritual family, so should we all prayerfully consider adopting children into our own physical families.

Clearly adoption—both in the physical sense and in the spiritual sense—is shown in a favorable light in Scripture. Both those who adopt and those who are adopted are receiving a tremendous blessing, a privilege exemplified by our adoption into God's family.

Question: What should be the order of priorities in our family?

Answer: The Bible does not lay out a step-by-step order for family relationship priorities. However, we can still look to the Scriptures and find general principles for prioritizing our family relationships. God obviously comes first: Deuteronomy 6:5, "Love the LORD your God with all your heart and with all your soul and with all your strength." All of one's heart, soul, and strength is to be committed to loving God, making Him the first priority.

If you are married, your spouse comes next. A married man is to love his wife as Christ loved the church (Ephesians 5:25). Christ's first priority—after obeying and glorifying the Father—was the church. Here is an example a husband should follow: God first, then his wife. In the same way, wives are to submit to their husbands "as to the Lord" (Ephesians 5:22). The principle is that a woman's husband is second only to God in her priorities.

If husbands and wives are second only to God in our priorities, and since a husband and wife are one flesh (Ephesians 5:31), it stands to reason that the result of the marriage relationship—children—should be the next priority. Parents are to raise godly children who will be the next generation of those who love the Lord with all their hearts (Proverbs 22:6; Ephesians 6:4), showing once again that God comes first. All other family relationships should reflect that.

Deuteronomy 5:16 tells us to honor our parents so that we may live long and so things will go well with us. No age limit is specified, which leads us to believe that as long as our parents are alive, we should honor them. Of course, once a child reaches adulthood, he is no longer obligated to obey them (*"Children,* obey your parents...*"*), but there is no age limit to honoring them. We can conclude from this that parents are next in the list of priorities after God, our spouses, and our children. After parents comes the rest of one's family (1 Timothy 5:8).

Following one's extended family in the list of priorities are fellow believers. Romans 14 tells us not judge or look down upon our brothers (v. 10) or do anything to cause a fellow Christian to "stumble" or fall spiritually. Much of the book of 1 Corinthians is Paul's instructions on how the church should live together in harmony, loving one another. Other exhortations referring to our brothers and sisters in Christ are "serve one another in love" (Galatians 5:13); "be kind and compassionate to one another, forgiving each other, just as in Christ God forgave you" (Ephesians 4:32); "encourage one another and build each other up" (1 Thessalonians 5:11); and "consider how we may spur one another on toward love and good deeds (Hebrews 10:24). Finally comes the rest of the world (Matthew 28:19), to whom we should bring the gospel, making disciples of Christ.

In conclusion, the scriptural order of priorities is God, spouse, children, parents, extended family, brothers and sisters in Christ, and then the rest of the world. While sometimes decisions must be made to focus on one person over another, the goal is to not be neglecting any of our relationships. The biblical balance is allowing God to empower us to meet all of our relationship priorities, inside and outside our families.

Question: What does it mean to honor my father and mother?

Answer: Honoring your father and mother is being respectful in word and action and having an inward attitude of esteem for their position. The Greek word for honor means "to revere, prize, and value." Honor is giving respect not only for merit but also for rank. For example, some Americans may disagree with the President's decisions, but they should still respect his position as leader of their country. Similarly, children of all ages should honor their parents, regardless of whether or not their parents "deserve" honor.

God exhorts us to honor father and mother. He values honoring parents enough to include it in the Ten Commandments (Exodus 20:12) and again in the New Testament: "Children, obey your parents in the Lord, for this is right. Honor your father and mother which is the first commandment with a promise, so that it may be well with you, and that you may live long on the earth" (Ephesians 6:1-3). Honoring parents is the only command in Scripture that promises long life as a reward. Those who honor their parents are blessed (Jeremiah 35:18-19). In contrast, those with a "depraved mind" and those who exhibit ungodliness in the last days are characterized by disobedience to parents (Romans 1:30; 2 Timothy 3:2).

Solomon, the wisest man, urged children to respect their parents (Proverbs 1:8; 13:1; 30:17). Although we may no longer be directly under their authority, we cannot outgrow God's command to honor our parents. Even Jesus, God the Son, submitted Himself to both His earthly parents (Luke 2:51) and His heavenly Father (Matthew 26:39). Following Christ's example, we should treat our parents the way we would reverentially approach our heavenly Father (Hebrews 12:9; Malachi 1:6).

Obviously, we are commanded to honor our parents, but how? Honor them with both actions and attitudes (Mark 7:6). Honor their unspoken as well as spoken wishes. "A wise son heeds his father's instruction, but a mocker does not listen to rebuke" (Proverbs 13:1). In Matthew 15:3-9, Jesus reminded the Pharisees of the command of God to honor their father and mother. They were obeying the letter of the law, but they had added their own traditions that essentially overruled it. While they honored their parents in word, their actions proved their real motive. Honor is more than lip service. The word "honor" in this passage is a verb and, as such, demands a right action.

We should seek to honor our parents in much the same way that we strive to bring glory to God—in our thoughts, words, and actions. For a young child, obeying parents goes hand in hand with honoring them. That includes listening, heeding, and submitting to their authority. After children mature, the obedience that they learned as children will serve them well in honoring other authorities such as government, police, and employers.

While we are required to honor parents, that doesn't include imitating ungodly ones (Ezekiel 20:18-19). If a parent ever instructs a child to do something that clearly contradicts God's commands, that child must obey God rather than his/her parents (Acts 5:28).

Honor begets honor. God will not honor those who will not obey His command to honor their parents. If we desire to please God and be blessed, we should honor our parents. Honoring is not easy, is not always fun, and certainly is not possible in our own strength. But honor is a certain path to our purpose in life—glorifying God. "Children, obey your parents in everything, for this pleases the Lord" (Colossians 3:20).

Question: How should a Christian deal with infertility?

Answer: The problem of infertility can be a very difficult one, especially for couples who have looked forward to children all their lives. Christian couples can find themselves asking "Why us, Lord?" Surely God wants Christians to be blessed with children to love and nurture. For physically healthy couples, one of the most heart-wrenching aspects of infertility is not knowing whether it is a temporary or permanent situation. If it is temporary, how long must they wait? If it is permanent, how do they know that, and what should be their course of action?

The Bible depicts the problem of temporary infertility in several stories:

> God promised Abraham and Sarah a child, but she did not bear a son, Isaac, until age 90.
>
> —Genesis 11:30

> Isaac, Rebekah's husband, prayed fervently, and God answered, resulting in the births of Jacob and Esau.
>
> —Genesis 25:21

> Rachel prayed, and at long last God "opened her womb." She bore two sons, Joseph and Benjamin.
>
> —Genesis 30:1; 35:18

> Manoah's wife, who was infertile for a time, gave birth to Samson.
>
> —Judges 13:2

459

Elizabeth in her old age gave birth to John the Baptist, the forerunner of Christ.

—Luke 1:7, 36

The barrenness of Sarah, Rebekah, and Rachel (the mothers of the Israelite nation) is significant in that their ability to finally bear children was a sign of the grace and favor of God. However, infertile couples must not assume that God is withholding His grace and favor, nor should they assume they are being punished in some way. Christian couples must cling to the knowledge that their sins are forgiven in Christ and that the inability to have children is not a punishment from God.

So what is an infertile Christian couple to do? It is good to seek advice from gynecologists and other fertility specialists. Both men and women should live a healthy lifestyle to prepare for pregnancy. The mothers of the Israelite nation prayed fervently for conception, so continuing to pray for a child is certainly not out of line. Primarily, though, we are to pray for God's will for our lives. If His will is for us to have a natural child, we will. If His will is that we adopt, foster-parent, or go childless, then that is what we should accept and commit to gladly doing. We know that God has a divine plan for each of His loved ones. God is the author of life. He allows conception and withholds conception. God is sovereign and possesses all wisdom and knowledge (see Romans 11:33-36). "Every good and perfect gift is from above..." (James 1:17). Knowing and accepting these truths will go a long way to filling the ache in the hearts of an infertile couple.

Question: What does the Bible say to do with a rebellious child?

Answer: The child who exhibits a rebellious streak may be doing so for a variety of reasons. Harsh, unloving, and critical parenting will nearly always result in rebellion of some sort. Even the most compliant child will rebel—inwardly or outwardly—against such treatment. Naturally, this type of parenting is to be avoided. In addition, a certain amount of rebellion against parents is natural in teenagers who are slowly pulling away from their families in the process of establishing lives and identities of their own.

Assuming that the rebellious child naturally possesses a strong-willed personality, he will be characterized by an inclination to test limits, an overriding desire for control, and a commitment to resisting all authority. In other words, rebellion is his middle name. In addition, these strong-willed, rebellious children are often very intelligent and can "figure out" situations with amazing speed, finding ways to take control of the circumstances and people around them. These kids can be, for their parents, an extremely trying and exhausting challenge.

Fortunately, it is also true that God has made children who and what they are. He loves them, and He has not left parents without resources to meet the challenge. There are biblical principles that address dealing with the rebellious, strong-willed child with grace. First, Proverbs 22:6 tells us to "train up a child in the way he should go: and when he is old, he will not turn from it." For all children, the way they should go is toward God. Teaching children in God's Word is crucial for all children, who must understand who God is and how to best serve Him. With the strong-willed child, understanding what motivates him—the desire for control—will go a long way to helping him find his "way." The rebellious child is one who must understand that he is not in charge of the world—God is—and that he simply must do things God's way. This requires parents to be absolutely convinced of this truth and to live accordingly. A parent who is himself in rebellion against God will not be able to convince his child to be submissive.

Once it has been established that God is the One making the rules, parents must establish in the child's mind that they are God's instruments and will do anything and everything necessary to carry out God's plan for their families. A rebellious child must be taught that God's plan is for the parents to lead and the child to follow. There can be no weakness on this point. The strong-willed child can spot indecisiveness a mile away and will jump at the opportunity to fill the leadership vacuum and take control. The principle of submitting to authority is crucial for the strong-willed child. If submission is not learned in childhood, the future will be characterized by conflicts with all authority, including employers, police, law courts, and military leaders. Romans 13:1-5 is clear that the authorities over us are established by God, and we are to submit to them.

Also, a strong-willed child will only willingly comply with rules or laws when they make sense to him. Give him a solid reason for a rule, constantly reiterating the truth that we do things the way God wants them done and that the fact is not negotiable. Explain that God has given parents the responsibility to love and discipline their children and that to fail to do so would mean the parents are disobeying Him. Whenever possible, however, give the child opportunities to help make decisions so that he does not feel completely powerless. For example, going to church is not negotiable because God commands us to gather together with other believers (Hebrews 10:25), but children can have a say (within reason) in what they wear, where the family sits, etc. Give them projects in which they can give input like planning the family vacation.

Further, parenting must be done with consistency and patience. Parents must try not to raise their voices or raise their hands in anger or lose their tempers. This will give the strong-willed child the sense of control he/she longs for, and he/she will quickly figure out how to control you by frustrating you to the point of making you react emotionally. Physical discipline often fails with these kids because they enjoy pushing parents to the breaking point so much that they feel a little pain is a worthwhile price to pay. Parents of strong-willed kids often report the kid laughs at them while they are being spanked, so spanking might not be the best method of discipline with them. Perhaps nowhere in life are the Christian fruits of the Spirit of patience and self-control (Galatians 5:23) more needed than with the strong-willed/rebellious child.

No matter how exasperating parenting these children can be, parents can take comfort in God's promise not to test us beyond our ability to bear it (1 Corinthians 10:13). If God gives them a strong-willed child, parents can be sure He has not made a mistake and will provide the guidance and resources they need to do the job. Perhaps nowhere in the life of a parent do the words "pray without ceasing" (1 Thessalonians 5:17) have more meaning than with the strong-willed youngster. Parents of these children have to spend lots of their time on their knees before the Lord asking for wisdom, which He has promised to provide (James 1:5). Finally, there is comfort in the knowledge that strong-willed children who are trained well often grow up to be high-achieving, successful adults. Many rebellious children have turned into bold, committed Christians who use their considerable talents to serve the Lord they have come to love and respect through the efforts of their patient and diligent parents.

Question: What are the roles of the husband and wife in a family?

Answer: Although males and females are equal in relationship to Christ, the Scriptures give specific roles to each in marriage. The husband is to assume leadership in the home (1 Corinthians 11:3; Ephesians 5:23). This leadership should not be dictatorial, condescending, or patronizing to the wife, but should be in accordance with the example of Christ leading the church. "Husbands, love your wives, just as Christ loved the church and gave himself up for her to make her holy, cleansing her by the washing with water through the word" (Ephesians 5:25-26). Christ loved the church (His people) with compassion, mercy, forgiveness, respect, and selflessness. In this same way husbands are to love their wives.

Wives are to submit to the authority of their husbands. "Wives, submit to your husbands as to the Lord. For the husband is the head of the wife as Christ is the head of the church, his body, of which he is the Savior. Now as the church submits to Christ, so also wives should submit to their husbands in everything" (Ephesians 5:22-24). Although women should submit to their husbands, the Bible also tells men several times how they are supposed to treat their wives. The husband is not to take on the role of the dictator, but should show respect for his wife and her opinions. In fact, Ephesians 5:28-29 exhorts men to love their wives in the same way that they love their own bodies, feeding and caring for them. A man's love for his wife should be the same as Christ's love for His body, the church.

"Wives, submit to your husbands, as is fitting in the Lord. Husbands, love your wives and do not be harsh with them" (Colossians 3:18-19). "Husbands, in the same way be considerate as you live with your wives, and treat them with respect as the weaker partner and as heirs with you of the gracious gift of life, so that nothing will hinder your prayers" (1 Peter 3:7). From these verses we see that love and respect characterize the roles of both husbands and wives. If these are present, then authority, headship, love, and submission will be no problem for either partner.

In regard to the division of responsibilities in the home, the Bible instructs husbands to provide for their families. This means he works and makes enough money to sufficiently provide all the necessities of life for his wife and children. To fail to do so has definite spiritual consequences. "If anyone does not provide for his relatives, and especially for his immediate family, he has denied the faith and is worse than an unbeliever" (1 Timothy 5:8). So, a man who makes no effort to provide for his family cannot rightly call himself a Christian. This does not mean that the wife cannot assist in supporting the family—Proverbs 31 demonstrates that a godly wife may surely do so—but providing for the family is not primarily her responsibility; it is her husband's. While a husband should help with the children and with household chores (thereby fulfilling his duty to love his wife), Proverbs 31 also makes it clear that the home is to be the woman's primary area of influence and responsibility. Even if she must stay up late and rise up early, her family is well cared for. This is not an easy lifestyle for many women—especially in affluent Western nations. However, far too many women are stressed out and stretched to the breaking point. To prevent such stress, both husband and wife should prayerfully reorder their priorities and follow the Bible's instructions on their roles.

Conflicts regarding the division of labor in a marriage are bound to occur, but if both partners are submitted to Christ, these conflicts will be minimal. If a couple finds arguments over this issue are frequent and vehement, or if arguments seem to characterize the marriage, the problem is a spiritual one. In such an instance, the partners should recommit themselves to prayer and submission to Christ first, then to one another in an attitude of love and respect.

Chapter 18

· ·

QUESTIONS ABOUT CREATION

CONTENTS

What does the Bible say about creation vs. evolution?...........................466

Do faith in God and science contradict? 468

What is the age of the earth? 469

Who was Cain's wife? Was Cain's wife his sister?..............................470

What does the Bible say about dinosaurs? Are there dinosaurs in the Bible? 471

Was Noah's flood global or local? 473

Why did God put the tree of knowledge of good and evil in the Garden of Eden? 474

What is the Intelligent Design Theory? 475

Does Genesis chapter 1 mean literal 24-hour days? 477

What does the Bible say about cavemen, prehistoric men, Neanderthals?...478

Why are there two different creation accounts in Genesis 1-2? 479

Is creationism scientific? 481

What is the Gap Theory? Did anything happen between Genesis 1:1 and 1:2? 483

What is theistic evolution?...485

Question: What does the Bible say about creation vs. evolution?

Answer: It is not the purpose of this answer to present a scientific argument in the creation vs. evolution debate. For scientific arguments for creation and/or against evolution, we highly recommend Answers in Genesis and the Institute for Creation Research. The purpose of this article is to explain why, according to the Bible, the creation vs. evolution debate even exists. Romans 1:25 declares, "They exchanged the truth of God for a lie, and worshiped and served created things rather than the Creator—who is forever praised. Amen."

A key factor in the debate is that the majority of scientists who believe in evolution are also atheists or agnostics. There are some who hold to some form of theistic evolution and others who take a deistic view of God (God exists but is not involved in the world, and everything proceeds along a natural course). There are some who genuinely and honestly look at the data and arrive at the conclusion that evolution betters fits with the data. However, these represent an insignificant percentage of the scientists who advocate evolution. The vast majority of evolutionary scientists hold that life evolved entirely without *any* intervention of a higher being. Evolution is by definition a naturalistic science.

For atheism to be true, there must be an alternate explanation—other than a Creator—for how the universe and life came into existence. Although belief in some form of evolution predated Charles Darwin, he was the first to develop a plausible model for the process of evolution—natural selection. Darwin once identified himself as a Christian but as a result of some tragedies that took place in his life, he later renounced the Christian faith and the existence of God. Evolution was invented by an atheist. Darwin's goal was not to disprove God's existence, but that is one of the end results of the theory of evolution. Evolution is an enabler of atheism. Evolutionary scientists likely would not admit that their goal is to give an alternate explanation of the origins of life, and thereby to give a foundation for atheism, but according to the Bible, that is exactly why the theory of evolution exists.

The Bible tells us, "The fool says in his heart, 'There is no God'" (Psalm 14:1; 53:1). The Bible also proclaims that people are without excuse for not believing in a Creator God. "For since the creation of the world God's invisible qualities—His eternal power and divine nature—have been clearly seen, being understood from what has been made, so that men are without excuse" (Romans 1:20). According to the Bible, anyone who denies the existence of God is a fool. Why, then, are so many people, including some Christians, willing to accept that evolutionary scientists are unbiased interpreters of scientific data? According to the Bible, they are all fools! Foolishness does not imply a lack of intelligence. Most evolutionary scientists are brilliant intellectually. Foolishness indicates an inability to properly apply knowledge. Proverbs 1:7 tells us, "The fear of the LORD is the beginning of knowledge, but fools despise wisdom and discipline."

Evolutionary scientists mock creation and/or intelligent design as unscientific and not worthy of scientific examination. In order for something to be considered a "science," they argue, it must be able to be observed and tested; it must be "naturalistic." Creation is by definition "supernatural." God and the supernatural cannot be observed or tested (so the argument goes); therefore, creation and/or intelligent design cannot be considered science. Of course, neither can evolution be observed or tested, but that does not seem to be an issue with evolutionists. As a result, all data is filtered through the preconceived, presupposed, and pre-accepted theory of evolution, without alternate explanations being considered.

However, the origin of the universe and the origin of life cannot be tested or observed. Both creation and evolution are faith-based systems in regards to origins. Neither can be tested because we cannot go back billions (or thousands) of years to observe the origin of the universe or of life in the universe. Evolutionary scientists reject creation on grounds that would logically force them to also reject evolution as a scientific explanation of origins. Evolution, at least in regard to origins, does not fit the definition of "science" any more than creation does. Evolution is supposedly the only explanation of origins that can be tested; therefore, it is the only theory of origins that can be considered "scientific." This is foolishness! Scientists who advocate evolution are rejecting a plausible theory of origins without even honestly examining its merits, because it does not fit their illogically narrow definition of "science."

If creation is true, then there is a Creator to whom we are accountable. Evolution is an enabler for atheism. Evolution gives atheists a basis for explaining how life exists apart from a Creator God. Evolution denies the need for a God to be involved in the universe. Evolution is the "creation theory" for the religion of atheism. According to the Bible, the choice is clear. We can believe the Word of our omnipotent and omniscient God, or we can believe the illogically biased, "scientific" explanations of fools.

Question: Do faith in God and science contradict?

Answer: Science is defined as "the observation, identification, description, experimental investigation, and theoretical explanation of phenomena." Science is a method that mankind can use to gain a greater understanding of the natural universe. It is a search for knowledge through observation. Advances in science demonstrate the reach of human logic and imagination. However, a Christian's belief in science should never be like our belief in God. A Christian can have faith in God and respect for science, as long as we remember which is perfect and which is not.

Our belief in God is a belief of faith. We have faith in His Son for salvation, faith in His Word for instruction, and faith in His Holy Spirit for guidance. Our faith in God should be absolute, since when we put our faith in God, we depend on a perfect, omnipotent, omniscient Creator. Our belief in science should be intellectual and nothing more. We can count on science to do many great things, but we can also count on science to make mistakes. If we put faith in science, we depend on imperfect, sinful, limited, mortal men. Science throughout history has been wrong about many things, such as the shape of the earth, powered flight, vaccines, blood transfusions, and even reproduction. God is never wrong.

Truth is nothing to fear, so there is no reason for a Christian to fear good science. Learning more about the way God constructed our universe helps all of mankind appreciate the wonder of creation. Expanding our knowledge helps us to combat disease, ignorance, and misunderstanding. However, there is danger when scientists hold their faith in human logic above faith in our Creator. These persons are no different from anyone devoted to a religion; they have chosen faith in man and will find facts to defend that faith.

Still, the most rational scientists, even those who refuse to believe in God, admit to a lack of completeness in our understanding of the universe. They will admit that neither God nor the Bible can be proved or disproved by science, just as many of their favorite theories ultimately cannot be proved or disproved. Science is meant to be a truly neutral discipline, seeking only the truth, not furtherance of an agenda.

Much of science supports the existence and work of God. Psalm 19:1 says, "The heavens declare the glory of God; the skies proclaim the work of His hands." As modern science discovers more about the universe, we find more evidence of creation. The amazing complexity and replication of DNA, the intricate and interlocking laws of physics, and the absolute harmony of conditions and chemistry here on earth all serve to support the message of the Bible. A Christian should embrace science that seeks the truth, but reject the "priests of science" who put human knowledge above God.

Question: What is the age of the earth?

Answer: Given the fact that, according to the Bible, Adam was created on the sixth day of our planet's existence, we can determine a biblically-based, approximate age for the earth by looking at the chronological details of the human race. This assumes that the Genesis account is accurate, that the six days of creation were literal 24-hour periods, and that there were no ambiguous gaps in the chronology of Genesis.

The genealogies listed in Genesis chapters 5 and 11 provide the age at which Adam and his descendants each fathered the next generation in a successive ancestral line from Adam to Abraham. By determining where Abraham fits into history chronologically and adding up the ages provided in Genesis 5 and 11, it becomes apparent that the Bible teaches the earth to be about 6000 years old, give or take a few hundred years.

What about the billions of years accepted by most scientists today and taught in the vast majority of our academic institutions? This age is primarily derived from two dating techniques: radiometric dating and the geologic timescale. Scientists who advocate the younger age of about 6000 years insist that radiometric dating is flawed in that it is founded upon a series of faulty assumptions, while the geologic timescale is flawed in that it employs circular reasoning. Moreover, they point to the debunking of old-earth myths, like the popular misconception that it takes long periods of time for stratification, fossilization and the formation of diamonds, coal, oil, stalactites, stalagmites, etc, to occur. Finally, young-earth advocates present positive evidence for a young age for the earth in place of the old-earth evidences which they debunk. Young-earth scientists acknowledge that they are in the minority today but insist that their ranks will swell over time as more and more scientists reexamine the evidence and take a closer look at the currently accepted old-earth paradigm.

Ultimately, the age of the earth cannot be proven. Whether 6000 years or billions of years, both viewpoints (and everything in between) rest on faith and assumptions. Those who hold to billions of years trust that methods such as radiometric dating are reliable and that nothing has occurred in history that may have disrupted the normal decay of radio-isotopes. Those who hold to 6000 years trust that the Bible is true and that other factors explain the "apparent" age of the earth, such as the global flood, or God's creating the universe in a state that "appears" to give it a very long age. As an example, God created Adam and Eve as fully-grown adult human beings. If a doctor had examined Adam and Eve on the day of their creation, the doctor would have estimated their age at 20 years (or whatever age they appeared to be) when, in fact, Adam and Eve were less than one day old. Whatever the case, there is always good reason to trust the Word of God over the words of atheistic scientists with an evolutionary agenda.

Question: Who was Cain's wife? Was Cain's wife his sister?

Answer: The Bible does not specifically say who Cain's wife was. The only possible answer was that Cain's wife was his sister or niece or great-niece, etc. The Bible does not say how old Cain was when he killed Abel (Genesis 4:8). Since they were both farmers, they were likely both full-grown adults, possibly with families of their own. Adam and Eve surely had given birth to more children than just

Cain and Abel at the time Abel was killed. They definitely had many more children later (Genesis 5:4). The fact that Cain was scared for his own life after he killed Abel (Genesis 4:14) indicates that there were likely many other children and perhaps even grandchildren of Adam and Eve already living at that time. Cain's wife (Genesis 4:17) was a daughter or granddaughter of Adam and Eve.

Since Adam and Eve were the first (and only) human beings, their children would have no other choice than to intermarry. God did not forbid inter-family marriage until much later when there were enough people to make intermarriage unnecessary (Leviticus 18:6-18). The reason that incest today often results in genetic abnormalities is that when two people of similar genetics (i.e., a brother and sister) have children together, there is a high risk of their recessive characteristics becoming dominant. When people from different families have children, it is highly unlikely that both parents will carry the same recessive traits. The human genetic code has become increasingly "polluted" over the centuries as genetic defects are multiplied, amplified, and passed down from generation to generation. Adam and Eve did not have any genetic defects, and that enabled them and the first few generations of their descendants to have a far greater quality of health than we do now. Adam and Eve's children had few, if any, genetic defects. As a result, it was safe for them to intermarry.

Question: What does the Bible say about dinosaurs? Are there dinosaurs in the Bible?

Answer: The topic of dinosaurs in the Bible is part of a larger ongoing debate within the Christian community over the age of the earth, the proper interpretation of Genesis, and how to interpret the physical evidences we find all around us. Those who believe in an older age for the earth tend to agree that the Bible does not mention dinosaurs, because, according to their paradigm, dinosaurs died out millions of years before the first man ever walked the earth. The men who wrote the Bible could not have seen living dinosaurs.

Those who believe in a younger age for the earth tend to agree that the Bible does mention dinosaurs, though it never actually uses the word "dinosaur." Instead, it uses the Hebrew word *tanniyn*, which is translated a few different ways in our English Bibles. Sometimes it's "sea monster," and sometimes it's "serpent." It is most commonly translated "dragon." The *tanniyn* appear to have been some sort of giant reptile. These creatures are mentioned nearly thirty times in the Old Testament and were found both on land and in the water.

In addition to mentioning these giant reptiles, the Bible describes a couple of creatures in such a way that some scholars believe the writers may have been describing dinosaurs. The behemoth is said to be the mightiest of all God's creatures, a giant whose tail is likened to a cedar tree (Job 40:15). Some scholars have tried to identify the behemoth as either an elephant or a hippopotamus. Others point out that elephants and hippopotamuses have very thin tails, nothing comparable to a cedar tree. Dinosaurs like the brachiosaurus and the diplodocus, on the other hand, had huge tails which could easily be compared to a cedar tree.

Nearly every ancient civilization has some sort of art depicting giant reptilian creatures. Petroglyphs, artifacts, and even little clay figurines found in North America resemble modern depictions of dinosaurs. Rock carvings in South America depict men riding diplodocus-like creatures and, amazingly, bear the familiar images of triceratops-like, pterodactyl-like, and tyrannosaurus rex-like creatures. Roman mosaics, Mayan pottery, and Babylonian city walls all testify to man's trans-cultural, geographically unbounded fascination with these creatures. Sober accounts like those of Marco Polo's *Il Milione* mingle with fantastic tales of treasure-hoarding beasts. In addition to the substantial amount of anthropic and historical evidences for the coexistence of dinosaurs and man, there are physical evidences, like the fossilized footprints of humans and dinosaurs found together at places in North America and West-Central Asia.

So, are there dinosaurs in the Bible? The matter is far from settled. It depends on how you interpret the available evidences and how you view the world around you. If the Bible is interpreted literally, a young earth interpretation will result, and the idea that dinosaurs and man coexisted can be accepted. If dinosaurs and human beings coexisted, what happened to the dinosaurs? While the Bible does not discuss the issue, dinosaurs likely died out sometime after the flood due to a combination of dramatic environmental shifts and the fact that they were relentlessly hunted to extinction by man.

Question: Was Noah's flood global or local?

Answer: The biblical passages regarding the flood make it clear that it was global. Genesis 7:11 states that "all the springs of the great deep burst forth, and the floodgates of the heavens were opened." Genesis 1:6-7 and 2:6 tell us that the pre-flood environment was much different from that which we experience today. Based on these and other biblical descriptions, it is reasonably speculated that at one time the earth was covered by some kind of water canopy. This canopy could have been a vapor canopy, or it might have consisted of rings, somewhat like Saturn's ice rings. This, in combination with a layer of water underground, released upon the land (Genesis 2:6) would have resulted in a global flood.

The clearest verses that show the extent of the flood are Genesis 7:19-23. Regarding the waters, "They rose greatly on the earth, and all the high mountains under the entire heavens were covered. The waters rose and covered the mountains to a depth of more than twenty feet. Every living thing that moved on the earth perished—birds, livestock, wild animals, all the creatures that swarm over the earth, and all mankind. Everything on dry land that had the breath of life in its nostrils died. Every living thing on the face of the earth was wiped out; men and animals and the creatures that move along the ground and the birds of the air were wiped from the earth. Only Noah was left, and those with him in the ark."

In the above passage, we not only find the word "all" being used repeatedly, but we also find "all the high mountains under the entire heavens were covered," "the waters rose and covered the mountains to a depth of more than twenty feet," and "every living thing that moved on the earth perished." These descriptions clearly describe a universal flood covering the whole earth. Also, if the flood was localized, why did God instruct Noah to build an ark instead of merely telling Noah to move and causing the animals to migrate? And why did He instruct Noah to build an ark large enough to house all of the different kinds of land animals found on the earth? If the flood was not global, there would have been no need for an ark.

Peter also describes the universality of the flood in 2 Peter 3:6-7, where he states, "By these waters also the world of that time was deluged and destroyed. By the same word the present heavens and earth are reserved for fire, being kept for the day of judgment and destruction of ungodly men." In these verses Peter compares the "universal" coming judgment to the flood of Noah's time and states that the world that existed then was flooded with water. Further, many biblical writers accepted the historicity of the worldwide flood (Isaiah 54:9; 1 Peter 3:20; 2 Peter 2:5; Hebrews 11:7). Lastly, the Lord Jesus Christ believed in the universal flood and took it as the type of the coming destruction of the world when He returns (Matthew 24:37-39; Luke 17:26-27).

There are many extra-biblical evidences that point to a worldwide catastrophe such as a global flood. There are vast fossil graveyards found on every continent and large amounts of coal deposits that would require the rapid covering of vast quantities of vegetation. Oceanic fossils are found upon mountain tops around the world. Cultures in all parts of the world have some form of flood legend. All of these facts and many others are evidence of a global flood.

Question: Why did God put the tree of knowledge of good and evil in the Garden of Eden?

Answer: God put the tree of knowledge of good and evil in the Garden of Eden to give Adam and Eve a choice to obey Him or disobey Him. Adam and Eve were free to do anything they wanted, except eat from the tree of knowledge of good and evil. Genesis 2:16-17, "And the LORD God commanded the man, 'You are free to eat from any tree in the garden; but you must not eat from the tree of the knowledge of good and evil, for when you eat of it you will surely die.'" If God had not given Adam and Eve the choice, they would have essentially been robots, simply doing what they were programmed to do. God created Adam and Eve to be "free" beings, able to make decisions, able to choose between good and evil. In order for Adam and Eve to truly be free, they had to have a choice.

There was nothing essentially evil about the tree or the fruit of the tree. It is unlikely that eating the fruit truly gave Adam and Eve any further knowledge. It was the act of disobedience that opened Adam and Eve's eyes to evil. Their sin of disobeying God brought sin and evil into the world and into their lives. Eating the fruit, as an act of disobedience against God, was what gave Adam and Eve knowledge of evil (Genesis 3:6-7).

God did not want Adam and Eve to sin. God knew ahead of time what the results of sin would be. God knew that Adam and Eve would sin and would thereby bring evil, suffering, and death into the world. Why, then, did God allow Satan to tempt Adam and Eve? God allowed Satan to tempt Adam and Eve to force them to make the choice. Adam and Eve chose, of their own free will, to disobey God and eat the forbidden fruit. The results—evil, sin, suffering, sickness, and death—have plagued the world ever since. Adam and Eve's decision results in every person being born with a sin nature, a tendency to sin. Adam and Eve's decision is what ultimately required Jesus Christ to die on the cross and shed His blood on our behalf. Through faith in Christ, we can be free from sin's consequences, and ultimately free from sin itself. May we echo the words of the Apostle Paul in Romans 7:24-25, "What a wretched man I am! Who will rescue me from this body of death? Thanks be to God—through Jesus Christ our Lord!"

Question: What is the Intelligent Design Theory?

Answer: The Intelligent Design Theory says that intelligent causes are necessary to explain the complex, information-rich structures of biology and that these causes are empirically detectable. Certain biological features defy the standard Darwinian random-chance explanation, because they appear to have been designed. Since design logically necessitates an intelligent designer, the appearance of design is cited as evidence for a designer. There are three primary arguments in the Intelligent Design Theory: 1) irreducible complexity, 2) specified complexity, and 3) the anthropic principle.

Irreducible complexity is defined as "...a single system which is composed of several well-matched interacting parts that contribute to the basic function, wherein the removal of any one of the parts causes the system to effectively cease functioning." Simply put, life is comprised of intertwined parts that rely on each other in order to be useful. Random mutation may account for the development of a new part, but it cannot account for the concurrent development of multiple parts necessary for a functioning system. For example, the human eye is obviously a very useful system. Without the eyeball, the optic nerve, and the visual cortex, a randomly mutated incomplete eye would actually be counterproductive to the survival of a species and would therefore be eliminated through the process of natural selection. An eye is not a useful system unless all its parts are present and functioning properly at the same time.

Specified complexity is the concept that, since specified complex patterns can be found in organisms, some form of guidance must have accounted for their origin. The specified complexity argument states that it is impossible for complex patterns to be developed through random processes. For example, a room filled with 100 monkeys and 100 computers may eventually produce a few words, or maybe even a sentence, but it would never produce a Shakespearean play. And how much more complex is biological life than a Shakespearean play?

The anthropic principle states that the world and universe are "fine-tuned" to allow for life on earth. If the ratio of elements in the air of the earth was altered slightly, many species would very quickly cease to exist. If the earth were a few miles closer or further away from the sun, many species would cease to exist. The existence and development of life on earth requires so many variables to be perfectly in tune that it would be impossible for all the variables to come into being through random, uncoordinated events.

While the Intelligent Design Theory does not presume to identify the source of intelligence (whether it be God or UFOs or something else), the vast majority of Intelligent Design theorists are theists. They see the appearance of design which pervades the biological world as evidence for the existence of God. There are, however, a few atheists who cannot deny the strong evidence for design, but are not willing to acknowledge a Creator God. They tend to interpret the data as evidence that earth was seeded by some sort of master race of extraterrestrial creatures (aliens). Of course, they do not address the origin of the aliens either, so they are back to the original argument with no credible answer.

The Intelligent Design Theory is not biblical creationism. There is an important distinction between the two positions. Biblical creation-ists begin with a conclusion that the biblical account of creation is reliable and correct, that life on Earth was designed by an intelligent agent—God. They then look for evidence from the natural realm to support this conclusion. Intelligent Design theorists begin with the natural realm and reach the conclusion that life on Earth was designed by an intelligent agent (whoever that might be).

Question: Does Genesis chapter 1 mean literal 24-hour days?

Answer: A careful examination of the Hebrew word for "day" and the context in which it appears in Genesis will lead to the conclusion that "day" means a literal, 24-hour period of time. The Hebrew word *yom* translated into the English "day" can mean more than one thing. It can refer to the 24-hour period of time that it takes for the earth to rotate on its axis (e.g., "there are 24 hours in a day"). It can refer to the period of daylight between dawn and dusk (e.g., "it gets pretty hot during the day but it cools down a bit at night"). And it can refer to an unspecified period of time (e.g., "back in my grandfather's day..."). It is used to refer to a 24-hour period in Genesis 7:11. It is used to refer to the period of daylight between dawn and dusk in Genesis 1:16. And it is used to refer to an unspecified period of time in Genesis 2:4. So, what does it mean in Genesis 1:5-2:2 when it's used in conjunction with ordinal numbers (i.e., the first day, the second day, the third day, the fourth day, the fifth day, the sixth day, and the seventh day)? Are these 24-hour periods or something else? Could *yom* as it is used here mean an unspecified period of time?

We can determine how *yom* should be interpreted in Genesis 1:5-2:2 simply by examining the context in which we find the word and then comparing its context with how we see its usage elsewhere in Scripture. By doing this we let Scripture interpret itself. The Hebrew word *yom* is used 2301 times in the Old Testament. Outside of Genesis 1, *yom* plus a number (used 410 times) always indicates an ordinary day, i.e., a 24-hour period. The words "evening" and "morning" together (38 times) always indicate an ordinary day. *Yom* + "evening" or "morning" (23 times) always indicates an ordinary day. *Yom* + "night" (52 times) always indicates an ordinary day.

The context in which the word *yom* is used in Genesis 1:5-2:2, describing each day as "the evening and the morning," makes it quite clear that the author of Genesis meant 24-hour periods. The references to "evening" and "morning" make no sense unless they refer to a literal 24-hour day. This was the standard interpretation of the days of Genesis 1:5-2:2 until the 1800s when a paradigm shift occurred within the scientific community, and the earth's sedimentary strata layers were reinterpreted. Whereas previously the rock layers were interpreted as evidence of Noah's flood, the flood was thrown out by the scientific community and the rock layers were reinterpreted as evidence for an excessively old earth. Some well-meaning but terribly mistaken Christians then sought to reconcile this new anti-flood, anti-biblical interpretation with the Genesis account by reinterpreting *yom* to mean vast, unspecified periods of time.

The truth is that many of the old-earth interpretations are known to rely upon faulty assumptions. But we must not let the stubborn close-mindedness of scientists influence how we read the Bible. According to Exodus 20:9-11, God used six literal days to create the world in order to serve as a model for man's workweek: work six days, rest one. Certainly God could have created everything in an instant if He wanted to. But apparently He had us in mind even before He made us (on the sixth day) and wanted to provide an example for us to follow.

Question: What does the Bible say about cavemen, prehistoric men, Neanderthals?

Answer: The Bible does not use the term "caveman" or "Neanderthals," and according to the Bible there is no such thing as "prehistoric" man. The term "prehistoric" means "belonging to the era before recorded history." It presupposes that the biblical account is merely a fabrication, because the book of Genesis records events which precede the creation of man (namely, the first five days of creation—man was created on the sixth day). The Bible is clear that Adam and Eve were perfect humans from the time of their creation and did not evolve from lower life forms.

With that said, the Bible does describe a period of traumatic upheaval upon the earth—the flood (Genesis 6-9), during which time civilization was utterly destroyed except for eight people. Humanity was forced to start over. It is in this historical context that some scholars believe men lived in caves and made use of stone tools. These men were not primitive; they were simply destitute. And they certainly were not half ape. The fossil evidence is quite clear: cavemen were human—men who lived in caves.

There are some fossilized ape remains which Darwinian paleo-anthropologists interpret as being some sort of transition between ape and men. Most people seem to think of these interpretations when they imagine cavemen. They picture furry half-men, half-ape creatures crouched in a cave next to a fire, drawing on the walls with their newly developed stone tools. This is a common misconception. And as far as Darwinian paleo-anthropology goes, we should keep in mind that these interpretations reflect a peculiar worldview and are not the result of the evidence. In fact, not only is there major opposition to these interpretations within the academic community, the Darwinists themselves do not entirely agree with each other on the details.

Unfortunately, the popular mainstream view promotes this idea that man and ape both evolved from the same ancestor, but this is certainly not the only plausible interpretation of the available evidence. In fact, the evidence in favor of this particular interpretation is lacking.

When God created Adam and Eve, they were fully developed human beings, capable of communication, society, and develop-ment (Genesis 2:19-25; 3:1-20; 4:1-12). It is almost entertaining to consider the lengths evolutionary scientists go to prove the existence of prehistoric cavemen. They find a misshapen tooth in a cave and from that create a misshapen human being who lived in a cave, hunched over like an ape. There is no way that science can prove the existence of cavemen by a fossil. Evolutionary scientists simply have a theory, and then they force the evidence to fit the theory. Adam and Eve were the first human beings ever created and were fully-formed, intelligent, and upright.

Question: Why are there two different creation accounts in Genesis chapters 1-2?

Answer: Genesis 1:1 says, "In the beginning, God created the heavens and the earth." Later, in Genesis 2:4, it seems that a second, different story of creation begins. The idea of two differing creation accounts is a common misinterpretation of these two passages which, in fact, describe the same creation event. They do not disagree as to the order in which things were created and do not contradict one another. Genesis 1 describes the "six days of creation" (and a seventh day of rest), Genesis 2 covers only one day of that creation week—the sixth day—and there is no contradiction.

In Genesis 2, the author steps back in the temporal sequence to the sixth day, when God made man. In the first chapter, the author of Genesis presents the creation of man on the sixth day as the culmination or high point of creation. Then, in the second chapter, the author gives greater detail regarding the creation of man.

There are two primary claims of contradictions between Genesis chapters 1-2. The first is in regard to plant life. Genesis 1:11 records God creating vegetation on the third day. Genesis 2:5 states that prior to the creation of man "no shrub of the field had yet appeared on the earth and no plant of the field had yet sprung up, for the LORD God had not sent rain on the earth and there was no man to work the ground." So, which is it? Did God create vegetation on the third day before He created man (Genesis 1), or after He created man (Genesis 2)? The Hebrew words for "vegetation" are different in the two passages. Genesis 1:11 uses a term that refers to vegetation in general. Genesis 2:5 uses a more specific term that refers to vegetation that requires agriculture, i.e., a person to tend it, a gardener. The passages do not contradict. Genesis 1:11 speaks of God creating vegetation, and Genesis 2:5 speaks of God not causing "farmable" vegetation to grow until after He created man.

The second claimed contradiction is in regard to animal life. Genesis 1:24-25 records God creating animal life on the sixth day, before He created man. Genesis 2:19, in some translations, seems to record God creating the animals after He had created man. However, a good and plausible translation of Genesis 2:19-20 reads, "Now the LORD God had formed out of the ground all the beasts of the field and all the birds of the air. He brought them to the man to see what he would name them, and whatever the man called each living creature, that was its name. So the man gave names to all the livestock, the birds of the air and all the beasts of the field." The text does not say that God created man, then created the animals, and then brought the animals to the man. Rather, the text says, "Now the LORD God had [already] created all the animals." There is no contradiction. On the sixth day, God created the animals, then created man, and then brought the animals to the man, allowing the man to name the animals.

By considering the two creation accounts individually and then reconciling them, we see that God describes the sequence of creation in Genesis 1, then clarifies its most important details, especially of the sixth day, in Genesis 2. There is no contradiction here, merely a common literary device describing an event from the general to the specific.

Question: Is creationism scientific?

Answer: There is currently a lot of debate over the validity of creationism, defined as "the belief that the universe and living organisms originate from specific acts of divine creation, as in the biblical account, rather than by natural processes such as evolution." Creation science is often dismissed by the secular community and accused of lacking scientific value. However, creationism is clearly compatible with a scientific approach to any topic. Creationism makes statements about real world events, places, and things. It is not concerned solely with subjective ideas or abstract concepts. There are established scientific facts that are consistent with creationism, and the way in which those facts relate to one another lends itself to a creationist interpretation. Just as other broad scientific ideas are used to lend coherence to a series of facts, so, too, does creationism.

How, then, is creationism—as opposed to "naturalism," defined as "a philosophical viewpoint according to which everything arises from natural properties and causes, and supernatural or spiritual explanations are excluded or discounted"—scientific? Admittedly, the answer depends on how you define "scientific." Too often, "science" and "naturalism" are considered one and the same, leaving creationist views out by definition. Such a definition requires an irrational reverence of naturalism. Science is defined as "the observation, identification, description, experimental investigation, and theoretical explanation of phenomena." Nothing requires science, in and of itself, to be naturalistic. Naturalism, like creationism, requires a series of presuppositions that are not generated by experiments.

They are not extrapolated from data or derived from test results. These philosophical presuppositions are accepted before any data is ever taken. Because both naturalism and creationism are strongly influenced by presuppositions that are neither provable nor testable, and enter into the discussion well before the facts do, it is fair to say that creationism is at least as scientific as naturalism.

Creationism, like naturalism, can be "scientific," in that it is compatible with the scientific method of discovery. These two concepts are not, however, sciences in and of themselves, because both views include aspects that are not considered "scientific" in the normal sense. Neither creationism nor naturalism is falsifiable; that is, there is no experiment that could conclusively disprove either one. Neither one is predictive; they do not generate or enhance the ability to predict an outcome. Solely on the basis of these two points, we see that there is no logical reason to consider one more scientifically valid than the other.

One of the major reasons naturalists give for rejecting creationism is the concept of miracles. Ironically, naturalists will typically say that miracles, such as special creation, are impossible because they violate the laws of nature, which have been clearly and historically observed. Such a view is ironic on several counts. As a single example, consider abiogenesis, the theory of life springing from non-living matter. Abiogenesis is one of the most thoroughly refuted concepts of science. Yet, a truly naturalistic viewpoint presumes that life on earth—self-replicating, self-sustaining, complex organic life—arose by chance from non-living matter. Such a thing has never been observed in all of human history. The beneficial evolutionary changes needed to progress a creature to a more complex form have also never been observed. So creationism actually holds the edge on evidence for "miraculous" claims in that the Scriptures provide documented accounts of miraculous happenings. To label creationism as unscientific on account of miracles demands a similar label for naturalism.

There are many facts that are used by both sides of the creation vs. naturalism debate. Facts are facts, but there is no such thing as a fact that absolutely requires a single interpretation. The divide between creationism and secular naturalism rests entirely on different interpretations. Regarding the evolution vs. creation debate specifically,

Charles Darwin himself made this point. In the introduction to *The Origin of Species*, he stated, "I am well aware that scarcely a single point is discussed in this volume on which facts cannot be adduced, often apparently leading to conclusions directly opposite to those at which I arrived." Obviously, Darwin believed evolution over creation, but he was willing to admit that interpretation was key to choosing a belief. One scientist might view a particular fact as supportive of naturalism; another scientist might view that same fact as supporting creationism.

Also, the fact that creationism is the only possible alternative to naturalistic ideas such as evolution makes it a valid topic, especially when this dichotomy has been admitted to by some of the leading minds of science. Many well-known and influential scientists state that the only possible explanations for life are naturalistic evolution or special creation. Not all scientists agree on which is true, but they almost all agree that one or the other must be.

There are many other reasons why creationism is a rational and scientific approach to learning. Among these are the concepts of realistic probability, the flawed evidential support for macro-evolution, the evidence of experience, and so forth. There is no logical basis to accept naturalistic presuppositions outright and flatly reject creationist presuppositions. Firm belief in creation is no barrier to scientific discovery. Simply review the accomplishments of men like Newton, Pasteur, Mendel, Pascal, Kelvin, Linnaeus, and Maxwell. All were clear and comfortable creationists. Creationism is not a "science," just as naturalism is not a "science." Creationism is, however, fully compatible with science itself.

Question: What is the Gap Theory? Did anything happen between Genesis 1:1 and 1:2?

Answer: Genesis 1:1-2 states, "In the beginning God created the heavens and the earth. Now the earth was formless and empty, darkness was over the surface of the deep, and the Spirit of God was hovering over the waters." The Gap Theory is the view that God created a fully functional earth with all animals, including the dinosaurs and other creatures we know only from the fossil record. Then, the theory goes, something happened to destroy the earth

483

completely—some speculate it was the fall of Satan to earth—so that the earth *became* without form and void. At this point, God started all over again, *re*creating the earth in its paradise form as further described in Genesis.

There are too many problems with this theory to describe adequately in a brief response, not the least of which is that if something important had occurred between the two verses, God would have told us so. God would not have left us to speculate in ignorance about such important events. Second, Genesis 1:31 says God declared His creation to be "very good," which He certainly could not say if evil had already entered the world via Satan's fall in the "gap." Along the same line, if the fossil record is to be explained by the millions of years in the gap, that means death, disease, and suffering were common many ages before Adam fell. But the Bible tells us that it was Adam's sin that introduced death, disease, and suffering to all life: "Sin entered the world through one man, and death through sin" (Romans 5:12).

Those who hold to the Gap Theory do so in order to reconcile the theories of modern scientists who hold to the old-earth theory—the belief that the earth is billions of years older than can be accounted for by adding up the genealogies of man found in the Bible. Even well-meaning evangelicals have bought into the old-earth theory, handling much of Genesis 1 allegorically, while attempting to hold to a literal interpretation of the rest of Scripture. The danger in this is in determining at what point to stop allegorizing and begin interpreting literally. Was Adam a literal person? How do we know? If he was not, then did he really bring sin into the human race, or can we allegorize that as well? And if there was no literal Adam to introduce the sin which we all inherit, then there was no reason for Jesus to die on the cross. A non-literal original sin denies the reason for Christ's coming in the first place, as explained in 1 Corinthians 15:22: "For as in Adam all die, even so in Christ all shall be made alive." At that point, Christianity itself becomes a hoax and the Bible just a nice book of stories and fables. Can we not see where this type of "reasoning" gets us?

Genesis 1 simply cannot be reconciled with the notion that creation occurred over long periods of time, nor that these periods occurred in the space between Genesis 1:1 and 1:2. What took place between Genesis 1:1 and 1:2? Absolutely nothing! Genesis 1:1 tells us that God created the heavens and the earth. Genesis 1:2 informs us that when He first created the earth, it was formless, empty, and dark; it was not finished and not yet inhabited by creatures. The rest of Genesis chapter 1 tells us how God completed the formless, empty, and dark earth by filling it with life, beauty, and goodness. The Bible is true, literal, and perfect (Psalm 19:7-9). Science has never disproved anything in the Bible and it never will. The Bible is supreme truth and therefore is the standard by which scientific theory should be evaluated, not the other way around.

Question: What is theistic evolution?

Answer: Theistic evolution is one of three major origin-of-life worldviews, the other two being atheistic evolution (also commonly known as Darwinian evolution and naturalistic evolution) and special creation.

Atheistic evolution says that there is no God and that life can and did emerge naturally from preexisting, non-living building blocks under the influence of natural laws (like gravity, etc), although the origin of those natural laws is not explained. Special creation says that God created life directly, either from nothing or from preexisting materials.

Theistic evolution says one of two things. The first option is that there is a God, but He was not directly involved in the origin of life. He may have created the building blocks, He may have created the natural laws, He may even have created these things with the eventual emergence of life in mind, but at some point early on He stepped back and let His creation take over. He let it do what it does, whatever that is, and life eventually emerged from non-living material. This view is similar to atheistic evolution in that it presumes a naturalistic origin of life.

The second alternative of theistic evolution is that God did not perform just one or two miracles to bring about the origin of life as we know it. His miracles were constant. He led life step by step down a path that took it from primeval simplicity to contemporary complexity, similar to Darwin's evolutionary tree of life (fish begot amphibians who begot reptiles who begot birds and mammals, etc). Where life was not able to evolve naturally (how does a reptile's limb evolve into a bird's wing naturally?), God stepped in. This view is similar to special creation in that it presumes that God acted supernaturally in some way to bring about life as we know it.

There are numerous differences between the biblical special creation perspective and the theistic evolution perspective. One significant difference concerns their respective views on death. Theistic evolutionists tend to believe that the earth is billions of years old and that the geologic column containing the fossil record represents long epochs of time. Since man does not appear until late in the fossil record, theistic evolutionists believe that many creatures lived, died, and became extinct long before man's belated arrival. This means that death existed before Adam and his sin.

Biblical creationists believe that the earth is relatively young and that the fossil record was laid down during and after Noah's flood. The stratification of the layers is thought to have occurred due to hydrologic sorting and liquefaction, both of which are observed phenomena. This puts the fossil record and the death and carnage which it describes hundreds of years after Adam's sin.

Another significant difference between the two positions is how they read Genesis. Theistic evolutionists tend to subscribe to either the day-age theory or the framework theory, both of which are allegorical interpretations of the Genesis 1 creation week. Young earth creationists subscribe to a literal 24-hour day as they read Genesis 1. Both of the theistic evolutionist views are flawed from a Christian perspective in that they do not line up with the Genesis creation account.

Theistic evolutionists imagine a Darwinian scenario in which stars evolved, then our solar system, then earth, then plants and animals, and eventually man. The two theistic evolution viewpoints disagree as to the role God played in the unfolding of events, but they generally agree on the Darwinian timeline. This timeline is in conflict with the Genesis creation account. For example, Genesis 1 says that the earth was created on day one and the sun, moon, and stars were not created until day four. Some argue that the wording of Genesis suggests the sun, moon, and stars were actually created on day one but they could not be seen through earth's atmosphere until day four, leading to their placement on day four. This is a bit of a stretch, as the Genesis account is pretty clear that the earth did not have an atmosphere until the second day. If the sun, moon, and stars were created on day one, they should have been visible on day one.

Also, the Genesis account clearly says that birds were created with sea creatures on day five while land animals were not created until day six. This is in direct opposition to the Darwinian view that birds evolved from land animals. The biblical account says that birds preceded land animals. The theistic evolutionist view says exactly the opposite.

One of the most unfortunate trends in modern Christianity is that of reinterpreting Genesis to accommodate evolutionary theories. Many well-known Bible teachers and apologists have caved in to the evolutionists and have come to believe that adhering to a literal interpretation of Genesis is somehow detrimental to the credibility of Christians. If anything, evolutionists lose respect for those whose belief in the Bible is so tenuous that they are willing to quickly compromise it. Although the number of true creationists may be dwindling in academia, several faithful organizations such as Answers in Genesis, the Creation Research Society, and the Institute for Creation Research have affirmed that the Bible is not only compatible with real science, but affirm that not a single word in the Bible has ever been disproved by true science. The Bible is God's living Word, given to us by the Creator of the universe, and His description of how He created that universe is not compatible with the theory of evolution, even a "theistic" understanding of evolution.

Chapter 19

. . . .

QUESTIONS ABOUT CULTS

AND RELIGIONS

CONTENTS

What is Christianity and what do Christians believe? 490

What is the definition of a cult? 491

What is the best way to evangelize someone who is in a cult or false
    religion? 492

How can I recognize a false teacher/false prophet?...................................493

Should Christians be tolerant of other people's religious beliefs? 494

Who are the Jehovah's Witnesses and what are their beliefs?.................495

Is Mormonism a cult? What do Mormons believe?..................................497

What is Buddhism and what do Buddhists believe?.................................499

What is Hinduism and what do Hindus believe?......................................503

What is Islam, and what do Muslims believe?...505

What is Judaism and what do Jews believe?...506

What is Christian Gnosticism? 509

What is Christian Science?...511

What is the Eastern Orthodox Church and what are the beliefs of
    Orthodox Christians? 512

What is the difference between religion and spirituality?.......................514

Is Scientology Christian or a cult? 515

Why are there so many religions? Do all religions lead to God?.............517

With all of the different religions, how can I know which one is
    correct? 518

Question: What is Christianity and what do Christians believe?

Answer: The core beliefs of Christianity are summarized in 1 Corinthians 15:1-4. Jesus died for our sins, was buried, was resurrected, and thereby offers salvation to all who will receive Him in faith. Unique among all other faiths, Christianity is more about a relationship than religious practices. Instead of adhering to a list of "do's and don'ts," the goal of a Christian is to cultivate a close walk with God. That relationship is made possible because of the work of Jesus Christ and the ministry of the Holy Spirit.

Beyond these core beliefs, there are many other items that are, or at least should be, indicative of what Christianity is and what Christianity believes. Christians believe that the Bible is the inspired, "God-breathed" Word of God and that its teaching is the final authority in all matters of faith and practice (2 Timothy 3:16; 2 Peter 1:20-21). Christians believe in one God that exists in three persons—the Father, the Son (Jesus Christ), and the Holy Spirit.

Christians believe that mankind was created specifically to have a relationship with God, but sin separates all men from God (Romans 3:23; 5:12). Christianity teaches that Jesus Christ walked this earth, fully God, and yet fully man (Philippians 2:6-11), and died on the cross. Christians believe that after His death, Christ was buried, He rose again, and now lives at the right hand of the Father, making intercession for the believers forever (Hebrews 7:25). Christianity proclaims that Jesus' death on the cross was sufficient to completely pay the sin debt owed by all men and this is what restores the broken relationship between God and man (Hebrews 9:11-14; 10:10; Romans 5:8; 6:23).

Christianity teaches that in order to be saved and be granted entrance into heaven after death, one must place one's faith entirely in the finished work of Christ on the cross. If we believe that Christ died in our place and paid the price of our own sins, and rose again, then we are saved. There is nothing that anyone can do to earn salvation. We cannot be "good enough" to please God on our own, because we are all sinners (Isaiah 53:6; 64:6-7). There is nothing more to be done, because Christ has done all the work! When He was on the cross, Jesus said, "It is finished" (John 19:30), meaning that the work of redemption was completed.

According to Christianity, salvation is freedom from the old sin nature and freedom to pursue a right relationship with God. Where we were once slaves to sin, we are now slaves to Christ (Romans 6:15-22). As long as believers live on this earth in their sinful bodies, they will engage in a constant struggle with sin. However, Christians can have victory in the struggle with sin by studying and applying God's Word in their lives and being controlled by the Holy Spirit—that is, submitting to the Spirit's leading in everyday circumstances.

So, while many religious systems require that a person do or not do certain things, Christianity is about believing that Christ died on the cross as payment for our own sins and rose again. Our sin debt is paid and we can have fellowship with God. We can have victory over our sin nature and walk in fellowship and obedience with God. That is true biblical Christianity.

Question: What is the definition of a cult?

Answer: When we hear the word "cult," we often think of a group that worships Satan, sacrifices animals, or takes part in evil, bizarre, and pagan rituals. However, in reality, most cults appear much more innocent. The specific Christian definition of a cult is "a religious group that denies one or more of the fundamentals of biblical truth." In simpler terms, a cult is a group that teaches something that will cause a person to remain unsaved if he/she believes it. As distinct from a religion, a cult is a group that claims to be part of the religion, yet denies essential truth(s) of that religion. A Christian cult is a group that denies one or more of the fundamental truths of Christianity, while still claiming to be Christian.

The two most common teachings of cults are that Jesus was not God and that salvation is not by faith alone. A denial of the deity of Christ results in Jesus' death not being a sufficient payment for our sins. A denial of salvation by faith alone results in salvation being achieved by our own works, something the Bible vehemently and consistently denies. The two most well-known examples of cults are the Jehovah's Witnesses and Mormons. Both groups claim to be Christian, yet both deny the deity of Christ and salvation by faith alone. Jehovah's Witnesses and Mormons believe many things that are in agreement with or similar to what the Bible teaches. However, the fact that they deny the deity of Christ and preach a salvation by works qualifies them as a cult. Many Jehovah's Witnesses, Mormons, and members of other cults are "good people" who genuinely believe they hold the truth. As Christians, our hope and prayer must be that many people involved in the cults will see through the lies and will be drawn to the truth of salvation through faith in Jesus Christ alone.

Question: What is the best way to evangelize someone who is in a cult or false religion?

Answer: The most important thing we can do for those involved in cults or false religions is pray for them. We need to pray that God would change their hearts and open their eyes to the truth (2 Corinthians 4:4). We need to pray that God would convince them of their need for salvation through Jesus Christ (John 3:16). Without the power of God and conviction of the Holy Spirit, we will never succeed in convincing anyone of the truth (John 16:7-11).

We also need to be living a godly Christian life, so those trapped in cults and religions can see the change God has made in our own lives (1 Peter 3:1-2). We need to pray for wisdom in how we can minister to them in a powerful way (James 1:5). After all of this, we must be bold in our actual sharing of the gospel. We must proclaim the message of salvation through Jesus Christ (Romans 10:9-10). We always need to be prepared to defend our faith (1 Peter 3:15), but we must do so with gentleness and respect. We can proclaim the doctrine correctly, win the war of words, and still impede the cause by an attitude of angry superiority.

Ultimately, we must leave the salvation of those to whom we witness up to God. It is God's power and grace that saves people, not our efforts. While it is good and wise to be prepared to give a vigorous defense and have knowledge of false beliefs, neither of these things will result in the conversion of those trapped in the lies of the cults and false religions. The best we can do is pray for them, witness to them, and live the Christian life in front of them, trusting that the Holy Spirit will do the work of drawing, convincing, and converting.

Question: How can I recognize a false teacher/false prophet?

Answer: Jesus warned us that "false Christs and false prophets" will come and will attempt to deceive even God's elect (Matthew 24:23-27; see also 2 Peter 3:3 and Jude 17-18). The best way to guard yourself against falsehood and false teachers is to know the truth. To spot a counterfeit, study the real thing. Any believer who "correctly handles the word of truth" (2 Timothy 2:15) and who makes a careful study of the Bible can identify false doctrine. For example, a believer who has read the activities of the Father, Son, and Holy Spirit in Matthew 3:16-17 will immediately question any doctrine that denies the Trinity. Therefore, step one is to study the Bible and judge all teaching by what the Scripture says.

Jesus said "a tree is recognized by its fruit" (Matthew 12:33). When looking for "fruit," here are three specific tests to apply to any teacher to determine the accuracy of his or her teaching:

1. What does this teacher say about Jesus? In Matthew 16:15-16, Jesus asks, "Who do you say I am?" Peter answers, "You are the Christ, the Son of the living God," and for this answer Peter is called "blessed." In 2 John 9, we read, "Anyone who runs ahead and does not continue in the teaching of Christ does not have God; whoever continues in the teaching has both the Father and the Son." In other words, Jesus Christ and His work of redemption is of utmost importance; beware of anyone who denies that Jesus is equal with God, who downplays Jesus' sacrificial death, or who rejects Jesus' humanity. First John 2:22 says, "Who is the liar? It is the man who denies that Jesus is the Christ. Such a man is the antichrist—he denies the Father and the Son."

2. Does this teacher preach the gospel? The gospel is defined as the good news concerning Jesus' death, burial, and resurrection, according to the Scriptures (1 Corinthians 15:1-4). As nice as they sound, the statements "God loves you," "God wants us to feed the hungry," and "God wants you to be wealthy" are *not* the complete message of the gospel. As Paul warns in Galatians 1:7, "Evidently some people are

493

throwing you into confusion and are trying to pervert the gospel of Christ." No one, not even a great preacher, has the right to change the message that God gave us. "If anybody is preaching to you a gospel other than what you accepted, let him be eternally condemned!" (Galatians 1:9).

3. Does this teacher exhibit character qualities that glorify the Lord? Speaking of false teachers, Jude 11 says, "They have taken the way of Cain; they have rushed for profit into Balaam's error; they have been destroyed in Korah's rebellion." In other words, a false teacher can be known by his pride (Cain's rejection of God's plan), greed (Balaam's prophesying for money), and rebellion (Korah's promotion of himself over Moses). Jesus said to beware of such people and that we would know them by their fruits (Matthew 7:15-20).

For further study, review those books of the Bible that were written specifically to combat false teaching within the church: Galatians, 2 Peter, 1 John, 2 John, and Jude. It is often difficult to spot a false teacher/false prophet. Satan masquerades as an angel of light (2 Corinthians 11:14), and his ministers masquerade as servants of righteousness (2 Corinthians 11:15). Only by being thoroughly familiar with the truth will we be able to recognize a counterfeit.

Question: Should Christians be tolerant of other people's religious beliefs?

Answer: In our age of "tolerance," moral relativism is touted as the supreme virtue. Every philosophy, idea, and faith system has equal merit, says the relativist, and is worthy of equal respect. Those who favor one faith system over another or—even worse—claim a knowledge of absolute truth are considered narrow-minded, unenlightened, or even bigoted.

Of course, different religions make mutually exclusive claims, and the relativist is unable to logically reconcile outright contradictions. For example, the Bible makes the claim that "man is destined to die once, and after that to face judgment" (Hebrews 9:27), while some Eastern religions teach reincarnation. So, do we die once or many times? Both teachings cannot be true. The relativist essentially redefines truth in order to create a paradoxical world where multiple, contradictory "truths" can co-exist.

Jesus said, "I am the way and the truth and the life. No one comes to the Father except through me" (John 14:6). A Christian has accepted Truth, not just as a concept, but as a Person. This acknowledgment of Truth distances the Christian from the so-called "open-mindedness" of the day. The Christian has publicly acknowledged that Jesus rose from the dead (Romans 10:9-10). If he truly believes in the resurrection, how can he be "open-minded" concerning an unbeliever's assertion that Jesus never rose again? For a Christian to deny the clear teaching of God's Word would indeed be a betrayal of God.

Note that we have cited the fundamentals of the faith in our examples so far. Some things (such as the bodily resurrection of Christ) are non-negotiable. Other things may be open to debate, such as who wrote the book of Hebrews or the nature of Paul's "thorn in the flesh." We should avoid becoming bogged down in disputations over secondary matters (2 Timothy 2:23; Titus 3:9).

Even when disputing/dialoguing over prominent doctrines, a Christian should exercise restraint and show respect. It is one thing to disagree with a position; it is quite another to disparage a person. We must hold fast to the Truth while showing compassion to those who question it. Like Jesus, we must be full of both grace and truth (John 1:14). Peter strikes a good balance between having the answer and having humility: "Always be prepared to give an answer to everyone who asks you to give the reason for the hope that you have. But do this with gentleness and respect" (1 Peter 3:15).

Question: Who are the Jehovah's Witnesses and what are their beliefs?

Answer: The sect known today as the Jehovah's Witnesses started out in Pennsylvania in 1870 as a Bible class led by Charles Taze Russell. Russell named his group the "Millennial Dawn Bible Study." Charles T. Russell began writing a series of books he called "The Millennial Dawn," which stretched to six volumes before his death and contained much of the theology Jehovah's Witnesses now hold. After Russell's death in 1916, Judge J. F. Rutherford, Russell's friend and successor, wrote the seventh and final volume of the "Millennial Dawn" series, "The Finished Mystery," in 1917. The Watchtower Bible and Tract Society was founded in 1886 and quickly became the vehicle through which the "Millennial Dawn" movement began distributing their views to others. The group was known as the "Russellites" until 1931 when, due to a split in the organization, it was renamed the "Jehovah's Witnesses." The group from which it split became known as the "Bible students."

What do Jehovah's Witnesses believe? Close scrutiny of their doctrinal position on such subjects as the deity of Christ, salvation, the trinity, the Holy Spirit, and the atonement shows beyond a doubt that they do not hold to orthodox Christian positions on these subjects. Jehovah's Witnesses believe Jesus is Michael the archangel, the highest created being. This contradicts many Scriptures which clearly declare Jesus to be God (John 1:1,14, 8:58, 10:30). Jehovah's Witnesses believe salvation is obtained by a combination of faith, good works, and obedience. This contradicts countless scriptures which declare salvation to be received by grace through faith (John 3:16; Ephesians 2:8-9; Titus 3:5). Jehovah's Witnesses reject the Trinity, believing Jesus to be a created being and the Holy Spirit to essentially be the inanimate power of God. Jehovah's Witnesses reject the concept of Christ's substitutionary atonement and instead hold to a ransom theory, that Jesus' death was a ransom payment for Adam's sin.

How do the Jehovah's Witnesses justify these unbiblical doctrines? First, they claim that the church has corrupted the Bible over the centuries; thus, they have re-translated the Bible into what they call the *New World Translation*. The Watchtower Bible and Tract Society altered the text of the Bible to make it fit their false doctrine, rather than basing their doctrine on what the Bible actually teaches. The *New World Translation* has gone through numerous editions, as the Jehovah's Witnesses discover more and more Scriptures that contradict their doctrines.

The Watchtower bases its beliefs and doctrines on the original and expanded teachings of Charles Taze Russell, Judge Joseph Franklin Rutherford, and their successors. The governing body of the Watchtower Bible and Tract Society is the only body in the cult that claims authority to interpret Scripture. In other words, what the governing body says concerning any scriptural passage is viewed as the last word, and independent thinking is strongly discouraged. This is in direct opposition to Paul's admonition to Timothy (and to us as well) to study to be approved by God, so that we need not be ashamed as we correctly handle the Word of God. This admonition, found in 2 Timothy 2:15, is a clear instruction from God to each of His children to be like the Berean Christians, who searched the Scriptures daily to see if the things they were being taught lined up with the Word.

There is probably no religious group that is more faithful than the Jehovah's Witnesses at getting their message out. Unfortunately, the message is full of distortions, deceptions, and false doctrine. May God open the eyes of the Jehovah's Witnesses to the truth of the gospel and the true teaching of God's Word.

Question: Is Mormonism a cult? What do Mormons believe?

Answer: The Mormon religion (Mormonism), whose followers are known as Mormons and Latter Day Saints (LDS), was founded less than two hundred years ago by a man named Joseph Smith. He claimed to have received a personal visit from God the Father and Jesus Christ who told him that all churches and their creeds were an abomination. Joseph Smith then set out to begin a brand-new religion that claims to be the "only true church on earth." The problem with Mormonism is that it contradicts, modifies, and expands on the Bible. Christians have no reason to believe that the Bible is not true and adequate. To truly believe in and trust God means to believe in His Word, and all Scripture is inspired by God, which means it comes from Him (2 Timothy 3:16).

Mormons believe that there are in fact four sources of divinely inspired words, not just one: 1) The Bible "as far as it is translated correctly." Which verses are considered incorrectly translated is not always made clear. 2) *The Book of Mormon*, which was "translated" by Smith and published in 1830. Smith claimed it is the "most correct book" on earth and that a person can get closer to God by following its precepts "than by any other book." 3) *The Doctrine and Covenants*, containing a collection of modern revelations regarding the "Church of Jesus Christ as it has been restored." 4) *The Pearl of the Great Price*, which is considered by Mormons to "clarify" doctrines and teachings that were lost from the Bible and adds its own information about the earth's creation.

Mormons believe the following about God: He has not always been the Supreme Being of the universe, but attained that status through righteous living and persistent effort. They believe God the Father has a "body of flesh and bones as tangible as man's." Though abandoned by modern Mormon leaders, Brigham Young taught that Adam actually was God and the father of Jesus Christ. In contrast, Christians know this about God: there is only one true God (Deuteronomy 6:4; Isaiah 43:10; 44:6-8), He always has existed and always will exist (Deuteronomy 33:27; Psalm 90:2; 1 Timothy 1:17), and He was not created but is the Creator (Genesis 1; Psalm 24:1; Isaiah 37:16). He is perfect, and no one else is equal to Him (Psalm 86:8; Isaiah 40:25). God the Father is not a man, nor was He ever (Numbers 23:19; 1 Samuel 15:29; Hosea 11:9). He is Spirit (John 4:24), and Spirit is not made of flesh and bone (Luke 24:39).

Mormons believe that there are different levels or kingdoms in the afterlife: the celestial kingdom, the terrestrial kingdom, the telestial kingdom, and outer darkness. Where mankind will end up depends on what they believe and do in this life. In contrast, the Bible tells us that after death, we go to heaven or hell based on whether or not we had faith in Jesus Christ as our Lord and Savior. To be absent from our bodies means, as believers, we are with the Lord (2 Corinthians 5:6-8). Unbelievers are sent to hell or the place of the dead (Luke 16:22-23). When Jesus comes the second time, we will receive new bodies (1 Corinthians 15:50-54). There will be a new heaven and new earth for believers (Revelation 21:1), and unbelievers will be thrown into an everlasting lake of fire (Revelation 20:11-15). There is no second chance for redemption after death (Hebrews 9:27).

Mormon leaders have taught that Jesus' incarnation was the result of a physical relationship between God the Father and Mary. Mormons believe Jesus is a god, but that any human can also become a god. Mormonism teaches that salvation can be earned by a combination of faith and good works. Contrary to this, Christians historically have taught that no one can achieve the status of God—only He is holy (1 Samuel 2:2). We can only be made holy in God's sight through faith in Him (1 Corinthians 1:2). Jesus is the only begotten Son of God (John 3:16), is the only one ever to have lived a sinless, blameless life, and now has the highest place of honor in heaven (Hebrews 7:26). Jesus and God are one in essence, Jesus being the only One existing before physical birth (John 1:1-8; 8:56). Jesus gave Himself to us as a sacrifice, God raised Him from the dead, and one day everyone will confess that Jesus Christ is Lord (Philippians 2:6-11). Jesus tells us it is impossible to get to heaven by our own works and that only by faith in Him is it possible (Matthew 19:26). We all deserve eternal punishment for our sins, but God's infinite love and grace have allowed us a way out. "For the wages of sin is death, but the gift of God is eternal life in Christ Jesus our Lord" (Romans 6:23).

Clearly, there is only one way to receive salvation and that is to know God and His Son, Jesus (John 17:3). It is not done by works, but by faith (Romans 1:17; 3:28). We can receive this gift no matter who we are or what we have done (Romans 3:22). "Salvation is found in no one else, for there is no other name under heaven given to men by which we must be saved" (Acts 4:12).

Although Mormons are usually friendly, loving, and kind people, they are deceived by a false religion that distorts the nature of God, the Person of Jesus Christ, and the means of salvation.

Question: What is Buddhism and what do Buddhists believe?

Answer: Buddhism is one of the leading world religions in terms of adherents, geographical distribution, and socio-cultural influence. While largely an "Eastern" religion, it is becoming increasingly popular and influential in the Western world. It is a unique world religion in its own right, though it has much in common with Hinduism in that both teach Karma (cause-and-effect ethics), Maya (the illusory nature of the world), and Samsara (the cycle of reincarnation). Buddhists believe that the ultimate goal in life is to achieve "enlightenment" as they perceive it.

Buddhism's founder, Siddhartha Guatama, was born into royalty in India around 600 B.C. As the story goes, he lived luxuriously, with little exposure to the outside world. His parents intended for him to be spared from the influence of religion and protected from pain and suffering. However, it was not long before his shelter was penetrated, and he had visions of an aged man, a sick man, and a corpse. His fourth vision was of a peaceful ascetic monk (one who denies luxury and comfort). Seeing the monk's peacefulness, he decided to become an ascetic himself. He abandoned his life of wealth and affluence to pursue enlightenment through austerity. He was skilled at this sort of self-mortification and intense meditation. He was a leader among his peers. Eventually, his efforts culminated in one final gesture. He "indulged" himself with one bowl of rice and then sat beneath a fig tree (also called the Bodhi tree) to meditate till he either reached "enlightenment" or died trying. Despite his travails and temptations, by the next morning, he had achieved enlightenment. Thus, he became known as the 'enlightened one' or the 'Buddha.' He took his new realization and began to teach his fellow monks, with whom he had already gained great influence. Five of his peers became the first of his disciples.

What had Gautama discovered? Enlightenment lay in the "middle way," not in luxurious indulgence or self-mortification. Moreover, he discovered what would become known as the 'Four Noble Truths'— 1) to live is to suffer (Dukha), 2) suffering is caused by desire (Tanha, or "attachment"), 3) one can eliminate suffering by eliminating all attachments, and 4) this is achieved by following the noble eightfold path. The "eightfold path" consists of having a right 1) view, 2) intention, 3) speech, 4) action, 5) livelihood (being a monk), 6) effort (properly direct energies), 7) mindfulness (meditation), and 8) concentration (focus). The Buddha's teachings were collected into the Tripitaka or "three baskets."

Behind these distinguishing teachings are teachings common to Hinduism, namely reincarnation, karma, Maya, and a tendency to understand reality as being pantheistic in its orientation. Buddhism also offers an elaborate theology of deities and exalted beings. However, like Hinduism, Buddhism can be hard to pin down as to its view of God. Some streams of Buddhism could legitimately be called atheistic, while others could be called pantheistic, and still others theistic, such as Pure Land Buddhism. Classical Buddhism, however, tends to be silent on the reality of an ultimate being and is therefore considered atheistic.

Buddhism today is quite diverse. It is roughly divisible into the two broad categories of Theravada (small vessel) and Mahayana (large vessel). Theravada is the monastic form which reserves ultimate enlightenment and nirvana for monks, while Mahayana Buddhism extends this goal of enlightenment to the laity as well, that is, to non-monks. Within these categories can be found numerous branches including Tendai, Vajrayana, Nichiren, Shingon, Pure Land, Zen, and Ryobu, among others. Therefore it is important for outsiders seeking to understand Buddhism not to presume to know all the details of a particular school of Buddhism when all they have studied is classical, historic Buddhism.

The Buddha never considered himself to be a god or any type of divine being. Rather, he considered himself to be a 'way-shower' for others. Only after his death was he exalted to god status by some of his followers, though not all of his followers viewed him that way. With Christianity however, it is stated quite clearly in the Bible that Jesus was the Son of God (Matthew 3:17: "And a voice from heaven said, 'This is my Son, whom I love; with him I am well pleased'") and that He and God are one (John 10:30). One cannot rightfully consider himself or herself a Christian without professing faith in Jesus as God.

Jesus taught that He is the way and not simply one who showed the way as John 14:6 confirms: "I am the way, the truth, and the life. No one comes to the Father except by me." By the time Guatama died, Buddhism had become a major influence in India; three hundred years later, Buddhism had encompassed most of Asia. The scriptures and sayings attributed to the Buddha were written about four hundred years after his death.

In Buddhism, sin is largely understood to be ignorance. And, while sin is understood as "moral error," the context in which "evil" and "good" are understood is amoral. Karma is understood as nature's balance and is not personally enforced. Nature is not moral; therefore, karma is not a moral code, and sin is not ultimately immoral. Thus, we can say, by Buddhist thought, that our error is not a moral issue since it is ultimately an impersonal mistake, not an interpersonal violation. The consequence of this understanding is devastating. For the Buddhist, sin is more akin to a misstep than a transgression against the nature of holy God. This understanding of sin does not accord with the innate moral consciousness that men stand condemned because of their sin before a holy God (Romans 1-2).

Since it holds that sin is an impersonal and fixable error, Buddhism does not agree with the doctrine of depravity, a basic doctrine of Christianity. The Bible tells us man's sin is a problem of eternal and infinite consequence. In Buddhism, there is no need for a Savior to rescue people from their damning sins. For the Christian, Jesus is the only means of rescue from eternal damnation. For the Buddhist there is only ethical living and meditative appeals to exalted beings for the hope of perhaps achieving enlightenment and ultimate Nirvana. More than likely, one will have to go through a number of reincarnations to pay off his or her vast accumulation of karmic debt. For the true followers of Buddhism, the religion is a philosophy of morality and ethics, encapsulated within a life of renunciation of the ego-self. In Buddhism, reality is impersonal and non-relational; therefore, it is not loving. Not only is God seen as illusory, but, in dissolving sin into non-moral error and by rejecting all material reality as maya ("illusion"), even we ourselves lose our "selves." Personality itself becomes an illusion.

When asked how the world started, who/what created the universe, the Buddha is said to have kept silent because in Buddhism there is no beginning and no end. Instead, there is an endless circle of birth and death. One would have to ask what kind of Being created us to live, endure so much pain and suffering, and then die over and over again? It may cause one to contemplate, what is the point, why bother? Christians know that God sent His Son to die for us, one time, so that we do not have to suffer for an eternity. He sent His Son to give us the knowledge that we are not alone and that we are loved. Christians know there is more to life than suffering, and dying, "… but it has now been revealed through the appearing of our Savior, Christ Jesus, who has destroyed death and has brought life and immortality to light through the gospel" (2 Timothy 1:10).

Buddhism teaches that Nirvana is the highest state of being, a state of pure being, and it is achieved by means relative to the individual. Nirvana defies rational explanation and logical ordering and therefore cannot be taught, only realized. Jesus' teaching on heaven, in contrast, was quite specific. He taught us that our physical bodies die but our souls ascend to be with Him in heaven (Mark 12:25). The Buddha taught that people do not have individual souls, for the individual self or ego is an illusion. For Buddhists there is no merciful Father in heaven who sent His Son to die for our souls, for our salvation, to provide the way for us to reach His glory. Ultimately, that is why Buddhism is to be rejected.

Question: What is Hinduism and what do Hindus believe?

Answer: Hinduism is one of the oldest known organized religions—its sacred writings date as far back as 1400 to 1500 B.C. It is also one of the most diverse and complex, having millions of gods. Hindus have a wide variety of core beliefs and exist in many different sects. Although it is the third largest religion in the world, Hinduism exists primarily in India and Nepal.

The main texts of Hinduism are the Vedas (considered most important), Upanishadas, the Mahabharata, and the Ramayana. These writings contain hymns, incantations, philosophies, rituals, poems, and stories from which Hindus base their beliefs. Other texts used in Hinduism include the Brahmanas, the Sutras, and the Aranyakas.

Though Hinduism is often understood as being polytheistic, supposedly recognizing as many as 330 million gods, it also has one "god" that is supreme—Brahma. Brahma is an entity believed to inhabit every portion of reality and existence throughout the entire universe. Brahma is both impersonal and unknowable and is often believed to exist in three separate forms: Brahma—Creator; Vishnu—Preserver; and Shiva—Destroyer. These "facets" of Brahma are also known through the many other incarnations of each. It is difficult to summarize Hindu theology since the various Hindu schools contain elements of almost every theological system. Hinduism can be:

1. Monistic—Only one thing exists; Sankara's school
2. Pantheistic—Only one divine thing exists so that God is identical to the world; Brahmanism
3. Panentheistic—The world is part of God; Ramanuja's School
4. Theistic—Only one God, distinct from Creation; Bhakti Hinduism.

Observing other schools, Hinduism can also be atheistic, deistic, or even nihilistic. With such diversity included under the title "Hindu," one may wonder what makes them "Hindu" in the first place? About the only real issue is whether or not a belief system recognizes the Vedas as sacred. If it does, then it is Hindu. If not, then it is not Hindu.

The Vedas are more than theology books. They contain a rich and colorful "theo-mythology," that is, a religious mythology which deliberately interweaves myth, theology, and history to achieve a story-form religious root. This "theo-mythology" is so deeply rooted in India's history and culture that to reject the Vedas is viewed as opposing India. Therefore, a belief system is rejected by Hinduism if it does not embrace Indian culture to some extent. If the system accepts Indian culture and its theo-mythical history, then it can be embraced as "Hindu" even if its theology is theistic, nihilistic, or atheistic. This openness to contradiction can be a headache for Westerners who seek logical consistency and rational defensibility in their religious views. But, to be fair, Christians are no more logical when they claim belief in Yahweh yet live life as practical atheists, denying Christ with their lives. For the Hindu the conflict is genuine logical contradiction. For the Christian, the conflict is more likely simple hypocrisy.

Hinduism views mankind as divine. Because Brahma is everything, Hinduism asserts that everyone is divine. Atman, or self, is one with Brahman. All of reality outside of Brahman is considered mere illusion. The spiritual goal of a Hindu is to become one with Brahma, thus ceasing to exist in its illusory form of "individual self." This freedom is referred to as "moksha." Until moksha is achieved, a Hindu believes that he/she will be repeatedly reincarnated in order that he/she may work towards self-realization of the truth (the truth being that only Brahman exists, nothing else). How a person is reincarnated is determined by karma, which is a principle of cause and effect governed by nature's balance. What one did in the past affects and corresponds with what happens in the future, past and future lives included.

Although this is just a brief synopsis, it is readily seen that Hinduism is in opposition to biblical Christianity on almost every count of its belief system. Christianity has one God who is both personal and knowable (Deuteronomy 6:5; 1 Corinthians 8:6); has one set of Scriptures; teaches that God created the earth and all who live upon it (Genesis 1:1; Hebrews 11:3); believes that man is created in God's image and lives only once (Genesis 1:27; Hebrews 9:27-28); and teaches that salvation is through Jesus Christ alone (John 3:16; 6:44; 14:6; Acts 4:12). Hinduism as a religious system fails because it fails to recognize Jesus as the uniquely incarnated God-Man and Savior, the one solely sufficient source of salvation for humanity.

Question: What is Islam, and what do Muslims believe?

Answer: The religion of Islam was begun early in the 7th century A.D. by a man named Muhammad. He claimed to have been visited by the angel Gabriel. During these angelic visitations, which continued for about 23 years until Muhammad's death, the angel purportedly revealed to Muhammad the words of God (called "Allah" in Arabic and by Muslims). These dictated revelations comprise the Qur'an, Islam's holy book. Islam teaches that the Qur'an is the final authority and the last revelation of Allah.

Muslims, the followers of Islam, believe the Qur'an to be the preexistent and perfect word of Allah. Further, many Muslims reject all other language versions of the Qur'an. A translation is not a valid version of the Qur'an, which only exists in Arabic. Although the Qur'an is the main holy book, the Sunnah is considered the second source of religious instruction. The Sunnah was written by Muhammad's companions about what Muhammad said, did, and approved.

The key beliefs of Islam are that Allah is the only true God and that Muhammad was Allah's prophet. By simply stating these beliefs, a person can convert to Islam. The word "Muslim" means "one who submits to Allah." Islam purports to be the one true religion from which all other religions are derived (including Judaism and Christianity).

Muslims base their lives on the five pillars:

1. The testimony of faith: "There is no true god but God (Allah), and Muhammad is the Messenger (Prophet) of God."
2. Prayer: five prayers must be performed every day.

3. Giving: one must give to the needy, as all comes from Allah.
4. Fasting: besides occasional fasting, all Muslims must fast during the celebration of Ramadan (the ninth month of the Islamic calendar).
5. Hajj: the pilgrimage to Mecca (Makkah) should be performed at least once in a lifetime (during the twelfth month of the Islamic calendar).

These five tenets, the framework of obedience for Muslims, are taken seriously and literally. A Muslim's entrance into paradise hinges on obedience to these five pillars.

In relation to Christianity, Islam has several similarities and significant differences. Like Christianity, Islam is monotheistic, but in opposition to Christianity, Islam rejects the concept of the Trinity. Islam accepts certain portions of the Bible, such as the Law and the Gospels, but rejects the majority of it as slanderous and uninspired.

Islam claims that Jesus was a mere prophet, not God's Son (only Allah is God, Muslims believe, and how could He have a Son?). Rather, Islam asserts that Jesus, though born of a virgin, was created just as Adam, from the dust of the earth. Muslims believe Jesus did not die on the cross; thus, they deny one of the central teachings of Christianity.

Finally, Islam teaches that paradise is gained through good works and obedience to the Qur'an. The Bible, in contrast, reveals that man cannot measure up to the holy God. Only because of His mercy and love can sinners be saved through faith in Christ (Ephesians 2:8-9).

Clearly, Islam and Christianity cannot both be true. Either Jesus was the greatest prophet, or Muhammad was. Either the Bible is the Word of God, or the Qur'an is. Salvation is either attained by receiving Jesus Christ as Savior or by observing the five pillars. Again, both religions cannot be true. This truth, the separation of the two religions in crucial areas, has eternal consequences.

Question: What is Judaism and what do Jews believe?

Answer: What is Judaism, and who or what is a Jew? Is Judaism simply a religion? Is it a cultural identity or just an ethnic group?

Are Jews a clan of people or are they a nation? What do Jews believe, and do they all believe the same things?

Dictionary definitions of a "Jew" include "a member of the tribe of Judah," "an Israelite," "a member of a nation existing in Palestine from the 6th century B.C to the 1st century A.D.," "a person belonging to a continuation through descent or conversion of the ancient Jewish people," and "one whose religion is Judaism."

According to rabbinical Judaism, a Jew is one who has a Jewish mother or one who has formally converted to Judaism. Leviticus 24:10 is often cited to give this belief credibility, although the Torah makes no specific claim in support of this tradition. Some rabbis say that it has nothing to do with what the individual actually believes. These rabbis tell us that a Jew does not need to be a follower of Jewish laws and customs to be considered Jewish. In fact, a Jew can have no belief in God at all and still be Jewish based on the above rabbinical interpretation.

Other rabbis make it clear that unless the person follows the precepts of the Torah and accepts the "Thirteen Principles of Faith" of Maimonides (Rabbi Moshe ben Maimon, one of the greatest medieval Jewish scholars), he cannot be a Jew. Although this person may be a "biological" Jew, he has no real connection to Judaism.

In the Torah—the first five books of the Bible—Genesis 14:13 teaches that Abram, commonly recognized as the first Jew, was described as a "Hebrew." The name "Jew" comes from the name of Judah, one of the twelve sons of Jacob and one of the twelve tribes of Israel. Apparently the name "Jew" originally referred only to those who were members of the tribe of Judah, but when the kingdom was divided after the reign of Solomon (1 Kings 12), the term referred to anyone in the kingdom of Judah, which included the tribes of Judah, Benjamin, and Levi. Today, many believe that a Jew is anyone who is a physical descendant of Abraham, Isaac, and Jacob, regardless of which of the original twelve tribes he descends from.

So, what is it that Jews believe, and what are the basic precepts of Judaism? There are five main forms or sects of Judaism in the world today. They are Orthodox, Conservative, Reformed, Reconstructionist, and Humanistic. The beliefs and requirements in each group differ dramatically; however, a short list of the traditional beliefs of Judaism would include the following:

God is the creator of all that exists; He is one, incorporeal (without a body), and He alone is to be worshipped as absolute ruler of the universe.

The first five books of the Hebrew Bible were revealed to Moses by God. They will not be changed or augmented in the future.

God has communicated to the Jewish people through prophets.

God monitors the activities of humans; He rewards individuals for good deeds and punishes evil.

Although Christians base much of their faith on the same Hebrew Scriptures as Jews do, there are major differences in belief: Jews generally consider actions and behavior to be of primary importance; beliefs come out of actions. This conflicts with conservative Christians for whom belief is of primary importance and actions are a result of that belief.

Jewish belief does not accept the Christian concept of original sin (the belief that all people have inherited Adam and Eve's sin when they disobeyed God's instructions in the Garden of Eden).

Judaism affirms the inherent goodness of the world and its people as creations of God.

Jewish believers are able to sanctify their lives and draw closer to God by fulfilling mitzvoth (divine commandments).

No savior is needed or is available as an intermediary.

The 613 commandments found in Leviticus and other books regulate all aspects of Jewish life. The Ten Commandments, as delineated in Exodus 20:1-17 and Deuteronomy 5:6-21, form a brief synopsis of the Law.

The Messiah (anointed one of God) will arrive in the future and gather Jews once more into the land of Israel. There will be a general resurrection of the dead at that time. The Jerusalem Temple, destroyed in A.D. 70 by the Romans, will be rebuilt.

Beliefs about Jesus vary considerably. Some view Him as a great moral teacher. Others see Him as a false prophet or as an idol of Christianity. Some sects of Judaism will not even say His name due to the prohibition against saying an idol's name.

The Jews are often referred to as God's chosen people. This does not mean that they are in any way to be considered superior to other groups. Bible verses such as Exodus 19:5 simply state that God has selected Israel to receive and study the Torah, to worship God only, to rest on the Sabbath, and to celebrate the festivals. Jews were not chosen to be better than others; they were simply selected to be a light to the Gentiles and to be a blessing to all the nations.

Question: What is Christian Gnosticism?

Answer: There is actually no such thing as Christian Gnosticism, because true Christianity and Gnosticism are mutually exclusive systems of belief. The principles of Gnosticism contradict what it means to be a Christian. Therefore, while some forms of Gnosticism may claim to be Christian, they are in fact decidedly non-Christian.

Gnosticism was perhaps the most dangerous heresy that threatened the early church during the first three centuries. Influenced by such philosophers as Plato, Gnosticism is based on two false premises. First, it espouses a dualism regarding spirit and matter. Gnostics assert that matter is inherently evil and spirit is good. As a result of this presupposition, Gnostics believe anything done in the body, even the grossest sin, has no meaning because real life exists in the spirit realm only.

Second, Gnostics claim to possess an elevated knowledge, a "higher truth" known only to a certain few. Gnosticism comes from the Greek word *gnosis* which means "to know." Gnostics claim to possess a higher knowledge, not from the Bible, but acquired on some mystical higher plain of existence. Gnostics see themselves as a privileged class elevated above everybody else by their higher, deeper knowledge of God.

To discredit the idea of any compatibility between Christianity and Gnosticism, one has only to compare their teachings on the main doctrines of the faith. On the matter of salvation, Gnosticism teaches that salvation is gained through the acquisition of divine knowledge which frees one from the illusions of darkness. Although they claim to follow Jesus Christ and His original teachings, Gnostics contradict Him at every turn. Jesus said nothing about salvation through knowledge, but by faith in Him as Savior from sin. "For it

509

is by grace you have been saved, through faith—and this not from yourselves, it is the gift of God—not by works, so that no one can boast" (Ephesians 2:8-9). Furthermore, the salvation Christ offers is free and available to everyone (John 3:16), not just a select few who have acquired a special revelation.

Christianity asserts that there is one source of Truth and that is the Bible, the inspired, inerrant Word of the living God, the only infallible rule of faith and practice (John 17:17; 2 Timothy 3:15-17; Hebrews 4:12). It is God's written revelation to mankind and is never superseded by man's thoughts, ideas, writings, or visions. The Gnostics, on the other hand, use a variety of early heretical writings known as the Gnostic gospels, a collection of forgeries claiming to be "lost books of the Bible." Thankfully, the early church fathers were nearly unanimous in recognizing these Gnostic scrolls as fraudulent forgeries that espouse false doctrines about Jesus Christ, salvation, God, and every other crucial Christian truth. There are countless contradictions between the Gnostic "gospels" and the Bible. Even when the so-called Christian Gnostics quote from the Bible, they rewrite verses and parts of verses to harmonize with their philosophy, a practice that is strictly forbidden and warned against by Scripture (Deuteronomy 4:2; 12:32; Proverbs 30:6; Revelation 22:18-19).

The Person of Jesus Christ is another area where Christianity and Gnosticism drastically differ. The Gnostics believe that Jesus' physical body was not real, but only "seemed" to be physical, and that His spirit descended upon Him at His baptism, but left Him just before His crucifixion. Such views destroy not only the true humanity of Jesus, but also the atonement, for Jesus must not only have been truly God, but also the truly human (and physically real) man who actually suffered and died upon the cross in order to be the acceptable substitutionary sacrifice for sin (Hebrews 2:14-17). The biblical view of Jesus affirms His complete humanity as well as His full deity.

Gnosticism is based on a mystical, intuitive, subjective, inward, emotional approach to truth which is not new at all. It is very old, going back in some form to the Garden of Eden, where Satan questioned God and the words He spoke and convinced Adam and Eve to reject them and accept a lie. He does the same thing today as he "prowls around like a roaring lion looking for someone to devour" (1 Peter 5:8). He still calls God and the Bible into question and catches in his web those who are either naïve and scripturally uninformed or who are seeking some personal revelation to make them feel special, unique, and superior to others. Let us follow the Apostle Paul who said to "test everything. Hold on to the good" (1 Thessalonians 5:21), and this we do by comparing everything to the Word of God, the only Truth.

Question: What is Christian Science?

Answer: Christian Science was begun by Mary Baker Eddy (1821-1910), who pioneered new ideas about spirituality and health. Inspired by her own experience of healing in 1866, Eddy spent years in Bible study, prayer, and research of various healing methods. The result was a system of healing she dubbed "Christian Science" in 1879. Her book, *Science and Health with Key to the Scriptures*, broke new ground in the understanding of the mind-body-spirit connection. She went on to found a college, a church, a publishing enterprise, and the respected newspaper "The Christian Science Monitor." Because of its similarity to other groups, many believe Christian Science to be a non-Christian cult.

Christian Science teaches that God—Father-Mother of all—is completely good and wholly spiritual and that all God's creation, including the true nature of every person, is the flawless spiritual likeness of the Divine. Since God's creation is good, evils such as disease, death, and sin cannot be a part of fundamental reality. Rather, these evils are the result of living apart from God. Prayer is a central way to come closer to God and heal human ills. This differs from the Bible, which teaches that man is born in sin inherited from Adam's fall and that sin separates us from God. Without God's saving grace through the death of Christ on the cross, we would never be healed of the ultimate sickness—sin.

Rather than teaching that Jesus heals our spiritual sickness (see Isaiah 53:5), Christian Scientists see Jesus' ministry as their own paradigm for healing, believing it demonstrates the centrality of healing in regard to salvation. Christian Scientists pray to realize more of the reality of God and God's love daily and to experience and help others experience the harmonizing, healing effects of this understanding.

For most Christian Scientists, spiritual healing is an effective first choice and, as a result, they turn to the power of prayer in lieu of medical treatment. Government authorities have occasionally challenged this approach, especially in circumstances when medical treatment is withheld from minors. However, there is no church policy mandating members' health-care decisions.

Christian Science has no ministers. Rather, the Bible and *Science and Health* act as pastor and preacher. Bible lessons are studied daily and read aloud on Sunday by two elected lay members of each local congregation. Christian Science churches also hold weekly testimonial meetings, at which congregation members relate experiences of healing and regeneration.

Of all the "Christian" cults in existence, "Christian Science" is the most inaccurately named. Christian Science is neither Christian or based on science. Christian Science denies all the core truths of what makes a system "Christian." Christian Science is, in fact, opposed to science and points to mystical new-age spirituality as the path for physical and spiritual healing. Christian Science should be recognized and rejected as the anti-Christian cult that it is.

Question: What is the Eastern Orthodox Church and what are the beliefs of Orthodox Christians?

Answer: The Eastern Orthodox Church is not a single church but rather a family of 13 self-governing bodies, denominated by the nation in which they are located (e.g., the Greek Orthodox Church, Russian Orthodox Church). They are united in their understanding of the sacraments, doctrine, liturgy, and church government, but each administers its own affairs.

The head of each Orthodox church is called a "patriarch" or "metropolitan." The patriarch of Constantinople (Istanbul, Turkey) is considered the ecumenical—or universal—patriarch. He is the closest thing to a counterpart to the Pope in the Roman Catholic Church. Unlike the Pope, who is known as VICARIUS FILIUS DEI (the vicar of the Son of God), the bishop of Constantinople is known as PRIMUS INTER PARES (the first amongst equals). He enjoys special honor, but he has no power to interfere with the 12 other Orthodox communions.

The Orthodox Church claims to be the one true church of Christ, and seeks to trace its origin back to the original apostles through an unbroken chain of apostolic succession. Orthodox thinkers debate the spiritual status of Roman Catholics and Protestants, and a few still consider them heretics. Like Catholics and Protestants, however, Orthodox believers affirm the Trinity, the Bible as the Word of God, Jesus as God the Son, and many other biblical doctrines. However, in doctrine, they have much more in common with Roman Catholics than they do with Protestant Christians.

Sadly, the doctrine of justification by faith is virtually absent from the history and theology of the Orthodox Church. Rather, Orthodoxy emphasizes *theosis* (literally, "divinization"), the gradual process by which Christians become more and more like Christ. What many in the Orthodox tradition fail to understand is that "divinization" is the progressive result of salvation, not a requirement for salvation itself. Other Orthodox distinctives that are in conflict with the Bible include:

The equal authority of church tradition and Scripture
Discouragement of individuals interpreting the Bible apart from tradition
The perpetual virginity of Mary
Prayer for the dead
Baptism of infants without reference to individual responsibility and faith
The possibility of receiving salvation after death
The possibility of losing salvation

While the Eastern Orthodox Church has claimed some of the church's great voices, and while there are many of the Orthodox traditions that have a genuine salvation relationship with Jesus Christ, the Orthodox church itself does not speak with a clear message that can be harmonized with the biblical gospel of Christ. The call of the Reformers for "Scripture alone, faith alone, grace alone, and Christ alone" is missing in the Eastern Orthodox Church, and that is too precious a treasure to do without.

Question: What is the difference between religion and spirituality?

Answer: Before we explore the difference between religion and spirituality, we must first define the two terms. Religion can be defined as "belief in God or gods to be worshipped, usually expressed in conduct and ritual" or "any specific system of belief, worship, etc., often involving a code of ethics." Spirituality can be defined as "the quality or fact of being spiritual, non-physical" or "predominantly spiritual character as shown in thought, life, etc.; spiritual tendency or tone." To put it briefly, religion is a set of beliefs and rituals that claim to get a person in a right relationship with God, and spirituality is a focus on spiritual things and the spiritual world instead of physical/earthly things.

The most common misconception about religion is that Christianity is just another religion like Islam, Judaism, Hinduism, etc. Sadly, many who claim to be adherents of Christianity do practice Christianity as if it were a religion. To many, Christianity is nothing more than a set of rules and rituals that a person has to observe in order to go to heaven after death. That is not true Christianity. True Christianity is not a religion; rather, it is having a right relationship with God by receiving Jesus Christ as the Savior-Messiah, by grace through faith. Yes, Christianity does have "rituals" to observe (e.g., baptism and communion). Yes, Christianity does have "rules" to follow (e.g., do not murder, love one another, etc.). However, these rituals and rules are not the essence of Christianity. The rituals and rules of Christianity are the result of salvation. When we receive salvation through Jesus Christ, we are baptized as a proclamation of that faith. We observe communion in remembrance of Christ's sacrifice. We follow a list of do's and don'ts out of love for God and gratitude for what He has done.

The most common misconception about spirituality is that there are many forms of spirituality, and all are equally valid. Meditating in unusual physical positions, communing with nature, seeking conversation with the spirit world, etc., may seem to be "spiritual," but they are in fact false spirituality. True spirituality is possessing the Holy Spirit of God as a result of receiving salvation through Jesus Christ. True spirituality is the fruit that the Holy Spirit produces in a person's life: love, joy, peace, patience, kindness, goodness, faithfulness, gentleness, and self-control (Galatians 5:22-23). Spirituality is all about becoming more like God, who is spirit (John 4:24) and having our character conformed to His image (Romans 12:1-2).

What religion and spirituality have in common is that they both can be false methods of having a relationship with God. Religion tends to substitute the heartless observance of rituals for a genuine relationship with God. Spirituality tends to substitute connection with the spirit world for a genuine relationship with God. Both can be, and often are, false paths to God. At the same time, religion can be valuable in the sense that it points to the fact that there is a God and that we are somehow accountable to Him. The only true value of religion is its ability to point out that we have fallen short and are in need of a Savior. Spirituality can be valuable in that it points out that the physical world is not all there is. Human beings are not only material, but also possess a soul-spirit. There is a spiritual world around us of which we should be aware. The true value of spirituality is that it points to the fact that there is something and someone beyond this physical world to which we need to connect.

Jesus Christ is the fulfillment of both religion and spirituality. Jesus is the One to whom we are accountable and to whom true religion points. Jesus is the One to whom we need to connect and the One to whom true spirituality points.

Question: Is Scientology Christian or a cult?

Answer: Scientology is a difficult religion to summarize. Scientology has gained popularity due to some Hollywood celebrities who have embraced it. Scientology was founded in 1953 by fiction author L. Ron Hubbard, just four years after he made the statement, "I'd like to start a religion—that's where the money is." That is where he found wealth, also—Hubbard became a multi-millionaire.

Scientology teaches that mankind is an immortal being (called a Thetan) not originally from this planet, and that man is trapped by matter, energy, space, and time (MEST). Salvation for a scientologist comes through a process called "auditing," whereby "engrams" (basically, memories of past pain and unconsciousness that create energy blockage) are removed. Auditing is a lengthy process and can cost hundreds of thousands of dollars. When all engrams are finally removed, the Thetan can once again control MEST instead of being controlled by it. Until salvation, each Thetan is constantly reincarnated.

Scientology is a very expensive religion to pursue. Every aspect of Scientology has some sort of fee associated with it. This is why Scientology's "pews" are filled only with the wealthy. It is also a very strict religion and very punitive against those who would try to leave behind its teachings and membership. Its "scriptures" are limited solely to the writings and teachings of L. Ron Hubbard.

Though scientologists will claim that Scientology is compatible with Christianity, the Bible counters each and every belief they hold to. The Bible teaches that God is the sovereign and only creator of the universe (Genesis 1:1); mankind was created by God (Genesis 1:27); the only salvation available to man is by grace through faith in the finished work of Jesus Christ (Philippians 2:8); salvation is a free gift that mankind can do nothing to earn (Ephesians 2:8-9); and Jesus Christ is alive and well and is seated at the right hand of God the Father even now (Acts 2:33; Ephesians 1:20; Hebrews 1:3), awaiting the time when He will gather His people to Himself to reside with Him for eternity in heaven. Everyone else will be cast into a very real hell, separated from God for eternity (Revelation 20:15).

Scientology categorically denies the existence of the God of the Bible, heaven, and hell. To a scientologist, Jesus Christ was simply a good teacher who unfortunately was wrongfully put to death. Scientology differs from biblical Christianity on every important doctrine. Some of the most important differences are summarized below.

God: Scientology believes that there are multiple gods and that some gods are above other gods. Biblical Christianity, on the other hand, recognizes the one and only true God who revealed Himself to us in the Bible and through Jesus Christ. Those who believe in Him cannot believe the false concept of God as taught in Scientology.

Jesus Christ: Like other cults, Scientology denies the deity of Christ. Instead of having a biblical view of who Christ is and what He did, they assign to Him the characteristics of some sort of lesser god who has obtained legendary status over the years. The Bible clearly teaches that Jesus was God in the flesh and through His incarnation He could act as a sacrifice for our sins. It is through Christ's death and resurrection that we can have the hope of eternal life with God (John 3:16).

Sin: Scientology believes in the inherent goodness of man and teaches that it is despicable and utterly beneath contempt to tell a man he must repent or that he is evil. On the other hand, the Bible teaches that man is a sinner and the only hope for him is that he receive Christ as his Lord and Savior (Romans 6:23).

Salvation: Scientology believes in reincarnation and that personal salvation in one's lifetime is freedom from the cycle of birth and death associated with reincarnation. They believe that religious practice of all faiths is the universal way to wisdom, understanding, and salvation. In contrast, the Bible teaches that there is only one way of salvation and that is through Jesus Christ. Jesus Himself said, "I am the way, the truth, and the life, no man comes to the Father except through me" (John 14:6).

Comparing the teachings of Scientology with the Bible, we see that the two have very little, if anything, in common. Scientology only leads away from God and eternal life. Scientology, while sometimes disguising its beliefs in Christian-sounding language, in fact diametrically opposes Christianity on every core belief. Scientology is clearly, and most definitely, not Christian.

Question: Why are there so many religions? Do all religions lead to God?

Answer: The existence of so many religions and the claim that all religions lead to God without question confuses many who are earnestly seeking the truth about God, with the end result sometimes being that some despair of ever reaching the absolute truth on the subject. Or they end up embracing the universalist claim that all religions lead to God. Of course, skeptics also point to the existence of so many religions as proof that either you cannot know God or that God simply does not exist.

Romans 1:19-21 contains the biblical explanation for why there are so many religions. The truth of God is seen and known by every human being because God has made it so. Instead of accepting the truth about God and submitting to it, most human beings reject it and seek their own way to understand God. But this leads not to enlightenment regarding God, but to futility of thinking. Here is where we find the basis of the "many religions."

Many people do not want to believe in a God who demands righteousness and morality, so they invent a God who makes no such requirements. Many people do not want to believe in a God who declares it impossible for people to earn their own way to heaven. So they invent a God who accepts people into heaven if they have completed certain steps, followed certain rules, and/or obeyed certain laws, at least to the best of their ability. Many people do not want a relationship with a God who is sovereign and omnipotent. So they imagine God as being more of a mystical force than a personal and sovereign ruler.

The existence of so many religions is not an argument against God's existence or an argument that truth about God is not clear. Rather, the existence of so many religions is demonstration of humanity's rejection of the one true God. Mankind has replaced Him with gods that are more to their liking. This is a dangerous enterprise. The desire to recreate God in our own image comes from the sin nature within us—a nature that will eventually "reap destruction" (Galatians 6:7-8).

Do all religions lead to God? Actually they do. All but one leads to His judgment. Only one—Christianity—leads to His forgiveness and eternal life. No matter what religion one embraces, everyone will meet God after death (Hebrews 9:27). All religions lead to God, but only one religion will result in God's acceptance, because only through His salvation through faith in Jesus Christ can anyone approach Him with confidence. The decision to embrace the truth about God is important for a simple reason: eternity is an awfully long time to be wrong. This is why right thinking about God is so critical.

Question: With all of the different religions, how can I know which one is correct?

Answer: There is no doubt that the number of different religions in the world makes it a challenge to know which one is correct. First, let's consider some thoughts on the overall subject and then look at how one might approach the topic in a manner that can actually get to a right conclusion about God. The challenge of different answers to a particular issue is not unique to the topic of religion. For example, you can sit 100 math students down, give them a complex problem to solve, and it is likely that many will get the answer wrong. But does this mean that a correct answer does not exist? Not at all. Those who get the answer wrong simply need to be shown their error and know the techniques necessary to arrive at the correct answer.

How do we arrive at the truth about God? We use a systematic methodology that is designed to separate truth from error by using various tests for truth, with the end result being a set of right conclusions. Can you imagine the end results a scientist would arrive at if he went into the lab and just started mixing things together with no rhyme or reason? Or if a physician just started treating a patient with random medicines in the hope of making him well? Neither the scientist nor the physician takes this approach; instead, they use systematic methods that are methodical, logical, evidential, and proven to yield the right end result.

This being the case, why think theology—the study of God—should be any different? Why believe it can be approached in a haphazard and undisciplined way and still yield right conclusions? Unfortunately, this is the approach many take, and this is one of the reasons why so many religions exist. That said, we now return to the question of how to reach truthful conclusions about God. What systematic approach should be used? First, we need to establish a framework for testing various truth claims, and then we need a roadmap to follow to reach a right conclusion. Here is a good framework to use:

1. Logical consistency—the claims of a belief system must logically cohere to each other and not contradict in any way. As an example, the end goal of Buddhism is to rid oneself of all desires. Yet, one must have a desire to rid oneself of all desires, which is a contradictory and illogical principle.
2. Empirical adequacy—is there evidence to support the belief system (whether the evidence is rational, externally evidential, etc.)? Naturally, it is only right to want proof for important claims being made so the assertions can be verified. For

example, Mormons teach that Jesus lived in North America. Yet there is absolutely no proof, archaeological or otherwise, to support such a claim.

3. Existential relevancy—the belief system must conform to reality as we know it, and it must make a meaningful difference in the life of the adherent. Deism, for example, claims that God just threw the spinning world into the universe and does not interact with those who live on it. How does such a belief impact someone in a day-to-day manner? In short, it does not.

The above framework, when applied to the topic of religion, will help lead one to a right view of God and will answer the four big questions of life:

1. Origin – where did we come from?
2. Ethics – how should we live?
3. Meaning – what is the purpose for life?
4. Destiny – where is mankind heading?

But how does one go about applying this framework in the pursuit of God? A step-by-step question/answer approach is one of the best tactics to employ. Narrowing the list of possible questions down produces the following:

1. Does absolute truth exist?
2. Do reason and religion mix?
3. Does God exist?
4. Can God be known?
5. Is Jesus God?
6. Does God care about me?

First we need to know if absolute truth exists. If it does not, then we really cannot be sure of anything (spiritual or not), and we end up either an agnostic, unsure if we can really know anything, or a pluralist, accepting every position because we are not sure which, if any, is right.

Absolute truth is defined as that which matches reality, that which corresponds to its object, telling it like it is. Some say there is no such thing as absolute truth, but taking such a position becomes self-defeating. For example, the relativist says, "All truth is relative," yet one must ask: is that statement absolutely true? If so, then absolute truth exists; if not, then why consider it? Postmodernism affirms no truth, yet it affirms at least one absolute truth: postmodernism is true. In the end, absolute truth becomes undeniable.

Further, absolute truth is naturally narrow and excludes its opposite. Two plus two equals four, with no other answer being possible. This point becomes critical as different belief systems and worldviews are compared. If one belief system has components that are proven true, then any competing belief system with contrary claims must be false. Also, we must keep in mind that absolute truth is not impacted by sincerity and desire. No matter how sincerely someone embraces a lie, it is still a lie. And no desire in the world can make something true that is false.

The answer of question one is that absolute truth exists. This being the case, agnosticism, postmodernism, relativism, and skepticism are all false positions.

This leads us to the next question of whether reason/logic can be used in matters of religion. Some say this is not possible, but—why not? The truth is, logic is vital when examining spiritual claims because it helps us understand why some claims should be excluded and others embraced. Logic is absolutely critical in dismantling pluralism (which says that all truth claims, even those that oppose each other, are equal and valid).

For example, Islam and Judaism claim that Jesus is not God, whereas Christianity claims He is. One of the core laws of logic is the law of non-contradiction, which says something cannot be both "A" and "non-A" at the same time and in the same sense. Applying this law to the claims Judaism, Islam, and Christianity means that one is right and the other two are wrong. Jesus cannot be both God and not God. Used properly, logic is a potent weapon against pluralism because it clearly demonstrates that contrary truth claims cannot both be true. This understanding topples the whole "true for you but not for me" mindset.

Logic also dispels the whole "all roads lead to the top of the mountain" analogy that pluralists use. Logic shows that each belief system has its own set of signs that point to radically different locations in the end. Logic shows that the proper illustration of a search for spiritual truth is more like a maze—one path makes it through to truth, while all others arrive at dead ends. All faiths may have some surface similarities, but they differ in major ways in their core doctrines.

The conclusion is that you can use reason and logic in matters of religion. That being the case, pluralism (the belief that all truth claims are equally true and valid) is ruled out because it is illogical and contradictory to believe that diametrically opposing truth claims can both be right.

Next comes the big question: does God exist? Atheists and naturalists (who do not accept anything beyond this physical world and universe) say "no." While volumes have been written and debates have raged throughout history on this question, it is actually not difficult to answer. To give it proper attention, you must first ask this question: Why do we have something rather than nothing at all? In other words, how did you and everything around you get here? The argument for God can be presented very simply:

> Something exists.
> You do not get something from nothing.
> Therefore, a necessary and eternal Being exists.

You cannot deny you exist because you have to exist in order to deny your own existence (which is self-defeating), so the first premise above is true. No one believes you can get something from nothing (i.e., that "nothing" produced the universe), so the second premise is true. Therefore, the third premise must be true—an eternal Being responsible for everything must exist.

This is a position no thinking atheist denies; they just claim that the universe is that eternal being. However, the problem with that stance is that all scientific evidence points to the fact that the universe had a beginning (the 'big bang'). And everything that has a beginning must have a cause; therefore, the universe had a cause and is not eternal. Because the only two sources of eternality are an eternal universe (proven to be untrue) or an eternal Creator, the only logical conclusion is that God exists. Answering the question of God's existence in the affirmative rules out atheism as a valid belief system.

Now, this conclusion says nothing about what kind of God exists, but amazingly enough, it does do one sweeping thing—it rules out all pantheistic religions. All pantheistic worldviews say that the universe is God and is eternal. And this assertion is false. So, Hinduism, Buddhism, Jainism, and all other pantheistic religions are ruled out as valid belief systems.

Further, we learn some interesting things about this God who created the universe. He is:

- Supernatural in nature (as He exists outside of His creation)
- Incredibly powerful (to have created all that is known)
- Eternal (self-existent, as He exists outside of time and space)
- Omnipresent (He created space and is not limited by it)
- Timeless and changeless (He created time)
- Immaterial (because He transcends space)
- Personal (the impersonal can't create personality)
- Necessary (as everything else depends on Him)
- Infinite and singular (as you cannot have two infinites)
- Diverse yet has unity (as nature exhibits diversity)
- Intelligent (supremely, to create everything)
- Purposeful (as He deliberately created everything)
- Moral (no moral law can exist without a lawgiver)
- Caring (or no moral laws would have been given)

This Being exhibits characteristics very similar to the God of Judaism, Islam, and Christianity, which interestingly enough, are the only core faiths left standing after atheism and pantheism have been eliminated. Note also that one of the big questions in life (origins) is now answered: we know where we came from.

This leads to the next question: can we know God? At this point, the need for religion is replaced by something more important—the need for revelation. If mankind is to know this God well, it is up to God to reveal Himself to His creation. Judaism, Islam, and Christianity all claim to have a book that is God's revelation to man, but the question is which (if any) is actually true? Pushing aside minor differences, the two core areas of dispute are 1) the New Testament of the Bible 2) the person of Jesus Christ. Islam and Judaism both claim the New Testament of the Bible is untrue in what it claims, and both deny that Jesus is God incarnate, while Christianity affirms both to be true.

There is no faith on the planet that can match the mountains of evidence that exist for Christianity. From the voluminous number of ancient manuscripts, to the very early dating of the documents written during the lifetime of the eyewitnesses (some only 15 years after Christ's death), to the multiplicity of the accounts (nine authors in 27 books of the New Testament), to the archaeological evidence—none of which has ever contradicted a single claim the New Testament makes—to the fact that the apostles went to their deaths claiming they had seen Jesus in action and that He had come back from the dead, Christianity sets the bar in terms of providing the proof to back up its claims. The New Testament's historical authenticity—that it conveys a truthful account of the actual events as they occurred—is the only right conclusion to reach once all the evidence has been examined.

When it comes to Jesus, one finds a very curious thing about Him—He claimed to be God in the flesh. Jesus own words (e.g., "Before Abraham was born I AM"), His actions (e.g., forgiving sins, accepting worship), His sinless and miraculous life (which He used to prove His truth claims over opposing claims), and His resurrection all support His claims to be God. The New Testament writers affirm this fact over and over again in their writings.

Now, if Jesus is God, then what He says must be true. And if Jesus said that the Bible is inerrant and true in everything it says (which He did), this must mean that the Bible is true in what it proclaims. As we have already learned, two competing truth claims cannot both be right. So anything in the Islamic Qur'an or writings of Judaism that contradict the Bible cannot be true. In fact, both Islam and Judaism fail since they both say that Jesus is not God incarnate, while the evidence says otherwise. And because we can indeed know God (because He has revealed Himself in His written Word and in Christ), all forms of agnosticism are refuted. Lastly, another big question of life is answered—that of ethics—as the Bible contains clear instructions on how mankind ought to live.

This same Bible proclaims that God cares deeply for mankind and wishes all to know Him intimately. In fact, He cares so much that He became a man to show His creation exactly what He is like. There are many men who have sought to be God, but only one God who sought to be man so He could save those He deeply loves from an eternity separated from Him. This fact demonstrates the existential relevancy of Christianity and also answers that last two big questions of life—meaning and destiny. Each person has been designed by God for a purpose, and each has a destiny that awaits him—one of eternal life with God or eternal separation from Him. This deduction (and the point of God's becoming a man in Christ) also refutes Deism, which says God is not interested in the affairs of mankind.

In the end, we see that ultimate truth about God can be found and the worldview maze successfully navigated by testing various truth claims and systematically pushing aside falsehoods so that only the truth remains. Using the tests of logical consistency, empirical adequacy, and existential relevancy, coupled with asking the right questions, yields truthful and reasonable conclusions about religion and God. Everyone should agree that the only reason to believe something is that it is true—nothing more. Sadly, true belief is a matter of the will, and no matter how much logical evidence is presented, some will still choose to deny the God who is there and miss the one true path to harmony with Him.

Chapter 20

. . . .

QUESTIONS ABOUT

FALSE DOCTRINE

CONTENTS

Is universalism/universal salvation biblical? 528

Is annihilationism biblical? 529

What is atheism? 531

What is agnosticism? 532

What is the preterist view of the end times? 534

What is open theism? 535

What is Arianism? 536

What is contemplative prayer? 537

What is contemplative spirituality? 538

What is dualism? 540

What is the JEDP Theory? 540

What is moral relativism? 542

What is pantheism? 543

What are Pelagianism and Semi-Pelagianism? 544

What is polytheism? 545

What does the Bible say about karma? 546

What does the Bible say about the prosperity gospel? 547

What is the Jesus Seminar? 549

What is the synoptic problem? 550

Question: Is universalism/universal salvation biblical?

Answer: Universalism is the belief that everyone will be saved. There are many people today who hold to universal salvation and believe that all people eventually end up in heaven. Perhaps it is the thought of men and women living a life of eternal torment in hell that causes some to reject the teaching of Scripture on this issue. For some it is an over-emphasis on the love and compassion of God—and the neglect of the righteousness and justice of God—that leads them to believe God will have mercy on every living soul. But the Scriptures do teach that some people will spend eternity in hell.

First of all, the Bible is clear that unredeemed men will dwell forever in hell. Jesus' own words confirm that the time spent in heaven for the redeemed will last as long as that of the unredeemed in hell. Matthew 25:46 says, "Then they [the unsaved] will go away to eternal punishment, but the righteous to eternal life." According to this verse, the punishment of the unsaved is just as eternal as the life of the righteous. Some believe that those in hell will eventually cease to exist, but the Lord Himself confirms that it will last forever. Matthew 25:41 and Mark 9:44 describe hell as "eternal fire" and "unquenchable fire."

How does one avoid this unquenchable fire? Many people believe that all roads—all religions and beliefs—lead to heaven, or they consider that God is so full of love and mercy that He will allow all people into heaven. God is certainly full of love and mercy; it was these qualities that led Him to send His Son, Jesus Christ, to earth to die on the cross for us. Jesus Christ is the exclusive door that leads to an eternity in heaven. Acts 4:12 says, "Salvation is found in no one else, for there is no other name under heaven given to men by which we must be saved." "There is one God and one mediator between God and men, the man Christ Jesus" (1 Timothy 2:5). In John 14:6, Jesus says, "I am the way and the truth and the life. No one comes to the Father except through me." John 3:16, "For God so loved the world that he gave his one and only Son, that whoever believes in him shall not perish but have eternal life." If we choose to reject God's Son, we do not meet the requirements for salvation (John 3:16, 18, 36).

With verses such as these, it becomes clear that universalism and universal salvation are unbiblical beliefs. Universalism directly contradicts what Scripture teaches. While many people accuse Christians of being intolerant and "exclusive," it is important to remember that these are the words of Christ Himself. Christians did not develop these ideas on their own; Christians are simply stating what the Lord has already said. People choose to reject the message because they do not want to face up to their sin and admit that they need the Lord to save them. To say that those who reject God's provision of salvation through His Son will be saved is to belittle the holiness and justice of God and negate the need of Jesus' sacrifice on our behalf.

Question: Is annihilationism biblical?

Answer: Annihilationism is the belief that unbelievers will not experience an eternity of suffering in hell, but will instead be "extinguished" after death. For many, annihilationism is an attractive belief because of the awfulness of the idea of people spending eternity in hell. While there are some passages that seem to argue for annihilationism, a comprehensive look at what the Bible says about the destiny of the wicked reveals the fact that punishment in hell is eternal. A belief in annihilationism results from a misunderstanding of one or more of the following doctrines: 1) the consequences of sin, 2) the justice of God, 3) the nature of hell.

In relation to the nature of hell, annihilationists misunderstand the meaning of the lake of fire. Obviously, if a human being were cast into a lake of burning lava, he/she would be almost instantly consumed. However, the lake of fire is both a physical and spiritual realm. It is not simply a human body being cast into the lake of fire; it is a human's body, soul, and spirit. A spiritual nature cannot be consumed by physical fire. It seems that the unsaved are resurrected with a body prepared for eternity just as the saved are (Revelation 20:13; Acts 24:15). These bodies are prepared for an eternal fate.

Eternity is another aspect which annihilationists fail to fully comprehend. Annihilationists are correct that the Greek word *aionion*, which is usually translated "eternal," does not by definition mean "eternal." It specifically refers to an "age" or "eon," a specific period of time. However, it is clear that in New Testament, *aionion* is sometimes used to refer to an eternal length of time. Revelation 20:10 speaks of Satan, the beast, and the false prophet being cast into the lake of fire and being tormented "day and night forever and ever." It is clear that these three are not "extinguished" by being cast into the lake of fire. Why would the fate of the unsaved be any different (Revelation 20:14-15)? The most convincing evidence for the eternality of hell is Matthew 25:46, "Then they [the unsaved] will go away to eternal punishment, but the righteous to eternal life." In this verse, the same Greek word is used to refer to the destiny of the wicked and the righteous. If the wicked are only tormented for an "age," then the righteous will only experience life in heaven for an "age." If believers will be in heaven forever, unbelievers will be in hell forever.

Another frequent objection to the eternality of hell by annihilationists is that it would be unjust for God to punish unbelievers in hell for eternity for a finite amount of sin. How could it be fair for God to take a person who lived a sinful, 70-year life, and punish him/her for all of eternity? The answer is that our sin bears an eternal consequence because it is committed against an eternal God. When King David committed the sins of adultery and murder he stated, "Against you, you only, have I sinned and done what is evil in your sight…" (Psalm 51:4). David had sinned against Bathsheba and Uriah; how could David claim to have only sinned against God? David understood that all sin is ultimately against God. God is an eternal and infinite Being. As a result, all sin against Him is worthy of an eternal punishment. It is not a matter of the length of time we sin, but the character of the God against whom we sin.

A more personal aspect of annihilationism is the idea that we could not possibly be happy in heaven if we knew that some of our loved ones were suffering an eternity of torment in hell. However, when we arrive in heaven, we will not have anything to complain about or be saddened by. Revelation 21:4 tells us, "He will wipe every tear from their eyes. There will be no more death or mourning or crying or pain, for the old order of things has passed away." If some of our loved ones are not in heaven, we will be in 100 percent complete agreement that they do not belong there and that they are condemned by their own refusal to accept Jesus Christ as their Savior (John 3:16; 14:6). It is hard to understand this, but we will not be saddened by the lack of their presence. Our focus should not be on how we can enjoy heaven without all of our loved ones there, but on how we can point our loved ones to faith in Christ so that they will be there.

Hell is perhaps a primary reason why God sent Jesus Christ to pay the penalty for our sins. Being "extinguished" after death is no fate to dread, but an eternity in hell most definitely is. Jesus' death was an infinite death, paying our infinite sin debt so that we would not have to pay it in hell for eternity (2 Corinthians 5:21). When we place our faith in Him, we are saved, forgiven, cleansed, and promised an eternal home in heaven. But if we reject God's gift of eternal life, we will face the eternal consequences of that decision.

Question: What is atheism?

Answer: Atheism is the view that God does not exist. Atheism is not a new development. Psalm 14:1, written by David in around 1000 B.C, mentions atheism: "The fool says in his heart, 'There is no God.'" Recent statistics show an increasing number of people claiming to be atheists, up to 10 percent of people worldwide. So why are more and more people becoming atheists? Is atheism truly the logical position atheists claim it to be?

Why does atheism even exist? Why doesn't God simply reveal Himself to people, proving that He exists? Surely if God would just appear, the thinking goes, everyone would believe in Him! The problem here is that it is not God's desire to just convince people that He exists. It is God's desire for people to believe in Him by faith (2 Peter 3:9) and accept by faith His gift of salvation (John 3:16). God clearly demonstrated His existence many times in the Old Testament (Genesis 6-9; Exodus 14:21-22; 1 Kings 18:19-31). Did the people believe that God exists? Yes. Did they turn from their evil ways and obey God? No. If a person is not willing to accept God's existence by faith, then he/she is definitely not ready to accept Jesus Christ as Savior by faith (Ephesians 2:8-9). God's desire is for people to become Christians, not just theists (those who believe God exists).

The Bible tells us that God's existence must be accepted by faith. Hebrews 11:6 declares, "And without faith it is impossible to please God, because anyone who comes to Him must believe that He exists and that He rewards those who earnestly seek Him." The

Bible reminds us that we are blessed when we believe and trust in God by faith: "Then Jesus told him, 'Because you have seen me, you have believed; blessed are those who have not seen and yet have believed'" (John 20:29).

The existence of God must be accepted by faith, but this does not mean belief in God is illogical. There are many good arguments for the existence of God. The Bible teaches that God's existence is clearly seen in the universe (Psalm 19:1-4), in nature (Romans 1:18-22), and in our own hearts (Ecclesiastes 3:11). With all that said, the existence of God cannot be proven; it must be accepted by faith.

At the same time, it takes just as much faith to believe in atheism. To make the absolute statement "God does not exist" is to make a claim of knowing absolutely everything there is to know about everything and of having been everywhere in the universe and having witnessed everything there is to be seen. Of course, no atheist would make these claims. However, that is essentially what they are claiming when they state that God absolutely does not exist. Atheists cannot prove that God does not, for example, live in the center of the sun, or beneath the clouds of Jupiter, or in some distant nebula. Since those places are beyond our capacity to observe, it cannot be proven that God does not exist. It takes just as much faith to be an atheist as it does to be a theist.

Atheism cannot be proven, and God's existence must be accepted by faith. Obviously, Christians believe strongly that God exists, and admit that God's existence is a matter of faith. At the same time, we reject the idea that belief in God is illogical. We believe that God's existence can be clearly seen, keenly sensed, and proven to be philosophically and scientifically necessary. "The heavens declare the glory of God; the skies proclaim the work of his hands. Day after day they pour forth speech; night after night they display knowledge. There is no speech or language where their voice is not heard. Their voice goes out into all the earth, their words to the ends of the world" (Psalm 19:1-4).

Question: What is agnosticism?

Answer: Agnosticism is the view that the existence of God is impossible to be known or proven. The word "agnostic" essentially means "without knowledge." Agnosticism is a more intellectually honest form of atheism. Atheism claims that God does not exist—an unprovable position. Agnosticism argues that God's existence cannot be proven or unproven, that it is impossible to know whether or not God exists. In this, agnosticism is correct. God's existence cannot be empirically proven or disproven.

The Bible tells us that we must accept by faith that God exists. Hebrews 11:6 says that "it is impossible to please God, because anyone who comes to him must believe that he exists and that he rewards those who earnestly seek him." God is spirit (John 4:24) so He cannot be seen or touched. Unless God chooses to reveal Himself, He is invisible to our senses (Romans 1:20). The Bible declares that the existence of God can be clearly seen in the universe (Psalm 19:1-4), sensed in nature (Romans 1:18-22), and confirmed in our own hearts (Ecclesiastes 3:11).

Agnostics are unwilling to make a decision either for or against God's existence. It is the ultimate "straddling the fence" position. Theists believe that God exists. Atheists believe that God does not exist. Agnostics believe that we should not believe or disbelieve in God's existence, because it is impossible to know either way.

For the sake of argument, let's throw out the clear and undeniable evidences of God's existence. If we put the positions of theism and agnosticism on equal footing, which makes the most "sense" to believe in regards to the possibility of life after death? If there is no God, theists and agnostics alike all simply cease to exist when they die. If there is a God, both theists and agnostics will have someone to answer to when they die. From this perspective, it definitely makes more "sense" to be a theist than an agnostic. If neither position can be proven or disproven, it seems wise to make every effort to thoroughly examine the position that may have an infinitely and eternally more desirable end result.

It is normal to have doubts. There are many things in this world that we do not understand. Often, people doubt God's existence because they do not understand or agree with the things He does and allows. However, as finite human beings we should not expect to be able to comprehend an infinite God. Romans 11:33-34 exclaims, "Oh, the depth of the riches of the wisdom and knowledge of God!

How unsearchable his judgments, and his paths beyond tracing out! 'Who has known the mind of the Lord? Or who has been his counselor?'" We must believe in God by faith and trust His ways by faith. God is ready and willing to reveal Himself in amazing ways to those who will believe in Him. Deuteronomy 4:29 proclaims, "But if from there you seek the Lord your God, you will find Him if you look for Him with all your heart and with all your soul."

Question: What is the preterist view of the end times?

Answer: The preterist interpretation of Scripture regards the book of Revelation as a symbolic picture of early church conflicts, not a description of what will occur in the end times. Preterism denies the future prophetic quality of most of the book of Revelation. In varying degrees, preterism combines the allegorical and symbolic interpretation with the concept that Revelation does not deal with specific future events. The preterist movement essentially teaches that all the end-times prophecies of the New Testament were fulfilled in A.D. 70 when the Romans attacked and destroyed Jerusalem and Israel.

The letters to the churches in Revelation 2 and 3 were written to real churches in the first century, and they have practical applications for churches today. But chapters 6-22, if interpreted in the same way as the rest of Bible prophecy, were written about events that are yet future. There is no reason to interpret the prophecies of Revelation allegorically. Previously fulfilled prophecies were fulfilled literally. For example, all of the Old Testament verses predicting the first coming of Christ were fulfilled literally in Jesus. Christ came at the time that He was predicted to come (Daniel 9:25-26). Christ was born of a virgin (Isaiah 7:14). He suffered and died for our sins (Isaiah 53:5-9). These are but a few examples of the hundreds of Old Testament prophecies God gave to the prophets that are recorded in Scripture and that were fulfilled literally. It simply does not make sense to try to allegorize unfulfilled prophecy or understand unfulfilled prophecy in any other way than by a normal reading.

Furthermore, preterism is entirely inconsistent in its interpretation of the book of Revelation. According to the preterist view of the end times, chapters 6-18 of Revelation are symbolic and allegorical, not describing literal events. However, chapter 19, according to preterists, is to be understood literally. Jesus Christ will literally and physically return. Then, chapter 20 is again interpreted allegorically by preterists, while chapters 21-22 are understood literally, at least in part, in that there will truly be a new heaven and new earth. No one denies that Revelation contains amazing and sometimes confusing visions. No one denies that Revelation describes some things figuratively. However, to arbitrarily deny the literal nature of select portions of Revelation is to destroy the basis of interpreting any of the book literally. If the seals, trumpets, bowls, witnesses, 144,000, beast, false prophet, millennial kingdom, etc., are allegorical or symbolic, on what basis do we claim that the second coming of Christ and the new earth are literal? That is the failure of preterism—it leaves the interpretation of Revelation to the opinions of the interpreter. Instead, we are to read it, believe it, and obey it—literally and exactly.

Question: What is open theism?

Answer: "Open theism," also known as "openness theology" and the "openness of God," is an attempt to explain the foreknowledge of God in relationship to the free will of man. The argument of open theism is essentially this: human beings are truly free; if God absolutely knew the future, human beings could not truly be free. Therefore, God does not know absolutely everything about the future. Open theism holds that the future is not knowable. Therefore, God knows everything that can be known, but He does not know the future.

Open theism bases these beliefs on Scripture passages which describe God "changing His mind" or "being surprised" or "seeming to gain knowledge" (Genesis 6:6; 22:12; Exodus 32:14; Jonah 3:10). In light of the many other Scriptures that declare God's knowledge of the future, these Scriptures should be understood as God describing Himself in ways that we can understand. God knows what our actions and decisions will be, but He "changes His mind" in regard to His actions based on our actions. God's disappointment at the wickedness of humanity does not mean He was not aware it would occur.

In contradiction to open theism, Psalm 139:4, 16 state, "Before a word is on my tongue you know it completely, O Lord...All the days ordained for me were written in your book before one of them came to be." How could God predict intricate details in the Old Testament about Jesus Christ if He does not know the future? How could God in any manner guarantee our eternal salvation if He does not know what the future holds?

Ultimately, open theism fails in that it attempts to explain the unexplainable—the relationship between God's foreknowledge and mankind's free will. Just as extreme forms of Calvinism fail in that they make human beings nothing more than pre-programmed robots, so open theism fails in that it rejects God's true omniscience and sovereignty. God must be understood through faith, for "without faith it is impossible to please God" (Hebrews 11:6a). Open theism is, therefore, not scriptural. It is simply another way for finite man to try to understand an infinite God. Open theism should be rejected by followers of Christ. While open theism is an explanation for the relationship between God's foreknowledge and human free will, it is not the biblical explanation.

Question: What is Arianism?

Answer: Arianism is named for Arius, a teacher in the early 4th century A.D. One of the earliest and probably the most important item of debate among early Christians was the subject of Christ's deity. Was Jesus truly God in the flesh or was Jesus a created being? Was Jesus God or just like God? Arius held that Jesus was created by God as the first act of creation, that Jesus was the crowning glory of all creation. Arianism, then, is the view that Jesus was a created being with divine attributes, but was not divine in and of Himself.

Arianism misunderstands references to Jesus' being tired (John 4:6) and not knowing the date of His return (Matthew 24:36). Yes, it is difficult to understand how God could be tired and/or not know something, but relegating Jesus to a created being is not the answer. Jesus was fully God, but He was also fully human. Jesus did not become a human being until the incarnation. Therefore, Jesus' limitations as a human being have no impact on His divine nature or eternality.

A second major misinterpretation in Arianism is the meaning of "firstborn" (Romans 8:29; Colossians 1:15-20). Arians understand "firstborn" in these verses to mean that Jesus was "born" or "created" as the first act of creation. This is not the case. Jesus Himself proclaimed His self-existence and eternality (John 8:58; 10:30). John 1:1-2 tells us that Jesus was "in the beginning with God." In Bible times, the firstborn son of a family was held in great honor (Genesis 49:3; Exodus 11:5; 34:19; Numbers 3:40; Psalm 89:27; Jeremiah 31:9). It is in this sense that Jesus is God's firstborn. Jesus is the preeminent member of God's family. Jesus is the anointed one, the "Wonderful Counselor, Mighty God, Everlasting Father, Prince of Peace" (Isaiah 9:6).

After nearly a century of debate at various early church councils, the Christian church officially denounced Arianism as a false doctrine. Since that time, Arianism has never been accepted as a viable doctrine of the Christian faith. Arianism has not died, however. Arianism has continued throughout the centuries in varying forms. The Jehovah's Witnesses and Mormons of today hold a very Arian-like position on Christ's nature. Just as the early church did, we must denounce any and all attacks on the deity of our Lord and Savior, Jesus Christ.

Question: What is contemplative prayer?

Answer: It is important to first define "contemplative prayer." Contemplative prayer is not just "contemplating while you pray." The Bible instructs us to pray with our minds (1 Corinthians 14:15), so, clearly, prayer does involve contemplation. However, praying with your mind is not what "contemplative prayer" has come to mean. Contemplative prayer has slowly increased in practice and popularity along with the rise of the emerging church movement—a movement which embraces many unscriptural ideas and practices. Contemplative prayer is one such practice.

Contemplative prayer, also known as "centering prayer," is a meditative practice where the practitioner focuses on a word and repeats that word over and over for the duration of the exercise. While contemplative prayer is done differently in the various groups that practice it, there are similarities. Contemplative prayer involves choosing a sacred word as the symbol of your intention to consent to God's presence and action within. Contemplative prayer usually includes sitting comfortably and with eyes closed, settling briefly and silently, introducing the sacred word as the symbol of your consent to God's presence and action within. When a contemplative pray-er becomes aware of thoughts, he/she is to return ever so gently to the sacred word.

Although this might sound like an innocent exercise, this type of prayer has no scriptural support whatsoever. In fact, it is just the opposite of how prayer is defined in the Bible. "Do not be anxious about anything, but in everything, by prayer and petition, with thanksgiving, present your requests to God." (Philippians 4:6). "In that day you will no longer ask me anything. I tell you the truth, my Father will give you whatever you ask in my name. Until now you have not asked for anything in my name. Ask and you will receive, and your joy will be complete" (John 16:23-24). These verses and others clearly portray prayer as being comprehendible communication with God, not an esoteric, mystical meditation.

Contemplative prayer, by design, focuses on having a mystical experience with God. Mysticism, however, is purely subjective, and does not rely upon truth or fact. Yet the Word of God has been given to us for the very purpose of basing our faith, and our lives, on Truth (2 Timothy 3:16-17). What we know about God is based on fact; trusting in experiential knowledge over the biblical record takes a person outside of the standard that is the Bible.

Contemplative prayer is no different than the meditative exercises used in Eastern religions and New Age cults. Its most vocal supporters embrace an open spirituality among adherents from all religions, promoting the idea that salvation is gained by many paths, even though Christ Himself stated that salvation comes only through Him (John 14:6). Contemplative prayer, as practiced in the modern prayer movement, is in opposition to biblical Christianity and should definitely be avoided.

Question: What is contemplative spirituality?

Answer: Contemplative spirituality is an extremely dangerous practice for any person who desires to live a biblical, God-centered life. It is most commonly associated with the emerging church movement, which is riddled with false teachings. It is also used by many different groups that have little, if any, connection with Christianity.

In practice, contemplative spirituality is primarily centered on meditation, although not meditation with a biblical perspective. Passages such as Joshua 1:8 actually exhort us to meditate: "Do not let this Book of the Law depart from your mouth; meditate on it day and night, so that you may be careful to do everything written in it. Then you will be prosperous and successful." Notice what the focus of meditation should be—the Word of God. Contemplative spirituality-driven meditation focuses on nothing, literally. A practitioner is exhorted to completely empty his/her mind, to just "be." Supposedly, this helps one to open up to a greater spiritual experience. However, we are exhorted in Scripture to transform our minds to that of Christ's, to have His mind. Emptying our minds is contrary to such active, conscious transformation.

Contemplative spirituality also encourages the pursuit of a mystical experience with God. Mysticism is the belief that knowledge of God, spiritual truth, and ultimate reality can be gained through subjective experience. This emphasis on experiential knowledge erodes the authority of Scripture. We know God according to His Word. "All Scripture is God-breathed and is useful for teaching, rebuking, correcting and training in righteousness, so that the man of God may be thoroughly equipped for every good work" (2 Timothy 3:16-17). God's Word is complete. There is no reason to believe that God adds additional teachings or truths to His Word through mystical experiences. Instead, our faith and what we know about God is based on fact.

The website for the Center for Contemplative Spirituality sums it up well: "We come from a variety of secular and religious back-grounds and we each seek to enrich our journey through spiritual practice and study of the world's great spiritual traditions. We desire to draw closer to the loving Spirit which pervades all creation and which inspires our compassion for all beings." There is absolutely nothing biblical about such goals. Studying the world's "spiritual traditions" is an exercise in futility because any spiritual tradition other than that which exalts Christ is falsehood. The only way to draw closer to God is through the path He has ordained—Jesus Christ and the Word.

Question: What is dualism?

Answer: In theology, the concept of dualism assumes that there are two separate entities—good and evil—which are equally powerful. In "Christian" dualism, God represents the good entity and Satan represents the evil entity.

However, the truth is that even though Satan has some power, he is no equal to God Almighty, for he was created by God as an angel before he rebelled (Isaiah 14:12-15; Ezekiel 28:13-17). As the Scripture says, "You, dear children, are from God and have overcome them, because the one who is in you is greater than the one who is in the world" (1 John 4:4). According to Scripture, there is no dualism, no two opposing forces of equal power called good and evil. Good, represented by God Almighty, is the most powerful force in the universe without exception. Evil, represented by Satan, is a lesser force that is no match for good. Evil will be defeated every time in any head-to-head match with good, for God Almighty, the essence of good, is all-powerful, whereas evil, represented by Satan, is not.

Whenever any doctrine portrays good and evil as two equal opposing forces, that doctrine contradicts the scriptural position that good, represented by God Almighty, is the dominant power in the universe. Since Satan was not, and never will be, equal to God, any doctrine that says he is can be marked as a false doctrine. The fact that Satan was thrown out of heaven for trying to rise above God does not mean Satan has given up trying to be equal or superior to God, as evidenced by the basic tenets of "dualism" that have come down largely through the philosophical stem of human wisdom.

There can be no dualism existing in any corner of our universe. There is only one power that is overriding, and that power is God Almighty as revealed to us in the Bible. According to the scriptural evidence, there is only one power that is omnipotent, not two. Thus, any doctrine of dualism which contends that there are two equal powers opposing each other (good and evil) is a false doctrine.

Question: What is the JEDP Theory?

Answer: In brief, the JEDP theory states that the first five books of the Bible, Genesis, Exodus, Leviticus, Numbers, and Deuteronomy, were not written entirely by Moses, who died in 1451 B.C, but also by different authors/compliers after Moses. The theory is based on the fact that different names for God are used in different portions of the Pentateuch, and there are detectable differences in linguistic style. The letters of the JEDP theory stand for the four supposed authors: the author who uses "Jehovah" for God's name, the author who uses *Elohim* for God's name, the author of Deuteronomy, and the priestly author of Leviticus. The JEDP theory goes on to state that the different portions of the Pentateuch were likely compiled in the 4th Century B.C, possibly by Ezra.

So, why are there different names for God in books supposedly written by a single author? For example, Genesis chapter 1 uses the name *Elohim* while Genesis chapter 2 uses the name *YHWH*. Patterns like this occur quite frequently in the Pentateuch. The answer is simple. Moses used God's names to make a point. In Genesis chapter 1, God is *Elohim*, the mighty Creator God. In Genesis chapter 2, God is *Yahweh*, the personal God who created and relates to humanity. This does not point to different authors but to a single author using God's various names to emphasize a point and describe different aspects of His character.

Regarding the different styles, should we not expect an author to have a different style when he is writing history (Genesis), writing legal statutes (Exodus, Deuteronomy), and writing intricate details of the sacrificial system (Leviticus)? The JEDP theory takes the explainable differences in the Pentateuch and invents an elaborate theory that has no basis in reality or history. No J, E, D, or P document has ever been discovered. No ancient Jewish or Christian scholar has even hinted that such documents existed.

The most powerful argument against the JEDP theory is the Bible itself. Jesus, in Mark 12:26, said, "Now about the dead rising—have you not read in the book of Moses, in the account of the bush, how God said to him, 'I am the God of Abraham, the God of Isaac, and the God of Jacob'?" Therefore, Jesus says plainly that Moses wrote the account of the burning bush in Exodus 3:1-3. Luke, in Acts 3:22, comments on a passage in Deuteronomy 18:15 and credits Moses as being the author of that passage. Paul, in Romans 10:5, talks about the righteousness Moses describes in Leviticus 18:5. Paul, therefore, testifies that Moses is the author of Leviticus. So, we have

Jesus showing that Moses was the author of Exodus, Luke (in Acts) showing that Moses wrote Deuteronomy, and Paul saying that Moses was the author of Leviticus. In order for the JEDP theory to be true, Jesus, Luke, and Paul must all either be liars or be in error in their understanding of the Old Testament. Let us put our faith in Jesus and the human authors of Scripture rather than the ridiculous and baseless JEDP theory (2 Timothy 3:16-17).

Question: What is moral relativism?

Answer: Moral relativism is more easily understood in comparison to moral absolutism. Absolutism claims that morality relies on universal principles (natural law, conscience). Christian absolutists believe that God is the ultimate source of our common morality, and that it is, therefore, as unchanging as He is. Moral relativism asserts that morality is not based on any absolute standard. Rather, ethical "truths" depend on variables such as the situation, culture, one's feelings, etc.

Several things can be said of the arguments for moral relativism which demonstrate their dubious nature. First, while many of the arguments used in the attempt to support relativism might sound good at first, there is a logical contradiction inherent in all of them because they all propose the "right" moral scheme—the one we all ought to follow. But this itself is absolutism. Second, even so-called relativists reject relativism in most cases. They would not say that a murderer or rapist is free from guilt so long as he did not violate his own standards.

Relativists may argue that different values among different cultures show that morals are relative to different people. But this argument confuses the actions of individuals (what they do) with absolute standards (whether they should do it). If culture determines right and wrong, how could we have judged the Nazis? After all, they were only following their culture's morality. Only if murder is universally wrong were the Nazis wrong. The fact that they had "their morality" does not change that. Further, although many people have different practices of morality, they still share a common morality. For instance, abortionists and anti-abortionists agree that murder is wrong, but they disagree on whether abortion is murder. So, even here, absolute universal morality is shown to be true.

Some claim that changing situations make for changing morality—in different situations different acts are called for that might not be right in other situations. But there are three things by which we must judge an act: the situation, the act, and the intention. For example, we can convict someone of attempted murder (intent) even if they fail (act). So situations are part of the moral decision, for they set the context for choosing the specific moral act (the application of universal principles).

The main argument relativists appeal to is that of tolerance. They claim that telling someone their morality is wrong is intolerant, and relativism tolerates all views. But this is misleading. First of all, evil should never be tolerated. Should we tolerate a rapist's view that women are objects of gratification to be abused? Second, it is self-defeating because relativists do not tolerate intolerance or absolutism. Third, relativism cannot explain why anyone should be tolerant in the first place. The very fact that we should tolerate people (even when we disagree) is based on the absolute moral rule that we should always treat people fairly—but that is absolutism again! In fact, without universal moral principles there can be no goodness.

The fact is that all people are born with a conscience, and we all instinctively know when we have been wronged or when we have wronged others. We act as though we expect others to recognize this as well. Even as children we knew the difference between "fair" and "unfair." It takes bad philosophy to convince us that we are wrong and that moral relativism is true.

Question: What is pantheism?

Answer: Pantheism is the view that God is everything and everyone and that everyone and everything is God. Pantheism is similar to polytheism (the belief in many gods), but goes beyond polytheism to teach that everything is God. A tree is God, a rock is God, an animal is God, the sky is God, the sun is God, you are God, etc. Pantheism is the supposition behind many cults and false religions (e.g., Hinduism and Buddhism to an extent, the various unity and unification cults, and "mother nature" worshippers).

Does the Bible teach pantheism? No, it does not. What many people confuse as pantheism is the doctrine of God's omnipresence.

Psalm 139:7-8 declares, "Where can I go from your Spirit? Where can I flee from your presence? If I go up to the heavens, you are there; if I make my bed in the depths, you are there." God's omnipresence means He is present everywhere. There is no place in the universe where God is not present. This is not the same thing as pantheism. God is everywhere, but He is not everything. Yes, God is "present" inside a tree and inside a person, but that does not make that tree or person God. Pantheism is not at all a biblical belief.

The clearest biblical arguments against pantheism are the countless commands against idolatry. The Bible forbids the worship of idols, angels, celestial objects, items in nature, etc. If pantheism were true, it would not be wrong to worship such an object, because that object would, in fact, be God. If pantheism were true, worshipping a rock or an animal would have just as much validity as worshipping God as an invisible and spiritual being. The Bible's clear and consistent denunciation of idolatry is a conclusive argument against pantheism.

Question: What are Pelagianism and Semi-Pelagianism?

Answer: Pelagius was a monk who lived in the late 300s and early 400s A.D. Pelagius taught that human beings were born innocent, without the stain of original or inherited sin. He believed that God created every human soul directly and therefore every human soul was originally free from sin. Pelagius believed that Adam's sin did not affect future generations of humanity. This view became known as Pelagianism.

Pelagianism contradicts many Scriptures and scriptural principles. First, the Bible tells us that we are sinful from the moment of conception (Psalm 51:5). Further, the Bible teaches that all human beings die as a result of sin (Ezekiel 18:20; Romans 6:23). While Pelagianism says that human beings are not born with a natural inclination towards sin, the Bible says the opposite (Romans 3:10-18). Romans 5:12 clearly states that Adam's sin is the reason sin infects the rest of humanity. Anyone who has raised children can attest to the fact that infants must be taught to behave; they do not have to be taught how to sin. Pelagianism, therefore, is clearly unscriptural and should be rejected.

Semi-Pelagianism essentially teaches that humanity is tainted by sin, but not to the extent that we cannot cooperate with God's grace on our own. Semi-Pelagianism is, in essence, partial depravity as opposed to total depravity. The same Scripture passages that refute Pelagianism will also refute Semi-Pelagianism. Romans 3:10-18 definitely does not describe humanity as only being partially tainted by sin. The Bible clearly teaches that without God "drawing" us, we are incapable of cooperating with God's grace. "No one can come to me unless the Father who sent me draws him" (John 6:44). Like Pelagianism, Semi-Pelagianism is unbiblical and should be rejected.

Question: What is polytheism?

Answer: Polytheism is the belief that there are many gods. Breaking the word down, "poly" comes from the Greek word for "many," and "theism" from the Greek word for "God." Polytheism has perhaps been the dominant theistic view in human history. The best-known example of polytheism in ancient times is Greek/Roman mythology (Zeus, Apollo, Aphrodite, Poseidon, etc.). The clearest modern example of polytheism is Hinduism, which has over 300 million gods. Although Hinduism is, in essence, pantheistic, it does hold to beliefs in many gods. It is interesting to note that even in polytheistic religions, one god usually reigns supreme over the other gods, e.g., Zeus in Greek/Roman mythology and Brahman in Hinduism.

Some argue that the Bible teaches polytheism in the Old Testament. Admittedly, several passages refer to "gods" in the plural (Exodus 20:3; Deuteronomy 10:17; 13:2; Psalm 82:6; Daniel 2:47). Ancient Israel fully understood that there was only one true God, but they often did not live as if they believed that to be true, continually falling into idolatry and the worship of foreign gods. So what are we to make of these and other passages that speak of multiple gods? It is important to note that the Hebrew word *elohim* was used to refer to the one true God and to false gods/idols. It functioned almost identically to the English word "God."

Describing something as a "god" does not mean you believe it to be a divine being. The vast majority of Old Testament Scriptures which speak of gods are speaking of false gods, those who claim to be gods but are not. This concept is summarized in 2 Kings 19:18,

"They have thrown their gods into the fire and destroyed them, for they were not gods but only wood and stone, fashioned by men's hands." Notice Psalm 82:6, "I said, 'You are "gods" you are all sons of the Most High.' But you will die like mere men; you will fall like every other ruler."

The Bible clearly teaches against polytheism. Deuteronomy 6:4 tells us, "Hear, O Israel: The LORD our God, the LORD is one." Psalm 96:5 declares, "For all the gods of the nations are idols, but the LORD made the heavens." James 2:19 says, "You believe that there is one God. Good! Even the demons believe that—and shudder." There is only one God. There are false gods and those who pretend to be gods, but there is only one God.

Question: What does the Bible say about karma?

Answer: Karma is a theological concept found in the Buddhist and Hindu religions. It is the idea that how you live your life will determine the quality of life you will have after reincarnation. If you are unselfish, kind, and holy during this lifetime, you will be rewarded by being reincarnated (reborn into a new earthly body) into a pleasant life. However, if you live a life of selfishness and evil, you will be reincarnated into a less-than-pleasant lifestyle. In other words, you reap in the next life what you sow in this one. Karma is based on the theological belief in reincarnation. The Bible rejects the idea of reincarnation; therefore, it does not support the idea of karma.

Hebrews 9:27 states, "Just as man is destined to die once, and after that to face judgment..." This Bible verse makes clear two important points which, for Christians, negate the possibility of reincarnation and karma. First, it states that we are "destined to die once," meaning that humans are only born once and only die once. There is no endless cycle of life and death and rebirth, an idea inherent in the reincarnation theory. Second, it states that after death we face judgment, meaning that there is no second chance, like there is in reincarnation and karma, to live a better life. You get one shot at life and living it according to God's plan, and that is it.

The Bible talks a lot about reaping and sowing. Job 4:8 says, "As I have observed, those who plow evil and those who sow trouble reap it." Psalm 126:5 says, "Those who sow in tears will reap with songs of joy." Luke 12:24 says, "Consider the ravens: They do not sow or reap, they have no storeroom or barn; yet God feeds them. And how much more valuable you are than birds!" In each of these instances, as well as all the other references to reaping and sowing, the act of receiving the rewards of your actions takes place in this life, not in some future life. It is a present-day activity, and the references make it clear that the fruit you reap will be commensurate with the actions you have performed. In addition, the sowing you perform in this life will affect your reward or punishment in the afterlife.

This afterlife is not a rebirth or a reincarnation into another body here on earth. It is either eternal suffering in hell (Matthew 25:46) or eternal life in heaven with Jesus, who died so that we might live eternally with Him. This should be the focus of our life on earth. The apostle Paul wrote in Galatians 6:8-9, "The one who sows to please his sinful nature, from that nature will reap destruction; the one who sows to please the Spirit, from the Spirit will reap eternal life. Let us not become weary in doing good, for at the proper time we will reap a harvest if we do not give up."

Finally, we must always remember that it was Jesus whose death on the cross resulted in the reaping of eternal life for us, and that it is faith in Jesus that gives us this eternal life. Ephesians 2:8-9 tells us, "For it is by grace you have been saved, through faith—and this not from yourselves, it is the gift of God—not by works, so that no one can boast." Therefore, we see that the concept of reincarnation and karma is incompatible with what the Bible teaches about life, death, and the sowing and reaping of eternal life.

Question: What does the Bible say about the prosperity gospel?

Answer: In the prosperity gospel, also known as the "Word of Faith," the believer is told to use God, whereas the truth of biblical Christianity is just the opposite—God uses the believer. Word of Faith or prosperity theology sees the Holy Spirit as a power to be put to use for whatever the believer wills. The Bible teaches that the Holy Spirit is a Person who enables the believer to do God's will. The prosperity gospel movement closely resembles some of the destructive greed sects that infiltrated the early church. Paul and the other apostles were not accommodating to or conciliatory with the false teachers who propagated such heresy. They identified them as dangerous false teachers and urged Christians to avoid them.

Paul warned Timothy about such men in 1 Timothy 6:5, 9-11. These men of "corrupt mind" supposed godliness was a means of gain and their desire for riches was a trap that brought about them "into ruin and destruction" (v. 9). The pursuit of wealth is a dangerous path for Christians and one which God warns about: "For the love of money is a root of all kinds of evil. Some people, eager for money, have wandered from the faith and pierced themselves with many griefs" (v. 10). If riches were a reasonable goal for the godly, Jesus would have pursued it. But He did not, preferring instead to have no place to lay His head (Matthew 8:20) and teaching His disciples to do the same. It should also be remembered that the only disciple concerned with wealth was Judas.

Paul said covetousness is idolatry (Ephesians 5:5) and instructed the Ephesians to avoid anyone who brought a message of immorality or covetousness (Ephesians 5:6-7). Prosperity teaching prohibits God from working on His own, meaning that God is not Lord of all because He cannot work until we release Him to do so. Faith, according to the Word of Faith doctrine, is not submissive trust in God; faith is a formula by which we manipulate the spiritual laws that prosperity teachers believe govern the universe. As the name "Word of Faith" implies, this movement teaches that faith is a matter of what we say more than who we trust or what truths we embrace and affirm in our hearts.

A favorite term in the Word of Faith movement is "positive confession." This refers to the teaching that words themselves have creative power. What you say, Word of Faith teachers claim, determines everything that happens to you. Your confessions, especially the favors you demand of God, must all be stated positively and without wavering. Then God is required to answer (as though man could *require* anything of God!). Thus, God's ability to bless us supposedly hangs on our faith. James 4:13-16 clearly contradicts this teaching: "Now listen, you who say, 'Today or tomorrow we will go to this or that city, spend a year there, carry on business and make money.' Why, you do not even know what will happen tomorrow. What is your life? You are a mist that appears for a little while and then vanishes." Far from speaking things into existence in the future, we do not even know what tomorrow will bring or even whether we will be alive.

Instead of stressing the importance of wealth, the Bible warns against pursuing it. Believers, especially leaders in the church (1 Timothy 3:3), are to be free from the love of money (Hebrews 13:5). The love of money leads to all kinds of evil (1 Timothy 6:10). Jesus warned, "Watch out! Be on your guard against all kinds of greed; a man's life does not consist in the abundance of his possessions" (Luke 12:15). In sharp contrast to the Word of Faith emphasis on gaining money and possessions in this life, Jesus said, "Do not store up for yourselves treasures on earth, where moth and rust destroy, and where thieves break in and steal" (Matthew 6:19). The irreconcilable contradictions between prosperity teaching and the gospel of our Lord Jesus Christ is best summed up in the words of Jesus in Matthew 6:24, "You cannot serve both God and money."

Question: What is the Jesus Seminar?

Answer: The "Jesus Seminar" was begun by New Testament "scholar" Robert Funk in the 1970s. It was Funk's desire to rediscover the "historical Jesus" that was hidden, he believed, behind almost 2000 years of Christian traditions, myths, and legends. The Jesus Seminar was created to examine the biblical gospels and other early Christian literature to discover who Jesus truly was and what He truly said. The Jesus Seminar was (and still is) comprised almost entirely of individuals who deny the inspiration, authority, and inerrancy of the Bible. The agenda of the Jesus Seminar is not to discover who the historical Jesus was. Rather, the purpose of the Jesus Seminar is to attack what the Bible clearly says about who Jesus is and what He taught.

The crowning publication of the Jesus Seminar is a work that goes through the four biblical gospels and the gospel of Thomas and proceeds to determine what Jesus truly said and taught. It divides Jesus' words from the gospels into categories based on how likely it is that Jesus truly said them. Words in red indicate words that Jesus most likely said. Words in pink represent words that Jesus possibly said. Words in grey indicate words that Jesus likely did not say, but are close to what He might have said. Words in black represent words that

Jesus definitely did not say. It is interesting to note that in this work from the Jesus Seminar there are more words in black than in red, pink, and grey combined. Almost the entire gospel of John is in black. It is also interesting that the gospel of Thomas is given a significantly higher percentage of red and pink words than the biblical gospels. It is absolutely ridiculous, even offensive, to think that a group of "scholars" today can more accurately determine what Jesus did and did not say than the authors of the gospels, who wrote in the same century in which Jesus lived, taught, died, and was resurrected.

The "scholars" of the Jesus Seminar do not believe in the deity of Christ, the resurrection of Christ, the miracles of Christ, or the substitutionary atonement death of Christ. Perhaps most significantly, they deny that the Holy Spirit is the author of all Scripture (2 Timothy 3:16-17), having moved the minds and hands of all the writers (2 Peter 1:20-21). Since the Jesus Seminar does not believe these Christian doctrines, they relegate anything that Jesus says in support of them as "black." Essentially, the agenda of the Jesus Seminar is, "I do not believe Jesus is God, so I am going to remove anything that records Jesus saying or teaching that He is God from the gospels." The claim that the purpose of the Jesus Seminar is to "discover the historical Jesus" is false and misleading. The true purpose of the Jesus Seminar is to promote the Jesus that the Jesus Seminar believes in instead of the Jesus of the Bible.

Question: What is the synoptic problem?

Answer: When the first three gospels are compared—Matthew, Mark, and Luke—it is unmistakable that the accounts are very similar to one another in content and expression. As a result, Matthew, Mark, and Luke are referred to as the "synoptic gospels." The word "synoptic" basically means "to see together with a common view." The many similarities between the synoptic gospels have led some to wonder if the gospel authors had a common source, another written account of Christ's birth, life, ministry, death, and resurrection from which they obtained the material for their gospels. Some argue that Matthew, Mark, and Luke are so similar that they must have used each other's gospels, or another common source. This supposed "source" has been given the title "Q" from the German word *quelle* which means "source."

Is there any evidence for a "Q" document? No, there is not. No portion or fragment of a "Q" document has ever been discovered. None of the early church fathers ever mentioned a gospel "source" in his writings. "Q" is the invention of liberal "scholars" who deny the inspiration of the Bible. They believe the Bible to be nothing more than a work of literature, subject to the same criticism given to other works of literature. Again, there is no evidence whatsoever for a "Q" document—biblically, theologically, or historically.

If Matthew, Mark, and Luke did not use a "Q" document, why are their Gospels so similar? There are several possible explanations. It is possible that whichever gospel was written first (likely Mark), the other gospel writers had access to it. There is absolutely no problem with the idea that Matthew and/or Luke copied some text from Mark's gospel and used it in their gospels. Perhaps Luke had access to Mark and Matthew and used texts from both of them in his own gospel. Luke 1:1-4 tells us, "Many have undertaken to draw up an account of the things that have been fulfilled among us, just as they were handed down to us by those who from the first were eyewitnesses and servants of the word. Therefore, since I myself have carefully investigated everything from the beginning, it seemed good also to me to write an orderly account for you, most excellent Theophilus, so that you may know the certainty of the things you have been taught."

Ultimately, the explanation as to why the Synoptic Gospels are so similar is that they are all inspired by the same Holy Spirit, and are all written by people who witnessed, or were told about, the same events. The gospel of Matthew was written by Matthew the apostle, one of the twelve who followed Jesus and were commissioned by Him. The gospel of Mark was written by John Mark, a close associate of the apostle Peter, another one of the twelve. The gospel of Luke was written by Luke, a close associate of the apostle Paul. Why would we not expect their accounts to be very similar to one another? Each of the gospels is ultimately inspired by the Holy Spirit (2 Timothy 3:16-17; 2 Peter 1:20-21). Therefore, we should expect coherence and unity.

Chapter 21

QUESTIONS ABOUT

LIFE DECISIONS

CONTENTS

Why should I not commit suicide? 554

What does the Bible say about a Christian going into debt? 555

Should Christians go to doctors? 557

Should a Christian exercise? 558

What does the Bible say about lawsuits/suing? 559

What does the Bible say about a Christian serving in the military? 560

What does the Bible say about how to find purpose in life? 562

Should a Christian go into business with an unbeliever? 563

What does the Bible say about a Christian staying single? 564

What does the Bible say about a Christian having plastic/cosmetic
 surgery? 565

Should a Christian get insurance? 567

Should a Christian take anti-depressants or other mental health
 medicines? 568

Should a Christian see a psychologist/psychiatrist? 569

What is the Christian view of retirement? 570

Was Jesus a vegetarian? Should a Christian be a vegetarian? 572

Should a Christian play video games? 573

Does God expect Christians to vote? 576

What does the Bible say about women working outside the home? 577

Why do people reject Jesus as their Savior? 578

Question: Why should I not commit suicide?

Answer: Our hearts go out to those who have thoughts of ending their own lives through suicide. If that is you right now, it may speak of many emotions, such as feelings of hopelessness and despair. You may feel like you are in the deepest pit, and you doubt there is any hope of things getting better. No one seems to care or understand where you are coming from. Life just is not worth living...or is it?

If you will take a few moments to consider letting God truly be God in your life right now, He will prove how big He really is, "for nothing is impossible with God" (Luke 1:37). Perhaps scars from past hurts have resulted in an overwhelming sense of rejection or abandonment. That may lead to self-pity, anger, bitterness, vengeful thoughts, or unhealthy fears that have caused problems in some of your most important relationships.

Why should you not commit suicide? Friend, no matter how bad things are in your life, there is a God of love who is waiting for you to let Him guide you through your tunnel of despair and out into His marvelous light. He is your sure hope. His name is Jesus.

This Jesus, the sinless Son of God, identifies with you in your time of rejection and humiliation. The prophet Isaiah wrote of Him in Isaiah 53:2-6, describing Him as a man who was "despised and rejected" by everyone. His life was full of sorrow and suffering. But the sorrows He bore were not His own; they were ours. He was pierced, wounded, and crushed, all because of our sin. Because of His suffering, our lives can be redeemed and made whole.

Friend, Jesus Christ endured all this so that you might have all your sins forgiven. Whatever weight of guilt you carry, know that He will forgive you if you humbly receive Him as your Savior. "...call upon me in the day of trouble; I will deliver you¼" (Psalm 50:15). Nothing you have ever done is too bad for Jesus to forgive. Some of His choicest servants committed gross sins like murder (Moses), murder and adultery (King David), and physical and emotional abuse (the apostle Paul). Yet they found forgiveness and a new abundant life in the Lord. "Therefore, if anyone is in Christ, he is a new creation; the old has gone, the new has come!" (2 Corinthians 5:17).

Why should you not commit suicide? Friend, God stands ready to repair what is "broken," namely, the life you have now, the life you want to end by suicide. In Isaiah 61:1-3, the prophet wrote, "The LORD has anointed me to preach good news to the poor. He has sent me to bind up the brokenhearted, to proclaim freedom for the captives and release from darkness for the prisoners, to proclaim the year of the Lord's favor…to comfort all who mourn, and provide for those who grieve…to bestow on them a crown of beauty instead of ashes, the oil of gladness instead of mourning, and a garment of praise instead of a spirit of despair."

Come to Jesus, and let Him restore your joy and usefulness as you trust Him to begin a new work in your life. He promises to restore the joy you have lost and give you a new spirit to sustain you. Your broken heart is precious to Him: "The sacrifices of God are a broken spirit; a broken and contrite heart, O God, you will not despise" (Psalm 51:12, 15-17).

Will you accept the Lord as your Savior and Shepherd? He will guide your thoughts and steps—one day at a time—through His Word, the Bible. "I will instruct you and teach you in the way you should go; I will counsel you and watch over you" (Psalm 32:8). "He will be the sure foundation for your times, a rich store of salvation and wisdom and knowledge; the fear of the LORD is the key to this treasure" (Isaiah 33:6). In Christ, you will still have struggles, but you will now have hope. He is "a friend who sticks closer than a brother" (Proverbs 18:24). May the grace of the Lord Jesus be with you in your hour of decision.

If you desire to trust Jesus Christ as your Savior, speak these words in your heart to God: "God, I need you in my life. Please forgive me for all that I have done. I place my faith in Jesus Christ and believe that He is my Savior. Please cleanse me, heal me, and restore my joy in life. Thank You for Your love for me and for Jesus' death on my behalf."

Have you made a decision to receive Jesus Christ as your personal Savior because of what you have read here? If so, please send us an email at questions@gotquestions.org.

Question: What does the Bible say about a Christian going into debt?

Answer: Paul's charge to us in Romans 13:8 to owe nothing but love is a powerful reminder of God's distaste for all forms of debt that are not being paid in a timely manner (see also Psalm 37:21). At the same time, the Bible does not explicitly command against all forms of debt. The Bible warns against debt, and extols the virtue of not going into debt, but does not forbid debt. The Bible has harsh words of condemnation for lenders who abuse those who are bound to them in debt, but it does not condemn the debtor.

Some people question the charging of any interest on loans, but several times in the Bible we see that a fair interest rate is expected to be received on borrowed money (Proverbs 28:8; Matthew 25:27). In ancient Israel the Law did prohibit charging interest on one category of loans—those made to the poor (Leviticus 25:35-38). This law had many social, financial, and spiritual implications, but two are especially worth mentioning. First, the law genuinely helped the poor by not making their situation worse. It was bad enough to have fallen into poverty, and it could be humiliating to have to seek assistance. But if, in addition to repaying the loan, a poor person had to make crushing interest payments, the obligation would be more hurtful than helpful.

Second, the law taught an important spiritual lesson. For a lender to forego interest on a loan to a poor person would be an act of mercy. He would be losing the use of that money while it was loaned out. Yet that would be a tangible way of expressing gratitude to God for His mercy in not charging His people "interest" for the grace He has extended to them. Just as God had mercifully brought the Israelites out of Egypt when they were nothing but penniless slaves and had given them a land of their own (Leviticus 25:38), so He expected them to express similar kindness to their own poor citizens.

Christians are in a parallel situation. The life, death, and resurrection of Jesus has paid our sin debt to God. Now, as we have opportunity, we can help others in need, particularly fellow believers, with loans that do not escalate their troubles. Jesus even gave a parable along these lines about two creditors and their attitude toward forgiveness (Matthew 18:23-35).

The Bible neither expressly forbids nor condones the borrowing of money. The wisdom of the Bible teaches us that it is usually not a good idea to go into debt. Debt essentially makes us a slave to the one who provides the loan. At the same time, in some situations going into debt is a "necessary evil." As long as money is being handled wisely and the debt payments are manageable, a Christian can take on the burden of financial debt if it is absolutely necessary.

Question: Should Christians go to doctors?

Answer: There are some Christians who believe that seeking medical attention is demonstrating a lack of faith in God. In the Word-Faith movement, consulting a doctor is often considered a lack of faith that will actually prevent God from healing you. In groups such as Christian Science, seeking the help of physicians is sometimes viewed as a barrier to using the spiritual energy God has given us to heal ourselves. The logic of these viewpoints is sorely lacking. If your car is damaged, do you take it to a mechanic or wait for God to perform a miracle and heal your car? If the plumbing in your house bursts, do you wait for God to plug the leak, or do you call a plumber? God is just as capable of repairing a car or fixing the plumbing as He is of healing our bodies. The fact that God can and does perform miracles of healing does not mean we should always expect a miracle instead of seeking the help of individuals who possess the knowledge and skill to assist us.

Physicians are referred to about a dozen times in the Bible. The only verse that could be taken out of context to teach that one should not go to physicians would be 2 Chronicles 16:12, "In the thirty-ninth year of his reign Asa was afflicted with a disease in his feet. Though his disease was severe, even in his illness he did not seek help from the LORD, but only from the physicians." The issue was not that Asa consulted physicians, but that "he did not seek help from the LORD." Even when visiting a doctor, our ultimate faith is to be in God, not the doctor.

There are many verses that speak of using "medical treatments" such as applying bandages (Isaiah 1:6), oil (James 5:14), oil and wine (Luke 10:34), leaves (Ezekiel 47:12), wine (1 Timothy 5:23), and salves, particularly the "balm of Gilead" (Jeremiah 8:22). Also, Luke, the author of Acts and the Gospel of Luke, is referred to by Paul as "the beloved physician" (Colossians 4:14).

Mark 5:25-30 relates the story of a woman who had trouble with continual bleeding, a problem that physicians could not heal even though she had been to many of them and had spent all of her money. Coming to Jesus, she thought that if she but touched the hem of His garment, she would be healed; she did touch His hem, and she was healed. Jesus, in answering the Pharisees as to why He spent time with sinners, said to them, "Those who are well have no need of a physician, but those who are sick" (Matthew 9:12). From these verses one might sift out the following principles:

1. Physicians are not God and should not be viewed as such. They can sometimes help, but there will be other times when all they will accomplish is the removal of money.
2. Seeking physicians and using "earthly" remedies are not condemned in Scripture. In fact, medical treatments are viewed favorably.
3. God's intervention in any physical difficulty should be sought (James 4:2; 5:13). He does not promise that He will answer the way we will always want (Isaiah 55:8-9), but we have the assurance that all He does will be done in love and thus in our best interest (Psalm 145:8-9).

So, should Christians go to doctors? God created us as intelligent beings and gave us the ability to create medicines and learn how to repair our bodies. There is nothing wrong with applying this knowledge and ability towards physical healing. Doctors can be viewed as God's gift to us, a means through which God brings healing and recovery. At the same time, our ultimate faith and trust is to be in God, not in doctors or medicine. As with all difficult decisions, we should seek God who promises to give us wisdom when we ask for it (James 1:5).

Question: Should a Christian exercise?

Answer: As with many things in life, there are extremes in the area of exercise. Some people focus entirely on spirituality, to the neglect of their physical bodies. Others focus so much attention on the form and shape of their physical bodies that they neglect spiritual growth and maturity. Neither of these indicates a biblical balance. First Timothy 4:8 informs us, "For physical training is of some value, but godliness has value for all things, holding promise for both the present life and the life to come." Notice that the verse does not negate the need for exercise. Rather, it says that exercise is valuable, but it prioritizes exercise correctly by saying that godliness is of greater value.

The apostle Paul also mentions physical training in illustrating spiritual truth in 1 Corinthians 9:24-27. He equates the Christian life to a race we run to "get the prize." But the prize we seek is an eternal crown that will not tarnish or fade. In 2 Timothy 2:5, Paul says, "Similarly, if anyone competes as an athlete, he does not receive the victor's crown unless he competes according to the rules." Paul uses an athletic analogy again in 2 Timothy 4:7: "I have fought the good fight, I have finished the race, I have kept the faith." While the focus of these Scriptures is not physical exercise, the fact that Paul uses athletic terminology to teach us spiritual truths indicates that Paul viewed physical exercise, and even competition, in a positive light. We are both physical and spiritual beings. While the spiritual aspect of our being is, biblically speaking, more important, we are to neglect neither the spiritual or physical aspects of our health.

So, clearly, there is nothing wrong with a Christian exercising. In fact, the Bible is clear that we are to take good care of our bodies (1 Corinthians 6:19-20). At the same time, the Bible warns against vanity (1 Samuel 16:7; Proverbs 31:30; 1 Peter 3:3-4). Our goal in exercise should not be to improve the quality of our bodies so that other people will notice and admire us. Rather, the goal of exercising should be to improve our physical health so we will possess more physical energy that we can devote to spiritual goals.

Question: What does the Bible say about lawsuits/suing?

Answer: The apostle Paul instructed the Corinthian believers to not go to court against one another (1 Corinthians 6:1-8). For Christians not to forgive each other and reconcile their own differences is to demonstrate spiritual defeat. Why would someone want to become a Christian if Christians have just as many problems and are just as incapable of solving them? However, there are some instances when a lawsuit might be the proper course of action. If the biblical pattern for reconciliation has been followed (Matthew 18:15-17) and the offending party is still in the wrong, in some instances a lawsuit might be justified. This should only be done after much prayer for wisdom (James 1:5) and consultation with spiritual leadership.

The whole context of 1 Corinthians 6:1-6 deals with disputes in the church, but Paul does reference the court system when he speaks of judgments concerning things pertaining to this life. Paul means that the court system exists for matters of this life that are outside the church. Church problems should not be taken to the court system, but should be judged within the church.

Acts chapters 21–22 talk about Paul being arrested and wrongfully accused of a crime he did not commit. The Romans arrested him and "the commander brought Paul inside and ordered him lashed with whips to make him confess his crime. He wanted to find out why the crowd had become so furious. As they tied Paul down to lash him, Paul said to the officer standing there, 'Is it legal for you to whip a Roman citizen who hasn't even been tried?'" Paul used the Roman law and his citizenship to protect himself. There is nothing wrong with using the court system as long as it is done with a right motive and a pure heart.

Paul further declares, "Actually, then, it is already a defeat for you, that you have lawsuits with one another. Why not rather be wronged? Why not rather be defrauded?" (1 Corinthians 6:7). The thing Paul is concerned with here is the testimony of the believer. It would be far better for us to be taken advantage of, or even abused, than it would be for us to push a person even further away from Christ by taking him/her to court. Which is more important—a legal battle or the battle for a person's eternal soul?

In summary, should Christians take each other to court over church matters? Absolutely not! Should Christians take each other to court over civil matters? If it can in any way be avoided, no. Should Christians take non-Christians to court over civil matters? Again, if it can be avoided, no. However, in some instances, such as the protection of our own rights (as in the example of the apostle Paul), it may be appropriate to pursue a legal solution.

Question: What does the Bible say about a Christian serving in the military?

Answer: The Bible contains plenty of information about serving in the military. While much of the Bible's references to the military in the

Bible are only analogies, several verses directly relate to this question. The Bible does not specifically state whether or not someone should serve in the military. At the same time, Christians can rest assured that being a soldier is highly respected throughout the Scriptures and know that such service is consistent with a biblical worldview.

The first example of military service is found in the Old Testament (Genesis 14), when Abraham's nephew Lot was kidnapped by Chedorlaomer, king of Elam, and his allies. Abraham rallied to Lot's aid by gathering 318 trained men of his household and defeating the Elamites. Here we see armed forces engaged in a noble task—rescuing and protecting the innocent.

Late in its history, the nation of Israel developed a standing army. The sense that God was the Divine Warrior and would protect His people regardless of their military strength may have been a reason why Israel was slow to develop an army. The development of a regular standing army in Israel came only after a strong, centralized political system had been developed by Saul, David, and Solomon. Saul was the first to form a permanent army (1 Samuel 13:2; 24:2; 26:2).

What Saul began, David continued. He increased the army, brought in hired troops from other regions who were loyal to him alone (2 Samuel 15:19-22) and turned over the direct leadership of his armies to a commander-in-chief, Joab. Under David, Israel also became more aggressive in its offensive military policies, absorbing neighboring states like Ammon (2 Samuel 11:1; 1 Chronicles 20:1-3). David established a system of rotating troops with twelve groups of 24,000 men serving one month of the year (1 Chronicles 27). Although Solomon's reign was peaceful, he further expanded the army, adding chariots and horsemen (1 Kings 10:26). The standing army continued (though divided along with the kingdom after the death of Solomon) until 586 B.C, when Israel (Judah) ceased to exist as a political entity.

In the New Testament, Jesus marveled when a Roman centurion (an officer in charge of one hundred soldiers) approached Him. The centurion's response to Jesus indicated his clear understanding of authority, as well as his faith in Jesus (Matthew 8:5-13). Jesus did not denounce his career. Many centurions mentioned in the New Testament are praised as Christians, God-fearers, and men of good character (Matthew 8:5; 27:54; Mark 15:39-45; Luke 7:2; 23:47; Acts 10:1; 21:32; 28:16).

The places and the titles may have changed, but our armed forces should be just as valued as the centurions of the Bible. The position of soldier was highly respected. For example, Paul describes Epaphroditus, a fellow Christian, as a "fellow soldier" (Philippians 2:25). The Bible also uses military terms to describe being strong in the Lord by putting on the whole armor of God (Ephesians 6:10-20), including the tools of the soldier—helmet, shield, and sword.

Yes, the Bible does address serving in the military, directly and indirectly. The Christian men and women who serve their country with character, dignity, and honor can rest assured that the civic duty they perform is condoned and respected by our sovereign God. Those who honorably serve in the military deserve our respect and gratitude.

Question: What does the Bible say about how to find purpose in life?

Answer: The Bible is very clear as to what our purpose in life should be. Men in both the Old and New Testaments sought for and discovered life's purpose. Solomon, the wisest man who ever lived, discovered the futility of life when it is lived only for this world. He gives these concluding remarks in the book of Ecclesiastes: "Here is the conclusion of the matter: Fear God and keep his commandments, for this is the whole duty of man. For God will bring every deed into judgment, including every hidden thing, whether it is good or evil" (Ecclesiastes 12:13-14). Solomon says that life is all about honoring God with our thoughts and lives and thus keeping His commandments, for one day we will stand before Him in judgment. Part of our purpose in life is to fear God and obey Him.

Another part of our purpose is to see life on this earth in perspective. Unlike those whose focus is on this life, King David looked for His satisfaction in the time to come. He said, "And I—in righteousness I will see your face; when I awake, I will be satisfied with seeing your likeness" (Psalm 17:15). To David, full satisfaction would come on the day when he awoke (in the next life) both beholding God's face (fellowship with Him) and being like Him (1 John 3:2).

In Psalm 73, Asaph talks about how he was tempted to envy the wicked who seemed to have no cares and built their fortunes upon the backs of those they took advantage of, but then he considered their ultimate end. In contrast to what they sought after, he states in verse 25 what mattered to him: "Whom have I in heaven but you? And earth has nothing I desire besides you" (verse 25). To Asaph, a relationship with God mattered above all else in life. Without that relationship, life has no real purpose.

The apostle Paul talked about all he had achieved religiously before being confronted by the risen Christ, and he concluded that all of it was like a pile of manure compared to the excellence of knowing Christ Jesus. In Philippians 3:9-10, Paul says that he wants nothing more than to know Christ and "be found in Him," to have His righteousness and to live by faith in Him, even if it meant suffering and dying. Paul's purpose was knowing Christ, having a righteousness obtained through faith in Him, and living in fellowship with Him, even when that brought on suffering (2 Timothy 3:12). Ultimately, he looked for the time when he would be a part of the "resurrection from the dead."

Our purpose in life, as God originally created man, is 1) glorify God and enjoy fellowship with Him, 2) have good relationships with others, 3) work, and 4) have dominion over the earth. But with man's fall into sin, fellowship with God is broken, relationships with others are strained, work seems to always be frustrating, and man struggles to maintain any semblance of dominion over nature. Only by restoring fellowship with God, through faith in Jesus Christ, can purpose in life be rediscovered.

The purpose of man is to glorify God and enjoy Him forever. We glorify God by fearing and obeying Him, keeping our eyes on our future home in heaven, and knowing Him intimately. We enjoy God by following His purpose for our lives, which enables us to experience true and lasting joy—the abundant life that He desires for us.

Question: Should a Christian go into business with an unbeliever?

Answer: The question of whether a Christian should go into business with an unbeliever is a common one. The most often-quoted

Scripture is "Do not be yoked together with unbelievers. For what do righteousness and wickedness have in common? Or what fellowship can light have with darkness?" (2 Corinthians 6:14). Many times, this verse is taken to be a prohibition against Christians marrying non-Christians. Marriage would definitely apply here, but there is nothing in the context to limit it to marriage. All types of "unequal yokes" are forbidden—marriages, intimate friendships, and, in many instances, business partnerships.

The command implies that a great difference exists between a believer and an unbeliever. Generally speaking, the motivations, goals, and methods of a Christian are incompatible with those of an unbeliever. Faith changes the character of a person. A Christian's highest ambition in life is to glorify the Lord Jesus and please Him in all things; an unbeliever is, at best, indifferent to such goals. If a Christian's methods and goals in business are identical to the methods and goals of an unbeliever, the Christian very likely needs to reevaluate and reconsider his/her priorities.

Second Corinthians 6:14 goes on to ask, "What fellowship can light have with darkness?" People are said to be "in fellowship" when they share something. Business partners are united in such a way that they must share things—what belongs to one also belongs to the other. This is precisely what is meant by "fellowship." With these principles in mind, it is best to avoid uniting with unbelievers in business. If a Christian is truly seeking to honor the Lord through the business, conflict with the unbelieving business partner is unavoidable. "Can two walk together, except they be agreed?" (Amos 3:3 KJV).

Question: What does the Bible say about a Christian staying single?

Answer: The question of a Christian staying single and what the Bible says about believers never marrying is often misunderstood. Paul tells us in 1 Corinthians 7:7-8: "I wish that all men were as I am. But each man has his own gift from God; one has this gift, another has that. Now to the unmarried and the widows I say: It is good for them to stay unmarried, as I am." Notice that he says some have the gift of singleness and some the gift of marriage. Although it seems that nearly everyone marries, it is not necessarily God's will for everyone.

Paul, for example, did not have to worry about the extra problems and stresses that come with marriage and/or family. He devoted his entire life to spreading the Word of God. He would not have been such a useful messenger if he had been married.

On the other hand, some people do better as a team, serving God as a couple and a family. Both kinds of people are equally important. It is not a sin to remain single, even for your entire life. The most important thing in life is not finding a mate and having children, but serving God. We should educate ourselves on the Word of God by reading our Bibles and praying. If we ask God to reveal Himself to us, He will respond (Matthew 7:7), and if we ask Him to use us to fulfill His good works, He will do that as well. "Do not conform any longer to the pattern of this world, but be transformed by the renewing of your mind. Then you will be able to test and approve what God's will is—his good, pleasing and perfect will" (Romans 12:2).

Singleness should not be viewed as a curse or an indication that there is "something wrong" with the single man or woman. While most people marry, and while the Bible seems to indicate that it is God's will for most people to marry, a single Christian is in no sense a "second class" Christian. As 1 Corinthians 7 indicates, singleness is, if anything, a higher calling. As with everything else in life, we should ask God for wisdom (James 1:5) concerning marriage. Following God's plan, whether that be marriage or singleness, will result in the productivity and joy that God desires for us.

Question: What does the Bible say about a Christian having plastic/cosmetic surgery?

Answer: The Bible does not specifically address a Christian having plastic surgery or cosmetic surgery. There is nothing in the Bible to indicate that plastic surgery is, in and of itself, wrong. However, there are several things that one needs to consider before deciding whether or not to undergo these procedures. Altering one's body is unnatural, and there are always risks of potential side effects, both physical and psychological. No one should allow himself to be put "under the knife" without first thoroughly researching all alternatives, risks, and side effects involved with the surgery. A person also needs to fully identify his or her motivation for desiring the surgery. For many with physical deformities—whether genetic or acquired—it is natural to want to fit into society and feel "normal." There are also cases of slight abnormalities that would cause someone to feel very uncomfortable with himself, such as a very large or misshapen nose. But many, if not most, plastic surgeries are attempts to meet emotional voids in physical ways, to attract attention, or to seek approval from others.

The most commonly performed cosmetic procedures include breast augmentation/lifts, liposuction (the removal of body fat), facelifts, eyelid lifts, buttock and other body lifts, leg vein treatments, botox/fat injections, and nose and face reshaping. Approximately two million people subject themselves to these kinds of procedures each year, shelling out money and sacrificing time and comfort. When vanity motivates a person to undergoing surgery, he/she has become his/her own idol. The Bible warns us not to be vain or conceited (Philippians 2:3-4) and not to draw attention to ourselves by the way we look (1 Timothy 2:9). Another concern would be the cost. This is a major consideration because most people have families, and the expense of plastic surgery should never come before the needs of the family. The Bible also tells us that we need to use wisely the money that God has entrusted to us (Proverbs 11:24-25; Luke 16:10-12).

The most important thing to do before making the decision to undergo plastic surgery would be to consult God about the issue. The Bible tells us that God cares about every worry and concern that we have, so we should take our problems to Him (1 Peter 5:7). Through the wisdom and guidance of the Holy Spirit and the Word of God, we have the ability to make decisions that will please and honor Him. "Charm is deceptive, and beauty is fleeting; but a woman who fears the LORD is to be praised" (Proverbs 31:30). Even the most skilled surgeon cannot hold back the hands of time, and all cosmetic surgeries will eventually have the same result—aging. Those lifted body parts will sag again, and those cosmetically altered facial features will eventually wrinkle. It is far better to work on beautifying the person underneath, "that of your inner self, the *unfading* beauty of a gentle and quiet spirit, which is of great worth in God's sight" (1 Peter 3:4).

Question: Should a Christian get insurance?

Answer: Christians often struggle with the question of whether to get insurance and if doing so demonstrates a lack of faith. This is a healthy struggle, and believers need to examine the Scriptures and come up with an answer they can defend biblically.

First, let us agree that insurance is not specifically mentioned in the Bible. If something is not specifically mentioned in the Word of God, then we must draw from the principles and teaching of the whole testimony of Scripture. After gleaning all applicable scriptural principles, different believers may come to different personal convictions. Romans chapter 14 says that such situations call for respect of others' convictions. In that same chapter, believers have a responsibility to make up our own minds (Romans 14:5). The wording of the text indicates that we are required to do a thorough study of the Word of God and then to form godly personal convictions. The final verse of that same chapter states that whatever we decide must be an act of faith.

Here are some of the biblical principles to guide us. We are to obey the authorities over us. Thus, when we are required by law to have insurance, such as auto liability, we must comply. We are to take care of our families. Thus, we should plan ahead for the future benefit of our families. This could also include preparing for the undesired and unforeseeable early demise of a parent. Life insurance can be seen as a lack of faith, love of money, prudent planning, or possibly wise stewardship of funds. Each person's conditions and convictions may differ in these areas. God certainly advocates planning ahead. The story of Joseph and his wise planning not only saved the nation of Egypt but also the people of Israel and the lineage of Christ (Genesis 41).

The bottom line is we must study the Word of God and call out to Him, asking what He would have us do in this and all areas of life. Hebrews 11:6 states that without faith it is impossible to please Him. This is the real question: "Will this please my Father in heaven?" Another verse to consider is James 4:17, which makes it clear that if we have a chance to do good, we must do it, or else we sin. Another verse that addresses this issue is 1 Timothy 5:8, which states that if we want to minister to others, we should start with our own families.

Insurance can be a good and proper tool to assist us to achieve these goals.

Question: Should a Christian take anti-depressants or other mental health medicines?

Answer: Panic attacks, anxiety disorders, phobias, and depression affect millions of people. Panic attacks can be particularly debilitating as they can strike a person with no warning. For most sufferers, what they experience is rooted in fear: fear of rejection, fear of acceptance, fear of responsibility, fear of the unknown. Something will trigger fear which drives the person to feel like he or she is losing control. Panic attacks are often both physically and psychologically intense.

Although medical experts believe that many times the above-mentioned ailments originate within a person's psyche, there are times when a chemical imbalance is the cause. If this is the case, medication is often prescribed to help counter the imbalance, which in turn treats the symptoms of the psychological ailment. Is this a sin? No. God has allowed man to grow in his knowledge of medicine, which God often uses in the healing process. Does God need man-made medicine in order to heal? Of course not! But God has chosen to allow the practice of medicine to progress, and there is no biblical reason not to avail ourselves of it.

However, there is a fine line between using medicine for healing purposes and continual reliance upon medicine for daily living. We need to recognize God as the Great Physician, and know that He alone holds the power to truly heal (John 4:14). We need to look to God first and foremost for our healing. Medicine used to treat a case of panic attack should only be used to the extent that it allows the sufferer to deal with the root cause of fear. It should be used to give back control to the sufferer. However, many sufferers take medicine in order to avoid dealing with the true cause of their ailment; this would be denying responsibility, denying God's healing, and possibly denying others the freedom of forgiveness or closure to some past event that could be contributing to the ailment. This, then, does become sin, as it is based on selfishness.

By taking medicine on a limited basis in order to treat the symptoms, then relying upon the Word of God and wise counsel to enact transformation in one's heart and mind, gradually the need for the medicine will diminish. The believer's position in Christ is affirmed, and God brings healing into those troubled areas of the heart and mind which are causing the ailment. God's Word has much to say about fear and its place in a believer's life. Reading through the following Scriptures and meditating on them is the universal cure. The following verses give confidence, and illuminate the truth behind what being a child of God entails: Proverbs 29:25; Matthew 6:34; John 8:32; Romans 8:28-39; 12:1-2; 1 Corinthians 10:13; 2 Corinthians 10:5; Philippians 4:4-9; Colossians 3:1-2; 2 Timothy 1:6-8; Hebrews 13:5-6; James 1:2-4; 1 Peter 5:7; 2 Peter 1:3-4; 1 John 1:9; 4:18-19.

God can heal supernaturally and miraculously. We should pray to that end. God also heals through medicine and doctors. We should pray to that end as well. Regardless of which direction God takes, our ultimate trust must be in Him alone (Matthew 9:22).

Question: Should a Christian see a psychologist/psychiatrist?

Answer: Many Christians struggle with the decision as to see a psychologist or psychiatrist as the key to overcoming mental illness. Christian psychologists, psychiatrists, and counselors are numerous, and Christians are seeking their advice regularly, most often for depression and anxiety. Part of the difficulty is that there are wide varieties of psychological disorders, some of which are emotional and some of which are physical, but all of which have a spiritual component.

A sinful lifestyle can be one cause of depression or anxiety. In the case of a true believer in Christ, the person needs to realize that God is waiting for him to confess his sins, repent of them, and return to Him. Doing so will result in the spiritual, mental, and emotional healing a person seeks. Demonic influence is another potential cause of mental illness (2 Corinthians 4:4). A Christian can be influenced and/or oppressed by demons to the point of mental illness. It is important to remember, though, that Christians cannot be possessed by demons or influenced beyond a bearable amount of temptation (1 Corinthians 10:13). This is because believers already possess the Spirit of God (Romans 8:9-11), and the Holy Spirit will not share His "residence" with demons.

Another thing people often do not take into account is that God has allowed mankind to invent and develop many different kinds of medicines for healing. If a person has a true mental illness caused by hormonal or chemical imbalances in the brain, medication may be necessary. It is no different from going to a doctor to get medicine for an injury or physical illness. Similarly, God has blessed some Christian counselors and psychologists with supernatural insight, the ability to accurately evaluate a person and get to the true root of the problem. To ignore such giftedness seems unwise.

Whether or not to seek help from a Christian psychologist is a personal decision. It is a matter of the conscience because the Bible does not specifically address the issue. Some things to consider are: Does my behavior affect others, especially my family? Is my illness causing me to be disobedient to God and refusing to allow the Holy Spirit to work through me? Is my witness for Christ suffering because of this disability? If a person knows he/she is sick, but refuses to get help for selfish reasons, that is sinful. If it is strongly against a person's belief system to seek psychiatric care, and he/she has spent time in prayer and meditation, he/she should discuss any alternatives with his/her doctor and pastor/minister.

It is not sinful to see a psychiatrist. Doing so does not show lack of faith in God, although we should always go to God first for healing and direction. He wants to be in charge of every part of our lives, and we should feel free to take our problems to Him in prayer for every situation and every circumstance. God often uses Christian psychologists and therapists to bring healing to His children. Seeing a trained Christian counselor or psychiatrist, however, is definitely preferable to a secular therapist who will give advice from a worldly viewpoint instead of a biblical one. Let David's words encourage us: "He lifted me out of the pit of despair, out of the mud and the mire. He set my feet on solid ground and steadied me as I walked along. He has given me a new song to sing, a hymn of praise to our God..." (Psalm 40:2-3, NLT).

Question: What is the Christian view of retirement?

Answer: As Christians approach retirement age, they often wonder what a Christian should do during the retirement years. Do Christians retire from Christian service when they retire from the workplace? How should a Christian view retirement?

1. Although there is no biblical principle that a person should retire from his work when he reaches a certain age, there is the example of the Levites and their work in the tabernacle. In Numbers 4, the Levite males are numbered for service in the tabernacle from ages 25-50 years old, and after age 50, they were to retire from regular service. They could continue to "assist their brothers" but could not continue to work (Numbers 8:24-26).

2. Even though we may retire from our vocations (even "full-time" Christian ministry), we should never retire from serving the Lord, although the way we serve Him may change. There is the example of two very old people in Luke 2:25-38 (Simeon and Anna) who continued to serve the Lord faithfully. Anna was an elderly widow who ministered in the temple daily with fasting and prayer. Titus 2 states that the older men and women are to teach, by example, younger men and women how to live.

3. One's older years are not to be spent solely in the pursuit of pleasure. Paul says that the widow who lives for pleasure is dead while she yet lives (1 Timothy 5:6). Contrary to biblical instruction, many people equate retirement with "pursuit of pleasure" if at all possible. This is not to say that retirees cannot enjoy golf, social functions, or pleasurable pursuits. But these should not be the primary focus of one's life at any age.

4. Second Corinthians 12:14 states that the parent ought to save up for the children. But by far the greatest thing to "save up" is one's spiritual heritage, which can be passed on to children, grandchildren, and great-grandchildren. Generations of descendants have been impacted by the faithful prayers of an elderly family "patriarch" or "matriarch." Prayer is perhaps the most fruitful ministry outlet for those who have retired.

The Christian never retires from Christ's service; he only changes the address of his workplace. In summary, as one reaches "retirement age" (whatever that is) the vocation may change but one's life work of serving the Lord does not change. Often it is these "senior saints" who, after a lifetime of walking with God, are able to convey the truths of God's Word by relating how God has worked in their lives. The psalmist's prayer should be our prayer as we age: "Even when I am old and gray, do not forsake me, O God, till I declare your power to the next generation, your might to all who are to come" (Psalm 71:18).

Question: Was Jesus a vegetarian? Should a Christian be a vegetarian?

Answer: Jesus was not a vegetarian. The Bible records Jesus eating fish (Luke 24:42-43) and lamb (Luke 22:8-15). Jesus miraculously fed the crowds fish and bread, a strange thing for Him to do if He was a vegetarian (Matthew 14:17-21). In a vision to the apostle Peter, Jesus declared all foods to be clean, including animals (Acts 10:10-15). After the flood in Noah's time, God gave humanity permission to eat meat (Genesis 9:2-3). God has never rescinded this permission.

With that said, there is nothing wrong with a Christian being a vegetarian. The Bible does not command us to eat meat. There is nothing wrong with abstaining from eating meat. What the Bible does say is that we should not force our convictions about this issue on other people or judge them by what they eat or do not eat. Romans 14:2-3 tells us, "One man's faith allows him to eat everything, but another man, whose faith is weak, eats only vegetables. The man who eats everything must not look down on him who does not, and the man who does not eat everything must not condemn the man who does, for God has accepted him."

Again, God gave humanity permission to eat meat after the flood (Genesis 9:3). In the Old Testament law, the nation of Israel was commanded not to eat certain foods (Leviticus 11:1-47), but there was never a command against eating meat. Jesus declared all foods, including all kinds of meat, to be clean (Mark 7:19). As with anything, each Christian should pray for guidance as to what God would have him/her eat. Whatever we decide to eat is acceptable to God as long as we thank Him for providing it (1 Thessalonians 5:18). "So whether you eat or drink or whatever you do, do it all for the glory of God" (1 Corinthians 10:31).

Question: Should a Christian play video games?

Answer: Completed nearly 2000 years ago, God's Word does not explicitly teach whether or not a Christian should play video games. But the Bible's principles still apply today regarding the best use of our time. When God shows us that a specific activity is controlling our lives, we should break away from it for a time. This "fast" could be from food, movies, TV, music, video games, anything that distracts our attention from knowing and loving God and serving His people. While some of these things may not be bad in and of themselves, they become idols if they distract us from our first love (Colossians 3:5; Revelation 2:4). Below are some principles to consider, whether the question is regarding video games, TV, movies, or any other earthly pursuit.

1. **Will video games edify or merely entertain me?** To edify means to build up. Will playing video games build up your love for God, knowledge of Him, and ministry to others? "'Everything is permissible'—but not everything is beneficial. 'Everything is permissible'—but not everything is constructive" (1 Corinthians 10:23-24; Romans 14:19). When God gives us relaxation time, we should find uplifting activities to enjoy. Do we choose permissible over praiseworthy activities? When we have a choice between good, better, and best, we should choose the best (Galatians 5:13-17).

2. **Will playing video games obey self-will or God's will?** God's will for His children can be summed up in His greatest commandment: "'Love the Lord your God with all your heart and with all your soul and with all your strength and with all your mind'; and, 'Love your neighbor as yourself'" (Luke 10:27). Our will has been polluted by sin. Because we have been saved from our selfish desires, we should surrender our will (Philippians 3:7-9). God's will transforms our will (Psalm 143:10). Progressively, His desires for us become our deepest desires as well.

573

Many people believe the will of God is boring and humiliating. They picture a monk in a lonely monastery or a resentful church janitor. On the contrary, people who follow God's will for their lives are the most joyful, adventurous people ever. Reading biographies of history's heroes such Hudson Taylor, Amy Carmichael, Corrie Ten Boom, and George Mueller will verify that. Certainly, these saints faced difficulty from the world, their own flesh, and the devil. They may not have had much of this world's possessions, but God accomplished great works through them. At first, His will seems impossible and too holy to be any fun, but God will give us the power to perform it and the desires to delight in it. "I delight to do Your will, O my God" (Psalm 40:8a; see Hebrews 13:21).

3. **Does the video game glorify God?** Some video games glorify violence, lewdness, and dumb decisions (e.g., "I'm out of the race, so I'll just wreck my car"). As Christians, our activities should bring glory to God (1 Corinthians 10:31) and help us to grow in the knowledge and grace of Christ.

4. **Will playing video games result in good works?** "For we are his workmanship, created in Christ Jesus for good works, which God prepared beforehand, that we should walk in them" (Ephesians 2:10; see also Titus 2:11-14 and 1 Peter 2:15). Laziness and selfishness violate God's purpose for us—to do good works to others (1 Corinthians 15:58; see also Galatians 6:9-10).

5. **Will playing video games exhibit self-control?** Many people have said that video games can become an addiction or an obsession. There is no room in the Christian life for such things. Paul compares the Christian life to an athlete disciplining his body so he may win the prize. Christians have a greater motivation to live a set-apart life of self-control—eternal reward in heaven (1 Corinthians 9:25-27).

6. **Will playing video games redeem the time?** You will give account for how you use your limited minutes. Spending hours at a time playing a video game can hardly be called a good use of time. "Be very careful, then, how you live—not as unwise

but as wise, making the most of every opportunity, because the days are evil. Therefore do not be foolish, but understand what the Lord's will is" (Ephesians 5:15-17). "Live for the rest of the time in the flesh no longer for human passions but for the will of God" (1 Peter 4:2; see also Colossians 4:5, James 4:14, and 1 Peter 1:14-22).

7. **Does it pass the test of Philippians 4:8?** "Finally, brothers, whatever is true, whatever is noble, whatever is right, whatever is pure, whatever is lovely, whatever is admirable—if anything is excellent or praiseworthy—think about such things" (Philippians 4:8). When you play video games, is your mind focused on godly or secular things?

8. **Will playing video games fit in with my life purpose?** Paul wrote that in the final days people would be "...lovers of pleasure rather than lovers of God" (2 Timothy 3:4). Western culture fits that description. We love to play. Non-Christians become addicted to entertainment such as movies, sports, and music because they do not have a purpose higher than to enjoy life before death. These amusements cannot truly satisfy (Ecclesiastes 2:1). When Christians become addicted to the same things as non-Christians, can we truly say that we are exhibiting the new life "in a crooked and depraved generation, in which you shine like stars in the universe" (Philippians 2:15)? Or do we prove to others that we are really no different than they are and that Christ has not made a significant difference in our lives?

Paul considered knowing, loving, and obeying God to be his highest priority. "I consider everything a loss compared to the surpassing greatness of knowing Christ Jesus my Lord, for whose sake I have lost all things. I consider them rubbish, that I may gain Christ....I want to know Christ and the power of his resurrection and the fellowship of sharing in his sufferings, becoming like him in his death," (Philippians 3:7-10). Will playing video games be showing my love for God or my love for the things of the world? (1 John 2:15-17).

9. **Will playing video games give me an eternal focus?** Christians have hope of eternal rewards in heaven if they are faithful on

earth (see Matthew 6:19-21 and 1 Corinthians 3:11-16). If we focus on living for eternity rather than the passing pleasures of earth, we will have surrendered resources, time, and hearts for ministry (Colossians 3:1-2, 23-24). If our possessions or activities cause us to lose our eternal rewards, of what worth are they (Luke 12:33-37)? Christians often try to serve both God and their own desires. But Jesus clearly stated, "No one can serve two masters" (Matthew 6:24). God gives us joy through times of work and rest (Ecclesiastes 5:19; Matthew 11:28-29; Colossians 3:23-24). We must find that balance between labor and recreation. When we do set aside time for relaxation as Jesus did (Mark 6:31), we should choose an edifying activity.

The question is not "Can I play video games?" but "Would video games be the best choice?" Will this edify me, show love to my neighbor, and glorify God? We are to pursue praiseworthy activities, not simply permissible ones. However He leads you, passionately follow Him above all else. Prepare for eternity. Every sacrifice will seem insignificant when we meet Jesus.

Question: Does God expect Christians to vote?

Answer: It is our contention that it is the duty and responsibility of every Christian to vote and to vote for leaders who promote Christian principles. God is most certainly in control, but that does not mean we should do nothing to further His will. We are commanded to pray for our leaders (1 Timothy 2:1-4). In terms of politics and leadership, there is evidence in Scripture that God has been displeased with our choices of leadership at times (Hosea 8:4). The evidence of sin's grip on this world is everywhere. Much of the suffering on earth is because of godless leadership (Proverbs 28:12). Scripture gives Christians instructions to obey legitimate authority unless it contradicts the Lord's commands (Acts 5:27-29; Romans 13:1-7). As born-again believers, we ought to strive to choose leaders who will be themselves led by our Creator (1 Samuel 12:13-25). Candidates or proposals that violate the Bible's commands for life, family, marriage, or faith should never be supported (Proverbs 14:34). Christians should vote as led through prayer and study of both God's Word and the realities of the choices on the ballot.

Christians in many countries in this world are oppressed and persecuted. They suffer under governments they are powerless to change and governments that hate their faith and silence their voices. These believers preach the gospel of Jesus Christ at risk of their own lives. In the U.S.A., Christians have been blessed with the right to speak about and choose their leaders without fearing for themselves or their families. In the U.S.A., in recent elections, about 2 of every 5 of self-professed Christians took that right for granted and did not vote. About 1 in 5 self-professed, eligible Christians are not even registered to vote.

In our day and age, there are many who want to drive the name and message of Christ completely out of the public arena. Voting is an opportunity to promote, protect, and preserve godly government. Passing up that opportunity means letting those who would denigrate the name of Christ have their way in our lives. The leaders we elect—or do nothing to remove—have great influence on our freedoms. They can choose to protect our right to worship and spread the gospel, or they can restrict those rights. They can lead our nation toward righteousness or toward moral disaster. As Christians, we should stand up and follow our command to fulfill our civic duties (Matthew 22:21).

Question: What does the Bible say about women working outside the home?

Answer: Whether or not a woman should work outside the home is a struggle for many couples and families. The Bible does have instructions regarding the role of women. In Titus 2:3-4, Paul gives these instructions as to how a young married woman is to be trained by older women: "...train the younger women to love their husbands and children, to be self-controlled and pure, to be busy at home, to be kind, and to be subject to their husbands so that no one will malign the Word of God." In this passage, the Bible is clear that when children are in the picture, that is where the young woman's responsibility lies. The older women are to teach the younger women and to live lives that glorify God. Keeping these responsibilities in mind, an older woman's time can be spent at the Lord's leading and her discretion.

Proverbs 31 speaks of "a wife of noble character." Starting at verse 11, the writer praises this woman as one who does everything in her power to care for her family. She works hard to keep her house and her family in order. Verses 16, 18, 24, and 25 show that she is so industrious that she also moonlights with a cottage industry that provides additional income for her family. This woman's motivation is important in that her business activities were the means to an end, not an end in themselves. She was providing for her family, not furthering her career, or working to keep up with the neighbors. Her employment was secondary to her true calling—the stewardship of her husband, children, and home.

The Bible nowhere forbids a woman from working outside the home. However, the Bible does teach what a woman's priorities are to be. If working outside the home causes a woman to neglect her children and husband, then it is wrong for that woman to work outside the home. If a Christian woman can work outside the home and still provide a loving, caring environment for her children and husband, then it is perfectly acceptable for her to work outside the home. With those principles in mind, there is freedom in Christ. Women who work outside the home should not be condemned, and neither should women who focus on the stewardship of the home be treated with condescension.

Question: Why do people reject Jesus as their Savior?

Answer: The decision to accept or reject Jesus as Savior is the ultimate life decision. Why do many people choose to reject Jesus as Savior? There are perhaps as many different reasons for rejecting Christ as there are people who reject Him, but the following four reasons can serve as general categories.

1.   Some people do not think they need a savior. These people consider themselves to be "basically good" and do not realize that they, like all people, are sinners who cannot come to God on their own terms. But Jesus said, "I am the way, the truth, and the life. No one comes to the Father except through me"

(John 14:6). Those who reject Christ will not be able to stand before God and successfully plead their own case on their own merits.

2. The fear of social rejection or persecution deters some people from receiving Christ as Savior. The unbelievers in John 12:42-43 would not confess Christ because they were more concerned with their status among their peers than doing God's will. These were the Pharisees whose love of position and the esteem of others blinded them, "for they loved the approval of men rather than the approval of God."

3. For some people, the things that the present world has to offer are more appealing than eternal things. We read the story of such a man in Matthew 19:16-23. This man was not willing to lose his earthly possessions in order to gain an eternal relationship with Jesus (see also 2 Corinthians 4:16-18).

4. Many people are simply resisting the Holy Spirit's attempts to draw them to faith in Christ. Stephen, a leader in the early church, told those who were about to murder him, "You stiff-necked people, with uncircumcised hearts and ears! You are just like your fathers: You always resist the Holy Spirit!" (Acts 7:51). The apostle Paul made a similar statement to a group of gospel rejecters in Acts 28:23-27.

Whatever the reasons why people reject Jesus Christ, their rejection has disastrous eternal consequences. "There is no other name under heaven given to men by which we must be saved" than the name of Jesus (Acts 4:12), and those who reject Him, for whatever reason, face an eternity in the "outer darkness" of hell where there will be "weeping and gnashing of teeth" (Matthew 25:30).

Chapter 22

TOPICAL BIBLE QUESTIONS

CONTENTS

What does the Bible say about suicide? 582

What does the Bible say about abortion? 583

What does the Bible say about the death penalty/capital punishment? ... 584

What does the Bible say about depression? How can a Christian overcome
  depression? 585

What does the Bible say about managing your finances? 586

What does the Bible say about healing? 587

What does the Bible say about war? 588

What does the Bible say on the importance of accountability? 590

What does the Bible say about anger? 591

What does the Bible say about fear? 593

What does the Bible say about what foods we should eat (kosher)? Are
  there foods a Christian should avoid? 595

What does the Bible say about ghosts/hauntings? 596

What does the Bible say about gossip? 597

What does the Bible say about jealousy? 599

What does the Bible say about laziness? 600

What does the Bible say about patience? 602

What does the Bible say about pride? 603

How should a Christian view self-esteem? 604

What does the Bible say about worry? 605

Question: What does the Bible say about suicide?

Answer: The Bible mentions six specific people who committed suicide: Abimelech (Judges 9:54), Saul (1 Samuel 31:4), Saul's armor-bearer (1 Samuel 31:4-6), Ahithophel (2 Samuel 17:23), Zimri (1 Kings 16:18), and Judas (Matthew 27:5). Five of them were wicked, sinful men (not enough is said regarding Saul's armor-bearer to make a judgment as to his character). Some consider Samson an instance of suicide (Judges 16:26-31), but Samson's goal was to kill the Philistines, not himself. The Bible views suicide as equal to murder, which is what it is—self-murder. God is the only one who is to decide when and how a person should die.

According to the Bible, suicide is not what determines whether a person gains entrance into heaven. If an unsaved person commits suicide, he has done nothing but "expedite" his journey to hell. However, that person who committed suicide will ultimately be in hell for rejecting salvation through Christ, not because he committed suicide. What does the Bible say about a Christian who commits suicide? The Bible teaches that from the moment we truly believe in Christ, we are guaranteed eternal life (John 3:16). According to the Bible, Christians can know beyond any doubt that they possess eternal life (1 John 5:13). Nothing can separate a Christian from God's love (Romans 8:38-39). If no "created thing" can separate a Christian from God's love, and even a Christian who commits suicide is a "created thing," then not even suicide can separate a Christian from God's love. Jesus died for all of our sins, and if a true Christian, in a time of spiritual attack and weakness, commits suicide, that would still be a sin covered by the blood of Christ.

Suicide is still a serious sin against God. According to the Bible, suicide is murder; it is always wrong. Serious doubts should be raised about the genuineness of faith of anyone who claimed to be a Christian yet committed suicide. There is no circumstance that can justify someone, especially a Christian, taking his/her own life. Christians are called to live their lives for God, and the decision on when to die is God's and God's alone. Although it is not describing suicide, 1 Corinthians 3:15 is probably a good description of what happens to a Christian who commits suicide: "He himself will be saved, but only as one escaping through the flames."

Question: What does the Bible say about abortion?

Answer: The Bible never specifically addresses the issue of abortion. However, there are numerous teachings in Scripture that make it abundantly clear what God's view of abortion is. Jeremiah 1:5 tells us that God knows us before He forms us in the womb. Psalm 139:13-16 speaks of God's active role in our creation and formation in the womb. Exodus 21:22-25 prescribes the same penalty—death—for someone who causes the death of a baby in the womb as for someone who commits murder. This clearly indicates that God considers a baby in the womb to be as human as a full-grown adult. For the Christian, abortion is not a matter of a woman's right to choose. It is a matter of the life or death of a human being made in God's image (Genesis 1:26-27; 9:6).

The first argument that always arises against the Christian stance on abortion is "What about cases of rape and/or incest?" As horrible as it would be to become pregnant as a result of rape and/or incest, is the murder of a baby the answer? Two wrongs do not make a right. The child who is a result of rape/incest could be given in adoption to a loving family unable to have children on their own, or the child could be raised by its mother. Again, the baby is completely innocent and should not be punished for the evil acts of its father.

The second argument that usually arises against the Christian stance on abortion is "What about when the life of the mother is at risk?" Honestly, this is the most difficult question to answer on the issue of abortion. First, let's remember that this situation is the reason behind less than one-tenth of one percent of the abortions done in the world today. Far more women have an abortion for convenience than women who have an abortion to save their own lives. Second, let's remember that God is a God of miracles. He can preserve the life of a mother and a child despite all the medical odds being against it. Ultimately, though, this question can only be decided between a husband, wife, and God. Any couple facing this extremely difficult situation should pray to the Lord for wisdom (James 1:5) as to what He would have them to do.

Over 95 percent of the abortions performed today involve women who simply do not want to have a baby. Less than 5 percent of abortions are for the reasons of rape, incest, or the mother's health at risk. Even in the more difficult 5 percent of instances, abortion should never be the first option. The life of a human being in the womb is worth every effort to allow the child to be born.

For those who have had an abortion, remember that the sin of abortion is no less forgivable than any other sin. Through faith in Christ, all sins can be forgiven (John 3:16; Romans 8:1; Colossians 1:14). A woman who has had an abortion, a man who has encouraged an abortion, or even a doctor who has performed one—can all be forgiven by faith in Jesus Christ.

Question: What does the Bible say about the death penalty/capital punishment?

Answer: The Old Testament law commanded the death penalty for various acts: murder (Exodus 21:12), kidnapping (Exodus 21:16), bestiality (Exodus 22:19), adultery (Leviticus 20:10), homosexuality (Leviticus 20:13), being a false prophet (Deuteronomy 13:5), prostitution and rape (Deuteronomy 22:4), and several other crimes. However, God often showed mercy when the death penalty was due. David committed adultery and murder, yet God did not demand his life be taken (2 Samuel 11:1-5, 14-17; 2 Samuel 12:13). Ultimately, every sin we commit should result in the death penalty because the wages of sin is death (Romans 6:23). Thankfully, God demonstrates His love for us in not condemning us (Romans 5:8).

When the Pharisees brought a woman who was caught in the act of adultery to Jesus and asked Him if she should be stoned, Jesus replied, "If any one of you is without sin, let him be the first to throw a stone at her" (John 8:7). This should not be used to indicate that Jesus rejected capital punishment in all instances. Jesus was simply exposing the hypocrisy of the Pharisees. The Pharisees wanted to trick Jesus into breaking the Old Testament law; they did not truly care about the woman being stoned (where was the man who was caught in adultery?) God is the One who instituted capital punishment: "Whoever sheds man's blood, by man his blood shall be shed, for in the image of God He made man" (Genesis 9:6). Jesus would support capital punishment in some instances. Jesus also demonstrated grace when capital punishment was due (John 8:1-11). The apostle Paul definitely recognized the power of the government to institute capital punishment where appropriate (Romans 13:1-7).

How should a Christian view the death penalty? First, we must remember that God has instituted capital punishment in His Word; therefore, it would be presumptuous of us to think that we could institute a higher standard. God has the highest standard of any being; He is perfect. This standard applies not only to us but to Himself. Therefore, He loves to an infinite degree, and He has mercy to an infinite degree. We also see that He has wrath to an infinite degree, and it is all maintained in a perfect balance.

Second, we must recognize that God has given government the authority to determine when capital punishment is due (Genesis 9:6; Romans 13:1-7). It is unbiblical to claim that God opposes the death penalty in all instances. Christians should never rejoice when the death penalty is employed, but at the same time, Christians should not fight against the government's right to execute the perpetrators of the most evil of crimes.

Question: What does the Bible say about depression? How can a Christian overcome depression?

Answer: Depression is a widespread condition, affecting millions of people, Christians and non-Christians alike. Those suffering from depression can experience intense feelings of sadness, anger, hopelessness, fatigue, and a variety of other symptoms. They may begin to feel useless and even suicidal, losing interest in things and people that they once enjoyed. Depression is often triggered by life circumstances, such as a loss of job, death of a loved one, divorce, or psychological problems such as abuse or low self-esteem.

The Bible tells us to be filled with joy and praise (Philippians 4:4; Romans 15:11), so God apparently intends for us all to live joyful lives. This is not easy for someone suffering from situational depression, but it can be remedied through God's gifts of prayer, Bible study and application, support groups, fellowship among believers, confession, forgiveness, and counseling. We must make the conscious effort to not be absorbed in ourselves, but to turn our efforts outward. Feelings of depression can often be solved when those suffering with depression move the focus from themselves to Christ and others.

Clinical depression is a physical condition that must be diagnosed by a physician. It may not be caused by unfortunate life circumstances, nor can the symptoms be alleviated by one's own will. Contrary to what some in the Christian community believe, clinical depression is not always caused by sin. Depression can sometimes be caused by a physical disorder that needs to be treated with medication and/or counseling. Of course, God is able to cure any disease or disorder. However, in some cases, seeing a doctor for depression is no different than seeing a doctor for an injury.

There are some things that those who suffer from depression can do to alleviate their anxiety. They should make sure that they are staying in the Word, even when they do not feel like it. Emotions can lead us astray, but God's Word stands firm and unchanging. We must maintain strong faith in God and hold even more tightly to Him when we undergo trials and temptations. The Bible tells us that God will never allow temptations into our lives that are too much for us to handle (1 Corinthians 10:13). Although being depressed is not a sin, one is still accountable for the response to the affliction, including getting the professional help that is needed. "Through Jesus, therefore, let us continually offer to God a sacrifice of praise—the fruit of lips that confess his name" (Hebrews 13:15).

Question: What does the Bible say about managing your finances?

Answer: The Bible has a lot to say about managing finances. Concerning borrowing, the Bible generally advises against it. See Proverbs 6:1-5; 20:16; 22:7, 26-27 ("The rich rule over the poor, and the borrower is servant to the lender.... Do not be a man who strikes hands in pledge or puts up security for debts; if you lack the means to pay, your very bed will be snatched from under you"). Over and over again, the Bible warns against the accumulation of wealth and encourages us to seek spiritual riches instead. Proverbs 28:20: "A faithful man will be richly blessed, but one eager to get rich will not go unpunished." See also Proverbs 10:15; 11:4; 18:11; 23:5.

Proverbs 6:6-11 offers wisdom concerning laziness and the financial ruin that inevitably results. We are told to consider the industrious ant who works to store up food for itself. The passage also warns against sleeping when we should be working at something profitable. A "sluggard" is a lazy, slothful person who would rather rest than work. His end is assured—poverty and want. At the other end of the spectrum is the one who is obsessed with gaining money. Such a one, according to Ecclesiastes 5:10, never has enough wealth to satisfy him and must be constantly grasping more and more. First Timothy 6:6-11 also warns against the trap of desiring wealth.

Rather than desiring to heap riches upon ourselves, the biblical model is one of giving, not getting. "Remember this: Whoever sows sparingly will also reap sparingly, and whoever sows generously will also reap generously. Each man should give what he has decided in his heart to give, not reluctantly or under compulsion, for God loves a cheerful giver" (2 Corinthians 9:6-7). We are also encouraged to be good stewards of what God has given us. In Luke 16:1-13, Jesus told the parable of the dishonest steward as a way of warning us against poor stewardship. The moral of the story is "So if you have not been trustworthy in handling worldly wealth, who will trust you with true riches?" (v. 11). We are also responsible to provide for our own household, as 1 Timothy 5:8 reminds us: "If anyone does not provide for his relatives, and especially for his immediate family, he has denied the faith and is worse than an unbeliever."

In summary, what does the Bible say about managing money? The answer can be summarized with a single word—wisdom. We are to be wise with our money. We are to save money, but not hoard it. We are to spend money, but with discretion and control. We are to give back to the Lord, joyfully and sacrificially. We are to use our money to help others, but with discernment and the guidance of God's Spirit. It is not wrong to be rich, but it is wrong to love money. It is not wrong to be poor, but it is wrong to waste money on trivial things. The Bible's consistent message on managing money is to be wise.

Question: What does the Bible say about healing?

Answer: Isaiah 53:5, which is then quoted in 1 Peter 2:24, is a key verse on healing, but it is often misunderstood and misapplied. "But he was pierced for our transgressions, he was crushed for our iniquities; the punishment that brought us peace was upon him, and by his wounds we are healed." The word translated "healed" can mean either spiritual or physical healing. However, the contexts of Isaiah 53 and 1 Peter 2 make it clear that it is speaking of spiritual healing. "He himself bore our sins in his body on the tree, so that we might die to sins and live for righteousness; by his wounds you have been healed" (1 Peter 2:24). The verse is talking about sin and righteousness, not sickness and disease. Therefore, being "healed" in both these verses is speaking of being forgiven and saved, not physically healed.

The Bible does not specifically link physical healing with spiritual healing. Sometimes people are physically healed when they place their faith in Christ, but this is not always the case. Sometimes it is God's will to heal, but sometimes it is not. The apostle John gives us the proper perspective: "This is the confidence we have in approaching God: that if we ask anything according to His will, He hears us. And if we know that He hears us—whatever we ask—we know that we have what we asked of Him" (1 John 5:14-15). God still performs miracles. God still heals people. Sickness, disease, pain, and death are still realities in this world. Unless the Lord returns, everyone who is alive today will die, and the vast majority of them (Christians included) will die as the result of a physical problem (disease, sickness, injury). It is not always God's will to heal us physically.

Ultimately, our full physical healing awaits us in heaven. In heaven, there will be no more pain, sickness, disease, suffering, or death (Revelation 21). We all need to be less preoccupied with our physical condition in this world and a lot more concerned with our spiritual condition (Romans 12:1-2). Then we can focus our hearts on heaven where we will no longer have to deal with physical problems. Revelation 21:4 describes the true healing we should all be longing for: "He will wipe every tear from their eyes. There will be no more death or mourning or crying or pain, for the old order of things has passed away."

Question: What does the Bible say about war?

Answer: Many people make the mistake of reading what the Bible says in Exodus 20:13, "You shall not kill," and then seeking to apply this command to war. However, the Hebrew word literally means "the intentional, premeditated killing of another person with malice; murder." God often ordered the Israelites to go to war with other nations (1 Samuel 15:3; Joshua 4:13). God ordered the death penalty for numerous crimes (Exodus 21:12, 15; 22:19; Leviticus 20:11).

So, God is not against killing in all circumstances, but only murder. War is never a good thing, but sometimes it is a necessary thing. In a world filled with sinful people (Romans 3:10-18), war is inevitable. Sometimes the only way to keep sinful people from doing great harm to the innocent is by going to war.

In the Old Testament, God ordered the Israelites to: "Take vengeance on the Midianites for the Israelites" (Numbers 31:2). Deuteronomy 20:16-17 declares, "However, in the cities of the nations the LORD your God is giving you as an inheritance, do not leave alive anything that breathes. Completely destroy them…as the LORD your God has commanded you." Also, 1 Samuel 15:18 says, "Go and completely destroy those wicked people, the Amalekites; make war on them until you have wiped them out." Obviously God is not against all war. Jesus is always in perfect agreement with the Father (John 10:30), so we cannot argue that war was only God's will in the Old Testament. God does not change (Malachi 3:6; James 1:17).

Jesus' second coming will be exceedingly violent. Revelation 19:11-21 describes the ultimate war with Christ, the conquering commander who judges and makes war "with justice" (v. 11). It's going to be bloody (v. 13) and gory. The birds will eat the flesh of all those who oppose Him (v. 17-18). He has no compassion upon His enemies, whom He will conquer completely and consign to a "fiery lake of burning sulfur" (v. 20).

It is an error to say that God never supports a war. Jesus is not a pacifist. In a world filled with evil people, sometimes war is necessary to prevent even greater evil. If Hitler had not been defeated by World War II, how many more millions would have been killed? If the American Civil War had not been fought, how much longer would African-Americans have had to suffer as slaves?

War is a terrible thing. Some wars are more "just" than others, but war is always the result of sin (Romans 3:10-18). At the same time, Ecclesiastes 3:8 declares, "There is…a time to love and a time to hate, a time for war and a time for peace." In a world filled with sin, hatred, and evil (Romans 3:10-18), war is inevitable. Christians should not desire war, but neither are Christians to oppose the government God has placed in authority over them (Romans 13:1-4; 1 Peter 2:17). The most important thing we can be doing in a time of war is to be praying for godly wisdom for our leaders, praying for the safety of our military, praying for quick resolution to conflicts, and praying for a minimum of casualties among civilians on both sides (Philippians 4:6-7).

Question: What does the Bible say on the importance of accountability?

Answer: With much temptation already in the world today, Satan is working overtime to create even more. We must have a brother or sister we can count on when we are facing temptations that threaten our spiritual lives. King David was alone the evening he was tempted into adultery by Satan. It may have appeared to be Bathsheba who tempted him (2 Samuel 11), but the Bible tells us we fight a war not of flesh but of the spirit, against powers and spiritual forces who threaten us (Ephesians 6:12).

Knowing we are in a battle against the forces of darkness, we should want as much help as we can gather around us. In Ephesians, Paul tells us that we must be equipped with all the power that God supplies to fight this battle. "Therefore put on the full armor of God, so that when the day of evil comes, you may be able to stand your ground, and after you have done everything, to stand" (Ephesians 6:13). Paul realized that even if we equip ourselves with everything God has to offer in defense of evil, we are still human and we may not always be able to resist Satan's temptations. We know without a doubt that temptation will come.

Satan knows our weaknesses, and he knows when we are vulnerable. He knows when a married couple is fighting and perhaps feeling that someone else might understand them better. He knows when a child has been punished by his parents and might be feeling spiteful. He knows when things are not going well at work and knows how that reminds us of the bar that is on the way home. Where do we find help if we have done all we can do to fight the battle? We want to do what is right in the sight of God, yet we are weak. What do we do?

Proverbs 27:17 says, "Iron sharpens iron; so a man sharpens his friend's countenance." A friend's countenance is a look or expression of encouragement or moral support. When is the last time you had a friend call you just to ask how you were doing? When is the last time you called a friend and asked her if she needed to talk? Encouragement and moral support from a friend are sometimes the missing ingredients in fighting the battle against Satan.

The writer of Hebrews summed it up when he said, "Let us consider how we may spur one another on toward love and good deeds. Let us not give up meeting together, as some are in the habit of doing, but let us encourage one another—and all the more as you see the Day approaching…" (Hebrews 10:19-26). Accountability is crucially important in the battle to overcome sin. An accountability partner can be there to encourage you, to rebuke you, to teach you, to rejoice with you, and to weep with you. Every Christian should have an accountability partner with whom they can pray, talk, confide, and confess.

Question: What does the Bible say about anger?

Answer: Handling anger is an important topic. Christian counselors report that 50 percent of people who come in for counseling have problems dealing with anger. Anger can shatter communication and tear apart relationships, and it ruins both the joy and health of many. Sadly, people tend to justify their anger instead of accepting responsibility for it. Everyone struggles, to varying degrees, with anger. Thankfully, God's Word contains principles regarding how to handle anger in a godly manner, and how to overcome sinful anger.

Anger is not always sin. There is a type of anger of which the Bible approves, often called "righteous indignation." God is angry (Psalm 7:11; Mark 3:5), and believers are commanded to be angry (Ephesians 4:26). Two Greek words are used in the New Testament for our English word "anger." One means "passion, energy" and the other means "agitated, boiling." Biblically, anger is God-given energy intended to help us solve problems. Examples of biblical anger include Paul's confronting Peter because of his wrong example in Galatians 2:11-14, David's being upset over hearing Nathan the prophet sharing an injustice (2 Samuel 12), and Jesus' anger over how some of the Jews had defiled worship at God's temple in Jerusalem (John 2:13-18). Notice that none of these examples of anger involved self-defense, but a defense of others or of a principle.

Anger turns to sin when it is selfishly motivated (James 1:20), when God's goal is distorted (1 Corinthians 10:31), or when anger is allowed to linger (Ephesians 4:26-27). Instead of using the energy generated by anger to attack the problem at hand, it is the person who is attacked. Ephesians 4:15-19 says we are to speak the truth in love and use our words to build others up, not allow rotten or destructive words to pour from our lips. Unfortunately, this poisonous speech is a common characteristic of fallen man (Romans 3:13-14). Anger becomes sin when it is allowed to boil over without restraint, resulting in a scenario in which hurt is multiplied (Proverbs 29:11), leaving devastation in its wake, often with irreparable consequences. Anger also becomes sin when the angry one refuses to be pacified, holds a grudge, or keeps it all inside (Ephesians 4:26-27). This can cause depression and irritability over little things, often things unrelated to the underlying problem.

We can handle anger biblically by recognizing and admitting our selfish anger and/or our wrong handling of anger as sin (Proverbs 28:13; 1 John 1:9). This confession should be both to God and to those who have been hurt by our anger. We should not minimize the sin by excusing it or blame-shifting.

We can handle anger biblically by seeing God in the trial. This is especially important when people have done something to offend us. James 1:2-4, Romans 8:28-29, and Genesis 50:20 all point to the fact that God is sovereign and in complete control over every circumstance and person that enters our path. Nothing happens to us that He does not cause or allow. And as these verses share, God is a good God (Psalm 145:8, 9, 17) who allows all things in our lives for our good and the good of others. Reflecting on this truth until it moves from our heads to our hearts will alter how we react to those who hurt us.

We can handle anger biblically by making room for God's wrath. This is especially important in cases of injustice, when "evil" men abuse "innocent" people. Genesis 50:19 and Romans 12:19 both tell us not play God. God is righteous and just, and we can trust Him who knows all and sees all to act justly (Genesis 18:25).

We can handle anger biblically by not returning evil for good (Genesis 50:21; Romans 12:21). This is key to converting our anger into love. As our actions flow from our hearts, so also our hearts can be altered by our actions (Matthew 5:43-48). That is, we can change our feelings toward another by changing how we choose to act toward that person.

We can handle anger biblically by communicating to solve the problem. There are four basic rules of communication shared in Ephesians 4:15, 25-32:

1. Be honest and speak (Ephesians 4:15, 25). People cannot read our minds. We must speak the truth in love.
2. Stay current (Ephesians 4:26-27). We must not allow what is bothering us to build up until we lose control. Dealing with and sharing what is bothering us before it gets to that point is important.
3. Attack the problem, not the person (Ephesians 4:29, 31). Along this line, we must remember the importance of keeping the volume of our voices low (Proverbs 15:1).
4. Act, not react (Ephesians 4:31-32). Because of our fallen nature, our first impulse is often a sinful one (v. 31). The time spent in "counting to ten" should be used to reflect upon the godly way to respond (v. 32) and to remind ourselves how anger is to be used to solve problems and not create bigger ones.

Finally, we must act to solve our part of the problem (Acts 12:18). We cannot control how others act or respond, but we can make the changes that need to be made on our part. Overcoming a temper is not accomplished overnight. But through prayer, Bible study, and reliance upon God's Holy Spirit, ungodly anger can be overcome. Just as we may have allowed anger to become entrenched in our lives by habitual practice, we must also practice responding correctly until it becomes a habit itself.

Question: What does the Bible say about fear?

Answer: The Bible mentions two specific types of fear. The first type is beneficial and is to be encouraged. The second type is a detriment and is to be overcome. The first type of fear is fear of the Lord. This type of fear does not necessarily mean to be afraid of something.

Rather, it is a reverential awe of God; a reverence for His power and glory. However, it is also a proper respect for His wrath and anger. In other words, the fear of the Lord is a total acknowledgement of all that God is, which comes through knowing Him and His attributes.

Fear of the Lord brings with it many blessings and benefits. It is the beginning of wisdom and leads to good understanding (Psalm 111:10). Only fools despise wisdom and discipline (Proverbs 1:7). Furthermore, fear of the Lord leads to life, rest, peace, and contentment (Proverbs 19:23). It is the fountain and life (Proverbs 14:27) and provides a security and a place of safety for us (Proverbs 14:26).

Thus, one can see how fearing God should be encouraged. However, the second type of fear mentioned in the Bible is not beneficial at all. This is the "spirit of fear" mentioned in 2 Timothy 1:7: "For God has not given us a spirit of fear, but of power and of love and of a sound mind" (NKJV). A spirit of fearfulness and timidity does not come from God.

However, sometimes we are afraid, sometimes this "spirit of fear" overcomes us, and to overcome it we need to trust in and love God completely. "There is no fear in love. But perfect love drives out fear, because fear has to do with punishment. The one who fears is not made perfect in love" (1 John 4:18). No one is perfect, and God knows this. That is why He has liberally sprinkled encouragement against fear throughout the Bible. Beginning in the book of Genesis and continuing throughout the book of Revelation, God reminds us to "Fear not."

For example, Isaiah 41:10 encourages us, "Do not fear, for I am with you; Do not anxiously look about you, for I am your God I will strengthen you, surely I will help you, Surely I will uphold you with My righteous right hand." Often we fear the future and what will become of us. But Jesus reminds us that God cares for the birds of the air, so how much more will He provide for His children? "So don't be afraid; you are worth more than many sparrows" (Matthew 10:31). Just these few verses cover many different types of fear. God tells us not to be afraid of being alone, of being too weak, of not being heard, and of lacking physical necessities. These admonishments continue throughout the Bible, covering the many different aspects of the "spirit of fear."

In Psalm 56:11 the psalmist writes, "In God I trust; I will not be afraid. What can man do to me?" This is an awesome testimony to the power of trusting in God. Regardless of what happens, the psalmist will trust in God because he knows and understands the power of God. The key to overcoming fear, then, is total and complete trust in God. Trusting God is a refusal to give in to fear. It is a turning to God even in the darkest times and trusting Him to make things right. This trust comes from knowing God and knowing that He is good. As Job said when he was experiencing some of the most difficult trials recorded in the Bible, "Though he slay me, yet will I trust in him" (Job 13:15 NKJV).

Once we have learned to put our trust in God, we will no longer be afraid of the things that come against us. We will be like the psalmist who said with confidence "…let all who take refuge in you be glad; let them ever sing for joy. Spread your protection over them, that those who love your name may rejoice in you" (Psalm 5:11).

Question: What does the Bible say about what foods we should eat (kosher)? Are there foods a Christian should avoid?

Answer: Leviticus chapter 11 lists the dietary restrictions God gave to the nation of Israel. The dietary laws included prohibitions against eating pork, shellfish, most insects, scavenger birds, and various other animals. The dietary rules were never intended to apply to anyone other than the Israelites. The purpose of the food laws was to make the Israelites distinct from all other nations. After this purpose had ended, Jesus declared all foods clean (Mark 7:19). God gave the apostle Peter a vision in which He declared that formerly unclean animals could be eaten: "Do not call anything impure that God has made clean" (Acts 10:15). When Jesus died on the cross, He fulfilled the Old Testament law (Romans 10:4; Galatians 3:24-26; Ephesians 2:15). This includes the laws regarding clean and unclean foods.

Romans 14:1-23 teaches us that not everyone is mature enough in the faith to accept the fact that all foods are clean. As a result, if we are with someone who would be offended by our eating "unclean" food, we should give up our right to do so as to not offend the other person. We have the right to eat whatever we want, but we do not have the right to offend other people, even if they are wrong. For the Christian in this age, though, we have freedom to eat whatever we wish as long as it does not cause someone else to stumble in his/her faith.

In the New Covenant of grace, the Bible is far more concerned with how much we eat than what we eat. Physical appetites are an analogy of our ability to control ourselves. If we are unable to control our eating habits, we are probably also unable to control other habits such as those of the mind (lust, covetousness, unrighteous hatred/anger) and unable to keep our mouths from gossip or strife. We are not to let our appetites control us; rather, we are to control them (Deuteronomy 21:20; Proverbs 23:2; 2 Peter 1:5-7; 2 Timothy 3:1-9; 2 Corinthians 10:5).

Question: What does the Bible say about ghosts/hauntings?

Answer: Is there such a thing as ghosts? The answer to this question depends on what precisely is meant by the term "ghosts." If the term means "spirit beings," the answer is a qualified "yes." If the term means "spirits of people who have died," the answer is "no." The Bible makes it abundantly clear that there are spirit beings, both good and evil. But the Bible negates the idea that the spirits of deceased human beings can remain on earth and "haunt" the living.

Hebrews 9:27 declares, "Man is destined to die once, and after that to face judgment." That is what happens to a person's soul-spirit after death—judgment. The result of this judgment is heaven for the believer (2 Corinthians 5:6-8; Philippians 1:23) and hell for the unbeliever (Matthew 25:46; Luke 16:22-24). There is no in-between. There is no possibility of remaining on earth in spirit form as a "ghost." If there are such things as ghosts, according to the Bible, they absolutely cannot be the disembodied spirits of deceased human beings.

The Bible teaches very clearly that there are indeed spirit beings who can connect with and appear in our physical world. The Bible identifies these beings as angels and demons. Angels are spirit beings who are faithful in serving God. Angels are righteous, good, and holy. Demons are fallen angels, angels who rebelled against God. Demons are evil, deceptive, and destructive. According to 2 Corinthians 11:14-15, demons masquerade as "angels of light" and as "servants of righteousness." Appearing as a "ghost" and impersonating a deceased human being definitely seem to be within the power and abilities that demons possess.

The closest biblical example of a "haunting" is found in Mark 5:1-20. A legion of demons possessed a man and used the man to haunt a graveyard. There were no ghosts involved. It was a case of a normal person being controlled by demons to terrorize the people of that area. Demons only seek to "kill, steal, and destroy" (John 10:10). They will do anything within their power to deceive people, to lead people away from God. This is very likely the explanation of "ghostly" activity today. Whether it is called a ghost, a ghoul, or a poltergeist, if there is genuine evil spiritual activity occurring, it is the work of demons.

What about instances in which "ghosts" act in "positive" ways? What about psychics who claim to summon the deceased and gain true and useful information from them? Again, it is crucial to remember that the goal of demons is to deceive. If the result is that people trust in a psychic instead of God, a demon will be more than willing to reveal true information. Even good and true information, if from a source with evil motives, can be used to mislead, corrupt, and destroy.

Interest in the paranormal is becoming increasingly common. There are individuals and businesses that claim to be "ghost-hunters," who for a price will rid your home of ghosts. Psychics, séances, tarot cards, and mediums are increasingly considered normal. Human beings are innately aware of the spiritual world. Sadly, instead of seeking the truth about the spirit world by communing with God and studying His Word, many people allow themselves to be led astray by the spirit world. The demons surely laugh at the spiritual mass-deception that exists in the world today.

Question: What does the Bible say about gossip?

Answer: The Hebrew word translated "gossip" in the Old Testament is defined as "one who reveals secrets, one who goes about as a tale-bearer or scandal-monger." A gossiper is a person who has privileged information about people and proceeds to reveal that information to those who have no business knowing it. Gossip is distinguished from sharing information by its intent. Gossipers have the goal of building themselves up by making others look bad and exalting themselves as some kind of repositories of knowledge.

In the book of Romans, Paul reveals the sinful nature and lawlessness of mankind, stating how God poured out His wrath on those who rejected His laws. Because they had turned away from God's instruction and guidance, He gave them over to their sinful natures. The list of sins includes gossips and slanderers (Romans 1:29b-32). We see from this passage how serious the sin of gossip is and that it characterizes those who are under God's wrath.

Another group who were (and still are today) known for indulging in gossip is widows. Paul cautions widows against entertaining the habit of gossip and of being idle. These women are described as "gossips and busybodies, saying things they ought not to" (1 Timothy 5:12-13). Because women tend to spend a lot of time in each other's homes and work closely with other women, they hear and observe situations which can become distorted, especially when repeated over and over. Paul states that widows get into the habit of going from home to home, looking for something to occupy their idleness. Idle hands are the devil's workshop, and God cautions against allowing idleness to enter our lives. "A gossip betrays a confidence; so avoid a man [or woman] who talks too much" (Proverbs 20:19).

Women are certainly not the only ones who have been found guilty of gossip. Anyone can engage in gossip simply by repeating something heard in confidence. The book of Proverbs has a long list of verses that cover the dangers of gossip and the potential hurt that results from it. "A man who lacks judgment derides his neighbor, but a man of understanding holds his tongue. A gossip betrays a confidence, but a trustworthy man keeps a secret" (Proverbs 11:12-13).

The Bible tells us that "a perverse man stirs up dissension, and a gossip separates close friends" (Proverbs 16:28). Many a friendship has been ruined over a misunderstanding that started with gossip. Those who engage in this behavior do nothing but stir up trouble and cause anger, bitterness, and pain among friends. Sadly, some people thrive on this and look for opportunities to destroy others. And when such people are confronted, they deny the allegations and answer with excuses and rationalizations. Rather than admit wrongdoing, they blame someone else or attempt to minimize the seriousness of the sin. "A fool's mouth is his undoing, and his lips are a snare to his soul. The words of a gossip are like choice morsels; they go down to a man's inmost parts" (Proverbs 18:7-8).

Those who guard their tongues keep themselves from calamity (Proverbs 21:23). So we must guard our tongues and refrain from the sinful act of gossip. If we surrender our natural desires to the Lord, He will help us to remain righteous. May we all follow the Bible's teaching on gossip by keeping our mouths shut unless it is necessary and appropriate to speak.

Question: What does the Bible say about jealousy?

Answer: When we use the word "jealous," we use it in a sense of being envious of someone who has something we do not have. This kind of jealousy is a sin and is not characteristic of a Christian; rather, it shows that we are still being controlled by our own desires (1 Corinthians 3:3). Galatians 5:26 says, "Let us not become conceited, provoking and envying each other."

The Bible tells us that we are to have the perfect kind of love that God has for us. "Love is patient, love is kind. It does not envy, it does not boast, it is not proud. It is not rude, it is not self-seeking, it is not easily angered, it keeps no record of wrongs." (1 Corinthians 13:4-5). The more we focus on ourselves and our own desires, the less we are able to focus on God. When we harden our hearts to the truth, we cannot turn to Jesus and allow Him to heal us (Matthew 13:15). But when we allow the Holy Spirit to control us, He will produce in us the fruit of our salvation, which is love, joy, peace, patience, kindness, goodness, faithfulness, gentleness, and self-control (Galatians 5:22-23).

Being jealous indicates that we are not satisfied with what God has given us. The Bible tells us to be content with what we have, for God will never fail or forsake us (Hebrews 13:5). In order to combat jealousy, we need to become more like Jesus and less like ourselves. We can get to know Him through Bible study, prayer, and fellowship with mature believers. As we learn how to serve others instead of ourselves, our hearts will begin to change. "Do not conform any longer to the pattern of this world, but be transformed by the renewing of your mind. Then you will be able to test and approve what God's will is—his good, pleasing and perfect will" (Romans 12:2).

Question: What does the Bible say about laziness?

Answer: Newton's first law of motion states that an object in motion tends to remain in motion, and an object at rest tends to remain at rest. This law applies to people. While some are naturally driven to complete projects, others are apathetic, requiring motivation to overcome inertia. Laziness, a lifestyle for some, is a temptation for all. But the Bible is clear that, because the Lord ordained work for man, laziness is sin. "Go to the ant, you sluggard! Consider her ways and be wise" (Proverbs 6:6).

The Bible has a great deal to say about laziness. Proverbs is especially filled with wisdom concerning laziness and warnings to the lazy person. Proverbs tells us that a lazy person hates work: "The sluggard's craving will be the death of him, because his hands refuse to work" (21:25); he loves sleep: "As a door turns on its hinges, so a sluggard turns on his bed" (26:14); he gives excuses: "The sluggard says, 'There is a lion in the road, a fierce lion roaming the streets'" (26:13); he wastes time and energy: "He who is slothful in his work is a brother to him who is a great waster" (18:9 KJV); he believes he is wise, but is a fool: "The sluggard is wiser in his own eyes than seven men who answer discreetly" (26:16).

Proverbs also tells us the end in store for the lazy: A lazy person becomes a servant (or debtor): "Diligent hands will rule, but laziness ends in slave labor" (12:24); his future is bleak: "A sluggard does not plow in season; so at harvest time he looks but finds nothing" (20:4); he may come to poverty: "The soul of the lazy man desires and has nothing; but the soul of the diligent shall be made rich" (13:4 KJV).

There is no room for laziness in the life of a Christian. A new believer is truthfully taught that "...it is by grace you have been saved, through faith—and this not from yourselves, it is the gift of God—not by works, so that no one can boast" (Ephesians 2:8-9). But a believer can become idle if he erroneously believes God expects no fruit from a transformed life. "For we are God's workmanship, created in Christ Jesus to do good works, which God prepared in advance for us to do" (Ephesians 2:10). Christians are not saved by works, but they do show their faith by their works (James 2:18, 26). Slothfulness violates God's purpose—good works. The Lord, however, empowers Christians to overcome the flesh's propensity to laziness by giving us a new nature (2 Corinthians 5:17).

In our new nature, we are motivated to diligence and productiveness out of a love for our Savior who redeemed us. Our old propensity toward laziness—and all other sin—has been replaced by a desire to live godly lives: "He who has been stealing must steal no longer, but must work, doing something useful with his own hands, that he may have something to share with those in need" (Ephesians 4:28). We are convicted of our need to provide for our families through our labors: "If anyone does not provide for his relatives, and especially for his immediate family, he has denied the faith and is worse than an unbeliever" (1 Timothy 5:8); and for others in the family of God: "You yourselves know that these hands of mine have supplied my own needs and the needs of my companions. In everything I did, I showed you that by this kind of hard work we must help the weak, remembering the words the Lord Jesus himself said: 'It is more blessed to give than to receive'" (Acts 20:34-35).

As Christians, we know that our labors will be rewarded by our Lord if we persevere in diligence: "Let us not become weary in doing good, for at the proper time we will reap a harvest if we do not give up. Therefore, as we have opportunity, let us do good to all people, especially to those who belong to the family of believers" (Galatians 6:9-10); "Whatever you do, work at it with all your heart, as working for the Lord, not for men, since you know that you will receive an inheritance from the Lord as a reward. It is the Lord Christ you are serving" (Colossians 3:23-24); "God is not unjust; he will not forget your work and the love you have shown him as you have helped his people and continue to help them" (Hebrews 6:10).

Christians should labor in God's strength to evangelize and disciple. The apostle Paul is our example: "We proclaim him [Christ], admonishing and teaching everyone with all wisdom, so that we may present everyone perfect in Christ. To this end I labor, struggling with all his energy, which so powerfully works in me" (Colossians 1:28-29). Even in heaven, Christians' service to God will continue, although no longer encumbered by the curse (Revelation 22:3). Free from sickness, sorrow, and sin—even laziness—the saints will glorify the Lord forever. "Therefore, my dear brothers, stand firm. Let nothing move you. Always give yourselves fully to the work of the Lord, because you know that your labor in the Lord is not in vain" (1 Corinthians 15:58).

Question: What does the Bible say about patience?

Answer: When everything is going our way, patience is easy to demonstrate. The true test of patience comes when our rights are violated—when another car cuts us off in traffic; when we are treated unfairly; when our coworker derides our faith, again. Some people think they have a right to get upset in the face of irritations and trials. Impatience seems like a holy anger. The Bible, however, praises patience as a fruit of the Spirit (Galatians 5:22) which should be produced for all followers of Christ (1 Thessalonians 5:14). Patience reveals our faith in God's timing, omnipotence, and love.

Although most people consider patience to be a passive waiting or gentle tolerance, most of the Greek words translated "patience" in the New Testament are active, robust words. Consider, for example, Hebrews 12:1: "Therefore since we also are surrounded with so great a cloud of witnesses, let us lay aside every weight and the sin which so easily besets us, and let us run with patience the race that is set before us" (NKJV). Does one run a race by passively waiting for slow-pokes or gently tolerating cheaters? Certainly not! The word translated "patience" in this verse means "endurance." A Christian runs the race patiently by persevering through difficulties. In the Bible, patience is persevering towards a goal, enduring trials, or expectantly waiting for a promise to be fulfilled.

Patience does not develop overnight. God's power and goodness are crucial to the development of patience. Colossians 1:11 tells us that we are strengthened by Him to "great endurance and patience," while James 1:3-4 encourages us to know that trials are His way of perfecting our patience. Our patience is further developed and strengthened by resting in God's perfect will and timing, even in the face of evil men who "succeed in their ways, when they carry out their wicked schemes" (Psalm 37:7). Our patience is rewarded in the end "because the Lord's coming is near" (James 5:7-8). "The Lord is good to those whose hope is in him, to the one who seeks him" (Lamentations 3:25).

We see in the Bible many examples of those whose patience characterized their walk with God. James points us to the prophets "as an example of patience in the face of suffering" (James 5:10). He also refers to Job, whose perseverance was rewarded by what the "Lord finally brought about" (James 5:11).

Abraham, too, waited patiently and "received what was promised" (Hebrews 6:15). Jesus is our model in all things, and He demonstrated patient endurance: "Who for the joy set before him endured the cross, scorning its shame, and sat down at the right hand of the throne of God" (Hebrews 12:2).

How do we display the patience that is characteristic of Christ? First, we thank God. A person's first reaction is usually "Why me?", but the Bible says to rejoice in God's will (Philippians 4:4; 1 Peter 1:6). Second, we seek His purposes. Sometimes God puts us in difficult situations so that we can be a witness. Other times, He might allow a trial for sanctification of character. Remembering that His purpose is for our growth and His glory will help us in the trial. Third, we remember His promises such as Romans 8:28, which tells us that "all things God works for the good of those who love him, who have been called according to his purpose." The "all things" include the things that try our patience.

The next time you are in a traffic jam, betrayed by a friend, or mocked for your testimony, how will you respond? The natural response is impatience which leads to stress, anger, and frustration. Praise God that, as Christians, we are no longer in bondage to a "natural response" because we are new creations in Christ Himself (2 Corinthians 5:17). Instead, we have the Lord's strength to respond with patience and in complete trust in the Father's power and purpose. "To those who by persistence in doing good seek glory, honor and immortality, he will give eternal life" (Romans 2:7).

Question: What does the Bible say about pride?

Answer: There is a difference between the kind of pride that God hates (Proverbs 8:13) and the kind of pride we feel about a job well done. The kind of pride that stems from self-righteousness is sin, and God hates it because it is a hindrance to seeking Him. Psalm 10:4 explains that the proud are so consumed with themselves that their thoughts are far from God: "In his pride the wicked does not seek him; in all his thoughts there is no room for God." This kind of haughty pride is the opposite of the spirit of humility that God seeks: "Blessed are the poor in spirit: for theirs is the kingdom of heaven" (Matthew 5:3). The "poor in spirit" are those who recognize their utter spiritual bankruptcy and their inability to come to God aside from His divine grace. The proud, on the other hand, are so blinded by their pride that they think they have no need of God or, worse, that God should accept them as they are because they deserve His acceptance.

Throughout Scripture we are told about the consequences of pride. Proverbs 16:18-19 tells us that "pride goes before destruction, a haughty spirit before a fall. Better to be lowly in spirit and among the oppressed than to share plunder with the proud." Satan was cast out of heaven because of pride (Isaiah 14:12-15). He had the selfish audacity to attempt to replace God Himself as the rightful ruler of the universe. But Satan will be cast down to hell in the final judgment of God. For those who rise up in defiance against God, there is nothing ahead but disaster (Isaiah 14:22).

Pride has kept many people from accepting Jesus Christ as Savior. Admitting sin and acknowledging that in our own strength we can do nothing to inherit eternal life is a constant stumbling block for prideful people. We are not to boast about ourselves; if we want to boast, then we are to proclaim the glories of God. What we say about ourselves means nothing in God's work. It is what God says about us that makes the difference (2 Corinthians 10:13).

Why is pride so sinful? Pride is giving ourselves the credit for something that God has accomplished. Pride is taking the glory that belongs to God alone and keeping it for ourselves. Pride is essentially self-worship. Anything we accomplish in this world would not have been possible were it not for God enabling and sustaining us. "What do you have that you did not receive? And if you did receive it, why do you boast as though you did not?" (1 Corinthians 4:7). That is why we give God the glory—He alone deserves it.

Question: How should a Christian view self-esteem?

Answer: Many define self-esteem as "feelings of worth based on their skills, accomplishments, status, financial resources, or appearance."

This kind of self-esteem can lead a person to feel independent and prideful and to indulge in self-worship, which dulls our desire for God. James 4:6 tells us that "God opposes the proud but gives grace to the humble." If we only trust in our earthly resources, we will inevitably be left with a sense of worth based on pride. Jesus told us, "You also, when you have done everything you were told to do, should say, 'We are unworthy servants; we have only done our duty'" (Luke 17:10).

This does not mean that Christians should have low self-esteem. It only means that our sense of being a good person should not depend on what we do, but rather on who we are in Christ. We need to humble ourselves before Him, and He will honor us. Psalm 16:2 reminds us, "I said to the Lord, 'You are my Lord; apart from you I have no good thing.'" Christians attain self-worth and esteem by having a right relationship with God. We can know we are valuable because of the high price God paid for us through the blood of His Son, Jesus Christ.

In one sense, low self-esteem is the opposite of pride. In another sense, low-self-esteem is a form of pride. Some people have low self-esteem because they want people to feel sorry for them, to pay attention to them, to comfort them. Low self-esteem can be a declaration of "look at me" just as much as pride. It simply takes a different route to get to the same destination, that is, self-absorption, self-obsession, and selfishness. Instead, we are to be selfless, to die to self, and to deflect any attention given to us to the great God who created and sustains us.

The Bible tells us that God gave us worth when He purchased us to be His own people (Ephesians 1:14). Because of this, only He is worthy of honor and praise. When we have healthy self-esteem, we will value ourselves enough to not become involved in sin that enslaves us. Instead, we should conduct ourselves with humility, thinking of others as better than ourselves (Philippians 2:3). Romans 12:3 warns, "Do not think of yourself more highly than you ought, but rather think of yourself with sober judgment, in accordance with the measure of faith God has given you."

Question: What does the Bible say about worry?

Answer: The Bible clearly teaches that Christians are not to worry. In Philippians 4:6, we are commanded, "Do not be anxious [do not worry] about anything, but in everything, by prayer and petition, with thanksgiving, present your requests to God." In this Scripture, we learn that we should bring all of our needs and concerns to God in prayer rather than worry about them. Jesus encourages us to avoid worrying about our physical needs like clothing and food. Jesus assures us that our heavenly Father will take care of all our needs (Matthew 6:25-34). Therefore, we have no need to worry about anything.

Since worrying should not be a part of a believer's life, how does one overcome worry? In 1 Peter 5:7, we are instructed to "cast all your anxiety on him because he cares for you." God does not want us to carry around the weight of problems and burdens. In this verse, God is telling us to give Him all of our worries and concerns. Why does God want to take on our problems? The Bible says it is because He cares for us. God is concerned about everything that happens to us. No worry is too big or too small for His attention. When we give God our problems, He promises to give us the peace which transcends all understanding (Philippians 4:7).

Of course, for those who do not know the Savior, worry and anxiety will be part of life. But to those who have given their lives to Him, Jesus promised, "Come to me, all you who are weary and burdened, and I will give you rest. Take my yoke upon you and learn from me, for I am gentle and humble in heart, and you will find rest for your souls. For my yoke is easy and my burden is light" (Matthew 11:28-30).

Chapter 23

MISCELLANEOUS
BIBLE QUESTIONS

CONTENTS

Who were the twelve disciples/apostles of Jesus Christ? 609

Are there such things as aliens or UFOs? 610

Does the Bible record the death of the apostles? How did each of the
   apostles die? 612

Why did God choose Israel to be His chosen people? 613

Why do Jews and Arabs/Muslims hate each other? 614

Do Christians have to obey the laws of the land? 615

What is the Christian view of psychics? 616

Does the Bible condone slavery? 618

What are the Ten Commandments? 619

Does God still give visions to people today? 621

Why did God command Abraham to sacrifice Isaac? 622

What were the Christian crusades? 624

What is the Great Commission? 625

What happened in the intertestamental period? 626

Should Christian women wear make-up or jewelry? 628

Who was Melchizedek? 628

Should a Christian listen to secular music? 629

What was the significance of the temple veil being torn in two when Jesus
   died? 631

What was Paul's thorn in the flesh? 633

What happened to the Ark of the Covenant? 634

Christian archeology—why is it important? 636

Can a Christian be cursed? 638

Who were the early church fathers? 639

Why did Judas betray Jesus? 640

What does it mean that Jesus fulfilled the law, but did not abolish it?....643

Are we to love the sinner but hate the sin? 644

Why did God harden Pharaoh's heart?....................................645

Who were the Sadducees and the Pharisees? 646

How does psychology work with biblical counseling? 649

How do I know which of God's promises are for me?...............652

Is there such a thing as absolute truth? 653

Question: Who were the twelve disciples/apostles of Jesus Christ?

Answer: The word "disciple" refers to a learner or follower. The word "apostle" means "one who is sent out." While Jesus was on earth, His twelve followers were called disciples. The twelve disciples followed Jesus Christ, learned from Him, and were trained by Him. After His resurrection and ascension, Jesus sent the disciples out to be His witnesses (Matthew 28:18-20; Acts 1:8). They were then referred to as the twelve apostles. However, even when Jesus was still on earth, the terms "disciples" and "apostles" were used somewhat interchangeably.

The original twelve disciples/apostles are listed in Matthew 10:2-4, "These are the names of the twelve apostles: first, Simon (who is called Peter) and his brother Andrew; James son of Zebedee, and his brother John; Philip and Bartholomew; Thomas and Matthew the tax collector; James son of Alphaeus, and Thaddaeus; Simon the Zealot and Judas Iscariot, who betrayed Him." The Bible also lists the twelve disciples/apostles in Mark 3:16-19 and Luke 6:13-16. A comparison of the three passages shows a couple of minor differences in the names. It seems that Thaddaeus was also known as "Judas, son of James" (Luke 6:16) and Lebbaeus (Matthew 10:3). Simon the Zealot was also known as Simon the Canaanite (Mark 3:18). Judas Iscariot, who betrayed Jesus, was replaced in the twelve apostles by Matthias (see Acts 1:20-26). Some Bible teachers view Matthias as an "invalid" apostle and believe that Paul was God's choice to replace Judas Iscariot as the twelfth apostle.

The twelve disciples/apostles were ordinary men whom God used in an extraordinary manner. Among the twelve were fishermen, a tax collector, and a revolutionary. The Gospels record the constant failings, struggles, and doubts of these twelve men who followed Jesus Christ. After witnessing Jesus' resurrection and ascension into heaven, the Holy Spirit transformed the disciples/apostles into powerful men of God who turned the world upside down (Acts 17:6). What was the change? The twelve apostles/disciples had "been with Jesus" (Acts 4:13). May the same be said of us!

Question: Are there such things as aliens or UFOs?

Answer: First, let's define "aliens" as "beings capable of making moral choices, having intellect, emotion, and a will." Next, a few scientific facts:

1. Men have sent spacecraft to nearly every planet in our solar system. After observing these planets, we have ruled out all but Mars and possibly a moon of Jupiter as being able to support life.
2. In 1976, the U.S.A. sent two landers to Mars. Each had instruments that could dig into the Martian sand and analyze it for any sign of life. They found absolutely nothing. In contrast, if you analyzed soil from the most barren desert on earth or the most frozen dirt in Antarctica, you would find it teeming with micro-organisms. In 1997, the U.S.A. sent Pathfinder to the surface of Mars. This rover took more samples and conducted many more experiments. It also found absolutely no sign of life. Since that time, several more missions to Mars have been launched. The results have always been the same.
3. Astronomers are constantly finding new planets in distant solar systems. Some propose that the existence of so many planets proves that there must be life somewhere else in the universe. The fact is that none of these has ever been proved to be anything close to a life-supporting planet. The tremendous distance between Earth and these planets makes it impossible to make any judgments regarding their ability to sustain life. Knowing that Earth alone supports life in our solar system, evolutionists want very badly to find another planet in another solar system to support the notion that life must have evolved. There are many other planets out there, but we certainly do not know enough about them to verify that they could support life.

So, what does the Bible say? The earth and mankind are unique in God's creation. Genesis 1 teaches that God created the earth before He even created the sun, the moon, or the stars. Acts 17:24, 26 states that "the God who made the world and everything in it is the Lord of heaven and earth and does not live in temples built by hands…he made every nation of men, that they should inhabit the whole earth; and he determined the times set for them and the exact places where they should live."

Originally, mankind was without sin, and everything in the world was "very good" (Genesis 1:31). When the first man sinned (Genesis 3), the result was problems of all sorts, including sickness and death. Even though animals have no personal sin before God (they are not moral beings), they still suffer and die (Romans 8:19-22). Jesus Christ died to remove the punishment that we deserve for our sin. When He returns, He will undo the curse that has existed since Adam (Revelation 21–22). Note that Romans 8:19-22 states that all of creation eagerly waits for this time. It is important to also note that Christ came to die for mankind and that He died only once (Hebrews 7:27; 9:26-28; 10:10).

If all of creation now suffers under the curse, any life apart from the earth would also suffer. If, for the sake of argument, moral beings do exist on other planets, then they also suffer; and if not now, then someday they will surely suffer when everything passes away with a great noise and the elements melt with fervent heat (2 Peter 3:10). If they had never sinned, then God would be unjust in punishing them. But if they had sinned, and Christ could die only once (which He did on earth), then they are left in their sin, which would also be contrary to the character of God (2 Peter 3:9). This leaves us with an unsolvable paradox—unless, of course, there are no moral beings outside of the earth.

What about non-moral and non-sentient life forms on other planets? Could algae or even dogs and cats be present on an unknown planet? Presumably so, and it would not do any real harm to any biblical text. But it would certainly prove problematic when trying answer questions like "Since all of creation suffers, what purpose would God have in creating non-moral and non-sentient creatures to suffer on distant planets?"

In conclusion, the Bible gives us no reason to believe that there is life elsewhere in the universe. In fact, the Bible gives us several key reasons why there cannot be. Yes, there are many strange and unexplainable things that take place. There is no reason, though, to attribute these phenomena to aliens or UFOs. If there is a discernable cause to these supposed events, it is likely to be spiritual, and more specifically, demonic, in origin.

Question: Does the Bible record the death of the apostles? How did each of the apostles die?

Answer: The only apostle whose death the Bible records is James (Acts 12:2). King Herod had James "put to death with the sword," likely a reference to beheading. The circumstances of the deaths of the other apostles are related through church tradition, so we should not put too much weight on any of the other accounts. The most commonly accepted church tradition in regard to the death of an apostle is that the apostle Peter was crucified upside-down on an x-shaped cross in Rome in fulfillment of Jesus' prophecy (John 21:18). The following are the most popular "traditions" concerning the deaths of the other apostles.

Matthew suffered martyrdom in Ethiopia, killed by a sword wound. John faced martyrdom when he was boiled in a huge basin of boiling oil during a wave of persecution in Rome. However, he was miraculously delivered from death. John was then sentenced to the mines on the prison island of Patmos. He wrote his prophetic book of Revelation on Patmos. The apostle John was later freed and returned to what is now modern-day Turkey. He died as an old man, the only apostle to die peacefully.

James, the brother of Jesus (not officially an apostle), was the leader of the church in Jerusalem. He was thrown from the southeast pinnacle of the temple (over a hundred feet down) when he refused to deny his faith in Christ. When they discovered that he survived the fall, his enemies beat James to death with a club. This is thought to be the same pinnacle where Satan had taken Jesus during the temptation.

Bartholomew, also known as Nathanael, was a missionary to Asia. He witnessed in present-day Turkey and was martyred for his preaching in Armenia, being flayed to death by a whip. Andrew was crucified on an x-shaped cross in Greece. After being whipped severely by seven soldiers, they tied his body to the cross with cords to prolong his agony. His followers reported that when he was led toward the cross, Andrew saluted it in these words: "I have long desired and expected this happy hour. The cross has been consecrated by the body of Christ hanging on it." He continued to preach to his tormentors for two days until he died. The apostle Thomas was stabbed with a spear in India during one of his missionary trips to establish the church there. Matthias, the apostle chosen to replace the traitor Judas Iscariot, was stoned and then beheaded. The apostle Paul was tortured and then beheaded by the evil Emperor Nero in Rome in A.D. 67. There are traditions regarding the other apostles as well, but none with any reliable historical or traditional support.

It is not so important how the apostles died. What is important is the fact that they were all willing to die for their faith. If Jesus had not been resurrected, the disciples would have known it. People will not die for something they know to be a lie. The fact that all of the apostles were willing to die horrible deaths, refusing to renounce their faith in Christ, is tremendous evidence that they had truly witnessed the resurrection of Jesus Christ.

Question: Why did God choose Israel to be His chosen people?

Answer: Speaking of the nation of Israel, Deuteronomy 7:7-9 tells us, "The LORD did not set His affection on you and choose you because you were more numerous than other peoples, for you were the fewest of all peoples. But it was because the LORD loved you and kept the oath He swore to your forefathers that He brought you out with a mighty hand and redeemed you from the land of slavery, from the power of Pharaoh king of Egypt. Know therefore that the LORD your God is God; He is the faithful God, keeping His covenant of love to a thousand generations of those who love Him and keep His commands."

God chose the nation of Israel to be the people through whom Jesus Christ would be born—the Savior from sin and death (John 3:16). God first promised the Messiah after Adam and Eve's fall into sin (Genesis chapter 3). God later confirmed that the Messiah would come from the line of Abraham, Isaac, and Jacob (Genesis 12:1-3). Jesus Christ is the ultimate reason why God chose Israel to be His special people. God did not need to have a chosen people, but He decided to do it that way. Jesus had to come from some nation of people, and God chose Israel.

However, God's reason for choosing the nation of Israel was not solely for the purpose of producing the Messiah. God's desire for Israel was that they would go and teach others about Him. Israel was to be a nation of priests, prophets, and missionaries to the world. God's intent was for Israel to be a distinct people, a nation who pointed others towards God and His promised provision of a Redeemer, Messiah, and Savior. For the most part, Israel failed in this task. However, God's ultimate purpose for Israel—that of bringing the Messiah into the world—was fulfilled perfectly in the Person of Jesus Christ.

Question: Why do Jews and Arabs/Muslims hate each other?

Answer: First, it is important to understand that not all Arabs are Muslims, and not all Muslims are Arabs. While a majority of Arabs are Muslims, there are many non-Muslim Arabs. Further, there are significantly more non-Arab Muslims in areas such as Indonesia and Malaysia than there are Arab Muslims. Second, it is important to remember that not all Arabs hate Jews, not all Muslims hate Jews, and not all Jews hate Arabs and Muslims. We must be careful to avoid stereotyping people. However, generally speaking, Arabs and Muslims have a dislike of and distrust for Jews, and vice-versa.

If there is an explicit biblical explanation for this animosity, it goes all the way back to Abraham. The Jews are descendants of Abraham's son Isaac. The Arabs are descendants of Abraham's son Ishmael. With Ishmael being the son of a slave woman (Genesis 16:1-16) and Isaac being the promised son who would inherit the blessings of Abraham (Genesis 21:1-3), obviously there would be some animosity between the two sons. As a result of Ishmael's mocking Isaac (Genesis 21:9), Sarah talked Abraham into sending Hagar and Ishmael away (Genesis 21:11-21). Likely, this caused even more contempt in Ishmael's heart towards Isaac. An angel prophesied to Hagar that Ishmael would "live in hostility toward all his brothers" (Genesis 16:11-12).

The religion of Islam, to which a majority of Arabs are adherents, has made this hostility more profound. The Qur'an contains somewhat contradictory instructions for Muslims regarding Jews. At one point it instructs Muslims to treat Jews as brothers and at another point commands Muslims to attack Jews who refuse to convert to Islam. The Qur'an also introduces a conflict as to which son of Abraham was truly the son of promise. The Hebrew Scriptures say it was Isaac. The Qur'an says it was Ishmael. The Qur'an teaches that it was Ishmael who Abraham almost sacrificed to the Lord, not Isaac (in contradiction to Genesis chapter 22). This debate over who was the son of promise contributes to the hostility today.

However, the ancient root of bitterness between Isaac and Ishmael does not explain all of the hostility between Jews and Arabs today. In fact, for thousands of years of Middle Eastern history, Jews and Arabs lived in relative peace and indifference towards each other. The primary cause of the hostility has a modern origin. After World War II, when the United Nations gave a portion of the land of Israel to the Jewish people, the land was at that time primarily inhabited by Arabs (the Palestinians). Most Arabs protested vehemently against the nation of Israel occupying that land. Arab nations united and attacked Israel in an attempt to drive them out of the land, but they were defeated. Ever since, there has been great hostility between Israel and its Arab neighbors. Israel exists on one tiny piece of land surrounded by much larger Arab nations such as Jordan, Syria, Saudi Arabia, Iraq, and Egypt. It is our viewpoint that, biblically speaking, Israel has a right to exist as a nation in its own land that God gave to the descendants of Jacob, grandson of Abraham. At the same time, we strongly believe that Israel should seek peace and display respect for its Arab neighbors. Psalm 122:6 declares, "Pray for the peace of Jerusalem: May those who love you be secure."

Question: Do Christians have to obey the laws of the land?

Answer: Romans 13:1-7 states, "Everyone must submit himself to the governing authorities, for there is no authority except that which God has established. The authorities that exist have been established by God. Consequently, he who rebels against the authority is rebelling against what God has instituted, and those who do so will bring judgment on themselves. For rulers hold no terror for those who do right, but for those who do wrong. Do you want to be free from fear of the one in authority? Then do what is right and he will commend you. For he is God's servant to do you good. But if you do wrong, be afraid, for he does not bear the sword for nothing. He is God's servant, an agent of wrath to bring punishment on the wrongdoer.

Therefore, it is necessary to submit to the authorities, not only because of possible punishment but also because of conscience. This is also why you pay taxes, for the authorities are God's servants, who give their full time to governing. Give everyone what you owe him: If you owe taxes, pay taxes; if revenue, then revenue; if respect, then respect; if honor, then honor."

This passage makes it abundantly clear that we are to obey the government God places over us. God created government to establish order, punish evil, and promote justice (Genesis 9:6; 1 Corinthians 14:33; Romans 12:8). We are to obey the government in everything—paying taxes, obeying rules and laws, and showing respect. If we do not, we are ultimately showing disrespect towards God, for He is the One who placed that government over us. When the apostle Paul wrote to the Romans, he was under the government of Rome during the reign of Nero, perhaps the most evil of all the Roman emperors. Paul still recognized the Roman government's rule over him. How can we do any less?

The next question is "Is there a time when we should intentionally disobey the laws of the land?" The answer to that question may be found in Acts 5:27-29, "Having brought the apostles, they made them appear before the Sanhedrin to be questioned by the high priest. 'We gave you strict orders not to teach in this Name,' he said. 'Yet you have filled Jerusalem with your teaching and are determined to make us guilty of this man's blood.' Peter and the other apostles replied: 'We must obey God rather than men!'" From this, it is clear that as long as the law of the land does not contradict the law of God, we are bound to obey the law of the land. As soon as the law of the land contradicts God's command, we are to disobey the law of the land and obey God's law. However, even in that instance, we are to accept the government's authority over us. This is demonstrated by the fact that Peter and John did not protest being flogged, but instead rejoiced that they suffered for obeying God (Acts 5:40-42).

Question: What is the Christian view of psychics?

Answer: The Bible strongly condemns spiritism, mediums, the occult, and psychics (Leviticus 20:27; Deuteronomy 18:10-13). Horoscopes, tarot cards, astrology, fortune tellers, palm readings, and séances fall into this category as well. These practices are based on the concept that there are gods, spirits, or deceased loved ones that can give advice and guidance. These "gods" or "spirits" are demons (2 Corinthians 11:14-15). The Bible gives us no reason to believe that deceased loved ones can contact us. If they were believers, they are in heaven enjoying the most wonderful place imaginable in fellowship with a loving God. If they were not believers, they are in hell, suffering the un-ending torment for rejecting God's love and rebelling against Him.

So, if our loved ones cannot contact us, how do mediums, spirit-ists, and psychics get such accurate information? There have been many exposures of psychics as frauds. It has been proven that psychics can gain immense amounts of information on someone through ordinary means. Sometimes by just using a telephone number through caller ID and an internet search, a psychic can get names, addresses, dates of birth, dates of marriage, family members, etc. However, it is undeniable that psychics sometimes know things that should be impossible for them to know. Where do they get this information? The answer is from Satan and his demons. "And no wonder, for Satan himself masquerades as an angel of light. It is not surprising, then, if his servants masquerade as servants of righteousness. Their end will be what their actions deserve" (2 Corinthians 11:14-15). Acts 16:16-18 describes a fortune teller who was able to predict the future until the apostle Paul rebuked a demon out of her.

Satan pretends to be kind and helpful. He tries to appear as some-thing good. Satan and his demons will give a psychic information about a person in order to get that person hooked into spiritism, something that God forbids. It appears innocent at first, but soon people can find themselves addicted to psychics and unwittingly allow Satan to control and destroy their lives. Peter proclaimed, "Be self-controlled and alert. Your enemy the devil prowls around like a roaring lion looking for someone to devour" (1 Peter 5:8). In some cases, the psychics themselves are deceived, not knowing the true source of the information they receive. Whatever the case and wherever the source of the information, nothing connected to spiritism, witchcraft, or astrology is a godly means of discovering information. How does God want us to discern His will for our life? God's plan is simple, yet powerful and effective: study the Bible (2 Timothy 3:16-17) and pray for wisdom (James 1:5).

Question: Does the Bible condone slavery?

Answer: There is a tendency to look at slavery as something of the past. But it is estimated that there are today over 12 million people in the world who are subject to slavery: forced labor, sex trade, inheritable property, etc. As those who have been redeemed from the slavery of sin, followers of Jesus Christ should be the foremost champions of ending human slavery in the world today. The question arises, though, why does the Bible not speak out strongly against slavery? Why does the Bible, in fact, seem to support the practice of human slavery?

The Bible does not specifically condemn the practice of slavery. It gives instructions on how slaves should be treated (Deuteronomy 15:12-15; Ephesians 6:9; Colossians 4:1), but does not outlaw slavery altogether. Many see this as the Bible condoning all forms of slavery. What many fail to understand is that slavery in biblical times was very different from the slavery that was practiced in the past few centuries in many parts of the world. The slavery in the Bible was not based exclusively on race. People were not enslaved because of their nationality or the color of their skin. In Bible times, slavery was more a matter of social status. People sold themselves as slaves when they could not pay their debts or provide for their families. In New Testament times, sometimes doctors, lawyers, and even politicians were slaves of someone else. Some people actually chose to be slaves so as to have all their needs provided for by their masters.

The slavery of the past few centuries was often based exclusively on skin color. In the United States, many black people were considered slaves because of their nationality; many slave owners truly believed black people to be inferior human beings. The Bible most definitely does condemn race-based slavery. Consider the slavery the Hebrews experienced when they were in Egypt. The Hebrew were slaves, not by choice, but because they were Hebrews (Exodus 13:14). The plagues God poured out on Egypt demonstrate how God feels about racial slavery (Exodus 7-11). So, yes, the Bible does condemn some forms of slavery. At the same time, the Bible does seem to allow for other forms. The key issue is that the slavery the Bible allowed for in no way resembled the racial slavery that plagued our world in the past few centuries.

In addition, both the Old and New Testaments condemn the practice of "man-stealing" which is what happened in Africa in the 19th century. Africans were rounded up by slave-hunters, who sold them to slave-traders, who brought them to the New World to work on plantations and farms. This practice is abhorrent to God. In fact, the penalty for such a crime in the Mosaic Law was death: "Anyone who kidnaps another and either sells him or still has him when he is caught must be put to death" (Exodus 21:16). Similarly, in the New Testament, slave-traders are listed among those who are "ungodly and sinful" and are in the same category as those who kill their fathers or mothers, murderers, adulterers and perverts, and liars and perjurers (1 Timothy 1:8-10).

Another crucial point is that the purpose of the Bible is to point the way to salvation, not to reform society. The Bible often approaches issues from the inside out. If a person experiences the love, mercy, and grace of God by receiving His salvation, God will reform his soul, changing the way he thinks and acts. A person who has experienced God's gift of salvation and freedom from the slavery of sin, as God reforms his soul, will realize that enslaving another human being is wrong. A person who has truly experienced God's grace will in turn be gracious towards others. That would be the Bible's prescription for ending slavery.

Question: What are the Ten Commandments?

Answer: The Ten Commandments are ten laws in the Bible that God gave to the nation of Israel shortly after the exodus from Egypt. The Ten Commandments are essentially a summary of the 613 commandments contained in the Old Testament Law. The first four commandments deal with our relationship with God. The last six commandments deal with our relationships with one another. The Ten Commandments are recorded in the Bible in Exodus 20:1-17 and Deuteronomy 5:6-21 and are as follows:

1. "You shall have no other gods before me." This command is against worshipping any god other than the one true God. All other gods are false gods.
2. "You shall not make for yourself an idol in the form of anything in heaven above or on the earth beneath or in the

waters below. You shall not bow down to them or worship them; for I, the LORD your God, am a jealous God, punishing the children for the sin of the fathers to the third and fourth generation of those who hate me, but showing love to a thousand generations of those who love me and keep my commandments." This command is against making an idol, a visible representation of God. There is no image we can create that can accurately portray God. To make an idol to represent God is to worship a false god.

3. "You shall not misuse the name of the LORD your God, for the LORD will not hold anyone guiltless who misuses His name." This is a command against taking the name of the Lord in vain. We are not to treat God's name lightly. We are to show reverence to God by only mentioning Him in respectful and honoring ways.

4. "Remember the Sabbath day by keeping it holy. Six days you shall labor and do all your work, but the seventh day is a Sabbath to the LORD your God. On it you shall not do any work, neither you, nor your son or daughter, nor your manservant or maidservant, nor your animals, nor the alien within your gates. For in six days the LORD made the heavens and the earth, the sea, and all that is in them, but he rested on the seventh day. Therefore the LORD blessed the Sabbath day and made it holy." This is a command to set aside the Sabbath (Saturday, the last day of the week) as a day of rest dedicated to the Lord.

5. "Honor your father and your mother, so that you may live long in the land the LORD your God is giving you." This is a command to always treat one's parents with honor and respect.

6. "You shall not murder." This is a command against the premeditated murder of another human being.

7. "You shall not commit adultery." This is a command against have sexual relations with anyone other than one's spouse.

8. "You shall not steal." This is a command against taking anything that is not one's own, without the permission of the person to whom it belongs.

9. "You shall not give false testimony against your neighbor." This is a command prohibiting testifying against another person falsely. It is essentially a command against lying.
10. "You shall not covet your neighbor's house. You shall not covet your neighbor's wife, or his manservant or maidservant, his ox or donkey, or anything that belongs to your neighbor." This is a command against desiring anything that is not one's own. Coveting can lead to breaking one of the commandments listed above: murder, adultery, and theft. If it is wrong to do something, it is wrong to desire to do that same something.

Many people mistakenly look at the Ten Commandments as a set of rules, that if followed, will guarantee entrance into heaven after death. In contrast, the purpose of the Ten Commandments is to force people to realize that they cannot perfectly obey the Law (Romans 7:7-11), and are therefore in need of God's mercy and grace. Despite the claims of the rich young ruler in Matthew 19:16, no one can perfectly obey the Ten Commandments (Ecclesiastes 7:20). The Ten Commandments demonstrate that we have all sinned (Romans 3:23) and are therefore in need of God's mercy and grace, available only through faith in Jesus Christ.

Question: Does God still give visions to people today?

Answer: Can God give visions to people today? Yes! Does God give visions to people today? Possibly. Should we expect visions to be an ordinary occurrence? No. As recorded in the Bible, God spoke to people many times by means of visions. Examples are Joseph, son of Jacob; Joseph, the husband of Mary; Solomon; Isaiah; Ezekiel; Daniel; Peter; and Paul. The prophet Joel predicted an outpouring of visions, and this was confirmed by the apostle Peter in Acts chapter 2. It is important to note that the difference between a vision and a dream is that a vision is given when a person is awake while a dream is given when a person is asleep.

In many parts of the world, God seems to be using visions and dreams extensively. In areas where there is little or no gospel message available, and where people do not have Bibles, God is taking His message to people directly through dreams and visions. This is entirely consistent with the biblical example of visions being frequently used by God to reveal His truth to people in the early days of Christianity. If God desires to communicate His message to a person, He can use whatever means He finds necessary—a missionary, an angel, a vision, or a dream. Of course, God also has the ability to give visions in areas where the gospel message is already readily available. There is no limit to what God can do.

At the same time, we must be careful when it comes to visions and the interpretation of visions. We must keep in mind that the Bible is finished, and it tells us everything we need to know. The key truth is that if God were to give a vision, it would agree completely with what He has already revealed in His Word. Visions should never be given equal or greater authority than the Word of God. God's Word is our ultimate authority for Christian faith and practice. If you believe you have had a vision and feel that perhaps God gave it to you, prayerfully examine the Word of God and make sure your vision is in agreement with Scripture. Then prayerfully consider what God would have you do in response to the vision (James 1:5). God would not give a vision to a person and then keep the meaning of the vision hidden. In Scripture, whenever a person asked God for the meaning of a vision, God made sure it was explained to the person (Daniel 8:15-17).

Question: Why did God command Abraham to sacrifice Isaac?

Answer: Abraham had obeyed God many times in his walk with Him, but no test could have been more severe than the one in Genesis 22. God commanded, "Take your son, your only son, Isaac, whom you love, and go to the region of Moriah. Sacrifice him there as a burnt offering" (Genesis 22:2a). This was an astounding request because Isaac was the son of promise. How did Abraham respond? With immediate obedience; early the next morning, Abraham started on his journey with two servants, a donkey and his beloved son Isaac, with firewood for the offering. His unquestioning obedience to God's confusing command gave God the glory He deserves and is an example to us of how to glorify God. When we obey as Abraham did, trusting that God's plan is the best possible scenario, we exalt His attributes and praise Him. Abraham's obedience in the face of this crushing command extolled God's sovereign love, His trustworthiness, and

His goodness, and it provided an example for us to follow. His faith in the God he had come to know and love placed Abraham in the pantheon of faithful heroes in Hebrews 11.

God uses Abraham's faith as an example to all who came after him as the only means of salvation. Genesis 15:6 says, "Abram believed the LORD, and he credited it to him as righteousness." This truth is the basis of the Christian faith, as reiterated in Romans 4:3 and James 2:23. The righteousness that was credited to Abraham is the same righteousness credited to us when we receive by faith the sacrifice God provided for our sins—Jesus Christ. "God made him who had no sin to be sin for us, so that in him we might become the righteousness of God" (2 Corinthians 5:21).

The Old Testament story of Abraham is the basis of the New Testament teaching of the atonement, the sacrificial offering of the Lord Jesus on the cross for the sin of mankind. Jesus said, many centuries later, "Your father Abraham rejoiced at the thought of seeing my day; he saw it and was glad" (John 8:56). Following are some of the parallels between the two biblical accounts:

- "Take your son, your only son, Isaac" (v. 2); "For God so loved the world that he gave his one and only Son…" (John 3:16).
- "Go to the region of Moriah. Sacrifice him there…" (v. 2); it is believed that this area is where the city of Jerusalem was built many years later, where Jesus was crucified outside its city walls (Hebrews 13:12).
- "Sacrifice him there as a burnt offering" (v. 2); "Christ died for our sins according to the Scriptures" (1 Corinthians 15:3).
- "Abraham took the wood for the burnt offering and placed it on his son Isaac" (v. 6); Jesus, "carrying his own cross. . ." (John 19:17).
- "But where is the lamb for the burnt offering?" (v. 7); John said, "Look, the Lamb of God, who takes away the sin of the world!" (John 1:29).
- Isaac, the son, acted in obedience to his father in becoming the sacrifice (v. 9); Jesus prayed, "My Father, if it is possible, may this cup be taken from me. Yet not as I will, but as you will" (Matthew 26:39).

- Resurrection – Isaac (figuratively) and Jesus in reality: "By faith Abraham, when God tested him, offered Isaac as a sacrifice. He who had received the promises was about to sacrifice his one and only son, even though God had said to him, 'It is through Isaac that your offspring will be reckoned.' Abraham reasoned that God could raise the dead, and figuratively speaking, he did receive Isaac back from death." (Hebrews 11:17-19); Jesus, "that he was buried, and that he was raised on the third day according to the Scriptures" (1 Corinthians 15:4).

Question: What were the Christian crusades?

Answer: The crusades have provided some of the most frequent arguments against the Christian faith. Some Islamic terrorists even claim that their terrorist attacks are revenge for what Christians did in the crusades. So, what were the crusades and why are they viewed as such a big problem for the Christian faith?

First of all, the crusades should not be referred to as the "Christian crusades." Most of the people involved in the crusades were not truly Christians, even though they claimed to be. The name of Christ was abused, misused, and blasphemed by the actions of many of the crusaders. Second, the crusades took place from approximately A.D. 1095 to 1230. Should the unbiblical actions of supposed Christians hundreds of years ago still be held against Christians today?

Third, not that this is an adequate excuse, but Christianity is not the only religion with a violent past. In actuality, the crusades were responses to Muslim invasions on what was once land occupied primarily by Christians. From approximately A.D. 200 to 900, the land of Israel, Jordan, Egypt, Syria, and Turkey was inhabited primarily by Christians. Once Islam became powerful, Muslims invaded these lands and brutally oppressed, enslaved, deported, and even murdered the Christians living in those lands. In response, the Roman Catholic Church and "Christian" kings/emperors from Europe ordered the crusades to reclaim the land the Muslims had taken. The actions that many so-called Christians took in the crusades were still deplorable. There is no biblical justification for conquering lands, murdering civilians, and destroying cities in the name of Jesus Christ. At the same time, Islam is not a religion that can speak from a position of innocence in these matters.

To summarize briefly, the crusades were attempts in the 10th through 12th centuries A.D. to reclaim land in the Middle East that had been conquered by Muslims. The crusades were brutal and evil. Many people were forced to "convert" to Christianity. If they refused, they were put to death. The idea of conquering a land through war and violence in the name of Christ is completely unbiblical. Many of the actions that took place in the crusades were completely antithetical to everything the Christian faith stands for.

How can we respond when, as a result of the crusades, the Christian faith is attacked by atheists, agnostics, skeptics, and those of other religions? We can respond in the following ways: 1) Do you want to be held accountable for the actions of people who lived 900+ years ago? 2) Do you want to be held accountable for the actions of everyone who claims to represent your faith? Trying to blame all of Christianity for the crusades is analogous to blaming all Muslims for Islamic terrorism.

Question: What is the Great Commission?

Answer: Matthew 28:19-20 contains what has come to be called the Great Commission: "Therefore go and make disciples of all nations, baptizing them in the name of the Father and of the Son and of the Holy Spirit, and teaching them to obey everything I have commanded you. And surely I am with you always, to the very end of the age." Jesus gave this command to the apostles shortly before He ascended into heaven, and it essentially outlines what Jesus expected the apostles, and those who followed them, to do in His absence.

It is interesting that in the original Greek, the only specific command in Matthew 28:19-20 is "make disciples." The Great Commission instructs us to make disciples while we are going throughout the world and while we are going about our daily activities. How are we to make disciples? By baptizing them and teaching them all that Jesus commanded. "Make disciples" is the command of the Great Commission. "As you are going," "baptizing," and "teaching" are the means by which we fulfill the command to "make disciples."

625

Many understand Acts 1:8 as part of the Great Commission as well, "But you will receive power when the Holy Spirit comes on you; and you will be my witnesses in Jerusalem, and in all Judea and Samaria, and to the ends of the earth." The Great Commission is enabled by the power of the Holy Spirit. We are to be Christ's witnesses, fulfilling the Great Commission in our cities (Jerusalem), in our states and countries (Judea and Samaria), and anywhere else God sends us (to the ends of the earth).

Question: What happened in the intertestamental period?

Answer: The time between the last writings of the Old Testament and the appearance of Christ is known as the "intertestamental" (or "between the testaments") period. Because there was no prophetic word from God during this period, some refer to it as the "400 silent years." The political, religious, and social atmosphere of Palestine changed significantly during this period. Much of what happened was predicted by the prophet Daniel. (See Daniel chapters 2, 7, 8, and 11 and compare to historical events.)

Israel was under the control of the Persian Empire from about 532-332 B.C. The Persians allowed the Jews to practice their religion with little interference. They were even allowed to rebuild and worship at the temple (2 Chronicles 36:22-23; Ezra 1:1-4). This period included the last 100 years of the Old Testament period and about the first 100 years of the intertestamental period. This time of relative peace and contentment was just the calm before the storm.

Alexander the Great defeated Darius of Persia, bringing Greek rule to the world. Alexander was a student of Aristotle and was well educated in Greek philosophy and politics. He required that Greek culture be promoted in every land that he conquered. As a result, the Hebrew Old Testament was translated into Greek, becoming the translation known as the Septuagint. Most of the New Testament references to Old Testament Scripture use the Septuagint phrasing. Alexander did allow religious freedom for the Jews, though he still strongly promoted Greek lifestyles. This was not a good turn of events for Israel since the Greek culture was very worldly, humanistic, and ungodly.

After Alexander died, Judea was ruled by a series of successors, culminating in Antiochus Epiphanes. Antiochus did far more than refuse religious freedom to the Jews. Around 167 B.C, he overthrew the rightful line of the priesthood and desecrated the temple, defiling it with unclean animals and a pagan altar (see Mark 13:14). This was the religious equivalent of rape. Eventually, Jewish resistance to Antiochus restored the rightful priests and rescued the temple. The period that followed was one of war, violence, and infighting.

Around 63 B.C, Pompey of Rome conquered Palestine, putting all of Judea under control of the Caesars. This eventually led to Herod being made king of Judea by the Roman emperor and senate. This would be the nation that taxed and controlled the Jews, and eventually executed the Messiah on a Roman cross. Roman, Greek, and Hebrew cultures were now mixed together in Judea.

During the span of the Greek and Roman occupations, two important political/religious groups emerged in Palestine. The Pharisees added to the Law of Moses through oral tradition and eventually considered their own laws more important than God's (see Mark 7:1-23). While Christ's teachings often agreed with the Pharisees, He railed against their hollow legalism and lack of compassion. The Sadducees represented the aristocrats and the wealthy. The Sadducees, who wielded power through the Sanhedrin, rejected all but the Mosaic books of the Old Testament. They refused to believe in resurrection and were generally shadows of the Greeks, whom they greatly admired.

This rush of events that set the stage for Christ had a profound impact on the Jewish people. Both Jews and pagans from other nations were becoming dissatisfied with religion. The pagans were beginning to question the validity of polytheism. Romans and Greeks were drawn from their mythologies towards Hebrew Scriptures, now easily readable in Greek or Latin. The Jews, however, were despondent. Once again, they were conquered, oppressed, and polluted. Hope was running low; faith was even lower. They were convinced that now the only thing that could save them and their faith was the appearance of the Messiah.

The New Testament tells the story of how hope came, not only for the Jews, but for the entire world. Christ's fulfillment of prophecy was anticipated and recognized by many who sought Him out. The stories of the Roman centurion, the wise men, and the Pharisee Nicodemus show how Jesus was recognized as the Messiah by those who lived in His day. The "400 years of silence" were broken by the greatest story ever told—the gospel of Jesus Christ!

Question: Should Christian women wear make-up or jewelry?

Answer: First Samuel 16:7b declares, "The LORD does not look at the things man looks at. Man looks at the outward appearance, but the LORD looks at the heart." First Timothy 2:9-10 tells us, "I also want women to dress modestly, with decency and propriety, not with braided hair or gold or pearls or expensive clothes, but with good deeds, appropriate for women who profess to worship God." Paul did not forbid women from wearing jewelry, makeup, or braided hair—rather he tells women to not let their outward appearance become more important than their inner beauty.

Peter reminds us of this spiritual fact: "Your beauty should not come from outward adornment, such as braided hair and the wearing of gold jewelry and fine clothes. Instead, it should be that of your inner self, the unfading beauty of a gentle and quiet spirit, which is of great worth in God's sight" (1 Peter 3:3-5). There is nothing wrong with wearing jewelry, makeup, or braided hair as long as it is done in a modest manner. A woman should not be so focused on her outward appearance that she neglects her inner spiritual life. The Bible focuses on the heart. If a woman is spending too much time and money on her appearance, the problem is that the woman's priorities are wrong. Expensive jewelry and clothing are the results of the problem, not the problem itself.

Question: Who was Melchizedek?

Answer: Melchizedek, whose name means "king of righteousness," was a king of Salem (Jerusalem) and priest of the Most High God (Genesis 14:18-20; Psalm 110:4; Hebrews 5:6-11; 6:20-7:28). Melchizedek's sudden appearance and disappearance in the book of Genesis is somewhat mysterious. Melchizedek and Abraham first met after Abraham's defeat of Chedorlaomer and his three allies. Melchizedek presented bread and wine to Abraham and his weary men, demonstrating friendship. He bestowed a blessing on Abraham in the name of El Elyon ("God Most High") and praised God for giving Abraham a victory in battle (Genesis 14:18-20).

Abraham presented Melchizedek with a tithe (a tenth) of all the items he had gathered. By this act Abraham indicated that he recognized Melchizedek as a fellow-worshiper of the one true God as well as a priest who ranked higher spiritually than himself. Melchizedek's existence shows that there were people other than Abraham and his family who served the one true God.

In Psalm 110, a messianic psalm written by David (Matthew 22:43), Melchizedek is seen as a type of Christ. This theme is repeated in the book of Hebrews, where both Melchizedek and Christ are considered kings of righteousness and peace. By citing Melchizedek and his unique priesthood as a type, the writer shows that Christ's new priesthood is superior to the old levitical order and the priesthood of Aaron (Hebrews 7:1-10).

Some propose that Melchizedek was actually a pre-incarnate appearance of Jesus Christ. While possible, this view is unlikely. Melchizedek was the king of Salem. Would Jesus Christ have come to earth and ruled as an earthly king over a city? Melchizedek is similar to Christ in that they are both priests and kings; therefore, Melchizedek could be called a "type" of Christ, but they are not the same person.

Question: Should a Christian listen to secular music?

Answer: Many Christians struggle with this question. Many secular musicians are immensely talented. Secular music can be very entertaining. There are many secular songs that have catchy melodies, thoughtful insights, and positive messages. In determining whether or not to listen to secular music, there are three primary factors to consider: 1) the purpose of music, 2) the style of music, and 3) the content of the lyrics.

1. **The purpose of music.** Is music designed solely for worship, or did God also intend music to be soothing and/or entertaining? The most famous musician in the Bible, King David, primarily used music for the purpose of worshipping

God (see Psalm 4:1; 6:1, 54, 55; 61:1; 67:1; 76:1). However, when King Saul was tormented by evil spirits, he would call on David to play the harp in order to soothe him (1 Samuel 16:14-23). The Israelites also used musical instruments to warn of danger (Nehemiah 4:20) and to surprise their enemies (Judges 7:16-22). In the New Testament, the apostle Paul instructs Christians to encourage one another with music: "Speak to one another with psalms, hymns and spiritual songs" (Ephesians 5:19). So, while the primary purpose of music does seem to be worship, the Bible definitely allows for other uses of music.

2. **The style of music.** Sadly, the issue of music styles can be very divisive among Christians. There are Christians who adamantly demand that no musical instruments be used. There are Christians who only desire to sing the "old faithful" hymns. There are Christians who want more upbeat and contemporary music. There are Christians who claim to worship best in a "rock concert" type of environment. Instead of recognizing these differences as personal preferences and cultural distinctions, some Christians declare their preferred style of music to be the only "biblical" one and declare all other forms of music to be unwholesome, ungodly, or even satanic.

   The Bible nowhere condemns any particular style of music. The Bible nowhere declares any particular musical instrument to be ungodly. The Bible mentions numerous kinds of string instruments and wind instruments. While the Bible does not specifically mention drums, it does mention other percussion instruments (Psalm 68:25; Ezra 3:10). Nearly all of the forms of modern music are variations and/or combinations of the same types of musical instruments, played at different speeds or with heightened emphasis. There is no biblical basis to declare any particular style of music to be ungodly or outside of God's will.

3. **The content of the lyrics.** Since neither the purpose of music nor the style of music determine whether a Christian should listen to secular music, the content of the lyrics must be considered. While not specifically speaking of music,

Philippians 4:8 is an excellent guide for musical lyrics: "Finally, brothers, whatever is true, whatever is noble, whatever is right, whatever is pure, whatever is lovely, whatever is admirable—if anything is excellent or praiseworthy—think about such things." If we should be thinking about such things, surely those are the things we should invite into our minds through music and lyrics. Can the lyrics in a secular song be true, noble, right, pure, lovely, admirable, excellent, and praiseworthy? If so, then there is nothing wrong with a Christian listening to a secular song of that nature.

However, much of secular music does not meet the standard of Philippians 4:8. Secular music often promotes immorality and violence while belittling purity and integrity. If a song glorifies what opposes God, a Christian should not listen to it. However, there are many secular songs with no mention of God that still uphold godly values such as honesty, purity, and integrity. If a love song promotes the sanctity of marriage and/or the purity of true love—even if it does not mention God or the Bible—it can still be listened to and enjoyed.

Whatever a person allows to occupy his mind will sooner or later determine his speech and his actions. This is the premise behind Philippians 4:8 and Colossians 3:2, 5: establishing wholesome thought patterns. Second Corinthians 10:5 says we should "take captive every thought and make it obedient to Christ." These Scriptures give a clear picture of the kind of music we should not listen to.

Obviously, the best kind of music is that which praises and glorifies God. Talented Christian musicians work in nearly every musical genre, ranging from classical to rock, rap, and reggae. There is nothing inherently wrong with any particular style of music. It is the lyrics that determine whether a song is "acceptable" for a Christian to listen to. If anything leads you to think about or get involved in something that does not glorify God, it should be avoided.

Question: What was the significance of the temple veil being torn in two when Jesus died?

Answer: During the lifetime of Jesus, the holy temple in Jerusalem was the center of Jewish religious life. The temple was the place where animal sacrifices were carried out and worship according to the Law of Moses was followed faithfully. Hebrews 9:1-9 tells us that in the temple a veil separated the Holy of Holies—the earthly dwelling place of God's presence—from the rest of the temple where men dwelt. This signified that man was separated from God by sin (Isaiah 59:1-2). Only the high priest was permitted to pass beyond this veil once each year (Exodus 30:10; Hebrews 9:7) to enter into God's presence for all of Israel and make atonement for their sins (Leviticus 16).

Solomon's temple was 30 cubits high (1 Kings 6:2), but Herod had increased the height to 40 cubits, according to the writings of Josephus, a first century Jewish historian. There is uncertainty as to the exact measurement of a cubit, but it is safe to assume that this veil was somewhere near 60 feet high. Josephus also tells us that the veil was four inches thick and that horses tied to each side could not pull the veil apart. The book of Exodus teaches that this thick veil was fashioned from blue, purple and scarlet material and fine twisted linen.

The size and thickness of the veil makes the events occurring at the moment of Jesus' death on the cross so much more momentous. "And when Jesus had cried out again in a loud voice, he gave up his spirit. At that moment the curtain of the temple was torn in two from top to bottom" (Matthew 27:50-51a).

So, what do we make of this? What significance does this torn veil have for us today? Above all, the tearing of the veil at the moment of Jesus' death dramatically symbolized that His sacrifice, the shedding of His own blood, was a sufficient atonement for sins. It signified that now the way into the Holy of Holies was open for all people, for all time, both Jew and Gentile.

When Jesus died, the veil was torn, and God moved out of that place never again to dwell in a temple made with hands (Acts 17:24). God was through with that temple and its religious system, and the temple and Jerusalem were left "desolate" (destroyed by the Romans) in A.D. 70, just as Jesus prophesied in Luke 13:35. As long as the temple stood, it signified the continuation of the Old Covenant. Hebrews 9:8-9 refers to the age that was passing away as the new covenant was being established (Hebrews 8:13).

In a sense, the veil was symbolic of Christ Himself as the only way to the Father (John 14:6). This is indicated by the fact that the high priest had to enter the Holy of Holies through the veil. Now Christ is our superior High Priest, and as believers in His finished work, we partake of His better priesthood. We can now enter the Holy of Holies through Him. Hebrews 10:19-20 says that the faithful enter into the sanctuary by the "blood of Jesus, by the new and living way which he opened for us through the veil, that is, through his flesh." Here we see the image of Jesus' flesh being torn for us just as He was tearing the veil for us.

The veil being torn from top to bottom is a fact of history. The profound significance of this event is explained in glorious detail in Hebrews. The things of the temple were shadows of things to come, and they all ultimately point us to Jesus Christ. He was the veil to the Holy of Holies, and through His death the faithful now have free access to God.

The veil in the temple was a constant reminder that sin renders humanity unfit for the presence of God. The fact that the sin offering was offered annually and countless other sacrifices repeated daily showed graphically that sin could not truly be atoned for or erased by mere animal sacrifices. Jesus Christ, through His death, has removed the barriers between God and man, and now we may approach Him with confidence and boldness (Hebrews 4:14-16).

Question: What was Paul's thorn in the flesh?

Answer: Countless explanations concerning the nature of Paul's thorn in the flesh have been offered. They range from incessant temptation, dogged opponents, chronic maladies (such as eye problems, malaria, migraine headaches, and epilepsy), to a speech disability. No one can say for sure what Paul's thorn in the flesh was, but it probably was a physical affliction.

What we do know about this thorn in the flesh comes from Paul himself in 2 Corinthians 12:7: "To keep me from becoming conceited because of these surpassingly great revelations, there was given me a thorn in my flesh, a messenger of Satan, to torment me." First, the purpose of the thorn in the flesh was to keep Paul humble. Anyone who had encountered Jesus and was spoken to and commissioned by Him (Acts 9:2-8) would, in his natural state, become "puffed up." Add to that the fact of being moved by the Holy Spirit to write much of the New Testament, and it is easy to see how Paul could become "haughty" (KJV) or "exalted above measure" (NKJV) or "too proud" (N.C.V.). Second, we know that the affliction came from or by a messenger of Satan. Just as God allowed Satan to torment Job (Job 1:1-12), God allowed Satan to torment Paul for God's own good purposes and always within God's perfect will.

It is understandable that Paul would consider this thorn a hindrance to wider or more effective ministry (Galatians 5:14-16) and that he would three times petition God for its removal (2 Corinthians 12:8). But Paul learned from this experience the lesson that dominates his writings: divine power is best displayed against the backdrop of human weakness (2 Corinthians 4:7) so that God alone is praised (2 Corinthians 10:17). Rather than removing the problem, God gave him grace and strength through it, and He declared that grace to be "sufficient."

Question: What happened to the Ark of the Covenant?

Answer: What happened to the Ark of the Covenant is a question that has fascinated theologians, Bible students, and archeologists for centuries. In the eighteenth year of his reign, King Josiah of Judah ordered the caretakers of the Ark of the Covenant to return it to the temple in Jerusalem (2 Chronicles 35:1-6; cf. 2 Kings 23:21-23). That is the last time the ark's location is mentioned in the Scriptures. Forty years later, King Nebuchadnezzar of Babylon captured Jerusalem and raided the temple. Less than ten years after that, he returned, took what was left in the temple, and then burnt it and the city to the ground. So what happened to the ark? Was it taken by Nebuchadnezzar? Was it destroyed with the city? Or was it removed and hidden safely away, as evidently happened when Pharaoh Shishak of Egypt raided the temple during the reign of Solomon's son Rehoboam? ("Evidently" because, if Shishak had managed to take the Ark, why did Josiah ask the Levites to return it? If the Ark was in Egypt—à la the plotline of *Raiders of the Lost Ark*—the Levites would not have possessed it and therefore could not have returned it.)

The non-canonical book of 2 Maccabees reports that just prior to the Babylonian invasion, Jeremiah, "following a divine revelation, ordered that the tabernacle and the ark should accompany him and... he went off to the mountain which Moses climbed to see God's inheritance [i.e., Mt. Nebo; cf. Deuteronomy 31:1-4]. When Jeremiah arrived there, he found a room in a cave in which he put the tent, the ark, and the altar of incense; then he blocked up the entrance" (2:4-5). However, "Some of those who followed him came up intending to mark the path, but they could not find it. When Jeremiah heard of this, he reproved them: 'The place is to remain unknown until God gathers his people together again and shows them mercy. Then the Lord will disclose these things, and the glory of the Lord will be seen in the cloud, just as it appeared in the time of Moses and when Solomon prayed that the Temple might be gloriously sanctified'" (2:6-8). It is not known if this secondhand (see 2:1) account is accurate; even if it is, we will not know until the Lord comes back, as the account itself claims.

Other theories concerning the whereabouts of the lost ark include Rabbis Shlomo Goren and Yehuda Getz's claim that it is hidden beneath the temple mount, having been buried there before Nebuchadnezzar could steal it away. Unfortunately, the temple mount is now home to the Dome of the Rock, an Islamic holy site, and the local Muslim community refuses to allow it to be excavated. So we cannot know if Rabbis Goren and Getz are correct.

Explorer Vendyl Jones, among others, believes that an artifact found among the Dead Sea Scrolls, the enigmatic "Copper Scroll" of Qumran Cave 3, is actually a treasure map of sorts detailing the location of a number of precious treasures taken from the temple before the Babylonians arrived, among them the lost Ark of the Covenant. Whether or not this is true remains to be seen, as no one has yet been able to locate all of the necessary geographical landmarks listed on the scroll. Interestingly, some scholars speculate that the Copper Scroll may actually be the record referred to in 2 Maccabees 2:1 and 4, which describes Jeremiah hiding the ark. While this is an interesting speculation, it remains unsubstantiated.

Former East African correspondent for "The Economist," Graham Hancock, published a book in 1992 entitled *The Sign and the Seal: The Quest for the Lost Ark of the Covenant,* in which he argued that the ark had been stowed away in Saint Mary of Zion's Church in Aksum, an ancient city of Ethiopia. Explorer Robert Cornuke of the B.A.S.E. Institute, also believes the Ark may now reside in Aksum. However, no one has yet found it there. Similarly, archaeologist Michael Sanders believes the ark is hidden away in an ancient Egyptian temple in the Israeli village of Djaharya, but he has yet to actually find it there.

A doubtful Irish tradition maintains that the Ark is buried under the Hill of Tara in Ireland. Some scholars believe that this is the source of the Irish "pot of gold at the end of the rainbow" legend. Even less believable are the claims of Ron Wyatt and Tom Crotser, Wyatt claiming to actually have seen the lost Ark of the Covenant buried under Mt. Calvary and Crotser claiming to have seen it on Mt. Pisgah near Mt. Nebo. Both of these men are held in low esteem by the archaeological community, and neither has been able to substantiate the wild claims with any evidence.

In the end, the ark remains lost to all but God. Interesting theories like the ones presented above continue to be offered, but the ark has yet to be found. The writer of 2 Maccabees may very well be right; we may not find out what happened to the lost Ark of the Covenant until the Lord Himself returns.

Question: Christian archeology—why is it important?

Answer: Archaeology comes from two compounded Greek words—*archae* meaning "ancient," and *logos* meaning "knowledge"; thus, "knowledge or study of the ancients." An archaeologist is much more than an Indiana Jones-type individual running around the world looking for old artifacts to place in a museum. Archeology is a science that studies ancient cultures by recovering and documenting materials from the past. Christian archeology is the science of studying ancient cultures that have impacted Christianity and Judaism and the Jewish and Christian cultures themselves. Not only are Christian archaeologists trying to discover new things about the past, they are trying to validate what we already know about the past and advance our understanding of the manners and customs of the peoples of the Bible.

The biblical text and other written records are the most important pieces of information we have about the history of ancient biblical peoples. But these records alone have left many unanswered questions. That is where Christian archeologists come in. They can fill in the partial picture that the biblical narrative provides. Excavations of ancient garbage dumps and abandoned cities have provided bits and pieces that give us clues to the past. The goal of Christian archeology is to verify the essential truths of the Old and New Testaments through the physical artifacts of ancient peoples.

Christian archeology did not become a scientific discipline until the 19th century. The building blocks of Christian archeology were laid by men such as Johann Jahn, Edward Robinson, and Sir Flinders Petrie. William F. Albright became the dominant figure in the 20th century. It was Albright who drew Christian archeology into the contemporary debates over the origins and reliability of the biblical narratives. It was Albright and his students who provided much of the physical evidence for the historical events described in the Bible. However, today it seems as though there are as many archeologists trying to disprove the Bible as there are those proving it to be accurate.

We do not have to go very far to find new attacks on Christianity from the secular world. An example is much of the programming on the Discovery Channel, such as "The Da Vinci Code" docudrama. Other offerings have dealt with historicity of Christ. One program, by James Cameron, argued that the tomb and burial box of Jesus had been found. From this "discovery" the conclusion was drawn that Jesus had not risen from the dead. What the program failed to say is that the box had been discovered years earlier and that it had already been proven not to be Christ's burial box. This knowledge was achieved through the hard work of Christian archeologists.

It is archaeological evidence that provides the best possible physical information on the life and times of the ancients. When proper scientific methods are applied to the excavation of ancient sites, information emerges that gives us a greater understanding of the ancient peoples and their culture and proofs that validate the biblical text. Systematic recordings of these findings, shared with experts worldwide, can give us the most complete information on the lives of those who lived in Bible times. Christian archeology is just one of the tools scholars can use to present a more complete defense of the biblical narrative and the gospel of Jesus Christ. Often, when sharing our faith, we are asked by non-believers how we know the Bible is true. One of the answers we can give is that, through the work of Christian archeologists, many of the facts of the Bible have been validated.

Question: Can a Christian be cursed?

Answer: The Bible tells us that "like a fluttering sparrow or a darting swallow, an undeserved curse does not come to rest" (Proverbs 26:2b). This means that foolish curses have no effect. God does not allow His children to be cursed. God is sovereign. No one has the power to curse one whom God has decided to bless. God is the only One able to pronounce judgment.

"Spells" in the Bible are always described negatively. Deuteronomy 18:10-11 numbers those who cast spells with those who commit other acts "detestable to the LORD" such as child sacrifice, witchcraft, sorcery, divination, or necromancy (consulting with the dead). Micah 5:12 says that God will destroy witchcraft and those who cast spells. Revelation 18 describes spells as part of the deception that will be used by the antichrist and his "great city of Babylon" (vv. 21-24). Though the end-times deception will be so great that even the elect would be deceived if God did not protect us (Matthew 24:24), God will utterly destroy Satan, the antichrist, and all who follow them (Revelation chapters 19-20).

The Christian has been born again as a new person in Jesus Christ (2 Corinthians 5:17), and we are in the constant presence of the Holy Spirit who lives within us and under whose protection we exist (Romans 8:11). We do not need to worry about anyone casting any sort of pagan spell on us. Voodoo, witchcraft, hexes, and curses have no power over us because they come from Satan, and we know that "the one who is in you [Christ] is greater than the one [Satan] who is in the world" (1 John 4:4). God has overcome him, and we have been freed to worship God without fear (John 8:36). "The Lord is my light and my salvation—whom shall I fear? The Lord is the stronghold of my life—of whom shall I be afraid?" (Psalm 27:1).

Question: Who were the early church fathers?

Answer: The early church fathers fall into three basic categories: apostolic fathers, ante-Nicene church fathers, and post-Nicene church fathers. The apostolic church fathers were the ones like Clement of Rome who were contemporaries of the apostles and were probably taught by them, carrying on the tradition and teaching of the apostles themselves. Linus, mentioned in 2 Timothy 4:21, became the bishop of Rome after Peter was martyred, and Clement took over from Linus. Both Linus and Clement of Rome, therefore, are considered apostolic fathers. However, there appear to be no writings of Linus that have survived, while many of the writings of Clement of Rome survived. The apostolic fathers would have largely passed from the scene by the beginning of the second century, except for those few who might have been disciples of John, such as Polycarp. The tradition is that the apostle John died in Ephesus around A.D. 98.

The ante-Nicene fathers were those who came after the apostolic fathers and before the Council of Nicea in A.D. 325. Such individuals as Iraenus, Ignatius, and Justin Martyr are ante-Nicene fathers.

The post-Nicene church fathers are those who came after the Council of Nicea in A.D. 325. These are such noted men as Augustine, bishop of Hippo, who is often called the father of the [Roman Catholic] Church because of his great work in Church doctrine; Chrysostom, called the "golden-mouthed" for his excellent oratorical skills; and Eusebius, who wrote a history of the church from the birth of Jesus to A.D. 324, one year before the Council of Nicea. He is included in the post-Nicene era since he did not write his history until after the Council of Nicea was held. Other post-Nicene fathers were Jerome, who translated the Greek New Testament into the Latin Vulgate, and Ambrose, who was largely responsible for the Emperor Constantine's conversion to Christianity.

So, what did the early church fathers believe? The apostolic fathers were very concerned about the proclamation of the gospel being just as the apostles themselves proclaimed it. They were not interested in formulating theological doctrine, for the gospel they had learned from the apostles was quite sufficient for them. The apostolic fathers were as zealous as the apostles themselves in rooting out and exposing any false doctrine that cropped up in the early church. The orthodoxy of the message was preserved by the apostolic fathers' desire to stay true to the gospel taught to them by the apostles.

The ante-Nicene fathers also tried to stay true to the gospel, but they had an additional worry. Now there were several spurious writings claiming to have the same weight as the established writings of Paul, Peter, and Luke. The reason for these spurious documents was evident. If the body of Christ could be persuaded to receive a false document, then error would creep into the church. So the ante-Nicene fathers spent a lot of their time defending the Christian faith from false doctrine, and this led to the beginnings of the formation of accepted church doctrine.

The post-Nicene fathers carried out the mission of defending the gospel against all kinds of heresies, so more and more the post-Nicene fathers grew interested in methods of defending the gospel and less interested in transmitting the gospel in a true and pure form. Thus, they began to fall away from the orthodoxy which was the hallmark of the apostolic fathers. This was the age of the theologian and endless discussion on arcane topics such as "how many angels can dance on the head of a pin."

The early church fathers are an example to us of what it means to follow Christ and defend the truth. None of the early church fathers were perfect, just as none of us are perfect. Some of the early church fathers held beliefs that most Christians today consider to be incorrect. What eventually developed into Roman Catholic theology had its roots in the writings of the post-Nicene fathers. While we can gain knowledge and insight by studying the early church fathers, ultimately our faith must be in the Word of God, not in the writings of early Christian leaders. Only God's Word is the infallible guide for faith and practice.

Question: Why did Judas betray Jesus?

Answer: While we cannot be absolutely certain why Judas betrayed Jesus, some things are certain. First, although Judas was chosen to be one of the Twelve (John 6:64), all scriptural evidence points to the fact that he never believed Jesus to be God. He even may not have been convinced that Jesus was the Messiah (as Judas understood it). Unlike the other disciples that called Jesus "Lord," Judas never used this title for Jesus and instead called him "Rabbi," which acknowledged Jesus as nothing more than a teacher. While other disciples at times made great professions of faith and loyalty (John 6:68; 11:16), Judas never did so and appears to have remained silent. This lack of faith in Jesus is the foundation for all other considerations listed below. The same holds true for us. If we fail to recognize Jesus as God incarnate, and therefore the only One who can provide forgiveness for our sins—and the eternal salvation that comes with it—we will be subject to numerous other problems that stem from a wrong view of God.

Second, Judas not only lacked faith in Christ, but he also had little or no personal relationship with Jesus. When the synoptic gospels list the Twelve, they are always listed in the same general order with slight variations (Matthew 10:2-4; Mark 3:16-19; Luke 6:14-16). The general order is believed to indicate the relative closeness of their personal relationship with Jesus. Despite the variations, Peter and the brothers James and John are always listed first, which is consistent with their relationships with Jesus. Judas is always listed last, which may indicate his relative lack of a personal relationship with Christ. Additionally, the only documented dialogue between Jesus and Judas involves Judas being rebuked by Jesus after his greed-motivated remark to Mary (John 12:1-8), Judas' denial of his betrayal (Matthew 26:25), and the betrayal itself (Luke 22:48).

Third, Judas was consumed with greed to the point of betraying the trust of not only Jesus, but also his fellow disciples, as we see in John 12:5-6. Judas may have desired to follow Jesus simply because he saw the great following and believed he could profit from collections taken for the group. The fact that Judas was in charge of the moneybag for the group would indicate his interest in money (John 13:29).

Additionally, Judas, like most people at the time, believed the Messiah was going to overthrow Roman occupation and take a position of power ruling over the nation of Israel. Judas may have followed Jesus hoping to benefit from association with Him as the new reigning political power. No doubt he expected to be among the ruling elite after the revolution. By the time of Judas' betrayal, Jesus had made it clear that He planned to die, not start a rebellion against Rome. So Judas may have assumed—just as the Pharisees did—that since He would not overthrow the Romans, He must not be the Messiah they were expecting.

There are a few Old Testament verses that point to the betrayal, some more specifically than others. Here are two:

"Even my close friend, whom I trusted, he who shared my bread, has lifted up his heel against me." (Psalm 41:9, see fulfillment in Matthew 26:14, 48-49). Also, "I told them, 'If you think it best, give me my pay; but if not, keep it.' So they paid me thirty pieces of silver. And the Lord said to me, 'Throw it to the potter'—the handsome price at which they priced me! So I took the thirty pieces of silver and threw them into the house of the Lord to the potter" (Zechariah 11:12-13; see Matthew 27:3-5 for the fulfillment of the Zechariah prophecy). These Old Testament prophecies indicate that Judas' betrayal was known to God and that it was sovereignly planned beforehand as the means by which Jesus would be killed.

But if Judas's betrayal was known to God, did Judas have a choice, and is he held responsible for his part in the betrayal? It is difficult for many to reconcile the concept of "free will" (as most people understand it) with God's foreknowledge of future events, and this is largely due to our limited experience of going through time in a linear fashion. If we see God as existing outside of time, since He created everything before "time" began, then we can understand that God sees every moment in time as the present. We experience time in a linear way—we see time as a straight line, and we pass from one point gradually to another, remembering the past we have already traveled through, but unable to see the future we are approaching. However, God, being the eternal Creator of the construct of time, is not "in time" or on the timeline, but outside of it. It might help to think of time (in relation to God) as a circle with God being the center and therefore equally close to all points.

In any case, Judas had the full capacity of making his choice—at least up to the point where "Satan entered into him" (John 13:27)—and God's foreknowledge (John 13:10, 18, 21) in no way supersedes Judas' ability to make any given choice. Rather, what Judas would choose eventually, God saw as if it was a present observation, and Jesus made it clear that Judas was responsible for his choice and would be held accountable for it. "I tell you the truth, one of you will betray me—one who is eating with me" (Mark 14:18). Notice that Jesus characterizes Judas' participation as a betrayal. And regarding accountability for this betrayal Jesus said, "Woe to that man who betrays the Son of Man! It would be better for him if he had not been born" (Mark 14:21). Satan, too, had a part in this, as we see in John 13:26-27, and he, too, will be held accountable for his deeds. God in His wisdom was able, as always, to manipulate even Satan's rebellion for the benefit of mankind. Satan helped send Jesus to the cross, and on the cross sin and death were defeated, and now God's provision of salvation is freely available to all who receive Jesus Christ as Savior.

Question: What does it mean that Jesus fulfilled the law, but did not abolish it?

Answer: In Matthew's record of what is commonly called the Sermon on the Mount, these words of Jesus are recorded: "Do not think that I have come to abolish the Law or the Prophets; I have not come to abolish them but to fulfill them. I tell you the truth, until heaven and earth disappear, not the smallest letter, not the least stroke of a pen, will by any means disappear from the Law until everything is accomplished" (Matthew 5:17-18).

It is frequently argued that if Jesus did not "abolish" the law, then it must still be binding. Accordingly, such components as the Sabbath-day requirement must be operative still, along with perhaps numerous other elements of the Mosaic Law. This assumption is grounded in a misunderstanding of the words and intent of this passage. Christ did not suggest here that the binding nature of the law of Moses would remain forever in effect. Such a view would contradict everything we learn from the balance of the New Testament (Romans 10:4; Galatians 3:23-25; Ephesians 2:15).

Of special significance in this study is the word rendered "abolish." It translates the Greek term *kataluo*, literally meaning "to loosen down." The word is found seventeen times in the New Testament. It is used, for example, of the destruction of the Jewish temple by the Romans (Matthew 26:61; 27:40; Acts 6:14), and of the dissolving of the human body at death (2 Corinthians 5:1). The term can carry the extended meaning of "to overthrow," i.e., "to render vain, deprive of success." In classical Greek, it was used in connection with institutions, laws, etc., to convey the idea of "to invalidate."

It is especially important to note how the word is used in Matthew 5:17. In this context, "abolish" is set in opposition to "fulfill." Christ came "...not to abolish, but to fulfill." Jesus did not come to this earth for the purpose of acting as an opponent of the law. His goal was not to prevent its fulfillment. Rather, He revered it, loved it, obeyed it, and brought it to fruition. He fulfilled the law's prophetic utterances regarding Himself (Luke 24:44). Christ fulfilled the demands of the Mosaic law, which called for perfect obedience under threat of a "curse" (see Galatians 3:10, 13). In this sense, the law's divine design will ever have an abiding effect. It will always accomplish the purpose for which it was given.

If, however, the law of Moses bears the same relationship to men today, in terms of its binding status, then it was not fulfilled, and Jesus failed at what He came to do. On the other hand, if the Lord did accomplish His goal, then the law was fulfilled, and it is not a binding legal institution today. Further, if the law of Moses was not fulfilled by Christ—and thus remains as a binding legal system for today—then it is not just partially binding. Rather, it is a totally compelling system. Jesus plainly said that not one "jot or tittle" (representative of the smallest markings of the Hebrew script) would pass away until all was fulfilled. Consequently, nothing of the law was to fail until it had completely accomplished its purpose. Jesus fulfilled the law. Jesus fulfilled all of the law. We cannot say that Jesus fulfilled the sacrificial system, but did not fulfill the other aspects of the law. Jesus either fulfilled all of the law, or none of it. What Jesus' death means for the sacrificial system, it also means for the other aspects of the law.

Question: Are we to love the sinner but hate the sin?

Answer: Many Christians use the cliché "Love the sinner, hate the sin." However, we must realize that this is an exhortation to us as imperfect human beings. The difference between us and God in regard to loving and hating is vast. Even as Christians, we remain imperfect in our humanity and cannot love perfectly, nor can we hate perfectly (in other words, without malice). But God can do both of these perfectly, because He is God. God can hate without any sinful intent. Therefore, He can hate the sin and the sinner in a perfectly holy way and still be willing to lovingly forgive at the moment of that sinner's repentance and faith (Malachi 1:3; Revelation 2:6; 2 Peter 3:9).

The Bible clearly teaches that God is love. First John 4:8-9 says, "Whoever does not love does not know God, because God is love. This is how God showed his love among us: He sent his one and only Son into the world that we might live through him." Mysterious but true is the fact that God can perfectly love and hate a person at the same time. This means He can love him as someone He created and can redeem, as well as hate him for his unbelief and sinful lifestyle. We, as imperfect human beings, cannot do this; thus, we must remind ourselves to "love the sinner, hate the sin."

How exactly does that work? We hate sin by refusing to take part in it and by condemning it when we see it. Sin is to be hated, not excused or taken lightly. We love sinners by being faithful in witnessing to them of the forgiveness that is available through Jesus Christ. A true act of love is treating someone with respect and kindness even though he/she knows you do not approve of his lifestyle and/or choices. It is not loving to allow a person to remain stuck in sin. It is not hateful to tell a person he/she is in sin. In fact, the exact opposites are true. We love the sinner by speaking the truth in love. We hate the sin by refusing to condone, ignore, or excuse it.

Question: Why did God harden Pharaoh's heart?

Answer: Exodus 7:3-4 says, "But I will harden Pharaoh's heart, and though I multiply my miraculous signs and wonders in Egypt he will not listen to you. Then I will lay my hand on Egypt and with mighty acts of judgment I will bring out my people the Israelites." It seems unjust for God to harden Pharaoh's heart and then to punish Pharaoh and Egypt for what Pharaoh decided when his heart was hardened. Why would God harden Pharaoh's heart just so He could judge Egypt more severely with additional plagues?

First, Pharaoh was not an innocent or godly man. He was a brutal dictator overseeing the terrible abuse and oppression of the Israelites, who likely numbered over 1.5 million people at that time. The Egyptian pharaohs had enslaved the Israelites for 400 years. A previous pharaoh—possibly even the pharaoh in question—ordered that male Israelite babies be killed at birth (Exodus 1:16). The pharaoh God hardened was an evil man, and the nation he ruled agreed with, or at least did not oppose, his evil actions.

Second, before the first few plagues, Pharaoh hardened his own heart against letting the Israelites go. "Pharaoh's heart became hard" (Exodus 7:13, 22; 8:19). "But when Pharaoh saw that there was relief, he hardened his heart" (Exodus 8:15). "But this time also Pharaoh hardened his heart" (Exodus 8:32). Pharaoh could have spared Egypt of all the plagues if he had not hardened his own heart. God was giving Pharaoh increasingly severe warnings of the judgment that was to come. Pharaoh chose to bring judgment on himself and on his nation by hardening his own heart against God's commands.

As a result of Pharaoh's hard-heartedness, God hardened Pharaoh's heart even further, allowing for the last few plagues (Exodus 9:12; 10:20, 27). Pharaoh and Egypt had brought these judgments on themselves with 400 years of slavery and mass murder. Since the wages of sin is death (Romans 6:23), and Pharaoh and Egypt had horribly sinned against God, it would have been just if God had completely annihilated Egypt. Therefore, God's hardening Pharaoh's heart was not unjust, and His bringing additional plagues against Egypt was not unjust. The plagues, as terrible as they were, actually demonstrate God's mercy in not completely destroying Egypt, which would have been a perfectly just penalty.

Romans 9:17-18 declares, "For the Scripture says to Pharaoh: 'I raised you up for this very purpose, that I might display my power in you and that my name might be proclaimed in all the earth.' Therefore God has mercy on whom He wants to have mercy, and He hardens whom He wants to harden." From a human perspective, it seems wrong for God to harden a person and then punish the person He has hardened. Biblically speaking, however, we have all sinned against God (Romans 3:23), and the just penalty for that sin is death (Romans 6:23). Therefore, God's hardening and punishing a person is not unjust; it is actually merciful in comparison to what the person deserves.

Question: Who were the Sadducees and the Pharisees?

Answer: The Gospels refer often to the Sadducees and Pharisees, as Jesus was in constant conflict with them. The Sadducees and

Pharisees comprised the ruling class of Israel. There are many similarities between the two groups but important differences between them as well.

The Sadducees: During the time of Christ and the New Testament era, the Sadducees were aristocrats. They tended to be wealthy and held powerful positions, including that of chief priests and high priest, and they held the majority of the 70 seats of the ruling council called the Sanhedrin. They worked hard to keep the peace by agreeing with the decisions of Rome (Israel at this time was under Roman control), and they seemed to be more concerned with politics than religion. Because they were accommodating to Rome and were the wealthy upper class, they did not relate well to the common man, nor did the common man hold them in high opinion. The common man related better to those who belonged to the party of the Pharisees. Though the Sadducees held the majority of seats in the Sanhedrin, history indicates that much of the time they had to go along with the ideas of the Pharisaic minority, because the Pharisees were popular with the masses.

Religiously, the Sadducees were more conservative in one main area of doctrine. The Pharisees gave oral tradition equal authority to the written Word of God, while the Sadducees considered only the written Word to be from God. The Sadducees preserved the authority of the written Word of God, especially the books of Moses (Genesis through Deuteronomy). While they could be commended for this, they definitely were not perfect in their doctrinal views. The following is a brief list of beliefs they held that contradict Scripture:

1. They were extremely self-sufficient to the point of denying God's involvement in everyday life.
2. They denied any resurrection of the dead (Matthew 22:23; Mark 12:18-27; Acts 23:8).
3. They denied any afterlife, holding that the soul perished at death, and therefore denying any penalty or reward after the earthly life.
4. They denied the existence of a spiritual world, i.e., angels and demons (Acts 23:8).

Because the Sadducees were more concerned with politics than religion, they were unconcerned with Jesus until they became afraid He might bring unwanted Roman attention. It was at this point that the Sadducees and Pharisees united and conspired to put Christ to death (John 11:48-50; Mark 14:53; 15:1). Other mentions of the Sadducees are found in Acts 4:1 and Acts 5:17, and the Sadducees are implicated in the death of James by the historian Josephus (Acts 12:1-2).

The Sadducees ceased to exist in A.D. 70. Since this party existed because of their political and priestly ties, when Rome destroyed Jerusalem and the temple in A.D. 70, the Sadducees were also destroyed.

The Pharisees: In contrast to the Sadducees, the Pharisees were mostly middle-class businessmen, and therefore were in contact with the common man. The Pharisees were held in much higher esteem by the common man than the Sadducees. Though they were a minority in the Sanhedrin and held a minority number of positions as priests, they seemed to control the decision making of the Sanhedrin far more than the Sadducees did, again because they had the support of the people.

Religiously, they accepted the written Word as inspired by God. At the time of Christ's earthly ministry, this would have been what is now our Old Testament. But they also gave equal authority to oral tradition and attempted to defend this position by saying it went all the way back to Moses. Evolving over the centuries, these traditions added to God's Word, which is forbidden (Deuteronomy 4:2), and the Pharisees sought to strictly obey these traditions along with the Old Testament. The Gospels abound with examples of the Pharisees treating these traditions as equal to God's Word (Matthew 9:14; 15:1-9; 23:5; 23:16, 23; Mark 7:1-23; Luke 11:42). However, they did remain true to God's Word in reference to certain other important doctrines. In contrast to the Sadducees, they believed the following:

1. They believed that God controlled all things, yet decisions made by individuals also contributed to the course of a person's life.

2. They believed in the resurrection of the dead (Acts 23:6).
3. They believed in an afterlife, with appropriate reward and punishment on an individual basis.
4. They believed in the existence of angels and demons (Acts 23:8).

Though the Pharisees were rivals of the Sadducees, they managed to set aside their differences on one occasion—the trial of Christ. It was at this point that the Sadducees and Pharisees united to put Christ to death (Mark 14:53; 15:1; John 11:48-50).

While the Sadducees ceased to exist after the destruction of Jerusalem, the Pharisees, who were more concerned with religion than politics, continued to exist. In fact, the Pharisees were against the rebellion that brought on Jerusalem's destruction in A.D. 70, and they were the first to make peace with the Romans afterward. The Pharisees were also responsible for the compilation of the Mishnah, an important document with reference to the continuation of Judaism beyond the destruction of the temple.

Both the Pharisees and the Sadducees earned numerous rebukes from Jesus. Perhaps the best lesson we can learn from the Pharisees and Sadducees is to not be like them. Unlike the Sadducees, we are to believe everything the Bible says, including the miraculous and the afterlife. Unlike the Pharisees, we are not to treat traditions as having equal authority as Scripture, and we are not to allow our relationship with God to be reduced to a legalistic list of rules and rituals.

Question: How does psychology work with biblical counseling?

Answer: Secular psychology, based primarily on the teachings of Sigmund Freud, Carl Jung, and Carl Rogers, has no place in biblical counseling. Nor does some of what is called "Christian counseling," because some of Christian counseling often has secular psychology, not the Bible, as its basis. This is not to say that someone who calls himself a Christian counselor is not also a biblical counselor, but too often Christian counselors are Christians who use secular psychology as their mode of operation.

Psychology is an academic discipline involving the scientific study of mental processes and behavior and the application of that knowledge to the various spheres of human activity. Psychology is humanistic in nature. Humanism affirms the worth and dignity of all people, based on the ability to determine right and wrong by appealing to universal human qualities, particularly rationality. Humanism rejects faith not based on reason, the supernatural, and the Bible. Therefore, psychology is man's way of trying to understand and repair the spiritual side of man without reference to, or recognition of, the spiritual. The Bible declares that mankind had a beginning different from any other created thing. Man was made in the image of God, and when God breathed into man the breath of life, he became a living soul (Genesis 1:26, 2:7). At its very core, the Bible deals with man's spirituality, beginning with his fall into sin and its consequences, particularly concerning man's relationship with God. It is the fall—sin—that separates us from God and requires a Redeemer to restore that relationship.

Secular psychology, on the other hand, is based on the idea that man is basically good and the answer to his problems lies within himself. With the help of the psychotherapist—and sometimes the Christian counselor—the patient delves into the maze of his own mind and "works through" his emotions in order to discover the cause of his own difficulties. The Bible, however, paints a very different picture of man's condition. Man is "dead in trespasses and sins" (Ephesians 2:1), and his heart is "deceitful and beyond all cure" (Jeremiah 17:9). He is the victim of "total depravity" (Romans 3:10-23). To delve into such a mind seeking mental health is an exercise in futility, very much like trying to find a rose growing at the bottom of a cesspool.

Man was created innocent, but he disobeyed God; his sin changed the first man, Adam, and all who came after him, resulting in physical and spiritual death (Genesis 2:17; 5:5; Romans 5:12; Ephesians 2:1). The answer to man's spiritual problems is to be born again—to be made alive spiritually (John 3:3, 6-7; 1 Peter 1:23). Man is born again by trusting in Jesus Christ. To trust in Jesus means to understand that He is God incarnate, God in human form (John 3:16; John 1:1-3). It means to understand and believe that Jesus paid for our sins when He died on the cross and that God demonstrated His acceptance of Christ as a sacrifice by raising Jesus from the dead (Romans 4:24-25).

Biblical counselors, as opposed to psychotherapists and some Christian counselors, see the Bible alone as the source of a comprehensive and detailed approach to counseling (2 Timothy 3:15-17; 2 Peter 1:4). Biblical counseling is committed to letting God speak for Himself through His Word and to handling the Word of Truth rightly (2 Timothy 2:15). Biblical counseling follows the Bible and seeks to minister the love of the true and living God, love that deals with sin and produces obedience.

Psychotherapy and some forms of Christian counseling are needs-based. The needs for self-esteem, love and acceptance, and significance tend to dominate. If these needs are met, it is believed, people will be happy, kind, and moral; if their needs are not met, people will be miserable, hateful, and immoral. Scripture teaches that it is God who changes our desires and that true happiness can only be found in the desire for God and godliness. People who crave self-esteem, love, and significance may be happy if they get it, but they will remain self-centered. On the other hand, people who desire God, godly wisdom, and God's glory will be satisfied, joyous, obedient, and profitable servants of God.

While secular psychotherapists attempt to help patients find the power to meet their own needs from within, most Christian counselors see Jesus Christ as the healer of the psyche. The patient is urged to realize how much he is loved by God, and the cross is presented as evidence of how valuable he/she is to God. The cross, therefore, exists to boost the patient's self-esteem and meet his need to be loved. But, in the Bible, Jesus Christ is the Lamb of God crucified in the place of sinners. The love of God actually demolishes self-esteem and makes unnecessary our incessant searching for it. God's love produces, instead, a great and grateful esteem for Jesus Christ, who loved us and gave His life for us—the Lamb of God who alone is worthy. The love of God does not satisfy our lust to be loved *as* we are; rather, God loves us *despite* who we are and teaches us to love God and neighbor (1 John 4:7-5:3).

When an inherently sinful person engages a secular psychologist or Christian counselor in order to have his felt needs met or to attain happiness, self-esteem and fulfillment, he will inevitably come away from such counseling unfulfilled. Jesus said we must die to self

651

and be born again. When we come to Him, it should be with the intention of putting off the old nature—not fixing it—and putting on the new nature, one that lives for Christ and seeks to serve Him out of love for what He has done. True biblical counselors seek to assist their clients to do just that, following the Bible and viewing counseling as a pastoral activity in which the goal is not self-esteem, but sanctification—growth in godliness and Christ-likeness.

Question: How do I know which of God's promises are for me?

Answer: There are literally hundreds of promises in the Bible. How can we know which promises apply to us, which promises we can claim? To frame this question another way, how can one tell the difference between general promises and specific promises? A general promise is one that is given by the Holy Spirit to every believer in every age. When the author penned the promise, he set no limitations on time period or recipient.

An example of a general promise is 1 John 1:9, "If we confess our sins, He is faithful and just to forgive us our sins and to cleanse us from all unrighteousness." This promise is based on the forgiving nature of God and is available to all believers everywhere. Another example of a general promise is Philippians 4:7, "And the peace of God, which transcends all understanding, will guard your hearts and your minds in Christ Jesus." This promise is made to all believers who, refusing to worry, bring their requests to God (v. 8). Other examples of general promises include Psalm 1:3; 27:10; 31:24; John 4:13-14 (note the word "whoever"); and Revelation 3:20.

A specific promise is one that is made to specific individuals on specific occasions. The context of the promise will usually make clear who the recipient is. For example, the promise of 1 Kings 9:5 is very specific: "I will establish your royal throne over Israel forever." The preceding and following verses make it clear that the Lord is speaking only to King Solomon.

Luke 2:35 contains another specific promise: "And a sword will pierce your own soul too." This prophecy/promise was directed to Mary and was fulfilled in her lifetime. While a specific promise is not made to all believers generally, the Holy Spirit can still use a specific promise to guide or encourage any of His children. For example, the promise of Isaiah 54:10 was written with Israel in mind, but the Holy Spirit has used these words to comfort many Christians today: "my unfailing love for you will not be shaken nor my covenant of peace be removed."

As he was led to take the gospel to the Gentiles, the apostle Paul claimed the promise of Isaiah: "I have made you a light for the Gentiles, that you may bring salvation to the ends of the earth" (Acts 13:47). Isaiah's promise was originally meant for the Messiah, but in it Paul found guidance from the Lord for his own life. When claiming a promise from Scripture, we should keep the following principles in mind:

1. Promises are often conditional. Look for the word "if" in the context.
2. God gives us promises to help us better submit to His will and trust Him. A promise does not make God bend to our will.
3. Do not assume to know precisely when, where, or how the promise will be fulfilled in your life.

Question: Is there such a thing as absolute truth?

Answer: In order to understand absolute or universal truth, we must begin by defining truth. Truth, according to the dictionary, is "conformity to fact or actuality; a statement proven to be or accepted as true." Some people would say that there is no true reality, only perceptions and opinions. Others would argue that there must be some absolute reality or truth.

One view says that there are no absolutes that define reality. Those who hold this view believe everything is relative to something else, and thus there can be no actual reality. Because of that, there are ultimately no moral absolutes, no authority for deciding if an action is positive or negative, right or wrong. This view leads to "situational ethics," the belief that what is right or wrong is relative to the situation. There is no right or wrong; therefore, whatever feels or seems right at the time and in that situation is right. Of course, situational ethics leads to a subjective, "whatever feels good" mentality and lifestyle, which has a devastating effect on society and individuals.

This is postmodernism, creating a society that regards all values, beliefs, lifestyles, and truth claims as equally valid.

The other view holds that there are indeed absolute realities and standards that define what is true and what is not. Therefore, actions can be determined to be either right or wrong by how they measure up to those absolute standards. If there are no absolutes, no reality, chaos ensues. Take the law of gravity, for instance. If it were not an absolute, we could not be certain we could stand or sit in one place until we decided to move. Or if two plus two did not always equal four, the effects on civilization would be disastrous. Laws of science and physics would be irrelevant, and commerce would be impossible. What a mess that would be! Thankfully, two plus two does equal four. There is absolute truth, and it can be found and understood.

To make the statement that there is no absolute truth is illogical. Yet, today, many people are embracing a cultural relativism that denies any type of absolute truth. A good question to ask people who say, "There is no absolute truth" is this: "Are you absolutely sure of that?" If they say "yes," they have made an absolute statement—which itself implies the existence of absolutes. They are saying that the very fact there is no absolute truth is the one and only absolute truth.

Beside the problem of self-contradiction, there are several other logical problems one must overcome to believe that there are no absolute or universal truths. One is that all humans have limited knowledge and finite minds and, therefore, cannot logically make absolute negative statements. A person cannot logically say, "There is no God" (even though many do so), because, in order to make such a statement, he would need to have absolute knowledge of the entire universe from beginning to end. Since that is impossible, the most anyone can logically say is "With the limited knowledge I have, I do not believe there is a God."

Another problem with the denial of absolute truth/universal truth is that it fails to live up to what we know to be true in our own consciences, our own experiences, and what we see in the real world. If there is no such thing as absolute truth, then there is nothing ultimately right or wrong about anything. What might be "right" for you does not mean it is "right" for me. While on the surface this type of relativism seems to be appealing, what it means is that everybody sets his own rules to live by and does what he thinks is right. Inevitably, one person's sense of right will soon clash with another's. What happens if it is "right" for me to ignore traffic lights, even when they are red? I put many lives at risk. Or I might think it is right to steal from you, and you might think it is not right. Clearly, our standards of right and wrong are in conflict. If there is no absolute truth, no standard of right and wrong that we are all accountable to, then we can never be sure of anything. People would be free to do whatever they want—murder, rape, steal, lie, cheat, etc., and no one could say those things would be wrong. There could be no government, no laws, and no justice, because one could not even say that the majority of the people have the right to make and enforce standards upon the minority. A world without absolutes would be the most horrible world imaginable.

From a spiritual standpoint, this type of relativism results in religious confusion, with no one true religion and no way of having a right relationship with God. All religions would therefore be false because they all make absolute claims regarding the afterlife. It is not uncommon today for people to believe that two diametrically opposed religions could both be equally "true," even though both religions claim to have the only way to heaven or teach two totally opposite "truths." People who do not believe in absolute truth ignore these claims and embrace a more tolerant universalism that teaches all religions are equal and all roads lead to heaven. People who embrace this worldview vehemently oppose evangelical Christians who believe the Bible when it says that Jesus is "the way, and the truth, and the life" and that He is the ultimate manifestation of truth and the only way one can get to heaven (John 14:6).

Tolerance has become the one cardinal virtue of the postmodern society, the one absolute, and, therefore, intolerance is the only evil. Any dogmatic belief—especially a belief in absolute truth—is viewed as intolerance, the ultimate sin. Those who deny absolute truth will often say that it is alright to believe what you want, as long as you do not try to impose your beliefs on others. But this view itself is a belief about what is right and wrong, and those who hold this view most definitely do try to impose it on others. They set up a standard of behavior which they insist others follow, thereby violating the very thing they claim to uphold—another self-contradicting position. Those who hold such a belief simply do not want to be accountable for their actions. If there is absolute truth, then there are absolute standards of right and wrong, and we are accountable to those standards. This accountability is what people are really rejecting when they reject absolute truth.

The denial of absolute truth/universal truth and the cultural relativism that comes with it are the logical result of a society that has embraced the theory of evolution as the explanation for life. If naturalistic evolution is true, then life has no meaning, we have no purpose, and there cannot be any absolute right or wrong. Man is then free to live as he pleases and is accountable to no one for his actions. Yet no matter how much sinful men deny the existence of God and absolute truth, they still will someday stand before Him in judgment. The Bible declares that "…what may be known about God is plain to them, because God has made it plain to them. For since the creation of the world God's invisible qualities—his eternal power and divine nature—have been clearly seen, being understood from what has been made, so that men are without excuse. For although they knew God, they neither glorified him as God nor gave thanks to him, but their thinking became futile and their foolish hearts were darkened. Although they claimed to be wise, they became fools" (Romans 1:19-22).

Is there any evidence for the existence of absolute truth? Yes. First, there is the human conscience, that certain "something" within us that tells us the world should be a certain way, that some things are right and some are wrong. Our conscience convinces us there is something wrong with suffering, starvation, rape, pain, and evil, and it makes us aware that love, generosity, compassion, and peace are positive things for which we should strive. This is universally true in all cultures in all times. The Bible describes the role of the human conscience in Romans 2:14-16: "Indeed, when Gentiles, who do not have the law, do by nature things required by the law, they are a law for themselves, even though they do not have the law, since they show that the requirements of the law are written on their hearts, their consciences also bearing witness, and their thoughts now accusing, now even defending them. This will take place on the day when God will judge men's secrets through Jesus Christ, as my gospel declares."

The second evidence for the existence of absolute truth is science. Science is simply the pursuit of knowledge, the study of what we know and the quest to know more. Therefore, all scientific study must by necessity be founded upon the belief that there are objective realities existing in the world and these realities can be discovered and proven. Without absolutes, what would there be to study? How could one know that the findings of science are real? In fact, the very laws of science are founded on the existence of absolute truth.

The third evidence for the existence of absolute truth/universal truth is religion. All the religions of the world attempt to give meaning and definition to life. They are born out of mankind's desire for something more than simple existence. Through religion, humans seek God, hope for the future, forgiveness of sins, peace in the midst of struggle, and answers to our deepest questions. Religion is really evidence that mankind is more than just a highly evolved animal. It is evidence of a higher purpose and of the existence of a personal and purposeful Creator who implanted in man the desire to know Him. And if there is indeed a Creator, then He becomes the standard for absolute truth, and it is His authority that establishes that truth.

Fortunately, there is such a Creator, and He has revealed His truth to us through His Word, the Bible. Knowing absolute truth/universal truth is only possible through a personal relationship with the One who claims to be the Truth—Jesus Christ. Jesus claimed to be the only way, the only truth, the only life and the only path to God (John 14:6). The fact that absolute truth does exist points us to the truth that there is a sovereign God who created the heavens and the earth and who has revealed Himself to us in order that we might know Him personally through His Son Jesus Christ. That is the absolute truth.

Appendix

STATEMENT OF FAITH

Section 1: The Bible

WE BELIEVE THE Bible, comprised of the Old and New Testaments, to be the inspired, infallible, and authoritative Word of God (Matthew 5:18; 2 Timothy 3:16-17). In faith we hold the Bible to be inerrant in the original writings, God-breathed, and the complete and final authority for faith and practice (2 Timothy 3:16-17). While still using the individual writing styles of the human authors, the Holy Spirit perfectly guided them to ensure they wrote precisely what He wanted written, without error or omission (2 Peter 1:21).

Section 2: God

We believe in one God, who is Creator of all (Deuteronomy 6:4; Colossians 1:16), who has revealed Himself in three distinct Persons—Father, Son, and Holy Spirit (2 Corinthians 13:14), yet who is one in being, essence, and glory (John 10:30). God is eternal (Psalm 90:2), infinite (1 Timothy 1:17), and sovereign (Psalm 93:1). God is omniscient (Psalm 139:1-6), omnipresent (Psalm 139:7-13), omnipotent (Revelation 19:6), and unchanging (Malachi 3:6). God is holy (Isaiah 6:3), just (Deuteronomy 32:4), and righteous (Exodus 9:27). God is love (1 John 4:8), gracious (Ephesians 2:8), merciful (1 Peter 1:3), and good (Romans 8:28).

Section 3: Jesus Christ

We believe in the deity of the Lord Jesus Christ. He is God incarnate, God in human form, the expressed image of the Father, who, without ceasing to be God, became man in order that He might demonstrate who God is and provide the means of salvation for humanity (Matthew 1:21; John 1:18; Colossians 1:15).

We believe that Jesus Christ was conceived of the Holy Spirit and was born of the virgin Mary; that He is truly fully God and truly fully man; that He lived a perfect, sinless life; that all His teachings are true (Isaiah 14; Matthew 1:23). We believe that the Lord Jesus Christ died on the cross for all humanity (1 John 2:2) as a substitutionary sacrifice (Isaiah 53:5-6). We hold that His death is sufficient to provide salvation for all who receive Him as Savior (John 1:12; Acts 16:31); that our justification is grounded in the shedding of His blood (Romans 5:9; Ephesians 1:17); and that it is attested by His literal, physical resurrection from the dead (Matthew 28:6; 1 Peter 1:3).

We believe that the Lord Jesus Christ ascended to heaven in His glorified body (Acts 1:9-10) and is now seated at the right hand of God as our High Priest and Advocate (Romans 8:34; Hebrews 7:25).

Section 4: The Holy Spirit

We believe in the deity and personality of the Holy Spirit (Acts 5:3-4). He regenerates sinners (Titus 3:5) and indwells believers (Romans 8:9). He is the agent by whom Christ baptizes all believers into His body (1 Corinthians 12:12-14). He is the seal by whom the Father guarantees the salvation of believers unto the day of redemption (Ephesians 1:13-14). He is the Divine Teacher who illumines believers' hearts and minds as they study the Word of God (1 Corinthians 2:9-12).

We believe that the Holy Spirit is ultimately sovereign in the distribution of spiritual gifts (1 Corinthians 12:11). We believe that the miraculous gifts of the Spirit, while by no means outside of the Spirit's ability to empower, no longer function to the same degree they did in the early development of the church (1 Corinthians 12:4-11; 2 Corinthians 12:12; Ephesians 2:20; 4:7-12).

Section 5: Angels and Demons

We believe in the reality and personality of angels. We believe that God created the angels to be His servants and messengers (Nehemiah 9:6; Psalm 148:2; Hebrews 1:14).

We believe in the existence and personality of Satan and demons. Satan is a fallen angel who led a group of angels in rebellion against God (Isaiah 14:12-17; Ezekiel 28:12-15). He is the great enemy of God and man, and the demons are his servants in evil. He and his demons will be eternally punished in the lake of fire (Matthew 25:41; Revelation 20:10).

Section 6: Humanity

We believe that humanity came into existence by direct creation of God and that humanity is uniquely made in the image and likeness of God (Genesis 1:26-27). We believe that all humanity, because of Adam's fall, has inherited a sinful nature, that all human beings choose to sin (Romans 3:23), and that all sin is exceedingly offensive to God (Romans 6:23). Humanity is utterly unable to remedy this fallen state (Ephesians 2:1-5, 12).

Section 7: Salvation

We believe that salvation is a gift of God's grace through faith in the finished work of Jesus Christ on the cross (Ephesians 2:8-9). Christ's death fully accomplished justification through faith and redemption from sin. Christ died in our place (Romans 5:8-9) and bore our sins in His own body (1 Peter 2:24).

We believe salvation is received by grace alone, through faith alone, in Christ alone. Good works and obedience are results of salvation, not requirements for salvation. Due to the greatness, sufficiency, and perfection of Christ's sacrifice, all those who have truly received Christ as Savior are eternally secure in salvation, kept by God's power, secured and sealed in Christ forever (John 6:37-40; 10:27-30; Romans 8:1, 38-39; Ephesians 1:13-14; 1 Peter 1:5; Jude 24). Just as salvation cannot be earned by good works, neither does it need good works to be maintained or sustained. Good works and changed lives are the inevitable results of salvation (James 2).

Section 8: The Church

We believe that the Church, the body of Christ, is a spiritual organism made up of all believers of this present age (1 Corinthians 12:12-14; 2 Corinthians 11:2; Ephesians 1:22-23; 5:25-27). We believe in the ordinances of believer's water baptism by immersion as a testimony to Christ and identification with Him, and the Lord's Supper as a remembrance of Christ's death and shed blood (Matthew 28:19-20; Acts 2:41-42; 18:8; 1 Corinthians 11:23-26). Through the church, believers are to be taught to obey the Lord and to testify concerning their faith in Christ as Savior and to honor Him by holy living. We believe in the Great Commission as the primary mission of the Church. It is the obligation of all believers to witness, by word and life, to the truths of God's Word. The gospel of the grace of God is to be preached to all the world (Matthew 28:19-20; Acts 1:8; 2 Corinthians 5:19-20).

Section 9: Things to Come

We believe in the blessed hope (Titus 2:13), the personal and imminent coming of the Lord Jesus Christ to rapture His saints (1 Thessalonians 4:13-18). We believe in the visible and bodily return of Christ to the earth with His saints to establish His promised millennial kingdom (Zechariah 14:4-11; 1 Thessalonians 1:10; Revelation 3:10; 19:11-16; 20:1-6). We believe in the physical resurrection of all men—the saints to everlasting joy and bliss on the New Earth, and the wicked to eternal punishment in the lake of fire (Matthew 25:46; John 5:28-29; Revelation 20:5-6, 12-13).

We believe that the souls of believers are, at death, absent from the body and present with the Lord, where they await their resurrection when spirit, soul, and body are reunited to be glorified forever with the Lord (Luke 23:43; 2 Corinthians 5:8; Philippians 1:23; 3:21; 1 Thessalonians 4:16-17). We believe that the souls of unbelievers remain, after death, in conscious misery until their resurrection when, with soul and body reunited, they shall appear at the Great White Throne judgment and shall be cast into the lake of fire to suffer everlasting punishment (Matthew 25:41-46; Mark 9:43-48; Luke 16:19-26; 2 Thessalonians 1:7-9; Revelation 20:11-15).

TOPICAL INDEX

12 disciples/apostles 609, 612-613
144,000 217-219
666 227-228
Abomination of
  desolation 208, 219-220
Abortion 583-584
Abraham.... 113-114, 137, 614, 622-623
Absolute truth 653-657
Accountability................. 314, 590-591
Adam and Eve 114, 179
Adoption 455-456
Afterlife 386-389
Age in relationships 442-443
Age of accountability 118-120
Age of the earth.......................469-470
Agnosticism 271, 532-534
Alcohol....................................372-373
Alexander the Great.................626-627
Aliens 610-612
Allah.......................................506-507
Amillennialism.........................288-290
Anabaptists............................. 190
Angel of death.......................... 250
Angel of the Lord 244-245
Angelology 279, 661
Angels
  Description of.......................234-235

Gender of.................................... 245
  Guardian.............................250-252
Anger.....................................591-593
Anglicans.................................... 190
Animal sacrifices 120-121
Animals in heaven 397-398
Animism.................................... 33
Annihilationism 529-531
Anthropic principle 476
Anthropology...........................279, 661
Anthropomorphism.......................... 23
Anti-depressants 568-569
Antichrist ..208, 216-217, 219, 227-228
Anxiety....................................605-606
Apocalypse 208, 220-221
Apocrypha..................................... 147
Apologetics 294-295
Apostasy...................................122-124
Archaeology 636-638
Archangels.................................... 246
Arianism...................................536-537
Ark of the Covenant 634-636
Armageddon 208, 221-222
Arminianism 281-282, 378
Arminius, Jacobus........................... 281
Artemis.....................................177-178
Assurance of salvation 111-112

Atheism.................. 11, 271, 531-532
Atonement theories 291-294
Augustine.........................639
Baptism
    Holy Spirit 79, 80-81
    Importance of 174-175
    Mode of 201
    Requirements for........................ 175
    Water 126-127, 174-175, 201
Baptismal regeneration 126-127
Battle of Armageddon 208, 221-222
Beast 208
Beer 372-373
Bible
    Accuracy...................... 140
    Authority of..........................148-149
    Authors of...... 136, 140-141, 153-154
    Brief summary 137-138
    Canonicity...........................144-147
    Divisions of................................ 136
    Illumination 191
    Inerrancy 142, 151, 154-157,
                            164-165
    Inspiration of.138-141, 147-149, 153
    Lost books of........................165-166
    Preservation of............. 141, 158-159
    Relevancy of 143, 151
    Study of 149-152, 191
Bible students............................. 496
Biblical counseling.................649-652
Biblical theology 279
Bibliology 279, 659
Bigamy.............................423-426
Birth control..........................453-455
Blasphemy of the Spirit.............382-383
Body of Christ.............................. 172
Body piercings..........................371-372
Book of Mormon............................. 497
Brahma 503
Buddhism.............. 499-503, 546
Business...........................563-564
Cain's wife................................470-471
Calvin, John 199
Calvinism...................... 281-282, 378
Canon of the Bible 144-147

Capital punishment 584-585
Carnality 322-323
Cavemen 478-479
Centering prayer 537
Cessationism.................................95-96
Cherubim................................247-248
Children of God.......................261-262
Christian 306-307, 334-336
Christian Science 511-512
Christianity 490-491
Christology 279, 660
Christophany 245
Church
    Attendance 180, 203-205
    Definition of 172
    Denominations............. 173, 189-191
    Discipline.............................185-186
    Government 186-188, 200
    Growth 188-189, 197
    History...............................196-200
    Local 172
    Looking for a 180-181
    Universal 172
    Purpose of 173-174
Classical apologetics 295
Clement of Rome 147, 639
Cloning 262-264
Cohabitation 432-433
Commercial theory 293
Communion..................... 173, 175-177
Conditional election 281
Conditional salvation........................ 282
Confession 125, 328-329
Constantine..................... 197-198, 639
Contemplative prayer 537-538
Contemplative spirituality........538-539
Contemporary theology.................. 279
Contraception 453-455
Contradictions
  in the Bible 142, 154-157, 164-165
Corporal punishment 450
Cosmetic surgery 565-566
Cosmological argument...................... 3
Council of Carthage........................ 147
Council of Hippo 147

Council of Laodicea 147
Courting 430-431
Creationism 466-468, 477-483
Cremation 264-265
Crucifixion, day of 56-58
Crusades 624-625
Cults 491-492
Curses 638
Darwin, Charles 483
Dating 430-431
David 119-120, 152
Da Vinci Code 46, 64-65
Day of the Lord 222-223
Dead Sea Scrolls 635
Death penalty 584-585
Deborah 178
Debt 555-556
Deism 520
Deliverance 105
Demonology 279
Demons 235, 243-244
Demon possession 237-240, 248-250
Depression 325-326, 554-555,
568, 585-586
Dichotomy 255-256
Dietary laws 595-596
Dinosaurs 471-472
Dionysus 46, 49
Disciplining children 450-452, 460-463
Discrepancies
in the Bible 142, 154-157, 164-165
Discrimination 259-260
Dispensationalism 284-285
Divine Comedy 400-401
Divorce and remarriage 411-414
DNA 262-264, 268, 469
Doctors 557-558
Dogmatic theology 279
Dramatic theory 292
Dualism 549
Early church fathers 639-640
Eastern Orthodoxy 512-513
Ecclesiology 279, 662
Eddy, Mary Baker 511
Election 118

Emergent church 538
End times
Preparation for 226-227
Prophesy 208
Signs of 209
Epiphanies, Antiochus 219, 627
Errors in the Bible 142, 154-157
Eschatology 226-227, 279, 662
Eternal security 107-109, 116-117,
122-124, 323
Ethics 295-297
Eusebius 639
Euthanasia 265-266
Evangelism 315-316
Evolution 466-468, 485-487
Example theory 293
Exercise 558-559
Exception clause 411-413
Excommunication 185-186
Existentialism 280
Exorcism 248-250
Ezekiel 72
Faith alone .. 106-107, 110-111, 126-127
Fallen angels 243-244
False teachers 493
False prophets 493
Family 456-457, 463-464
Fasting 316-317, 353-355
Fathers 447-449
Fear 593-595
Filioque clause 87
Finding a husband 433-436, 438-440
Finding a wife 436-440
Five pillars of Islam 505-506
Flood 473-474
Foreknowledge 118
Food 595-596
Forgiveness 124-125, 317-318
Free will 14, 117-118, 269-270
Fruit of the Spirit 86, 88, 91
Full armor of God 320
Futurism 217
Gambling 374-375
Gap theory 483-485
Gay marriage 409-411

General revelation................299-301
Geologic timescale........................ 470
Ghosts.................................596-597
Gift of tongues 96-102
Glorification..........................108-109
Gluttony.....................................377
Gnosticism.............................509-511
Gnostic gospels.............................. 45
God
    Attributes of 6, 12, 14, 17
    Character of................................. 5
    Definition of 4
    Existence of 2, 4
    Fear of.. 18
    Gender of.................................... 22
    Holiness of...............................8, 17
    Immutability of 7, 14, 16, 19
    Love of.................................16, 21
    Names of...................................... 6
    Nature of...................................... 5
    Relationship with 5
    Sovereignty of..................7, 117-118
    Voice of..........................17, 321-322
    Work of....................................... 5
    Wrath of................................. 15, 17
God-shaped hole......................270-271
Gospel of John 162
Gospel of Luke.............................. 162
Gospel of Mark 161
Gospel of Matthew......................... 161
Gossip 597-599
Governmental theory..................... 294
Great commission............ 174, 625-626
Great tribulation 208
Great White Throne... 55, 208, 395-397
Grim reaper................................. 250
Guardian angels 250-252
Guatama, Siddhartha 499
Guilt..................................331-333
Habakkuk.................................... 34
Hades... 55
Hamartiology 279
Healing................................587-588
Heaven 389-391, 398-401
Hell................... 54-55, 392-394

Henotheism....................................31
Hermeneutics................................ 192
Hinduism 503-505, 545
Hippolytus 147
Historical theology........................279
Historicism..................................217
Hitler, Adolph 217
Holy Spirit
    Baptism of............................79, 80-81
    Blasphemy of 79-80
    Deity of............................ 10, 78, 87
    Filling of......................79, 81-82, 86
    Fruit of......................86, 88, 91, 107
    Gifts of.................... 83-85, 91, 94-95
    Grieving..............................89, 93
    Identity of.................................... 78
    Indwelling 78-79, 92-93
    Personality of................................ 78
    Praying in 352-353
    Quenching..............................89, 93
    Reception of 78-79
    Role of 90
Homosexuality.......... 368-369, 409-411
Honoring parents.....................457-459
Hubbard, L. Ron 515
Horus 47-48
Huldah 178
Hypocrisy.........................34, 323-325
Hypostatic union 63
Idealism..................................... 217
Idolatry..31
Ignatius 147
Image of God 23, 254-255, 276
Infertility 459-460
Inherited sins 377-378
Insurance 567
Intelligent design 475-477
Interracial marriage 408-409
Intertestamental period 626-628
Irenaeus....................................... 147
Irreducible complexity.................... 475
Irresistible grace........................... 282
Isaac 614, 622-623
Ishmael.......................................614
Isis 47

Islam............................ 33, 505-506, 614
Israel......................... 302-304, 613-614
Jacob.. 35
Jealousy...................................... 30, 599
JEDP theory 540-542
Jehovah's Witnesses................ 189, 218,
                                          495-497, 537
Jesus Christ
  Birth of...................................... 47, 70
  Evidence for 42, 44
  Death of.................... 68, 71, 631-633
  Deity of.. 10, 39, 40-41, 53, 63, 65-66
  Genealogies of 62
  Impeccability of.............................. 60
  Miracles of 42
  Prophecies of................ 70-71, 74-75
  Rejection of 578-579
  Resurrection of.... 43, 51-52, 132-133
  Second coming...... 214-215, 223-224
  Siblings of....................................... 67
  Sinlessness of.......................54, 59, 60
  Son of God.................................... 53
  Son of man 72
  Temptation of 61
  Timing of.....................................72-75
  Who is 38
Jesus Seminar............................549-550
Jewelry 628
Job 12
Josephus, Flavius 44
Joy 325-326
Judaism 506-508
Judas......................................53, 640-643
Judgment Seat of Christ... 208, 394-395
Justification............... 107-108, 127-128
Karma............................... 499, 546-547
Knowing God's will 310, 348-349
Krishna.. 49
Lamb of God 69-70
Latter Day Saints (LDS) 497
Law........... 310-311, 615-616, 643-644
Lawsuits 559-560
Law of Christ 311
Laziness......................................600-602
Legalism 333-334

Levels of heaven........................400-401
Levels of hell 401-402
Lewis, C.S....................................38-39
License to sin 116-117
Life after death 386-389
Lifespan..................... 257-258, 260-261
Limited atonement........................... 281
Local church 172, 180-181
Lord's prayer 340-341, 352
Lord's supper 173, 175-177
Lost books of the Bible 165-166
Lottery..374-375
Love........................... 431-432, 644-645
Luther, Martin. 166, 169, 190, 199, 217
Lutherans 189-190
Make-up 628
Managing finances....................586-587
Mark of the beast 227-228
Marriage ... 406-408, 415-420, 421-422,
                                          433-434, 440-442
Martyrdom 43
Mary, mother of Jesus 54, 67
Masturbation..............................370-371
Meaning of life 307-309, 562-563
Meditation..................................326-327
Melchizedek................................628-629
Michael the archangel..................... 246
Midtribulationalism..................212-213
Military..560-562
Millennial kingdom..................215-216
Millennium 215-216
Miracles.. 23
Miraculous gifts 95-96
Miriam... 178
Mithras...46, 48
Money 555-556, 586-587
Monotheism....................................8, 31
Moral argument 3
Moral influence theory 293
Moral absolutism 542
Moral relativism....... 280, 542-543, 655
Mormonism 189, 497-499
Moses 35, 137
Mothers....................................449-450
Muhammad.................................506-507

Muratorian canon 147
Music 629-631
Mystical theory 292
Mysticism 538-539
Natural disasters 26
Naturalism 280, 481-482
Neanderthals 478
Nephilim 240-243
New Earth 208, 391
New Heaven 208, 391
New Jerusalem 209
New Testament
   Canon of 146
   Differences with Old 159-161
   Reliability of 50, 163
New World Translation 496
Never heard gospel 115-116
Nirvana 502
Old Testament
   Canon of 146
   Differences with New 159-161
Ontological argument 2
Open theism 535-536
Organized religion 182-183
Original sin 378-379
Orthodox 512-513
Osiris 46-47
Pantheism 503, 543-544
Paradise 55, 403
Parenting 446-447
Partial depravity 281
Passover 69, 175
Paterology 279, 659
Patience 602-603
Paul the Apostle 633-634
Pelagianism 379, 544-545
Penal substitution theory 294
Perseverance of the saints 282
Pets in heaven 397-398
Pharaoh 645-646
Pharisees 646-649
Phoebe 178-179
Plastic surgery 565-566
Plato 509
Pneumatology 279, 660

Polity 186-188, 200
Polycarp 147
Polygamy 423-426
Polytheism 31, 545-546
Pornography 369-370
Postmillennialism 290-291
Postmodernism 521, 654
Posttribulationalism 212-213
Pragmatism 280
Prayer
   Answered 342-343
   Corporate 344-346
   God's will 348-349
   Hindrances 357-359
   Importance of 313, 339-340
   In Jesus' name 342
   In the Spirit 352-353
   In tongues 98-101
   Intercessory 360-361
   Of salvation 338-339
   Power of 347-348
   Proper 351-352
   Repeated 343-344
   Silent 350-351
   Unbeliever 29
   Walking 356-357
   With fasting 353-355
   Without ceasing 355-356
Predestination 118, 282-284
Prejudice 259-260
Premarital intimacy 430
Premarital sex 428-430, 432-433
Premillennialism 285-288
Presbyterian church 189-190
Presuppositional apologetics 295
Preterism 217, 534-535
Pretribulationalism ... 212-213, 223-224
Pre-wrath rapture 212-213
Pride 603-604
Priscilla and Aquila 178
Prodigal children 452-453
Progressive revelation 14, 27
Promises of God 652-653
Prosperity gospel 547-549
Providence 297-299

Psychiatrists 569-570
Psychics........................... 597, 616-617
Psychologists...........................569-570
Psychology 649-652
Q gospel 551
Qur'an 506-507, 614
Racism.......................................259-260
Radiometric dating 469-470
Ransom 130, 292
Rapture.................... 208, 210, 223-224
Rebellious children 460-463
Recapitulation theory 292
Reconciliation 128-129
Redemption...................... 108, 129-130
Reformation 106, 166-169, 190,
                                              198-199
Reincarnation...........................500, 546
Religion 514-515, 517-525
Repentance................ 29, 106, 130-131
Replacement theology 302-304
Resistible grace............................... 282
Retirement.................................570-572
Roman Catholic Church...........67, 106,
              166-169, 190, 198, 346, 512
Russell, Charles Taze 495
Sabbath day.................. 57-58, 202-203
Sadducees..................................646-649
Salvation...................................104-106
Sanctification 323
Satan......................... 235-237, 243-244
Scandals....................................194-196
Science 168-169, 181-183
Scientology...............................515-516
Self-esteem 604-605
Semi-pelagianism......................544-545
Separation 183-185
Seraphim 248
Seventy weeks................................. 211
Seven bowls..............................228-229
Seven deadly sins 367-368
Seven seals 228-229
Seven trumpets 228-229
Sex before marriage .. 428-430, 432-433
Sex in marriage 423
Sexism... 27

Sheol.. 55
Sin
    Continuing in........................329-331
    Definition of 61, 364-366
    Equality 368
    Knowing 366-367
    Overcoming..........................311-314
    Unto death...........................381-382
Singleness.................................564-565
Slain in the Spirit 91-92
Slavery......................................618-619
Smith, Joseph 497
Smoking 375-376
Sola Scriptura 166-169
Sons of God..............................240-241
Soteriology 279, 661
Soul 256-257, 273-275
Soul mates................................434-435
Soul sleep..................................402-403
Speaking in tongues...................96-102
Special revelation 299-301
Specified complexity........................ 476
Spirit...256-257
Spirit baptism..........................79, 80-81
Spirit filling 79, 81-82, 86
Spirituality................ 327-328, 514-515
Spiritual gifts.............. 83-85, 91, 94-95
Spiritual growth 318-319
Spiritual warfare.......................319-321
Submission...............................414-415
Substitutionary
    atonement..................... 112-113, 294
Suicide............................. 554-555, 582
Synoptic gospels 162, 550-551
Synoptic problem......................550-551
Systematic theology 279-280
Tattoos......................................371-372
Teleological argument.......................... 3
Ten Commandments 619-621
Tertullian... 49
Theistic evolution 485-487
Theodicy 13
Theology 278-280
Theology proper 279, 659
Theophany 245

Tithing......................................314-315
Tolerance.................. 494-495, 543, 655
Torah 507-508
Total depravity 281
Tower of Babel................................258
Traducianism 274
Tree of knowledge.....................474-475
Tribulation 208, 210-212, 224
Trichotomy................................255-256
Trinity........................ 7, 8, 66, 301-302
UFOs............................... 476, 610-612
Unconditional election 281
Unequally
  yoked.............420-421, 428, 563-564
Unforgivable sin.........................382-383
Universalism 528-529
Universal church............................ 172
Universal truth.........................653-657
Unlimited atonement......................281
Unpardonable sin.....................382-383

Utopianism...................................... 280
Vegetarianism...........................572-573
Verbal plenary inspiration 148
Video games.............................573-576
Virgin birth.. 54
Visions.....................................621-622
Voting.......................................576-577
War..588-590
Watchtower Society 496
Wesley, John............................ 190, 281
Wine...372-373
Women in ministry..................177-180
Women working.......................577-578
Word-Faith movement 547-549, 557
Worldview................................280-281
Worry 605-606
YHWH...41-42
Young, Brigham............................. 498
Zeitgeist..47-49

SCRIPTURE INDEX

Genesis

1:1.....4, 5, 6, 9, 26, 479, 485, 505, 516
1:1-2 483
1:1, 26..9
1:2.....................9, 10, 235, 254, 485
1:6-7 ....257, 473
1:11...480
1:14-18 399
1:16...477
1:24-25 480
1:25...397
1:26.............9, 235, 254, 259, 308, 650
1:26-27 ....23, 255, 259, 262, 378,
                           397, 583, 661
1:26-28 6
1:27.....................271, 276, 505, 516
1:27-28 280
1:28.....................................254, 453
1:28-29 263
1:30...397
1:31.....................254, 276, 484, 611
2:2-3 274
2:4.......................................477, 479
2:5...480
2:6...473
2:7...................254, 255, 264, 274, 397

2:15...308
2:16-17 474
2:17.......................................272, 650
2:18.............................254, 406, 420
2:18-20 414
2:18-25 308
2:19...480
2:19-20 480
2:19-25 479
2:20...406
2:21-24 ....411, 421
2:22...417
2:23-24 ....406, 407
2:24..............409, 412, 413, 417, 418,
                          421, 422, 425, 431, 432
2:31...407
3:1-5 237
3:1-14 236
3:1-20 479
3:6-7 475
3:8.............................254, 300, 308
3:15.....................114, 176, 242, 280
3:17-18 6
3:21...120
3:22...9
3:24...247
4:1...454

4:1-12 479
4:4-5 120
4:8......................................470
4:14....................................471
4:17....................................471
4:19....................................423
5:1-32 257
5:3.............................274, 378
5:4......................................471
5:5......................................650
5:32............................260, 261
6:1-4 ....240, 241, 242
6:3................................260, 261
6:4................................241, 242
6:5-7 ....240, 242
6:6..............................20, 535
6:11-22 242
6:17....................................397
7:6......................................260
7:11....................257, 473, 477
7:13....................................259
7:15, 22 397
7:19-23 473
8:20-21 120
9:1-2 263
9:2-3 572
9:3......................................572
9:6...............378, 583, 584, 585, 616
9:7......................................424
11:1-9 258
11:7..9
11:10-32 257
11:24..................................260
11:30..................................459
12:1-3 ....215, 286, 613
12:2-3 136,
14:13..................................507
14:18-20 ....628, 629
14:20..........................6, 380
15:1....................................300
15:6............................113, 623
15:9-17 287
16:1-16 614
16:7-12 244
16:11-12 614

16:13......................................6
17:1..6
17:8....................................209
18:1....................................300
18:25..........................453, 592
19:1-5 241
19:1-13 368
19:10-12 245
19:24......................................9
21:1-3 ....454, 614
21:9....................................614
21:11-21 614
21:14-19 29
21:17-18 244
22:2....................................622
22:11-18 244
22:12..................................535
23:19..................................265
25:21..................................459
25:21-22 454
28:12..................................300
30:1....................................451
30:1-2 454
33:5....................................454
35:4....................................265
35:18..........................257, 459
38:9-10 370
38:10..................................454
45:5....................................298
49:3....................................537
50:19..................................592
50:20..........................298, 592
50:21..................................592

Exodus

1:15-22 455
1:16....................................645
2:1-10 455
3:1-3 541
3:1-4 300
3:2......................................244
3:2, 4-5 8
3:13-14 162
3:14......................17, 39, 276, 278

4:10, 13..6
7:3-4 645
7:13, 22...646
7:17...187
8:15...646
8:19...646
8:32...646
9:12...646
9:27...7, 659
10:20, 27...646
11:5...537
12:11-13 69
13:14...618
14:21-22 531
19:5...509
20:1-17 ....508, 619
20:3...545
20:3-5 6
20:4-5 31
20:5......................30, 31, 380, 381
20:8-11 202
20:9-11 478
20:12...457
20:13...588
21:12...584
21:12, 15...588
21:16...584, 619
21:22-25 583
22:19...584, 588
24:1, 9...187
25:17-22 247
26:1, 31...247
29:38-42 69
30:10...632
31:2-5 93
31:3...312
32:14..20, 535
33:19-23 35
33:20...35
34:5-7 300
34:6...8, 14
34:19...537
36:8...247

Leviticus

4:35...120
5:10...120
10:9...372
11:1-47 572
16:15...121
16:20-22 121
16:29-31 57
17:7...238
17:11...143
18:5...541
18:6-18 471
18:22...368, 409
19:28...371
20:10...584
20:11...588
20:13...584
20:27...616
23:24-32, 39 57
24:10...507
24:15..40, 53
25:35-38 556
25:38...556
27:30...315

Numbers

3:40...537
6:3...372
8:24-26 571
11:16, 24-25 187
13:33...243
14:18...14
16:22...255
16:30-34 26
18:26...315
23:19..7, 20, 498
24:2...312,
27:18...9
31:2...589

Deuteronomy

3:11...243
4:2...510, 648

4:9, 15, 23.................................450
4:10...449
4:29............................115, 283, 534
4:30...211
4:31..14
4:35...................................32, 276
5:6-21................................508, 619
5:16...456
6:4..................7, 8, 32, 498, 546, 659
6:5.................................447, 456, 505
6:6-7.......................................449
6:7-9.......................................446
7:3-4.......................................408
7:7-9.......................................613
8:18...298
9:7...................................364, 377
10:12, 20-21.............................19
10:17................................259, 545
11:17..26
12:32.......................................510
13:2...545
13:4...419
13:5...584
14:24.......................................315
15:12-15..................................618
17:14-20..................................425
18:10-11..................................638
18:10-13..................................616
18:15.......................................541
19:15.......................................163
20:16-17..................................589
21:20................................377, 596
22:4...584
24:1-4......................................411
25:4...146
25:5-6......................................454
29:6...372
30:1-10....................................215
30:3-5......................................287
31:1-4......................................635
32:3-5......................................392
32:4...................................7, 659
32:17.......................................238
33:27..................................7, 498

Joshua

1:1...17
1:8....................................152, 539
1:18..................................364, 377
4:13...588
11:21-22..................................243

Judges

2:1-4.......................................244
4:15...221
5:23...244
6:11-24....................................244
6:17-22....................................321
6:18...17
6:36-40....................................321
7:16-22....................................630
9:54...582
13:2...459
13:3-22....................................245
13:4, 7, 14...............................372
13:22..35
16:26-31..................................582

1 Samuel

1:6-8.......................................454
2:2...498
3:1-10......................................321
3:11...17
10:10.......................................312
12:13-25..................................576
12:23.......................................361
13:2...561
15:3...588
15:18.......................................589
15:29.................................7, 498
16:7...............................559, 628
16:13..93
16:14..93
16:14-15..................................238
16:14-23..................................630
18:10-11..................................238
19:9-10....................................238
24:2...561

26:2..561
28:6...35
28:8-17 390
31:4..582
31:4-6 582
31:8..221

2 Samuel

2:1..17
5:3..187
6:14..87
7:8-16 288
7:10-17 287
7:22...5, 7
11:1..561
11:1-5, 14-17 584
12:8..423
12:13..584
12:14..185
12:16..354
12:21-23 119
12:23..390
15:19-22 561
17:4, 15..187
17:23..582
23:5..288
24:16..245

1 Kings

3:5..300
6:2..632
6:23-35 247
7:29-36 247
8:6-7 247
9:5..652
10:26..561
11:3..423
11:3-4 425
16:18.......................................264, 582
18:16-46 325
18:19-31 531
19:3-5 325
19:5-7 251

19:19-21 325
21:17-29 30

2 Kings

6:13-17 251
19:18..545
19:35..250
21:6..264
23:10..183
23:16-20 264
23:21-23 634
23:29-30 221

1 Chronicles

20:1-3 561
28:18..247

2 Chronicles

3:7-14 247
3:10-13 247
5:7-8 247
16:12..557
16:14..265
31:5..315
35:1-6 634
35:22..221
36:22-23 626

Ezra

1:1-4 626
3:10..630

Nehemiah

2:5..74
4:20..630
9:6..661
9:17..15

Esther

4:16..354

Job

1:1-12	634
1:6	234, 240
1:6-7	237
1:21	12
2:1	234, 240
3:11	325
4:8	546
4:18	251
13:15	12, 595
14:1-2, 14	386
15:15	251
26:13	10
30:23	266
30:25	257
33:26	325
36:27-29	143
38:4-7	236
38:6-7	234
38:7	240
40:1	17
40:15	472
42:7	6
42:8	360

Psalms

1:2	327
1:3	652
2:7, 12	9
2:12	113
4:1	630
4:8	297
5:2	346
5:5	5
5:11	595
6:1, 54-55	630
7:11	591
8:5	276
10:4	603
12:6	136, 155
14:1	2, 4, 466, 531
16:2	605
16:10	159

16:10-11	55
17:6	348
17:15	562
18:2	41
18:30	7, 244
19:1	469
19:1-4	2, 299, 532, 533
19:7	155
19:7-9	485
19:8	325
19:14	82, 326
22:1	159
22:7-8	159
22:12-17	176
22:14-18	68, 159
22:16-18	71
22:26	275
23:6	275
24:1	6, 498
24:3-4	216
27:1	638
27:4	345
27:10	652
28:4	395
31:19	8
31:24	652
32:3-5	332
32:8	152, 555
34:17	348
37:4	309, 310, 414, 438
37:4-5	85
37:7	602
37:18, 37	450
37:21	556
40:2-3	570
40:8	574
41:9	642
42:5	325
43:5	257
45:6-7	9
49:7-9	275
50:15	554
50:21	4
51:1-2	349
51:4	392, 393, 530

51:5................118, 364, 378, 379, 544
51:10-12 9
51:11..93,
51:11-12 396
51:12..................................123, 332
51:12, 15-17 555
53:1..466
55:6-8 325
56:11..595
61:1..630
62:12..395
63:1-8 345
66:7..297
66:18..357
67:1..630
68:25..630
69:21..159
71:18..572
76:1..630
76:10..392
78:5-6 449
82:6....................................545, 546
85:2..332
86:5, 15..15
86:5..332
86:8......................................7, 498
89:3-4 ....136, 288
89:27..537
89:48..265
90:2......................7, 393, 498, 659
90:3-12 272
90:10..261
93:1......................................7, 659
94:12..451
95:1..41
95:3..7
96:5..546
102:25-27 143
102:26, 27......................................7
103:8-12 332
103:12..328
103:19..297
103:20..234
104:10-32 271
104:14-15 372

104:30..10
106:37..239
108:4..15
110:4..628
111:10..594
113:9..454
117:2..7
119:9, 11....................................152
119:11..112
119:89..156
119:99..152
119:160......................................144
122:6..360
126:5..546
127:3-5 ....449, 454
130:4......................................5, 41
130:7..41
130:7-8 130
139:1-5 7
139:1-6 659
139:4, 16....................................535
139:7-8 ....78, 544
139:7-12 5
139:7-13 ....7, 659
139:13-16 ....263, 454, 583
139:14..............................256, 266
139:17-24 269
139:23..350
139:23-24 332
143:10..573
145:8..15
145:8-9 558
145:8-9, 17 592
145:18..344
148:1-2 234
148:2..661

Proverbs

1:6..152
1:7............................19, 451, 467, 594
1:8..458
3:5..439
3:5-6 ....13, 414, 434, 440
3:6..438

3:11-12	331
4:23	255
5:19	429
5:21	7
6:1-5	586
6:6	600
6:6-11	586
6:16-19	366, 367, 393
6:23	451
6:25-28	370
8:13	603
10:9	450
10:15	586
11:3	450
11:4	586
11:12-13	598
11:24-25	566
12:1	451
12:24	600
13:1	451, 458
13:4	600
13:11	374, 375
13:24	446, 450, 451
14:26	594
14:27	594
14:34	576
15:1	593
15:5	451
16:9	299
16:18	195
16:18-19	604
16:28	598
16:33	374
17:6	454
18:7-8	599
18:8, 17	195
18:9	600
18:11	586
18:24	555
19:18	447, 450
19:23	594
20:1	372, 598
20:4	600
20:16	586
20:19	598

20:30	451
21:1	298
21:23	599
21:25	600
22:6	447, 449, 456, 461
22:7, 26-27	586
22:15	450, 451
23:2	377, 596
23:5	374, 586
23:13-14	450
23:20-21	377
23:29-35	373
26:2	638
26:13	600
26:14	600
26:16	600
27:17	191, 314, 590
28:7	377
28:8	556
28:12	576
28:13	592
28:20	586
29:11	592
29:15	451
29:15-17	450
29:25	569
30:2-4	9
30:5	155
30:6	510
30:17	458
31:4	372
31:10-31	422
31:30	559, 566

Ecclesiastes

1:2	307
1:6-7	143
1:9	151
1:12-18	273
2:1	575
2:1-11	273
2:12-23	273
3:8	589
3:11	2, 115, 270, 273, 307, 532, 533

3:12-13 273
4:9-12 325
4:11-12 314
5:10......................................374, 587
5:19......................................576
7:14......................................266
7:20......................12, 105, 338, 621
8:8..266
9:3..270
9:7..372
12:7......................................274, 275
12:13....................................271
12:13-14 ....273, 562

Isaiah

1:6..557
2:12......................................211, 222
2:17......................................223
5:11, 22...............................372
5:25......................................393
6:1-7 248
6:2..248
6:2-4 248
6:3........................8, 196, 234, 659
6:7..248
6:8..9
7:3..17
7:14...................54, 70, 214, 291, 534
7:18-25 222
9:2..159
9:3-7 216
9:6........................39, 65, 71, 537
9:6-7.....................................144, 214
10:27....................................223
11:1-10 ....136, 216
11:6......................................397
11:6-9 289
13:6, 9.................................222
13:6-9 211
13:6-22 223
14:12....................................236
14:12-14 ....236, 243
14:12-15 ....235, 236, 237,
                                   364, 540, 604

14:12-17 661
14:13-14 236
14:15....................................237
14:22....................................604
24:9......................................372
28:7......................................372
28:11......................................97
29:9......................................372
29:18....................................289
32:1......................................216
32:17-18 216
33:6......................................555
35:1-2 289
35:8......................................216
37:16....................................498
38:16....................................451
40:1-2 216
40:25....................................7, 498
40:28......................................6, 7
41:10....................................594
42:5..5, 274
42:8......................................347
43:10....................................498
44:6-8 498
44:24......................................42
45:22-23 41
46:10-11 21
48:16......................................9
49:1-5 263
50:6..71
52:14......................................68
52:19....................................159
53:2-6 554
53:3, 5...................................68
53:3-7 71
53:4-7 176
53:4-9 291
53:5....................113, 386, 511, 587
53:5-6 660
53:5-9 534
53:6......................................151, 490
53:7..70
53:10......................................69
54:9......................................474
54:10....................................653

55:6-7 393
55:8-9 ....244, 558
55:11.................................17, 372
56:12...372
59:1-2 632
59:2...357
60:19...6
61:1...9, 10,
61:1-3 555
61:7, 10.......................................216
63:1...221
64:6...110
64:6-7 490
65:16...216
65:17-25 280
65:20-22 289
65:25...397
66:1...398

Jeremiah

1:2...155
1:5...454, 583
8:22...557
11:19...70
12:3...350
13:17...257
15:2...257
17:9.............................270, 379, 650
23:5-8 289
23:20...7
23:23...7
29:7...360
29:13...8, 30
30:7.....................208, 211, 224, 230
30:19-31, 40 223
31:9...537
31:31-34 215
31:33...216
31:34...41
32:17, 27...7
33:15-21 216
35:18-19 458

Ezekiel

1:5...247
1:6, 11, 23.................................247
1:8...248
1:10...247
1:28...91
8:3-4 300
10:7-8, 21 248
10:14...247
11:19...335
13:5...222
18:20.............................380, 381, 544
20:18-19 458
20:30...370
20:42-44 287
28:12-14 236
28:12-15 ....235, 237, 247, 661
28:12-18 ....236, 243
28:13-17 540
28:15...236
28:16-17 237
30:2-19 223
30:3...222
33:11...387
47:1-12 289
47:12...557

Daniel

2:47...545
6:20-23 251
7:13-14 72
7:13-14, 27 289
7:24-25 216
7:25...212
8:15-17 622
8:17-18 91
9:3...354
9:12...230
9:20-27 213
9:24...211
9:24-27 ....74, 211, 218
9:25-26 534
9:27.....................208, 212, 213, 219

10:7-9 91
10:13..246
10:14..209
10:21...............................246, 251
11:41..209
12:1......................211, 230, 246, 251
12:2...............................275, 392
12:2-3..275
12:11-12 212

Hosea

1:4..9
8:4...576
8:5...393
11:9..498
13:6..195
13:14...41

Joel

1:15.............................211, 222, 223
2:1...222
2:1, 11...222
2:1-31 211
2:13..15, 222
2:28-29 ....97, 216
3:14.............................211, 222, 223

Amos

3:3..407, 564
5:18, 20...............................222, 223
9:11..216
9:11-15 289
9:13-15 216
9:14..372

Obadiah

15..222

Jonah

3:5-10 29
3:10......................................20, 535

Micah

4:2-4 216
5:2...71, 159
5:12..638

Habakkuk

1:13..8

Zephaniah

1:7...222
1:7, 14...222
1:14-15 223
1:15..211

Zechariah

1:12..245
3:1...245
8:3...216
9:9..71
10:3..393
11:12-13 642
12:1..274
12:8..245
12:10....................41, 71, 214, 218
12:10-14 215
14:1.......................................222, 223
14:4..214
14:4, 9..289
14:4-11 662

Malachi

1:3...645
1:6...458
2:10...32
2:15..422
2:16.........................411, 413, 435
3:6...................5, 7, 19, 276, 589, 659
4:5...222

Matthew

1:6...62
1:12...62
1:16...62
1:18................................54, 455
1:20...54
1:20-21....................................251
1:21...............................10, 660
1:22-23...................................144
1:23..................54, 291, 660
1:25...68
2:11...40
2:13-15.....................................67
2:20-23.....................................67
3:2...............................269, 331
3:7...122
3:8...131
3:12...392
3:16-17.....................5, 9, 493
3:17...501
4:1...61
4:1-11.....................................320
4:3...236
4:4...............................151, 273
4:17.............................269, 331
5:3...604
5:14-16....................................185
5:17...............................196, 644
5:17-18..........................148, 643
5:18...............................159, 659
5:21-28...................................368
5:23-24...................................350
5:27-30...................................370
5:28...370
5:32...411
5:34-35...................................398
5:43-48...................................593
5:44...............................349, 360
5:45...............................271, 297
5:48...7
6:2, 5, 16..............................323
6:5-6..349
6:5-8..344
6:6...............................339, 351

6:6-7..341
6:8...345
6:9-13...........................340, 352
6:10...347
6:12...318
6:14-15...................................318
6:16-18...................................317
6:19...549
6:19-21...................................576
6:24..................375, 549, 576
6:25-34...................................606
6:34...569
7:7...................314, 339, 565
7:7-8..165
7:7-11...........................313, 344
7:13-14...................................402
7:15-20..........................194, 494
7:16...122
7:19...122
7:21...123
7:22-23...................................124
7:23...324
7:24-27...................................152
8:5...562
8:5-13......................................561
8:20...548
8:29...234
9:12...558
9:14...648
9:22...569
9:27...161
9:32-33...................................237
9:35...42
10:1...............................235, 314
10:2-4............................609, 641
10:3...609
10:31.......................................594
10:37.......................................431
11:21...5
11:23...55
11:27...10
11:28-29.........................111, 576
11:28-30............309, 326, 606
12:22.......................................237
12:22-32.........................79, 382

12:24................................8, 382
12:24-26 351
12:31................................80, 382
12:31-32 80
12:33..493
12:34..368
12:40..................................56, 58
12:46..67
13:1-9 123
13:15..599
13:18-30 324
13:42..387
13:55..67
13:56..67
14:15..164
14:17-21 572
14:18-21 64
14:22..163
14:25..42
14:33..40
15:1-9 648
15:3-9 458
15:18-19 379
16:15..51
16:15-16 493
16:18........................55, 188, 196
16:21..................................42, 57
16:21-22 114
16:23..238
16:24-25 309
17:3-4 390
17:6..91
17:14-18 239
17:14-21 ....249, 339
17:18..237
18:10................................250, 251
18:15-17 ....196, 559
18:15-20 185
18:19-20 345
18:20..42
18:23-35 ....318, 358, 556
19:4-6 411
19:5................412, 417, 420, 431, 432
19:6..............................406, 411, 413
19:8..411

19:9........................200, 411, 412, 413
19:16..621
19:16-23 ....272, 579
19:17..110
19:24-25 106
19:26..499
19:28..216
20:28..130
21:9..161
21:12-13 59
21:22..30
22:21..577
22:23................................419, 647
22:23-28 419
22:30....................240, 241, 245, 419
22:37..433
22:37-39 311
22:40..311
22:43..629
23:5..648
23:13-33 324
23:16, 23..................................648
23:35..145
24:4-30 224
24:5-8 209
24:15................................212, 219
24:15-30 224
24:22, 31..........................118, 283
24:23-27 493
24:24..638
24:29-30 224
24:30..214
24:31..215
24:36....................226, 234, 536
24:37-39 474
24:40-41 224
25:27..556
25:30..579
25:31-36 396
25:31-46 ....212, 396
25:37..216
25:41....................392, 528, 661
25:41-46 662
25:46..............275, 387, 389, 392, 396,
528, 530, 547, 596, 662

26:14, 48-49 642
26:25..641
26:26-29 176
26:28..368, 414
26:29...373
26:30...175
26:31-46 66
26:39...458, 623
26:41...........................313, 339, 349
26:61..643
26:63..53
26:64..53
26:65-66 53
27:3-5 642
27:5...582
27:40..643
27:45-46 7
27:46..56, 68
27:50-51 632
27:54..562
27:60-66 265
28:1-20 51
28:5-7 52
28:5, 9, 16-17 57
28:6..660
28:9, 17...40
28:18-20 ....84, 118, 174, 179,
                          295, 395, 609
28:19.................................9, 42, 457
28:19-20 ....115, 315, 625, 662
28:20..42

Mark

1:27...235
1:35..66, 339
1:40-42 42
2:3..42
3:5...59, 591
3:16-19 ....609, 641
3:18..609
3:22-30 ....79, 382
3:30..80, 382
3:31...67

5:1-20 237
5:25-30 557
5:35..42
6:31..576
6:46..66
6:48-50 164
7:1-23 ....627, 648
7:6...458
7:19..572, 595
7:20-23 324
7:24-30 30
7:26-30 ....237, 340
8:31...57
9:38...249
9:43-48 662
9:44..528
9:44, 46, 48...89
9:44-49 392
10:7-9 434
10:45...65, 161
11:15-18 59
11:24..348
11:25..349
12:18-27 647
12:25..502
12:26..541
13:14..627
13:20, 27...................................118, 283
13:31..141
14:17-25 176
14:18..642
14:21..643
14:24..197
14:53..648, 649
15:1...648, 649
15:39-45 562
15:42..57
16:1...57
16:1-20 51
16:5..241
16:9...52
16:15..227
16:19..398

Luke

1:1-4 ....162, 551
1:7, 24-25 454
1:7, 36..460
1:11-20 251
1:15..263
1:27, 34..54
1:32-33 215
1:35..................................53, 54, 64
1:37..................................347, 554
1:42..454
1:52..297
2:4-7 67
2:13..234
2:25-38 571
2:35..652
2:36-38 339
2:37..................................316, 354
2:38..130
2:51..458
3:8-14 130
3:23......................................62, 63
3:23-38 62
3:27..62
3:31..62
4:14-19 9
4:33-35 239
4:33-36 237
5:33..316
6:12-13 339
6:13-16 609
6:14-16 641
6:16..609
6:35..................................431, 442
7:2...562
7:11-15 42
7:34..184
8:19...67
8:27-33 239
8:28-31 234
8:31..387
8:52..402
9:22...57
9:23-26 124

10:2..............................339, 349, 573
10:7..146
10:15..55
10:17...249
10:27...573
10:34...557
11:2-4 340
11:4..................................413, 648
11:5-12 343
11:7..351
11:13...344
11:18-19 249
11:42...648
12:5...18
12:15...549
12:16-21 272
12:24...547
12:26...257
12:33-37 576
12:51-53 315
13:35...632
14:25-33 124
15:10...246
15:11-32 452
15:13-15 272
16:1-13 587
16:10-12 566
16:19-31 ....25, 273, 390, 403
16:19-26 662
16:22...234
16:22-23 ....388, 403, 498
16:22-24 596
16:23..55
16:23-24 392
16:24...389
16:26..55
17:3-4 318
17:10...605
17:26-27 474
18:1..................................347, 350
18:1-7 343
18:1-8 ....313, 339
18:9-14 345
18:27...441
18:35-43 340

19:10..............................280
19:13..............................226
19:47...............................60
21:36..............................220
22:3...............................237
22:7-22 176
22:8-15 572
22:19-21 175
22:42........................10, 358
22:48..............................641
23:43..............55, 308, 403, 662
23:46...............................56
23:47..............................562
23:52-54 57
23:56...............................57
24:1-53 51
24:13...............................58
24:13-35 52
24:21...............................58
24:22...............................58
24:39..............................498
24:42-43 572
24:44..............................644
24:52...............................40

John

1:1...............10, 39, 41, 72, 162,
1:1-2 537
1:1-3 650
1:1-8 499
1:1, 14............9, 35, 40, 53, 54, 64,
                                65, 279, 301
1:2................................42
1:3................................10
1:4...............................271
1:12..............17, 110, 111, 261, 306,
                                308, 338, 660
1:12-13 270
1:14.............5, 39, 54, 63, 72, 137,
                                162, 495
1:17..............................334
1:18.........................7, 35, 660
1:29.............69, 110, 121, 301, 623
1:36...............................69

2:1-11 373
2:7................................42
2:13-18 591
2:13-22 59
2:17...............................59
3:3...............................306
3:3, 6-7 650
3:3-5 408
3:3-8 430
3:5-16 79
3:6................................10
3:7...............................306
3:15-16 271
3:16............8, 12, 15, 17, 21, 25, 28,
     52, 58, 80, 105, 108, 111, 114, 116,
     118, 126, 152, 164, 173, 259, 261,
     283, 302, 316, 338, 382, 394, 399,
     492, 496, 499, 505, 510, 517, 528,
     530, 531, 582, 584, 613, 623, 650
3:16-17 10
3:16, 18, 36..............388, 392, 528
3:17..............................106
3:36.............22, 58, 80, 105, 387, 389
4:2................................72
4:6...........................64, 536
4:13-14 652
4:14..............................568
4:24...5, 7, 23, 254, 256, 498, 515, 533
4:42..........................10, 162
5:17...............................10
5:18..............................146
5:19-27 65
5:21...............................42
5:28-29 662
5:36...............................10
5:40..............................269
6:11...............................42
6:23-27 313
6:27................................9
6:28-29 110
6:35..............................104
6:37-40 661
6:38...............................66
6:44............5, 111, 131, 283, 505, 545
6:63..............................170

6:64...640
6:67-69 156
6:68...641
6:71...53
7:1-10...67
7:37-39...82
8:1-11...584
8:7..584
8:12..104
8:32...28, 569
8:36..638
8:42..261
8:44..261
8:56...499, 623
8:58...............38, 40, 42, 63, 64, 162,
                    245, 279, 537
8:59...38
9:4..226
9:7...42
9:31..29
9:38..40
10:9..104
10:10.....................188, 271, 309, 597
10:11, 14...104
10:27...321
10:27-30 661
10:28...323
10:28-29 ....109, 112, 116
10:29...122
10:30................24, 38, 40, 63, 64, 65,
                    66, 279, 501, 537, 589, 659
10:33...38, 40
11:16...641
11:25-26 ....104, 387
11:38-44 42
11:41-42 66
11:43..64
11:43-44 42
11:48-50 ....648, 649
11:52...261
12:1-8 641
12:5-6 641
12:6..238
12:28-29 192
12:31...236

12:42-43 579
13:10, 18, 21...................................642
13:21-30 176
13:26-27 643
13:27...642
13:29...641
13:34...259
14:1-4 398
14:2..399
14:6......5, 39, 104, 106, 116, 119, 151,
           153, 271, 281, 308, 338, 382, 399,
           402, 495, 501, 505, 517, 528,
           530, 538, 579, 633, 655, 657
14:9...137, 221
14:10...10
14:13...30
14:13-14 ....342, 347, 352
14:16...................10, 78, 81, 87, 90, 92
14:16-17 ....9, 85, 319
14:26....................10, 39, 78, 87, 297
14:31...17
15:1-11 326
15:7...........................30, 343, 357
15:10...65
15:13...105
15:14-15 276
15:15...6, 129
15:16...270, 346
15:18-19 411
15:26....................10, 78, 87, 90
16:7...10
16:7-11 ....90, 492
16:12-15 10
16:13.....................90, 149, 327
16:13-14 10
16:14...91
16:23...346
16:23-24 538
17:3............................8, 271, 499
17:12...53
17:17...158, 510
17:21-22 191
17:22-23 346
19:7...53
19:17...623

19:28......................................64
19:30....................................490
19:37......................................41
20:1.......................................58
20:1-21:25.............................51
20:16, 20.............................391
20:21......................................10
20:28............39, 40, 41, 144, 162, 279
20:29.............................2, 532
20:30....................................163
20:30-31 162
21:1-14..................................52
21:12....................................391
21:18....................................612

Acts

1:6-8 52
1:8....................84, 116, 118, 174, 179,
315, 609, 626, 662
1:9-10 660
1:11......................................214
1:14................................67, 339
1:20-26 609
1:23, 26...............................188
2:1-4 ....96, 196
2:4.............................101, 285
2:6-8 99
2:6-12 98
2:11......................................97
2:20.....................................222
2:22................................25, 96
2:27-31 55
2:33.....................................516
2:36.....................................131
2:38.............................130, 131
2:41......................................101
2:41-42 662
2:41-47 183
2:42.....................................339
2:42-47 ....181, 189
2:46-47 203
3:1.................................313, 339
3:19................106, 130, 131, 269, 331
3:21.....................................289

3:22.....................................541
4:1......................................648
4:12...............106, 119, 153, 160, 308,
338, 499, 505, 528, 579
4:13.....................................609
4:23-31 339
4:29.....................................349
4:31.....................................313
5:1-10 ....324, 381, 382
5:3-4 ....9, 78, 87, 660
5:17.....................................648
5:27-29 ....576, 616
5:28.....................................459
5:29.....................................426
5:31.........................41, 42, 131
5:40-42 616
6:3, 5...................................188
6:4................................313, 339
6:14.....................................643
7:48-49 398
7:51.....................................579
7:52-53 251
7:55-56 398
7:59.....................................346
8:5......................................197
8:5-25 101
8:26............................17, 234, 251
9:1-2 197
9:1-6 51
9:2-8 634
9:15......................................17
10:1.....................................562
10:1-6 30
10:2......................................30
10:3.....................................234
10:10-15 572
10:15....................................595
10:34....................................259
10:38.....................................10
10:43..............................125, 638
10:44-46 101
10:44-47 102
10:47....................................102
11:17....................................102
11:18.............................130, 131

11:26..306
11:30..187
12:1-2...648
12:2..612
12:5..361
12:5-10..234
12:18..593
13:1..188
13:1-3....................................313, 339
13:4..316
13:22..435
13:38.......................................42, 378
13:47..653
14:3..96
14:23......................................187, 316
15:2..187
15:2-16:4.......................................187
15:7-11..102
15:19-20..202
15:20.....................................429, 432
15:22, 30..188
16:6-10...298
16:16-18.................................237, 617
16:30-31...106
16:31.............108, 110, 111, 126, 660
16:31, 34...144
16:31-34..101
17:6..609
17:11......................................157, 170
17:18-20...51
17:24..632
17:24, 26...610
17:30......................................130, 338
17:31..5
18:8..662
18:24-28...193
18:26..178
18:28..146
19:6..101
19:11-16...249
19:13-16...321
20:7..203
20:17..187
20:21..130
20:28.......................................40, 130

20:34-35..601
21:20..101
21:32..562
23:1..255
23:6..649
23:8..647
24:15..529
26:20..130
26:28..306
27:23-24..234
28:16......................................197, 562
28:23-27..579

Romans

1:7..9
1:16......................................106, 284
1:17..499
1:18...15, 22
1:18-22.......................270, 532, 533
1:18-32..410
1:19-20.....................................6, 398
1:19-21..517
1:19-22..656
1:20...................3, 115, 300, 467, 533
1:20-21..269
1:21-23..115
1:24-27..369
1:24-32..115
1:25..3, 466
1:26-27..................................368, 409
1:29..432
1:29-32..598
1:30..458
1:31..410
2:4..131
2:5..397
2:6..395, 397
2:7..603
2:11..259
2:14-16..656
3:9-18, 23......................................112
3:10..110
3:10-18.................xi, 12, 69, 151, 544,
                                            545, 589

3:10-23 650
3:11.. 115
3:13-14 592
3:19... 160
3:19-20 74
3:21-26 ....7, 127
3:22...499
3:23..................3, 21, 22, 70, 105, 110,
        129, 269, 283, 338, 378,
        392, 490, 621, 646, 661
3:24... 129
3:25-26 22
3:28...107, 499
4:3...623
4:3-8 ....113, 117
4:24-25 650
4:25...386
5:1.........................107, 108, 128, 325
5:3...266
5:6-8 152
5:8.....................12, 17, 21, 22, 25, 39,
        68, 105, 111, 117, 126,
        151, 164, 183, 490, 584
5:8-9 661
5:9...106, 660
5:10...................................6, 106, 129
5:12.....................255, 364, 378, 484,
        490, 544, 650
5:12-18 379
5:12, 17, 19..54
5:12, 19...379
5:13...364
5:14...364
5:17...5, 129
5:18-19 128
6:1-2 ....117, 329
6:1-4 ....81, 395
6:1-10 81
6:3-4 ....126, 174, 201
6:3-5 127
6:4..81, 335
6:4-5 105
6:5-6 335
6:11-15 330
6:13...260

6:15-22 491
6:15-23 117
6:19...369
6:23............3, 12, 21, 22, 70, 105, 106,
        112, 151, 250, 283, 325, 338,
        364, 365, 368, 392, 490, 499,
        517, 544, 584, 646, 661
7:2.. 407
7:7-9 311
7:7-11 621
7:14-25 88
7:23...379
7:24-25 475
8:1.....................13, 332, 335, 394, 584
8:1, 38-39 661
8:3... 69
8:7...270
8:9..........79, 82, 88, 90, 92, 102, 660
8:9-11 ....239, 365, 569
8:11...638
8:13...358
8:14-17 262
8:15...455
8:16...261
8:17...219
8:19-21 26
8:19-22 611
8:21...203
8:26.............................98, 99, 346, 353
8:26-27 ....78, 339, 350, 361
8:28...............................27, 350, 603, 659
8:28-29 592
8:28-30 252
8:28-39 569
8:29...............................118, 335, 536
8:29-30 ....118, 122, 282, 283
8:30...................................108, 109
8:33...118, 283
8:34...360, 660
8:37...336
8:37-39 323
8:38-39 ....19, 109, 116, 582
9:5...9
9:8...261
9:11..118, 283

690

9:15......................................5
9:17-18 646
9:20..................................156
10:1.........................349, 360
10:4.................311, 371, 595, 643
10:5..................................541
10:9....................................13
10:9-10 ....118, 164, 283,
                        316, 492, 495
10:9-10, 13 106
10:9-13 151
11:5..................................118
11:5-7, 28 283
11:6..................................110
11:7..................................118
11:17-31 225
11:25-27 218
11:26................................223
11:28................................118
11:33................................284
11:33-34 ....7, 11, 14, 533
11:33-36 ....118, 278, 460
12:1-2 ....323, 422, 434, 515, 588
12:2..........18, 256, 310, 370, 565, 599
12:3..................................605
12:3-6 94
12:3-8 ....83, 94, 188, 449
12:5..................................335
12:8..................................616
12:9-10 431
12:10........................173, 180
12:19................................592
12:21................................292
13:1..................................296
13:1-2 416
13:1-4 589
13:1-5 461
13:1-7 ....416, 426, 452, 453,
                        576, 584, 585, 615
13:8..................................555
13:14................................184
14:1..................................333
14:1-23 595
14:2-3 572
14:4..................................334

14:5.................184, 202, 203, 567
14:10................................334
14:10-12 ....394, 397
14:19................................573
14:21................................367
14:23.................366, 371, 372, 430
15:1..................................367
15:11................................585
15:13................................326
15:14........................173, 180
15:30................................361
16:5..................................172

1 Corinthians

1:2..................................499
1:14..................................127
1:17..................................127
2:9.............................386, 400
2:9-12................................660
2:10....................................78
2:10-11................................78
2:11..................................256
2:12-13..............................148
2:13-14..............................170
2:14............................192, 256
2:14-16..............................170
3:1..................................256
3:1-3................................322
3:2-3................................193
3:3..................................599
3:5-8..................................85
3:7..................................189
3:8..................................189
3:11..................................188
3:11-15..............................208
3:11-16..............................576
3:12..................................401
3:15............................323, 582
3:16..............................9, 239
3:18..................................440
4:7..................................604
4:9..................................234
5:1.............................429, 432

5:1-5 382
5:1-13 185
5:5..186
5:6-7 185
5:7..177
5:7-8 185
5:9-10 184
6:1-6 560
6:1-8 559
6:7..560
6:9...................368, 369, 370, 409
6:9-10 ....366, 369
6:9-11 332
6:9, 13..................................431
6:11.......................................369
6:12..............367, 370, 373, 375, 376
6:13, 18........................429, 432
6:14.......................................386
6:18................................431, 432
6:19................................238, 239
6:19-20 ....90, 130, 296, 366,
                        371, 372, 376, 559
6:20......................................376
7:1-5 ....316, 370
7:1-16 440
7:2.....................417, 428, 429, 432
7:2-16 409
7:3-5 422
7:5..423
7:7-8 ....414, 564
7:9..414
7:12-14 420
7:12-15 413
7:12-16 200
7:15.......................................412
7:17.......................................420
7:29-34 422
7:32-35 413
7:32-36 414
7:39.......................................439
8:4...8
8:6..............................10, 32, 505
8:9..203
8:9-13 373
9:4-27 395

9:24-27 559
9:25-27 574
10:4...41
10:8................................429, 432
10:12......................................324
10:13............62, 314, 462, 569, 586
10:20......................................239
10:23-24 573
10:31......348, 366, 371, 372, 373, 376,
                433, 435, 573, 574, 592
11:2-3 414
11:3................................446, 463
11:5.......................................179
11:10......................................234
11:23-26 ....173, 662
11:23-29 176
11:26......................................176
11:27-29 176
11:28-32 382
11:30......................................381
12:3...90
12:4-7 201
12:4-11 660
12:7.....................83, 94, 100, 201
12:7-11 ....78, 83, 95
12:8-10 96
12:8-11 94
12:11.................94, 98, 100, 660
12:12-13 80
12:12-14 ....660, 662
12:12-27 174
12:13........78, 81, 88, 90, 102, 172, 173
12:14-20 180
12:21-26 180
12:27......................................180
12:28......................................150
12:28-30 ....96, 100
12:28-31 84
12:29-31 102
12:30..97
12:31..85
12:31-14:1 85
13:1..100
13:4-5 599
13:4-7 ....431, 442

13:4-8 16
13:8..97
13:10..97
14:4..100
14:4-17 ....98, 99
14:6..97
14:10..98
14:12..83
14:12-13 84
14:13..97
14:13-17 ....99, 100
14:13, 27..99
14:14..99, 353
14:15.......................................352, 353, 537
14:19..97
14:22..97, 100
14:27-28 ....98, 353
14:33..98, 616
15:1-4 ....490, 493
15:1-5 43
15:1-8 127
15:3...117, 623
15:3-4 115
15:4..624
15:4-7 391
15:5-7 52
15:6...141, 402
15:12-15 52
15:12-19 275
15:14...132
15:15...132
15:16-19 52
15:17...132
15:18...132
15:19...132
15:20..52, 132
15:20-22 386
15:20-23 52
15:22...379, 484
15:24-34 52
15:26, 54-56 266
15:29-31 133
15:33...428, 440
15:35-49 52
15:35-58 ....265, 391

15:45...264
15:47...390
15:49, 53..390
15:50-54 ....210, 223, 224, 388, 498
15:51-52 ....210, 230
15:51-53 211
15:51-54 208
15:54-55 132
15:55...132
15:50-58 52
15:58................52, 133, 226, 574, 602
16:1-2 315
16:2...203, 315

2 Corinthians

1:3..5
1:22...82, 93, 238
2:5-8 186
2:10-11 238
3:17..203
4:4..................235, 236, 316, 492, 569
4:7...634
4:16-18 579
4:17-18 398
5:1...643
5:1-4 398
5:5...238
5:6-8 ....388, 402, 498, 596
5:8...247, 662
5:10...208, 394, 396
5:17.........88, 107, 108, 117, 131, 201,
        240, 255, 293, 319, 322, 330,
   333, 334, 369, 554, 601, 603, 638
5:18..129
5:18-19 129
5:19...10
5:19-20 662
5:21.........39, 41, 56, 60, 68, 105, 110,
       111, 112, 117, 121, 126, 127,
            164, 338, 365, 368, 381,
                       394, 531, 623
6:2...387
6:14................407, 408, 428, 437, 564
6:14-15 ....420, 430, 439

6:14-17 184
6:15-17 428
8:19 188
9:6-7 587
9:7 .... 204, 315
10:5 .... 351, 631
10:13 604
10:17 634
11:2 .... 31, 662
11:3 234
11:3-4 238
11:13-15 238
11:14 494
11:14-15 .... 195, 235, 596, 617
11:15 494
12:1-7 300
12:1-9 399
12:2 400
12:4 403
12:7 .... 235, 633
12:8 634
12:10 326
12:12 .... 25, 95, 660
12:14 571
12:21 .... 429, 432
13:4 326
13:5 .... 123, 331
13:14 .... 9, 42, 659

Galatians

1:1-2 172
1:3 42
1:7 493
1:9 494
1:15 .... 297, 454
1:19 67
2:11-14 591
2:13 324
3:2 82,
3:3 116
3:10, 13 644
3:13 .... 129, 130
3:13-14 5
3:20 8

3:22 146
3:22-23 74
3:23-25 .... 311, 371, 643
3:24 .... 74, 107, 311, 333
3:24-26 .... 595, 595
3:26 262
3:26-28 28
3:27 127
3:28 .... 183, 260
4:4 .... 54, 72
4:5 .... 129, 130
4:5-6 262
5:1 203
5:13 .... 180, 457
5:13-15 203
5:13-17 573
5:14-16 634
5:16 370
5:16, 25 86
5:16-25 312
5:16-26 319
5:19 .... 423, 429, 432
5:19-21 .... 88, 117, 330, 366
5:19-23 .... 131, 318
5:20 .... 30, 431
5:22 .... 326, 377, 450, 602
5:22-23 .... 88, 91, 92, 107, 117,
 122, 179, 324, 328, 330,
 421, 422, 442, 515, 599
5:22-24 86
5:23 462
5:26 599
6:1 196
6:2 311
6:7 269
6:7-8 518
6:8-9 547
6:9-10 .... 574, 601

Ephesians

1:2 42
1:3 .... 256, 335
1:5 .... 262, 456
1:5, 11 .... 118, 282

1:6-8 ....328, 329
1:7.......6, 106, 129, 366, 368, 378, 414
1:9-11 303
1:11.......................................5, 118, 283
1:13.................................82, 106, 327
1:13-14 ....79, 82, 88, 93, 102,
              122, 219, 660, 661
1:14..605
1:17..660
1:18-23 188
1:20..516
1:22...................................181, 186
1:22-23 ....172, 662
2:1.................................293, 335, 650
2:1-2 379
2:1-5 256
2:1-5, 12 661
2:1-10 151
2:2...................................236, 249
2:3..261
2:4-5 5
2:5..335
2:5, 8.....................................106
2:8....................111, 306, 338, 659
2:8-9 ....107, 108, 116, 126, 164,
         183, 199, 249, 255, 496, 506,
         510, 516, 531, 547, 600, 661
2:8-10 322
2:9..110
2:10..............................107, 574, 600
2:14.......................................259
2:15...................311, 372, 595, 643
2:20...................................25, 660
3:5...10
3:10.......................................234
3:20.......................................340
4:5...................................81, 191
4:6..32
4:7-12 660
4:8..399
4:8-10 55
4:10-12 94
4:11...................................187, 188
4:11-12 150
4:12.......................................95

4:14.......................................173
4:15...............................181, 186, 411
4:15-19 592
4:15, 25...................................593
4:15, 25-32 593
4:17-19 89
4:17-24 249
4:19.......................................370
4:23.......................................249
4:24...................................255, 270
4:25..89
4:26....................................59, 591
4:26-27 ....89, 592, 593
4:27.......................................249
4:28...................................89, 601
4:29...................................89, 366
4:29, 31...................................593
4:29-32 450
4:30....................78, 82, 89, 93, 125,
              191, 327, 328
4:31..89
4:31-32 593
4:32....................89, 173, 180, 196,
         260, 317, 412, 413, 457
5:1-2 450
5:3..........371, 423, 429, 430, 432, 433
5:3-5 89
5:5..548
5:6-7 548
5:15-17 575
5:18...................82, 86, 327, 373
5:18-21 312
5:19...................256, 416, 630
5:19-20 204
5:19-21 86
5:19-33 415
5:20...................................346, 415
5:21...................................415, 446
5:22...................................407, 456
5:22-23 406
5:22-24 ....359, 437, 463
5:22-31 440
5:22-33 ....179, 406, 422, 425,
              426, 433, 434
5:23-33 ....409, 415

5:23	463
5:24	415, 446
5:25	406, 456
5:25-26	463
5:25-27	185, 662
5:25-29	446
5:25-31	407
5:25-33	414, 437
5:28-29	406, 463
5:31	406, 412, 417, 456
6:1-3	458
6:4	422, 447, 448, 449, 450, 452, 456
6:9	259, 618
6:10	249
6:10-12	319
6:10-18	239, 249, 319
6:10-20	562
6:12	590
6:12-18	313
6:13	590
6:13-18	320
6:16	89
6:16-18	361
6:17	152, 313
6:18	98, 313, 352, 353, 355
6:18-19	339

Philippians

1:1	187
1:6	122, 299
1:19	87, 105, 360
1:23	388, 402, 596, 662
2:3	605
2:3-4	358, 566
2:5	430
2:5-6	144
2:5-8	41
2:5-11	64, 66
2:6-8	301
2:6-11	490, 499
2:8	516
2:10-11	41
2:14	421

2:15	575
2:25	562
3:3	326
3:7-9	573
3:7-10	575
3:9-10	563
3:21	662
4:4	585, 603
4:4-9	569
4:6	344, 345, 347, 355, 538, 605
4:6-7	173, 339, 341, 350, 352, 590
4:7	129, 606, 652
4:8	370, 575, 631
4:13	88, 336, 369

Colossians

1:9	256
1:11	602
1:14	125, 130, 584
1:15	660
1:15-17	246
1:15-20	536
1:16	261, 275, 659
1:16-17	10, 26, 42, 143
1:17	5, 271
1:18	181, 183, 186
1:18-20	129
1:19	60
1:20-21	129
1:28-29	601
2:9	6, 9, 61, 144
2:12	81, 127
2:13	256
2:16	203
2:16-17	202
2:20-23	334
3:1-2	569
3:1-2, 23-24	576
3:1-6	295
3:2, 5	631
3:5	423, 429, 431, 432, 573
3:12	118, 283
3:13	41, 196, 317
3:16	199, 256, 312

3:17..367
3:18..446
3:18-19 ....426, 440, 463
3:20..459
3:21..447
3:23-24 ....576, 601
4:1...618
4:2...350, 355
4:2-3 361
4:3...349
4:5...366, 575
4:10..161
4:14..162, 557
4:16..145, 147

1 Thessalonians

1:4...118, 283
1:6...326
1:10..662
3:5...236
4:3.....................................423, 429, 432
4:3-4 370
4:13-17 ....224, 303, 388
4:13-18 ....133, 208, 210, 211, 213,
            223, 224, 230, 247, 303, 662
4:16..246, 265
4:16-17 ....210, 662
4:17..224
4:18..210
5:2...211, 230
5:9.....................................106, 211, 213, 224
5:11.............................173, 204, 346, 457
5:12-24 343
5:14..602
5:17...............350, 351, 355, 357, 462
5:18..572
5:19..........................82, 93, 312, 328
5:21..511
5:22..........................184, 432, 433
5:27..145, 147

2 Thessalonians

1:6..22

1:7-9 662
1:9...392
1:11..345
2:2...222, 223
2:3...209
2:3-4 ....216, 228
2:3-10 208
2:4 224
2:16..345
3:1...349

1 Timothy

1:5..18
1:8-10 619
1:17................................5, 7, 498, 659
2:1...360
2:1-3 349
2:1-4 576
2:2...360
2:5.................5, 8, 32, 121, 360, 528
2:6...121, 130
2:9...566
2:9-10 628
2:11-12 ....177, 178
2:11-14 ....177, 178, 179
2:13..414
3:1-13 ....179, 196
3:2...200
3:2-4 425
3:2, 8...187
3:2, 12..425
3:3...549
3:6...236
3:8-13 187
3:11..437
3:15..181
3:16..54, 155
4:1...209
4:1-5 238
4:8...558
4:12..443
4:14...84
5:1, 19..187
5:6...571

5:8.................457, 464, 567, 587, 601
5:12-13 598
5:17...187
5:18...146
5:19...195
5:20...196
5:21.........................118, 244, 283
5:23.......................................373, 557
6:5, 9-11 548
6:6-11 587
6:10.........................374, 375, 549

2 Timothy

1:6..84
1:6-8 569
1:7.......................................450, 594
1:9...106
1:10...502
2:5.......................................395, 559
2:10.............................6, 118, 283
2:13-14 177
2:15.................142, 149, 157, 167, 191,
                    192, 493, 497, 651
2:22...431
2:23...495
2:26...234
3:1-7 290
3:1-9 ....209, 377, 596
3:2...458
3:4...575
3:12...563
3:15...................................16, 146, 152
3:15-17 ....139, 161, 181, 510, 651
3:16........136, 144, 146, 148, 149, 150,
            153, 159, 161, 166, 490, 497
3:16-17 ....17, 18, 96, 142, 148, 157,
            158, 165, 166, 204, 278, 300,
        312, 319, 321, 327, 433, 449, 538,
            539, 542, 550, 551, 617, 659
4:1..41
4:2...168
4:7...559
4:7-8 401
4:8...395

4:16...360
4:21...639

Titus

1:1.......................................118, 283
1:2...321
1:5.......................................186, 187
1:5-7 187
1:6...425
1:6-9 179
2:1-5 440
2:3-4 577
2:3-5 180
2:4.......................................449, 450
2:4-5 ....446, 449
2:11-14 574
2:13....................39, 40, 41, 144, 214,
                    224, 226, 662
2:14...129
3:5....................10, 106, 110, 126,
                    306, 496, 660
3:9...495

Hebrews

1:1-2 115
1:1-3 301
1:2...221
1:3...53, 516
1:6...234
1:8.............................9, 40, 41, 144
1:8-9 9
1:13-14 246
1:14.........................234, 241, 251, 661
2:4..25
2:9, 14-15 266
2:14-17 ....54, 510
2:17..64
2:18..61
3:13...180
4:1..6
4:10...111
4:12.................143, 152, 156, 256, 257,
                    300, 312, 510

4:14-16 ....30, 633
4:15...61, 292
4:15-16 340
4:16...344
5:6-11 628
5:8...66
6:1...379
6:4-6 124
6:10...601
6:12...439
6:15...603
6:19-20 398
6:20-7:28 628
7:1-10 629
7:4-9 380
7:25...490, 660
7:26...54, 499
7:27...121, 611
8:1-2 398
8:8-13 177
8:12...401
8:13...632
9:1-9 632
9:5...247
9:7...632
9:8-9 632
9:11-14 490
9:14...379
9:22...120
9:24...398
9:25-28 177
9:26 28 611
9:27...........................265, 387, 402, 494,
                          498, 518, 546, 596
9:27-28 505
9:28...114
10:1-10 114
10:4-10 160
10:10...490, 611
10:12...110
10:19...355
10:19-20 633
10:19-22 399
10:19-26 591
10:24.......................180, 314, 346, 457

10:24-25 ....204, 205
10:25..............................180, 447, 462
10:26-29 124
10:31...18
11:3...505
11:6..........................2, 4, 34, 359, 531,
                          533, 536, 567
11:7...474
11:17-19 624
11:25...272
12:1...389, 602
12:2...110, 603
12:5-11 ....18, 19, 323, 331, 450
12:6...5, 15, 19
12:9...274, 451, 458
12:11...447, 451
12:28-29 18
12:29...8
13:4...423, 429
13:5.............................19, 374, 375, 549
13:5-6 ....252, 569, 599
13:12...623
13:15...586
13:20...41
13:21...574

James

1:2-4 ....331, 569, 592
1:2-5 18
1:3-4 602
1:5 ....170, 265, 266, 315, 316, 343,
            347, 348, 414, 462, 492, 558,
            560, 565, 583, 617, 622
1:6...348
1:6-7 359
1:12...395
1:13...61
1:17....................................6, 16, 19, 460, 589
1:19-20 60
1:20...592
1:21...414
1:25...152
1:27...174
2:1-10 408

2:8...259
2:10.......................................311
2:14, 17, 20, 26......................107
2:14-26..................................131
2:17-18..................................107
2:18, 26.................................600
2:19.........................32, 234, 546
2:20-26..................................107
2:23.......................................623
2:24.......................................107
2:26.......................................256
3:1-9.....................................395
3:9...255
4:2..................................340, 558
4:3..................................349, 358
4:4...261
4:6..................................195, 605
4:7..........................239, 249, 414
4:10.......................................344
4:13-16..................................548
4:14.......................................575
4:17.......................................567
5:7-8.....................................602
5:10.......................................603
5:11.......................................603
5:13................................349, 558
5:14.........................187, 360, 557
5:16.........................314, 347, 349
5:16-18..................................340
5:17...26

1 Peter

1:1...118
1:1-2......................................283
1:1-16....................................331
1:2....................9, 10, 118, 306, 650
1:3.............................8, 659, 660
1:5...661
1:6...603
1:6-7..18
1:12................................234, 246
1:14-16..................................184
1:14-18..................................129
1:14-22..................................575

1:16.......................................425
1:18-19.........................108, 240
1:18-21....................................70
1:23................................306, 650
2:1...324
2:2...170
2:6-8.......................................41
2:9..................................118, 283
2:15.......................................574
2:17................................416, 589
2:22...60
2:24..............113, 291, 587, 588, 661
2:25.......................................187
3:1...421
3:1-2................................316, 492
3:1-7.......................................440
3:3-4.......................................559
3:3-5.......................................628
3:4...566
3:7..................................359, 463
3:8-9.......................................450
3:15..............174, 179, 294, 295, 315,
                    316, 411, 492, 495
3:16...18
3:18.......................................113
3:18-20....................................55
3:20.......................................474
3:21.......................................127
4:2...575
4:8...196
4:15.......................................453
4:16.......................................306
5:1-4......................................187
5:4...................................41, 395
5:7.........................566, 569, 606
5:8...........195, 235, 244, 249, 511, 617
5:8-9......................................239

2 Peter

1:1...........................39, 40, 144
1:3...18
1:3-4......................................569
1:3-8......................................318
1:4..................................335, 651

1:5-7 ....377, 596
1:5-8 122
1:10...................................118, 283
1:20-21 ....286, 490, 550, 551
1:21..........10, 136, 148, 149, 155, 659
2:1...22
2:5...474
2:19..................................370, 373
2:20...430
3:3...493
3:6-7 473
3:9............22, 131, 394, 531, 611, 645
3:10...............................222, 611
3:15-16 146
3:16...192

1 John

1:5..5
1:5-8 328
1:7...421
1:7-9 56
1:8...............................12, 312, 322
1:8-9 325
1:9..............17, 93, 125, 318, 328, 329,
      332, 347, 359, 365, 370, 376,
            383, 569, 592, 652
2:1...332
2:2..................21, 39, 41, 68, 119, 161,
      338, 365, 368, 394, 660
2:4, 10...306
2:15-17 575
2:16..................................62, 370, 423
2:19......................109, 124, 323
2:22...493
2:27...297
3:1-10 261
3:1, 23-24 17
3:2.................................390, 400, 562
3:4.................................364, 377
3:6...............................109, 117
3:6-9 117
3:8...261
3:10...261

3:11...173
3:20...418
3:21-22 344
3:23...269
4:1...334
4:1-3 238
4:2...72
4:4.................235, 240, 540, 638
4:7-5:3 651
4:8.................................16, 659
4:8-9 645
4:8, 16..21
4:10...16
4:11-12 191
4:12...180
4:14...10
4:18...594
4:18-19 569
4:19...152
5:3...311
5:4-5 325
5:11-13 111
5:13..................................323, 582
5:14...358
5:14-15 ....29, 30, 313, 314, 339,
            342, 344, 351, 588
5:16...381
5:20...9

2 John

9 493

Jude

3 ....144, 200, 334
6 ....234, 235, 241
7 ....429, 432
9 319
11...494
17-18 493
20..................................98, 346, 353
24.................................116, 661
24-25 109

Revelation

1:1	10
1:3	217
1:7	41, 214, 224
1:17	41, 91
1:18	403
1:19	230
2:4	573
2:6	645
2:8	41
2:10	395
2:14-15	184
2:23	395
3:10	213, 224, 662
3:20	652
4:6-9	248
4:11	10, 275
5:9	41, 130
5:9-10	129
5:8-13	234
6:1-2	228
6:1-17	228
6:2	225
6:3-4	228
6:4	225
6:5-6	225, 228
6:7-8	228
6:8	225
6:9-11	228
6:12-14	228
6:16-17	228
6:17	218, 222
7:1	208, 234
7:2	245
7:4	218
7:9	218, 420
7:14	208
8:1-5	228
8:2	234
8:3	245
8:6-21	228
8:7	229
8:8-9	229
8:10-11	229
8:12	229
9:1	387
9:1-11	229
9:12-21	229
10:7	245
11:2-3	212
11:8	209
11:15-19	228, 229
12:4	235, 243
12:4-9	235
12:7-8	320
12:9	235
12:10	236, 332
12:12	234
12:17	234
13:5	212
13:5-8	217
13:14	220
13:15-18	227
13:18	228
14:4	218
14:9, 11	227
14:10-11	392
15:1-8	228, 229
15:2	227
16:1-21	228, 229
16:2	227, 229
16:3	229
16:4-7	229
16:5-7	229
16:8-9	229
16:10-11	229
16:12-14	229
16:14	222
16:15-21	229
16:16	221
16:19	221
17:7	216
17:8	395
18:6	395
18:21-24	638
19:6	5, 7, 659
19:7-9	407
19:10	40
19:11-16	215, 224, 225, 662

19:11-21 ....208, 589
19:14...224
19:20...227
20:1-3 221
20:1-5 303
20:1-6 ....208, 662
20:1-7 ....287, 303
20:2-7 ....215, 216
20:3.......................................236, 285
20:4.......................................218, 227
20:4-6 ....212, 285, 290
20:5-6 662
20:6...400
20:7-10 ....208, 221, 395
20:7-15 395
20:10...............236, 387, 392, 530, 661
20:10-15 208
20:11-15 .... 5, 55, 250, 308, 365,
                    388, 389, 395, 396, 402,
                    403, 498, 662
20:12.......................................395, 402
20:12-13 662
20:13-14 403

20:13-15 402
20:15.......................................396, 516
21:1.................389, 391, 397, 403, 498
21:3...219
21:4.........266, 308, 398, 400, 530, 588
21:7...308
21:10-27 399
21:11...399
21:12...400
21:14...400
22:1-2 400
22:3...601
22:5...399
22:7...217
22:9...234
22:10...217
22:12.......................................395, 401
22:13...41
22:18.......................................145, 217
22:18-19 510
22:18-20 157
22:19...217

PW